Atlantic Spain and Portugal

La Coruña to Gibraltar

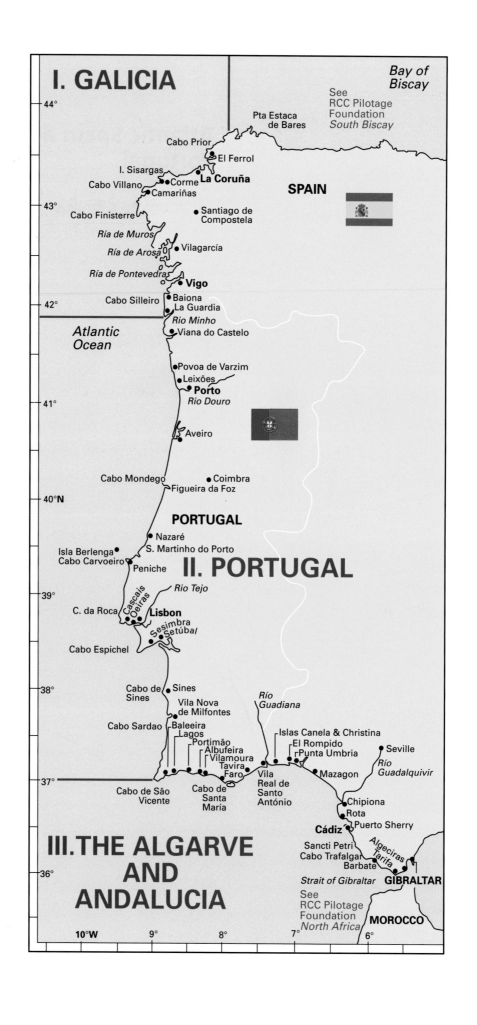

I. GALICIA

Bay of Biscay

See RCC Pilotage Foundation *South Biscay*

Pta Estaca de Bares

Cabo Prior

El Ferrol

I. Sisargas

Cabo Villano

Corme

La Coruña

Camariñas

SPAIN

Cabo Finisterre

Santiago de Compostela

Ría de Muros

Ría de Arosa

Vilagarcía

Ría de Pontevedra

Vigo

Cabo Silleiro

Baiona

La Guardia

Rio Minho

Atlantic Ocean

Viana do Castelo

Povoa de Varzim

Leixões

Porto

Rio Douro

Aveiro

Cabo Mondego

Coimbra

Figueira da Foz

PORTUGAL

Nazaré

S. Martinho do Porto

Isla Berlenga

Cabo Carvoeiro

Peniche

II. PORTUGAL

Rio Tejo

C. da Roca

Cascais

Oeiras

Lisbon

Sesimbra

Setúbal

Cabo Espichel

Cabo de Sines

Sines

Vila Nova de Milfontes

Río Guadiana

Cabo Sardao

Baleeira

Lagos

Portimão

Albufeira

Vilamoura

Tavira

Faro

Islas Canela & Christina

El Rompido

Punta Umbria

Seville

Río Guadalquivir

Vila Real de Santo António

Mazagon

Cabo de São Vicente

Cabo de Santa María

Chipiona

Rota

Puerto Sherry

Cádiz

III. THE ALGARVE AND ANDALUCIA

Sancti Petri

Cabo Trafalgar

Barbate

Algeciras

Tarifa

GIBRALTAR

Strait of Gibraltar

See RCC Pilotage Foundation *North Africa*

MOROCCO

44°
43°
42°
41°
40°N
39°
38°
37°
36°

10°W   9°   8°   7°   6°

Atlantic Spain and Portugal

La Coruña to Gibraltar

ROYAL CRUISING CLUB
PILOTAGE FOUNDATION

Martin Walker (Galicia)
Anne Hammick (Portugal and Andalucía)

Imray Laurie Norie & Wilson

Published by
Imray Laurie Norie & Wilson Ltd
Wych House The Broadway St Ives
Cambridgeshire PE27 5BT England
☎ +44 (0)1480 462114
Fax +44 (0) 1480 496109
Email ilnw@imray.com
www.imray.com
2006

First edition 1988
Second edition 1990
Third edition 1995
Fourth edition 2000
Fifth edition 2006

ISBN 0 85288 893 7

British Library Cataloguing in Publication Data.
A catalogue record for this title is available from
the British Library.

Printed in Singapore by Star Standard Industries

CORRECTIONAL SUPPLEMENTS

This pilot book may be amended at intervals by the issue of
correctional supplements. These are published on the internet at
our web site www.imray.com and also via www.rccpf.org.uk and
may be downloaded free of charge. Printed copies are also
available on request from the publishers at the above address.
Like this pilot, supplements are selective. Navigators requiring
the latest definitive information are advised to refer to official
hydrographic office data.

www.rccpf.org.uk includes a photo library for some ports in
this book. It includes additional material and will publish
appropriate updating photographs received in digital form
from yachtsmen or the authorities.

CAUTION

Whilst every care has been taken to ensure that the information
contained in this book is accurate, the RCC Pilotage Foundation, the
authors and the publishers hereby formally disclaim any and all
liability for any personal injury, loss and/or damage howsoever
caused, whether by reason of any error, inaccuracy, omission or
ambiguity in relation to the contents and/or information contained
within this book. The book contains selected information and thus is
not definitive. It does not contain all known information on the
subject in hand and should not be relied on alone for navigational
use: it should only be used in conjunction with official hydrographic
data. This is particularly relevant to the plans, which should not be
used for navigation.

The RCC Pilotage Foundation, the authors and publishers believe
that the information which they have included is a useful aid to
prudent navigation, but the safety of a vessel depends ultimately on
the judgment of the skipper, who should assess all information,
published or unpublished.

WAYPOINTS

This edition of the *Atlantic Spain and Portugal* pilot includes
waypoints. The RCC PF consider a waypoint to be a position likely
to be helpful for navigation if entered into some form of electronic
navigation system for use in conjunction with GPS. In this pilot they
have been derived from official charts. Key harbour positions have
been verified during visits by the authors. All waypoints are given to
datum WGS 84 and every effort has been made to ensure their
accuracy. Nevertheless, for each individual vessel, the standard of
onboard equipment, aerial position, datum setting, correct entry of
data and operator skill all play a part in their effectiveness. In
particular it is vital for the navigator to note the datum of the chart
in use and apply the necessary correction if plotting a GPS position
on the chart.

We emphasise that we regard waypoints as an aid to navigation
for use as the navigator decides. We hope that the waypoints in
this pilot will help ease that navigational load.

POSITIONS

Positions given in the text and on plans are intended purely as an
aid to locating the place in question on the chart.

PLANS

The plans in this guide are not to be used for navigation – they are
designed to support the text and should always be used together
with navigational charts. Every effort has been made to locate
harbour and anchorage plans adjacent to the relevant text.

All bearings are given from seaward and refer to true north. Scales
are indicated on the plans. Symbols are based on those used by the
British Admiralty: users are referred to *Symbols and Abbreviations
(NP 5011)*.

Contents

THE RCC PILOTAGE FOUNDATION

In 1976 an American member of the Royal Cruising Club, Dr Fred Ellis, indicated that he wished to make a gift to the Club in memory of his father, the late Robert E Ellis, of his friends Peter Pye and John Ives and as a mark of esteem for Roger Pinckney. An independent charity known as the RCC Pilotage Foundation was formed and Dr Ellis added his house to his already generous gift of money to form the Foundation's permanent endowment. The Foundation's charitable objective is 'to advance the education of the public in the science and practice of navigation', which is at present achieved through the writing and updating of pilot books covering many different parts of the world.

The Foundation is extremely grateful and privileged to have been given the copyrights to books written by a number of distinguished authors and yachtsmen including the late Adlard Coles, Robin Brandon and Malcolm Robson. In return the Foundation has willingly accepted the task of keeping the original books up to date and many yachtsmen and women have helped (and are helping) the Foundation fulfil this commitment. In addition to the titles donated to the Foundation, several new books have been created and developed under the auspices of the Foundation. The Foundation works in close collaboration with three publishers – Imray Laurie Norie and Wilson, Adlard Coles Nautical and On Board Publications – and in addition publishes in its own name short run guides and pilot books for areas where limited demand does not justify large print runs. Several of the Foundation's books have been translated into French, German and Italian.

The Foundation runs its own website at www.rccpf.org.uk which not only lists all the publications but also contains free downloadable pilotage information.

The overall management of the Foundation is entrusted to trustees appointed by the Royal Cruising Club, with day-to-day operations being controlled by the Director. All these appointments are unpaid. In line with its charitable status, the Foundation distributes no profits; any surpluses are used to finance new books and developments and to subsidise those covering areas of low demand.

RCC PILOTAGE FOUNDATION PUBLICATIONS

Imray
The Baltic Sea
Norway
North Brittany and the Channel Islands
Faroe, Iceland and Greenland
Isles of Scilly
The Channel Islands
North Biscay
South Biscay
Atlantic Islands
Atlantic Spain & Portugal
Mediterranean Spain
 Costas del Sol & Blanca
Mediterranean Spain
 Costas del Azahar,
 Dorada & Brava
Islas Baleares
Corsica and North Sardinia
North Africa
Chile

Adlard Coles Nautical
Atlantic Crossing Guide
Pacific Crossing Guide

On Board Publications
South Atlantic Circuit
Havens and Anchorages for the South American Coast

The RCC Pilotage Foundation
RCC PF Website www.rccpf.org.uk
Cruising Guide to West Africa
South Georgia
Supplements
Passage planning guides

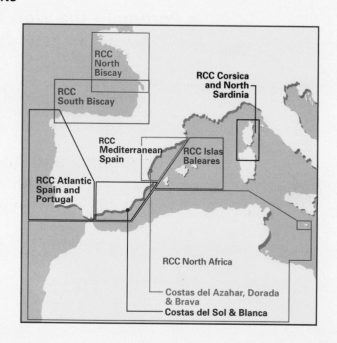

Foreword

Thousands of yachtsmen have cause to thank Oz Robinson, whose work led to *Atlantic Spain and Portugal* first being published in 1988. I have twice had it on board; the first time as a 'just in case pilot' as I sailed directly from Plymouth to Gibraltar and next in 1999 when I slowly cruised Galicia, sped past Portugal as far as Lagos under spinnaker, and then enjoyed the cruising and inshore delights of the Algarve and Andalucía.

There is something for everyone along this varied 700 mile coastline, with opportunities for both gentle and demanding navigation, good food ashore and cultural high spots close inland. Galicia is excellent for a summer cruise or to explore at the start of a longer term voyage towards the Mediterranean or the Canaries and beyond. By the time a crew have reached Gibraltar they will have had ample opportunity to prove their preparedness and plenty of places to seek technical help if required.

Anne Hammick revised the fourth edition and I am grateful to her for again revising the whole coast from Foz do Minho to Gibraltar. I was happy to take on Galicia. Although much of the original work has stood the test of time, these are complicated waters and much busier than 20 years ago. In this edition we have restructured the book, made full use of excellent aerial photographs by Patrick Roach, and introduced more plans and waypoints. These are both to aid description of the pilotage aspects and for use as the skipper so decides – attention is drawn to the appropriate caution.

There has been much harbour development as one runs southwards from La Coruña, and Galicia in particular is seeing rapid change. Therefore, whilst we aim to issue updating supplements on the Imray website, we have also opened a photo library for this book at www.rccpf.org.uk. It currently includes additional photographs of harbours and anchorages in Galicia but our intention is to publish updating photographs sent in from yachtsmen on their travels. We expect that, in this age of digital cameras and easy communications, this will provide a more speedy updating opportunity in parallel with the official publications.

Martin Walker
Director
RCC Pilotage Foundation
March 2006

Acknowledgements

Galicia

This edition builds on the earlier work of Oz Robinson and Anne Hammick and I am grateful to her for passing on the Spanish *Avisos* and comments which she had received since the last edition was published in 2000. Notes were included from Mike Johnston, Jens and Ellen Barndorf, Ian and Judy Jenkins, JR Owen, Martin Farnworth, Pat and Pippa Purdy, Sally and John Milton, Kreale Talbot. All were valuable and I hope that fellow yachtsmen will continue to contribute in such a way.

I recced the whole coastline from El Ferrol to La Guardia, in August 2005, revisiting old haunts and discovering new opportunities. Prior to departure I had studied the detailed aerial photographs taken by Patrick Roach in 2004 – many of which appear in this book. They were invaluable in indicating major changes and new harbours, although such is the continuing pace of development that some of his photographs have been marked to show what has been happening in the subsequent 12 months. Marina staff were all most friendly, helpful and keen to answer my queries.

Also available to me were detailed notes made a few weeks before my visit by Roddy Innes as he cruised steadily south in his Rustler 36, *Jessamy*. He confirmed my memories of cruising the area, gave good tips on what was changing and who to talk to and provided a fund of photographs. He has been kind enough to let them be used both in this book and on the Pilotage Foundation website as additional material. I fear he and his crew spent much time visiting harbours obtaining information when a quiet anchorage may have been more appealing, but the book is the better for it.

Restructuring a book of this nature would not have been possible without the enthusiastic advice and cooperation of Willie Wilson who, with the rest of the team at Imray, continues to play such a valuable role in bringing pilot books to the cruising world. I thank them for their support and patience.

I hope those who use this book will enjoy Galicia, and onwards, as much as I did.

Martin Walker
RCC Pilotage Foundation
March 2006

Portugal and Andalucía

No book is ever a singlehanded effort, and acknowledgements generally centre on those people whose input has directly contributed to the contents of the volume in question. However, in this instance my primary thanks must go to my sister Liz. Had she not been willing to undertake far more than her share of the workload during a very difficult year of parental illness I would undoubtedly have had to pull out of this project long before it was completed.

Torn between family commitments and the demands of a book covering nearly 700 miles of very varied coastline, it was a relief to hand the updating of the entire Galicia section over to Martin Walker, Director of the Pilotage Foundation. I hope that the inevitable differences in our writing styles will not cause problems for the reader, and am confident that the skills of the Imray production team of Julia Knight (typesetting), Elaine Sharples, Debbie Stapleford and Chris Holley (plans) and Elinor Cole (page layouts) will have done much to smooth the passage. I would also like to thank Willie Wilson, MD of Imray Laurie Norie & Wilson Ltd, for his sympathetic and tactful advice on more than one occasion during the past year.

On a more traditional note – and in the realisation that someone will always, inevitably, be left out – I would particularly like to thank the following for taking the trouble to write or email me and/or the publishers with new or corrected information: Brian Alexander (*Captain's Lady*); Signe & Gaute Birkeland (*Pernoll*); Michelle & Jean Marie Boveroux (*Belinda*); Anna Brunyee (*Marguerite*); John Clow (*Capercaillie of Clyde*); Mike Dorsett (*White Princess*); Mike Dwyer (*Allegro III*); John & Suzanne Dyer (*Demara*); Andrew Edsor; Lisa Farrow-Gillespie (*Heartsong III*); Martin Farnworth (*Cinnabar of Dundee*); John & Fay Garey (*Subtle*); Yvonne Habermann & Bartek Schade (*Tadorna*); Michael & Sally Hadley of Nazaré; Dr Alan Hirsh; Dr Jörg Peter Hombusch (*Miriquidi*); Graham Hutt, Editor *North Africa*; Roddy Innes (*Jessamy*); Ian & Judy Jenkins (*Pen Azen*); Graham & Avril Johnson (*Dream Away*); Mike Johnston (*Arran Comrades*); Scott Kuhner (*Tamure*); Jackie & Chris Lambertsen (*Shibumi*); The late John Lawson, Editor *South Biscay*; Michael Lewin-Harris (*Natanis*); David Lumby, Viana do Castelo; John & Sally Melling (*Taraki*); Wolfgang Michalsky, El Rompido; Keith

Nethercot; Martin Northey, Albufeira; John Owen (*Tanna*); Mike Parkin (*Nina Tamara*); Peter Passano (*Sea Bear*); John Petch; Peter Poole (*Holly*); Kit Power (*Kwai Muli*); Alistair Pratt (*Copihue II*); François Salle, Portugal; Heidi & Lester Smith (*Tatsu*); Ray & Jo Staines (*Cegonha*); Major V Stevenson, RM (*Moonshadow*); Kneal Talbot (*Sally E*); Donald Tew (*Mary Helen*); Sue Thatcher (*Tamar Swallow*); Colin Thomas, Gibraltar; Nick Thomas (*Tokomaru 2*); Douglas Thomson (*Tomcat of Kip*) and finally David & Jackie (*Mary Kate*) whom I met in Puerto Gelves, Seville and whose surname I carelessly omitted to note down.

It hardly needs stating that feedback from fellow yachtsmen and women is an essential part of updating any cruising guide, and both the publishers and the editors are delighted to receive comments from those 'in the field'. If writing or emailing (contact details on the back cover) it is particularly helpful to include the size and type of one's vessel – or whether the visit was by land – and the month / year in question. If commenting on more than one place, it makes our job infinitely easier if the harbours are in book order and page referenced. Many thanks in anticipation!

Finally I would like to thank Mike Grubb, Willy Ker, John Power and Ros Hogbin for agreeing to proofread the Portugal and Andalucía sections at very short notice. All are highly experienced navigators in whom I have great confidence, but I should stress that their remit does not include checking hard facts – merely ensuring that what I have written makes sense, is unambiguous and that the text tallies with the plans and photographs. Any factual errors are my responsibility alone.

Anne Hammick
Falmouth, Cornwall
February 2006

Key to symbols used on the plans

	English	Portuguese	Spanish
	harbourmaster	*diretor do porto/capitania*	*capitán de puerto/capitanía*
	fuel (diesel, petrol)	*gasoleo, gasolina*	*gasoil, gasolina*
(25T)	travel-lift	*pórtico elevador*	*pórtico elevado*
	yacht club	*club náutico, club naval*	*club náutico*
	anchorage	*fundeadouro*	*fondeadero*
	visitors' moorings		*amarradero, ancladero*
	slipway	*carreira*	*varadero*

Introduction

The character of the Atlantic coasts of Spain and Portugal varies widely between the sheer cliffs north of Cabo Finisterre and the flat sandy lagoons of the Faro area. Their attraction for the cruising yachtsman is equally variable. The aim of this book is to indicate both the nature of the cruising grounds and harbours of the regions and how they may be approached. It does not pretend to be a comprehensive guide and should not be used without the appropriate charts. Excellent travel guides are available for crews who make time to explore this historic region.

Local place names are used except for a few cities and towns, such as Lisbon and Seville, which are widely known by their anglicised form. In Galicia the Gallego form of the name is generally given. Gallego, an ancient language which falls somewhere between Castilian Spanish and Portuguese, is still in everyday use; while away from major routes, road signs rarely use Castilian Spanish. Other non-English words used will be found in the glossary.

Gibraltar is included in this book as it remains an important refuge or staging post for those bound for the Mediterranean or heading south towards the Canaries and beyond.

The cruising grounds

In cruising terms, the Atlantic coast of Spain and Portugal falls naturally into three regions:

Galicia The Rías Altas between El Ferrol and Cabo Finisterre and the Rías Bajas from Finisterre to the Portuguese border at the Rio Miño – Part I.

The Portuguese coast from the Spanish border south to Cabo de São Vicente – Part II.

The eastward trending coast from Cabo de São Vicente to Gibraltar, (in Portugal the Algarve and in Spain part of Andalucía) – Part III.

Galicia

Rías Altas

Of all the regions, this is the one most exposed to the Atlantic climate. It also has a dramatic coastline, especially in the west and the individual rias are suited to day sailing. In fine summer weather the cruise from La Coruña round to Finisterre calling at the Rías de Corme and de Camariñas is an interesting and pleasant sail, but in stormy conditions the coast is one to avoid – not for nothing is it known locally as the Costa del Morte (Coast of Death). With the exception of La Coruña, which has pretty well everything necessary for the yachtsman (as has nearby Sada Marina) plus a long and distinguished history, the small harbours of the Rías Altas have limited facilities for yachts, but they are well set in striking surroundings.

Rías bajas

Some consider the Rías Bajas to be the best cruising area of all and spend weeks pottering about the ports and anchorages, taking advantage of good communications and safe harbours and marinas to explore Galicia (and in particular to visit Santiago de Compostela). Less exposed to the Atlantic weather than the Rías Altas, the great inlets have beaches, interesting towns, and opportunities for rock-hopping for those wishing to test their pilotage. There are many restaurants and hotels, while excellent Atlantic fish and local shellfish are readily available.

The region suffers more from fog than the Rías Altas, yet the Azores high pressure system can on occasion produce a clear weather northeasterly blow of Force 5–6 which may last for several days – but there is always shelter to be found within a short distance.

Atlantic Portugal

This coast is not a cruising man's paradise but it includes some remarkable places to visit, notably Porto and Lisbon for their history, and Aveiro and the Rio Sado for their sandbanks and swamps. The coast itself is on the whole low – the hills are inland and in summer may be lost in the haze – and in places there are miles of featureless beach.

The harbours are commercial or fishing in origin, but most are making increasing concessions to yachts. Many have hazards of one sort or another in the entrance; Leixões and Sines are notable exceptions. The most common is a bar which alters with the winter storms and which, although safe enough for freighters, can be dangerous for the smaller vessel if there is a swell running – and be worse if it is running across the tidal stream. The bars are associated with rivers and conditions are generally worse on the ebb.

Another major feature of this region is the Portuguese trade winds. Many take advantage of these prevailing northerly winds to slide south past the coast as quickly as possible. Making the passage northwards is tedious even in summer.

Algarve and Andalucía

The southern coasts of Portugal and Spain offer easier cruising than the Portuguese/Atlantic margin. Having rounded the corner at Cabo de São Vicente, the influences of the Mediterranean and the Moor begin to show. Harbours are generally more frequent and better equipped and, with a couple of exceptions, are easier to enter than those on the Atlantic coast.

The Algarve is crowded, both summer and winter, and its harbours busy. The shallow lagoons of Faro and Olhão, the quiet Río Guadiana and the relatively busy Río Guadalquivir, are the best areas for wildlife.

A particular hazard of this coast is the tunny net, which can stretch several miles out to sea at right angles to the shoreline, and is strong enough to foul the propeller of a small coaster. Currently five or six are set annually. Details and locations are given in the text.

Overall passage planning

A passage planning guide providing an overview of the route (Route 7) from the English Channel to Gibraltar is available at www.rccpf.org.uk.

Sailing and navigation

Winds and climate

Weather systems

The northern part of the region is influenced by North Atlantic weather systems. In winter, fronts and occasionally secondary depressions may cross the area. Winds are variable but those between southwest and northwest are more common. In summer, land and sea breezes can be expected inshore but the influence of the Azores Highs tends to produce winds from the north; this northerly tendency starts about April and as summer progresses and latitude decreases these winds develop into the Portuguese trades. At the height of summer in the south of the region, the Portuguese trades remain dominant offshore west of 20°W, while eastwards their influence is felt along the coast from São Vicente towards Faro, often reinforced in the afternoons by the land effect. This influence wanes until, by Cádiz, summer afternoons may produce a westerly sea breeze. Cádiz can also be affected by a *levante* coming out of the Mediterranean. Towards the Strait of Gibraltar the winds tend to be either easterly or westerly, the former more common in summer and the latter in winter.

Gales

Gales are rare in the summer. The better known are the *levante* and *poniente*, the easterly and westerly gales of the Strait of Gibraltar, and the *nordeste pardo*, a cloudy northeaster of the Finisterre area. In theory the *vendavale*, a southwesterly blow in Galicia, is unlikely to occur in summer but exceptions do occur. Tarifa, protruding into the Strait of Gibraltar, will frequently experience very strong local winds and yachts should be prepared for this.

Rainfall

Galicia is the wet corner of Spain – it has much the same climatic feel as southwest England. To the south, whilst winters may be like June in the English Channel, in summer rainfall decreases and temperatures rise until, around Cádiz, Mediterranean levels are reached.

Fog

Sea temperatures in summer range from 17°C in Galicia to 21° at Gibraltar, and in winter from 12° to 14°. The chances of coastal fog along the west coast of the peninsula are greatest in July and August when incidence may rise as high as one day in ten. In the larger rias of southern Galicia it occasionally lasts for a week at a stretch in summer. It is much rarer along the southwest coast.

Currents and tides

Currents

Currents are much affected by recent winds and may set in any direction. The trend along the Atlantic coast is from north to south, though north of Finisterre there can be an easterly set into the Bay of Biscay. East of São Vicente the upper layers of the sea re-supply the Mediterranean with water lost through evaporation. The current sets towards the Strait at about 0.5 knot at the western end, increasing to around 2 knots through the Strait itself, to which a tidal element may have to be added – see page 302–4. However, prolonged easterly winds can produce a reverse current, which is said to set into the bays as far west as São Vicente.

Tidal streams

Information on tidal streams is confusing. Off the Rías Bajas the flood is supposed to run north and off Peniche, in Portugal, to the southeast. The only reasonably safe assumption is that the flood tide sets into the Galician rias and the ebb drains them. The same is generally true of a Portuguese rio, but this is less than a certainty and depends on the amount of water coming down the rio itself. The Rio Douro is a particular example of this. In the Strait of Gibraltar, tidal streams can exceed 3 knots at springs.

Tide times

The standard ports for the area are La Coruña, Lisbon, Cádiz and Gibraltar and quoted time and height differences for other harbours are related to them. An excellent source of tidal information for those with internet access is the UK Hydrographic Office's user-friendly (and free) Easytide programme at www.ukho.gov.uk which gives daily tidal data for almost all major harbours and many minor ones.

	La Coruña	Vigo	Lisbon	Faro	Cádiz	Gibraltar
Springs	3.3	2.9	3.3	2.8	2.8	0.9
Neaps	1.3	1.4	1.6	1.2	1.3	0.4

Lights and buoyage

All buoys and lights in this area adhere to the IALA A system, based on the direction of the main flood tide. In Portugal and Spain, heights of lights are measured from mean sea level. They therefore generally appear in Iberian publications as a metre or so higher than in British Admiralty publications.

The four-figure international numbering system has been used to identify lights in text and on plans. In addition to being shown on the plans, details of the main leading lights and, in Galicia, the outer breakwater light are given in the text. All bearings are given from seaward and refer to true north.

Charts

Current British Admiralty information is largely obtained from Spanish and Portuguese sources. The Spanish and Portuguese Hydrographic Offices issue their own charts (often to a much larger scale than Admiralty coverage and corrected by their own *Notices*) but they can be difficult to obtain outside the peninsula. *Notices to Mariners* to update Admiralty charts will be found on www.ukho.gov.uk; the Spanish and Portuguese equivalents – *Avisos* – on www.armada.mde.es/ihm and www.hidrografico.pt/hidrografico respectively.

A full list of charts – Admiralty, Spanish, Portuguese and Imray – will be found in Appendix I but note that the Portuguese Instituto Hidrográfico tends to announce new charts up to three years before they are published; where this is the case the new number is given in brackets.

Before departure Spanish and Portuguese charts (as well as fully corrected Admiralty publications) can be obtained through

Imray Laurie Norie & Wilson Ltd,
Wych House, The Broadway, St Ives,
Huntingdon, Cambs PE27 5BT
☎ 01480 462114 *Fax* 01480 496109
www.imray.com

In Spain Spanish charts can be ordered from

Instituto Hidrográfico de la Marina,
Plaza de San Severiano 3, DP 11007 Cádiz
☎ 956 599409 *Fax* 956 599396

In Galicia there are Spanish chart agents in La Coruña, Vilagarcía de Arosa and Vigo; in Andalucía in Huelva, Seville, Cádiz and Algeciras. A few marina offices are also willing to order charts for visiting yachts.

In Portugal only two companies, both in Lisbon, sell charts. Full contact details are given in the Facilities section for Lisbon.

In Gibraltar fully corrected Admiralty charts and other publication are available from the Gibraltar Chart Agency, and YachtScene Publications are official agents for Spanish charts – contact details are given under Gibraltar.

Horizontal chart datum and satellite derived positions

An increasing number of charts are now based on WGS84 datum and this is used for all positions in this book. However, most Portuguese charts are still to be converted and navigators are advised to check the chart datum if plotting satellite derived data. Harbour positions have been checked using GPS to WGS84 but Waypoints have not been verified at sea. They have been derived from current charts, including *C-Map NT+*, and are offered as an aid to rapid orientation within the book as well as a contribution to safe navigation. They are not intended to replace normal planning or visual observation; unless specifically stated in the text, none should be linked to form routes without verification that it is safe to do so. The full list of waypoints forms Appendix II.

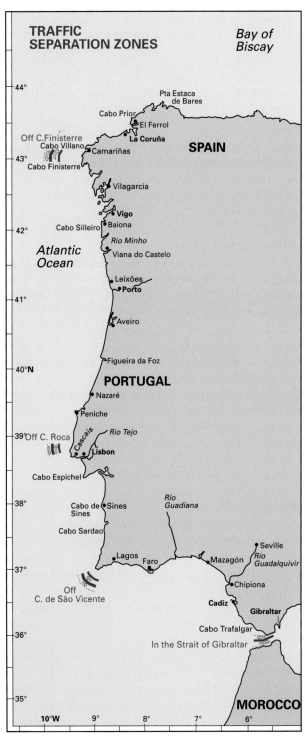

Magnetic variation

In 2006 the magnetic variation down the Atlantic coast was 5°W±30' reducing to 3°W on the approach to Gibraltar.

Traffic Separation Zones

Traffic Separation Zones exist off Cabo Finisterre, on the approaches to Ría de Vigo, off Cabo da Roca, off Cabo de São Vicente and in the Strait of Gibraltar. Each has a wide Inshore Traffic Zone and yachts are strongly advised to avoid crossing the main shipping lanes if at all possible.

Visual harbour signals

Although in theory both Spain and Portugal still use visual signals to indicate whether a harbour is safe to enter, in relatively few cases do they appear to be used. It must be remembered that signals indicating the state of a harbour bar are intended for commercial traffic, and that conditions deemed safe for a big ship are not necessarily safe for a yacht.

Time

Spain keeps Standard Euro Time (UT+1), advanced one hour in summer to UT+2, while Portugal keeps UT, advanced one hour in summer to UT+1. (effectively the same as BST). It is particularly important to allow for this difference when using tidal data based on Lisbon in the Spanish *rías bajas*.

Nomenclature

Two likely pitfalls for the unwary English speaker in Iberia are the words 'marina' and 'yacht'. In both Spain and Portugal *marina* or *marinha* implies simply 'marine' (as in *marina mercante* – merchant navy) and does not necessarily imply a purpose-built yacht harbour which, unless it is unusually large and has all facilities, is more likely to be designated a *puerto deportivo* in Spain, and either *porto desportivo* or *doca de recreio* in Portugal. Similarly, the description 'yacht' is usually taken to mean a good-sized motorboat, particularly in the south. A sailing boat of whatever size is a *barco de vela* or, in Portugal, a *barco à vela*.

Google Earth

The Google Earth satellite photographs of this area are somewhat dated, and generally of low definition, but the images available provide an interesting overview of the area.

Coast radio stations

Details of coast radio stations will be found in the Admiralty Leisure publication *NP 289* and in the text. Locations are shown on the plan below, outstations are controlled by La Coruña, Lisboa and Malaga. On receipt of traffic, Spanish coast radio stations will call vessels once on Ch16; after that the vessel's call-sign will be included in scheduled MF traffic lists.

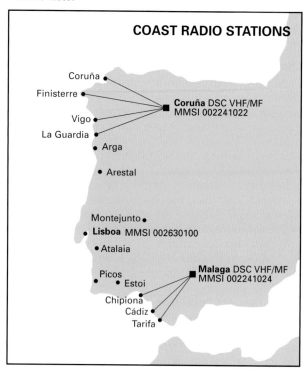

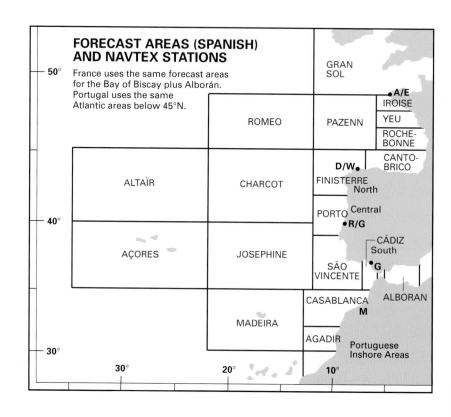

Navtex Schedules 518kHz		* Weather Bulletins
A	Corsen	0000*, 0400, 0800, 1200*, 1600, 2000
D	Coruña	0030, 0430, 0830*, 1230, 1630, 2030*
R	Monsanto	0250*, 0650*, 1050*, 1450*, 1850*, 2250*
G	Tarifa	0100, 0500, 0900*, 1300, 1700, 2100*
M	Casablanca (proposed)	

Navtex on 490kHz

E	Corsen	in French
W	Coruña	in Spanish
G	Monsanto	in Portuguese

Poor reception may be a problem in the Galician rias or in harbours throughout the area.

GALICIA *Radio Weather Bulletins* and *Navigational Warnings*

Coruña Finisterre	1698kHz and 1764kHz	0703*, 1303*, 1903*
Coruña	VHF Ch 26	0840*, 1240*, 2010*
Coruña MRSC	VHF Ch 10	0005*, 0205, 0405*, 0605 0805*, 1005, 1205*, 1405 1605*, 1805, 2005*, 2205
Finisterre	VHF Ch 22	0840*, 1240*, 2010*
Finisterre MRCC	VHF Ch 11	0033, 0233*, 0433, 0633* 0833, 1033*, 1233, 1433* 1633, 1833*, 2033, 2233*
Vigo	VHF Ch 65	0840*, 1240*, 2010*
Vigo MRSC	VHF Ch 10	0015*, 0215, 0415*, 0615 0815*, 1015, 1215*, 1415 1615*, 1815 2015*, 2215
La Guardia	VHF Ch 21	0840*, 1240*, 2040*

PORTUGAL *Radio Weather Bulletins and Navigational Warnings*

Portugal coastal waters up to 20M offshore are in three zones:

Zona Norte	Rio Minho to Cabo Carvoeiro (40°N)
Zona Centro	Cabo Carvoeiro to Cabo São Vicente
Zona Sul	Cabo São Vicente to Rio Guadiana

Forecasts and navigational warnings: in Portuguese and English

RT(MF)	2657kHz	0905, 2105
VHF	Ch 11	0705, 0905, 1905, 2105 Norte & Centro 0805, 0905, 2005, 2105 Centro & Sul

ANDALUCIA *Radio Weather Bulletin* and *Navigational Warnings*

Huelva MRSC	VHF Ch 10	0315*, 0515*, 0715*, 1115*, 1515*, 1915*, 2315*
Chipiona Tarifa	1656kHz and 1704 kHz	0733*, 1233*, 1933*
Cádiz	VHF Ch 26	0833* 1133*, 2003, 2033*
Tarifa	VHF Ch 81	0733*, 0833, 1233* 1933*, 2003*
Tarifa MRCC	VHF Ch 10, 67	Ev Hrs +15* On Receipt
Algeciras MRSC	VHF Ch 74	0315*, 0515*, 0715*, 1115*, 1515*, 1915*, 2314*

Weather forecasts

It should be noted that although marinas generally display weather information, yachts may find difficulty receiving official forecasts when in harbour or anchored in quiet bays. Yachts heading for the Mediterranean may later find that reception there can be erratic. Attention is therefore drawn to the use of weatherfax and RTTY messages from DWD and the usefulness of GRIB files.

Navtex Stations and forecast areas

(Spanish areas are shown on the diagram opposite) France uses the same forecast areas for the Bay of Biscay plus Alborán.

Portugal uses the same Atlantic areas below 45°N.

Weatherfax and RTTY

Northwood (RN) broadcasts a full set of UK Met Office charts out to 5 days ahead on 2618.5,4610,8040 and 11086.5kHz. (Schedule at 0236, surface analysis at 3 hourly intervals from 0300 to 2100 and 2300.)

Deutscher Wetterdienst broadcasts German weather charts on 3855,7880,13882.5kHz. (Schedule at 1111, surface analysis at 0430, 1050,1600,2200.)

DWD broadcasts forecasts using RTTY on 4583, 7646, and 10001.8kHz (in English at 0955 and 2155) 11039 and 14467.3kHz (in German at 0820, 1429, 2020). Alternatively, a dedicated receiver will record automatically – see 'weatherman' on www.nasamarine.com

Inmarsat

Broadcast times for weather for METAREA III are 1000 and 2200.

GRIB

This service enables arrow diagram forecasts for up to 5 days ahead, and other information, to be obtained in email form (or by marine HF and HAM radio). The data are highly compressed so that a great deal of information can be acquired quickly, even using a mobile phone connected to laptop. For details of one popular service email query@saildoc.com subject 'any'.

Gibraltar weather forecasts – VHF (FM)

LT	BFBS 1			BFBS2	Gibraltar BC		
	Mon-Fri	Sat	Sun	Mon-Fri	Mon-Fri	Sat	Sun
0530					X	X	
0630					X	X	X
0730					X	X	X
0745	X						
0845	X	X	X				
0945		X	X				
1005	X						
1030					X		
1200				X			
1202		X	X				
1230					X	X	X
1602		X					
1605	X						

Also storm warnings on receipt
			1438 AM
	93.5 FM	89.4 FM	91.3 FM
	97.8 FM	99.5 FM	92.6 FM

Includes high and low water times   100.5 FM

Weather forecasts on the Internet

Excellent weather-related information can be found on the internet. As sites change and new ones come on stream, skippers are urged to use the internet as a supplementary source of information and to ensure that official forecasts can be obtained on board.

As a good start try www.franksingleton.clara.net as well as:

UK Met Office	www.metoffice.com
Spanish Met Office	www.inm.es/
Portuguese Met Office	www.meteo.pt
US National Weather Service	www.noaa.gov/
Yahoo! Weather	www.yahoo.com

Weather forecasts ashore or by telephone

Nearly all marina offices display a weather forecast and synoptic chart(s), usually updated daily; though often in the local language the vocabulary is limited and can easily be deciphered.

For a more general indication of trends try the weather map in a local newspaper e.g. *El País, Voz de Galicia* or *El Correo Galicia* (Spain) or *Jornal de Notícias or Público* (Portugal).

In Spain, recorded marine weather bulletins are provided by the Instituto Nacional de Meteorología for Galicia and the north coast, and Andalucía and beyond. The service is only available within the country, but can be accessed by vessels equipped with Autolink. The bulletin is read in Spanish.

Galicia ☎ 906 365 372
High seas bulletin for Finisterre, etc.
Coastal waters bulletin for the coasts of Coruña and Pontevedra, etc.

Andalucía ☎ 906 365 373
High seas bulletin for São Vicente, Cádiz, etc.
Coastal waters bulletin for the coasts of Huelva, Cádiz, Ceuta, etc.

Spanish television shows a useful synoptic chart with its land weather forecast every evening after the news at about 2120 weekdays, 1520 Saturday and 2020 Sunday.

In Portugal, recorded marine weather bulletins are available, in Portuguese, on the following numbers:

Spanish border to Lisbon
Inshore ☎ 0601 123 123 Offshore ☎ 0601 123 140

Lisbon to Cabo de São Vicente
Inshore ☎ 0601 123 124 Offshore ☎ 0601 123 141

Cabo de São Vicente to the Spanish border
Inshore ☎ 0601 123 125 Offshore ☎ 0601 123 142.

Weather forecasts by radio

A variety of weather forecasts are available by radio, though relatively few in English. It should be noted that all times quoted for weather messages, navigational warnings and traffic lists are in Universal Time (UT) unless otherwise stated. This contrasts with harbour and marina radio schedules, which are generally governed by office hours and are therefore given in Local Time (LT).

BBC Radio 4

Shipping forecasts are broadcast on 198kHz (1515m) at 0048, 0520, 1201 and 1754 UK local time (BST in summer, UT in winter). The relevant areas are Biscay, Fitzroy and Trafalgar but the latter is only included in the 0048 forecast. While undoubtedly useful, particularly in Galicia, the areas covered are large, reception may be difficult and forecasts may have little relevance to local conditions.

Radio France International

Weather information is broadcast at 1140 UT daily, (timed to fit the vagaries of programming and therefore not always punctual). The following receiving frequencies vary according to location: English Channel and Bay of Biscay 6175kHz; North Atlantic east of 50°W 11700, 15530, 17575kHz. Although in French, the format is straightforward: gale warnings, synopsis, development and 24 hour area forecasts.

Radio Nacional de España

Weather information is broadcast at 1000 and 1300 LT via from: La Coruña 639kHz; Seville 684kHz.

Sociedad España de Radio

A programme containing information for commercial fishing operations, plus weather forecasts and sea conditions, is broadcast between 0600 and 0700 LT and again in condensed form at 2205 LT from: La Coruña 1080kHz; Vigo 1026kHz; Huelva 100.5MHz; Cádiz 1485kHz; Seville 792kHz.

Radiodifusão Portuguesa

Broadcasts a forecast for the coastal waters of Portugal at 1100 daily on the following frequencies: 650kHz, 666kHz, 720kHz, 1287kHz, 94.7MHz, 96.4MHz, 97.6MHz, 97.9MHz.

Practicalities

Entry and regulations

Under EU regulations, EU registered boats arriving in another EU country are not required to fly the Q flag unless they have come directly from a non-EU country (which could be Gibraltar), have non-EU nationals aboard, or are carrying dutiable goods. Yachts registered outside the EU should always fly the Q flag on arrival. All visiting yachts should fly the relevant national courtesy flag.

Spain

On first arrival in the country check with immigration, most easily done via a yacht club or marina office. Ship's papers, insurance documents and passports should be to hand. It is also a requirment that at least one member of the crew has a VHF radio operator's certificate. At subsequent ports it is not necessary to seek out officialdom, though one may occasionally be approached for information. This relaxed attitude is more noticeable in Galicia than Andalucía, where smuggling is more common and there is greater public awareness of Gibraltar as a political issue. It should be noted that Spain requires all vessels over 6m to carry proof of third party insurance in Spanish. UK marine insurers are aware of this and will provide the appropriate certificate free of charge on request. Skippers should be aware that differing initial length of stay and visa requirements apply according to crew nationalities and also that anyone staying in Spain for more than 183 days in any 12-month period is liable to Spanish tax legislation. A note on this, and VAT, is included in Appendix V. Officials may not recognize time spent in Gibraltar as being out of Spain.

Portugal

As of 2005, yachtsmen were still required, in theory, to notify the authorities on arrival in every harbour, whether entering Portugal for the first time or from elsewhere within it – and to do so immediately upon coming ashore. This should not present problems at one of the increasing number of marinas. In general, produce passports, ship's papers (including proof of VAT status and insurance documents) complete a *Movimento de Embarcacoes de Recreio* form and state an intended departure date. In most harbours there is no requirement for formal outward clearance. Skippers should also carry an International Certificate of Competence or equivalent. In UK this is administered by the Royal Yachting Association www.rya.org.uk/cruising or email cruising@rya.org.uk. At Least one crew member must have a VHF operator's certificate.There is no limitation on length of stay for a VAT paid or exempt yacht. However, visiting yachts spending more than 183 day a year in Portugal are liable to tax (see pages 118 and 204 for details).

Gibraltar

Although Gibraltar is a British Territory, it is not part of the EU. Fly the Q Flag on approach and clear customs at marinas. See page 316 for details.

Day signals / anchor lights

Over the past few years, a number of skippers in both Spanish and Portuguese waters have faced an on the spot fine for not displaying a black ball or white light when at anchor and a cone when motor sailing (€40 at last report). Yachts have also been fined for not flying a courtesy flag.

Drugs

Drug running is a serious problem along the entire Iberian coast. The authorities may board yachts at any time, including on passage, though normally this is confined to 'interesting' yachts, with the names of others merely being noted down. In both countries, yachtsmen are asked to inform the authorities of any yacht that merits a particular interest – and presumably of any other goings-on which appear suspicious.

Laying up

Yachts can safely be left afloat, whether laid up or over-wintering, in most of the larger marinas described. It should be clear from the text when this is not the case.

Facilities, chandlery and repairs

In Galicia, the facilities for yachts are extensive, travel lifts frequent and good English is spoken in at least one marina per ría. Facilities are therefore not listed in detail here, but they are in a most useful publication *Galicia Sailing Facilities* available at major marinas or downloadable from www.turgalicia.es. In the Portugal and Andalucía sections in the text.

Chandleries

Well-stocked yachting chandleries are not always easy to find in either Spain or Portugal, and by no means all marinas have one on site. Amongst the best are those at Sada, La Coruña, Vilagarcía de Arosa, Vigo and Baiona (Galicia). Viana do Castelo, Leixões, Cascais and Lisbon (Atlantic Portugal) Lagos, Portimão and Vilamoura (Algarve); Isla Christina, Punta Umbria, Chipiona, Seville, Puerto Sherry and Barbate (Andalucía). Gibraltar's chandleries are some of the best in Iberia, as well as being duty-free. Basic boat tackle is more widely available.

Repairs

There are numerous boatyards throughout all the regions, mainly geared to fishing and other commercial vessels but able to do basic work on yachts. However, for major repairs or other work reportedly good yards are currently located at Sada, Vilagarcía de Arosa and Vigo (Galicia); Lisbon and Seixal (Atlantic Portugal); Lagos, Portimõa and Vilamoura (Algarve); El Rompido, Seville (Puerto Gelves) and Puerto Sherry (Andalucía); and, of course, Gibraltar. Note that if taking expensive electrical or mechanical equipment ashore for repair, particularly in Portugal, it is wise to first inform the *GNR–Brigada Fiscal*. Possession of a receipt will confirm that the equipment was bought elsewhere. With the availability of cheap flights it might be preferable to fly back to one's own country rather than attempt to deal with repairs by post.

Fuel

Diesel is widely available (except to yachts visiting fishing harbours); petrol rather less so. In both countries fishermen have access to diesel at a lower rate of tax than do yachtsmen, but whereas in Spain this invariably means two separate pumps, in Portugal it all comes out of the same pump – simply at a different price. Fuel supplies are generally clean, but it can do no harm to filter all fuel taken aboard as a matter of course. Credit cards are generally – but not always – accepted when paying for fuel and it is essential to confirm the local situation before going ahead.

Standard grade paraffin (*parafina*) is virtually unobtainable in much of Spain, though the more expensive medicinal grade is stocked by most pharmacies. In Portugal *petróleo para iluminãçao* (lamp oil) is widely available.

Drinking water

Water is available at all marinas and on many fuelling pontoons. It is usually included in the price of berthing. In those harbours where a piped supply is not available for yachts, a public tap can generally be found, when a good supply of 5 or 10-litre plastic cans will be useful. Though water quality throughout the peninsula is generally good, bottled water is widely available.

Bottled gas

Camping Gaz exchanges are widely available, usually from *ferreterías* (ironmongers), filling stations or supermarkets – in 2·7kg bottles identical to those used in the UK.

Getting other cylinders refilled is much more of a problem, particularly if the cylinder is more than five years old. Boats heading south for extended cruising might consider carrying the appropriate adaptor and regulator and buying local gas on arrival in Spain or elsewhere.

Calor Gas dealers in the UK can advise on installations and supply the necessary parts. Contact

Southampton Calor Gas Centre Ltd, Third Avenue, Millbrook Trading Estate, Southampton SO15 0JX
☎ 02380 788155 *Fax* 02380 774768
email socal@tcp.co.uk
www.calorgas.co.uk

Also useful is their free leaflet *LPG (Bottled Gas) for Marine Use.*

Electricity

Electricity is available on nearly all marina pontoons, generally via standard marina sockets, although adaptors should be carried to cope with the European domestic type socket. Mains electricity is 220 volt 50Hz; yachts equipped with 110 volt 60Hz equipment will require a transformer. (These are best bought before arrival; they are readily obtainable from builders merchants in UK.)

Holding Tanks

Since 2004 it has been compulsory for Spanish flagged vessels to fit holding tanks. Although pump-out facilities are still rare there is a determination to protect the water quality for both the fishing and tourist industries. Skippers should be aware that Spanish legislation on prevention of sewage does not permit sewage to be discharged in port areas, protected zones, rivers, or bays. Crumbled and disinfected sewage may be discharged from 4 miles off shore by vessels exceeding 4 knots.

Marina charges

It is not practicable to list the varying rates at all the different marinas and harbours. An indication is given for Galicia in Appendix VI and for Portugal to Gibraltar within the text.

Charges will often be based on length x beam and skippers should carry documentation which records both of these (SSR documentation does not).

Marina office hours (local time)

In Spain (both Galicia and Andalucía) it is normal for marina offices to be closed during the siesta period, any time between 1200 and 1700, though seldom for as long as this. In Portugal a shorter lunch break – often from 1230 until 1400 – is the norm. While the majority of marinas have 24-hour security, most offices are closed overnight, sometimes from as early as 1800.

While this latter can cause problems when wishing to leave, a firmly locked office is more likely to disrupt things on first arrival, particularly if an electronic card is needed to open an access gate to the pontoons. In Portugal, where marina offices are increasingly handling clearance procedures, it can also frustrate a quick shopping trip into town or a well-deserved meal ashore.

Sometimes security guards have authority to issue pass cards, often they do not. There is no guarantee that a guard will re-admit an unknown yachtsman to the marina pontoons, particularly if not carrying the yacht's papers and a passport or other identity document.

Security

Crime afloat is not a major problem in most areas. It is sensible to take much the same precautions as at home – to lock up if leaving the yacht unattended, to padlock the outboard to the dinghy, and to secure the dinghy (particularly if an inflatable) with chain or wire rather than line, both to the yacht and when left ashore.

General and nautical information

Embassies, consulates and national tourist offices are listed in Appendix IV.

A useful website on Spain is:
www.DocuWeb.ca/Si/Spain

Sailors should be aware of the excellent information available on, or linked through www.noonsite.com www.cruising-association.com and, for Galicia, www.turgalicia.es

Websites relevant to Portugal and Andalucía are listed in Appendix VII.

Medical

No inoculations are required before visiting either Spain or Portugal. Minor ailments may best be treated by consulting a *farmacía* (often able to dispense drugs which in some other countries would be on prescription), or by contact with an English-speaking doctor established via the *farmacía*, marina office, tourist office or possibly a hotel. In Spain the emergency telephone number is 091; in Portugal it is 112.

All EU nationals should carry a European Health Insurance Card issued in the UK by the Department of Health ☎ 0845 606 2030, www.dh.gov.uk/travellers. This entitles one to free medical treatment under reciprocal agreements with the National Health Service. Private medical treatment is likely to be available but may be expensive.

Money

The unit of currency is the Euro. Major credit cards are widely used although it is wise to check this particularly before refuelling. Bank hours are normally 0830 to 1400 Mondays to Fridays with a few also open 0830 to 1300 on Saturdays; most banks have ATMs.

Mail

Nearly all marinas are willing to hold mail for visiting yachts but it is wise to check first. All mail should be clearly labelled with both the name of the recipient and the yacht, but avoiding honorifics such as Esq, which may cause confusion and misfiling. In Portugal it is technically illegal for uncollected mail to be held for more than five days without being returned, though most marinas will stretch this period. Far better to address an outer envelope directly to the marina office, with a short covering note asking for the envelope enclosed to be held pending the yacht's arrival.

Letters also may be sent *Poste Restante* to any post office in either country, though again they are likely to be returned if not collected promptly. In Spain they should be addressed with the surname of the recipient followed by *Lista de Correos* and the town and province. In Portugal, *Posta Restante* is used, and the collection counter labelled *Encomendas*. A passport is likely to be needed on collection. Post Offices are signed: in Spain PTT on a yellow background, in Portugal postal services are indicated by *Correios* on a red background

Telephones

Telephone kiosks are common, both local and international, and most carry instructions in English. The majority use phonecards (widely available from post offices, newsagents and tobacconists), though coin-operated kiosks can also be found. Country code numbers are: Spain +34, Portugal +351, Gibraltar +350 (Gibraltar from Spain 9567).

Fax and email

Nearly all marinas have fax machines and will send and receive faxes for visiting yachts. A small charge is usually made. Internet connection facilities are becoming more widespread. Telephone and Fax numbers as well as email addresses and websites are listed for each harbour or marina.

Transport

In both Spain and Portugal almost every community has some form of public transport, if only one bus a day. Local buses and trains can provide a view of the interior not otherwise available without hiring a car, although the latter offer good value and the road network in Galicia is very good.

There are rail connections to El Ferrol, La Coruña, Pontevedra, Vigo, Porto, Lisbon, Lagos, Faro, Tavira, Vila Real de Santo António, Huelva, Seville, Cádiz and Algeciras. Other towns may be served by branch lines. Long distance coaches are also popular, and on a par with the railways for cost.

International airports serve La Coruña, Santiago de Compostela, Vigo, Porto, Lisbon, Faro, Seville, Jerez de la Frontera and Gibraltar. Recent years have seen a rapid increase in the availability of low cost flights.

National holidays and fiestas

Fiestas are extremely popular throughout both Spain and Portugal, often celebrating the local saint's day or some historical event. Some local *fiestas* occurring during the sailing season are mentioned in the text.

Spain

1 January	New Year's Day
6 January	Epiphany
	Good Friday
	Easter Monday
1 May	May Day/Labour Day
(early/mid June)	Corpus Christi
24 June	Día de San Juan (the King's name saint)
25 July	Día de Santiago (celebrated throughout Northwest Spain as 'Galicia Day')
15 August	Feast of the Assumption
12 October	National Day
1 November	All Saints' Day
6 December	Constitution Day
8 December	Immaculate Conception
25 December	Christmas Day

When a national holiday falls on a Sunday, the autonomous region may either celebrate it the following day or use it to celebrate a regional festival.

Portugal

1 January	New Year's Day
	Good Friday
25 April	National or Libertyl Day
1 May	Labour Day
(early/mid June)	Corpus Christi
10 June	Portugal Day (Camões Day)
15 August	Feast of the Assumption
5 October	Republic Day
1 November	All Saints' Day
1 December	Restoration of Independence Day
8 December	Feast of the Immaculate Conception
25 December	Christmas Day

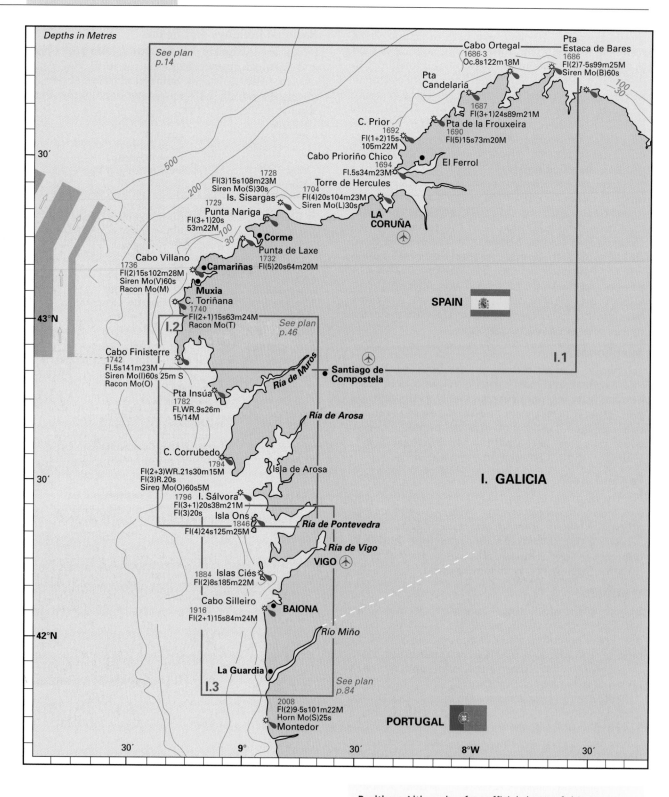

Depths in Metres

See plan p.14

Cabo Ortegal
1686·3
Oc.8s122m18M

Pta Estaca de Bares
1686
Fl(2)7·5s99m25M
Siren Mo(B)60s

Pta Candelaria
1687
Fl(3+1)24s89m21M

C. Prior
1692
Fl(1+2)15s
105m22M

Pta de la Frouxeira
1690
Fl(5)15s73m20M

Cabo Prioriño Chico
1694
Fl.5s34m23M

El Ferrol

1728
Fl(3)15s108m23M
Siren Mo(S)30s

Is. Sisargas

Torre de Hercules
1704
Fl(4)20s104m23M
Siren Mo(L)30s

LA CORUÑA

1729
Punta Nariga
Fl(3+1)20s
53m22M

Corme

Punta de Laxe
1732
Fl(5)20s64m20M

Cabo Villano
1736
Fl(2)15s102m28M
Siren Mo(V)60s
Racon Mo(M)

Camariñas

Muxia
C. Toriñana
1740
Fl(2+1)15s63m24M
Racon Mo(T)

SPAIN

I.2

See plan p.46

I.1

Cabo Finisterre
1742
Fl.5s141m23M
Siren Mo(I)60s 25m S
Racon Mo(O)

Pta Insúa
1782
Fl.WR.9s26m
15/14M

Ría de Muros

Santiago de Compostela

Ría de Arosa

C. Corrubedo
1794
Fl(2+3)WR.21s30m15M
Fl(3)R.20s
Siren Mo(O)60s5M

Isla de Arosa

I. GALICIA

1796 I. Sálvora
Fl(3+1)20s38m21M
Fl(3)20s

Isla Ons
1846
Fl(4)24s125m25M

Ría de Pontevedra

Ría de Vigo

VIGO

1884 Islas Cíes
Fl(2)8s185m22M

Cabo Silleiro
1916
Fl(2+1)15s84m24M

BAIONA

Río Miño

La Guardia

I.3

See plan p.84

2008
Fl(2)9·5s101m22M
Horn Mo(S)25s
Montedor

PORTUGAL

30' 9° 30' 8°W 30'

43°N 30' 42°N 30'

Photos on page 11 (MW)
Top Torre de Hercules at La Coruña
Middle left Wonderfully fresh sea food in Combarro
Right Granaries on stilts (*horreos*) at Combarro
Bottom left Typical ria fishing boat at Freixo
Right Daymark and main anchorage at Islas Cíes

Positions Although a few official charts of this area have yet to be converted from Datum ED50, skippers should note that all positions in this book are to WGS84. All were derived using C-Map electronic charts and Admiralty charts. Harbour positions have been verified using a handheld GPS. Waypoints have not been verified at sea. They have been included to help with planning and orientation. Much of this coast demands visual pilotage and skippers must satisfy themselves that it is safe to sail directly between any two waypoints.

I. Galicia
La Coruña to the Portuguese border

GALICIA

La Coruña to the Portuguese border

The *Rías Altas* and *Rías Bajas* of Galicia offer varied cruising in an attractive setting. They are well worth visiting in their own right and changing crew there is straightforward. They also offer a safe cushion to yachtsmen on the haul south from northern European waters to the Mediterranean or before heading out into the Atlantic. There is challenging pilotage for those who relish it, good anchorages, and many welcoming marinas where boats may be safely secured while the crew explore ashore or leave for extended periods.

Steady development since the mid-1980s is receiving a major boost with the injection of significant EU infrastructure funding. The fishing fleets are exceptionally well provided for; good roads allow rapid travel around the area and, in their wake, have brought major construction of homes and hotels – particularly in the more southern rías. Some beaches are therefore now barred off to protect swimmers, with traditional anchorage positions being pushed slightly offshore. Increasing prosperity is leading to modern, busy marinas.

The northern rías, the *Rías Altas*, are generally small with longer distances of often high, rugged and exposed coastline in between shelter. In onshore winds this coast becomes a dangerous lee shore while the lights of high-sited lighthouses may be lost to view in fog. Nevertheless, in settled weather this area can provide attractive cruising.

South of Cabo Finisterre, and beyond the offshore dangers north of Ría de Muros, the four rías of Muros, Arosa, Pontevedra and Vigo offer more sheltered cruising with a variety of anchorages and harbours to visit. With few exceptions the rías are wide and deep, and the hazards well marked, although this is not always the case further off the beaten track and sometimes close to harbours. Lights, buoys and beacons are generally well maintained, although many could do with a lick of paint.

Hazards

Apart from the clearly recorded Traffic Separation Zone (which lies well off shore) the main hazards are the weather and *viveros* (mussel rafts). Weather forecasts are readily obtainable but local conditions may change rapidly and it would be advisable to have a clear escape plan when visiting some of the more interesting anchorages. In the summer months, rías which start the day in brilliant summer conditions may be plunged into lingering local fog which may make passage through the *viveros* somewhat challenging.

The areas on the plans marked as viveros cannot be definitive; some are shown on the air photographs but, although many are well established and remain year after year, a few may be removed and others established elsewhere. Some

Toriñana lighthouse on the western edge of the Coast of Death

GALICIA

Islas Cíes anchorage 4 (Isla del Faro page 101)

Monument to the fishermen of Aguiño

In addition to the offshore fishing boats, and the *viveros* support boats, large fleets of small fishing boats, some with a clam cage handle stretching up to 20 metres behind them, may be encountered hard at work or jostling to unload their catch. Life in this area revolves around the fishing fleets and they dominate the harbours. Skippers will wish to respect this when planning their local cruising routes and crew will enjoy the abundant fresh seafood which is obtainable everywhere.

Swell

The exposed coastline is subject to Atlantic swells from the westerly quadrant, sometimes originating hundreds of miles offshore and building from an apparently flat sea. Swell is often, though not always, the harbinger of an approaching frontal system.

Winds

In summer the dominance of the Azores high pressure area, usually combined with low pressure over the Iberian peninsula, leads to prevailing northeasterlies in the northern part of the area, gaining a more northerly component south of Cabo Finisterre. However, land or sea breeze effects may dictate conditions locally, sometimes leading to a 180° shift in wind direction during the warmer parts of the day.

Gales are infrequent during the summer but may occur, notably the *nordeste pardo*, a cloudy northeaster of the Finisterre area. In theory the southwesterly *vendavale* is also uncommon at this time of year.

In winter, Galicia's weather is largely determined by the passage of North Atlantic frontal systems bringing strong southwesterlies, doubtless why the Bay of Biscay gained its fearsome reputation in the days of the square-riggers.

viveros will be found in the more northern rías but the majority are further south, with over 3,000 rafts said to be in Ría de Arosa alone. They are serviced by a large fleet of support vessels and the anchor cables run almost vertically downwards to permit access. It is possible to sail between them and anchoring between them and the shore is generally possible. However, although the outer perimeters of the rafts are usually marked by yellow buoys, and often lit, they do offer a very significant obstacle - particularly at night. An idea of the scale and layout of the viveros may be gleaned from Google Earth.

I.1 Galicia – Rías Altas

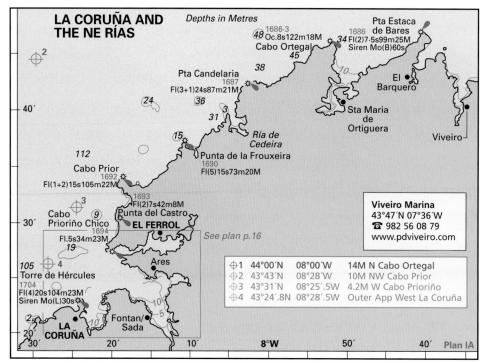

LA CORUÑA AND THE NE RÍAS

Depths in Metres

Pta Estaca de Bares
1686 *34* Fl(2)7·5s99m25M
Siren Mo(B)60s

1686·3 *48* Oc.8s122m18M
Cabo Ortegal
45

38
Pta Candelaria
1687
Fl(3+1)24s87m21M

24
36

31 3

El Barquero

Sta Maria de Ortiguera

15
Ría de Cedeira

Viveiro

112
Cabo Prior
1692
Fl(1+2)15s105m22M

Punta de la Frouxeira
1690
Fl(5)15s73m20M

3
Cabo Prioriño Chico
1694
Fl.5s34m23M

1693
Fl(2)7s42m8M
Punta del Castro
9
EL FERROL

See plan p.16

19

Viveiro Marina
43°47′N 07°36′W
☎ 982 56 08 79
www.pdviveiro.com

105 4
Torre de Hércules
1704
Fl(4)20s104m23M
Siren Mo(L)30s

Ares

2
LA CORUÑA
20′

Fontan/ Sada

⊕1	44°00′N	08°00′W	14M N Cabo Ortegal
⊕2	43°43′N	08°28′W	10M NW Cabo Prior
⊕3	43°31′N	08°25′.5W	4.2M W Cabo Prioriño
⊕4	43°24′.8N	08°28′.5W	Outer App West La Coruña

30′ 20′ 10′ 8°W 50′ 40′ **Plan IA**

Coastguard
La Coruña
☎ 981 209 541/548
Sea Rescue Service
☎ 900 202 202

MRSC Coruña   Ch 10
MRCC Finisterre   Ch 11

Weather
Navtex (D)
Coruña Ch 26 at
  0840, 1240, 2010
Finisterre Ch 22 at
  0840, 1240, 2010

For details of rías to the
northeast of La Coruña
refer to Imray/RCC pilot
South Biscay by
John Lawson

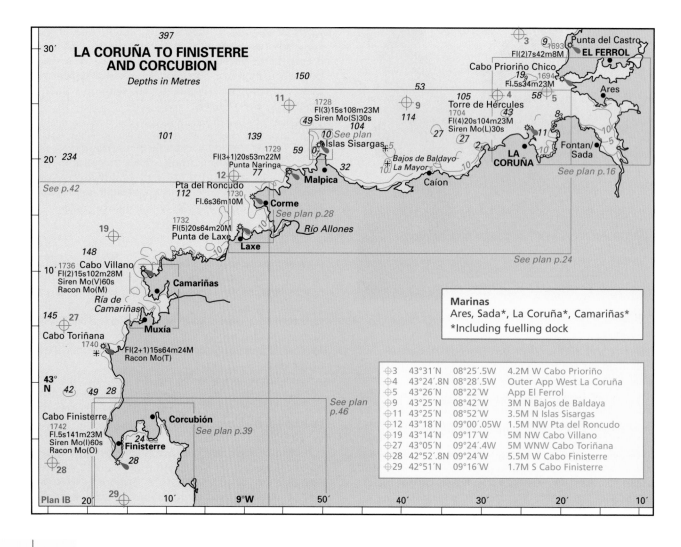

LA CORUÑA TO FINISTERRE AND CORCUBION

Depths in Metres

397

30′

3 9 Punta del Castro
1693
Fl(2)7s42m8M
EL FERROL

150

Cabo Prioriño Chico
19 1694
Fl.5s34m23M

53
105 4 58 5
Torre de Hércules
1704
Fl(4)20s104m23M
Siren Mo(L)30s

Ares

11
1728
Fl(3)15s108m23M
49 Siren Mo(S)30s
104

9
114

101
139
59 10 See plan
Islas Sisargas

27
27
LA CORUÑA

234

1729
Fl(3+1)20s53m22M
Punta Naringa
12 77

Fontan/ Sada

20′
See p.42

Pta del Roncudo
112
1730
Fl.6s36m10M

32
Bajos de Baldaya
La Mayor

Malpica

Caión

See plan p.16

Corme

See plan p.28

19
1732
Fl(5)20s64m20M
Punta de Laxe

Río Allones

Laxe

See plan p.24

148

10 1736 Cabo Villano
Fl(2)15s102m28M
Siren Mo(V)60s
Racon Mo(M)

Camariñas

Ría de Camariñas

145 27
Cabo Toriñana

Muxia

1740
Fl(2+1)15s64m24M
Racon Mo(T)

Marinas
Ares, Sada*, La Coruña*, Camariñas*
*Including fuelling dock

43° N
42 49 28

Cabo Finisterre
1742
Fl.5s141m23M
Siren Mo(I)60s
Racon Mo(O)

Corcubión

See plan p.46

See plan p.39

24
Finisterre

28

28

⊕3	43°31′N	08°25′.5W	4.2M W Cabo Prioriño
⊕4	43°24′.8N	08°28′.5W	Outer App West La Coruña
⊕5	43°26′N	08°22′W	App El Ferrol
⊕9	43°25′N	08°42′W	3M N Bajos de Baldaya
⊕11	43°25′N	08°52′W	3.5M N Islas Sisargas
⊕12	43°18′N	09°00′.05W	1.5M NW Pta del Roncudo
⊕19	43°14′N	09°17′W	5M NW Cabo Villano
⊕27	43°05′N	09°24′.4W	5M WNW Cabo Toriñana
⊕28	42°52′.8N	09°24′W	5.5M W Cabo Finisterre
⊕29	42°51′N	09°16′W	1.7M S Cabo Finisterre

Plan IB 20′ 29 10′ 9°W 50′ 40′ 30′ 20′ 10′

Visibility

The chances of coastal fog are greatest in July and August when the incidence may rise as high as one day in ten or twelve (many yachtsmen would argue that this is conservative), with many more days of early morning mist which then disperses. In the *Rías Bajas* visibility of less than 2M may occasionally last for a week at a stretch.

Currents

Off the *Rías Altas* currents may set easterly into the Bay of Biscay. South of Cabo Finisterre the general trend is southwards, seldom reaching more than ½ knot.

Tides

Tidal predictions for the *Rías Altas* use La Coruña as the Standard Port; those for the *Rías Bajas* use Lisbon. When calculating Spanish tides using Lisbon data, note that allowance has already been made for the difference in time zone (Spanish time being UT+1, Portuguese time UT, both advanced one hour in summer – see page 4.)

If La Coruña tide tables are not available, as a very rough guide high water occurs at approximately 0510 and 1650 at springs ±20 minutes; and 1045 and 2330 at neaps ±50 minutes. The same figures for Lisbon are approximately 0410 and 1630 ±30 minutes, and 0920 and 2230 ±1 hour 10 minutes.

Ranges are near 3m at springs and 1.4m at neaps, but both time and height may be affected by wind, particularly in the *Rías Bajas*.

The flood stream sets north and northeast around the coast. Unlike some of the rios of Portugal and southern Spain, all Galicia's rías are fully tidal, certainly as far as a yacht is likely to penetrate.

Where no tidal data is given for an individual harbour it will be found under the preliminary notes for the ría as a whole.

Climate

Galicia is the wet corner of Spain – it has much the same climatic feel as southwest England, though on average is rather warmer. Mean air temperature varies from around 20°C in August to 9°C in January, sea temperature from 17°C in summer to 12°C in winter.

Marinas

Marinas are available in Ares, Sada, La Coruña and Camariñas and each of the four southern rías. Weather information is posted daily and internet facilities are generally available to visiting yachtmen.

Language

Galicia is a popular holiday area but few foreigners visit the rías. Although English and other languages are spoken in the major marina offices, visiting yachtsmen who do not speak Spanish should arm themselves with the necessary phrasebook.

Visits

Ashore La Coruña is an excellent place from which to hire a car to explore or recce ahead. The whole rugged and attractive area from La Coruña to Finisterre can be covered in a day, and the ancient cathedral city of Santiago de Compostela visited in another (see also page 77).

Berthing Costs

Contact details are provided for most ports so that applicable costs can be checked in advance if desired. An indication of 2005 berthing costs is given at Appendix VI where it will be seen that joining a *Pasaporte* system may provide discounts.

Facilities

Galicia is no longer a remote cruising area. The large number of fishing fleets means that emergency and basic technical and harbour support is widely available. For normal routine work or chandlery seek advice from the multiligual staff of the major marinas. Sada offers the most comprehensive support in the north: Portosin, Vilagarcia, Sanxenxo, Cangas, Punta Lagoa, Vigo, Baiona in the four southern rías. Easy refuelling places are indicated by * at the start of the sections. Water, food shops and restaurants are widely available.

GALICIA

Rías Altas

1.1 La Coruña area
    El Ferrol, Ares, Sada
    1. La Coruña
1.2 La Coruña to Laxe (Lage)
    2. Malpica
    Ría de Corme and Lage
    3. Corme
    4. Laxe

1.3 Laxe to Finisterre
    5. Camelle
    Ría de Camariñas
    6. Camariñas
    7. Muxia
1.4 Finisterre and Seno de Corcubion
    8. Finisterre
    9. Corcubión

I.1.1 Approaches to Rías El Ferrol, Ares, Betanzos and La Coruña

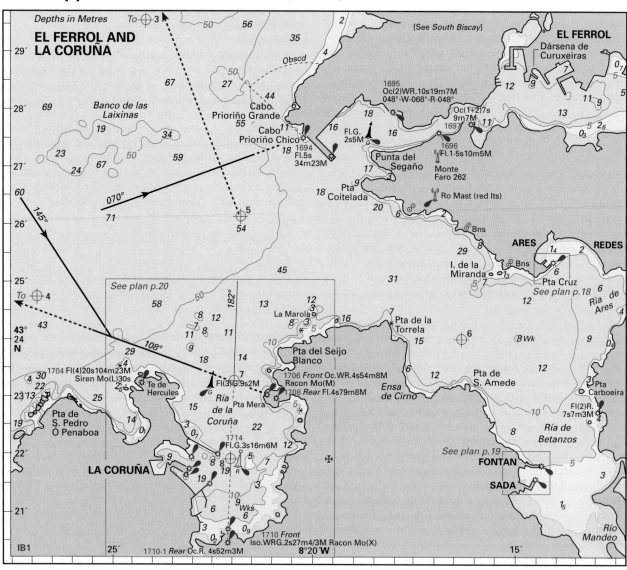

⊕3	43°31′N	08°25′.5W	4.2M W Cabo Prioriño
⊕4	43°24′.8N	08°28′.5W	Outer App West La Coruña
⊕5	43°26′N	08°22′W	App El Ferrol
⊕6	43°24′N	08°16′W	App for Ares and Marina Sada
⊕7	43°23′.2N	08°22′.1	Ría de La Coruña
⊕8	43°21′.9N	08°22′.2	Off breakwater La Coruña

Charts	Approach	Rías
Admiralty	1111, 1094	1110, 1117, 1118
Spanish	928, 412A	4122, 4123, 4125, 4126
Imray	C18, C48	C18, C48

Tides
See La Coruña page 21.

This group of rías includes the major commercial and naval port of El Ferrol, the small friendly marina at Ares and the major marinas at Sada and La Coruña.

Hazards

In rough weather the sea breaks over two banks about 1M off the coast north of Cabo Prioriño –

Bajos Tarracidos and Cabaleiro – and a third, Banco de las Laixinas some 2–4M west of that cape. Under such conditions it is advisable to approach these rías from the west and remain well clear of Banco de las Laixinas. Clearing lines are shown on the plan.

Approach

From the north under settled conditions The route from ⊕3 to ⊕5 (5.5M) clears the dangers. From the area of ⊕5 set course as appropriate or look south for ⊕7 and ⊕8 to pick up the leading lights for La Coruña (1706 and 1708).

From the west (the all-weather route) The route from ⊕4 to ⊕5 (5M) will keep a yacht south of Banco de las Laixinas. If bound for La Coruña ⊕4 to ⊕7 lie on the leading marks (1710 and 1710-1) now see plan page 20.

Local cruising and alternatives to La Coruña

The rías outside La Coruña offer pleasant cruising. They are covered briefly here (pages 17–19) but see RCCPF *South Biscay* for fuller details.

El Ferrol
(suggest emergency use only)

Chart Admiralty 1094

El Ferrol is a huge commercial and naval harbour with a new container ship terminal being constructed beyond a prominent new mole in the approach to the ría.

Approach

Follow the main ship channel taking note of the starboard hand mark off Punta del Segano.

Berthing

A berth might be possible to find in La Grana (43°28′.6N 08°15′.5W) in Dársena de Curuxeiros (43°28′.5N 08°14′.5W) or anchor clear of the moorings NE side of Castillo de San Felipe (43°28′.5N 08°16′W) or south side in Ensenada de Bano.

Green buoy

The new outer mole at El Ferrol and the approach to the narrows

El Ferrol from the west with the forts of San Felipe to port and La Palma to starboard in the narrows

La Grana   Dársena de Curuxeiros

Ría de Ares

Club Náutico Ría de Ares
Breakwater head location 43°25'.34N 08°14'.27W
☎/*Fax* 981 11 10 12
Email secretaria@náuticoares.com
www.náuticoares.com
VHF Ch 09

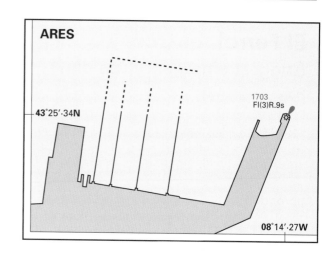

Well protected from northeasterlies and a welcoming marina

Approach

The approach from the west (⊕5) is straightforward but in any swell, the shallow area Bajo la Miranda lying 0.6M SW of Punta Miranda should be given a generous clearance (⊕6 is 0.8M south of the shoal area).

Anchorages

The anchorages off Ares and Redes should be comfortable in a north or northeast wind provided fish farms do not limit swinging room. The mooring buoys off Ares are all private but the Ares Yacht Club may be able to arrange short-term use.

Ares Marina

Ares Marina has visitors' berths, minimum depth 2.5m, and provides good protection except in a northwest wind. The proposed extension is likely to be completed in 2006 and will provide increased berthing and protection. The club is very welcoming and has excellent domestic facilities and restaurant/cafeteria but no fuel. Local shops.

Ares Marina

Ría de Betanzos

Charts
Admiralty	1094
Spanish	4125
Imray	C48

Sada Marina
South Mole head location (red beacon)
43°21′.58N 08°14′.68W
☎ 981 619 015 *Fax* 981 619 287
Email marinasada@igatel.net
www.marinasada.com
VHF Ch 09

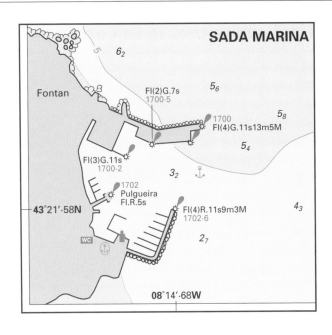

Holiday area with a major full service marina

Approach and anchorage

The approach is straightforward and it is possible to anchor off Banobre opposite Fontán Sada or clear of the harbour entrance itself. South of here the ría shoals rapidly.

Sada Marina

Sada Marina lies to port on entry to the main harbour and offers all services; it is a suitable place to overwinter and is within easy reach of La Coruña.

Sada Marina and Fontán Harbour from the south

Final approaches to La Coruña (A Coruña)

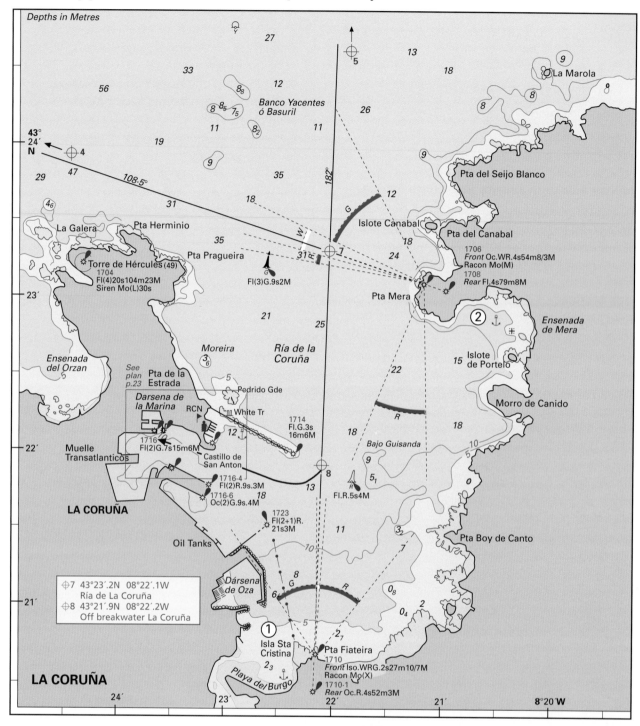

Depths in Metres

27

33

56

8₈

12

Banco Yacentes
ó Basuril

8 8₅ 7₅

8₂

11

11

43°
24′
N

19

9

29

47

108.5°

31

35

18

G

12

13

18

9

La Marola

8

8

9

Pta del Seijo Blanco

4₆

La Galera

Pta Herminio

35

Torre de Hércules (49)
1704
Fl(4)20s104m23M
Siren Mo(L)30s

Pta Pragueira

31

182°

W

R

7

Islote Canabal

18

24

Pta del Canabal

1706
Front Oc.WR.4s54m8/3M
Racon Mo(M)
1708
Rear Fl.4s79m8M

Pta Mera

②

Ensenada
de Mera

G
Fl(3)G.9s2M

23′

21

25

Moreira
3₆

Ría de la
Coruña

15 Islote
de Portelo

Ensenada
del Orzan

See
plan
p.23

Pta de la
Estrada

5

Pedrido Gde

22

R

Morro de Canido

Darsena de
la Marina

RCN

White Tr

1714
Fl.G.3s
16m6M

18

18

Bajo Guisanda

10

5

Muelle
Transatlanticos

1716
Fl(2)G.7s15m6M

12

Castillo de
San Anton

9

5₁

22′

1716·4
Fl(2)R.9s.3M
1716·6
Oc(2)G.9s.4M

18

8

R
Fl.R.5s4M

13

LA CORUÑA

1723
Fl(2+1)R.
21s3M

11

3₂

Pta Boy de Canto

Oil Tanks

10

7

8

0₈

⊕7 43°23′.2N 08°22′.1W
      Ría de La Coruña
⊕8 43°21′.9N 08°22′.2W
      Off breakwater La Coruña

Dársena
de Oza

8

G

R

6₄

0₄

2

5

2₇

①

Isla Sta
Cristina

Pta Fiateira
1710
Front Iso.WRG.2s27m10/7M
Racon Mo(X)
1710·1
Rear Oc.R.4s52m3M

21′

LA CORUÑA

2₃

Playa del Burgo

24′

23′

22′

21′

8°20′W

Lights
Pta Mera Ldg Lts 108°30′
1706 *Front* Oc.WR.4s54m8/3M White 8-sided tower
1708 *Rear* Fl.4s79m8M White 8-sided tower
Pta Fiateira LdgLts 182°
1710 *Front* Iso.WRG.2s27m10/7M Red and white
      chequered square tower
1710.1 *Rear* Oc.R.4s52m3M Red and white chequered
      square tower
1714 **Breakwater head** 43°21′.9N 08°22′.47W
      Fl.G.3s16m6M Truncated conical tower

Torre de Hércules

Coruña breakwater tower

1. La Coruña (A Coruña)

Location
43°21′.9N 08°22′.47W
(Outer breakwater light)
43°22′.0N 08°23′.70W
(Dársena Deportiva)

Shelter Excellent inside

Warning
Banco Yacentes must be avoided and the leading lines followed in heavy weather or swell

Tides
Standard Port La Coruña
Heights in metres

MHWS	MHWN	MLWN	MLWS
3.8	2.8	1.5	0.5

Charts

	Approach	Harbour
Admiralty	1111, 1094	1110
Spanish	928, 412A	4126
Imray	C18, C48	C18, C48

Berthing
Marina – Entry beacons are red and green pillars

Facilities
All, including charts and chandlery

Weather *see below*

Radio
Port Control Ch 12
Marina Ch 09

Communications
Marinas
Dársena de la Marina
☎ 981 914 142 *Fax* 981 914 144
www.darsenacoruna.com
Email info@darsenacoruna.com
Marina A Coruña
☎ 981 217 678 *Fax* 981 217 679
www.marinacoruna.com
Email
administracion@marinacoruna.com

Navtex
518kHz (D) at 0030, 0430, 0830*, 1230, 1630, 2030*
(*weather only*)
490kHz (W) (Spanish) at 0340, 0740, 1140, 1540, 1940, 2340

Weather bulletins
MF 1698kHz at 0703, 1303, 1903
VHF Ch 26 at 0840, 1240, 2010
MRSC Ch 10 at 0005, 0405, 0805, 1205, 1605, 2005

Navigational warnings
MF 1698kHz at 0703, 1903
VHF Ch 26 at 0840, 2010
MRSC Ch 10 at 0205, 0605, 1005, 1405, 1805, 2205

Primary working freqs
c/s Coruña Radio
Manual Ch 26 Tx 1698 Rx 2123
Autolink Ch 28 Tx 2806 Rx 3283
DSC Ch 70 2187.5kHz

GALICIA

A major city port with modern marina facilities

La Coruña is the major city of northern Galicia, offering good communications by motorway or airport. It has a busy commercial port and a modern welcoming marina. The old city is picturesque with narrow paved streets, houses with characteristic glassed-in balconies, and numerous small restaurants and cafés. North of the town the Torre de Hércules, begun by the Romans, is the oldest functioning lighthouse in the world. In addition to local attractions, La Coruña is a good place to leave a boat or visit inland. With a hire car, one can explore, in a day, the whole coastline down to Finisterre, or visit the cathedral city of Santiago de Compostela in another.

Approach

For the outer approach refer to pages 16 and 20, and note that Banco Yacentes must be avoided. The lit yellow buoy to the north of this bank is reported as small and difficult to identify.

From the north: Canal del Este (potentially dangerous in high SW or NW winds). The track of 182° follows the leading lines of Pta Fiateira through ⊕5, ⊕7 and ⊕8. The white tower on the mole will be conspicuous on this approach. After passing the outer mole turn onto 280° for the marinas.

From the west: Canal del Oeste This is the big ship route and the safest in bad weather. ⊕4 is on the extended leading line on 108° through ⊕7, to Pta Mera. Conspicuous will be the Torre de Hércules followed by the white tower on the mole. Once clear of the green channel mark Fl(3)G.9s course may be altered towards the mole end or the Pta Fiateira leading line.

Berthing, moorings and anchorage

After rounding the breakwater, head towards Castillo de St Anton (on approx 280°). Until recently visitors were directed to the major marina at Dársena Deportiva de La Coruña (see plan) where there are 44 reserved visitors' berths including 4 for vessels up to 30m. Now Marina A Coruña is also available. Both marinas are on VHF Ch 9.

It is still possible to anchor in the protection of the breakwater in 10–12m mud with patchy holding and foul bottom – trip line advisable.

Dársena Deportiva entrance from the clubhouse   *RI*

Torre de Hércules

La Coruña from the western approach

La Coruña from the west with a small boat leaving Dársena Deportiva

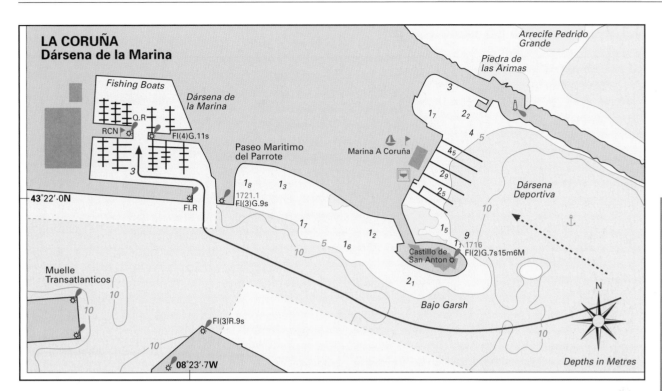

Dársena Deportiva

Entry to Dársena Deportiva is straightforward: turn to port after passing the narrow entrance. Call ahead on Ch 09 or secure alongside the main building and enquire at the office. Note that the Real Club Náutico is very formal.

Facilities

Although the travel-lift and diesel remain at the old site, most yacht support facilities are available within or close to the welcoming marina which

provides an excellent fact sheet for visitors. Town plans are readily available and the tourist office is at the NW corner of the marina. There is an internet café off Plaza de Maria Pito just west of the Plaza.

New RCN building from the north   *MW*

New Marina A Coruña   *RI*

Alternative anchorages

(See plan page 20)

1. **Playa del Burgo** 43°20′.7N 08°20′.6W
   Off the east end of the Playa del Burgo, partly sheltered by the Isla de Santa Cristina, in 2–3m with good holding over sand and weed. Dinghies can be left on the sandy beach. There is a small restaurant ashore and a supermarket one road further back. The ferry to La Coruña departs from the tiny pier every hour, and must not be impeded.

2. **Ensenada de Mera** 43°22′.8N 08°20′.4W
   In the Ensenada de Mera, protected from northwest clockwise to south. Beware the unmarked rock some distance from the mole, which only shows near low water. Anchor as moorings and depth permit in 3–4m over sand and weed, surrounded by a crescent of sandy beach (a line of closely spaced yellow buoys may define the swimming area). The village is very much a holiday resort, with restaurants and limited shopping plus a ferry to/from La Coruña.

I.1.2 La Coruña to Laxe (Lage)

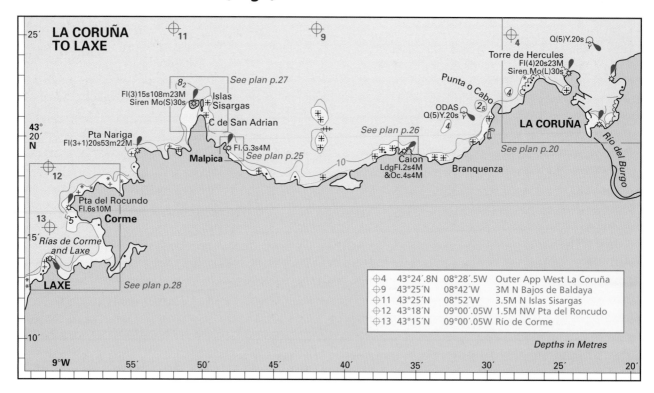

Chart legend:

```
LA CORUÑA
TO LAXE
```

Fl(3)15s108m23M
Siren Mo(S)30s

Islas Sisargas
See plan p.27
C de San Adrian

Pta Nariga
Fl(3+1)20s53m22M

Malpica

Fl.G.3s4M

See plan p.25

Caion
LdgFl.2s4M
&Oc.4s4M

Branquenza

See plan p.26

ODAS
Q(5)Y.20s

Punta o Cabo

Torre de Hercules
Fl(4)20s23M
Siren Mo(L)30s

Q(5)Y.20s

LA CORUÑA

See plan p.20

Río del Burgo

Pta del Rocundo
Fl.6s10M

Corme

Rías de Corme
and Laxe

LAXE   See plan p.28

⊕4	43°24′.8N	08°28′.5W	Outer App West La Coruña
⊕9	43°25′N	08°42′W	3M N Bajos de Baldaya
⊕11	43°25′N	08°52′W	3.5M N Islas Sisargas
⊕12	43°18′N	09°00′.05W	1.5M NW Pta del Roncudo
⊕13	43°15′N	09°00′.05W	Río de Corme

Depths in Metres

Lights
1704 **Torre de Hércules** Fl(4)20s104m23M Tall Square tower, 8-sided top
1728 **Sisarga** Fl(3)15s108m23M 8-sided tower and building
1729 **Pta Nariga** Fl(3+1)20s53m22M Round tower on building
1730 **Pta del Roncondo** Fl.6s36m10M White round tower

Tides
See La Coruña standard port page 21

Charts
Admiralty 1111, 3633, 1094, 1113, 3764
Spanish   412, 928
Imray   C18, C48

Overview

Only in the most settled weather will yachtsmen wish to close the coast between La Coruña and Corme. Most will choose to keep offshore. It would be unwise to go rock hopping without a large-scale chart. Heavy swell builds rapidly in a northerly wind. Malpica offers some protection but with extensive unmarked dangerous shallows to the east. There are shallows off Isla Sisargas with its massive lighthouse. Beyond that the wind farms start high above Pta Nariga and continue southwards. Malpica is a typical fishing harbour: shallow at the head and subject to swell around the breakwater; a launching ramp, crane and inner harbour, high walls, full of fishing boats and fuel not available to yachts. Refined for the fishing industry and generally of only limited use to the leisure sailor who may have difficulty finding a place to secure.

West from Cabo de San Adrián towards Pta Nariga and wind farm   *MW*

Malpica. Typical fishing harbour   *MW*

2. Malpica

Location
43°19´.31N 08°48´.12W

Charts
Admiralty 3633
Spanish 412
Imray C48

Light
Breakwater Fl.G.3s18m4M. Green column

Facilities
Expect none except in emergency

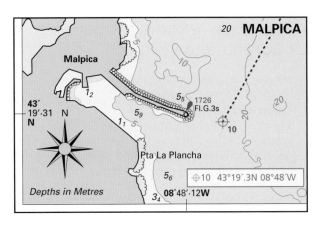

A harbour devoted to fishing

Malpica is a fishing port on a rugged coastline, and a minor tourist outlet for La Coruña. The harbour is colourful and there are good beaches nearby. The 420m mole is backed by a high wall over which heavy spray breaks in gales. There is good protection from south through west and north and northeast but a swell builds rapidly in a northerly wind and a northeasterly swell may come some way round the corner of the mole. The main harbour is full of fishing boat moorings. The small inner harbour is not open to yachts, neither is the fuel station.

The town has everyday provisions and restaurants.

Malpica from the west

Approach

From the east The unmarked Bajos de Baldayo must be avoided. There is a fair-weather inside route about 0.7M offshore. Normally keep at least 5M off shore (⊕9) before turning southwest (towards ⊕10) for the harbour.

Round the mole head well clear of the shore as there are reported to be unmarked rocks near the entrance.

From the west Other than Isla Sisargas there are no offshore hazards.

Anchorage

Anchor in the entrance clear of the fishing boats or negotiate the temporary use of a buoy or space against the very high harbour wall.

GALICIA

Alternative anchorages between La Coruña and Corme

Depending on the conditions there are five other potential anchorages in this area:

1. **Caion** 43°19′.2N 08°36′.1W
   The tiny harbour of Caion is tucked to the east of Punta Insua de Caion and should be approached on the leading line on 147°. Something of a Malpica in miniature, the harbour faces east with a high stone breakwater offering protection from north through west to south. Strictly a fair weather spot; although lit, it should not be approached in darkness. It may be possible to lie alongside for a short period if the fishing boats are out and there is no swell.

2. Off the beach immediately west of Malpica sheltered from the south.

3. **Playa de Seaya SE of Cabo de San Adrián** 43°19′.8N 08°49′.6W
   Sheltered from the south and west.

4. **Islas Sisargas**

5. **Ensenada de Bazio** (entrance 43°19′.2N 08°52′.85W)
   The bay is 3M SW of Isla Sisargas and is overlooked by cliffs and the Punta Nariga wind farm. A ledge runs out from the eastern headland leaving a usable width of about 250m in the entrance. The bay, which is open to the NW and subject to swell from that quarter, opens out inside and provides shelter for small fishing vessels to lie to summer moorings, with more craned ashore. A concrete mole, slipway and green light structure lie in the SW corner.

   There is a fine sandy beach at the head of the bay, but otherwise the bottom is rock and sand.

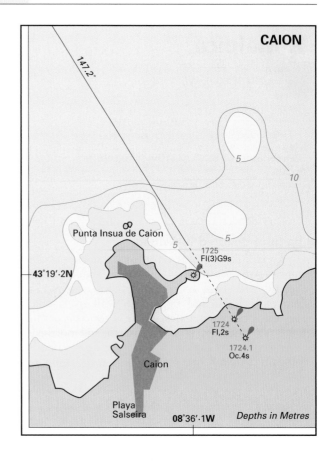

Caion from the north

Islas Sisargas

(landing 43°21'.47N 08°50'.30W)

The Islas Sisargas landing, in the cone between Sisarga Grande and Sisarga Chica (sometimes referred to as Sisarga Pequeña) is sheltered from the north. The gap between the two islands is very narrow, and virtually non-existent at low water. Anchor southeast of the stone quay in 3–4m: holding is variable over sand and rock. There are steps at the quay, and a track leading up to the lighthouse on the island's summit. The islands are a seabird reserve, and audible from a considerable distance.

The Sisargas channel is hazardous. Both east and west winds can produce breakers and there are strong tidal streams. The approaches, which should not be attempted without large-scale charts (e.g. inset to Spanish 928), are as follows:

a. From the northwest, keeping the prominent headland of Atalaya de Malpica in line with Punta del Castro on 133°.
b. From the southwest, keeping to the south of La Carreira and Laxe de Barizo.
c. From the east, either by following a leading bearing of 265° towards the rock Pedro do Lobo and changing towards Punta del Rostro when this bears 309°, or by eye. The channel is about 400m wide and closer to Punta del Castro than Isla Sisarga Chica (which has a rock, La Chan, awash some 250m to the south).

Lighthouse

Landing

Islas Sisargas from Cabo de San Adrián   MW

GALICIA

Corme and Laxe (Lage)

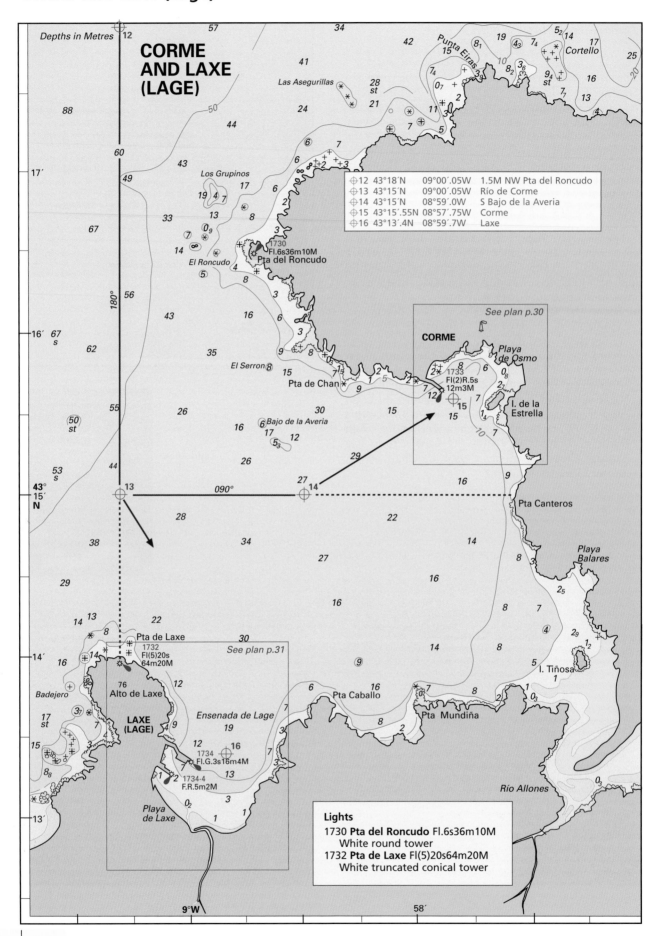

Depths in Metres

**CORME
AND LAXE
(LAGE)**

⊕12	43°18′N	09°00′.05W	1.5M NW Pta del Roncudo
⊕13	43°15′N	09°00′.05W	Río de Corme
⊕14	43°15′N	08°59′.0W	S Bajo de la Averia
⊕15	43°15′.55N	08°57′.75W	Corme
⊕16	43°13′.4N	08°59′.7W	Laxe

Los Grupinos

El Roncudo

1730
Fl.6s36m10M
Pta del Roncudo

El Serron

Pta de Chan

Bajo de la Averia

CORME

Playa de Osmo

1733
Fl(2)R.5s
12m3M

I. de la Estrella

See plan p.30

090°

180°

Pta Canteros

Playa Balares

I. Tiñosa

Pta de Laxe

1732
Fl(5)20s
64m20M

Alto de Laxe

Badejero

**LAXE
(LAGE)**

Ensenada de Lage

1734
Fl.G.3s16m4M

1734·4
F.R.5m2M

Playa
de Laxe

See plan p.31

Pta Caballo

Pta Mundiña

Río Allones

Las Asegurillas

Punta Eiras

Cortello

Lights
1730 **Pta del Roncudo** Fl.6s36m10M
White round tower
1732 **Pta de Laxe** Fl(5)20s64m20M
White truncated conical tower

9°W

58′

Ría de Corme y Laxe

Entrance
22°43´.15N 09°00´.63W

Tides
Standard port La Coruña
Mean time differences
HW +0045; LW +0045
Heights in metres

MHWS	MHWN	MLWN	MLWS
3.7	2.8	1.5	0.5

Charts
Admiralty 3633, 1113
Spanish 928
Imray C48

Warning
Note offlyers off Pta del Roncudo and Pta de Laxe;
also note Bajo de la Avería to the southwest of
Pta de Chan.

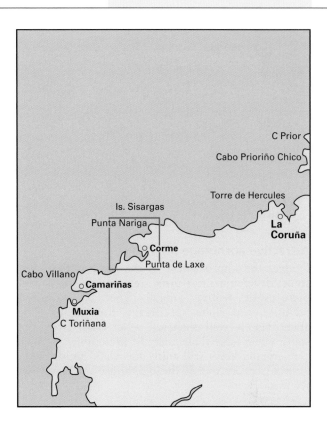

A pleasant ría

For many, the Ría de Corme y Laxe offers welcome
anchorage following the 35M coastal passage from
La Coruña. The two could hardly be more different
with the busy city being exchanged for dramatic
scenery, quiet beaches and the chance to explore, by
dinghy, the beautiful Río Allones as it winds its way
5M up to the picturesque old bridge at Pontecesco.

If heading north, into prevailing north or
northwest winds, then departure from here, rather
than La Coruña, avoids giving away considerable
ground to windward.

Approach

From the north Islas Sisargas, Pta Nariga and Pta del
Roncudo are well marked (plan page 24). Round Pta
del Roncudo with an offing of at least 1M and make
track of 180° towards Pta de Laxe (⊕12 to ⊕13).
In heavy weather the seas break on all the banks in
the area and it is advisable to pass west and south of
Bajo de la Averia (5m).

For Corme, head initially for Pta Canteros (and
⊕14) to clear the bank and then for ⊕15 or the
outer mole.

For Laxe (Lage), head for ⊕16 or the outer mole,
keeping 500m offshore to clear the outlying rocks of
Pta de Laxe.

From the south Keep 1M off the coast northeast of
Cabo Villano, with its attendant windfarm (plan
page 34). Keep out 500m or more rounding Pta de
Laxe, and follow the coast around at that distance to
pick up Laxe breakwater, or head east until Corme
breakwater bears 050°.

Corme. Anchorage between *viveros* and the harbour   *MW*

Laxe. Anchorage off the small boat pontoon   *RI*

3. Corme

Location
43°15'.64N 08°57'.78W

Charts
Admiralty   1113
Spanish   928
Imray   C48

Tides
See ría page 29

Final approaches ⊕
⊕15 from ⊕14

Light
Breakwater beacon Fl(2)R.5s12m3M Red Column

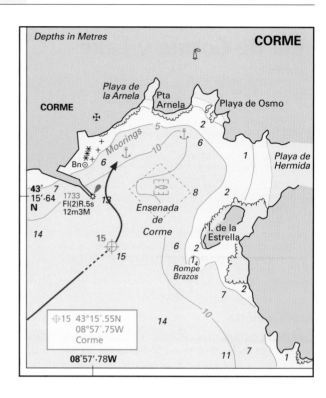

Attractive anchorage off village

Despite the improvement in the road system, and some development, Corme remains a small and picturesque fishing village. There are limited facilities and none specifically for yachts. The anchorage is well sheltered other than from the south when Laxe (Lage) may be preferable.

Energetic crews will enjoy the walk amidst wild granite scenery out to the lighthouse on Punta del Roncudo.

Approach

See under Ría approaches page 29. Note the recommended route to the anchorage which passes between the breakwater and two small green buoys 'guarding' the *viveros*.

Anchorage

Fishing boats use the inside of the breakwater, while the small area to the northeast is filled with moorings. There are rocks inshore of the moorings, marked by an unlit green beacon.

Anchor to the west of the *viveros* in 10m or less, or further round the bay towards the beaches.

Facilities

Adequate shopping, restaurants, hotels and a bank.

Corme from the south

4. Laxe (Lage)

Location
43°13´.37N 08°59´.97W

Charts
Admiralty 1113
Spanish 928
Imray C48

Tides
See ría page 29

Final approaches ⊕
⊕16 from ⊕13

Light
Breakwater beacon Fl.G.3s15m4M Green column

Communications
Club Náutico de Laxe
Fax 981 728 255
Email náuticolaxe@hotmail.com

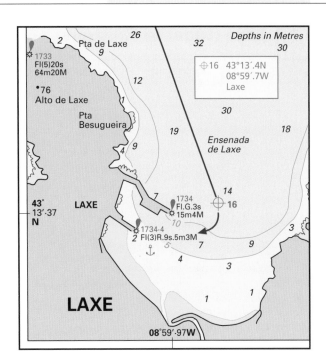

Limited facilities for yachts

Laxe (the common name) is a holiday resort around a fishing village. There is a long sandy beach to the south and the 14th-century church of Santiago de Lage overlooks the harbour. This is a popular area for sailing dinghies. There is a street market on Fridays. Good walks, impressive scenery.

Approach

See under Ría approaches page 29.

Anchorage

The 300m breakwater offers good shelter in most conditions, though swell may work in. In fair weather, and south or west winds, anchor off the beach near the south mole but clear of the harbour approach in 5m or less over sand. Small buoys may impede swinging room. This would become untenable in a north wind when Corme will provide better shelter. Fishing boats enter day and night, timber ships berth along the north mole.

There are many small-craft moorings within the harbour, some trail floating lines.

Facilities

It may be possible to berth at the end of the small boat pontoon to take on water. Water on the quay, shops, hardware store, banks, restaurants and bars.

Laxe from the southwest

I.1.3 Laxe (Lage) to Finisterre

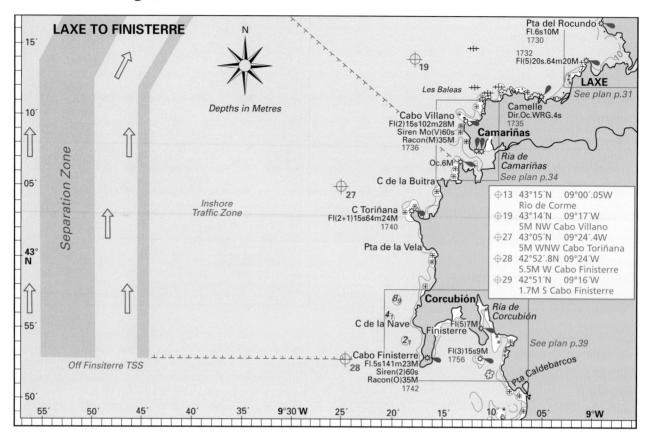

Lights

1730 **Pta del Rocundo** Fl.6s36m10M Round tower on building
1732 **Pta de Laxe** Fl(5)20s64m20M White truncated conical tower
1736 **Cabo Villano** Fl(2)15s102m28M 8-sided tower, grey cupola
1737 **Pta de la Barca** Oc.4s12m6M Grey truncated conical tower
1740 **Cabo Toriñana** Fl(2+1)15s64m24M White round tower
1742 **Cabo Finisterre** Fl.5s141m23M 8-sided granite tower and dwelling

Charts

Admiralty 1111, 3633, 3764
Spanish 927
Imray C48

Warning
A local magnetic anomaly has been reported within a radius of 13M of Cabo Toriñana

Overview

This rugged coast amply justifies its name as Costa del Morte. Other than the delightful ría of Camariñas and Muxia the yachtsman should make passage well out to sea. If sailing between Corme/Laxe and Camariñas, do not cut the corner, avoid Camelle. Do not link ⊕13 and ⊕20 except via ⊕19. Stay away from Cabo Toriñana where, even on the calmest days the Atlantic swell crashes on the outlying rocks off the lighthouse sitting on the edge of the barren peninsula.

Traffic Separation Zone

A very busy 19M wide Traffic Separation Zone lies off Cape Finisterre. Yachts are strongly advised to use the Inshore Traffic Zone, also 19M wide.

Finisterre Vessel Traffic Services (Finisterre VTS)
Monitors all traffic and can give advice to particular vessels or of those nearby.

Provides regular navigational and weather information; see page 39.

c/s Finisterre Traffic (Finisterre Trafico)
VHF Ch 11, 16 (74)
☎ 981 76 73 20 & 76 77 38

Cabo Toriñana Lighthouse on the most western point of mainland Europe

5. Camelle

Location (see plan on page 32)
  43°11'.34N 09°05'.19W (outer breakwater green
  column)
Charts
  Admiralty 1111, 3633
  Spanish   927
  Imray   C48

No place for sailing yachts

Camelle is a small harbour lying between Laxe (Lage) and Camariñas. Any rock hopping, inquisitive yachtsman considering making this a lunchtime stop is strongly advised to remain well offshore. In winds from the north to west this is a dangerous lee shore.

Swell works into the outer harbour which is narrow and with isolated rocks inside the breakwater; the inner harbour is shallow, except by the quay but that lies beyond a criss-cross of mooring lines lying on and beneath the surface. The harbour is recorded here only as a place to avoid – unless coming by land to beach comb in which case it has a charm of its own.

Camelle   *MW*

Shoreside in Rías Altas

All photos MW

One of hundreds of wind generators

Eucalyptus alternate with firs throughout the hills

Typical Galician house

Typical granite grain store

GALICIA

Ría de Camariñas

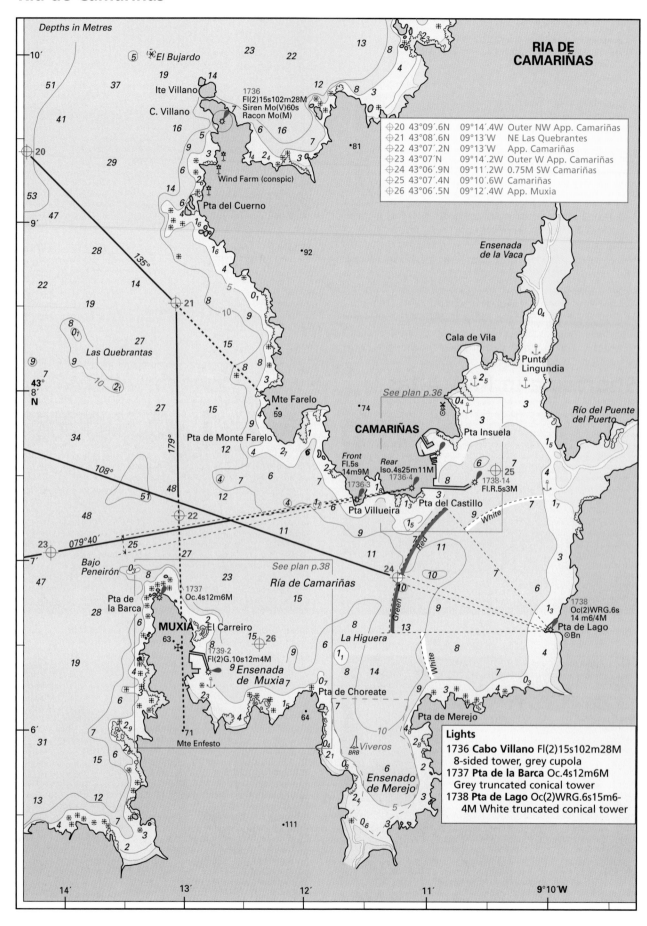

Depths in Metres

RIA DE CAMARIÑAS

1736
Fl(2)15s102m28M
Siren Mo(V)60s
Racon Mo(M)

⊕20	43°09´.6N	09°14´.4W	Outer NW App. Camariñas
⊕21	43°08´.6N	09°13´W	NE Las Quebrantes
⊕22	43°07´.2N	09°13´W	App. Camariñas
⊕23	43°07´N	09°14´.2W	Outer W App. Camariñas
⊕24	43°06´.9N	09°11´.2W	0.75M SW Camariñas
⊕25	43°07´.4N	09°10´.6W	Camariñas
⊕26	43°06´.5N	09°12´.4W	App. Muxia

El Bujardo
Ite Villano
C. Villano
Wind Farm (conspic)
Pta del Cuerno
Las Quebrantas
Mte Farelo
Pta de Monte Farelo
Ensenada de la Vaca
Cala de Vila
Punta Lingundia
Río del Puente del Puerto

See plan p.36
CAMARIÑAS
Pta Insuela
Front
Fl.5s
14m9M
Rear
Iso.4s25m11M
1736·4
1738·14
Fl.R.5s3M
1736·3
Pta Villueira
Pta del Castillo
White
Red
Green
White

Bajo Peneirón
See plan p.38
Ría de Camariñas
24
1737
Oc.4s12m6M
Pta de la Barca
MUXIA
El Carreiro
1739·2
Fl(2)G.10s12m4M
Ensenada de Muxia
Pta de Choreate
Pta de Merejo
La Higuera
1738
Oc(2)WRG.6s
14 m6/4M
Pta de Lago
Bn

Mte Enfesto
Viveros
BRB
Ensenado de Merejo

Lights
1736 **Cabo Villano** Fl(2)15s102m28M
8-sided tower, grey cupola
1737 **Pta de la Barca** Oc.4s12m6M
Grey truncated conical tower
1738 **Pta de Lago** Oc(2)WRG.6s15m6-
4M White truncated conical tower

Ría de Camariñas

Location
43°07´.28N 09°13´.00W

Tides
Standard port La Coruña
Mean time differences
HW +0005; LW –0005
Heights in metres

MHWS	MHWN	MLWN	MLWS
3.8	2.8	1.5	0.5

Charts
Admiralty 1111, 3633, 1113
Spanish   927
Imray   C48

Warning
Note hazards of El Bujardo, Las Quebrantas, Bajo Peneiron and the shallows southwest of Monte Farelo, and further note the warning below regarding Leixon de Juanboy. The only sound signal in the area is on Cabo Villano.

West of the plan, and lying between the two leading lines shown, is the small but dangerous shoal of Leixon de Juanboy – position 43°07´.48N 09°14´.97W.

Approach ⊕
⊕20 43°09´.6N 09°14´.4W or ⊕23 43°07´N 09°14´.2W
Entrance ⊕22 43°07´.2N 09°13´W

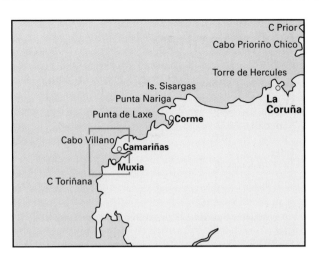

Well placed, scenic and useful ría

Many would consider the Ría de Camariñas amongst Galicia's loveliest, with the added advantage that it contains anchorages protected from almost every direction. However, the Ría itself is fully exposed to winds and seas from the northwest and may be inaccessible in rough weather. The two towns meet the daily needs of the cruising yachtsman; Camariñas has a well established welcoming marina and Muxia is improving its protection within the harbour. Crews can dig for their shellfish lunch on the beaches or walk through the unspoilt countryside.

Approach

Full use should be made of the leading lines by both day and night; ⊕ are positioned to ease the recognition of the key lights and headlands, although night entry by first timers is not recommended.

From the north Keep well off Cabo Villano, with its wind farm, to avoid El Bujardo, a pinnacle rock awash at low tide. Either stay well off shore, to avoid Las Quebrantas, until Pta de Lago bears 108° (white sector) or come inside that bank tracking via ⊕20, ⊕21, ⊕22 as indicated on the plan page 34.

From the southwest Keep well off Cape Toriñana and do not cut the corner around Pta de la Barca. ⊕23 lies on the leading line to Pta Villueira. Follow until Pta de Lago bears 108° (white sector) or route through ⊕22.

From ⊕22, or the crossing of the leading lines, maintain the line towards ⊕24 and Pta de Lago until shaping course for Camariñas or Muxia.

Camariñas rear leading light 1736.4 on Pta Villueira line *MW*

New southern mole at Muxia (Aug 05) with the high octagonal Cabo Villano lighthouse and wind farm in the distance   *MW*

Alternative anchorages

The plan shows anchorages north and east of Camariñas which may offer solitude, shelter from north or northeast winds or the chance to enjoy the fine beaches. Excellent shelter and good holding has been reported here.

A settled weather anchorage off the mouth of the Río del Puente del Puerto offers the chance to dinghy 2M up the river to the town (of the same name) with its shops, restaurants, banks etc.

6. Camariñas

Location
North side Ría de Camariñas and Muxia
43°07′.47N 09°10′.70W

Charts
Admiralty   3633, 1113
Spanish   927
Imray   C48

Tides
See ría page 35

Final approaches ⊕
⊕25 (037°/0.7M from ⊕24)

Light
Breakwater beacon Fl.R.5s3M Red concrete beacon

Fuel
Available

Communications
Club Náutico de Camariñas
☎ 981 737 130 *Fax* 981 736 1325
Email cnc@cibergal.com
www.come.to/cncam
VHF Ch 09

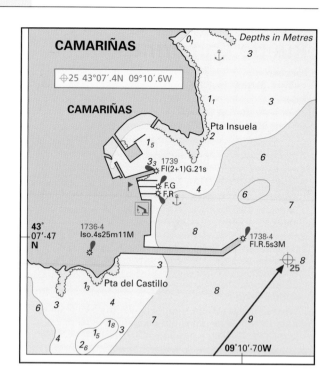

Welcoming and efficient marina

Camariñas has an attractive harbour enclosed by a long breakwater which gives excellent shelter from all directions other than east and northeast. There is talk of building a mole extending southeast from Pta Insuela to improve protection from that quarter. Shelter from these winds can be found across the ría. The Club Náutico Camariñas has an active dinghy club and a long well-deserved reputation for making visiting yachtsmen welcome.

Approach

See page 34 for approach to the ría; make the final approach to off the Camariñas breakwater from ⊕24. Note shallows extend south of the rear light on Pta del Castillo.

Berthing and anchorage

Visiting yachts are berthed on substantial finger pontoons with visitors generally towards the outer ends. Catamarans and larger yachts use the T ends. At the busiest time of the year it may be necessary to anchor off. Holding is reported to be excellent in 4–5m sand and mud. The berthing master's office is the small wooden hut at the top of the centre pontoon. The fuelling pontoon is immediately beneath that.

Facilities

The club marina provides, or can arrange, most support facilities but it does not have a travel-lift. There are several walls in the old harbour where it might be possible to dry out. Fuel is available on site for normal top up; larger quantities will be readily arranged for delivery by tanker to the main quay – yachts would find this position bumpy in an east wind. Otherwise the nearest alongside fuel pumps are in La Coruña or Muros.

Apart from providing showers, the club has an excellent small bar/restaurant, which was due to be extended by 2006, and two computers for visiting yachtsmen.

The town of Camariñas has a market and shops for reprovisioning. Tourism is increasing and cafés and restarants are close to the harbour.

The marina at Camariñas   *MW*

Camariñas harbour looking west

Major refuels   Marina office, refuel, club with showers/bar/restaurant   Old harbour

Camariñas. Club Náutico Camariñas from the outer mole looking northwest   *MW*

7. Muxia (Mugia)

Location
South side Ría de Camariñas 43°06'.43N 09°12'.92W

Charts
Admiralty 3633, 1113
Spanish 927
Imray C48

Tides
See ría page 35

Final approaches ⊕
⊕26 43°06'.5N 09°12'.4W (150°/0.9M from ⊕22 43°07'.2N 09°13'W)

Lights
Breakwater beacon Fl(2)G.10s12m4M Concrete beacon, green top

Facilities
Being developed (Aug 2005)

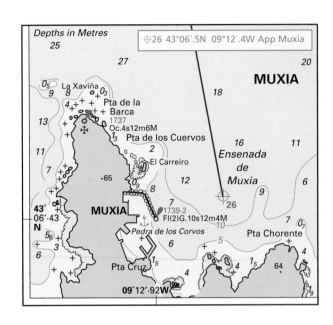

Fishing harbour with improving shelter

This is a minor fishing harbour but with some developing tourism. There are some old buildings amidst the modern blocks; the 17th-century church of La Virgen de la Barca on the northern point has ship models suspended from its arches. A mole system was in the latter stages of construction in August 2005. There is a clean sandy beach to the south of the harbour and fine views over the ría from Punta de la Barca.

Approach

See under ría on page 35 and note warnings.

Anchorage (and berthing)

Anchor in harbour if space or over sand southeast of the outer mole. Space outside is limited and the position likely to be untenable in northerly winds. A pontoon with some visitors berths is due to be provided within the current workings.

Facilities

Several small supermarkets, restaurants, bars, banks, hardware store and post office.

Muxia from the north

I.1.4 Finisterre and Seno de Corcubión

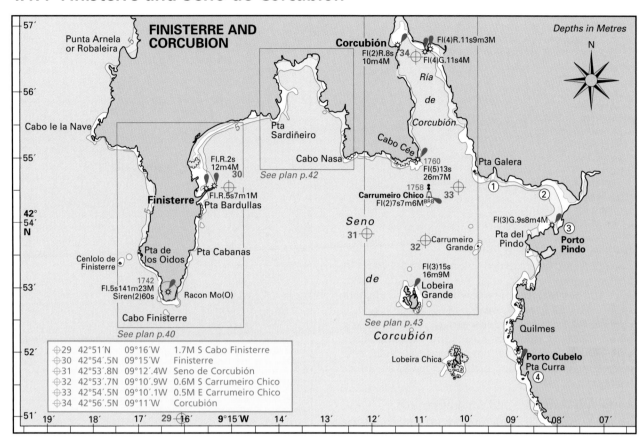

FINISTERRE AND CORCUBION

Depths in Metres

⊕29	42°51′N	09°16′W	1.7M S Cabo Finisterre
⊕30	42°54′.5N	09°15′W	Finisterre
⊕31	42°53′.8N	09°12′.4W	Seno de Corcubión
⊕32	42°53′.7N	09°10′.9W	0.6M S Carrumeiro Chico
⊕33	42°54′.5N	09°10′.1W	0.5M E Carrumeiro Chico
⊕34	42°56′.5N	09°11′W	Corcubión

GALICIA

Lights
1742 **Cabo Finisterre** Fl.5s141m23M 8-sided granite tower and dwelling
1758 **Carrumeiro Chico** Fl(2)7s7m6M Black balls on black beacon, red band
1760 **Cabo Cée** Fl(5)13s26m7M 8-sided tower on white dwelling (to the south see plan page 43)
1782 **Punta Insúa** Fl(3)WR.9s26m15/14M 6-sided tower and house

Finisterre (Fisterra)

42°54′N 9°15′W

Tides
Standard port Lisbon
Mean time differences
HW +0105 ±0010; LW +0130 ±0010
(the above allows for the difference in time zones)
Heights in metres

MHWS	MHWN	MLWN	MLWS
3.3	2.6	1.2	0.5

Note
A considerable inshore set may be encountered south of Cabo Finisterre with a westerly wind and flood tide

Charts
Admiralty   3764
Spanish   927, 9270
Imray   C48

Navtex
518kHz (D) at 0030, 0430, 0830*, 1230, 1630, 2030*
(*weather only)

Weather bulletins
MF 1764kHz at 0703, 1303, 1903
VHF Ch 22 at 0840, 1240, 2010
MRCC Ch 11 at 0233, 0633, 1033,1433, 1833, 2233

Navigational warnings
MF 1764kHz at 0703, 1903
VHF Ch 22 at 0840, 2010
MRCC Ch 11 at 0033, 0433, 0833, 1233, 1633, 2033

Primary working frequencies
c/s Coruña Radio
Manual Ch 22 Tx 1764 Rx 2108
Autolink Ch 27 Tx 2596 Rx 3280
DSC Ch 70 2187.5kHz

Cabo Finisterre
Traffic Separation Zone. See page 32

Overview

The area northeast and east of Cabo Finisterre offers a variety of anchorages depending on the direction of the wind and, to the east, interesting pilotage for rock-hopping sailors armed with Admiralty chart 3764.

Passage planning

Unless intending to explore the area covered by the above plan, yachtsmen are advised to keep well offshore. ⊕19, ⊕27, ⊕28, ⊕35 may act as a guide (see pages 32 and 46). Refer to page 40 if rounding Cabo Finisterre from the north.

8. Finisterre

Location
Cabo Finisterre light 42°52'.94N 09°16'.32W
Finisterre breakwater 42°54'.56N 09°15'.36W

Tides
See page 39

Charts
Admiralty   3764
Spanish   9270
Imray   C48

Final approach ⊕
⊕30 42°54'.5N 09°15'W Finisterre

Light
Breakwater end beacon Fl.R.4s12m4M

Facilities
Little for yachts

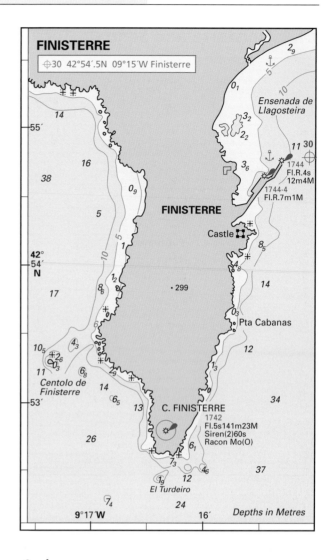

A picturesque fishing harbour

The harbour is crowded with fishing boats. It provides good shelter from west and south but is open to the northeast. The town has the usual small shops, bars and restaurants; it becomes crowded in summer with tourists. Most go to the lighthouse where there is a small restaurant and stunning views and walks on a fine day. Finisterre has two interesting churches, one 12th century and the other baroque.

Rounding Finisterre and final approach.

From the north The main options are either to keep 2M off and avoid the 2m patch La Carraca and, 1M to the southeast, Centolo de Finisterre (an island some 20m high), or to come inside both – much will depend upon the weather. At the point there is a similar option: either pass more than 0.5M off or about 200m off in order to avoid El Turdeiro shoal – a large-scale chart is needed for the latter passage. Once round, keep at least 300m off until reaching Finisterre breakwater (1744).

From the south Give Punta Insúa (1782) a 5M offing to clear Bajo de los Meixidos and head straight for Finisterre mole. On a night approach, take the outside passages and keep at least 300m away from the east coast.

Anchorage

There is a small boat pontoon, the harbour is full of moorings and anchoring abeam the breakwater may be uncomfortable, particularly in north or northeast winds. A popular anchorage, which provides protection from the summer northerly winds is off the sandy beach of Ensenada de Llagosteira. The southwest end is foul.

Finisterre from the southeast

Finisterre lighthouse from the south. Finisterre harbour and anchorage visible east and north

Anchorage north of Finisterre   *MW*

Finisterre lighthouse   *MW*

Ensenada del Sardiñeiro

(See plan page 39)

Entrance
42°55.5N 09°13´.40W

Tides
See page 39

Charts
Admiralty   3764
Spanish   9270
Imray   C48

An unspoilt anchorage

Although open to the south, this unspoilt anchorage provides good protection from west through north to east. Both Playa Sardiñeiro and Playa Esordi are good bathing beaches.

Approach

Approach is straightforward but care is required to avoid the shallow patch of La Eyra.

Ensenada del Sardiñeiro anchorage   *RI*

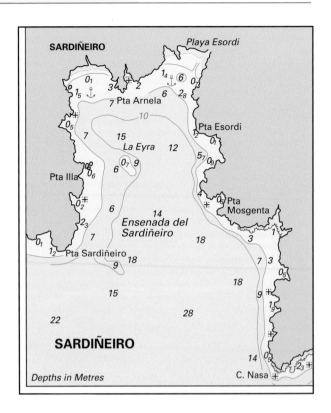

Anchorage

Anchor in either bay to suit conditions. Both offer good holding in sand, though Playa Sardiñeiro generally has the least swell.

Facilities

The village, with supermarkets, restaurants and camp site, straddles the road between Corcubión and Finisterre.

Pta Arnela (centre) divides the two anchorages of Ensenada del Sardiñeiro, seen from the S

9. Corcubión

Locations (see plan page 39)
Mouth of ría (⊕33) 42°54′.5N 09°10′.1W
Corcubión fish quay 42°56′.6N 09°11′.35W

Tides
See page 39

Charts
Admiralty 3764
Spanish 9270
Imray C48

Warning
There are considerable hazards on the approach to the ría and south and east of it

Port radio
Corcubión Practicos VHF Ch 14,16

Facilities
Usual village shops and restaurants.

Little used by yachts

Most of the more sheltered spots in Ría de Corcubión are occupied by small craft moorings. In the past Corcubión enjoyed considerable importance, not least because its relatively narrow entrance was overlooked by twin forts which allowed it to be defended in a way not possible in most other rías.

The small town, which is on the west bank of the ría, is a summer holiday resort with banks, shops, restaurants and bars. In contrast, there is a large industrial plant on the east side of the ría polluting the atmosphere with coal dust.

Waterborne processions mark the fiesta of the Virgen del Carmen on 16 July (also at Muros and in many other harbours). Cee, a larger town at the head of the estuary, can be reached on foot or by bus.

Approach

From the west See page 40 regarding rounding Finisterre.

From the south Give Punta Insúa an offing of at least 5M to clear Bajo de los Meixidos, or if using the inner passage, hold the course towards Finisterre (and ⊕29) until the passage between Carrumeiro Chico and Isolote Lobeira Grande can be approached from the southwest. ⊕31, ⊕32, ⊕33 and ⊕34 indicate the safe route.

Anchorages

(See photograph page 44.) Although it may be possible to lie alongside the fishing quay this becomes uncomfortable as soon as wind builds up. Be prepared to anchor. Anchorages in the ría, none of which offer shelter from southerly winds, are:

1. In the small bay north of Punta de Quenje. Inshore is occupied by moorings, but some shelter will still be gained outside them – even so it would be uncomfortable in winds from south through east to north. There is a restaurant on the beach fringing the bay, and considerable recent development to the south.

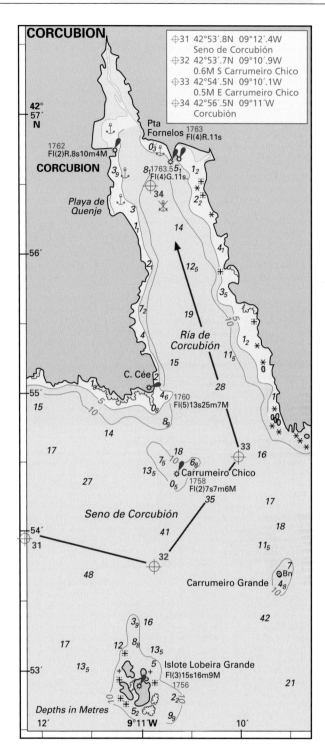

2. Southeast of the main quay in 8–10m is probably the best bet, as it has yet to be filled with moorings.
3. North of the main quay in 3–4m, between the many small-craft moorings and the shoal water to the north. Holding is poor. If not busy it might be possible to lie alongside briefly.
4. In the northeast corner of the ria between the commercial quay and Punta Fornelos. Depths shoal rapidly once within the 5m line. This anchorage provides shelter in strong north winds.

The bottom in all these anchorages is a mixture of rock and sand and the holding is variable.

Corcubión   Fishing quay   Cée Shipyard   Industry

The upper reaches of Ría de Corcubión

Anchorages and harbours east and south of Ría Corcubión

Yachts rarely visit the area surrounded by reefs and rocky outcrops off the coast heading south from Ría Corcubión. Given settled weather, chart 3764 and an escape plan, there are several anchorages worth visiting.

1. **Off Playa Gures** 42°54′.6N 09°08′.9W

Anchor in sand, avoiding the weed patches, with shelter from the north but with a possibility of squally winds.

2. **Ensenada de Ezaro** 42°54′N 09°08′W

This is a beautiful bay with fine beaches but totally exposed to the west. The rocky banks of Los Bois and El Asno might complicate a hasty departure.

3. **Porto del Pindo** Breakwater green column at 42°53′.81N 09°08′.04W

The harbour is open to the north but, with eyeball navigation on the approach, temporary space might be found near the head of the mole. The inner harbour is full of moorings. Pindo has restaurants and limited supplies.

4. **Porto Cubelo** Breakwater green column at 42°48′.45N 09°08′.13W

This harbour is best approached from the north/northeast to avoid the numerous rocks and reefs to the northwest and west. A short stop near the end of the breakwater, on a calm sunny day when eyeball navigation is possible, might be considered.

Looking north over Pta del Pindo and the harbour (3) to Ensenada de Ezaro (2). Playa Gures (1) is just to the west

Porto Cubelo (4)

I.2 Finisterre to Isla Ons (Ría de Muros and Ría de Arosa)

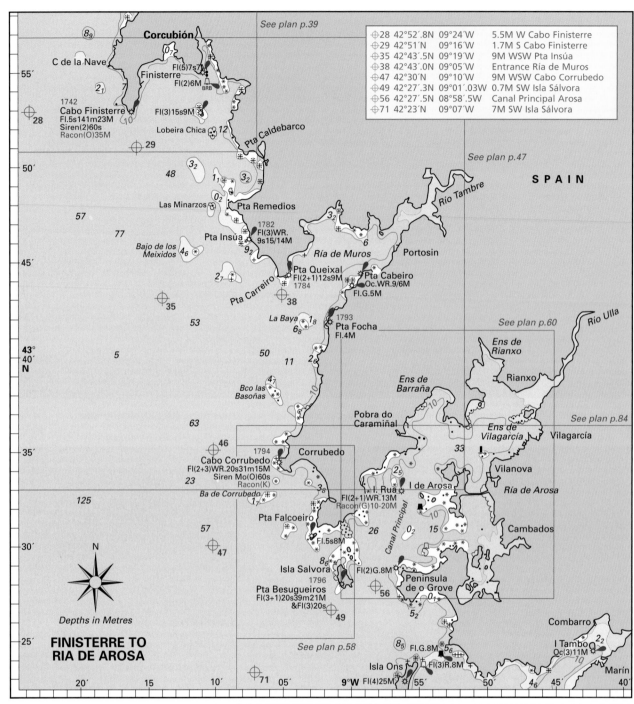

See plan p.39
See plan p.47
See plan p.60
See plan p.84
See plan p.58

⊕28 42°52′.8N	09°24′W	5.5M W Cabo Finisterre
⊕29 42°51′N	09°16′W	1.7M S Cabo Finisterre
⊕35 42°43′.5N	09°19′W	9M WSW Pta Insúa
⊕38 42°43′.0N	09°05′W	Entrance Ría de Muros
⊕47 42°30′N	09°10′W	9M WSW Cabo Corrubedo
⊕49 42°27′.3N	09°01′.03W	0.7M SW Isla Sálvora
⊕56 42°27′.5N	08°58′.5W	Canal Principal Arosa
⊕71 42°23′N	09°07′W	7M SW Isla Sálvora

Corcubión
C de la Nave
Finisterre
Fl(5)7s7M
Fl(2)6M BRB
2₁
1742 Cabo Finisterre
Fl.5s141m23M
Siren(2)60s
Racon(O)35M
Fl(3)15s9M
Lobeira Chica 12
Pta Caldebarco
0₇
10
SPAIN
48 3₂
1₁ 3₂
0₂
Las Minarzos
Pta Remedios
57
77
Bajo de los Meixidos 4₆
1782 Fl(3)WR. 9s15/14M
Pta Insúa 9₂
Río Tambre
3₂
6
Ría de Muros
Portosin
Pta Carreiro
2₇
Pta Queixal
Fl(2+1)12s9M
1784
38
Pta Cabeiro
Oc.WR.9/6M
Fl.G.5M
53
35
La Baya 1₈
6₈
1793
Pta Focha
Fl.4M
Río Ulla
Ens de Rianxo
43° 40′ N
5
50
11
2₆
Rianxo
Ens de Barraña
Bco las Basoñas 4₇
Ens de Vilagarcía
Vilagarcía
63
Pobra do Caramiñal
46
1794 Cabo Corrubedo
Fl(2+3)WR.20s31m15M
Siren Mo(O)60s
Racon(K)
23
Corrubedo
33
Vilanova
Ba de Corrubedo 1₇
3₈
2₅
I. Rua
Fl(2+1)WR.13M
Racon(G)10-20M
I de Arosa
Ría de Arosa
125
Pta Falcoeiro
26
0₂
15
Cambados
57
47
Fl.5s8M
8₆
N
Isla Salvora
Fl(2)G.8M
Peninsula de o Grove
0₁
1796
Pta Besugueiros
Fl(3+1)20s39m21M
&Fl(3)20s
49
56
5₂
Combarro
I Tambo 2₂
Oc(3)11M
Depths in Metres
8₅ Fl.G.8M 5₆
10
Marín
25′ FINISTERRE TO RIA DE AROSA
71 05′
9°W
Isla Ons
Fl(3)R.8M
55′
50′
4₆ 45′
40′
Fl(4)25M
20′ 15 10′

Lights
1742 **Cabo Finisterre** Fl.5s141m23M 8-sided granite tower and dwelling
1782 **Pta Insúa** Fl(3)WR.9s26m15/14M 6-sided tower and house
1784 **Pta Queixal** Fl(2+1)12s26m9M 6-sided granite tower and dwelling
1793 **Pta Focha** Fl.5s28m4M White tower and round dwelling
1794 **Cabo Corrubedo** Fl(2+3)WR.20s31m15M Round tower on white dwelling
1796 **Isla Sálvora** Fl(3+1)20s39m21M White 8-sided tower, red band
1847.3 **Isla Ons** Fl.R.4s126m25M 8-sided white tower

Coastguard
Fisterra ☎ 981 767 500

Sea Rescue Service
☎ 900 202 202
MRCC Finisterre Ch 11

Weather
Navtex (D)
Finisterre Ch 22 at 0840, 1240, 2919

Pta Insúa   *MW*

Pta Queixal   *MW*

Corrubedo   *MW*

Corrubedo daymark   *MW*

Approaches to Ría de Muros

Tides

Standard port Lisbon
Mean time differences (at Muros)
HW +0100 ±0010; LW +0125 ±0010
(the above allows for the difference in time zones)
Heights in metres

MHWS	MHWN	MLWN	MLWS
3.5	2.7	1.3	0.5

Charts

	Approach	Ría
Admiralty	3633, 3764	1756
Spanish	415	415A
Imray	C48	

Warning

Note the dangerous breaking shoals of Los Meixidos, Los Biuyos, Baco las Basoñas, La Baya

A scenic ría

Ría Muros is the least developed of the rías. It has good anchorages, old towns and a welcoming marina at Portosin.

Approach

The safest approach, and in particular by night, is from the westsouthwest towards ⊕38. Keep 5M off Pta Insúa or 3M off Cabo Corrubedo. In fairweather:

From the north Canal de Los Meixidos may be used (⊕29, ⊕36, ⊕37, ⊕38) Do not cut inside the prominent rock off Pta Carreiro.

From the south Canal de Las Basoñas, the passage inside the banks, may be used.

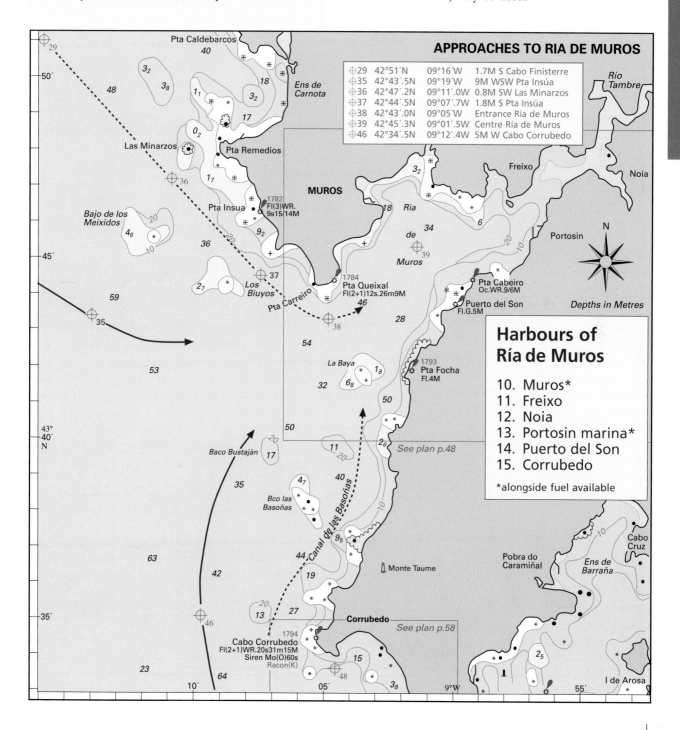

APPROACHES TO RIA DE MUROS

⊕29	42°51′N	09°16′W	1.7M S Cabo Finisterre
⊕35	42°43′.5N	09°19′W	9M WSW Pta Insúa
⊕36	42°47′.2N	09°11′.0W	0.8M SW Las Minarzos
⊕37	42°44′.5N	09°07′.7W	1.8M S Pta Insúa
⊕38	42°43′.0N	09°05′W	Entrance Ría de Muros
⊕39	42°45′.3N	09°01′.5W	Centre Ría de Muros
⊕46	42°34′.5N	09°12′.4W	5M W Cabo Corrubedo

Harbours of Ría de Muros

10. Muros*
11. Freixo
12. Noia
13. Portosin marina*
14. Puerto del Son
15. Corrubedo

*alongside fuel available

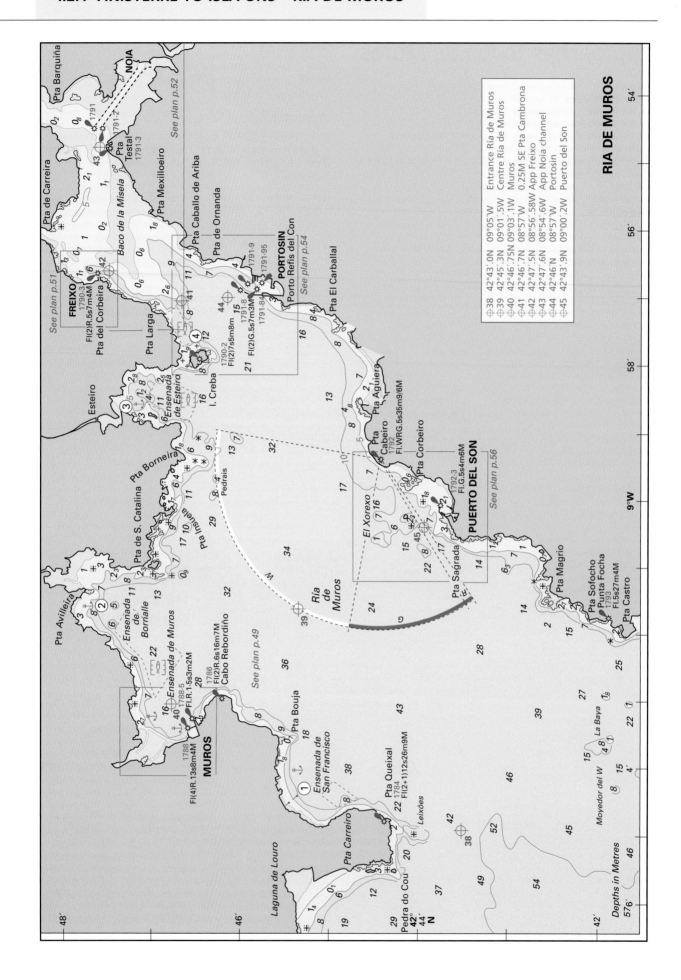

RIA DE MUROS

⊕38	42°43'.0N	09°05'W	Entrance Ría de Muros
⊕39	42°45'.3N	09°01'.5W	Centre Ría de Muros
⊕40	42°46'.75N	09°03'.1W	Muros
⊕41	42°46'.7N	08°57'.7W	0.25M SE Pta Cambrona
⊕42	42°47'.5N	08°56'.58W	App Freixo
⊕43	42°47'.6N	08°54'.6W	App Noia channel
⊕44	42°46'.N	08°57'.W	Portosin
⊕45	42°43'.9N	09°00'.2W	Puerto del Son

10. Muros

Location
42°46′.66N 09°03′.30W

Tides
See page 47

Charts
Admiralty 1756
Spanish 415A
Imray C48

Final approaches ⊕
⊕40 42°46′.75N 09°03′.1W

Lights
Breakwater beacon Fl(4)R.13s8m4M White round tower

Fuel
Available

Communications
☎/Fax 981 826 140
Email muros@portosdegalicia.com

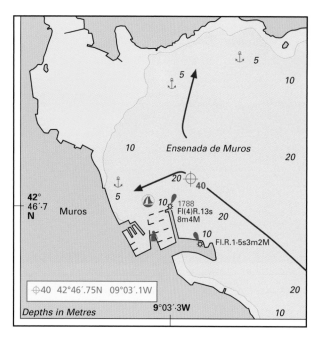

A pleasant fishing town with increasing tourism and probable future marina

The whole feeling of Galicia changes as one rounds the Lauro peninsula past Pta Queixal and enters the warmer, softer ría with its immediate sense of increased shelter and temperature, tourism and prosperity. Inland, the fields of sweet-corn give way to massed vineyards. Muros is a picturesque old fishing town with colonnaded pavements, narrow streets, covered and open-air markets, a Romanesque church and a number of bars and restaurants. It has long been popular with cruising yachtsmen due to both its atmosphere and its facilities. Waterborne processions mark the fiesta of the Virgen del Carmen on 16 July, a practice which has spread throughout the area. The town is popular with tourists.

Approach

Head northeast from the mouth of the ría until Cabo Rebordiño lighthouse comes into view, then steer to clear it by 200m or so. Note recommended track. If approaching by night be aware that there are isolated unlit rafts inside 20m.

Muros harbour and anchorages from the southeast

Popular anchorage in Ensenada de Muros looking
southwest towards the town and harbour.   *MW*

Proposed changes to Muros harbour   *RI*

Berthing and anchorage

A visitor is unlikely to find space on the small
pontoons in the inner harbour. It may be possible to
secure temporarily, between fishing boats, to the
north breakwater where the short stub near the
outer end lessens the effect of swell. There are
proposals to extend the central mole and convert the
inner and outer harbours to pontoon berths.

Currently most yachts will go to anchor unless
they can borrow one of the few private buoys west
of the harbour entrance. Here the bottom of black
mud (and rubbish) drops sharply from 3m to 10m
and a trip line is recommended. The more popular
anchorages are in Ensenada de Muros. Here it is
quieter, cleaner, more scenic – and a longer haul to
town by dinghy. The bay is bounded on the east side
by Isla de San Anton; one can eyeball in to anchor
either side of it.

Facilities

Diesel and water from the CEPSA pump on the inner
mole, where there is reportedly less than 1m at low
tide. The water, from a manhole, is metered. The
attendant is usually on duty from 1000–1300,
weekdays only, but in contrast to many fishing
harbours there is no apparent problem in selling fuel
to yachts.

Repairs would undoubtedly be possible in an
emergency, but work and chandlery is geared
generally to fishing boats. There is a tidal scrubbing
berth at a quay some 600m north of the harbour, on
hard sand with about 2.5m at high water springs. It
is well sheltered other than from southwesterly
swell.

The town is well provided with shops of all kinds,
banks, hotels, restaurants and pavement cafés. There
are excellent ones by the harbour. There is a good
produce market, plus a fish market on the quay.
Supermarkets and a good hardware store will be
found near the north end of the town, some distance
away from the harbour.

Alternative anchorages

(See plan page 48)

1. **Ensenada de San Francisco** 42°45′.4N 09°04′.30W
   In strong northerly winds, the Ensenada de San
   Francisco 1.5M southwest of Muros provides
   good shelter. Anchor in the northern part of the bay
   in 7m or less with excellent holding over sand. Land
   on the beach, where there are shops and cafés.

   In 1999 it was reported that an anchor trapping
   pipe of some kind ran out into the bay from a
   point near the 'lollipop' lights on the road,
   terminating near the 10m line (see plan page 48).
   No more is known of its position or purpose.

2. **Ensenada de Bornalle** 42°47′.60N 09°01′.7W
   In the northwest corner of the Ensenada de
   Bornalle, nearly 2M northeast of Muros, in 5m or
   less. There is a good bathing beach and a
   freshwater stream, but holding is variable due to
   large patches of very dense weed. The massed
   ranks of *viveros* in the entrance to the bay give
   some protection from southwesterly swell.

3. In the **Ensenada de Esteiro** 42°47′.20N 08°58′.50W
   about 4M east of Muros, well protected from
   west through north to east. The bay is effectively
   divided into two by a central rocky promontory
   (with shallow off-liers) and anchorage can be had
   on either side in 3–4m over sand and weed,
   avoiding the rock patches. There is a private quay
   on the west shore of the western arm and the
   entire surroundings are somewhat built up. Both
   arms of the bay shelter small but attractive
   beaches and there are normally some *viveros*
   moored in the entrance.

4. Close **northeast of Isla Crebra** 42°46′.60N
   08°57′.6W, now lit at its southerly extreme
   (Fl(2)7s5m8M Metal post 3m) and easily
   identified by the red-roofed building on its
   summit. Anchor north of the Vella rocks and clear
   of the *viveros* in 2–4m, sheltered from southwest
   to north. This is an isolated anchorage in the ría,
   with no facilities and notices forbidding landing.

11. Freixo (Freijo)

(See plan page 52)

Location
42°47´.62N 08°56´.62W

Tide
See page 47

Charts
Admiralty 1756
Spanish   415A
Imray   C48

Final approaches ⊕
⊕42 but not direct from ⊕41

Light
Breakwater beacon Fl(2)R.5s7m4M Red and white

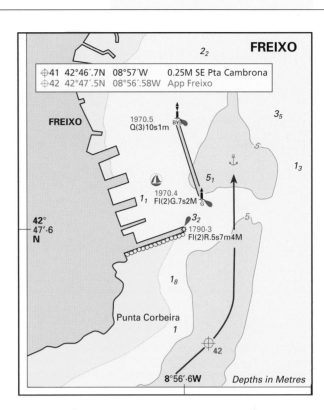

Approach (see plan page 52 and chart 1756)

The deep water shallows as the *viveros* to the northwest of Isla Creba are passed. From ⊕41 pick up the channel as it follows the west bank past the reef extending from Pta Larga. Watch the depth gauge as the channel edge shifts.

Straggling Village with active boat yard

Freixo (Freijo) offers a sheltered anchorage, in 5m mud, and minor food shops and restaurants ashore.

Freixo from the south

Approaches to Freixo and Noia

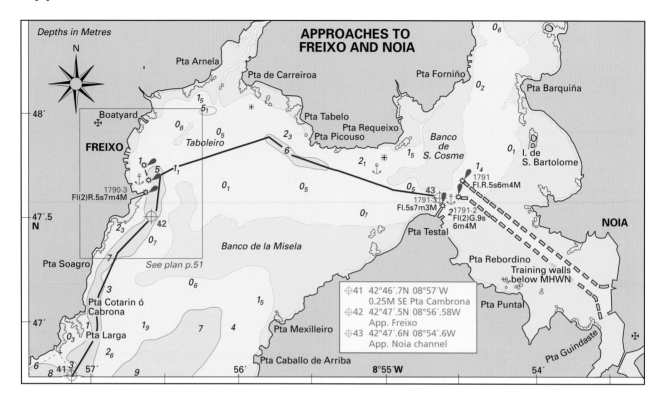

Depths in Metres

APPROACHES TO FREIXO AND NOIA

Pta Arnela
Pta de Carreiroa
Boatyard
FREIXO
Taboleiro
Pta Tabelo
Pta Requeixo
Pta Picouso
Pta Forniño
Pta Barquiña
Banco de S. Cosme
I. de S. Bartolome
1790·3 Fl(2)R.5s7m4M
1791 Fl.R.5s6m4M
43
1791·3 Fl.5s7m3M
1791·2 Fl(2)G.9s 6m4M
NOIA
42
Banco de la Misela
Pta Testal
Pta Soagro
See plan p.51
Pta Rebordino
Training walls below MHWN
Pta Puntal
Pta Cotarin ó Cabrona
Pta Larga
Pta Mexilleiro
Pta Caballo de Arriba
Pta Guindaste

⊕41 42°46′.7N 08°57′W 0.25M SE Pta Cambrona
⊕42 42°47′.5N 08°56′.58W App. Freixo
⊕43 42°47′.6N 08°54′.6W App. Noia channel

See page 51 for Freixo and page 53 for Noia.
The latter can only be reached by dinghy having left the mother ship at anchor at
1. Freixo
2. Southeast of Pta Picouso
3. Off Pta Testal

Tides
 West winds may increase tidal heights in the upper parts of the ría by up to 0.6m, but tidal flow in general is weak.

Training wall
 Beacons are red and white and green and white. Pta Testal beacon is green and white. All are lit.

Freixo. Anchor beyond the wave-breaker – 5m mud   *MW*

The anchorage at Pta Testal   *RI*

Looking northwest between the Noia training walls. Two yachts are at anchor southeast of Pta Picouso   *MW*

12. Noia (Noya)

Location
Noia lies 1M southeast between training walls from Pta Testal (⊕43) at 42°47′N 08°53′.5W

Old town and port now inaccessible to most yachts

The harbour and approaches to Noia are now severely silted but at high water it is still possible for a yacht drawing less than 2m to get within 1M of the town. Then continue by dinghy, or land at the quay at Punta Testal and walk into town, a distance of about 2.5km (taxis are available in the main square for the return journey). Punta Testal is fringed by clear sandy beach, where a yacht able to take the ground could dry out.

Noia, nicknamed 'Little Florence', was an important port in the 15th century and its picturesque, narrow streets and many old buildings and churches reflect its history. A fiesta is held on 24 August.

Approach

Leave Freixo after half flood, or as draught allows. From the 5m patch north of the Freixo molehead head for Punta Tabelo until the 5–6m trench is reached. Follow the trench past Punta Picouso. When it starts to shoal, head just south of the tip of the Punta Testal sand, where red and green buoys mark the start of the channel to the north hand south training wall lights, the northern side of the channel being marked with yellow buoys.

Anchorage (see plan page 52)

Anchor south of Pta Picouso or between the south training wall and Pta Testal molehead. The latter offers more shelter but is a holiday area, the water is shallower and there are many small boat moorings. There is little room for more than one visiting boat to anchor.

Facilities

All the domestic facilities of a bustling small town.

The route to Noia – Pta Testal in foreground

GALICIA

13. Portosin

Location
42°45′.94N 08°56′.91W

Tides
See page 47

Charts
Admiralty 1756
Spanish 415A
Imray C48

Final approaches ⊕
⊕44

Light
Breakwater beacon Fl(3)G.9s Green round tower

Facilities
Good marina and technical support facilities available

Fuel
Diesel on site (depth may be limited at low tide)

Communications
Club Náutico Portosin
☎ 981 766 583 *Fax* 981 766 389
Email info@portosin.com
www.cnportosin.com
VHF Ch 09

Weather
Forecasts posted daily in the marina

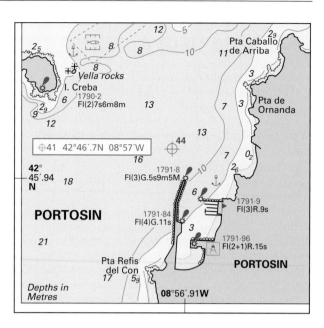

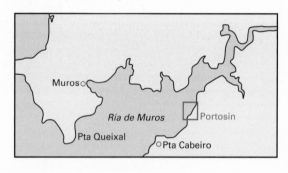

An efficient and pleasant marina

The large harbour houses an established marina and *club náutico* which has long received unanimous praise from visitors. The town is without any great charm, but the marina has an attractive setting backed by wooded hills and with a good beach nearby. A yacht can be left afloat in total safety here, whether exploring ashore or changing crew.

Approach

Head up the middle of the ría to the harbour (App ⊕44) which is on the south shore opposite Isla Crebra. The marina is to port on entering harbour.

Berthing and anchorage

Unless a berth has been pre-arranged, visitors should secure to an outer pontoon. Most berths are bows-on with a mooring line provided astern and yachts up to 20m can be accommodated in depths 2–5m. Shelter is good though some surge may be experienced in northeasterlies.

Office hours are 1000–1030 and 1530–2000 weekdays, 1030–1330 Saturdays, closed Sundays. Charges are based on LOA × beam. The staff are very welcoming and helpful and a range of European languages is spoken.

Anchorage

Yachts may anchor immediately north of the mole in 5–6m, sheltered from northeast through to south or southwest. Holding is reported to be good in sand.

Facilities

Facilities are very good within the marina, both for boat support and domestically. The club has a good bar and restaurant. The town has all normal requirements and a produce market on Saturdays. Portosin is the closest marina to leave a boat whilst visiting Santiago de Compostela (see page 77).

Ashore in Portosin

Portosin offers a welcome break for yachts which have crossed Biscay and rounded Finisterre. The Marina is secure and well placed, has helpful multi-lingual office staff, good showers and laundry facilities, and a club restaurant. It is a useful place to pause to restock, change crew or explore ashore. Boats may be left for extended periods. Hire cars may be arranged from here.

Portosin itself has only modest shops but the head of the ría old town of Noia (declared an Area of Historical Importance) is a short bus trip away. Noia offers supermarkets, an excellent covered market and a weekly general street market. Santiago de Compostela, its airport and the excellent 'Atlantic' motorway, are less than an hour away.

Portosin marina lies to port after entering harbour *MW*

Portosin from the west

Alternative anchorage

42°46´.6N 08°58´.2W

The bay east of Punta Aguieira (1.5M southwest of Portosin) offers an attractive anchorage when the wind is in the southern quadrant. Depths are said to be greater than shown on Admiralty *1756* (shoaling to 2m some way off the beach), and it may be possible to tuck in behind the isthmus running out to the almost-islet of Punta Aguiera and thus avoid any swell running into the ría. Holding is good over sand off an inviting sandy beach.

Typical covered market with fruit, meat and fish, other foodstuffs and general goods   *RI*

Galicia has excellent fish stalls   *RI*

14. Puerto del Son (El Son)

Location
42°43´.74N 09°00´.05W

Tides
See page 47

Charts
Admiralty 1756
Spanish 415B
Imray C48

Final approaches ⊕
⊕45 42°43´.9N 09°00´.2W but from the west and only with great care

Lights
Breakwater beacon Fl.G.5s4m6M Green and white round concrete tower
Pta Cabeiro Oc.WR.3s36m9/6M Grey truncated pyramidal tower

Small fishing harbour

A yachtsman might find shelter here. The village has basic shops and there are good beaches nearby.

Approach

The bay between Puerto del Son and Punta Cabeiro is shallow and largely foul although under ideal conditions it is possible to approach the harbour breakwater on a heading of 180°. A safer route is from the southwest with Pta Cabeiro bearing 056.5° (the narrow-beam red sector of the light) until the end of Puerto del Son breakwater bears 170°.

Alternatively, approach ⊕45 from a westerly direction taking note of El Xorexo reef to the north and the shallows of Bajo Angostin.

Anchorage

Anchor in the outer harbour clear of the approach channel to the fishermen's quays. The likely spot will be abeam the distinctive orange lifeboat. In quiet periods it may be possible to lie alongside the quay for a short while.

Facilities

Water on the quay, shop, restaurants, post office but little else.

Many harbours have lifeboats   *MW*

Puerto del Son from the northwest

15. Corrubedo

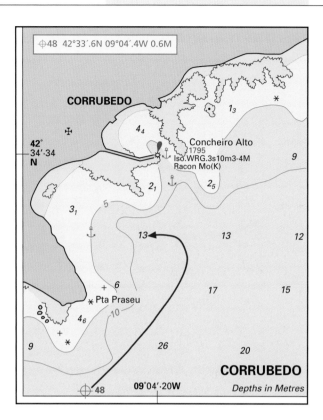

Location
42°34´.34N 09°04´20W

Tides
See page 47

Charts
Admiralty 1734 (essential)
Spanish 415B
Imray C48

Final approaches ⊕
⊕46 42°34´.5N 09°12´.4W 5M W Cabo Corrubedo but only in good conditions and with great care

Lights
Breakwater beacon Iso.WRGs.3s White truncated conical tower
Cabo Corrubedo Fl(2+3)WR.20s31m15M Round tower and daymark (see photographs page 46)

Warning
Yachtsmen should avoid this area in poor weather conditions and at night

A small fishing harbour offering little space or protection

Corrubedo should be visited in fair weather only and using chart 1734. The approaches should only be attempted in calm weather and daylight. If a southerly develops it would be necessary to clear out. There are basic shops and restaurants ashore. To the east lie vast sand dunes and nature trails.

Approach

(See chart 1734 for offshore dangers, not all are recorded here. See page 46 for photograph of lighthouse and daymark.)

From the north Cabo Corrubedo itself has rocks awash up to 600m offshore and there is an isolated reef, La Marosa, 1M south of the lighthouse and about 0.7M off the shoreline. The passage between is feasible, keeping 4.5M offshore, in some 25m, to avoid the covering reefs off Punta Posalgueiro. Continue on this line (through ⊕48) until Corrubedo breakwater bears 350°.

From the south (plan page 58) Either keep 4.5M offshore until Cabo Corrubedo bears at least 050° and then pass between La Marosa and the shore as described above, or take the inshore passage. For the latter, route between ⊕50 and ⊕48 or take a departure from the westernmost rock of Isla Sagres and pick up a course of 356° (the centre of narrow white sector of Corrubedo breakwater light) for 4M to Corrubedo.

Anchorage

The bay to the southwest of the harbour may offer more room and greater comfort than the harbour itself but note the swell in the photo.

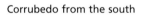

Corrubedo from the south

Northern approaches to Ría de Arosa

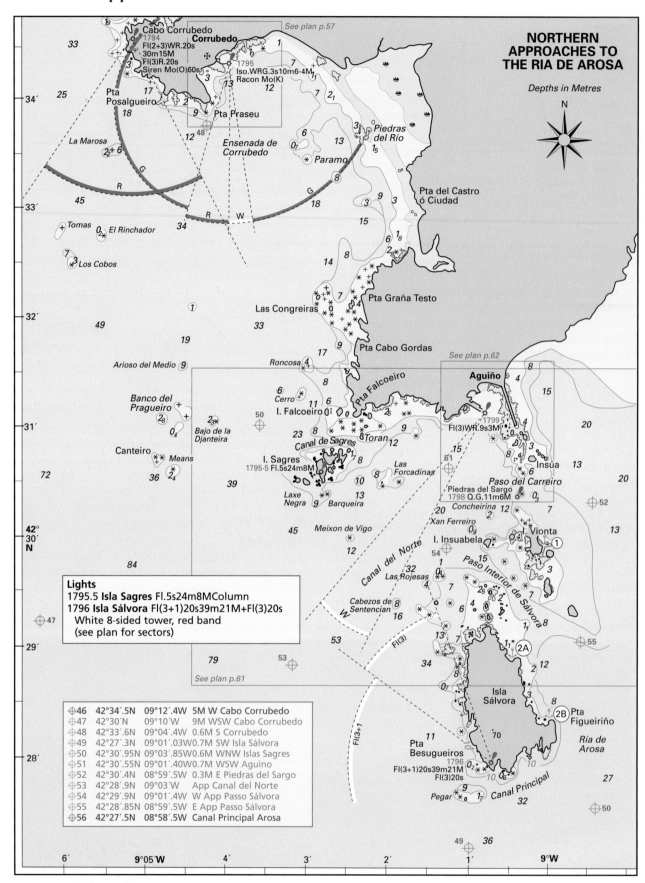

NORTHERN APPROACHES TO THE RIA DE AROSA

Depths in Metres

See plan p.57

Cabo Corrubedo
1794
Fl(2+3)WR.20s
30m15M
Fl(3)R.20s
Siren Mo(O)60s

Corrubedo
1795
Iso.WRG.3s10m6-4M
Racon Mo(K)

Pta Posalgueiro

Pta Praseu

La Marosa

Ensenada de Corrubedo

Piedras del Río

Paramo

Pta del Castro ó Ciudad

Tomas

El Rinchador

Los Cobos

Pta Graña Testo

Las Congreiras

Pta Cabo Gordas

Arioso del Medio

Roncosa

See plan p.62

Aguiño

Banco del Pragueiro

Cerro

Pta Falceiro

I. Falceiro

1799
Fl(3)WR.9s3M

Bajo de la Djanteira

Canal de Sagres

Toran

Insua

Canteiro

Means

I. Sagres
1795·5 Fl.5s24m8M

Las Forcadinas

Paso del Carreiro

Piedras del Sargo
1798 Q.G.11m6M

Laxe Negra

Barqueira

Concheirina

Xan Ferreiro

Vionta

Meixon de Vigo

I. Insuabela

Paso Interior de Sálvora

Lights
1795.5 **Isla Sagres** Fl.5s24m8MColumn
1796 **Isla Sálvora** Fl(3+1)20s39m21M+Fl(3)20s
White 8-sided tower, red band
(see plan for sectors)

Canal del Norte

Las Rojesas

Cabezos de Sentencian

Fl(3)

Isla Sálvora

See plan p.61

Fl(3+1)

Pta Figueiriño

2B

Ría de Arosa

Pta Besugueiros
1796
Fl(3+1)20s39m21M
Fl(3)20s

Pegar

Canal Principal

⊕46	42°34′.5N	09°12′.4W	5M W Cabo Corrubedo
⊕47	42°30′N	09°10′W	9M WSW Cabo Corrubedo
⊕48	42°33′.6N	09°04′.4W	0.6M S Corrubedo
⊕49	42°27′.3N	09°01′.03W	0.7M SW Isla Sálvora
⊕50	42°30′.95N	09°03′.85W	0.6M WNW Islas Sagres
⊕51	42°30′.55N	09°01′.40W	0.7M WSW Aguino
⊕52	42°30′.4N	08°59′.5W	0.3M E Piedras del Sargo
⊕53	42°28′.9N	09°03′W	App Canal del Norte
⊕54	42°29′.9N	09°01′.4W	W App Passo Sálvora
⊕55	42°28′.85N	08°59′.5W	E App Passo Sálvora
⊕56	42°27′.5N	08°58′.5W	Canal Principal Arosa

Ría de Arosa and approaches

Tides
Standard port Lisbon
Mean time differences (at Vilagarcía)
HW +0050 ±0015; LW +0115 ±0005
(the above allows for the difference in time zones)
Heights in metres

MHWS	MHWN	MLWN	MLWS
3.5	2.8	1.3	0.5

Charts
	Approach	Ría
Admiralty	3633, 1734	1768, 1764
Spanish	41B, 925, 926	415B, 415C, 9261, 9263
Imray	C48	C48

Lights
1796 **Isla Sálvora** Fl(3+1)20s39m21M White 8-sided tower, red band
1800 **Bajo Pombeiriño** Fl(2)G.12s14m8M White truncated conical tower, green band
1798 **Piedras del Sargo** Q.G.12m6M White truncated conical tower, green band
1816 **Bajo La Loba** Q.G.9m3M Grey truncated conical beacon tower, green top
1818 **Isla Rúa** Fl(2+1)WR.21s25m13M Grey round tower and dwelling
1824 **Bajo Piedra Seca** Fl(3)G.15s11m8M White truncated conical tower, green band
1826 **Punta del Caballo, Isla Arosa** Fl(4)11s12m10M 8-sided grey tower, white building
1828 **Bajo Sinal de Ostreira** Fl(3)R.9s9m3M White truncated conical tower, red top

The largest Galician Ría

The largest of the Galician rías and perhaps the most attractive for cruising, Ría de Arosa has many pleasant anchorages to explore and some interesting challenges in the way of pilotage. Not surprisingly it is also very popular with the Spanish, both afloat and on the many beaches. Food and other basics may be obtained in most of the small harbours on its shores, though the widest choice is undoubtedly to be had at Vilagarcía de Arosa, an otherwise unappealing town.

The variety of anchorages is such that shelter from any wind direction can be found relatively easily. The simplest harbours to enter in darkness are Santa Uxia de Riveira, Pobra do Caramiñal and Vilagarcía de Arosa – night approaches to other places would be easier with local knowledge, not least because of the dangers posed by unlit *viveros*, of which the Ría Arosa is particularly full.

In addition to the harbours detailed in the following pages, a number of nominal *puertos* exist, usually consisting of a short breakwater (sometimes lit) behind which small fishing vessels lie on moorings. Few can be approached by a keel yacht at all states of the tide. Similarly, not all the possible anchorages in this large ría can be described, though an attempt has been made to include those most popular.

Approach (overview plan page 46)

The easiest and safest approach to the ría, particularly at night or in poor conditions, is from the southwest through the Canal Principal. This leads between Isla Sálvora and Pombeiriño, at the northwest point of the Península de o Grove. Isla Rúa light can be seen from well out to sea, and from offshore is safe to approach on a bearing of between 010° and 025°.

Coming from the north on passage, clear Cabo Corrubedo by 5M to avoid the dangers of Bajos de Corrubedo. When past them, steer to round Isla Sálvora giving the lighthouse a berth of 1M to avoid the Pegar rock group and enter by the Canal Principal. Alternatively ⊕46, ⊕47, ⊕56 apply.

The inshore route passes close round Cabo Corrubedo between the offshore rocks and La Marosa, then continues eastwards until Corrubedo breakwater bears 350°. Then turn south onto 170°, towards Laxe Negra, the low-lying, westernmost rock of the Sagres group, generally with surf breaking on it. Strong and unpredictable currents can run strongly through both these channels, which should not be attempted in less than perfect weather, when they provide an interesting exercise in pilotage.

Refer to page 61 for passages south of Aguiño.

Harbours of Ría de Arosa

16. Aguiño
17. St Uxia de Riveira*
18. A Pobra do Caramiñal*
19. Puerto de Cruz
20. Rianxo
21. Vilagarcía Marina*
22. Vilanova Marina
23. O Grove
24. Cambados*
25. San Vicente*

*Fuel available alongside

Anchorage at Isla de Arosa   *MW*

RIA DE AROSA

Warning
The numerous *viveros* moored near to and sometimes infringing on the channel north of Isla Rúa make it inadvisable to beat up the channel at night or in poor visibility. Their pattern shows up well on Google Earth, as do the shallows to the east of O Grove.

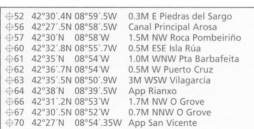

⊕52	42°30′.4N 08°59′.5W	0.3M E Piedras del Sargo
⊕56	42°27′.5N 08°58′.5W	Canal Principal Arosa
⊕57	42°30′N 08°58′W	1.5M NW Roca Pombeiriño
⊕60	42°32′.8N 08°55′.7W	0.5M ESE Isla Rúa
⊕61	42°35′N 08°54′W	1.0M WNW Pta Barbafeita
⊕62	42°36′.7N 08°58′W	0.5M W Puerto Cruz
⊕63	42°35′.5N 08°50′.9W	3M WSW Vilagarcía
⊕64	42°38′N 08°39′.5W	App Rianxo
⊕66	42°31′.2N 08°53′W	1.7M NW O Grove
⊕67	42°30′.5N 08°52′W	0.7M NNW O Grove
⊕70	42°27′N 08°54′.35W	App San Vicente

Pombeiriño light with Aguiño in the distance   *MW*

16. Aguiño

Location
42°31′.12N 09°00′.95W

Tides
See page 59

Charts
Admiralty 1734 (essential)
Spanish 415B
Imray C48

Final approaches ⊕
⊕51 42°30′.65N 09°01′.40W
SW Aguiño then 030°/0.6M
to breakwater

Light
Breakwater beacon
Fl(3)WR.9s3M Red post

Warning
Strong and unpredictable currents can run strongly
through the channels which should not be attempted
in less than perfect weather or at night

Facilities
Geared for the fishing fleet, usual town facilities

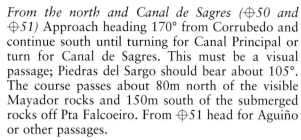

Fishing harbour

Aguiño is dedicated to fishing – primarily for
shellfish. It lies at the head of numerous reefs and
islands which form a National Park.

Approaches

There are four approaches or passages to or past
Aguiño. (⊕ are used for reference; do not link for
direct routing without plotting; visual pilotage is
vital. The plan should not be used for navigation.)

*From the north and Canal de Sagres (⊕50 and
⊕51)* Approach heading 170° from Corrubedo and
continue south until turning for Canal Principal or
turn for Canal de Sagres. This must be a visual
passage; Piedras del Sargo should bear about 105°.
The course passes about 80m north of the visible
Mayador rocks and 150m south of the submerged
rocks off Pta Falcoeiro. From ⊕51 head for Aguiño
or other passages.

To/from the Ría – Paso del Carreiro (⊕51 and ⊕52)
Piedras del Sargo light is prominent (white
tower/green band). The passage is about 250m wide;
keep 150m north of the tower to avoid its two
offlying rocks. If heading up Ría de Arosa from this
passage, beware Bajo Trouza del Sur to port; Isla
Rúa, a distinctive clump of rocks with a prominent
lighthouse, is 3M up the ría. ⊕60 is abeam.

Canal del Norte (⊕53 and ⊕51) The centre line of
the white sector is 032° to Aguiño breakwater light

Passo Interior de Sálvora (⊕54 and ⊕55) This route
is suited to local fishermen or devoted rock-hoppers.

Anchorage

The Las Centolleiras reef continues to be filled in to
form a causeway protecting the harbour from the
east. As a result the harbour is reasonably sheltered,
though the entrance is exposed to the southwest.
The best anchorage is occupied by smallcraft
moorings. Anchor about 150m north or northeast of
the breakwater as space allows in 2–4m over sand,
keeping clear of the approach to the fishermen's
quay on the inside of the breakwater.

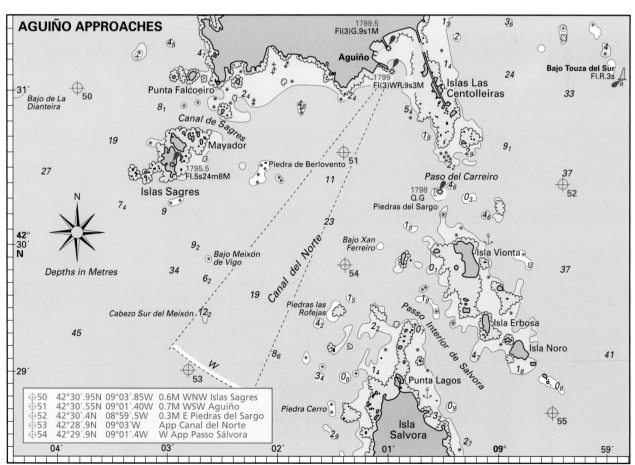

AGUIÑO APPROACHES

⊕50	42°30′.95N	09°03′.85W	0.6M WNW Islas Sagres
⊕51	42°30′.55N	09°01′.40W	0.7M WSW Aguiño
⊕52	42°30′.4N	08°59′.5W	0.3M E Piedras del Sargo
⊕53	42°28′.9N	09°03′W	App Canal del Norte
⊕54	42°29′.9N	09°01′.4W	W App Passo Sálvora

GALICIA

Looking WSW over Aguiño towards Canal de Sagres

Alternative anchorages

(See plan page 58)

The following isolated anchorages offer interesting daytime exploring in settled weather, but have intricate approaches and in an easterly (not uncommon in the rías) would be difficult to leave. None are recommended for an overnight stop.

1. **Isla Vionta**, (northeast coast 42°30′N 9°00′W). Off the small beach over sand, rock and weed.
2. **Isla Sálvora**. The island is a military area and landing is discouraged, though there appears to be no objection to picnicking on Playa dos Bois. A polite approach to the guards may result in an invitation to visit the *castillo* and other places of interest.
   A. *Playa dos Bois* (northeast coast 42°28′.9N 9°00′.5W). Off the beach over sand and weed.
   B. *Playa del Castillo* (east coast 42°28′.4N 9°00′W). Off a short stone mole at the southern end of a pair of small sandy beaches, in 4–5m over sand, rock and weed. The *castillo* which gives the bay its name is a low stone affair with a tiled roof.

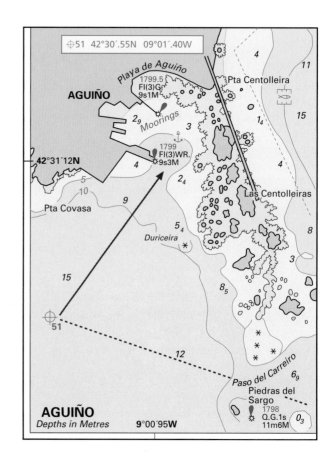

Fishing for shellfish is the priority at Aguiño

Aguiño fisherman. Work continues beyond to enhance
protection from the east

Shellfish drags. The pole may be up to 25m long and trail
behind the fishing boat; give a wide berth.

All photos MW

GALICIA

17. Sta Uxia de Riveira (Ribeira)

(Old charts may refer to St Eugenia)

Location
42°33'.75N 08°59'.26W

Charts and tides
See ría page 59

Harbour chart
Admiralty 1755

Final approach ⊕
⊕59 42°33'.7N 08°59'W
App Sta Uxia de Riveira

Light
Marina breakwater beacon
Fl(2+1)G.15s3M GRG pillar
See plan for main harbour lights

Fuel
Available

Communications
Club Náutico Deportivo de Ribeira
☎ 981 874 739 *Fax* 981 873 801
Email náutico@riveira.com
www.náuticodeRiveira.com
VHF Ch 09

Facilities
Good

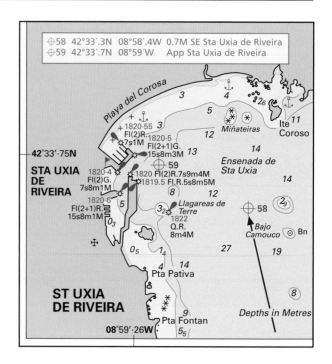

Llagareas de Terre in foreground and the port and marina of Riveira

Small club marina next to large commercial harbour

The main harbour caters for coasters, fishing boats and small local boats. It is well marked and has a substantial breakwater. Yachts go to the marina immediately to the north which offers shelter.

Approach

Riveira lies in the bay to the west of the prominent Isla Rúa. Approach is straightforward via ⊕57, ⊕58, ⊕59. Head up the ría towards Isla Rúa until clear of Bajo Touza del Sur to the southeast of Castineira. As the bay opens, identify the harbour wall, and off-lying red topped tower of Llagareos de Terre Q.R, before closing the marina breakwater.

Berthing and anchorage

Visitors may be directed to lie bow to one of the inner pontoons in the northern part of the marina where depths are at least 5m. Boats of up to 16m can be accommodated. The outer pontoon is likely to be untenable in a northeaster.

Anchorage is possible off Playa del Corosa to the northeast of the marina in 3–5m over sand and mud.

Marina breakwater head with anchorage off beach beyond

Facilities

On-site club facilities are good, although very little English is spoken. Technical support is available in the area and the club has a pleasant restaurant The marina is close to the large town with a wide choice of restaurants and all normal facilities. There is a good supermarket reasonably close by, plus a produce and fish market.

GALICIA

Alternative anchorages

1. **Northeast of Isolote Coroso**
   42°33′.95N 08°58′.05W
   In 3-4m over sand, surrounded by smooth, pinkish boulders. Approach only in good light. Use chart 1755.

2. **Ensenada de Palmeira** 42°34′.90N 08°57′.04W
   Use chart 1734 or 1764. There are isolated rocks shown in the east of part of the bay. Immediately west is the small village and harbour of Palmeira. It has little space and the shallow approach should be checked by dinghy before considering entering above half tide for minor provisions or a meal ashore. On the outer breakwater is one of a number of monuments seen on this coast to the many people who have emigrated from Galicia.

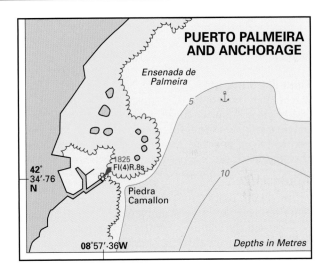

Palmeira outer harbour pontoon   *MW*

Monument to emigrants pointing west, Palmeira   *MW*

18. A Pobra do Caramiñal (Puebla del Caramiñal)

Location
42°36'.25N 08°56'.00W

Charts and tides
See ría page 59
Harbour chart Admiralty
1755

Final approaches ⊕
⊕61 42°35'N 08°54'W
1.0M WNW Pta Barbafeita
⊕62 42°36'.7N 08°54'W
0.5M W Puerto Cruz

Lights
Harbour breakwater
  Fl(3)G.9s9m5M White and
  green round tower
Marina mole head Fl(2+1)R.12s3M White and red round
  tower (low red green red pillar at pontoon head)

Fuel
Yes

Communications
Club Náutico do Caramiñal
☎ 981 877 317 *Fax* 981 878 455
VHF Ch 09

Facilities
Good and being further improved

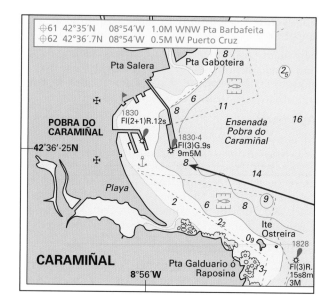

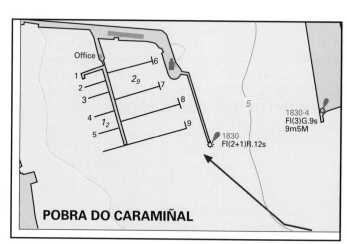

Well-liked marina

Yachtsmen welcome the substantial pontoons at Pobra (as it is known locally) which provides normal marina facilities alongside a useful town. It is well protected by the big ship breakwater from north through west, but exposed to the southeast.

Approach

From abeam Isla Rúa (⊕60) maintain 030° towards ⊕61 to clear the buoyed dangers of Sinal del Maño to port and the shallows off Isla Arosa to starboard.

Head north (towards ⊕62) until a clear passage to Pobra can be seen between the *viveros* heading about 285° which will clear the dangers and *viveros* between Islote Ostreira and the harbour.

Anchorage and berthing

Yachts may anchor off the beach clear of the marina entrance. If berthing has not been pre-arranged in the marina secure to a pontoon and check at the marina office at the top of the gangway.

Facilities

Marina facilities are good and the town offers all the normal support. There is an excellent modern supermarket in what appears to be a rundown yellow building overlooking the anchorage

Alternative anchorage

Southeast of Pobra towards Islote Ostreira inside the *viveros* in 3-5m.

Yacht at anchor beyond marina entrance   *MW*

Final approach to Pobra do Caramiñal

Marina from the outer breakwater across a mussel boat inbound from a day at the *viveros*   MW

19. Puerto de Cruz

Location
42°36´.89N 08°53´.43W

Charts and tides
See ría page 59

Final approach ⊕
⊕62 42°36´.7N 08°54´W
0.5M W Puerto Cruz
(0.45M SW of
breakwater)

Light
Breakwater beacon
Fl.G.5s3M White and
green round tower

Facilities
The village has a small
supermarket, restaurants and a bank

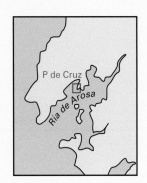

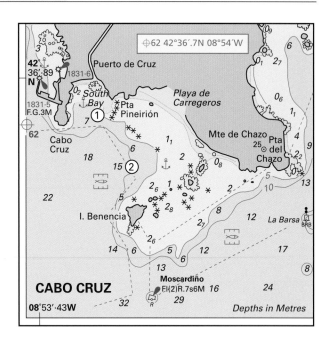

A busy fishing village

A fishing village in an attractive setting, where wooden vessels are hauled out on the quay for painting and repair.

The harbour gives shelter from all winds other than north, while the open bays to the south provide shelter from west through north to east. The village depends for its livelihood on the cultivation and canning of mussels, and there are many *viveros* close offshore.

Approach

There is much foul ground to the southeast of Cabo Cruz, and the safe approach lies west of the distinctive humped Isla Benencia (about 0.7M southeast of Cabo Cruz), 16m high with a rocky

Puerto de Cruz from the east with Pobra de Caramiñal on the far shore

The harbour and fishing boats at anchor, Puerto de Cruz

ridge and a reef extending south-southwest from its southern tip. ('Findlay' or 'Moscardiño' on Admiralty *1768*) marks the southern end of the foul ground.

Head north up the ría keeping west of Isla Benencia or make for the breakwater from ⊕62 heading 060° for 0.45M.

Alternative anchorages

East of Cabo Cruz

1. **South Bay** 42°36′.74N 08°53′.05W
   Anchor in the centre of the bay clear of the fishing boat moorings in 5m over sand and weed, exposed to southeast round to southwest. There are rocks in the eastern part of the bay off Punta Pineirón.
2. **Playa de Carregeros** 42°36′.38N 08°52′.55
   Anchor in the angle between the southeast end of the beach and Isla Benencia with its associated reef, in 2–3m over sand. There is reasonable clearance between the island and an isolated half-tide rock to the northeast, but approach should only be made

Escarabote   *MW*

Anchorages
Although the harbour offers shelter from the south (and would be untenable in winds from the north) finding space to anchor is likely to be difficult. Anchor northeast of the breakwater in 5–10m mud as space allows.

in flat conditions and good light. Protection is excellent from north to east, while both the reef (largely exposed at low tide) and the closely-packed *viveros* give some shelter from the south.

Northwest of Cabo Cruz

3. **Playa Barrana (Escarabote)** (see plan page 60 and chart 1764)
   Holding is good in 3m over mud and sand. The bay is exposed from the southeast through to southwest. Escarabote offers a place to land; small yachts might anchor near the harbour mouth.

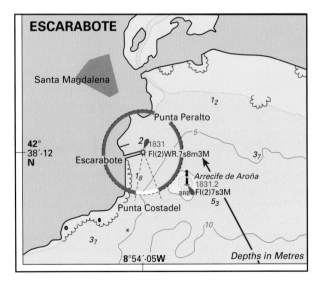

20. Rianxo (Rianjo)

Location
42°39′.00N 08°49′.40W

Charts and tides
See ría page 59, and chart 1764

Final approaches ⊕
⊕64 42°38′N 08°49′.5W (0.7m south of harbour)

Lights
Breakwater elbow Q(9)15s3M ⟂ card bn
Entrance beacons Fl(3)G Green pillar
Fl(3)R.11s Metal post
Note Works in progress 2005/2006

Fuel
None

Communications
Club Náutico de Rianxo
☏ 981 866 107 *Fax* 981 860 620

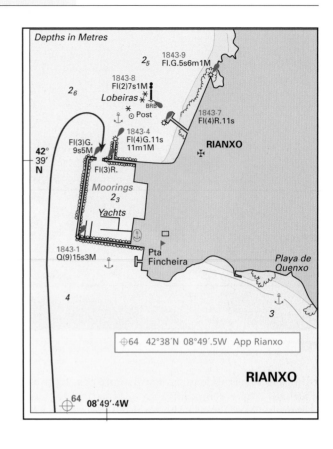

RIANXO

A protected fishing harbour with facilities for yachts

The upgrading programme sweeping Galicia's harbours reached Rianxo in mid 2005. The harbour entrance is now on the north side and the old entrance is closed. The current yacht pontoons will be upgraded but remain broadly in the same place as shown. The majority of the harbour remains in active use by the fishing fleet.

A sardine festival is celebrated in June, while in September the week-long fiesta of Santa Maria de Guadaloupe takes place, with entertainment every evening culminating in an all-night event.

The historic town of Padrón lies 16km away by road. Called Iris Flavia by the Romans, it was important in the middle ages and still displays the stone post to which, legend claims, the boat bearing the remains of St James the Great was moored in the headwaters of the ría. The relics were subsequently lost and rediscovered before coming to rest at what is now Santiago de Compostela.

Approach

Come up the centre of the ría and continue past ⊕63 for 0.35M until ⊕64 (and Rianxo) bears 010° and a clear but watchful approach can be made through the mass of *viveros*. Head north 0.75M from ⊕64 and follow the mole around to the entrance on the north side. A W cardinal beacon is on the SW corner of the harbour.

Berthing and anchorage

Proceed with care on entering harbour as many fishing boats lie to moorings and depths are reported to range from 4 to 2m. Secure to the marina pontoons and seek advice from the security box at the gangway to the pontoons.

Anchoring is not permitted in the harbour but is possible north of the entrance and west of the Lobeiras rocks.

Facilities

There is adequate technical and domestic support available within, or close to, the harbour and the small club is welcoming. The town offers all the normal facilities of a small town, including a good fish market.

New entrance

Closed

Rianxo from the south. The only entrance is from the north

Looking WNW out of the new harbour entrance   *MW*

West cardinal beacon on breakwater SW corner   *MW*

21. Vilagarcía (Villagarcía de Arosa)

Location
42°36´.04N 8°46´.20W

Tides
See page 59

Charts
Admiralty 1764, 1762
Spanish 415C
Imray C48

Final approaches ⊕
⊕65 42°36´.2N 08°46´.6W

Lights
1840.5 **Muelle head** Iso.2s2m10M Round masonry tower
Marina entrance beacons 3-sided towers, red and green, flashing Q.R and Q.G

Facilities
Good marina and technical support facilities available

Fuel
Diesel and petrol

Communications
Marina Vilagarcía
☎ 981 511 175 *Fax* 981 512 792
Email marinavilagarcia@marinavilagarcia.com
www.marinavilagarcia.com
VHF Ch 09

Facilities
Very good

Weather
Forecasts posted daily in the marina

An efficient and welcoming marina

Vilagarcía Marina is self-contained within the arms of the commercial port and is run pleasantly and efficiently by the port authority. The modern office building includes a restaurant and showers; the staff are particularly helpful and will advise, or arrange, lift out or technical support or handle travel or hotel services. There is a pleasant Club de Mar on the outer mole. Yachts may safely be left here while visiting Santiago de Compostela or else laid up. Vilagarcía is a good place for crew change or reprovisioning.

Approach

Approach up the centre of the ría. From abeam Isla Rúa ⊕60, use ⊕61, ⊕64 and ⊕65 which follow a track of 030° from Isla Rúa to clear the northeast hazards of Isla de Arosa and then 075° between the vast *viveros* fields.

Berthing

Do not anchor in the harbour. Call ahead by radio and be prepared to turn immediately to starboard after passing through the narrow marina entrance. Unless ordered to the fuel jetty, expect to secure to finger pontoons (the outer pontoon near the entrance is reported to be untenable in strong northerly winds). Charges in 2005 were €0.36 per m² low season, €0.42 per m² high season

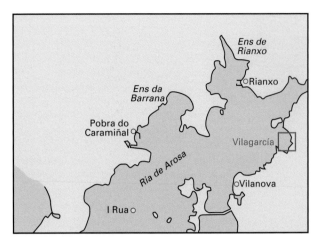

APPROACHES TO VILAGARCIA
08°46´.20W

Vilagarcía marina *MW*

Port office, showers and restaurant *MW*

Green buoy   Vilagarcía Marina   Vilaxoan

The oil tank quay continues to be developed. The marina may be screened on the approach but will become obvious once the course is set to round the green buoy north of that quay

Entrance to Vilagarcía marina   *RI*

Alternative anchorages

1. **Vilaxoan (Villajuan)** 42°35′.41N 08°47′.47W
   Small fishing harbour southwest of Vilagarcía. (See main air photo.) It may be possible to anchor in the shelter of the breakwater or moor alongside the inner quay.

2. **South of Carril** 42°36′.7N 08°46′.85W and the nearby Bahia de Tierra beacon (white tower red band)
   Approach from the southwest and keep clear of the El Porron beacon (yellow lattice metal tower). Keep well clear of the lines of stakes which mark the shell fish beds. Enter the harbour only by dinghy.

Carril. Anchor and take the dinghy to harbour

Isla de Arosa Anchorages

Location
42°34′N 08°52′W

Tides
See page 59

Charts
Admiralty 1764, 1755

Final approaches ⊕
⊕61 42°35′N 08°54′W (1.0M WNW Pta Barbafeita)

Port O Xufre and fuel jetty (Anchorage 1)　　　*MW*

Anchorages, good beaches, dense fishing activity

The Isla de Arosa comprises two islands connected by an isthmus on which the holiday and fishing village of San Xulian (San Julian) sits. It is connected to the mainland by the long El Vado bridge which is conspicuous from the north. The west coast has a number of islets and parts require very careful navigation. The northern approach is clear until closing the shore. The *viveros* are numerous, as are their support boats, but there are clear routes around and between them.

Isla de Arosa Anchorages

1. **Porto O Xufre (Ensenada Norte de San Xulian)** 42°34′.0N 08°52′.1W
This is a friendly, bustling little harbour with a small boat marina and many moored fishing boats. Finding space to anchor (in sand/mud/stones) will be difficult. Fuel is available on the jetty where sports boats, fishing boats and cars squeeze in as best they can. Good supermarket south of the pier.

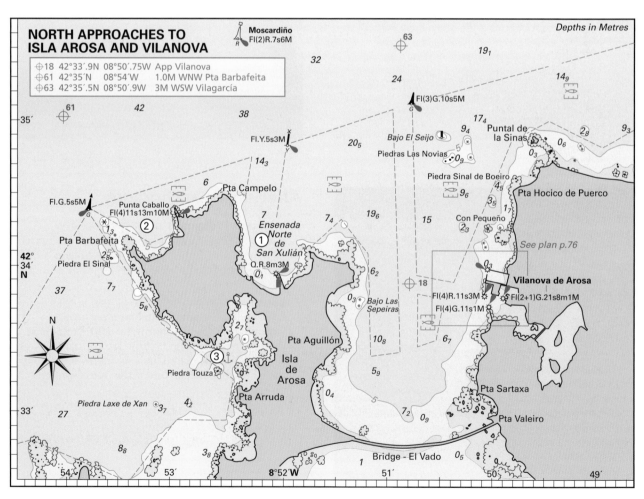

Pta Caballo lighthouse is set back from giant granite rocks. Anchor in the bay beyond (Anchorage 2)   *MW*

Seek space to anchor beyond moorings (Anchorage 3) *MW*

2. Southwest of Pta Caballo off the beach
42°34´.15N 08°53´.22W
A long sandy beach generally clear of the fishing fleet. Approach from the north to anchor in 5–10m clear of the shoreline rocks.

3. Ensenada Sur de San Xulian
42°33´.38N 08°52´.56W
A small harbour, guarded by rocks and filled with small boats. Under good light one might work in and find space before the moorings to anchor. This is a quiet harbour with shoreside restaurants and calm compared to the main port just the other-side of the isthmus to the north. There is good shelter except from the southwest.

Looking east from San Xulian with anchorages 1 and 3 left and right of the isthmus. The route through the *viveros* to Vilanova – central on the far shore – can be seen. Vilagarcía is at top left

22. Vilanova Marina

Location
42°33′.97N
08°50′.04W

Tides
See page 59

Charts
Admiralty 1764,
1755
Spanish 415C
Imray C48

Final approach ⊕
⊕18 42°33′.9N
08°50′.75W (0.5m
west of entrance)

Harbour entrance
Mole heads carry
green and white
and red and white
pillars and lights.

New Marina (under construction 2005)

At the end of August 2005, construction of a new marina at Vilanova was well under way with earthworks seemingly complete, pontoons ready for launching and piling in progress. The shallow water shown on charts appears to have been dredged. Further details of depths and facilities are not yet available but the impression given was of a significant and well equipped marina being rapidly developed.

Approaches to Vilanova

Follow the centre of the ría as if for Vilagarcía (⊕60, ⊕61, ⊕63) and at ⊕63, north of El Seijo green buoy, turn south and follow the passage 1.5M through the *viveros* until ⊕18, when Vilanova bears east.

North harbour will become a marina; south harbour is busy with fishing boats from *viveros*

Vilanova under construction (August 2005)   *MW*

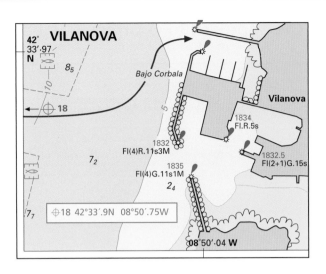

Santiago de Compostela

Since the discovery of the tomb of St James at the beginning of the 9th century Santiago de Compostela has been the focus for thousands of pilgrims to what became the most import Christian site after Jerusalem and Rome. No lesser numbers come today, many on foot following the old medieval routes, and thousands by air.

The cathedral is magnificent and the old city built of local granite glistens in the rain. It is compact and can be explored in a few hours. Those looking for accommodation can stay in style at the Hostal de los Reyes Catolics, now a Parador Hotel.

The fiesta of St James (celebrated throughout the province as Galicia Day) takes place on 25th July with associated cultural events for a week or so on either side. When this date falls on a Sunday the entire year is declared a 'Holy Year' and the fiesta celebrated with even greater enthusiasm. A visit to the basilica on holy days, when the huge incense burner is swung over the crowd by eight priests, is not to be missed.

MW

The approach to O Grove, Cambados and Toxa anchorages

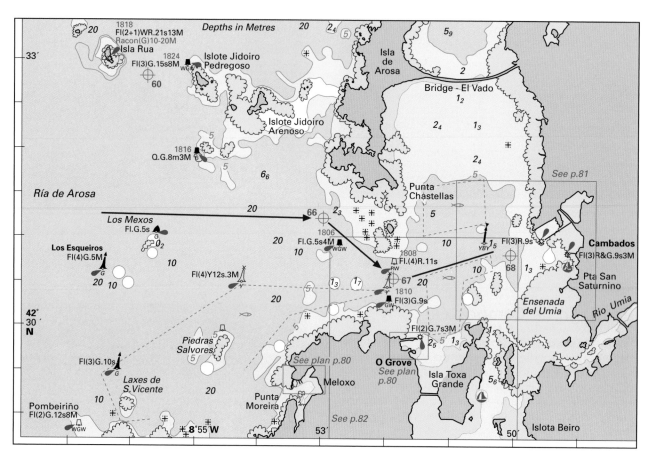

Lights
1816 **Bajo La Loba** Q.G.9m3M Grey truncated conical
   tower, green top
1806 **Bajo Praguero** Fl.G.5s9m4M White truncated
   conical tower, green band
1808 **Bajo Lobeira de Cambados, S** Fl(4)R.11s11m5M
   White truncated conical tower, red top
1810 **Bajo Golfeira** Fl(3)G.9s11m4M White truncated
   conical tower, green top

⊕60 42°32'.8N 08°55'.7W 0.5M ESE Isla Rúa
⊕66 42°31'.2N 08°53'W   1.7M NW O Grove
⊕67 42°30'.5N 08°52'W   0.7M NNW O Grove
⊕68 42°30'.9N 08°50'.0W Ensenada de Cambados

Location
   Centred on 42°30'.5N 08°51'.2W
Tides
   See page 59
Charts
   Admiralty 1764, 1755
   Spanish   4152
   Imray   C48
Approach
   ⊕66 42°31'.2N 08°53'W 1.7M NW O Grove
   ⊕67 42°30'.5N 08°52'W 0.7M NNW O Grove
   ⊕68 42°30'.9N 08°50'.0W Ensenada de Cambados

A chance to stray from the beaten track

O Grove is popular with tourists in season and
numerous tripper boats operate from here.

Cambados is a sophisticated old town with limited
mooring facilities for yachtsmen.

Toxa (Isla Toxa Grande) is for the smart set and
offers pleasant anchorages.

Approach

The area north of the Peninsula de O Grove and approaching Cambados has numerous shallows, rocks and fields of *viveros*. Although it is well marked, the repetitive nature of the area means it is important for navigators to absorb the key features and maintain a plot. Newcomers may find waypoint navigation, whilst monitoring the physical marks, of benefit.

Leave the centre of the ría south of Isla Rúa, heading east for ⊕66 and passing around midway between La Loba in the north and Los Mexos in the south. Both are clearly marked dangers. Note plan page 78 and use chart 1764. From ⊕66 (use chart 1755) track 132°/1M to ⊕67, leaving the beacons of Bajo Praguero to starboard and Lobeira de Cambos to port.

For O Grove Maintain a broad heading southeast, to leave Viveros yellow buoy to starboard, and then run down the line of *viveros* to O Grove harbour.

For Cambados Track between *viveros* on about 075°/1.5M to ⊕68.

For the Toxa anchorages head almost to Cambados before working south through the shallows.

Local boats use a route westwards through the *viveros* from north of Golfeira beacon, passing north or south of Piedras Salvores.

Boats heading north (from ⊕66) can track up the west coast of Isla de Arosa to exit over the shallows east of Isolote Carmallon towards Piedra Touza.

Looking northeast from Peninsula de O Grove. Left is O Grove harbour, right is the bridge to Isla Toxa Grande with an anchorage lying between that island and the small one beyond (Isla Toxa Pequeña). On the far shore in the centre is Cambados

Alternative anchorage

The large bay to the north between Isla de Arosa and the mainland shoals gradually towards the shores and the bridge. It has fine beaches. Anchor in 2–4m.

23. Puerto O Grove (San Martin del Grove)

(See plan page 78)

Location
42°29´.88N 08°51´.52W

Tides
See page 59

Charts
Admiralty   1764, 1755
Spanish   415C
Imray   C48
Final approaches ⊕
⊕67

Light
Breakwater Fl(2)G.7s Green round tower

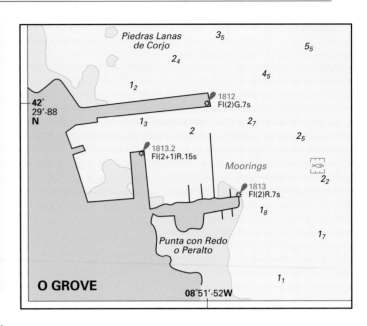

A shallow fishing and tripper boat harbour

O Grove is a major holiday resort and the shallow fishing harbour has been developed for fast tripper boats to visit the offlying islands.

Approach

Route around *viveros* fields from the north, from ⊕67 between the beacons of Lobeira de Cambados and Golfeira (see pages 78–9). Do not cut the corner, rocks protrude well beyond the line between Golfeira and the harbour.

Mooring and anchorage

There is little room for shallow-draught boats to anchor in the harbour, and very limited space outside as the water shoals rapidly immediately south of the harbour. Pick up a mooring buoy outside the harbour but do not leave the boat unattended for long.

Facilities

Water on the quay, usual shops and many restaurants. A seafood festival takes place at O Grove on 14 September.

O Grove from the west. Avoid anchoring in the busy route between harbour entrance and the tripper jetty, lower right

Alternative anchorage

Porto de Meloxo (Melojo) 42°29´.32N 08°53´.51W (Breakwater end with red light) is a fishing harbour on the northwest of the peninsula and exposed to the west. The harbour is full of fishing boats on moorings. One might negotiate to borrow a mooring or anchor outside, although the harbour and the small village appears to have little to offer the yachtsman.

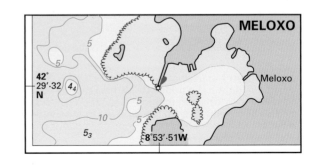

24. Cambados (Puerto de Tragove and Cambados Old Harbour)

(See also plan page 78)

Location
42°30′.91N 08°49′.58W

Tides
See page 59

Charts
Admiralty 1764, 1755
Spanish   415C
Imray   C48

Final approaches ⊕
  ⊕68 42°30′.9N 08°50′.0W Ensenada de Cambados

Light
Breakwater Fl(3)G.9s Green round tower

Fuel
Old harbour.

Old town, shallow harbours

The modern harbour (Puerto de Tragove) is large but shallow and supports the major mussel industry. The old harbour (Cambados-San Tome) is small and shallow but has fuel.

Cambados is a small town with an attractive and historic central square and imposing buildings. It is the home of O Albariño, considered by many to be Galicia's best wine. A *sardiñada* (sardine festival) is held on 25 July (Galicia Day) and a wine festival on the first Sunday in August.

Cambados harbours from the northwest

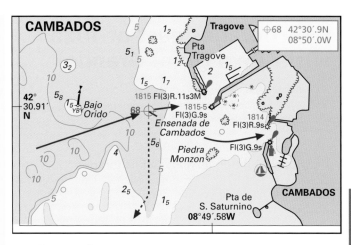

Approach

See page 78–9.

Anchorage and berthing

Main Harbour (Tragove Marina) The harbour shallows rapidly from the major fishing boat pontoon. Only the outer sides of the yacht pontoon should be considered; inside is very rocky. Lying to anchor, facing the harbour mouth, with stern to the pontoon offers greatest depth. Anchoring may be possible behind the fishing boats depending on the random moorings and the busy boat traffic.

Old Harbour (Cambados Marina) This is small, attractive, well placed for the town and claims depths of 2.3m – significantly more than charted. Approach and enter with caution, and check at the fuel dock for mooring opportunities on wall or pontoon. Boats which take the ground may find space beyond the pontoons.

Anchorages east of Toxa (Isla Toxa (Toja) Grande)

(See page 78 and use chart 1755)

Warning
Silting has been reported in the approaches to the anchorages.

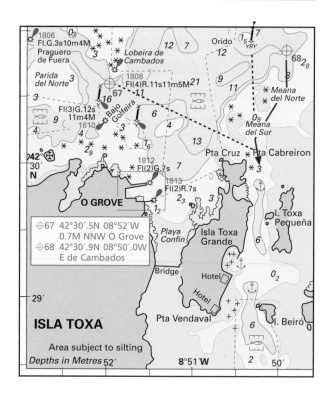

Careful navigation leading to anchorages

Toxa is a smart, well groomed island. The bridge access to the west crosses over drying sands; the anchorages all lie to the east.

Approach

The routes cross sandbanks and should only be made on a rising tide.

From the main channel north of O Grove (shallow-draught vessels) From ⊕67 head on a bearing of about 108° to cross the bank north of Toxa at least 100m offshore; turn to 175° when deep water is reached. On no account attempt to pass inside the rock off Pta Cabreiron.

From off Cambados From Orido buoy head for the middle of the gap between Toxa Grande and Toxa Pequeña on 175°.

From ⊕68 (the 'normal, deeper route'). Head south from ⊕68 on westing 08°50' until on a line of 210° Cambados main harbour entrance and Punta Cabreiron, and then onto 175° shortly before reaching Punta Cabreiron.

Anchorages (and berthing)

See plan, eyeball to avoid shallows and kelp; anchor in 3–5m over sand.

Occasionally space may be available on Marina Isla da Toja jetty ☎ 616 954 252, *Fax* 956 512 792.

Looking SW over Toxa Grande with Toxa Pequeña on the left. Anchorage areas may be seen on the left, south of the small Marina Isla da Toja jetty, and near the *viveros*

25. San Vicente del Mar (Porto Pedras Negras)

Location
42°27′.47N 08°55′.06W

Charts and tides
See ría page 59

Final approaches ⊕
⊕70 42°27′N
08°54.35′W
(0.7M southwest of harbour)

Lights
Breakwater beacon
Fl(4)WR.11s5m4/3M
Red post
Approach buoys
Fl(2)G.9s Green buoy
Fl(3)R.9s Red buoy

Fuel
Yes

Communications
☎ 986 738 325 *Fax* 986 738 325
Email club.náutico.s.v@wanadoo.es
www.cnsvicente.com
VHF Ch 09

Facilities
Good on site, including club restaurant

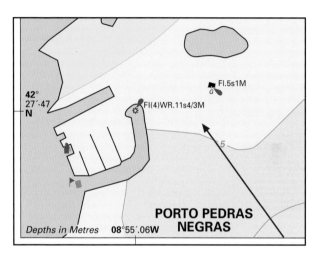

A small, smart marina with good facilities

There is little outside the marina except houses, hotels and a small supermarket. This is a place to relax, enjoy the stunning walk to Pta Miranda or visit the beach.

Approach

If coming from Ría de Arosa keep clear outside the *viveros* of the northwest shores of Peninsula de O Grove and the Roca Pombeirino beacon. Keep at least 800m offshore rounding the complete headland before heading towards the long sandy beach La

Lanzada and ⊕70. This is in the white sector of the breakwater light and between the red and green buoys. Then head direct to harbour.

Berthing and anchoring

Call ahead for a berth or use the first pontoon. There is no space to anchor in the harbour but there are numerous options off the beach to the east, over sand in depths to suit.

San Vicente from the west

GALICIA

I.3 Ría de Arosa to Baiona

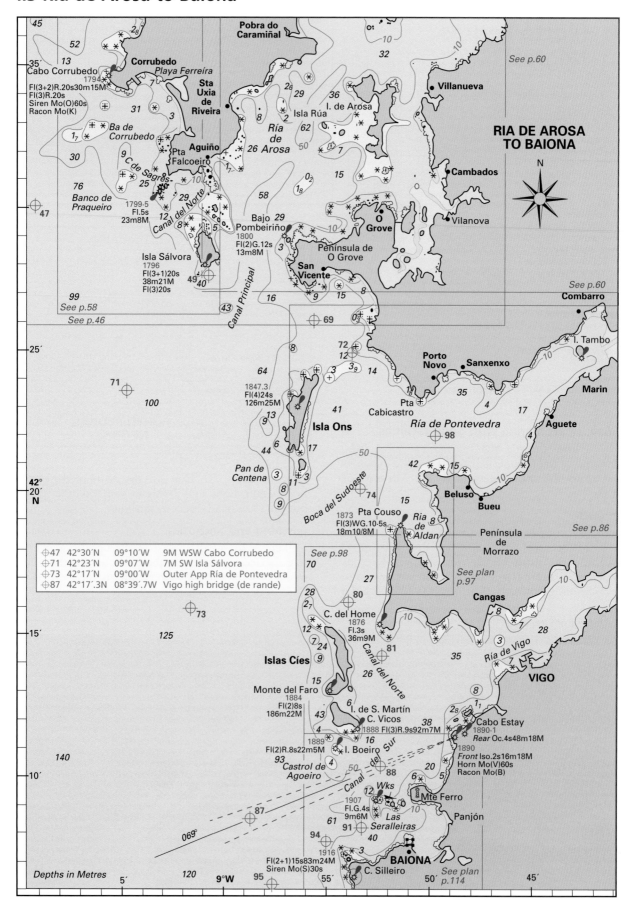

RIA DE AROSA TO BAIONA

N

Depths in Metres

⊕47	42°30′N	09°10′W	9M WSW Cabo Corrubedo
⊕71	42°23′N	09°07′W	7M SW Isla Sálvora
⊕73	42°17′N	09°00′W	Outer App Ría de Pontevedra
⊕87	42°17′.3N	08°39′.7W	Vigo high bridge (de rande)

See p.60
See p.60
See p.86
See p.98
See plan p.97
See p.58
See p.46
See plan p.114

Approaches to Ría de Pontevedra

Location
42°22′N 08°53′W

Tides
Standard port Lisbon
Mean time differences (at Marín)
HW +0100 ±0010; LW +0125 ±0005
(the above allows for the difference in time zones)
Heights in metres

MHWS	MHWN	MLWN	MLWS
3.3	2.6	1.2	0.5

Charts

	Approach	Ria
Admiralty	3633	1732, 1733, 1734
Spanish	416,	416A
Imray	C48	C48

A fast-developing ría

A new fast road to Sanxenxo brings development in its wake, both with tourism and the upgrading of harbour facilities. Senxenxo is a major marina: Cambarro, on the northern shore towards the head of the ría, remains unspoilt. It is worth visiting by sea or land, preferably for a leisurely lunch in one of its numerous restaurants. Pontevedra itself lies upriver and is reachable only by small yacht. The Spanish Naval College has its home and marina at Marin but this is not open to visitors.

Approach

From the north or Ría de Arosa ⊕69, ⊕72, ⊕98 through Paso de Fagilda marked by a red buoy Bajo Fagilda in the north and a beacon on Bajo Picamillo in the south. This tower may be passed up to 0.5M either side or else the route west of Los Camoucos tower may be used (Canal de los Camoucos). Refer to large scale chart.

From the southwest The main channel ⊕73, ⊕74, through Boca del Sudoeste between Isla Ons and the mainland.

From the south and Ría de Vigo ⊕81, ⊕80, ⊕74, through Canal del Norte between Islas Cíes and the mainland.

Note The entrance to the ría proper lies between the unmarked Punta Cabicastro, which has a rock off it, and Cabo de Udra which is surrounded by foul ground (see plan page 86).

Isla Ons (Almacen) looking north over Paso de Fagilda

Coastguard
Vigo ☎ 981 297 403
Sea Rescue Service ☎ 900 202 202
MRCC Finisterre Ch 11
MRSC Vigo Ch 10

Navtex
518kHz (D) at 0030, 0730, 0830*1230, 1630, 2030*
(*weather only)

Weather bulletins VHF
Vigo Ch 65 at 0840, 1240, 2010
MRSC Vigo Ch 10 at 0015, 0415, 0815, 1215, 1615, 2015

Navigational warnings VHF
Vigo Ch 65 at 0840, 2010
MRSC Ch 10 at 0215, 0615, 1015, 1415, 1815, 2215

Primary working freqs
c/s Coruña Radio
Vigo Manual Ch 65
Autolink Ch 62 Tx 2596 Rx 3280
DSC Ch 70 2187.5kHz

Lights (opposite page)
1796 **Isla Sálvora** Fl(3+1)20s39m21M Round tower on white dwelling
1847.3 **Isla Ons** Fl.R.4s126m25M 8-sided white tower
1884 **Monte del Faro** Fl(2)8s186m22M Tower and cabin
1916 **Cabo Silleiro** Fl(2+1)15s84m24M While 8-sided tower, red bands on dwelling

Isla Ons and the harbours of Ría de Pontevedra

Isla Ons
Porto Novo and Sanxenxo
26. Porto Novo
27. Sanxenxo Marina*
28. Combarro and Pontevedra
29. Marin
30. Aguete*
31. Bueu and Beluso
Ría de Alden

*Fuel available alongside

⊕47	42°30′N	09°10′W	9M WSW Cabo Corrubedo
⊕56	42°27′.5N	08°58′.5W	Canal Principal Arosa
⊕69	42°26′N	08°55′.3W	0.9M S Pta Miranda
⊕71	42°23′N	09°07′W	7M SW Isla Sálvora
⊕72	42°24′.5N	08°53′.47W	Canal de la Fagilda
⊕73	42°17′N	09°00′W	Outer App Ría de Pontevedra
⊕74	42°20′.2N	08°53′W	Entrance Ría de Pontevdra
⊕76	42°24′.1N	08°42′.6W	App Marin
⊕80	42°15′.65N	08°53′.3W	N Canal del Norte
⊕81	42°14′.45N	08°52′.65W	S Canal del Norte
⊕88	42°10′N	08°52′.7W	Canal del Sur
⊕89	42°08′.5N	08°58′W	Outer App Canal del Sur
⊕91	42°07′.95N	08°53′W	0.8M SSW Islotes Las Serralleiras
⊕95	42°06′.5N	08°56′.6W	2M W Cabo Silleiro

GALICIA

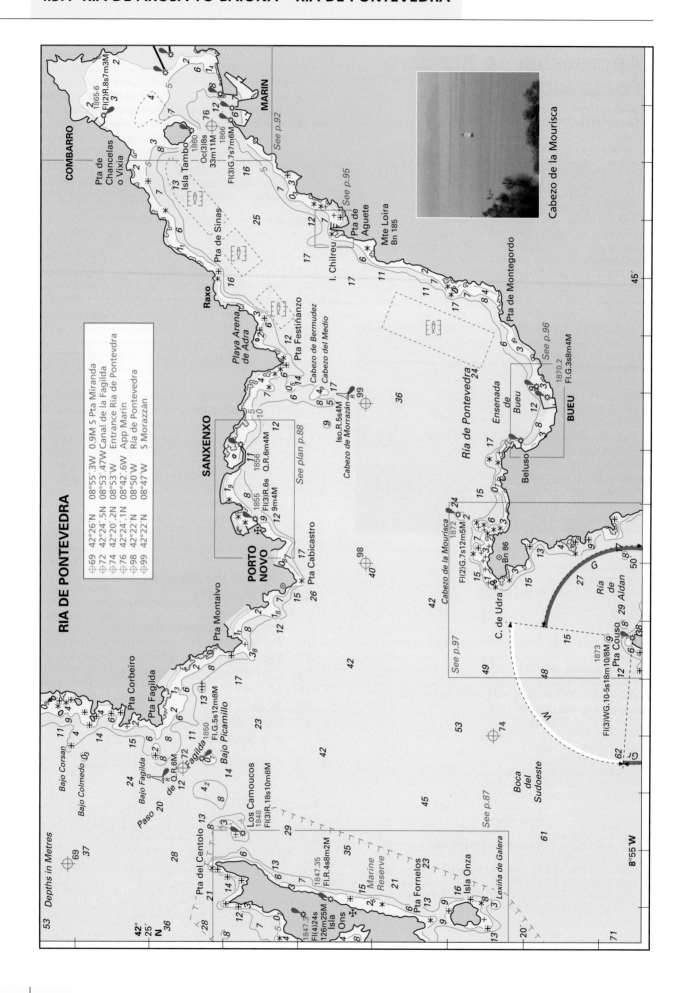

Cabezo de la Mourisca

COMBARRO

MARIN

See p.92

See p.95

Pta de Chancelas o Vixia

Pta de Sinas

Isla Tambo

1865·6
Fl(2)R.8s7m3M
3

Oc(3)8s
33m11M

1866
Fl(3)G.7s7m6M

1860

Raxo

Playa Arena de Adra

Pta Festiñanzo

Cabezo de Bermudez

Cabezo del Medio

Cabezo de Morrazán

Iso.R.5s4M

Pta de Aguete

I. Chilreu

Mte Loira
Bn 185

Pta de Montegordo

See p.96

1870·2
Fl.G.3s8m4M

BUEU

Ensenada de Bueu

Ría de Pontevedra

Beluso

SANXENXO

PORTO NOVO

1856
Q.R.6m4M

1855
Fl(3)R.6s
9m4M

See plan p.88

Pta Cabicastro

Pta Montalvo

RIA DE PONTEVEDRA

⊕69	42°26′N	08°55′·3W	0.9M S Pta Miranda
⊕72	42°24′·5N	08°53′·47W	Canal de la Fagilda
⊕74	42°20′·2N	08°53′W	Entrance Ria de Pontevedra
⊕76	42°24′·1N	08°42′·6W	App Marin
⊕98	42°22′N	08°50′W	Ria de Pontevedra
⊕99	42°22′N	08°47′W	S Morazzán

Pta Corbeiro

Pta Fagilda

Bajo Corsan

Bajo Colmedo

Bajo Fagilda

Paso de

1850
Fl.G.5s12m8M

Bajo Picamillo

Los Camoucos
1848
Fl(3)R.18s10m8M

Pta del Centolo

Marine Reserve

Pta Fornelos

Isla Onza

Lexiña de Galera

1847·35
Fl.R.4s8m2M

1847·3
Fl(4)24s
126m25M
Isla Ons

Cabezo de la Mourisca

1872
Fl(2)G.7s12m5M

Bn 86

C. de Udra

See p.97

1873
Fl(3)WG.10·5s18m10/8M

Pta Couso

Ría de Aldan

Boca del Sudoeste

See p.87

Depths in Metres

42° 25′ N

8°55′W

45′

20′

Isla Ons

Location
42°22'.62N 08°55'.77W

Charts
Admiralty 1732, 1734
Spanish 416A
Imray C48

Facilities
Bars and restaurants at Almacen, camp site

National Park, limited anchorages

Isla Ons helps protect the Ría de Pontevedra from westerly seas and winds. It is a rugged and attractive island with few permanent inhabitants. It is much visited by campers in the summer, tripper boats from Ría de Arosa and Ría de Pontevedra, and regular ferries from Porto Novo, Sanxenxo and Marin. All land at Almacén. Shelter is limited on the east coast which offers the only normal anchorages. Landing is forbidden on the small southern island of Onza (Onceta) which is a bird sanctuary.

Approach

See Ría de Pontevedra page 85 and close the island from the east.

Anchorages

Anchorages should be vacated if the wind gains an easterly component

1. **Almacén** 42°22'.62N 08°55'.77W
   The mole at Almacén is not a good place to lie. There is little room and frequent ferries. Visitors' buoys may be positioned either side of the mole head. Reefs extend north and south of the entrance but it is possible to anchor east-northeast of the mole head in 12m or more over rock and weed.

2. **Playa de Melide** 42°23'.33N 08°55'.43W
   The beach is about 1M north of Almacén mole. Anchor in 4m over sand, rock and weed. The anchorage is sheltered from north through west to southwest. The beach is favoured by nudists.

3. **Southern Bay** 42°21'.23N 08°56'.47W
   A short stay possibility in a light northerly is the small bay between Punta Fedoranto and Punta Rab d'Egua on the south coast.

Lights (opposite page)
1847.3 **Isla Ons** Fl(4)24s126m25M 8-sided white tower
   Bajo Fagilda Q.R.6M Red buoy
1848 **Los Camoucos** Fl(3)R.18s11m8M Tower
1850 **Bajo Picamillo** Fl.G.5s11m8M Tower
1860 **Isla Tampo** Oc(3)8s34m12M White round
   brick tower
1872 **Cabesa de la Mourisca** Fl(2)G.7s11m5M Tower
1873 **Pta Couso** Fl(3)WG.10.5s10m10/8M White
   truncated tower, green top

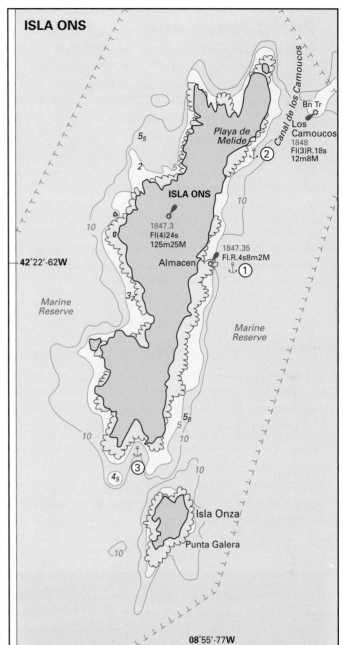

The anchorage at Almacén with Isla Ons lighthouse above

Porto Novo and Sanxenxo

Location
42°23′.5N 08°48′.7W (between ports)

Charts and tides
See page 85

Approach ⊕
⊕75 42°23′.4N 08°48′.6W

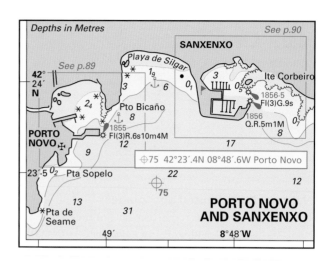

Club marina and major marina in holiday area

The VRG (Via Rapida Galicia) connects the Sanxenxo area to the main Motorway Atlantic and the cities of Santiago de Compostela and the rest of Galicia. Holidaymakers and business firms pour down this road making this part of Galicia both thriving and developing. The yachtsman can now choose between seeking space at the club marina of Port Novo, making use of the vast Sanxenxo marina or anchoring in between them off Playa de Silgar.

Approach

Approach is straightforward (although headlands should be given an offing of at least 200m) except from the east where shallows extend up to 600m southwest off Pta Festiñanzo. In normal weather a yacht may safely pass about midway between the warning Cabezo de Morrazan port hand buoy and the shore.

Berthing and anchorage

From ⊕75 head left for the small club marina of Porto Novo, ahead to anchor, or right to the major full service marina of Sanxenxo.

Playa Silgar anchorage   *MW*

Playa Silgar anchorage between Sanxenxo and Porto Novo

26. Porto Novo

Location
42°23′.64N 08°49′.12W

Charts and tides
See ría page 85

Chart
Admiralty 1732

Final approach⊕
⊕75 42°23′.4N 08°48′.6W (0.45M SE of harbour)

Light
Marina breakwater beacon Fl(3)R.6s3M Red tower

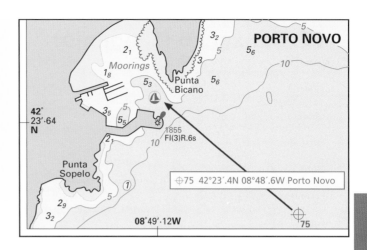

Attractive fishing harbour with club marina

Porto Novo is a fishing village and holiday resort with an easy approach.

The Club Náutico de Portonovo has a small club house with facilities at the end of the inner quay from which sprouts the boat pontoons.

Approach

See pages 84–5 and 88.

Berthing and anchorage

No anchoring in the harbour: secure to an outer pontoon and seek a berth. Take care not to become locked out of the pontoon by the gangway security gate.

Ashore

There are the usual shops. A number of restaurants, with fresh food at good prices, overlook the 110-tonne travel-lift, the harbour and the fine beach.

GALICIA

Porto Novo from the southeast

27. Sanxenxo (Sangenjo)

Locations
42°23′.80N 08°48′.06W

Tides
See page 85

Chart
Admiralty 1732

Final approaches ⊕
⊕75 42°23′.4N 08°48′.6W (0.6M SW of harbour)

Light
Breakwater beacon Q.R Red and white round tower

Facilities
Major marina, technical support facilities available

Fuel
Diesel

Communications
Nauta Sanxenxo
☎ 986 720 059 *Fax* 986 720 009
Email 986720059@infonegocio.com
www.rcnsangenjo.com
Wi-Fi
VHF Ch 09

Weather forecasts
Posted daily in the marina

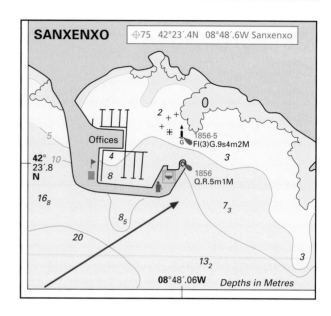

An easily accessible major marina (pronounced Sanshensho)

By August 2005 the large and well protected Sanxenxo Marina – now with 450 berths of between 8 and 45m – was in the final stages of shoreside development. Visitors should be aware of three areas. **The mole head** (with fuel dock, lift, workshops and ferry pontoon); **the central quay** (orange roofs with the harbour office, domestic facilities, shops and restaurants) and **the western end** (the prominent RCN Club house next to a large covered carpark).

Sanxenxo town is a major holiday resort.

Approach

Straightforward – see pages 84–85 and 88. Be aware of the ferries, to the ría and the outlying islands, which operate from a small pontoon on the very end of the main breakwater.

Berthing and anchoring

There is no anchoring allowed in the harbour. The marina staff are friendly, helpful and speak good English. Call ahead for a berth. Alternatively, proceed between the two parts of the marina towards the central mole and the arrivals pontoon. At crowded times it may be necessary to moor initially along the extended fuel pontoon but it is a very long walk from here to the office marina facilities.

Ashore

Routine shops and numerous restaurants are close to the marina. There is a major supermarket about a mile away at the roundabout leading to the fast road out of town – the green signed VRG.

Beware ferry when rounding the outer mole   *MW*

Sanxenxo fuel dock and technical area   *MW*

GALICIA

Sanxenxo in August 2004. By August 2005 the orange roofed buildings were fully operational (see text). The white covered car park has been extended north; the yellow sided building having been removed and replaced with the imposing RCN clubhouse on the outer corner left

Real Club Náutico de Sanxenxo   *MW*

Alternative anchorage

Anchorage is possible off the north shore beyond Cabo de Morrazán, particularly off Raxo quay (red beacon) (42°24'.1N 08°45'28W).

Raxo anchorage looking towards Isla Tambo and Marin *MW*

28. Combarro

Location
42°25′.62N 08°42′.22W

Charts and Tides
See ría page 85

Charts
Admiralty 1733
Spanish 416A
Imray C48

Final approaches ⊕
⊕77 42°25′.5N 08°42′W

Lights
Marina breakwater
beacon Fl(2)R.6s3M
Red round tower

Fishing harbour, anchorage, gem of a village

It would be a shame to visit this part of Galicia and miss seeing Combarro. This restored old fishing village, of massive granite and surrounded by vineyards, is both picturesque and serves excellent seafood. In addition to the attractions of the village, all routine shops are available plus a morning fruit market in the square.

Approach

The best approach is from east of Isla Tambo.

Anchorage

Anchor off the two moles in 2–3m. Depths shallow quickly towards the old village. Thick weed can prove a problem and it may take a few tries to get the anchor properly set in thick mud; then, holding is reported to be excellent.

Combarro old village at low tide   *MW*

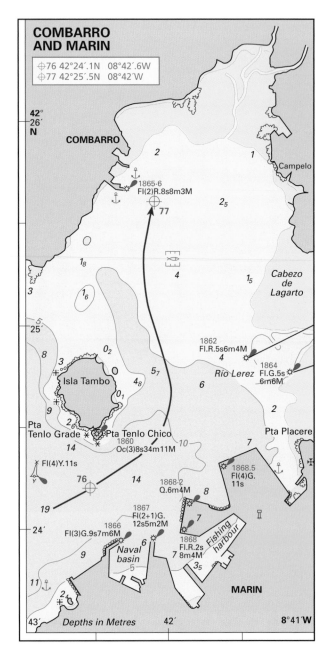

Squid. If you like seafood you will love Combarro   *MW*

Combarro

Río Lerez to Pontevedra

The Pontevedra Naval Club and marina, at the ancient historic provincial capital, Pontevedra, lies about 2.5M upriver from the training walls to the east of Isla Tambo. The limiting factor for yachts is 2m draught and 12m air height.

Normal facilities are available including fuel. ☎ 986 861 022.

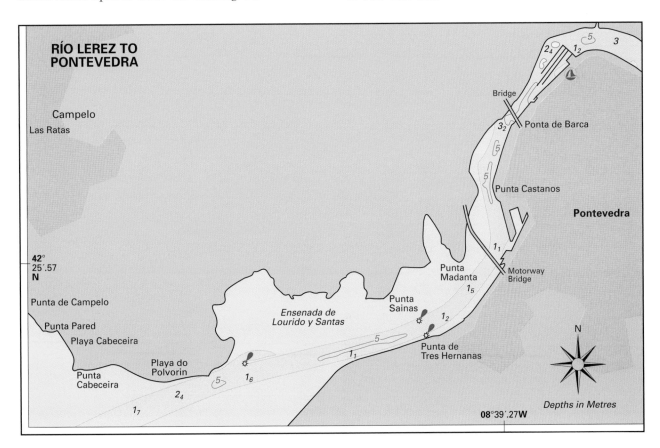

29. Marin

(See plan page 92)

Location
42°24´N 08°42´W

Charts
Admiralty 1733
Spanish 416A
Imray C48

Approaches ⊕
⊕76 42°24´.1N
08°42´.6W

Consider only as a port of refuge

Marin is a commercial fishing and naval port and the home of the Spanish Naval College. The west basin (with its marina) and offlying Isla Tomba are restricted military areas. Two other pontoon areas are for small local boats only.

Anchorages

Shelter from strong southerlies might be sought off Playa Placere (42°24´.5N 08°41´.4W) before the shallows which protrude immediately north of that area. In other winds, anchoring in the lee of Isla Tomba might be more satisfactory. Note from charts 1732 and 1733, that a cable runs from the yellow lightbuoy to the southwest of Isla Tomba to Pta Placere.

Traditional craft near Isla Tampo   *MW*

Marin, looking northeast with the Naval College in the foreground

30. Aguete

Location
42°22′.56N 08°44′.20W

Charts and tides
See ría page 85

Charts
Admiralty 1732
Spanish 416A
Imray C48

Final approach ⊕
⊕78 42°22′.8N 08°44′.W

Lights
Pontoon wave breaker
Green/white post
Lit green buoy 0.1M off marina promontory

Fuel
Yes

Communications
☎ 986 702 373 *Fax* 986 702 708
Email rcma@ctv.es
www.ctv.es/users/rcma

Note On-site GPS survey indicates slight error in position on official charts.

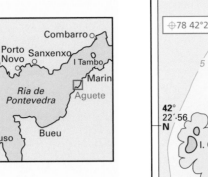

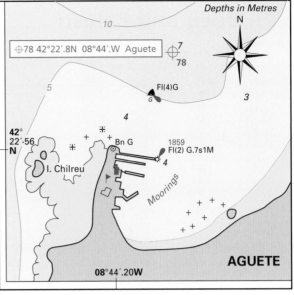

Small friendly club marina

Aguete is the recreational marina for Marin, situated in an attractive bay with steep hill behind. The Real Club de Mar de Aguete welcomes visitors and has an attractive clubhouse, with restaurant, overlooking the harbour.

Aguete is one of the many harbours in Galicia to celebrate the fiesta of the Virgen del Carmen on 16 July with a waterborne procession. A lifesize statue of the Virgin is taken on a tour of the harbour in the club launch accompanied by local craft of all sizes decked out with flags and bunting.

Approach

The approach (to ⊕78) is straightforward from west to northeast; rocks off Punta de Aguete are marked by a green buoy (see note above).

Berthing and anchoring

The outer separated pontoons act as a wave breaker. Berth on the first pontoon behind the wave breaker or anchor off the beach clear of the moorings. Even in calm weather, some swell from passing boats works in as the harbour and moorings are fully exposed to the north.

GALICIA

Aguete from the northeast, Cabo de Udra at the top left *MW*

31. Bueu and Beluso

Location
Bueu 42°19′.79N 08°47′.01W
Beluso 42°20′.01N 08°47′.90W

Charts and tides
See ría page 85

Charts
Admiralty 1732
Spanish 416A
Imray C48

Final approaches ⊕
⊕79 43°20′.2N
08°47′.2W

Lights
Breakwater Bueu
Fl.G.3s4M Green column
Breakwater Beluso
Fl(3)G.9s3M Green
column

Communications (Beluso)
☎ 902 400 870
Fax 981 545 324

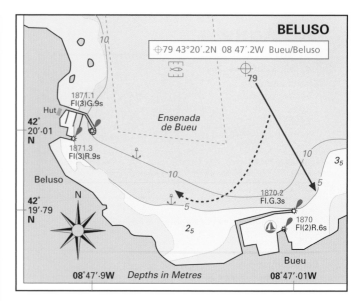

Busy fishing harbour/small marina

Bueu is a small fishing and market town with shops, restaurants, market and good beaches. 0.6M west is the small marina of Beluso with one nearby restaurant.

Approach

Straightforward from the north down a wide fairway between *viveros* to ⊕79; offlying rocks of Isolote El Caballo de Bueu to the west. There is a clear route inside the viveros between harbours.

Berthing and anchorage

No space is reserved for yachts in Bueu. There may be room to anchor outside the harbour mouth and small moorings in 4–6m over mud. Try the outside pontoon in Beluso or anchor midway between harbours in 3–5m over sand and mud. The *viveros* appear to dampen the swell from the north.

Bueu fishing harbour looking southeast

Beluso. Use the outer pontoon or anchor off

Ría de Aldan

Locations
42°19´.6N 08°51´.2W

Charts and tides
See ría page 85

Chart
Admiralty 1732

Overview

The Ría de Aldan, between Punta Couso and Cabo de Udra is worth a visit in suitable conditions for its rocky shores and small secluded beaches. There are good walks through the woods on the peninsula up ancient, steep, stone-paved tracks.

There are numerous *viveros* lining the west side of the ría but space should be found inside them. The eastern side of the bay is deeper and somewhat prone to swell.

Ría de Aldan should be avoided if winds build from the north or northwest. Under other conditions it offers anchorage in several of the small bays on the west side of the ría (but note the offlying rocks) or in the southeast corner towards the head of the bay. There are moorings here and a large rock which tends to merge into the background. Anchorage may be found off the ramp in 10m mud.

Approach

From down Ría de Pontevedra Cabo de Udra is foul and passage south of Cabezo de la Mourisca beacon inadvisable. (Photo page 86).

From the south Pta Couso should be given a good berth.

Aldan

The short mole at Aldan (42°16´.95N 08°49´.37W red beacon) offers little protection for yachts but one can anchor off, or on the opposite shore, to seek provisions from the developing village.

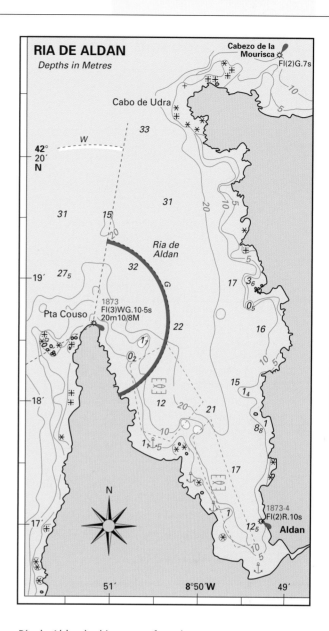

Ría de Aldan looking east of north

GALICIA

I.3.2 Ría de Vigo and Ensenada de Baiona

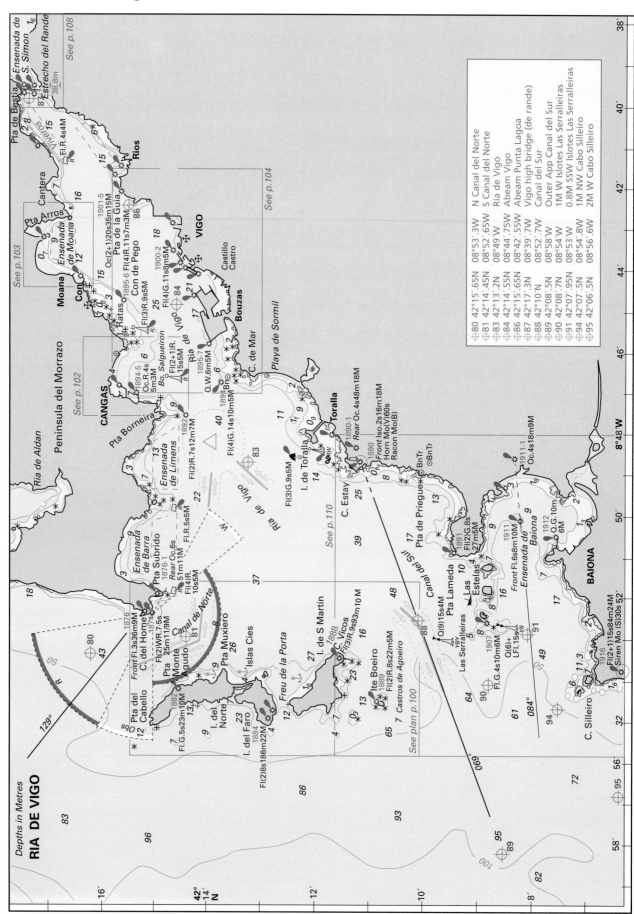

⊕80	42°15´.65N	08°53´.3W	N Canal del Norte
⊕81	42°14´.45N	08°52´.65W	S Canal del Norte
⊕83	42°13´.2N	08°49´.W	Ría de Vigo
⊕84	42°14´.55N	08°44´.75W	Abeam Vigo
⊕86	42°15´.65N	08°42´.55W	Abeam Punta Lagoa
⊕87	42°17´.3N	08°39´.7W	Vigo high bridge (de rande)
⊕88	42°10´.N	08°52´.7W	Canal del Sur
⊕89	42°08´.5N	08°58´.W	Outer App Canal del Sur
⊕90	42°08´.7N	08°54´.W	1M W Islotes Las Serralleiras
⊕91	42°07´.95N	08°53´.W	0.8M SSW Islotes Las Serralleiras
⊕94	42°07´.5N	08°54´.8W	1M NW Cabo Silleiro
⊕95	42°06´.5N	08°56´.6W	2M W Cabo Silleiro

Ría de Vigo

Tides
Standard port Lisbon
Mean time differences (at Vigo)
HW +0050 ±0010; LW +0115 ±0010
(the above allows for the difference in time zones)
Heights in metres

MHWS	MHWN	MLWN	MLWS
3.4	2.7	1.3	0.5

Charts	*Approach*	*Ria*
Admiralty	3633	1730, 1731
Spanish	417	416B
Imray	C18, C48	C18, C48

Note A traffic separation scheme operates through Canal de Norte and Canal del Sur. If waypoint navigating using ⊕87, ⊕88, ⊕83 use the cross track error function to avoid tracking along the centre line of the scheme.

There are sound signals on Cabo Silleiro and Cabo Estay.

Warning
Ría de Vigo and Ensenada de Baiona are separated by the Islas Las Estelas and Isolas Serrolleiras with their offlying, extensive and dangerous reefs and individual rocks. North/south passage between islands is not recommended without local knowledge, or in fair weather and using Spanish chart 4167.

Avoid the shallows around Isla de Toralla

A partly industrial ría but with good marinas and attractive anchorages

Industrial dockland Vigo dominates the upper part of the ría and its suburbs and dormitory towns spread down both sides. With them come harbours, ferries and marinas. There is peace as well, both in the tranquillity of Ensenada de Simon above the giant Rande Suspension bridge, or off a sandy beach of the Islas Cíes which protect the ría from the worst effects of Atlantic storms. There are shallows off most headlands; they are marked by buoys or beacons on both sides of the ría.

Approach

From the north or the northern rías Canal de Norte is well marked and free from dangers. (If coming from seaward note the dangers extending well north of Isla del Norte (Islas Cíes), if approaching from Ría de Pontevedra do not cut the corner off Pta Couso.) ⊕80 and ⊕81 are positioned on the mainland side of the TSS at 160°. Pick up the line of red buoys after clearing Cabo del Home and Pta Subrido or head up ría on 095° from ⊕81.

From the west or south ⊕89 and ⊕88 lie on the Canal del Sur Cabo Estay 069° leading lights switching, to ⊕88, ⊕83 on 041°. These ⊕ are on the TSS centre line, track to starboard.

From Baiona In fair weather and towards high tide, Canal de la Porta, between Monte Ferro and the easternmost of the three Estelas Islands, may be used. There is a 0.9m patch in the middle of this channel and a separate 1.6m patch about 0.1M further NW. Favour the west side, use Spanish chart 4167 and then keep 1M clear of the headland, and Cabo Estay, before heading up Ría de Vigo.

Marinas

There are main marinas at Cangas, Vigo and Baiona and smaller ones as listed later.

Approach lights (opposite page)
Canal de Norte
1874 **Cabo del Home** Fl(2)WR.7.5s26m11/9M Red tower
1876 **Ldg Lts 129°** *Front* Fl.3s37m9M White round tower
1876.1 **Punta Subrido** *Rear* Oc.6s52m11M White round tower
1882 **Monte Agudo** Fl.G.5s24m10M White tower
Canal del Sur
1890 **Cabo Estay Ldg Lts 069°20′** *Front* Iso.2s17m18M Red truncated tower, white bands
1890.1 **Cabo Estay** *Rear* Oc.4s49m18M As above
Vigo Narrows
1892 **Bajo Borneira No.6** Fl(2)R.7s12m5M Red and white tower
1894 **Bajo Tofiño No.3** Fl(4)G.14s10m5M Red and white tower
Baiona approaches
1911 **Cabezo de San Juan** Fl.6s8m10M White truncated tower
1911.1 **Playa de Panjon** Oc.4s18m9m White truncated tower on 8-sided base
Islas Cíes
1884 **Monte Faro** Fl(2)8s186m22M Tower and cabin

Islas Cíes and the harbours of Ría de Vigo
    Islas Cíes
32. Cangas*
33. Vigo (3 Marinas*)
34. Punta Lagoa*
    Ensenada de San Simón
35. Baiona*

*Fuel available alongside

Anchorages at Islas Cíes

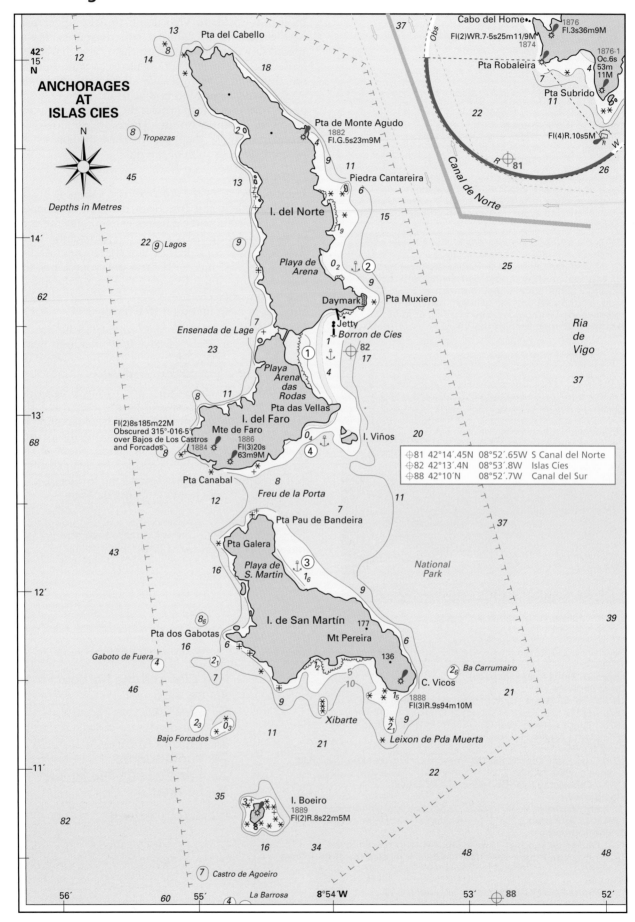

ANCHORAGES AT ISLAS CIES

N

Depths in Metres

42° 15' N

Cabo del Home
Fl(2)WR.7·5s25m11/9M
1876 Fl.3s36m9M
1874
Pta Robaleira
1876·1 Oc.6s 53m 11M
Pta Subrido
Fl(4)R.10s5M
R ⊕ 81

Canal de Norte
Obs

13
Pta del Cabello
12
14
18
9
Tropezas
8
45
Pta de Monte Agudo
1882 Fl.G.5s23m9M
9
11
Piedra Cantareira
13
6
I. del Norte
15
22 9 Lagos
9
9
Playa de Arena
0 2 ⚓ 2
9
Ensenada de Lage
7
Daymark
Pta Muxiero
Jetty
Borron de Cíes
62
23
1
17
82
1
(1)
4
Playa Arena das Rodas
8
11
Pta das Vellas
I. del Faro
I. Viños
20
Fl(2)8s185m22M
Obscured 315°-016·5' over Bajos de Los Castros and Forcados
Mte de Faro
1886 Fl(3)20s 63m9M
0 4
68
8
(1884)
(4)
Pta Canabal
8
Freu de la Porta
11
12
7
Pta Pau de Bandeira
Pta Galera
(3)
Playa de S. Martin
1 6
National Park
16
I. de San Martín
Mt Pereira
177
9
Ria de Vigo
37
25
37

⊕81 42°14'.45N 08°52'.65W S Canal del Norte
⊕82 42°13'.4N   08°53'.8W   Islas Cíes
⊕88 42°10'N   08°52'.7W   Canal del Sur

43
Pta dos Gabotas
16
8 6
6
136
C. Vicos
2 6 Ba Carrumairo
21
Gaboto de Fuera
4
2 1
5
10
1888 Fl(3)R.9s94m10M
1 5
46
7
9
Xibarte
2 1
2 3
0 3
11
Leixon de Pda Muerta
Bajo Forcados
21
39
22
35
I. Boeiro
1889 Fl(2)R.8s22m5M
3
8
82
16
34
48
48
(7) Castro de Agoeiro
56'   60   55'   La Barrosa   8°54'W   53'   ⊕88   52'

Islas Cíes

Location
42°13´.00N 08°54´.00W

Tides
See page 99

Charts
Admiralty   1730
Spanish   416B
Imray   C48

Daymark
42°13´.65N 08°53´.78W

A nature reserve with good anchorages

The Islas Cíes are mountainous, wooded and very attractive. The whole area is a Nature Park, and in addition a large part of Isla del Norte, Isla del Faro and all of Isla de San Martín are bird sanctuaries (mostly herring gulls, lesser black-backed gulls and shags, plus a few guillemots) where access is forbidden. However, there are good tracks on Isla del Norte and Isla del Faro, which are linked by a narrow sandy isthmus, and it is worth studying the map displayed at the northern end of Playa Arena das Rodas.

There are no cars on the islands and few permanent inhabitants, but in summer many campers and day visitors come by ferry from Vigo, Baiona and Cangas to enjoy the clean sandy beaches so time a visit for midweek if possible. In terms of their surroundings the anchorages, which are on the east side of the islands, are amongst the best in the rías, but all are open to the east.

Approach

Initially to ⊕82 or Daymark. Monte del Faro is easily identified, standing on the highest point of the central island, Isla del Faro, as is the long beach lining the isthmus between Isla del Faro and Isla del Norte.

The four anchorages, the daymark and the lighthouse atop Isla del Faro may all be seen

Anchorages

1. **Off Playa Arena das Rodas** 42°13´.36N 08°53´.89W Anchor over sand, rock and weed towards the middle of the beach as depth allows. Borron de Cíes, a submerged rock some 20m across, lies about 200m south of the stone mole. It shows at low water and is marked by a beacon (tall black pole, 2 balls, light). Avoid anchoring too close to the mole, which is in constant use by tourist ferries. It is possible for a shallow-draught boat to anchor inshore of the rocks, though in summer the beach itself is buoyed-off for swimming.

   Good anchorage, clear of both rocks and ferries, is to be found with the western white tower on Cabo del Home framed in the centre of a cleft in the rocks at the end of Punta Muxiero. Holding is good in sand.
2. In southerlies, anchor in the bay (42°13´.93N 08°53´.89W) north of Punta Muxiero and its daymark.
3. In south to northwest conditions, better anchorage is to be had on the north coast of Isla de San Martín off the Playa de San Martín (42°12´.23N 08°54´.18W), in 3–5m over rock and sand. This is a particularly quiet and attractive spot although without access to facilities of any kind. The island is a bird sanctuary where landing is forbidden.
4. In east winds some shelter may be found in a small bay on the south coast of the Isla del Faro immediately west, and in the lee, of Isla Viños (42°12´.88N 08°54´.09W). It is occasionally used by fishing boats and there is not much room. The Monte Faro jetty some 600m to the west is used by fishing boats and the occasional ferry, and yachts are not welcome.

Facilities

A few restaurants and a small supermarket at Playa Arena das Rodos and a good visitors' centre above the campsite.

GALICIA

32. Cangas

Location
42°15'.63N
08°46'.95W

Charts and tides
See ría page 99

Charts
Admiralty 1730, 1731
Spanish 416B
Imray C48

Final approach ⊕
⊕85 42°15'.5N
08°46'.7W Cangas

Light
Outer breakwater
beacon Fl(2)R.7s3M
Red round tower

Fuel
Yes

Communications
Club Náutico de Rodeira
☎ 986 305 618 *Fax* 986 305 618
Email náuticorobeira@navgalia.com

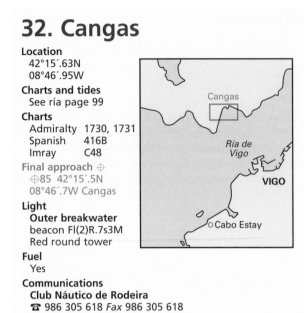

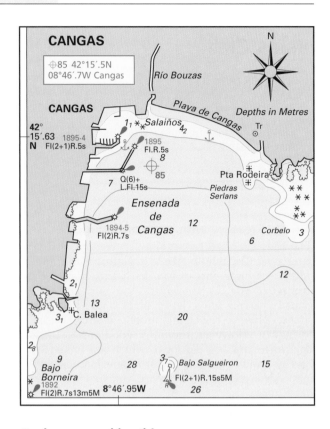

Cheerful welcome from modernising marina

Cangas is a fishing and industrial town with a good and improving marina. There are regular ferries to Vigo. There is a seafront market on Friday.

Approach

Buoys mark the extent of the rocks off the headlands to east and west. If coming up the ría, Ensenada de Barra offers a good anchorage in 6m over sand and weed, open southwest to east. Approach Cangas between Piedra Barneira and Bajo Salgueiron – line of 010° to ⊕85. Alternatively head northwest from the centre of Vigo passing midway between the buoys off headland. Do not close the buoy.

Cangas from the east

Anchorage and berthing

On rounding the breakwater there are three sections to the harbour, fishing boats to main harbour left, ferries to the right hand pier and yachts to the marina in the middle harbour. Alternatively anchor off Playa de Cangas in 5–6m over sand.

Marina facilities are developing quickly with a additional pontoon being added in 2005; there are plans for further expansion on the water. Ashore the domestic facilities and restaurant are in the end of the main blue roofed building on the centre mole. The main club house is next to the Shell fuel station immediately outside the harbour road entrance.

Alternative anchorages/berthing up ría

1. **Ensenada de Moana** 42°16′.76N 08°43′.38W
   Anchor in mud and sand inside the *viveros*. On the west of the bay the harbours of Con and Moana are small and crowded but a new marina is in build close northwest of the Moana ferry jetty 42°16′.4N 08°44′.09W. Entry will be from the northeast.

2. **Domaio Marina** 42°17′.3N 08°40′.5W
   Two miles beyond Moana, anchorage is just possible inside the *viveros* between the tiny Puerto de Domaio and a large factory. Also here is a (possibly private) marina with good pontoons and protection from the swell. In August 2005 it had no shoreside facilities, security gates preventing access to pontoons.

Marina in build at Moana (August 2005)   *MW*

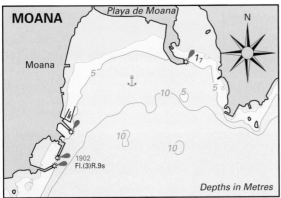

MOANA

Depths in Metres

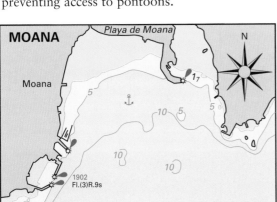

Domaio Marina from the east

Domaio Marina   *MW*

GALICIA

33. Vigo

Location
Centred 42°14′N
08°45′W

Tides
See page 99

Charts
Admiralty 1730, 1731
Spanish 416B
Imray C48

Final approach ⊕
⊕84 42°14′.55N
08°44′.75W abeam Vigo

Facilities
Vigo has all the nautical and shoreside facilities expected of a major seafaring city

Approach

Proceed up the centre of the ría for ⊕84 or head for Monte de la Guia (⊕86).

A lively modern city

Vigo has an ancient history and strong maritime connection. Its wharfs stretch for two miles handling cargo, deep-sea fishing and cruise ships as well as building coasters and fishing vessels. Full facilities available, plus a Sea Museum.

Marinas

There are three marinas in Vigo that will accept visiting yachts if space is available. A fourth, major marina, is at the end of the docks (off ⊕86) under the wooded Monte de la Guia. Other marinas will be seen – particularly by Bouzas bridge – but they are shallow.

1. **Liceo Maritimo** 42°13′.65N 08°45′.0W

   A long established marina, close to shipyards, some way from town.
   ☎/Fax 986 239 955

2. **Marina Davila Sport** 42°13′.9N 08°44′.5W

   Deep water, long pontoon, technical support, long way from town. Developing quickly.
   ☎ 986 244 612 Fax 986 206 809
   Email marina@davilasport.es
   www.davila.verticalia.com

East of Muelle Transatlanticos (now used by cruise liners)

3. **Real Club Náutico de Vigo** 42°14′.57N 08°43′.43W

   Long established but very congested marina with little space to manoeuvre. Pre-booking advised. Good facilities on site and easy access to the city.

   Approach square on and beware ferries emerging from the right. Secure to reception/fuel pontoon on the starboard side immediately before the entrance and seek instructions.
   ☎ 986 449 694 Fax 986 449 695
   Email puertocnv@yahoo.com

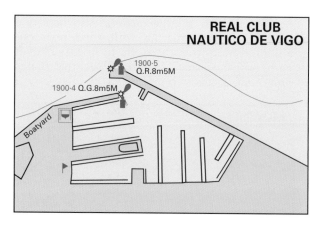

Liceo Maritimo looking south

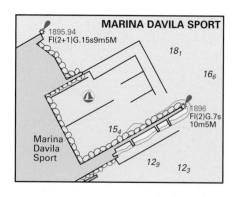

Marina Davila Sport looking south

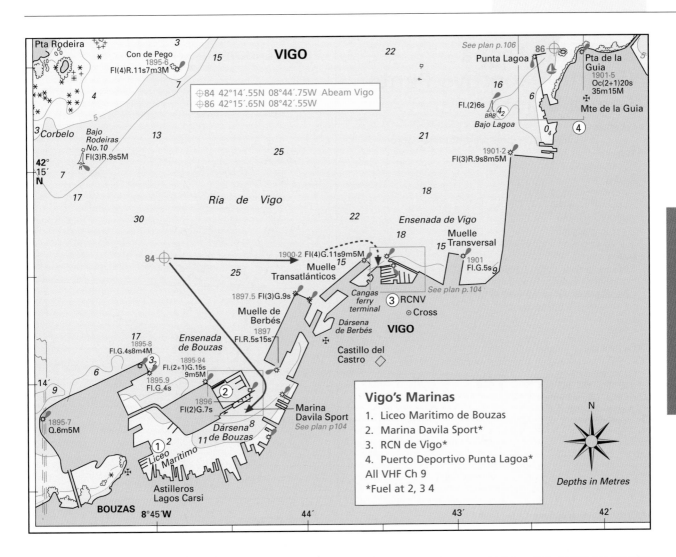

Pta Rodeira

Con de Pego
1895·6
Fl(4)R.11s7m3M

3

15

VIGO

22

See plan p.106

Punta Lagoa

86

Pta de la
Guia
1901·5
Oc(2+1)20s
35m15M

⊕84 42°14'.55N 08°44'.75W Abeam Vigo
⊕86 42°15'.65N 08°42'.55W

16

Fl.(2)6s
BRB

6

42

Bajo Lagoa

Mte de la Guia

4

3 Corbelo   Bajo
Rodeiras
No.10
Fl(3)R.9s5M

13

25

21

1901·2
Fl(3)R.9s8m5M

0,4

4

**42°
15'
N**

7

17

Ría   de   Vigo

18

30

22

Ensenada de Vigo

18

Muelle
Transversal

15

1901
Fl.G.5s

84 ⊕

1900·2 Fl(4)G.11s9m5M

Muelle
Transatlánticos

15

25

Cangas
ferry
terminal

RCNV
⊙ Cross

See plan p.104

1897.5 Fl(3)G.9s

Muelle de
Berbés

Dársena
de Berbés

VIGO

1897
Fl.R.5s15s7

17
1895·8
Fl.G.4s8m4M

*Ensenada
de Bouzas*

1895·94
Fl.(2+1)G.15s
9m5M

Castillo del
Castro

6

3,

1895.9
Fl.G.4s

2

Vigo's Marinas

1. Liceo Maritimo de Bouzas
2. Marina Davila Sport*
3. RCN de Vigo*
4. Puerto Deportivo Punta Lagoa*
All VHF Ch 9
*Fuel at 2, 3 4

N

14'

9

1896
Fl(2)G.7s

Marina
Davila Sport
See plan p104

1895·7
Q.6m5M

Dársena
de Bouzas

8

11

1

2

Liceo   Marítimo

Depths in Metres

Astilleros
Lagos Carsi

BOUZAS

8°45'W

44'

43'

42'

RCN de Vigo Marina

GALICIA

34. Punta Lagoa (Puerto Deportivo Punta Lagoa Vigo)

Location
42°15′.55N 08°42′.30W Close west of Islote Cabron

Tides
See page 99

Charts
Admiralty 1730, 1731
Spanish   416B
Imray   C48

Final approach ⊕
⊕86 42°15′.65N 08°45′.55W Abeam Punta Lagoa

Lights
Pta de la Guia Oc(2+1)20s36m15M White round masonry tower
Breakwater 42°15′.52N 08°42′.45W Q.G.3M Green post
Entrance Yes (green post)

Fuel
Yes

Pump out
Yes

Communications
☎ 986 374 305 *Fax* 986 410 096
Email lagoa@yatesport.es
www.yatesport.es
VHF Ch 09

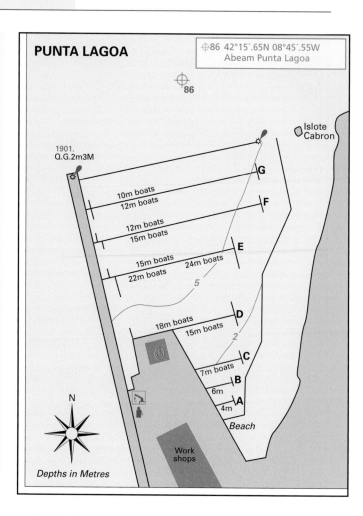

Major new marina

This major marina nestles between the wooded slopes of the prominent Monte de la Guia and a long breakwater stretching out from the now absorbed Punta Lagoa. One looks down ría from here across the full frontage of Vigo and out to Islas Cíes.

Although still under construction in August 2005, much of the infrastructure was in place and work continues apace with the final piling for the shallow inshore berths to be completed. Of the 355 berths planned 10% were already occupied, fuel, water, pump out and travel-lift were available and technical firms were starting up in the workshops.

Technical and domestic services on site will be comprehensive. However, at the end of 2005 it was a steep and tedious walk out to the nearest shops and restaurants.

Approach

Head up ría for ⊕86 on about 070°. Punta de la Guia is high, tree-clad and prominent as it sticks out into the ría beyond all the docks industry and the city of Vigo. Beyond it is the high bridge (⊕87).

Berthing

Call ahead. Boats up to 24m can be accommodated. Depths reduce from some 4m at the entrance to 2m after pontoon D. The *Tarifas 2005* published by Marinas de Galicia suggest prices will be double the rate of other major marinas at €0.50 per m² low season and €1.00 per m² high season.

Inner shallow section being piled. The green workshops are prominent   *MW*

Harbourmaster's office with fuel and pump-out by the travel-lift   *MW*

Halfway down the substantial breakwater. In Aug 2005 it had a temporary light at the head, as did the entrance MW

Pontoon F for 15m boats with pontoon G 12 and 10m boats and then the outer low pontoon. Right of that is Islote Cabron *MW*

On the shore – Rías Bajas

MW

A typical beach – clean sand, interesting rocks and rock pools, roped off area for swimming with clearly marked access route for small craft. Many have paths or board walks behind *MW*
Inset Shoreside board walk *RI*

Ensenada de San Simón

(at the top of Ría de Vigo)

Location
Entry 42°17′.3N 08°39′.6W

Charts
Admiralty 1730, 1731
Spanish 416B
Imray C48

Peace

Sail under the 38.8m high Rande suspension bridge (⊕87) and leave Vigo behind. Ensenada de San Simón tends to be shallow, particularly in the northern part, and peaceful.

Anchorages and berthing

Harbours are very shallow, berth may be sought in the new club marina of San Adrián and the following are suggested anchorages.

1. On the south shore beyond the cranes off Punta Soutelo before the shallows in 3–4m mud. Beware the shallows extending off the mouth of the Ría de Redondela and the training walls which cover at half tide.
2. Southwest of the reef which extends south from the Islas de San Simón (two islands linked by a distinctive bridge). Anchor clear of the beacon – 3m mud in or work in between moorings towards the sand shore. There is a restaurant on the spit of beach, and a bakery and shop 400m inland, or take the dinghy to the small harbour of Cesantes (food shops but up a steep hill).
3. South of Pta Pereiro with its pontoons shielded in shallow water behind Islote Pedro.
4. San Adrián. 42°18′.14N 08°39′.27W village mole, red beacon. Anchor off the pier in 4m, small restaurant by the dock, or try the new club marina.

From the west Isla de San Simón is above the left hand bridge tower. Anchorage 1 is beyond the cranes to the right; anchorage 2 is south of the islands.

Marina and clubhouse at San Adrián   *MW*

Punta Lagoa   Vigo

⚓ 4

From the northeast San Adrián anchorage 4 off quay, and San Adrián Marina under construction
in 2004. Punta Lagoa marina is beyond the prominent tree-clad hill on the left down the ría.

I.3.3 Approaches to Baiona

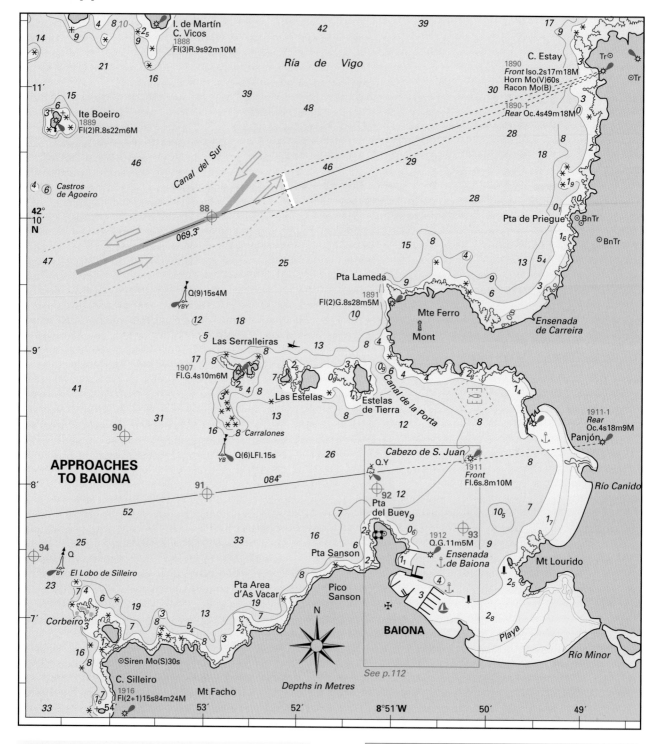

Lights

Canal del Sur Ldg Lts 069°20′
1890 **Cabo Estay** *Front* Iso.2s17m18M Red truncated
   pyramid tower red bands
1890.1 **Cabo Estay** *Rear* Oc.4s49m18M as above
Baiona approach Ldg Lts 084°
1911 **Cabezo de san Juan** *Front* Fl.6s8m10M White
   truncated conical tower
1911.1 **Playa de Panjón** *Rear* Oc.4s18m9M White
   truncated tower on 8-sided base
1916 **Cabo Silleiro** Fl(2+1)15s84m24M White 8-sided
   tower, red bands ,on dwelling

⊕88	42°10′N	08°52′.7W	Canal del Sur
⊕90	42°08′.7N	08°54′W	1M W Islotes Las Serralleiras
⊕91	42°07′.95N	08°53′W	0.8M SSW Islotes Las Serralleiras
⊕92	42°08′N	08°51′W	0.3M WNW Punta del Buey
⊕93	42°07′.6N	08°50′.3W	App Baiona
⊕94	42°07′.5N	08°54′.8W	1M NW Cabo Silleiro

35. Baiona (Bayona)

Location
42°07′.47N 08°50′.55W

Tides
Standard port Lisbon
Mean time differences
HW +0045 ±0010; LW +0110 ±0010
(the above allows for the difference in time zones)
Heights in metres

MHWS	MHWN	MLWN	MLWS
3.5	2.7	1.3	0.5

Charts
Admiralty 3633
Spanish 4167
Imray C48

Final approaches⊕
⊕93 (northeast of breakwater)

Light
Breakwater beacon Q.G.5M Green and white tower

Facilities
Two marinas, technical support, good shops

Fuel
Fuel at both sites

Communications
Monte Real Club de Yates
☎ 986 385 000 *Fax* 986 355 061
Email mrcyb@mrcyb.com
www.mrcyb.com
Wi-Fi
VHF Ch 09 *'Use club title'*
Porto Deportivo Baiona
☎ 986 385 107 *Fax* 986 356 489
Email puertobaiona@puertobaiona.com
www.puertobaiona.com
Wi-Fi
VHF Ch 06 *Baiona Sport Harbour*

Weather forecasts
Posted daily in the marinas

A popular harbour for yachtsmen

Long a favourite harbour with British yachtsmen, Baiona is easily approached by day or night. It is well sheltered other than from strong winds with an easterly component, which are rare in summer. The facilities of the imposing Monte Real Club de Yates are made available to visiting yachtsmen who berth in their marina or use their moorings.

The town is attractive and thriving as a tourist resort, with well protected beaches and a secure place in history as Columbus' first mainland landfall in 1493 after returning from the New World, commemorated by a replica of the *Pinta* permanently berthed in the harbour. The old part of the town is surprisingly uncommercialised compared to the tourist shops along the front, and a cool place to take a leisurely stroll on a hot day. Medieval walls surround the Parador Conde do Gondomar on the northern headland, commanding the harbour and its approaches, and there are pleasant walks among the pine forests beyond, where stands the enormous statue of the Virgen de la Roca.

Approach
⊕91 lies on the leading line of 084° through Cabezo de San Juan and Panjón.

From the north In fair weather keep west of Westing 08°57′ to clear the hazards northwest of Islas Cíes, before setting heading for Cabo Silleiro ⊕94 and then Ensenada de Baiona (or use ⊕90, ⊕91, ⊕92). In foul weather, stay further west for ⊕89 before turning for Baiona.

From Ría de Vigo With settled weather and with good visibility Canal de la Porta may be used (but see warning on page 99). Otherwise ⊕88, ⊕90, ⊕91, ⊕92, ⊕93 indicate a route around the dangers of Las Serralleiras and the Las Estelas group of islands and rocks.

From the south Stay off shore, coming no closer than 2m off Cabo Silleiro (⊕95 then ⊕94) before turning onto the approach. ⊕94, ⊕91, ⊕92, ⊕93 apply.

Anchoring and berthing
The western part of Ensenada de Baiona is fully occupied with marinas and moorings. One is unlikely to find room to anchor without impeding fairways. There is space to anchor to the east of Puerto Deportivo.

The Monte Real Club de Yates may be able to loan a mooring for a short period.

Both marinas are welcoming, efficient and speak good English.

Monte Real Club de Yates The MRCY is a long established club in a superb situation on the harbour ramparts of the headland. The old defensive walls tower above it and house the Parador. The club restaurant provides good food and an excellent view over the harbour. Visitors are welcome and are expected to match the dress code of members. Office and domestic facilities are on the lower level beneath the restaurant.

Puerto Deportivo de Baiona, Baiona Sports Harbour The modern marina has become popular and is a little closer to town than the MRCY. It is still being developed. The wave breaker, and comprehensive marina buildings, shown at the root of the marina in advertising material, are expected to be built in

The Parador Conde do Gondomar now guards the approach to Baiona

GALICIA

Baiona, Puerto Deportivo and MRCY from the northeast

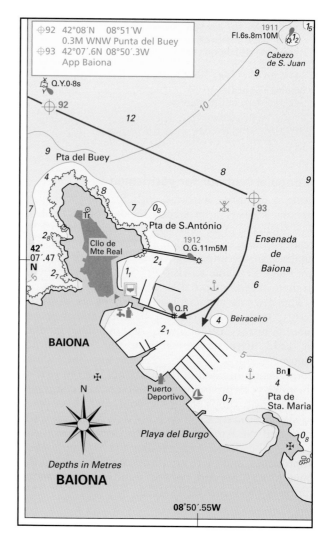

2006. However, fuel, travel-lift and onsite chandlers are fully functioning and English is spoken by the helpful staff.

Facilities

Baiona is an excellent port of call whether arriving from transatlantic passage, working north or heading south. Technical support is either readily available or can be obtained from Vigo. Baiona offers the chance to relax, to wait out inclement weather and to re-provision.

Alternative anchorage

(See plan page 110)

(42°08′.5N 08 43′.4W)

In settled or easterly conditions it is possible to anchor off the small town of Panjón (Panxón) on the eastern side of the Ensenada de Baiona, with some protection from northwest round to south. The short stone mole (Fl(2)R.10s12m5M Red column 7m) shelters a small harbour packed with moorings, but it provides convenient steps while the Club Náutico de Panjón at its root has showers, a restaurant and bar. South of the harbour is a long sandy beach, the Playa de América. Basic shopping is available in the town, which is dominated by a spectacular church.

A calm day at the headland guarding Baiona, rocks extend offshore *MW*

MRCY Peppers. Beware a local tradition of slipping in a green chilli to catch the unwary *MW*

Baiona anchorage *MW*

Office and chandlery at the root of Puerto Deportivo, to be replaced by a 2,000m² marina complex, restaurant and bank *RI*

Approach to MRCY *MW*

Replica of the *Pinta* *MW*

36. La Guardia

(See plans page 84 and 110)

41°54′.04N 08°52′.90W

Tides
Standard port Lisbon
Mean time differences
HW +0050 ±0010; LW +0115 ±0010
(the above allows for the difference in time zones)
Heights in metres

MHWS	MHWN	MLWN	MLWS
3.3	2.6	1.2	0.4

Charts
Admiralty 3633
Spanish 417
Imray C48

Final approach ⊕
⊕96, ⊕97

Lights
North breakwater Fl(2)R.7s5M Red truncated conical tower
Cabo Silleiro Fl(2+1)15s84m24M

Navtex
518kHz (D) at 0030, 0630, 0830*, 1230, 1630, 2030*
(*weather only)

Weather bulletins VHF
Vigo Ch 65
La Guardia Ch 21 at 0840, 1240, 2010
Vigo MRSC Ch 10 at 0015, 0415, 0815, 1215, 1615, 2015

Navigational warnings VHF
Vigo Ch 65
La Guardia Ch 21 at 0840, 2010
MRSC Vigo Ch 10 at 0215, 0615, 1015, 1415, 1815, 2215

Primary working frequencies
c/s Coruña Radio
Manual: Vigo Ch 65; La Guardia Ch 21
Autolink: Vigo Ch 62 Tx 2596 Rx 3280
DSC Ch 70 2187.5kHz

Facilities
Normal fish harbour/town facilities

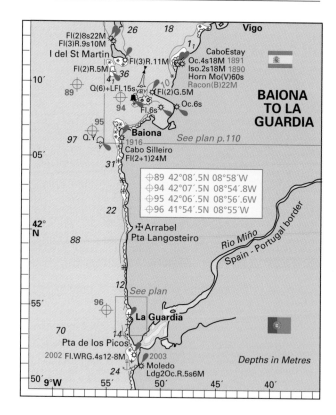

A harbour of limited use to yachtsmen

A border town and centre of seafood gastronomy in an attractive setting, La Guardia has more shops, restaurants, hotels and banks than might be expected. It is a busy fishing port with few opportunities to anchor in the harbour, and despite a mole partially closing the entrance from the north heavy swells from the west can set in. A visit in settled conditions can be rewarding, but be prepared to leave at once if conditions deteriorate.

Monte de Santa Tecla, which rises steeply behind the town, repays the effort of the 350m climb. Near the summit is a remarkable Roman-Celtic hut settlement, though somewhat over-restored, and beyond this a series of large stone crosses leads to a tiny church, a restaurant and a hotel. In clear weather there are magnificent views south to the Río Miño, and Portugal, and as far north as the Islas Cíes.

Several fiestas take place in La Guardia during the course of the year, including that of the Virgen del Carmen on 16 July, and those of Monte de Santa Tecla during the second week of August.

The hazards off Cabo Silleiro

GALICIA

Stay at least a mile offshore until La Guardia has been identified close north of Monte de Santa Tecla. There are two chimneys on the coast just north of La Guardia. From the north, note ⊕89, ⊕96. From Baiona or Ría de Vigo ⊕94, ⊕96 apply.

From the south. Keep at least 1M off. Conical Monte de Santa Tecla stands out prominently with a clutch of stone buildings and radio aerials on the summit – and the two chimneys near the shore.

Do not approach La Guardia at night, in thick foggy weather, or if there is any noticeable swell.

Entrance

Make final approach to ⊕97 from ⊕96 or the west. The gap between the two moleheads is no more than 70m wide: enter on approximately 105°, staying near the centre as neither wall goes down sheer. Favour the north side of the harbour once inside, and keep well outside a line drawn from the molehead to the corner of the inner wharf in order to clear Barquiña, a rocky shoal some 20m outside this line.

Depths shoal from 8m at the entrance to 0.5m off the quay at the head of the harbour, and on either side it shoals rapidly.

Anchorage and mooring

Very little space remains in which to anchor, as the centre of the harbour is taken up by closely packed fishing boat moorings, while to the south the fairway to the quay must not be obstructed. North of the moorings the water is shallow with an uneven, rocky floor likely to foul an anchor – should it hold at all.

Enlist the help of local fishermen, who may be able to advise if a mooring is free. It is essential to ask (preferably attempting some Spanish) rather than to help oneself.

Approach

From the north The coast south from Baiona or Cabo Silleiro holds nothing for the yachtsman bar potential hazards. Rocks awash extend up to 0.7M to the northwest of Cabo Silleiro. Swell builds up to crash on what is generally a lee shore and fog can obscure the shoreline although the tops of the hills behind may be in the clear. Straggling buildings run along the coast road as far as the village of Arrabel with its ancient church.

La Guardia

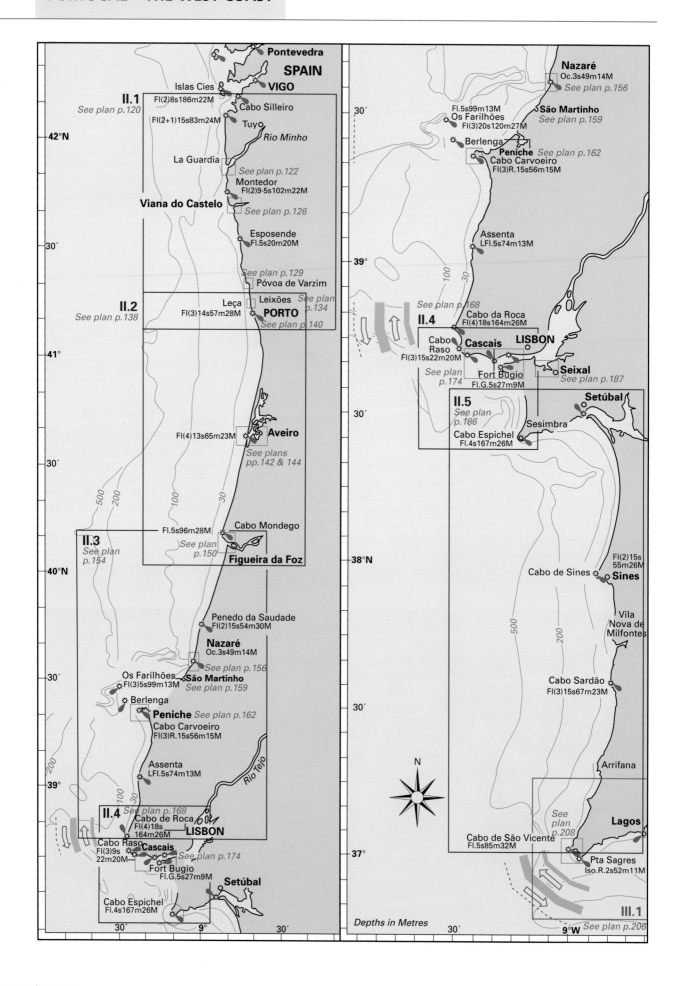

II. Portugal – The West Coast
Foz do Minho to Cabo de São Vicente

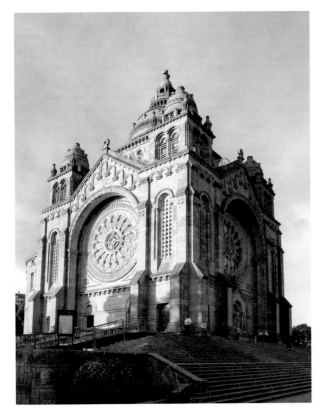

The impressive Basílica Senhora da Agonia which overlooks the town of Viana do Castelo   *AH*

Lisbon is famous for its trams, used by local people every day as well as by tourists bent on sightseeing   *AH*

Colourful fishing craft in the Ria de Aveiro   *Roddy Innes*

PORTUGAL – THE WEST COAST

Foz do Minho to Cabo de São Vicente

Until recently many yachtsmen have viewed the west coast of Portugal as best avoided, or to be skirted at some distance offshore en route to the Algarve or beyond. This is their loss, as it has much to offer including pockets of stunning scenery, busy wildlife habitats and history by the bucketful. The increased accuracy of weather forecasts and almost universal use of GPS have played their part, since west-facing entrances can become dangerous in onshore swell, while long stretches of the coast are low and featureless and in summer may be lost in the haze.

Facilities for yachts are much improved over just a decade ago, with some provision for visiting yachts in almost every harbour. However, local yacht ownership is increasing in tandem, and in most places it is wise to telephone ahead to check that a berth will be available. Neither is berthing the relatively cheap option it once was – a situation compounded by there being relatively few all-weather anchorages – with high season marina fees for a yacht of 10–12m in 2005 varying from around €15 per night in Póvoa de Varzim and Sines to more than €30 per night in Figueira da Foz and Cascais. Comparable rates for a yacht of 12–15m were just over €20 per night in Póvoa de Varzim and Sines, rising to around €45 per night in Figueira da Foz and Cascais. The majority of marinas do not accept payment by credit card (*cartão de crédito*) due to the stiff levy charged by most card companies, and neither is there always a cash dispenser (*caixa automática*) nearby. Fuel must nearly always be paid for in cash, even in those harbours where plastic is accepted in the marina office.

All yachts, both locally-owned and visitors, spending more than 183 days in Portuguese waters are liable for a 'long stay' tax, calculated using a formula based on displacement in metric tons, engine capacity and age. In 2003 (the last date for which figures were available) a yacht of 8 tons displacement with a 40hp engine would have paid €121.92 if registered in 1986 or earlier, €74.80 if registered since 1986. Figures for a yacht of 16 tons displacement with a 90 hp engine were €304.72 and €176.56 respectively. Collection is in the hands of the local *GNR–Brigada Fiscal*, and though non-payment can in theory lead to a fine of around €150.00 it is often poorly publicised. A certificate and receipt are issued on payment, valid for one year from the date of arrival in Portuguese waters (including the Azores and Madeira).

A few harbours have hazards of one sort or another on their approach, most commonly a bar which alters with the winter storms and can be dangerous if there is a swell running, particularly if it meets an ebbing tidal stream. Even though most river mouths are now dredged and no longer pose a threat in terms of depth – those of the Rio Minho in the north and Vila Nova de Milfontes in the south being notable exceptions – nearly all can be dangerous in heavy weather, and on average at least one yacht is lost (or at least capsized) each year while attempting to enter a harbour on the Portuguese Atlantic coast in the wrong conditions.

Caution

Nearly all charts of the area, both British Admiralty and Portuguese, still use ED50 datum, whereas both the plans and waypoints in the following pages have been converted to WGS84 (the necessary shift is generally stated on a published chart, and in addition several hundred known positions were verified by handheld GPS during research).

Great care has been taken over the creation of waypoints, together with their associated courses and distances. However it remains the responsibility of the individual navigator to satisfy him or herself of each one's validity before placing any reliance on it.

Hazards – lobster and fish pots

Clusters of fish pots may be met with at intervals all along the Portuguese coast and particularly around the approaches to harbours. Others are laid well out to sea in surprising depths, and although most are reasonable well marked with flags, a minority rely on dark coloured plastic containers or even branches.

Swell

Swell along this coast originates well offshore and as a result is seldom absent. In many ways it poses a greater danger than the wind, not least because it is extremely easy to underestimate its extent while still

The anchorage at Portinho de Arrábida (page 191) photographed from the cliffs above. The shadow of Baixo do Alpertuche can be seen at centre right, with some of the sandbanks fringing the entrance to Setúbal on the left *AH*

in deep water and be taken by surprise by its height and power on closing the coast. In winter it can come from anywhere between southwest and northwest; in summer it is more likely to come from northwest, with heavy swell occurring about 10% of the time.

Winds

In April the prevailing northerly Portuguese trades – the *nortada* – begin to set in, generally blowing at around 15–25 knots (force 4–6), and becoming more firmly established from north to south as the season advances. In winter, fronts and occasionally secondary depressions may cross the area. Summer gales are unusual – in winter, onshore gales can close some harbours for days.

Particular mention should be made of the strength of the afternoon sea breezes. From early summer onwards these start to blow at around 1200 each day, regularly reaching 25 knots (force 6) and occasionally 30 knots (force 7) and continuing to blow until sundown. Typically they pick up from the east, swinging north and increasing during the afternoon. For this reason passages north, particularly in smaller yachts or if lightly crewed, are most easily made in short daily hops between dawn and midday with afternoons spent in harbour.

However it should be stressed that while these are the typical conditions, others can and do override them from time to time. In particular, September will occasionally see southwesterly winds gusting to 35 knots (force 8) blow without respite for a week or more, in which case the only prudent course is to stay put.

Winds are frequently stronger in river mouths and in the lee of headlands (due to the katabatic effects) and allowance should be made for this if entering under sail.

'Accessorise your fishing boat with a matching tender...' as always in Portugal, primary colours rule supreme   AH

Visibility

Poor visibility (less than 2M) can occur any time of year but there is a steep increase in its incidence (from 3% to 10%) 60M either side of Lisbon in July and an increase of approximately the same order further north in August and September. By October, all areas have returned to the 2%–4% level. Coastal fog can occur at any time but generally comes with light onshore winds.

Shelter

Many Portuguese harbours provide excellent shelter once inside, but in strong onshore winds only Leixões, Nazaré, Peniche, Cascais, Lisbon and Sines are likely to be safe to enter. In really strong winds even the entrance to the Rio Tejo (Lisbon) can become dangerous.

Currents

The set of the current depends upon the recent dominant wind, but the basic trend is from north to south. Its speed averages about 0.5 knot, though this can double in summer when the *nortada* has been blowing for some time.

Tides

Tidal predictions throughout Portugal use Lisbon as the Standard Port, Volume 2 of the Admiralty *Tide Tables: The Atlantic and Indian Oceans including tidal stream predictions (NP 202)*, published annually, covering the entire coastline. Alternatively consult the UK Hydrographic Office's EasyTide programme at www.ukho.gov.uk – see page 2 – which gives daily tidal data for all major harbours.

The mean tidal range at Lisbon is 3·3m at springs and 1·6m at neaps, but both height and time of tide along the coast can be affected by wind. Offshore tidal streams are very weak and surprisingly little is known about them – at Cabo Carvoeiro it is said to flood to the southeast, roughly the opposite to the stream off Galicia, but it is not known where the change takes place.

Climate

Rain occurs mainly between November and March, with cloud following the same pattern. Cool in winter, warm in summer, cooler in the north, warmer in the south. July averages for Lisbon are 14–36°C with 57% humidity; in January 3–16°C with 75% humidity.

Maritime radio stations and weather/navigational services

Many Portuguese Maritime radio stations and those broadcasting weather and navigational information are situated between, rather than at, ports or harbours. Details will be found under the nearest harbour to the station. All Maritime radio stations are remotely controlled from Lisbon. Broadcast times are quoted in UT, but all other times (office hours etc) are given in LT.

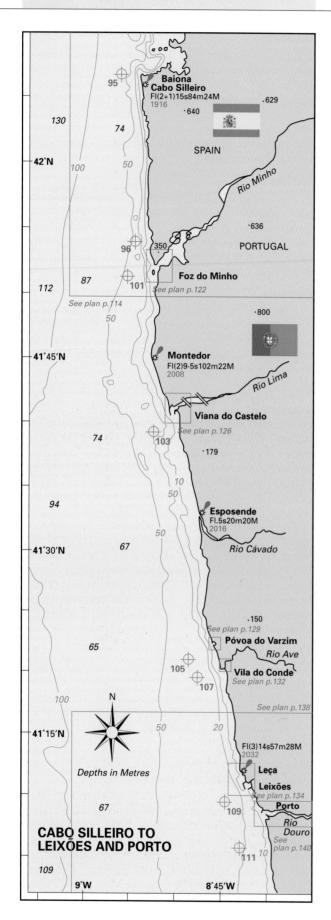

II.1 Foz do Minho to Leixões

⊕95	42°06′.5N	8°56′.6W	2M W of Cabo Silleiro
⊕96	41°45′.5N	8°55′.1W	1.6M WNW La Guardia
⊕101	41°51′.3N	8°54′.9W	Foz do Minho approach
⊕103	41°39′.2N	8°52′.5W	Viana do Castelo approach
⊕105	41°21′.2N	8°48′.7W	Póvoa de Varzim approach
⊕107	41°19′.7N	8°47′.5W	Vila do Conde approach
⊕109	41°09′.2N	8°44′.7W	Leixões approach
⊕111	41°08′.4N	8°43′W	Porto & the Rio Douro approach

PRINCIPAL LIGHTS

1916 **Cabo Silleiro** Fl(2+1)15s84m24M
   White 8-sided tower, red bands on dwelling
2008 **Montedor** Fl(2)9.5s102m22M
   Horn Mo 'S' (···)25s 800m WSW
   Square masonry tower and building 28m
2016 **Esposende** Fl.5s20m20M Horn 20s 100m S
   Red tower on white base and building 15m
2032 **Leça** Fl(3)14s57m28M
   White tower, narrow grey bands, red lantern 46m

Ports

37.   Foz do Minho
38.   Viana do Castelo*
39.   Póvoa de Varzim*
40.   Vila do Conde
41.   Leixões*

* Fuel available alongside

The elegant front leading light on the corner of
the Castelo de Santiago at Viana do Castelo   *AH*

37. Foz do Minho

Waypoints and distances
⊕95 42°06′.5N 8°56′.6W (2M W of Cabo Silleiro)
⊕101 – 41°51′.3N 8°54′.9W (approach)
⊕102 – 41°51′.04N 8°52′.48W (entrance)

Courses and distances
⊕95 (Cabo Silleiro) – F101 = 15.3M, 175° or 355°
⊕101 – ⊕102 = 1.8M, 098° or 278°
⊕101 – ⊕103 (Viana do Castelo) = 14M, 173° or 353°

Tides
Standard port Lisbon
Mean time differences (at La Guardia)
HW –0010 ±0010; LW +0015 ±0010
Heights in metres

MHWS	MHWN	MLWN	MLWS
3.3	2.6	1.2	0.4

Charts

	Approach	Entrance/river
Admiralty	3633	
Imray	C19, C48	
Portuguese	23202, (23201), 24201	51, (26301)

Principal lights
2002 Insua Nova Fl.WRG.4s16m12/8/9M
357°-W-204°-G-270°-R-357°
White conical tower on square base 7m
2003 Ldg Lts 100°
Front Moledo Oc.R.5s12m6M
White, red and yellow column on beach 3m
2003.1 *Rear* 25m from front Oc.R.5s16m6M
White, red and yellow column behind beach 7.5m
1926 Piedra Cabrón (Bajo de las Oliveiras)
Fl(2)5s3M Black beacon, red band, ⦂ topmark

Night entry
Not feasible, though in calm conditions it might be possible to anchor in the entrance

Maritime radio station
Arga (41°48′.4N 8°41′.6W)
Remotely controlled from Lisbon)
Manual – VHF Ch 16, 24, 25, 28. *Autolink* – VHF Ch 83.

Attractive river with several anchorages but a difficult entrance

The Rio Minho (or Río Miño to those further north) forms part of the boundary between Spain and Portugal. It gives its name to Portugal's northern province, where the hilly landscape with its numerous villages and their vines, eucalyptus and fruit trees is as pretty as its produce is good.

The Minho valley itself is particularly attractive – though increasingly built-up near its mouth – and, with local knowledge and a current large-scale chart or plan, a yacht of modest draught can navigate a considerable distance up the river. Dinghies, multihulls and monohulls able to take the ground can penetrate as far as Valença on the Portuguese shore – Túy (Tui) on the Spanish side – where there are bridges with an estimated clearance 15m.

The shallow river mouth (*foz*) is continually changing in shape, particularly regarding the position of the deep channel, and local knowledge should be enlisted if at all possible.

Approach

If coastal sailing, the Rio Minho's northern approach is dominated by the 350m Monte de Santa Tecla, topped by grey stone buildings and an aerial. On the mountain's western flank lies a conspicuous factory with two tall chimneys. South of the entrance a narrow strip of land fronted by a wide sandy beach separates the sea from hills which rise to some 700m about 8km inland, while the entrance itself is guarded by the low-lying Insua Nova with its stone fortress.

The mouth of the Rio Minho, with Insua Nova in the foreground and Bandeira rock clearly visible

PORTUGAL – THE WEST COAST

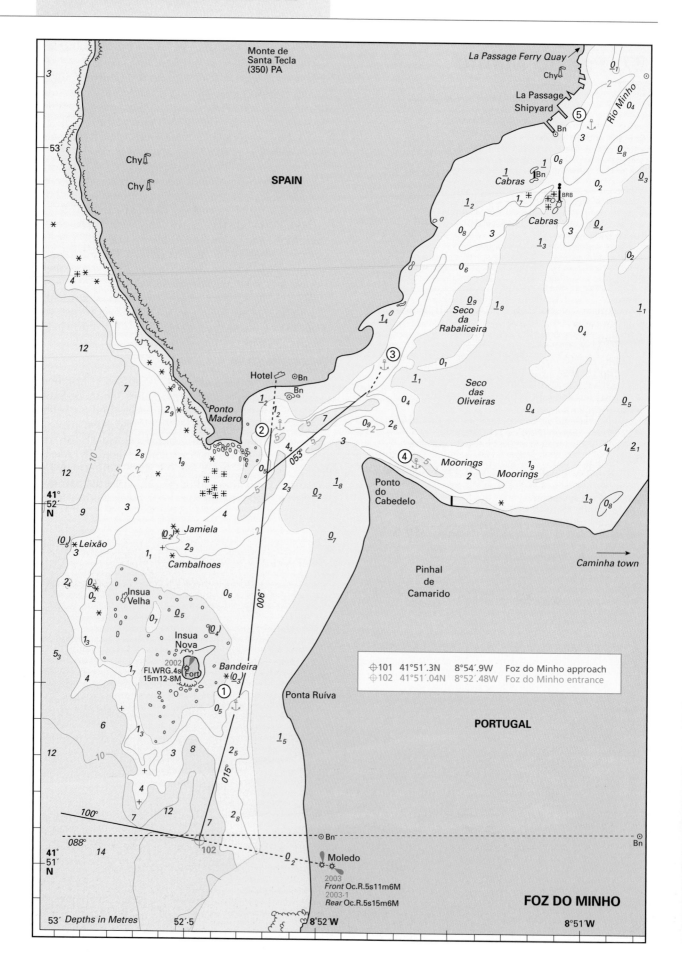

⊕101	41°51′.3N	8°54′.9W	Foz do Minho approach
⊕102	41°51′.04N	8°52′.48W	Foz do Minho entrance

Monte de
Santa Tecla
(350) PA

La Passage Ferry Quay

Chy

La Passage
Shipyard

SPAIN

Chy

Chy

Rio Minho

Cabras

Cabras

Seco
da
Rabaliceira

Seco
das
Oliveiras

Hotel

Bn

Bn

Ponto
Madero

Moorings

Moorings

Ponto
do
Cabedelo

Caminha town

Jamiela

Leixão

Cambalhoes

Pinhal
de
Camarido

Insua
Velha

Insua
Nova

Fl.WRG.4s
15m12-8M
2002
Fort

Bandeira

PORTUGAL

Ponta Ruíva

Moledo
2003
Front Oc.R.5s11m6M
2003-1
Rear Oc.R.5s15m6M

FOZ DO MINHO

53′ Depths in Metres

52′.5

8°52′W

8°51′W

From offshore, ⊕101 lies some 2M off the coast. A course of 097° for 1.8M leads to ⊕102, after which refer to the plan on page 122.

A fish farm which incorporates a floating platform, marked by a south cardinal post, topmark, Q(6)+LFl.6M, lies at 41°49′.3N 8°55′.6W (2M south-southwest of ⊕101).

Entrance

The entrance is difficult and can be dangerous, and has claimed more than one yacht as well as innumerable local craft. It is an option only in calm weather with little or no swell. Once inside, should westerly winds or swell get up a yacht can remain trapped inside for days, though well protected. There are many rocks, shoals and banks in the approaches and the river itself, the sands shift, and the currents run hard in the narrow entrance particularly after rain. Once in the channel there are no buoys or other channel markers.

If possible enter at about half flood, when Bandeira rock, 150m east of Insua Nova, will be visible. At the same time some protection will be offered by the rocky shoals which largely block the north entrance (itself not a viable proposition without informed local knowledge).

If coming from the north keep at least 0.5M off Insua Nova and continue south until, by turning onto the Moledo leading line[2003] on 100°, one passes south of its fort by some 0.5M. If in doubt there is good water to the south. If coming from the south keep a good 0.5M offshore until able to turn onto 100°, as above. Although the Moledo leading marks are lit, night approach is out of the question. The nearby pair of beacons on 088° – see plan – may also be useful but the rear beacon, nearly a mile inland, is difficult to identify.

When the east side of Insua Nova bears 000°, turn onto approximately 015° to pass as close to the island as Bandeira rock allows. The sandbank off Ponta Ruíva opposite is growing westwards by the year, yet remains very steep-to and in the least swell is likely to be indicated by breaking water. If feasible, anchor about 250m southeast of the fort and

reconnoitre by dinghy before pushing on. After leaving Bandeira rock close to port head straight for the conspicuous hotel on the Spanish shore on a bearing of approximately 006°, ignoring the leading marks to the east of the hotel. At approximately 41°52′.08N – or as depths begin to shoal off the rocky patch south of Ponto Madero – alter course to 053°, roughly parallel to the Spanish shore. South of the point depths shoal quickly inside the 5m contour. If heading towards Caminha town, the channel lies approximately 200m off the southern shore. It shoals after the shore turns northeast.

If continuing north-northeast favour the north shore, keeping to the middle of the gap between the two Cabras (goat) rocks, awash at high tide but the southern group marked by a lit red and black beacon, topmark. Note that a group of smaller rocks lie close north of the marked pair. More substantial beacons some 0.5M upstream indicate the ferry channel between the small towns of Camposancos and Caminha.

Anchorages near the Foz

1. As already mentioned, temporary anchorage is possible 250m southeast of the fort on Insua Nova. Holding is good over clean sand, protected from west through north to southeast, but it is too exposed for an overnight stay in all but the very calmest conditions
2. South of the hotel on the Spanish side of the entrance, protected from the west by Ponto Madero, in 2–3m.
3. Between the Seco das Oliveiras sandbank and the Spanish shore in 2–3m.
4. Off the southern shore east of Ponta do Cabedelo, outside the smallcraft moorings.
5. Abeam of the La Passage shipyard, but keeping clear of the dredged ferry channel, indicated by beacons.

The Rio Minho seen from the heights of Monte de Santa Tecla to the north. The two sets of Cabras rocks are clearly visible at half left   *AH*

PORTUGAL – THE WEST COAST

The long white sand beach south of the Rio Minho   *AH*

Formalities

Little notice is likely to be taken of a visiting yacht, though officials from the *Polícia Marítima* and/or the *GNR–Brigada Fiscal* may arrive alongside if in the area. There is a *Capitania* near the Caminha ferry berth which should be visited if anchored in the vicinity, but the nearby *Alfândega* (customs) office has long been closed.

Facilities and communications

On the Portuguese shore a restaurant and a campsite with a small general store will be found near anchorage No.4 above. Caminha itself (within walking distance) has a post office, shops, a market, banks, restaurants and several public telephones. Taxis are available, with bus and train services to Valença, Vigo and Porto.

On the Spanish side there is a small shipyard building trawlers at La Passage and a few buildings near the ferry landing at Goyan, but otherwise little between La Guardia and Túy.

Adjacent anchorage

41°49′N 08°52′.2W (approach)

Ancora, with its small stone fort and miniature harbour, lies just over 2M south of Foz de Minho entrance. There is no room to seek protection inside the tiny harbour – even local craft are hauled high up a wide concrete apron – but in the right conditions anchoring is possible in 2–3m just off the breakwater. However, even if the morning breeze is offshore, by lunchtime the nortada may well make the anchorage untenable and the yacht should never be left unattended.

If intent on exploration, remain at least 0.5M offshore until the harbour has been identified, then pick up the leading marks on 071° (two red and white posts on white pyramid bases). The cross on the hill above is almost in line. Although lit, Fl(2)R.5s11m9M and Fl(2)G.5s10m6M, on no account should the coast be closed in darkness.

The town has shops and restaurants.

The mouth of the Rio Minho from the southwest. On the right is the small harbour at Ancora, about 3M south of the Foz do Minho

38. Viana do Castelo

Waypoints
⊕103 – 41°39´.2N 8°52´.5W (approach)
⊕104 – 41°40´.34N 8°50´.43W (entrance)

Courses and distances
⊕95 (Cabo Silleiro) – ⊕103 = 27.5M, 174° or 354°
⊕101 (Foz do Minho) – ⊕103 = 14M, 173° or 353°
⊕103 – ⊕104 = 1.9M, 054° or 234°
⊕103 – ⊕105 (Póvoa de Varzim) = 18M, 171° or 351°
⊕103 – ⊕109 (Leixões) = 30.6M, 169° or 349°

Tides
Standard port Lisbon
Mean time differences (at La Guardia)
HW –0010 ±0010; LW +0015 ±0005
Heights in metres

MHWS	MHWN	MLWN	MLWS
3.5	2.7	1.4	0.5

Or refer to EasyTide at www.ukho.gov.uk (see page 2)

Charts

	Approach	Harbour
Admiralty	3633, 3634, 3257	3257
Imray	C19, C48	C48
Portuguese	23202, (23201), 24201	26401

Principal lights
2012.8 **Outer breakwater** Fl.R.3s9M Horn 30s
   White tower, red bands 10m
2012 **Fishing harbour Ldg Lts** 012°
   Front Castelo de Santiago
   Iso.R.4s14m23M 241°-vis-151°
   Red tower in corner of castle, white lantern 6m
2012.1 *Rear* **Senhora da Agonia** 400m from front
   Oc.R.6s33m23M 005°-vis-020°
   Red tower beside prominent church, white lantern 9m
Note The above lights lead from the main channel into
the fishing harbour and should NOT be followed through
the entrance itself
2012.6 **East (inner) breakwater** Fl.G.3s9M
   White tower, green bands 6m
2012.4 **Sectored entrance light** Oc.WRG.4s15m8-6M
   035°-G-005°-W-010°-R-025°-obscd-350°
2013 **Fishing harbour, port side** Iso.R.4m3M
   White column, red bands 2m
2013.5 **Fishing harbour, starboard side**
   Iso.G.4m3M White column, green bands 2m

Night entry
   Well lit (though buoys may occasionally be missing), and
   straightforward in all normal conditions

Harbour communications
   Port Authority ☎ 258 359500 *Fax* 258 359535
   Email ipn@ipnorte.pt
   www.ipnorte.pt
   VHF Ch 11, 16 (call *Capimarviana*) (0900–1200,
   1400–1700 weekdays only)
   VianaMarina ☎/*Fax* 258 359546
   Email marina@ipnorte.pt
   www.ipnorte.pt/i/portorecreio.htm
   VHF Ch 12.

Commercial harbour with small marina beside old and attractive town

Near the mouth of the Rio Lima, Viana do Castelo
will provide a welcome break if slogging north and
an fine introduction to Portugal if heading south. In
the 16th century the town grew rich from trade with
Brazil and from cod fishing on the Newfoundland
Banks, where the Portuguese swapped local fortified
wine for nets brought out by fishermen from
England's West Country. This returned to England as
'Portuguese wine' later abbreviated to 'Port wine'.

English merchants came to Viana do Castelo to
develop the trade, which moved to Vila Nova de
Gaia on the Rio Douro, opposite Porto, when the
harbour at Viana silted up. In the meantime the
town's citizens had built the beautiful grey granite
and white stucco houses which make the old town so
attractive today.

Employment these days is provided by a large
commercial harbour on the south bank of the river
and one of Portugal's most extensive shipbuilding
yards on the north bank close inside the entrance
(the *Gil Eannes*, built there in 1955 and long in
service to the Portuguese Grand Banks fishing fleet is
now on permanent display in the old commercial
basin). There is also an active though reduced fishing
fleet, some local industry and a growing tourist
industry.

One of the major *festas* of the Minho area is the
romaria dedicated to Nossa Senhora da Agonía
which takes place in Viana do Castelo over the
weekend nearest to 20 August – well worth
considering if heading south in late summer. At any
time of year the energetic will enjoy the steep walk
up to the Basílica on Monte de Santa Luzia which
commands superb views in all directions, though for
an edifice which looks as though it should have
graced the town for centuries it is surprisingly
modern, having been completed in the early 20th
century. For genuinely old buildings stroll through
the town centre to admire the renaissance fountain,
almshouses and nearby *Câmara Municipal* (town
hall).

The small VianaMarina lies, quite literally, under the road
and railway bridge

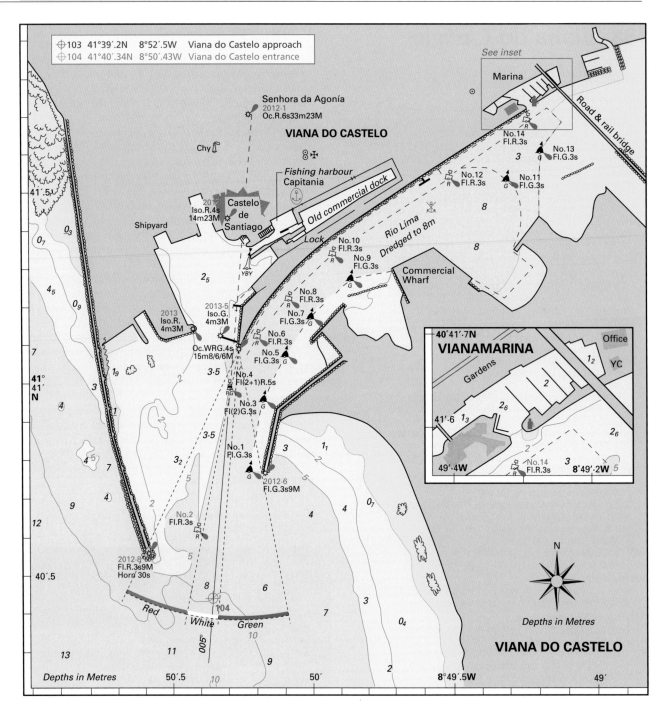

```
⊕103  41°39´.2N   8°52´.5W   Viana do Castelo approach
⊕104  41°40´.34N  8°50´.43W  Viana do Castelo entrance
```

Senhora da Agonía
2012·1
Oc.R.6s33m23M

VIANA DO CASTELO

Chy

Fishing harbour
Capitania

Castelo
de
Santiago

2012
Iso.R.4s
14m23M

Shipyard

Old commercial dock

Lock

Rio Lima
Dredged to 8m

No.10
Fl.R.3s

No.9
Fl.G.3s

Commercial
Wharf

Marina

No.14
Fl.R.3s

No.13
Fl.G.3s

No.12
Fl.R.3s

No.11
Fl.G.3s

Road & rail bridge

2013
Iso.R.
4m3M

2013·5
Iso.G.
4m3M

Oc.WRG.4s
15m8/6/6M

No.8
Fl.R.3s

No.7
Fl.G.3s

No.6
Fl.R.3s

No.5
Fl.G.3s

No.4
Fl(2+1)R.5s

No.3
Fl(2)G.3s

No.1
Fl.G.3s

2012·6
Fl.G.3s9M

No.2
Fl.R.3s

2012·8
Fl.R.3s9M
Horn 30s

Red   White   Green

104

40°41´.7N
VIANAMARINA
Gardens
Office
YC
No.14
Fl.R.3s
49´.4W   8°49´.2W

Depths in Metres

VIANA DO CASTELO

Depths in Metres   50´.5   50´   8°49´.5W   49´

Approach

If coastal sailing, note that hazards lie close offshore both north and south of Viana do Castelo – for peace of mind keep outside the 20m line.

From offshore, ⊕103 lies 1.9M southwest of the entrance, a course of 054° leading to ⊕104, close outside the harbour mouth.

The major lights are Montedor to the north, Senhora da Agonia at Viana itself, and Esposende. There are a pair of leading lights at Neiva, 3.5M to the south, which are not relevant to Viana.

Two floating platforms, possibly linked and both marked by black posts with • topmarks, Q(3)15s, are positioned some 3.6M west-northwest of the harbour entrance at 41°41´.7N 8°55´.2W and

41°41´.6N 8°54´.7W respectively. Their purpose is unknown but they should clearly be avoided.

Entrance

From the north, take a wide swing eastwards at least 500m south of the outer breakwater. At night, do not turn into the harbour until within the white sector of the entrance light (see plan), to pass up the centre of the buoyed channel to pass up the centre of the buoyed channel.

From the south, head in from the 20m line with the radio aerial on Faro de Anha bearing around 080° until within the white sector, then proceed as above. The entrance is kept dredged to 8m, making it safe in all but the severest weather or swell.

The south-facing entrance to Viana do Castelo

Leaving the entrance to the fishing dock to port, follow the buoyed channel northeast past the commercial wharf, to the marina entrance on the north bank, just short of the bridge and marked by a tall signal mast. Ten buoys are shown as marking the channel between the fishing dock and marina entrance, though it appears rare for all to be in place and working at any given time. Thus while night entry is perfectly feasible it should be undertaken with some caution.

Beyond the commercial wharf depths decrease from 8m to 3m, shoaling to less than 2.5m in the marina approach. Beware strong crosscurrents at the marina entrance on both the flood and the ebb.

Anchoring in the river is prohibited, but towage is available if required.

Berthing

VianaMarina lies about 1.5M upriver from the entrance, beneath (literally) the two-tier road and rail bridge (designed by Gustaf Eiffel of Tower fame). The town is a short walk away through pleasant public gardens which also contain a children's playground.

The marina contains some 160 berths of which around 20 are nominally reserved for visiting yachts of up to 14m. In addition there is a single berth capable of taking a 20m vessel. There is no reception pontoon, and until recently visitors berthed bow or stern-to anywhere on the westernmost of the four pontoons where there appeared a chance of squeezing in (many of the 'visitors' appear to have stayed long-term). A pickup line is provided, but all the fingers serve private berths. Far more appealing is the right-angled pontoon to be found on the port side just inside the entrance, though again there are no fingers and a pick-up line must be used.

The office claims never to close, and in 2005 the high season (15 May–15 September) rate for a visiting yacht of 10–12m was €17.61 per night, rising to €23.72 for 12–15m, inclusive of water, electricity and tax. Multihulls paid a 50% surcharge. Unusually, a 15% discount was available to those who opted to do without water and electricity, and useful discounts were available if paying for longer periods in advance. Payment must be made in cash – no credit cards are accepted.

Despite its proximity to the road and rail bridge, if the marina can be said to suffer a noise problem it comes from the busy road which parallels it within feet of its landward side. If berthed for any length of time, particularly in northerly winds, a fair measure of dust and dirt should be anticipated.

Plans to build a second marina, the Marina Oceânica, in the old commercial dock have been under discussion for some time and it is hoped that work will start within the next few years. With a surface area of 34,000m² it is easy to enter, enjoys excellent protection and has more than adequate depths. It is bordered to the south by acres of semi-derelict land on which the usual shoreside facilities could be built and to the northwest by the Castelo de Santiago with a small grassy park beyond. Initially it is planned to install around 120 berths, most of them for larger yachts, with facilities including a travel-lift. Further information will be found on the port's excellent website (with English version) at www.ipnorte.pt.

Formalities

The marina office will be found in the large new building at the east end of the basin. Although for many yachts this will be their first (or last) Portuguese harbour, formalities are kept to a minimum with computer-generated forms distributed automatically to the various officials. The usual passports, ship's papers and insurance documents will be required. Normally no other offices need be visited, though skippers of non-EU registered yachts, or with non–EU nationals amongst their crew, should check current requirements. Yachts which arrive outside office hours may be visited by a member of the *GNR–Brigada Fiscal*.

Facilities

Boatyard No boatyard at the marina, but extensive shipyards west of the fishing dock where commercial vessels, as well as GRP and timber fishing boats, are built. In an emergency there is little doubt that yacht repairs in most materials could be undertaken. Enquire at the marina office.

Travel-lift Not as such, but the marina has a mobile crane capable of lifting at least 20 tonnes, with larger ones available in the new commercial harbour on the south bank of the river. Yachts of suitable underwater shape may also use the tidal grid. A travel-lift is planned for the Marina Oceânica (see page 127) but no timescale is in place.

Engineers Costa & Rego Lda, ☎ 235 844250/1, situated between the river and the old commercial basin, are precision engineers and machinists. They can arrange engine repairs and will copy any unobtainable metal parts.

Next to them will be found Mechanica Magalhães (run by two brothers, it is sometimes referred to as Magalhães & Magalhães Lda), ☎ 258 823950, mobile 93 8344 797. Neither speak much English but the marina staff are happy to translate if necessary.

Finally Manuel Carvalhosa & Ca Lda, ☎/*Fax* 058 832133, mobile 96 9024 743, has been recommended as 'fast, efficient and reliable' for work on diesel engines/electrics/fabrication/ welding etc.

Electronic and radio repairs Arrange through the marina office, who may well suggest Engineering Pires, mobile 91 7540 233.

Sail repairs Minor repairs may also be done locally (enquire at the marina office). For anything major try Pires de Lima in Porto (see page 137).

Chandlery A good range will be found at Angelo Silva Lda, ☎ 258 801460 *Fax* 258 801469 *Email* geral@nautigas.pt, overlooking the old commercial basin. Items not in stock can be ordered from a wide variety of suppliers. Ferraz & Ferraz Lda just beyond sells some chandlery in addition to all kinds of fishing tackle.

A chandlery is planned for the large building where the marina office is situated.

Water On the pontoons.

Showers Immaculate showers and toilets at the back of the block housing the marina office. The latter are open to all, the former accessed by key on payment of around €1 a time.

Launderette A washer and a dryer are provided in both the men's and the ladies' ablutions areas. There are several commercial launderettes in the town.

Electricity On the pontoons.

Fuel Diesel and petrol at the fuelling pontoon on the starboard side just inside the marina entrance.

Bottled gas Camping Gaz is readily available. Angelo Silva Lda (see Chandlery above) can arrange for other bottles to be refilled, but allow a minimum of 24 hours.

Clube náutico Small but friendly *clube náutico* at the east end of the marina basin, which welcomes visiting yachtsmen.

Weather forecast At the marina office.

Banks Several in the town, nearly all with cash dispensers.

Shops/provisioning Good shopping of all kinds in the town, including several supermarkets, with a hypermarket about 1.5km inland.

Produce market Fish and produce market daily, plus open-air general market on Friday near the Castelo de Santiago at the seaward end of the town.

Cafés, restaurants and hotels A wide choice in and around the town. The *clube náutico* has a bar overlooking the marina which also serves light meals.

Medical services Hospital etc in the town.

Communications

Post office In the town.

Mailing address The marina office will hold mail for visiting yachts – c/o Instituto Portuário do Norte, Marina de Viana do Castelo, Rua da Lima, 4900-405 Viana do Castelo, Portugal. It is important that the envelope carries the name of the yacht in addition to that of the addressee.

Internet access At least three venues, including several terminals in the nearby youth hostel (the rather boxy building just upstream of the two-tier bridge) and eps@ço.net on Rua General Luis do Rêgo (open 0900–1900 weekdays, 0900–1800 Saturday, closed Sunday), which also has printers.

Public telephones In the entrance to the *clube náutico* and elsewhere.

Fax service At the marina office, *Fax* 258 359546.

Car hire/taxis In the town. Taxis can be ordered from the marina office.

Buses and trains To Porto, Vigo and beyond.

Air services International airport at Porto some 50km away.

Not feasible – Esposende

Esposende (41°32′.5N 8°47′.5W), just under 10M south of Viana do Castelo, should be mentioned in passing – literally. A long sandbank blocks the mouth of the Rio Cávado, leaving a very shallow entrance some 50m wide which gives onto an equally shallow lagoon where a few small boats are moored. Shoals and isolated rocks (the Cavalos de Fão and Baixo da Foz) extend up to 1.5M offshore opposite the lighthouse. Give it a wide berth.

Esposende – not recommended for any vessel larger than a canoe

39. Póvoa de Varzim

Waypoints
⊕105 – 41°21′.2N 8°48′.7W (approach)
⊕106 – 41°22′.15N 8°46′.14W (entrance)

Courses and distances
⊕95 (Cabo Silleiro) – ⊕105 = 45.7m, 173° or 353°
⊕103 (Viana do Castelo) – ⊕105 = 18M, 171° or 351°
⊕105 – ⊕106 = 2.1M, 064° or 244°
⊕105 – ⊕107 (Vila do Conde) = 1.8M, 149° or 329°
⊕105 – ⊕109 (Leixões) = 12.4M, 166° or 346°

Tides
Standard port Lisbon
Mean time differences
HW –0010 ±0010; LW +0015 ±0005
Heights in metres

MHWS	MHWN	MLWN	MLWS
3.5	2.7	1.4	0.5

Or refer to EasyTide at www.ukho.gov.uk (see page 2)

Charts

	Approach	Harbour
Admiralty	3634	
Imray	C19, C48	C48
Portuguese	23202, (23201), 24201	(27501)

Principal harbour lights
2020.4 **North breakwater** Fl.R.3s14m12M
White tower, red bands 5m Siren 40s
Note The breakwater projects some distance beyond the light structure
2020.6 **South breakwater** LFl.G.6s13m4M
White post, green bands 4m

Night entry
Straightforward, though care must be taken to observe the small, unlit, starboard hand buoys

Maritime radio station
Apúlia – *Digital Selective Calling* (MF)
MMSI 002630200 (planned)

Harbour communications
Marina da Póvoa ☎ 252 688121 *Fax* 252 688123
Email marinadapova@telepac.pt
www.clubenavalpovoense.com
VHF Ch 09, 12,16 (0900–1200, 1400–1700).

⊕105 41°21′.2N 8°48′.7W Póvoa de Varzim approach
⊕106 41°22′.15N 8°46′.14W Póvoa de Varzim entrance

The semi-circular harbour at Póvoa de Varzim, seen from a little west of south. The Marina da Póvoa can been seen in the foreground, with the fishing boat berths beyond

Small, friendly marina in busy fishing harbour

Coming in from the sea, the view of Póvoa de Varzim's newer high-rise buildings belies the interesting old town which lies to the east and south. Hotels and a casino front the beach, but the harbour still boasts an active fishing fleet and the Marina da Póvoa has gained a well-deserved reputation for friendly and efficient service since its opening in 1999.

A colourful *romaria* is held on 15 August each year to commemorate those lost at sea, while the Museu Municipal de Etnografica e História on Rua do Visconde de Azevedo often has interesting displays relating to local fishing and other maritime pursuits in its handsome 18th century headquarters.

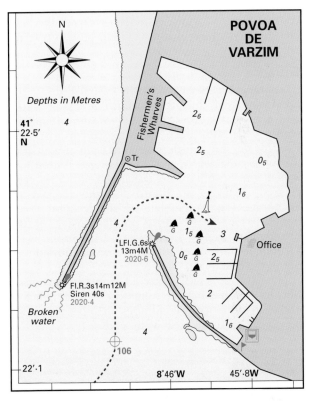

Approach

If coastal sailing, the coast between Viana do Castelo and Esposende has offlying dangers and should be given 2M clearance. From Esposende southwards there are sandy beaches and rocks with further isolated hazards all the way to Leixões – for relaxed sailing keep outside the 20m contour. Four yellow pillar buoys – two Fl.2.5s3M, × topmarks, one Fl(2)5s6M, ⁙ topmark, and one unlit – lie north of Póvoa de Varzim between 41°27′N and 41°27′.6N and 8°47′.6W and 8°50′.6W to mark submarine cables.

From offshore, ⊕105 lies 2.1M west-southwest of the entrance, a course of 064° leading to ⊕106, close outside the harbour mouth.

A distinctive white apartment block stands a short distance north of the harbour. The latter may be identified by its tower – reminiscent of an airport control tower – which also serves as an excellent landmark. A range of fish-handling buildings stand behind it.

Entrance

If approaching from the north swing wide of the breakwater end and its associated breaking water, and note that it is also foul up to 30m off on the south side. Approach heading north-northeast towards the spur which projects at right angles from the north breakwater, giving the latter a 50m offing. When the southern breakwater head has been cleared, turn to starboard for the marina or anchorage leaving the line of small, unlit, green buoys (which mark shoals on the inside of the breakwater) well to starboard and the (unlit) west cardinal to port. As of 2005 there was a minimum of 3m in the entrance.

The harbour is well protected from the northwest, but the entrance may be rough if the swell is heavy and even in moderate conditions breaking water can be expected off the breakwater end.

Berthing

The Marina da Póvoa offers 241 berths on its six pontoons, about a third of which can accommodate yachts of 10m or more in depths of at least 2.4m – the four largest berths, for yachts of up to 18m, carry at least 3m at all times. Around 40 berths are reserved for visitors.

The marina lies in the shelter of the south breakwater, and even in gale force west-northwesterlies experiences remarkably little movement inside. All berths are provided with finger pontoons of appropriate length.

On arrival yachts should berth on the short hammerhead by the marina office. Office hours are 0900–2000 daily in summer, 0900–1230 and 1400–1730 in winter, with a night watchman providing 24 hour security. As already noted the staff were quick to establish a high reputation for efficient, helpful service and nearly all speak good English.

In 2005 the daily rate for a visiting yacht of 10.5–12m was €15 per night, rising to €23 for 12–15m, inclusive of water, electricity and tax. Multihulls normally paid a 50% surcharge. Generous discounts were available for stays of a month or more. Payment must be made in cash – no credit cards are accepted.

Anchorage

As of 2004 anchoring in the harbour was still permitted, though not encouraged, provided neither the marina approach nor the many fishing boat movements to and from the north breakwater were impeded. The most obvious spot is in the northeast of the harbour, clear of the yacht and smallcraft moorings, in about 3m over mud and sand. Depths shoals gradually at some distance from the shore.

The friendly and well-run Marina da Póvoa

Hauling a fishing boat ashore in days gone by, as depicted on tiles near the root of the main breakwater. The church on the skyline appears in the photograph opposite *AH*

Formalities

If berthed in the marina visit the office taking passports, ship's papers and insurance documents. A single form must be completed, which is then photocopied and circulated by the marina to the GNR–*Brigada Fiscal*, *Alfândega* and *Polícia Marítima*. This procedure must be observed whether entering Portugal for the first time or arriving from elsewhere within the country. Even if not using the marina it is still necessary to observe clearance formalities.

Facilities

Boatyard Several concerns operate within the marina's secure area – ask at the office. There is a large area of open space fronting the marina, part of which is designated for use as hardstanding. A small covered workshop has been provided in the central marina building, next to the main gate.

Travel-lift A 32-tonne capacity hoist operates in the southern part of the secure area.

Engineers, electronic and radio repairs All skills available amongst those who service the fishing fleet – enquire at the marina office. A professional diver is also available.

Sail repairs Nothing nearby – try Pires de Lima in Porto (see page 137).

Chandlery Náutica Vaga, tucked away behind the old fort opposite the fishing harbour, has only limited stock. For anything major contact Angelo Silva Lda in Viana do Castelo or Nautileça in Leixões (see pages 128 and 137 respectively).

Water On the pontoons.

Showers In the central marina building.

Launderette In the central marina building.

Electricity At every berth.

Fuel No fuel at the marina, the original plan to install pumps on the reception pontoon having been shelved indefinitely. However diesel can be obtained in the fishing harbour (no minimum quantity) and small quantities of petrol, for outboards or generators, from the marina office.

Bottled gas Camping Gaz exchanges are readily available in the town, and Calor Gas bottles can be refilled. Ask at the office for directions

Clube naval The Clube Naval Povoense, which in 2004 celebrated its centenary, has large premises overlooking the south breakwater, where members' dinghies and jet-skis are stored on the ground floor with a bar and restaurant above. Visiting yachtsmen are made particularly welcome.

Weather forecast 48 hour forecast posted daily outside the marina office.

Banks In the town, about ten minutes' walk.

Shops/provisioning Good range in the town, with a large supermarket about 2km distant.

Produce market In the town.

Cafés, restaurants and hotels Wide variety in the town, as well as a restaurant at the *clube naval*.

Medical services Well equipped first aid post in the marina's central building, with doctors and a hospital in the town.

Communications

Post offices In the town.

Mailing address The *clube naval* will hold mail for visiting yachts – c/o Marina da Póvoa, Rua da Ponte No.2, Apartado 24, 4491 Póvoa de Varzim, Portugal. It is important that the envelope carries the name of the yacht in addition to that of the addressee.

Internet access At least three possibilities in the town, including the Diana-Bar on the beach just north of the harbour (about 10 minutes' walk from the marina), which is open 1000–2200 and also features comfortable seating and a small library in several languages including English.

Public telephones At the marina's central building, with cards available from the office.

Fax service At the marina office, *Fax* 252 688123.

Car hire/taxis In the town. A taxi can be ordered via the marina office. Bicycles (some with small trailers) can be hired from an office at the root of the main breakwater.

Buses and trains To Porto, Viana do Castelo etc. Several yachtsmen have recommended the 'direct' bus as a convenient way to visit Porto, while in due course the new metro is to extend north from the city all the way to Póvoa and beyond.

Air services International airport at Porto some 20km away. When complete, the new *metro* (see above) will provide easy access for crew changes.

40. Vila do Conde

Waypoints
⊕107 – 41°19′.7N 8°47′.5W (approach)
⊕108 – 41°20′.1N 8°44′.88W (entrance)

Courses and distances
⊕105 (Póvoa de Varzim) – ⊕107 = 1.8M, 149° or 329°
⊕107 – ⊕108 = 2M, 079° or 259°
⊕107 – ⊕109 (Leixões) = 10.7M, 169° or 349°

Tides
See Póvoa de Varzim, page 129

Charts

	Approach	Harbour
Admiralty	3634	
Imray	C19, C48	
Portuguese	23202, (23201), 24201	(27501)

Principal lights
2023.7 **Breakwater** Fl.R.4s8m9M Siren 30s
  Red column, white bands 8m
2023 **Outer Ldg Lts 079°**
  Front **Azurara** Iso.G.4s9m6M
  White post, red bands 7m, at rear of beach
2023.1 *Rear* 370m from front Iso.G.4s26m6M
  Square white tower, red bands and ▲ 6m
2024 **Inner Ldg Lts 357°** *Front* Barra Oc.R.3s6m6M
  White column, red bands 3m
2024.1 *Rear* 86m from front Oc.R.3s7m6M
  White column, red bands 5m

Night entry
Not feasible without local knowledge

Harbour communications
Capimarviconde VHF Ch 11, 16 (0900–1200, 1400–1700 Mon–Fri).

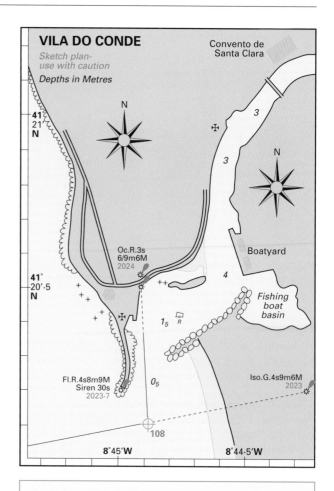

Looking into Vila do Conde from the southwest, with the white bulk of the Convento de Santa Clara clearly visible just left of centre

| ⊕107 | 41°19′.7N | 8°47′.5W | Vila do Conde approach |
| ⊕108 | 41°20′.1N | 8°44′.88W | Vila do Conde entrance |

PORTUGAL – THE WEST COAST

Narrow river offering possible anchorage

A small and difficult harbour only suitable for entry in calm weather, in daylight and towards high tide. The town has a thriving fishing fleet, a growing tourist industry and has long been known for its lace-making. A crafts fair is held over the last week of July and first week of August, while motor races take place along the seafront roads in early June and mid July.

The old town, dominated by the imposing Convento de Santa Clara, lies some distance upstream from the entrance, just below the bridge. Azurara, the village at the entrance, has a Manueline fortified church, a small stone fort and an attractive rocky beach where, until only a decade ago, seaweed was still collected for removal on horse-drawn sleds. Sadly but inexorably the area around the harbour is becoming filled with breeze-block developments, but even in 2005 some of the old cod-drying wires were still to be seen.

If berthed in Póvoa de Varzim for more than a few days, perhaps while waiting for suitable weather to head north or south, a walk to Vila do Conde and back would make an interesting afternoon's excursion.

Plans for a marina – or more probably a single pontoon – were mentioned in the late 1990s. However there is no sign of work starting and, with empty berths available less than 2M to the north at Póvoa de Varzim, there seems little prospect that it will, at least in the foreseeable future.

Approach and entrance

The entrance lies at the southern end of the line of high-rise blocks strung out along the beach between Póvoa and Vila do Conde. The low breakwater is some 350m long and has a small chapel dedicated to Senhora da Gaia at its root.

Fishing boats alongside the public quay, with the distinctive white dome of the 17th century Capela do Socorro beyond. (The angular construction is a piece of sculpture, not an ice chute!) *AH*

From offshore the outer leading marks, on 079°, clear the mole but are difficult to identify from offshore. ⊕107 lies on this line and 2M offshore. The inner pair, on 357°, lead over the bar – which may shoal to 0.5m at low water springs – but as the bar shifts these do not always indicate best water. ⊕108 lies at the intersection of the two leading lines.

Once round the eastern (inner) mole the channel swings to pass south of a small, L-shaped sandbank, marked by a single red buoy. A sizeable fishing boat basin, not available to yachts, lies to the east of the bend.

Tidal streams in the relatively narrow entrance can run strongly on both ebb and flood.

Anchorage

Continue upriver to anchor just short of the road bridge in 3–4m, taking care to buoy the anchor as the bottom is mainly foul. On the north bank there is an unusual fortified church with an almost Moorish white dome, while the entire area is overshadowed by the vast bulk of the Convento de Santa Clara. Traces of the old shipyard which long operated between the two can still be made out, though now supplanted by the impressive building and repair yard overlooking the fishing boat basin.

Facilities and communications

Food shops, banks and restaurants are all available, with a produce market on Fridays. There is a post office, with public telephones throughout the town and a regular bus service north to Póvoa de Varzim and south to Porto. On completion the Porto *metro* will provide an additional, and considerably faster, service.

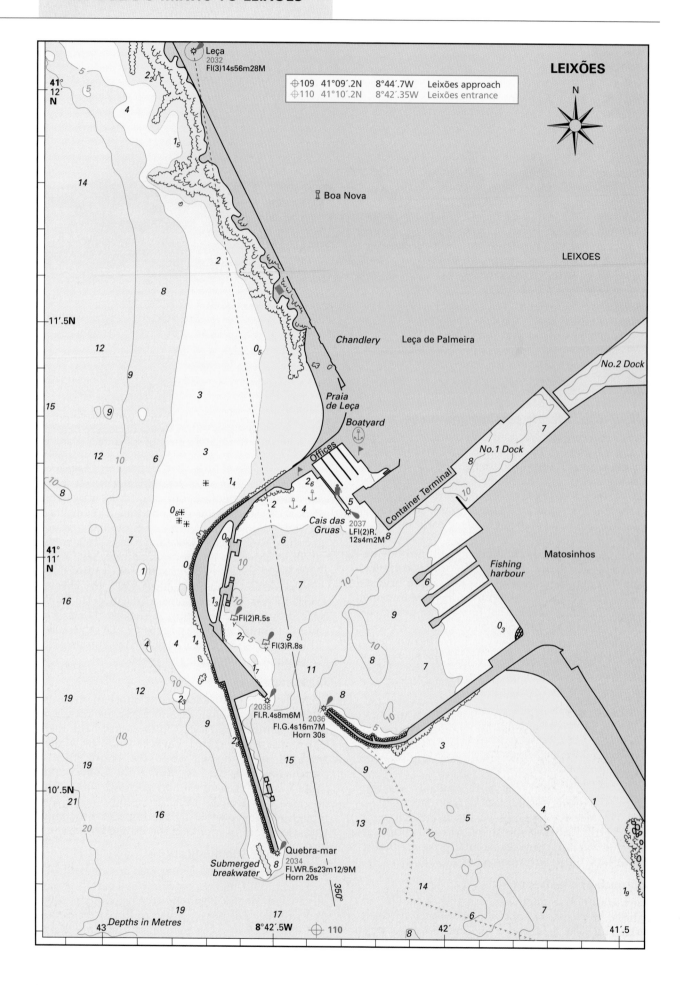

LEIXÕES

N

Leça
2032
Fl(3)14s56m28M

| ⊕109 | 41°09´.2N | 8°44´.7W | Leixões approach |
| ⊕110 | 41°10´.2N | 8°42´.35W | Leixões entrance |

41°
12´
N

Boa Nova

LEIXOES

11´.5N

Chandlery   Leça de Palmeira

No.2 Dock

Praia
de Leça

Boatyard

No.1 Dock

Offices

Container Terminal

Cais das   2037
Gruas   LFl(2)R.
12s4m2M

41°
11´
N

Matosinhos

Fishing
harbour

Fl(2)R.5s

FI(3)R.8s

2038
Fl.R.4s8m6M

2036
Fl.G.4s16m7M
Horn 30s

10´.5N

350°

Quebra-mar
2034
Submerged   Fl.WR.5s23m12/9M
breakwater   Horn 20s

Depths in Metres

8°42´.5W   ⊕ 110   42´   41´.5

41. Leixões

Waypoints

⊕109 – 41°09′.2N 8°44′.7W (approach)
⊕110 – 41°10′.2N 8°42′.35W (entrance)

Courses and distances

⊕103 (Viana do Castelo) – ⊕109 = 30.6M, 169° or 349°
⊕105 (Póvoa de Varzim) – ⊕109 = 12.4M, 166° or 346°
⊕107 (Vila do Conde) – ⊕109 = 10.7M, 169° or 349°
⊕109 – ⊕110 = 2M, 061° or 241°
⊕109 – ⊕111 (Porto and the Rio Douro) = 1.5M, 122° or 302°
⊕109 – ⊕113 (Ria de Aveiro) = 31.7M, 185° or 005°
⊕109 – ⊕116 (Figueira da Foz, via F115) = 61.7M, 189°&162° or 342°&009°
⊕109 – ⊕118 (Nazaré) = 95.1M, 190° or 010°

Tides

Standard port Lisbon
Mean time differences
HW –0015 ±0010; LW +0005 ±0005
Heights in metres

MHWS	MHWN	MLWN	MLWS
3.5	2.7	1.3	0.5

Or refer to EasyTide at www.ukho.gov.uk (see page 2)

Charts	Approach	Harbour
Admiralty	3634	3258
Imray	C19, C48	C19, C48
Portuguese	23202, (23201), 24201	26402

Principal lights

2034 West breakwater head (Quebramar)
Fl.WR.5s23m12/9M 001°-R-180°-W-001°
Horn 20s Grey tower 10m
2038 West breakwater spur
Fl.R.4s8m6M Red lantern 4m
2036 South breakwater
Fl.G.4s16m7M 328°-vis-285° Horn 30s
Hexagonal tower, green lantern 10m
2037 Marina mole (Cais das Gruas)
LFl(2)R.12s4m2M White post, red bands 3m

Night entry

Straightforward – the entrance is wide and the harbour well-lit. However it might be wise to anchor until daylight rather than enter the crowded marina

Weather bulletins and navigational warnings

Weather bulletins in Portuguese and English for the Rio Minho to Cabo de São Vicente within 20 miles offshore: VHF Ch 11 at 0705, 1905 UT
Navigational warnings in Portuguese and English within 200 miles offshore: VHF Ch 11 at 0705, 1905 UT

Harbour communications

Marina Porto Atlântico ☎ 229 964895 *Fax* 229 964899
Email info@marinaportoatlantico.net
www.marinaportoatlantico.net (with English translation)
VHF Ch 09, 16 (0900–1230 & 1400–2000 daily 16 June–15 Sept, otherwise 0900–1230 & 1400–1830 Mon–Sat).

The large commercial harbour at Leixões from a little west of south

A secure marina and adjacent anchorage which can be entered in all weather conditions

Leixões (pronounced 'layshoinsh'), with its wide entrance, is by far the best port of refuge on this stretch of the coast and can be entered in almost any weather. The busy commercial port is centred on oil, fishing and general trade, while the Marina Porto Atlântico in its northwest corner was one of the first yacht harbours to be established on the Portuguese Atlantic coast. The marina provides good shelter and is an excellent base from which to explore the fascinating city of Porto, easily accessible by bus, taxi or *metro*. The facilities available are much better than those on offer in Porto, but the nearby towns of Leça de Palmeira and Matosinhos cannot compete with the older city in terms of general shopping, historical interest and tourist sights. Those cruising with small children may be interested to know that the infant school on the road which runs north past the marina allows visiting youngsters to use the play area in its grounds.

Perhaps inevitably, bearing in mind its position in the corner of a commercial harbour, the marina sometimes suffers from poor water quality, but efforts are being made to overcome this. In autumn 2004 the marina was badly affected by an oil leakage from the nearby refinery – the first time this had happened in 30 years. It remained closed for refurbishment throughout 2005 but should, by the 2006 season, be fully operational with new pontoons and improved shoreside facilities. As in many Portuguese marinas all the personnel have been consistently praised by visiting yachtsmen for their helpfulness and efficiency, and all office staff (though not all the *marineros*) spoke good English.

Approach

Compared to the coastline further north, the area around Leixões is somewhat featureless. The oil refinery 1.5M north is a good mark by day or night, with the powerful Leça light lying between it and the harbour.

A spherical yellow outfall buoy (Fl.Y.4s6M Horn 30s) and a yellow tanker discharge 'superbuoy' (Fl(3)15s6M Horn (3)30s) lie 2.2M northwest of the west breakwater at 41°12′.5N 8°44′.7W and 41°12′.2N 8°45′W respectively. If in the vicinity after dark, note that both have occasionally been reported as unlit, and that other unlit yellow buoys have been reported nearby. A prohibited zone extends 1000m in all directions from the superbuoy, which is located about 1.6M offshore and well outside the 20m depth contour.

Harbour regulations state that vessels must give the outside of the west breakwater a berth of at least 1M, but few fishing boats appear to observe this. There are, however, shoals up to 200m off the seaward side of this breakwater as well as obstructions off its end. There are fewer hazards if approaching from the south, though several lit yellow buoys may be encountered within 1M of the shore. The buildings of Porto can be seen from a good distance, with the entrance to Leixões 2M northwest.

From offshore, ⊕109 lies 2M west-southwest of the entrance, a course of 061° leading to ⊕110, close outside the harbour mouth.

Entrance

The breakwater light may be difficult to identify against shore lights, but from south of the harbour – or ⊕110 – Leça light on 350° leads between the breakwater spur and the south breakwater, after which the marina will become visible. During westerly gales the swell at the entrance may be heavy, but it decreases rapidly once inside. Floating debris can be a hazard when crossing the harbour, and it is also best to avoid entry in the early evening when the many fishing trawlers are heading out to sea.

Berthing

The three yacht clubs and the Marina Porto Atlântico are all located around the old fishing harbour at the northwest of the main harbour, behind a short mole (the Cais das Gruas). The narrow entrance (less than 50m wide) faces southeast, but even so considerable swell may work in during strong southwesterlies. Boats berthed near the entrance will obviously bear the brunt.

The marina, which has been dredged to 5m, can berth about 240 boats alongside narrow finger pontoons. It is crowded with local craft, but it is claimed that space can always be found for a visitor, even if this means rafting up at the reception and fuel berths. It is said to be able to accommodate one or two yachts of up to 30m, though it is difficult to see where.

Secure to the reception pontoon (to port on entry) and visit the marina office at the root of the marina mole. Office hours are 0900–1230 and 1400–2000 daily from 16 June until 15 September, closing at 1830 and all day Sunday outside the high season. In 2004 (the marina was closed during 2005 – see above) the rate for a visiting yacht of 10.5–12m at any time of year was €17 per night, rising to €22.50 for 12–15m, inclusive of water, electricity and tax. Multihulls paid a 50% surcharge. Payment must be made in cash – no credit cards are accepted.

Anchorage

A designated public anchorage exists just outside the marina, in the angle formed by the marina mole and the breakwater, in 5m or more. Holding, particularly near the mole, is reported to be good over mud. There is a single ladder on the outside of the marina mole at which a dinghy might be left (though note the 3m spring range), while the short pontoon belonging to the Yate Clube de Porto is closed off by security gates from early evening. It is normally possible to leave a dinghy in the marina, in which case a small charge is made.

Formalities

Visit the marina office taking passports and ship's papers, whether berthed in the marina or anchored off. A single form (in quintuplicate, but on self-carbonated paper) must be completed, copies of which are then circulated by the marina to the *GNR–Brigada Fiscal*, *Alfândega* and *Polícia Marítima*. This procedure must be observed whether entering the country for the first time or arriving from elsewhere within it. There is no charge, and though an intended departure date must be stated there is no need for formal outward clearance.

Facilities

Boatyard The boatyard next to the marina is able to handle repairs in GRP, wood, steel and aluminium.
Travel-lift No travel-lift, but 6.3-tonne capacity crane at the boatyard. The nearest large (ie 32-tonne capacity) travel-lift is at Póvoa de Varzim, 12M north.
Engineers, electronic and radio repairs Inboard and outboard engine specialists, and electrical and electronic workshops, are all available, though geared more to commercial vessels than yachts. Ask at the marina office. Lisbon-based NautiRadar Lda (see page 184) has a local agent, Antonio Rocha ☎ 229 381391.
Sailmaker The Pires de Lima loft, Rua Joaquim Vieira Moutinho 35, 4460 Santa Cruz de Bispo, ☎ 229 952218 *Fax* 229952 209 *Email* ukportugal@mail.telepac.pt, is situated a taxi-ride away near the airport. Sails are both made and repaired.
Chandlery Nautileça, ☎/*Fax* 229 951463, will be found about 50m north of the main harbour gates. A wide stock is held and anything not immediately available can be ordered. A family-run firm, Nautileça is open 0900–1900 daily throughout the year and the owner's son speaks excellent English.
Charts Portuguese charts and other publications may be available from 'Sailing', at Traversa des Laranjeiras 34, Foz do Douro, 4100 Porto, ☎ 226 179936 *Fax* 226 103716.
Liferaft servicing Can be arranged via the Nautileça chandlery, see above.
Water On the pontoons.
Showers At the marina – free if occupying a berth, but charged for if anchored off. The Yate Clube de Porto also has showers, which it may be possible to use by arrangement.
Laundry In the town. Washing left at the marina office will normally be returned within 24 hours, clean, dry and ironed.
Electricity On the pontoons.
Fuel At the reception pontoon, to port just inside the entrance. Available 0900–1200 and 1400–1700 weekdays, 0900–1200 Saturday, closed Sunday.
Bottled gas Cylinders taken to the Petrogal refinery about 2km north of the marina will be exchanged or refilled as necessary.
Clube náuticos The Yate Clube de Porto, the Clube Vela Atlântico and the Clube Náutico de Leça all overlook the harbour and marina.
Weather forecast Posted daily at the marina office.
Banks In Leça da Palmeira (about 1km away), Matosinhos and Porto.
Shops/provisioning Good shopping locally, and a very wide choice in Porto.
Produce market In Matosinhos, a taxi-ride away – or at least for the return, if heavy laden.
Cafés, restaurants and hotels Numerous in Leça da Palmeira and Porto, but nearly all at some distance from the harbour. However the Yate Clube de Porto has a formal restaurant as well as a very pleasant terrace bar.
Medical services In Leça da Palmeira, with a large modern hospital in Porto.

Communications

Post offices In Leça da Palmeira, Matosinhos and Porto.
Mailing address The marina office will hold mail for visiting yachts – c/o Marina Porto Atlântico, Molhe Norte de Leixões, 4450-718 Leça da Palmeira, Portugal. It is important that the envelope carries the name of the yacht in addition to that of the addressee.
Internet access A public computer terminal (for which a small charge will be made) should be installed in the marina office in time for the 2006 season.
Public telephones In the marina and elsewhere, with cards on sale at the office.
Fax service At the marina office, *Fax* 229 964899.
Car hire/taxis Both can be arranged via the marina office, though there is a good chance of flagging down a taxi on the main road outside the harbour gates.
Buses Numbers 44 and 76 both run into Porto (a city not to be missed) every 15/20 minutes. A convenient bus stop will be found on the main road just outside the harbour gates.
Trains Stations at Leça da Palmeira and Porto, both of which can be reached by bus. The new *metro* line, inaugurated in 2004, links Matosinhos to the city centre. Unlike most of its fellows, much of the line is above ground and a good part of that runs, tram-like, along city streets, making it scenic as well as practical.
Air services Porto International Airport lies about 6km northeast of the harbour and is (or soon will be) reachable by *metro*.

Looking northeast across the Marina Porto Atlântico at Leixões, unusually empty following a nearby fire – see text

II.2 Porto to Figueira da Foz

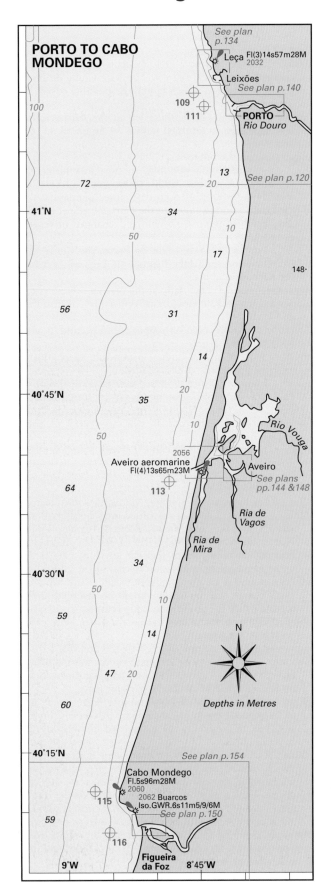

PORTO TO CABO MONDEGO

Leça Fl(3)14s57m28M 2032
Leixões
See plan p.134
See plan p.140

109
111

PORTO
Rio Douro

See plan p.120

100
72
13
20
41°N
34
10
50
17
148·
56
31
14
40°45'N
35
20
10
50
2056
Aveiro aeromarine Fl(4)13s65m23M
Aveiro
See plans pp.144 & 148
113
64
Rio Vouga
Ria de Vagos
Ria de Mira
34
40°30'N
50
59
10
14
N
47 20
60
Depths in Metres
40°15'N
See plan p.154
Cabo Mondego Fl.5s96m28M
2060
115
2062 Buarcos Iso.GWR.6s11m5/9/6M
See plan p.150
59
116
Figueira da Foz
9°W
8°45'W

⊕109	41°09'.2N	8°44'.7W	Leixões approach
⊕111	41°08'.4N	8°43'W	Porto & the Rio Douro approach
⊕113	40°37'.6N	8°48'.5W	Ria de Aveiro approach
⊕115	40°11'.4N	8°56'.5W	1.7M W of Cabo Mondego
⊕116	40°08'.4N	8°55'.2W	Figueira da Foz approach

PRINCIPAL LIGHTS

2032 **Leça** Fl(3)14s57m28M
   White tower, narrow grey bands, red lantern 46m
2056 **Aveiro** Fl(4)13s65m23M
   Red tower, white bands and building 62m
2060 **Cabo Mondego** Fl.5s96m28M Horn 30s
   Square white tower and building, red cupola 15m
2062 **Buarcos** Iso.GWR.6s11m5/9/6M
   004°-G-028°-W-048°-R-086°
   White tower, red bands 7m

Ports

42. Porto and the Rio Douro
     Aveiro anchorages
43. Figueira da Foz*

* Fuel available alongside

The faded tower of the powerful lighthouse at Aveiro *AH*

42. Porto and the Rio Douro

Waypoints
⊕111 – 41°08′.4N 8°43′W (approach)
⊕112 – 41°08′.7N 8°40′.8W (entrance)

Courses and distances
⊕109 (Leixões) – ⊕111 = 1.5M, 122° or 302°
⊕111 – ⊕112 = 1.7M, 080° or 260°
⊕111 – ⊕113 (Ria de Aveiro) = 31.1M, 188° or 008°
⊕111 – ⊕116 (Figueira da Foz, via ⊕115) = 61.1M, 190°&162° or 342°&010°

Tides
Standard port Lisbon
Mean time differences (at entrance)
HW 0000 ±0010; LW +0020 ±0005
Heights in metres

MHWS	MHWN	MLWN	MLWS
3.2	2.5	1.3	0.5

Mean time differences (at Porto)
HW 0000; LW +0040
Heights in metres

MHWS	MHWN	MLWN	MLWS
3.3	2.6	1.3	0.5

Or refer to EasyTide at www.ukho.gov.uk (see page 2)

Charts

	Approach	*River*
Admiralty	3634	3258
Imray	C19, C48	
Portuguese	23202, (23201), 24201	26402

Principal lights
2046 **Felgueiras (north breakwater)**
Fl.R.5s16m9M 265°-vis-134° Siren (2)30s
Hexagonal stone tower, red windows and lantern 11m
2048 **Bar Ldg Lts 079°**
Front **Cantareira** Oc.R.6s11m9M
Thin white column, red bands, white gallery and lantern, close to red-roofed building with tower 6m
2048.1 *Rear* **Sobreiras** 562m from front Oc.R.6s32m9M
Red and white banded square on wall 4m
(Difficult to identify even in clear conditions)

Night entry
Not feasible – divert to Leixões instead

Harbour communications
Capimardouro VHF Ch 11, 16 (0900–1200, 1400–1700 Mon–Fri).

A fascinating old city, but with a shallow entrance and very limited berthing possibilities

The second city of Portugal, Porto's historic involvement with the rest of Europe, the Americas and the East makes for a fascinating tale. The reverberations remain in its architecture, its customs and its behaviour as well as in its present commercial life, all of which makes for a vibrant city, full of contrasts and well worth exploring (though with the ever-improving transport links, many may feel this best enjoyed with the yacht safely tucked up in the Marina Porto Atlântico at Leixões – see page 135).

Although various plans have been put forward to build a marina on the Rio Douro, as of 2005 the river was in constant use by tourist boats, visiting yachts were not encouraged, and it appeared highly unlikely that any marina or other yacht-friendly facility would materialise within the foreseeable future.

A highlight of any visit to the city must be a visit to one or more of the port warehouses at Vila Nova de Gaia, on the south bank opposite the Cais da Estiva, for a guided tour and tasting. That provided by Taylor's – correctly Taylor Fladgate and Yeatman – is particularly recommended and well repays the uphill approach.

The entrance to the Rio Douro from the southwest, with the Fogomanados de Fora rocks visible in the foreground

PORTUGAL – THE WEST COAST

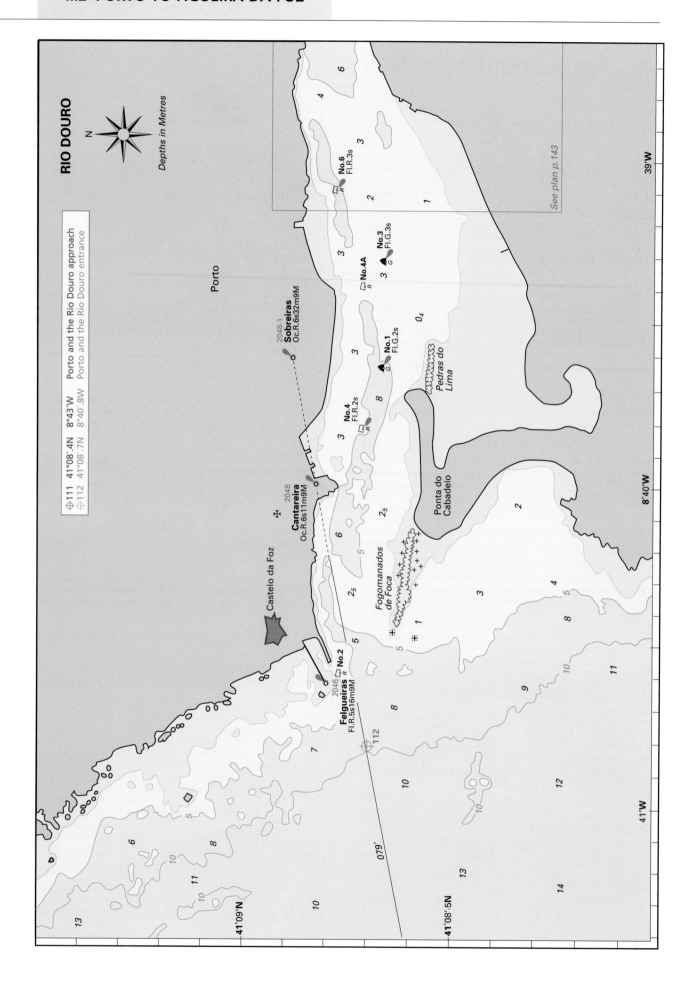

RIO DOURO

N

Depths in Metres

⊕111 41°08'.4N 8°43'W   Porto and the Rio Douro approach
⊕112 41°08'.7N 8°40'.8W Porto and the Rio Douro entrance

Porto

See plan p.143

No.6
Fl.R.3s
R

No.3
Fl.G.3s
G

No.4A
R

No.1
Fl.G.2s
G

Pedras do Lima

2048·1
Sobreiras
Oc.R.6s32m9M

No.4
Fl.R.2s
R

2048
Cantareira
Oc.R.6s11m9M

Castelo da Foz

Ponta do Cabadelo

Fogomanados de Foca

No.2
R
2046
Felgueiras
Fl.R.5s16m9M

112

079°

8°40'W

41°W

39'W

41°09'N

41°08'.5N

The Ponte da Arrábida, furthest downstream of the Rio Douro's many bridges

Approach

If coastal sailing, the low hills along the coast between Leixões and Porto extend south beyond the mouth (*foz*) of the Rio Douro. Further south the foreshore is flat, with sandy beaches and marshes behind, and from that direction the buildings on the hill immediately north of the Rio Douro are conspicuous.

From offshore, ⊕111 lies 1.7M southwest of the rivermouth, a course of 080° leading to ⊕112, about 300m from the Felgueiras breakwater and light structure. These, together with a short inner mole, mark the north side of the entrance.

Entrance

The bar is dangerous in strong winds or when there is heavy swell, with a 6–7 knot current on the spring ebb which may be even stronger after rain. In winter, storms may close the entrance for weeks. To add to the challenge both the narrows and the 'bag' inside are frequently crowded with dozens of small, open boats lying at anchor whilst their owners fish. It hardly needs saying that entry should only be attempted in daylight and settled weather.

Ideally, identify the leading lights on 079° while still at least 0.5M offshore and follow them in towards the low promontory at Cantareira. However they are notoriously difficult to identify even in ideal conditions, in which case home in on ⊕112 from anywhere in the western quadrant, alter onto 079°, and favour the northern shore towards Cantareira. As of 2005 the bar was claimed to carry at least 3m at MLWS, but this figure fluctuates from year to year. Cantareira mole has a rocky shoal off its southeast tip marked by a port-hand buoy – skirt this buoy closely to keep well clear of the opposing Ponta do Cabadelo, a long sandspit which has extended north and east over the past decade.

Once in the Rio Douro, the channel as far as the Ponte de Arrábida (60.5m clearance) is well buoyed and should present no problems. Beyond the bridge there are only four more buoys, but at least 6m should be found in mid-channel up to the Ponte Dom Luís I (8.8m).

On departure, having dropped downstream on the ebb it may be wise to wait for a little more water over the bar, in which case one experienced cruising couple recommend anchoring on the south side of the fairway, east of buoy No.3 and clear of fishing boat moorings and the nearby quay. They report the holding to be reasonably good in 3–4m over a mixed bottom which shoals fairly quickly nearer the land.

Looking downstream past the Cais de Estiva from the Ponte Dom Luís I bridge. Traditional port barges (many of them replicas) are moored on the left *AH*

The Ponte Dom Luís I bridge, just upstream from the Cais de Estiva and the head of navigation for masted yachts

Berthing

As mentioned previously, yachts are not encouraged to enter the Rio Douro, and those visitors who make the effort are permitted little time to savour it. The quays on both sides of the river are rented out to the many concerns operating tourist boats, some of which have installed floating pontoons. These are, of course, private and should not be used even temporarily.

As of 2005 it was still generally possible for a visiting yacht to secure for a short period to the high and sometimes dirty wall of the Cais de Estiva (warehouse quay) on the north bank about 400m downstream of the Ponte Dom Luís I, which though equipped with sizeable bollards has no ladders. However, the tourist boats have first rights, and it would be unwise to leave a yacht unattended even

The Cais de Estiva, see from the Ponte Dom Luís I bridge *AH*

for short periods. Overnight berthing is no longer permitted, and weekends should also be avoided, particularly in the holiday season.

A possible alternative, though again discouraged by the authorities, is to anchor just below the bridge – only feasible in settled weather around neap tides and when there has been no rain further up the Douro valley. Use heavy ground tackle with plenty of scope, but allow a full swinging circle. The ebb runs hard and a fresh breeze against it can cause a very nasty lop, dangerous for a small dinghy. The yacht should not be left unattended in these conditions (or some would say at all).

Caution

Little secret is made of the fact that the Rio Douro still carries much of Porto's raw sewage out to sea, and several crews have become ill after handling lines which have been in the water. Scrupulous washing is therefore essential.

Formalities

It is unlikely that any official notice will be taken of a yacht berthed for a few hours, but passports and ship's papers should be available for inspection if required.

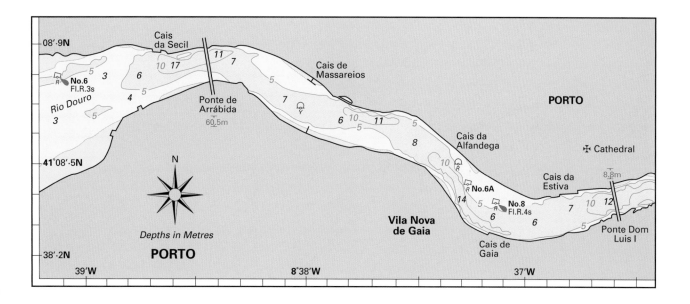

Facilities

The historic Cais de Estiva and its surroundings are being increasingly promoted as a tourist venue, with a growing number of bars, cafés and tourist shops in evidence. Do not expect anything of a more serious nature – even fresh water is difficult to obtain – and all practical needs are much better served at the Marina Porto Atlântico in Leixões.

Communications

Post offices plus numerous telephone kiosks in the city, with internet access also available (at OnWeb, opposite the *Câmara Municipal* on Avenida dos Aliados, amongst others). There are both international and national air, rail and bus connections, plus the usual taxis and car rental. For travel within the city, mention should be made of the new *metro* line, as yet unfinished but already providing a useful link from the city centre to Matosinhos close south of Leixões (see page 137).

Upriver

Motorboats, or yachts with masts which can be lowered, can explore as far as Barca de Alva, 200km upstream, following cruise boats into the large locks. The approaches require care and 6 knots of boat speed in some conditions, while it may take a week to work through the inevitable red tape before departure.

The upper reaches of the Rio Douro are particularly attractive, and if unable to venture by yacht it could be worth jumping ship to spend a few days aboard one of the many hotel-boats which ply the river.

Not feasible – Lagoa de Esmoriz

The Lagoa de Esmoriz (40°57.6´.5N 8°39´.5W), close south of Espinho and some 11M south of Porto, bears more than a passing resemblance to Esposende – see page 128 – but on an even smaller scale. Sail on by.

Thousands of barrels of port mature at Vila Nova da Gaia on the south bank of the river *AH*

Port maturing in the 19th century warehouses of Taylor Fladgate and Yeatman in Vila Nova da Gaia *AH*

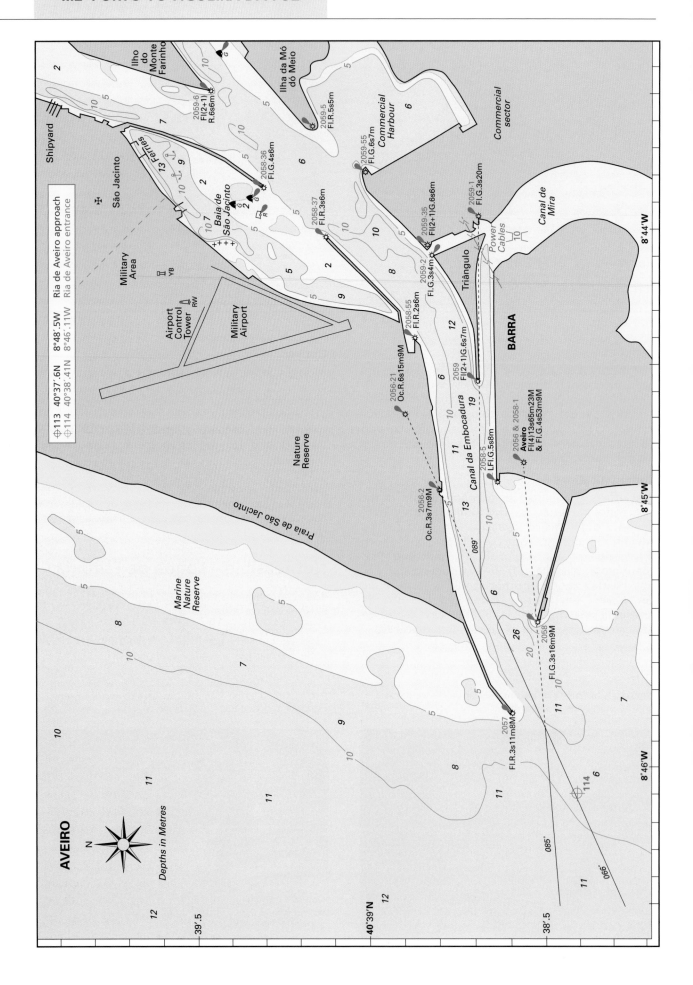

AVEIRO

N

Depths in Metres

Shipyard

Ilho do Monte Farinho

São Jacinto

Ferries

Baia de São Jacinto

Military Area

Airport Control Tower

Military Airport

Nature Reserve

Marine Nature Reserve

Praia de São Jacinto

Ilha da Mó dô Meio

Commercial Harbour

Commercial sector

Canal de Mira

Triângulo

BARRA

Canal da Embocadura

Aveiro

Power Cables

2059.6 Fl(2+1) R.6s6m
2059.5 Fl.R.5s5m
2058.36 Fl.G.4s6m
2058.37 Fl.R.3s6m
2059.55 Fl.G.6s7m
2059.2 Fl.G.3s4m
2059.35 Fl(2+1)G.6s6m
2059.1 Fl.G.3s20m
2058.55 Fl.R.2s6m
2059 Fl(2+1)G.6s7m
2056.21 Oc.R.6s15m9M
2056.2 Oc.R.3s7m9M
2058.5 L.Fl.G.5s8m
2056 & 2058.1 Fl(4)13s65m23M & Fl.G.4s53m9M
2057 Fl.R.3s11m8M
2058 Fl.G.3s16m9M

089°
085°
066°

113 40°37'.6N 8°48'.5W Ria de Aveiro approach
114 40°38'.41N 8°46'.11W Ria de Aveiro entrance

RW
YB

40°39'N

39'.5

38'.5

8°44'W
8°45'W
8°46'W

Ria de Aveiro

Waypoints
⊕113 – 40°37′.6N 8°48′.5W (approach)
⊕114 – 40°38′.41N 8°46′.11W (entrance)

Courses and distances
⊕109 (Leixões) – ⊕113 = 31.7M, 185° or 005°
⊕111 (Porto and the Rio Douro) – ⊕113 = 31.1M,
188° or 008°
⊕113 – ⊕114 = 2M, 066° or 246°
⊕113 – ⊕116 (Figueira da Foz, via ⊕115) = 30.1M,
193°&162° or 342°&013°

Tides
Standard port Lisbon
Mean time differences (at entrance)
HW +0005 ±0005; LW +0010 ±005
Heights in metres

MHWS	MHWN	MLWN	MLWS
3.2	2.6	1.4	0.7

Or refer to EasyTide at www.ukho.gov.uk (see page 2)

Charts

	Approach	River
Admiralty	3634	3227
Imray	C19, C49	
Portuguese	23202, 24201, 24202	26403

Principal lights
2056 **Aveiro** Fl(4)13s65m23M
Red tower, white bands and building 62m
2057 **North breakwater** Fl.R.3s11m8M Horn 15s
White tower, red bands 6m
2058 **South breakwater** Fl.G.3s16m9M
White tower, green bands 12m (20m from outer end)
2058 **Outer Ldg Lts 085°** *Front* South breakwater
2058.1 *Rear* 850m from front Fl.G.4s53m9M
065.4°-vis°-105.4° Shares tower with Aveiro (above),
at 50m

2058.55 **Entrance channel north side**
Fl.R.2s6m3M Red tower 4m
2056.2 **Entrance Ldg Lts 066°** *Front* Oc.R.3s7m9M
060.6°-vis-070.6° Red column 4m
2056.21 *Rear* 440m from front Oc.R.6s15m9M
060.6°-vis-070.6° Red column 13m
2058.5 **South inner mole** LFl.G.5s8m3M
White tower, green bands 4m
2059 **Triangle – west corner** Fl(2+1)G.6s7m6M
Green tower, red band 4m
2059 **Inner Ldg Lts 089°**
Front Triangle – west corner (above)
2059.1 *Rear* **Fuerte de Barra** 870m from front
Fl.G.3s20m6M 084.5°-vis°-094.5° White tower 19m
Plus numerous lit and unlit beacons and buoys on the
Canal Principal de Navegação, leading to the Canal das
Pirâmides lock – see plan page 148

Night entry
Not recommended, even in light conditions. Although
the entrance is well lit this does not extend to any of
the yacht berths or anchorages

Maritime radio station
Arestal (40°46′.8N 8°21′4W)
Remotely controlled from Lisbon)
Manual – VHF Ch 16, 24, 25, 26. *Autolink* – VHF Ch 85.

Harbour communications
Capimaraveiro VHF Ch 11, 16 (0900–1200, 1400–1700
Mon–Fri)
Associação Aveirense de Vela de Cruzeiro (AVELA)
☎ 234 42214, *Email* avela@avela.pt
www.avela.pt (in Portuguese only).

Windswept channels and lagoons, inside an ever-changing entrance

The Aveiro estuary is made up of salt marshes and
sand spits, low lying and often deceptive. The ria has
been developed as an oil, timber and general port
but it is possible to escape into unspoilt, almost
desolate, surroundings. There are strong tidal
streams and the entrance can be dangerous on the
ebb, in spite of having been dredged to a reported
10m or more. In September 1999 a yacht was lost
while attempting to enter at night in a 3m swell
which doubtless increased to many times this height
in the entrance.

The town of Aveiro, some 12km from the
entrance, prospered from trade with the New World
until a storm in the 16th century effectively closed
the entrance. It was re-opened early in the 19th
century and Aveiro recovered its prosperity. Today it
combines modern business and industry with
reminders of the past, and is one of the more
attractive towns along the coast. The Festa da Ria
takes place during the last two weeks of August.

Much work has been done to improve the port
commercially and to channel the river, though many
of the dyked areas shown as dry land on Admiralty
3227 – including some reclaimed salt-pans – are now
back underwater. There are very limited facilities for
yachts, and the two small marinas in the Canal de
Mira to the south (see plan) are not only shallow but
inaccessible to most cruising yachts due to the
8–10m power cables which cross the Canal at its
northern end.

Approach

If coastal sailing from the north, from the Rio Douro
to Espinho the coast is backed by low hills some
7km inland and has isolated rocks inshore. South
from Espinho one continuous beach backed by sand
dunes and lagoons – known locally as the *Costa de
Prata* or 'silver coast' – stretches for over 50M to
Cabo Mondego, with the Barra de Aveiro rather less
than halfway down its length. A dangerous wreck
lies just over 2M southwest of the entrance at
approximately 40°36′.7N 8°47′W.

From offshore, ⊕113 lies 2M west-southwest of the
entrance, from which a course of 066° leads to
⊕114, on the leading line and about 500m from the
north breakwater head.

Entrance

As already stressed, the potential dangers of the
entrance should not be underestimated. Winds from
between northwest and southwest can quickly
produce a vicious sea, at its worst on the ebb tide –
which may reach 8 knots in the entrance at springs
following heavy rain. The ebb runs for about seven
hours and the flood for five, the best time to enter or
leave being shortly before high water. If coming from
the north, give the end of the north breakwater a
wide berth, as shoals often build around its tip,
while least depths – and hence the worst seas – are
also to be found in this area.

There are two leading lines for the outer entrance.
The northern line, on 085.4°, consists of the south
breakwater light structure in line with Aveiro

The potentially dangerous entrance to the Ria de Aveiro from the southwest

lighthouse and should be visible from some distance offshore. The southern line, on 065.6° and consisting of two red columns, is much harder to pick out and, even if identified, flatter water is likely to be found further south. A third leading line, on 089.5°, has been established inside the entrance, but is intended mainly for commercial traffic heading for the Canal de Mira.

Once the protection of the river mouth is gained, while the tide may still run strongly, there should never be less than 7m depths and frequently much more. Leave the Triângulo to starboard and continue up the Canal de Embocadura. In contrast to some Portuguese harbours the channels buoys appear to be well maintained.

Anchorages and berthing (see plans pp. 144 and 148)

1. Good anchorage will be found in the Baía de São Jacinto, about 1.5M northeast of the river mouth. The entrance is shallow although there are good depths once inside, and it is essential to observe the buoyage – currently red and green buoys to port and starboard on entering, with a further green buoy marking the western edge of the north shoal. The outer moles are both lit (F.R and F.G), but movement after dark is not recommended. Strong currents, with unpredictable eddies, run across and into the entrance on both the flood and the ebb.

   If the inner buoy is not in place and no local craft on hand to offer a lead in, after passing between the entrance buoys head for a conspicuous yellow and black water tower on approximately 330°. Remain on this bearing until past the shallowest part of the bar (0.5–1m at datum). When the base pier (often with small military craft alongside) bears 015° head in towards it, following the shore in 5–6m towards the ferry pier.

   Anchor between the pier and the outer mole in 10–12m. The bottom is somewhat uneven, with holding poor in places and excellent in others – a few years ago one yacht reported holding absolutely firm while laid over by gusts exceeding 50 knots. Some local moorings occupy the north end of the bay, behind which are steps and a broad slipway. The ferry pier carries prominent 'no mooring' notices, and though it might be possible to land by dinghy at the smallcraft pontoon beyond, there is no possibility of lying alongside, even for a few minutes.

   São Jacinto is very much a holiday town, with numerous cafés and restaurants, small shops, a post office and several public telephones. There is nothing specifically for yachts, though a small shipyard lies just to the north. There is a nature reserve along the beach to the west but the large military area, including the airfield, is off limits.

2. It is also possible to anchor further north in the Canal de Ovar, a lagoon separated from the sea by a sandbank carrying the access road to São Jacinto. Tidal currents weaken beyond São Jacinto, and though relatively shallow (2.5–3m) where the Canal is wide, the narrow stretches contain pools with 5–7m. If very shoal draught or able to take the ground it is possible to work a good distance up the channel.

3. Space may be found for a small visiting yacht at the Marina da Costa Nova on the Canal Mira, but air height is restricted to an estimated 8–10m by the power cables already mentioned. The channel is indicated by buoys and posts.

4. Yachts have in the past anchored in the Canal Principal de Navagação, a buoyed channel carrying 3–4m and leading to the town of Aveiro (see plan overleaf). However tidal currents are strong and it would be difficult to find swinging room without impeding local traffic. The Clube Naval de Aveiro and neighbouring Sporting Clube de Aveiro have no more than 1m at their quays – local smallcraft are craned ashore when not in use – but for short periods it may be possible to lie alongside the jetty at either the Ria–Marine or Fracon yards – see under Facilities, below. Berthing at any of the fishermen's or commercial quays is strongly discouraged.

5. Space may be found alongside the 200m pontoon recently installed by AVELA (the Associação Aveirense de Vela de Cruzeiro) in the Canal de Veia, close to the Canal das Pirâmides lock. Though privately owned, visiting yachts are said to be made welcome. Water and electricity are installed, though it would plainly be tactless to help oneself prior to making contact with a representative of the club. Although AVELA has premises on the semi-derelict land behind the pontoon (until recently a fishing quay) they appear to be little used.

Although power cables cross the Canal just downstream of the pontoon, they have a reported air height of 18m so will worry few yachts.

Salt pans – many now flooded and derelict – line the north bank of the Canal Principal de Navagação. The new AVELA pontoon lies at centre left

Visiting yachts are no longer permitted to enter the Canal das Pirâmides, which runs through the centre of the old town of Aveiro, but it would make an interesting dinghy excursion. The Canal is administered by the Associação Turistica Vigilância, with the lock reported to open for one hour either side of high water and on demand at other times – most often for small tourist vessels with which a dinghy could double up (the lock measures 18m by 5m). Strong tidal eddies may be encountered at the entrance.

The Canal and Baia de São Jacinto, with several yachts in the anchorage described opposite

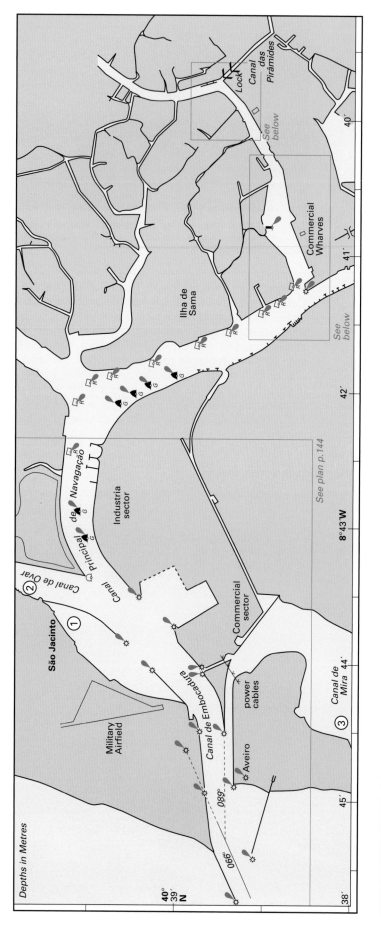

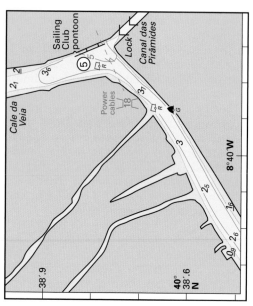

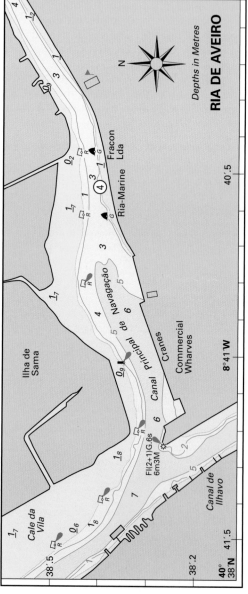

RIA DE AVEIRO

Yachts alongside the AVELA pontoon, close to the Canal
das Pirâmides lock and within walking distance of the town
centre   *AH*

Formalities

The *GNR–Brigada Fiscal* and possibly the *Polícia
Marítima* may visit if anchored in the Baía de São
Jacinto or moored at the AVELA pontoon.

Facilities

Boatyard Fracon Lda ☎ 234 422297 *Fax* 234 420561
Email fracon@fracon.pt website www.fracon.pt on the
Canal Principal de Navegação can handle repairs in all
materials including GRP in large covered workshops.
Staff are helpful with some English and German
spoken, and security appears to be good. There is
plenty of outdoor hardstanding for potential winter
lay-up.
Ria–Marine Lda, ☎ 234 384049/426686, just
downstream of Fracon, can handle work on yachts of
all sizes in GRP, wood and steel. Little or no English is
spoken. In the mid 1990s the yard was given
responsibility for rebuilding Portugal's last surviving
East Indiaman, the *D Fernando II e Glória*, for the
Lisbon Maritime Museum, a commission which they
carried out to a high standard.
Travel-lift Not as such, but Fracon has a 10-tonne capacity
crane and can arrange for a 30 tonner to visit, and also
has a marine railway (unsuitable for deep keels).
Ria–Marine can haul yachts of all sizes by crane or on
one of their two marine railway.
Engineers, mechanics, electricians At both Fracon and
Ria–Marine as well as Quatro-Ventos (see *Chandlery*,
below).

Sail repairs Can be organised via Quatro-Ventos, below.
Chandlery Good range at Quatro-Ventos, 230 Avenida
Fernandes Lavrador, Praia da Barra (accessible by ferry
from the São Jacinto anchorage), ☎ 243 394654, *Fax*
234 394 655, e-mail quatro-ventos@quatro-
ventos.com, website www.quatro-ventos.com. Owner
Augusto Pereir (who also runs a sailing school and is an
agent for Bénéteau) is reported to be helpful and
efficient, and to speak fluent English and French. He
can arrange for maintenance and repairs to anything
from engines to sails etc.
Charts Portuguese charts and other publications may be
available from Bolivar, on Rua da Aviação Naval 51,
3810 Aveiro.
Water On the AVELA pontoon, or by can from the Clube
Naval de Aveiro or one of the boatyards.
Showers May be available at the Clube Naval de Aveiro or
at one of the yards.
Electricity On the AVELA pontoon, though see above.
Fuel By can from a filling station in Aveiro. In an
emergency it might be possible to buy a few litres from
Fracon's own supply, but they are not officially licensed
to sell retail.
Clube naval The Clube Naval de Aveiro and the Sporting
Clube de Aveiro both have premises on the Canal
Principal de Navegação, but only the former appears to
be open regularly.
Banks In Aveiro.
Shops/provisioning Good shopping in Aveiro, but a much
more restricted choice in São Jacinto.
Cafés, restaurants and hotels Wide choice in Aveiro, with
plenty of cafés and restaurants (but apparently no
hotels) in São Jacinto.
Medical services In Aveiro.

Communications

Post offices In both Aveiro and São Jacinto
Telephones Public telephones in both towns.
Car hire/taxis In Aveiro.
Ferries Regular ferries from the pier at São Jacinto across
the Canal de Embocadura to Barra, on the south side of
the estuary, and tourist excursions downstream from
Aveiro via the Canal das Pirâmides.
Trains Direct rail link to Oporto, amongst other
destinations.
Air services Porto International Airport lies about 70km to
the north.

Forest fires plagued northern Portugal in 2005 – here a
seaplane scoops up water to douse the flames   *RI*

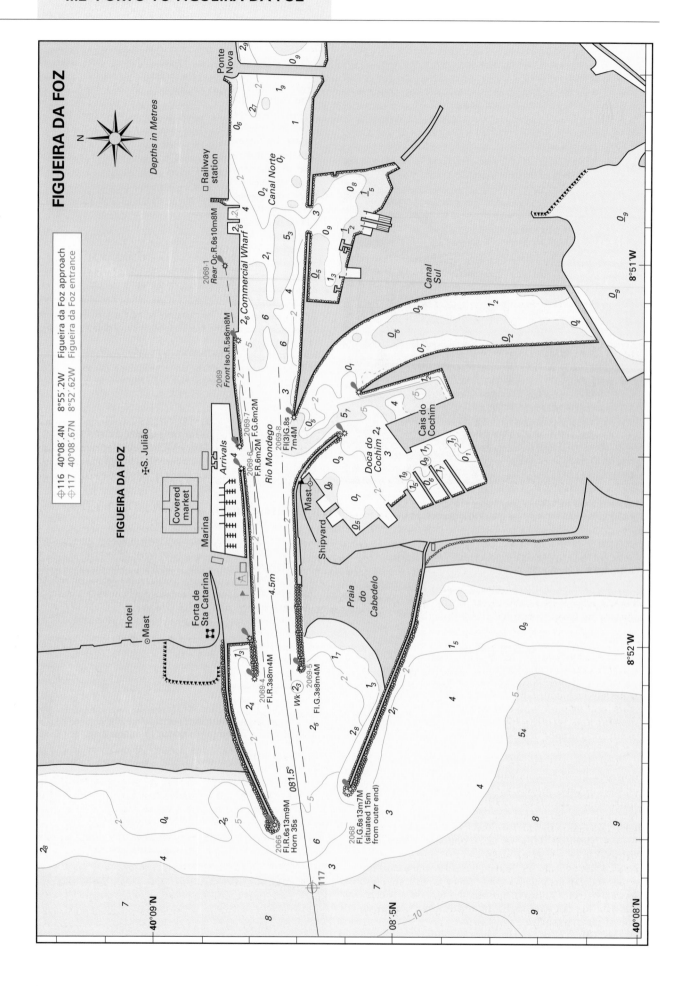

FIGUEIRA DA FOZ

N

Depths in Metres

□ Railway station

⊕116	40°08'·4N	8°55'·2W	Figueira da Foz approach
⊕117	40°08'·67N	8°52'·62W	Figueira da Foz entrance

FIGUEIRA DA FOZ

✠S. Julião

Hotel
⊙Mast

Forta de Sta Catarina

Covered market

Marina

Arrivals

Rio Mondego

4·5m

081·5°

2066
Fl.R.6s13m9M
Horn 35s

2069·4
Fl.R.3s8m4M

Wk

2069·5
Fl.G.3s8m4M

2068
Fl.G.6s13m7M
(situated 15m
from outer end)

Ponte Nova

Canal Norte

2069·1
Rear Oc.R.6s10m8M

Commercial Wharf

2069
Front Iso.R.5s6m8M

2069·7 F.G.6m2M
2069·6 F.R.6m2M

2069·8
Fl(3)G.8s
7m4M

Shipyard

Mast

Doca do
Cochim

Cais do
Cochim

Canal Sul

Praia
do
Cabedelo

117

8°51'W

8°52'W

43. Figueira da Foz

Waypoints
⊕15 – 40°11′.4N 8°56′.5W (1.7M W of Cabo Mondego)
⊕116 – 40°08′.4N 8°55′.2W (approach)
⊕117 – 40°08′.67N 8°52′.62W (entrance)

Courses and distances
⊕109 (Leixões) – ⊕116 (via ⊕115) = 61.7M, 189°&162°
or 342°&009°
⊕111 (Porto and the Rio Douro) – ⊕116 (via F115) =
61.1M, 190°&162° or 342°&010°
⊕113 (Ria de Aveiro) – ⊕116 (via F115) = 30.1M,
193°&162° or 342°&013°
⊕116 – ⊕117 = 2M, 082° or 262°
⊕116 – ⊕118 (Nazaré) = 34M, 196° or 016°

Tides
Standard port Lisbon
Mean time differences
HW –0010 minutes ±0010; LW +0015 minutes ±0005
Heights in metres

MHWS	MHWN	MLWN	MLWS
3.5	2.6	1.3	0.6

Or refer to EasyTide at www.ukho.gov.uk (see page 2)

Charts	Approach	Harbour
Admiralty	3634, 3635	3228
Imray	C19, C49	C19, C49
Portuguese	34, 23202, 24202	64, 26404

Principal lights
2066 **North breakwater** Fl.R.6s13m9M Horn 35s
White tower, red bands 9m
2068 **South breakwater** Fl.G.6s13m7M
White tower, green bands 7m (15m from outer end)
Note Destroyed late in 2005. A temporary light with the
same characteristics has been erected 30m from the
end of the breakwater
2069 **Ldg Lts 081.5°** *Front* Iso.R.5s6m8M
White column, red bands 4m
2069.1 *Rear* 239m from front Oc.R.6s10m8M
White column, red bands 7m
2069.4 **North inner mole** Fl.R.3s8m4M
Red tower, white bands 4m
2069.5 **South inner mole** Fl.G.3s8m4M
Green tower, white bands 5m
2069.6 **Marina, west mole** F.R.6m2M Red column 3m
2069.7 **Marina, east mole** F.G.6m2M Green column 3m
2069.8 **Confluência** Fl(3)G.8s7m4M
Green tower, red band 4m

Night entry
Straightforward other than in heavy onshore swell. The
marina entrance is well lit with the reception/fuel berth
opposite. However anchored smallcraft may be
encountered in the entrance – see below

Harbour communications
Instituto Portuário e dos Transportes Marítimos (IPTM)
☎ 233 402910 *Fax* 233 402920
Email geral.ffoz@imarpor.pt Ch 11, 16
Marina da Figueira da Foz ☎ 233 402918
VHF Ch 11, 16.

Small but pricey marina opposite large commercial port

Figueira da Foz is on the north bank of the longest
river to rise in Portugal, and although a modern town
with good facilities depending largely on shipbuilding
and tourism for its income, a large part of the
attractive old town remains. The city of Coimbra,
some 48km upstream, is worth visiting by bus or
train. The university, transferred there from Lisbon in
1320, is partially disfigured by some unsightly
modern faculty blocks but the old city, including the
crenellated 12th century cathedral, is memorable.

Approach

Figueira da Foz lies 2.5M south of Cabo which at a
distance, from both north and south, can be
mistaken for an island. The shore to the south of the
town forms a continuous low, sandy, beach backed
by one of the largest coniferous forests in Europe.
The major mark to the south is Penedo da Saudade,
25M distant.

From offshore, ⊕116 lies 2M west of the entrance,
a course of 082° leading to ⊕117, close outside the
breakwaters. The pale grey suspension bridge 1.5M
upriver from the entrance is conspicuous.

Entrance

Regular dredging of the previously shallow bar has
greatly improved the entrance and a minimum of 5m
should be found at all times. However in strong
onshore winds it can still be dangerous – a British
yacht was lost in 1997, and waves frequently break
all the way across the gap. At springs the ebb can
run at up to 7 knots, particularly if there has been
heavy rain inland, though this rate is unlikely to be
reached during the summer.

Danger signals are displayed if necessary from
Forte de Santa Catarina (on the north side of the
entrance) as follows: black ball or vertical green, red,
green lights – entrance closed; black ball at half-mast
or vertical green, flashing red, green lights – entrance
dangerous. These signals – which are near some
strong sodium lights and are difficult to see from
offshore – are mandatory and instructions may also
be given by radio. If no signals are displayed the
entrance is considered to be safe – at least for large
commercial vessels.

Care must be taken to avoid the many local
fishermen who anchor in the main channel
apparently at random, peacefully line-fishing from
small rowing boats and motor vessels. Although
most either depart before dusk or show lights, this
should not be relied upon. It is reported that nets are
sometimes strung across the river, in which case a
yacht will be guided through the gaps by hand
signals.

Berthing

The entrance to the Marina da Figueira da Foz lies
on the port hand about 0.7M inside the river mouth
– beware of cross-currents, particularly on the ebb.
Secure to the reception pontoon opposite the
entrance, and during office hours (0830–1230 and
1400–2200 daily) wait for the berthing master to
walk down from his office at the west end of the
basin. Outside these times the *Polícia Marítima*
allocate berths.

The marina consists of a single long pontoon from
which seven spurs run southward. All are fitted with
individual finger pontoons and the two easternmost
– some 36 berths – are reserved for visitors, though
more will be fitted in elsewhere if necessary. Though
easy of access, both eastern spurs are reported to
suffer from strong cross-currents and swell on the
ebb, and it is a longish walk to the shoreside
facilities. This area is nominally dredged to 4.5m

and able to take yachts of up to 25m LOA, though some would consider this optimistic.

In 2005 the high season (15 May–15 September) rate for a visiting yacht of 10–12m was €30.80 per night, rising to €44 for 12–15m, inclusive of water, electricity and tax. Multihulls paid a 50% surcharge. Unusually, payment could be made by credit card. (If driven to protest, it should be remembered that the marina officials do not set the prices.)

Formalities

It is no longer necessary for EU registered yachts to visit the *GNR–Brigada Fiscal* and *Polícia Marítima* except if arriving outside office hours. However skippers of non–EU registered yachts, or with non–EU nationals amongst their crew, would be wise to walk up and make themselves known.

Facilities

Boatyard Not as such, though there are several concerns which could handle minor work. Papiro, ☎ 233 411849, at the west end of the basin advertises GRP work, including osmosis treatment, but appears fairly small.

There is a wide concrete slipway in the southwest corner of the basin where yachts of medium draught can dry out for scrubbing. A pressure washer (with operator) can be hired – enquire at the marine office. As with all such facilities it would plainly be wise to inspect thoroughly at low water before committing oneself.

Travel-lift None at present, though it is possible that a 50-tonne lift may be installed in the commercial area on the south side of the river. Enquire at the marina office.

Engineers, electronic and radio repairs Available in the commercial harbour – enquire at the marina office.

Sailmaker/sail repairs Sails in need of repair are normally sent to Lisbon for attention – ask at the marina office.

Chandlery Limited stocks at Figueira Iates at the west end of the basin. Papiro (see above) stocks a full range of International Paints including antifouling, thinners etc.

Water On the pontoons, with a generous number of long hoses.

Showers Round the back of the *clube náutico* building (close to the security gate), with keypad access.

Launderette Next to the showers, but with only one washer and no dryer.

Electricity On the pontoons.

Fuel Diesel and petrol from a self-service pump on the reception pontoon, wich takes credit cards including VISA and MasterCard. Instructions are in Portuguese and English. The pump is reported to be somewhat temperamental, making it wise to fuel-up during office hours in case assistance is required.

Looking east-northeast past the outer breakwaters at Figueira da Foz, with the marina at centre and the impressive Ponte Nova on the right

The pleasant but expensive Marina da Figueira da Foz, with the town's park and the double-gabled covered market behind

Bottled gas Camping Gaz from Alavanca (which also stocks an enormous range of tools), on the road leading east from the marina basin.

Clube náutico The Clube Náutico de Figueira da Foz, which celebrated its 20th anniversary in 2004, has a small clubhouse adjacent to the marina office. The children's play area behind the building is a particularly nice touch.

Weather forecast Posted daily outside the marina office.

Banks In the town.

Figueira da Foz is a spacious and attractive town   *RI*

Shops/provisioning Good shopping of all types in the town. The nearest supermarket will be found across the road and slightly west from the marina gate, up a small side street.

Produce market The impressive covered market opposite the marina is amongst the best of its genre, and sells consumables of all types, clothing, souvenirs etc.

Cafés, restaurants and hotels The *clube náutico* has a pleasant bar/restaurant with indoor and outdoor tables, with others across the road from the marina entrance and dozens in the town proper.

Medical services In the town.

Communications

Post office Just off the square of public gardens which face the yacht basin.

Mailing address The marina office will hold mail for visiting yachts – c/o Instituto Portuário do Centro, AP 2008–3080, Figueira da Foz, Portugal. It is important that the envelope carries the name of the yacht in addition to that of the addressee.

Internet access Several possibilities, including WebSymbol on Rua dos Bombeiros, which also sells computer equipment and expendables.

Public telephones At the post office.

Fax service The marina office will receive faxes for yachts, Fax 233 402920, but they must be sent from the post office.

Car hire/taxis In the town.

Buses and trains In the town. The station is less than 0.5km east of the marina.

II.3 Figueira da Foz to Cabo da Roca

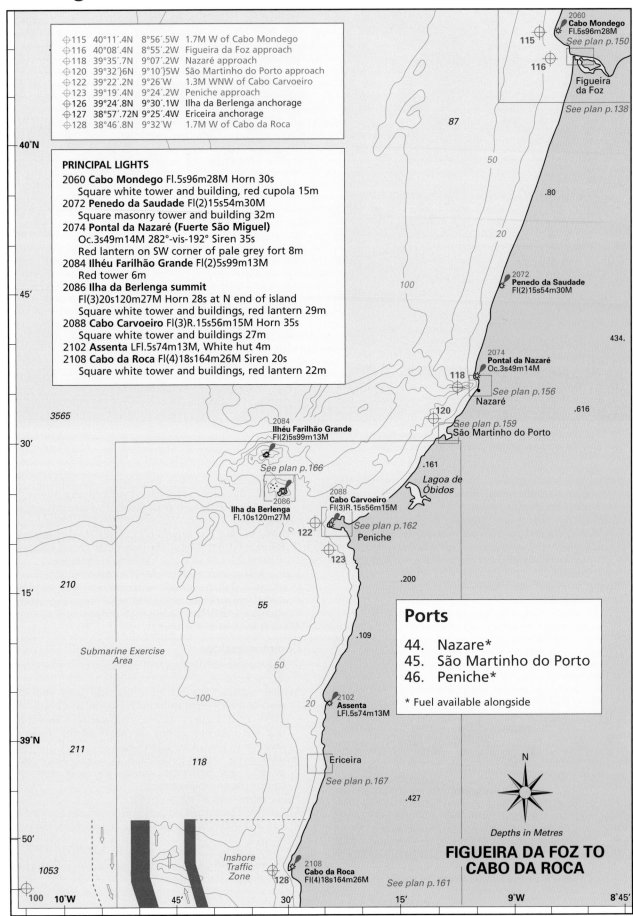

⊕115   40°11′.4N   8°56′.5W   1.7M W of Cabo Mondego
⊕116   40°08′.4N   8°55′.2W   Figueira da Foz approach
⊕118   39°35′.7N   9°07′.2W   Nazaré approach
⊕120   39°32′}6N   9°10′}5W   São Martinho do Porto approach
⊕122   39°22′.2N   9°26′W   1.3M WNW of Cabo Carvoeiro
⊕123   39°19′.4N   9°24′.2W   Peniche approach
⊕126   39°24′.8N   9°30′.1W   Ilha da Berlenga anchorage
⊕127   38°57′.72N 9°25′.4W   Ericeira anchorage
⊕128   38°46′.8N   9°32′W   1.7M W of Cabo da Roca

PRINCIPAL LIGHTS

2060 **Cabo Mondego** Fl.5s96m28M Horn 30s
  Square white tower and building, red cupola 15m
2072 **Penedo da Saudade** Fl(2)15s54m30M
  Square masonry tower and building 32m
2074 **Pontal da Nazaré (Fuerte São Miguel)**
  Oc.3s49m14M 282°-vis-192° Siren 35s
  Red lantern on SW corner of pale grey fort 8m
2084 **Ilhéu Farilhão Grande** Fl(2)5s99m13M
  Red tower 6m
2086 **Ilha da Berlenga summit**
  Fl(3)20s120m27M Horn 28s at N end of island
  Square white tower and buildings, red lantern 29m
2088 **Cabo Carvoeiro** Fl(3)R.15s56m15M Horn 35s
  Square white tower and buildings 27m
2102 **Assenta** LFl.5s74m13M, White hut 4m
2108 **Cabo da Roca** Fl(4)18s164m26M Siren 20s
  Square white tower and buildings, red lantern 22m

Ports

44. Nazare*
45. São Martinho do Porto
46. Peniche*

* Fuel available alongside

Depths in Metres

**FIGUEIRA DA FOZ TO
CABO DA ROCA**

44. Nazaré

Waypoints
⊕118 – 39°35′.7N 9°07′.2W (approach)
⊕119 – 39°35′.48N 9°04′.74W (entrance)

Courses and distances
⊕109 (Leixões) – ⊕118 = 95.1M, 190° or 010°
⊕116 (Figueira da Foz) – ⊕118 = 34M, 196° or 016°
⊕118 – ⊕119 = 1.9M, 097° or 277°
⊕118 – ⊕120 (São Martinho do Porto) = 4M,
    219° or 039°
⊕118 – ⊕123 (Peniche, via ⊕122 Cabo Carvoeiro) =
    22.9M, 227°&153° or 333°&047°

Tides
Standard port Lisbon
Mean time differences
HW –0020 ±0010 LW 0000 ±0005
Heights in metres

MHWS	MHWN	MLWN	MLWS
3.3	2.6	1.3	0.6

Or refer to EasyTide at www.ukho.gov.uk (see page 2)

Charts

	Approach	Harbour
Admiralty	3635	
Imray	C19, C49	C49
Portuguese	34, 23202, 24202, 24203	34, (26302)

Principal lights
2074.3 **North breakwater** LFl.R.5s14m9M
    White tower, red bands 7m
2074.5 **South breakwater** LFl.G.5s14m8M
    White tower, green bands 7m

Night entry
Straightforward, though the small marina is crowded
and it may be necessary to raft up to a fishing boat until
daylight.

Harbour communications
Porto de Recreio da Nazaré ☎ 262 561401
mobile 96 8074 254 (Celtic Marine Services)
Fax 262 561402 *Email* celticmarin@clix.pt
VHF Ch 09, 16 (0900–1900 weekdays only)

Small marina in busy fishing harbour with safe, all-weather entry

Old Nazaré (O Sítio), whose citizens claim
Phoenician origin, occupies a fine position looking
south over the beach that provided – and still
provides – the shelter needed for its day to day life.
The town now relies largely on tourism for its
prosperity, but the lower town on the beach keeps
some of its old atmosphere.

The harbour is a purpose built, well sheltered
fishing port with no hazards on the approach –
indeed it is claimed that Nazaré's harbour is never
closed, even in conditions in which it would be
foolhardy to attempt any of those further north
other than Leixões. This is due to the Canhão da
Nazaré, a deep trench which runs close offshore and
markedly reduces swell, doubtless aided by the
natural headlands to north and south.

Though useful as a port of refuge and sheltering a
small but friendly marina, many would claim that
the harbour itself is somewhat bleak. It is also more
than 1.5km from the town itself, though there is a
bus service. (The surroundings are very flat,
however, and Nazaré is one of those places where
bicycles come into their own).

The imposing west front of 15th century Batalha Abbey,
easily accessible from Nazaré   *AH*

Wash from returning fishing boats occasionally
causes problems – one must remember that the first
boat home gets the best prices – and more than one
yachtsman has also remarked less than politely on
the siren which signals a boat's return (and so a
catch to be auctioned), though it seldom sounds
after midnight. The upside is that visitors are
welcome to go and watch the sale, and may well be
given some smaller fry to take back aboard.

Possibly the most compelling reason to visit
Nazaré is as a base from which to visit a number of
Portugal's most famous cultural sites, including
Fatima, Obidos, Alcobaça and Caldas da Rainha, all
of which can be reached by public transport.
However the top 'must see' is undoubtedly the early
15th century abbey of Batalha – literally Battle
Abbey – built to commemorate Dom João I's victory
over the Spanish in 1385. As well as being a
masterpiece of Manueline architecture, it contains
the tomb of Prince Henry the Navigator, younger
son of Dom João and his English wife Philippa of
Lancaster . . . and honorary patron saint of all pilot
book writers. The slightly tortuous 90-minute bus
journey via Leiria will be amply rewarded.

Approach

The low-lying beach which reaches from Figueira da
Foz to the light at Penedo da Saudade gives way to a
more broken coastline backed by low hills leading
south to the Pontal da Nazaré, with a light on the
wall of its fort, São Miguel. The point has rocks
200m offshore to the southwest, but within a further

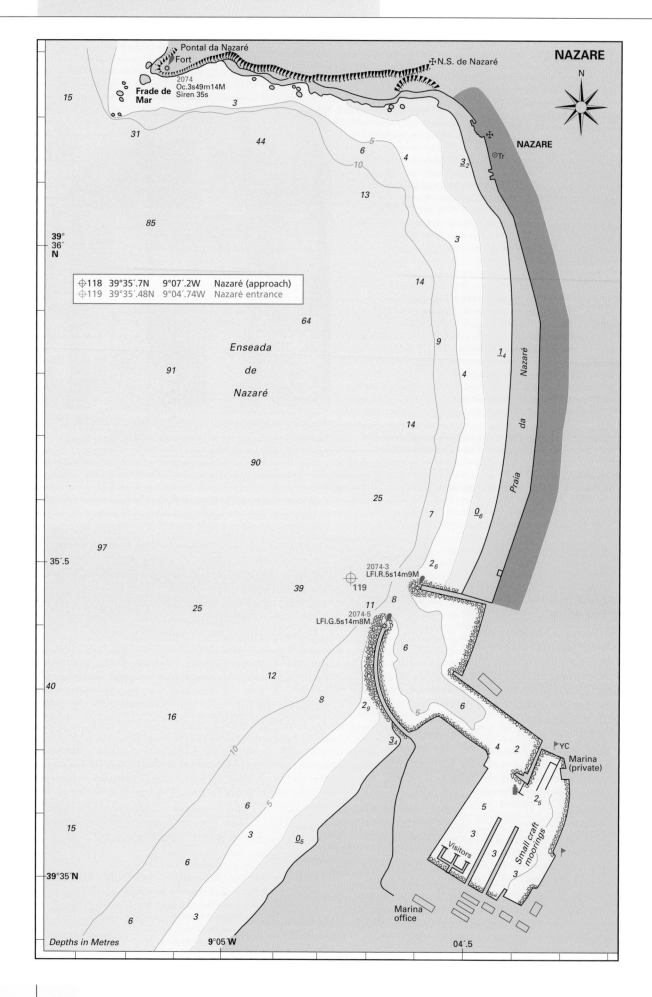

NAZARE

Pontal da Nazaré
Fort

✛ N.S. de Nazaré

N

2074
Oc.3s49m14M
Siren 35s

Frade de Mar

NAZARE

⊙ Tr

15

31

3

44

5

6

4

$\underline{3}_2$

10

13

3

39°36′ N

85

14

⊕	118	39°35′.7N	9°07′.2W	Nazaré (approach)
⊕	119	39°35′.48N	9°04′.74W	Nazaré entrance

64

9

1_4

Enseada

de

91

Nazaré

4

14

90

Praia   da   Nazaré

25

7

$\underline{0}_6$

97

35′.5

2074·3
LFl.R.5s14m9M

2_6

⊕
119

39

11

8

2074·5
LFl.G.5s14m8M

6

25

6

40

12

8

5

6

16

2_9

4   2

▷ YC

10

$\underline{3}_4$

Marina
(private)

6

2_5

5

15

6

3

5

Visitors

3

Small craft moorings

3

3

$\underline{0}_5$

39°35′ N

6

Marina
office

6

3

Depths in Metres

9°05′ W

04′.5

The inner harbour at Nazaré, with the small Porto de Recreio da Nazaré just visible through a gap in the clouds

60m the bottom drops to 50m or more. If approaching from this direction it is worth standing on until the harbour entrance bears 120° before turning, to avoid concentrations of pot buoys in the northeast part of the bay.

The coast 4M south of Nazaré loses its sand dunes and becomes rocky. South of São Martinho, towards the Lagoa de Obidos, there is a rugged stretch of higher coast. South of this the coast is again a sandy beach, here backed by cliffs, as far as Cabo Carvoeiro. Fishing nets may be laid on a line parallel to and up to 4M off this stretch of shore. On final approach from the south, particularly in thick weather, note that the Canhão da Nazaré underwater canyon trends north of east into the Enseada da Nazaré, and that its 100m line comes within 600m of the shore.

From offshore, ⊕118 lies 2M from the coast. A course of 097° leads to ⊕119, directly outside the harbour mouth.

Entrance

Straightforward, between the moles – though watch for fishing boats travelling at speed.

Berthing

There are two marinas in the harbour, both small. Visiting yachts should head for the three pontoons in the southwest corner, known as the Porto de Recreio da Nazaré. Although officially administered by the Instituto Portuário e dos Transportes Marítimos, in practice the marina's reception and information

office is run by Captain Michael Hadley and his wife Sally, for whom nothing is too much trouble.

Yachts are generally met on arrival and directed to a berth but failing this, or outside office hours (officially 0900–1900, but often much later in summer), any suitable spot may be used. Depths are said to be a minimum of 3m throughout the marina. Fourteen of the 52 berths are nominally reserved for visitors, all alongside either main or finger pontoons, but by dint of rafting up both at the marina and on the adjacent fishing boat jetties, nearly 50 visitors have been squeezed in on occasion – a good excuse for a party, one suspects. There is talk of extending the marina, possibly by dredging part of the large empty area between the marina and the office – it is, after all, only sand – but no date has been set.

In 2005 the high season (May–September) rate for a visiting yacht of 10–12m was €23.80 per night, rising to €29.75 for 12–15m, inclusive of water, showers, electricity and tax. Multihulls of the same lengths paid €27.85 and €38.68 respectively. Payment must be made in cash – no credit cards are accepted.

The second marina mentioned above is private, consisting of two pontoons used by members of the Clube Naval de Nazaré, which has premises on the east side of the harbour. There is very seldom space for visitors.

Security throughout the entire port area is excellent though relaxed, with a watchman permanently on duty at the main gate and access to the pontoons via electronic card.

The yacht pontoons at Nazaré – referred to by some as 'Mike's marina'   *AH*

Anchorage

Anchoring is not permitted in the harbour or its approaches. However in settled weather it is possible to anchor anywhere along the beach off the lower town, protected from the prevailing northerlies by the Pontal da Nazaré. Holding is good over sand.

Formalities

Nazaré does not yet have the 'single form' system (see page 7), but there is a *GNR–Brigada Fiscal* office in the same building as the marina office and normally no other officials need be seen.

Facilities

The first place to enquire about almost any need is at the marina reception and information office, mentioned above. Sailors themselves – they were returning home after some years cruising in the Eastern Mediterranean when bad weather sent them into Nazaré, supposedly for a single night – Michael and Sally have amassed an impressive fund of knowledge. They can advise on anything from major repair work by local contractors to the local bus timetable, and Sally will translate into Portuguese if necessary. Almost as an aside they produce a very useful information sheet in a dozen or more languages, and find space for a multi-lingual book-swap.

Boatyard Near the main gate to the port area, and able to handle repairs in GRP and steel, painting etc. However visitors (particularly those who do not speak Portuguese) would be well advised to approach them through the marina office.

Travel-lift 80-tonne capacity hoist, backed by a large area of concrete hard-standing which serves both fishing boats and yachts (most of the latter in cradles with additional props). Electricity is laid on, and owners are free both to work on their own boats and to live aboard whilst ashore.

Engineers, electronic and radio repairs Again, all services are available but contact is best made via the marina office.

Sailmaker/sail repairs The nearest sailmakers are in Lisbon – again, enquire at the marina office.

Chandlery Some basic chandlery is held by Naval-Ship, but most items will probably have to be ordered from Lisbon or beyond.

Water On the pontoons.

Showers In the main building, and due for renovation when visited in September 2004.

Launderette Washing machine next to the showers, but no dryer. There is a full-service launderette in the town.

Electricity On the pontoons.

Fuel Diesel and petrol pumps on the short hammerhead pontoon next to the *clube naval* marina, run by the nearby BP garage (who accept credit cards) and said to operate around the clock.

Bottled gas Camping Gaz available in the town, but no possibility of getting other bottles refilled.

Clube naval The small Clube Naval de Nazaré has premises on the east side of the harbour.

Weather forecast Posted daily outside the marina office.

Banks In the town, with a cash dispenser at the marina.

Shops/provisioning Well-stocked mini-market facing the marina (where fresh bread is available twice a day), with good general shopping in Nazaré itself.

Produce market Good market in the town, open 0700–1300 daily in summer, closed Mondays in the winter. A large open market is held every Friday just behind the produce hall.

Cafés, restaurants and hotels Café/bar at the mini-market and another beside the *clube naval* pontoons, with a wide choice in the thriving holiday resort. Not surprisingly, all menus feature fish prominently.

Medical services In Nazaré, but visit the marina office for advice and assistance.

Communications

Post offices In the town, though stamped mail can be left at the marina office for posting.

Mailing address Mail is best sent via Michael and Sally Hadley – c/o Celtic Marine, Caixa Postal 1, Porto da Nazaré, 2450-075 Nazaré, Portugal. It is important that the envelope carries the name of the yacht in addition to that of the addressee.

Internet access One terminal in the marina office on payment of a small fee, or free access at the Cultural Centre in the town (but often a long queue).

Public telephone Kiosks near the marina security gate and at the mini-market, which also sells the necessary card.

Fax service At the marina office *Fax 262 561 402*.

Car hire/taxis Best arranged via the marina office, from which bicycles can also be hired.

Buses Regular buses into Nazaré (though the walk is less than a mile over flat ground). A timetable is displayed outside the marina office. Express buses connect Nazaré with Lisbon airport (about 90 minutes), Porto etc.

The tomb of Prince Henry the Navigator, honorary patron saint of pilot book writers, inside Batalha Abbey   *AH*

45. São Martinho do Porto

Waypoints
⊕120 – 39°32´.6N 9°10´.5W (approach)
⊕121 – 39°30´.76N 9°08´.9W (entrance)

Courses and distances
⊕118 (Nazaré) – ⊕120 = 4M, 219° or 039°
⊕120 – ⊕121 = 2.2M, 146° or 326°
⊕120 – ⊕123 (Peniche, via ⊕122 Cabo Carvoeiro) =
   19M, 229°&153° or 333°&049°

Peniche

Tides
See Nazaré, page 155

Charts

	Approach	Harbour
Admiralty	3635	
Imray	C19, C49	
Portuguese	34, 23202, 24202, 24203	34, (27501)

Principal lights
2076 **Ponta do Santo Antonío**
   Iso.R.6s33m9M Siren 60s
   White tower, red, bands
   Obscured on a bearing of more than 165°
2078 **Ldg Lts 145°** *Front* **Carreira do Sul** Iso.R.1.5s9m9M
   White column, red bands 6m
2078.1 *Rear* 129m from front Oc.R.6s11m9M
   White column, red bands, on square white base 8m

Night entry
   Not feasible without local knowledge

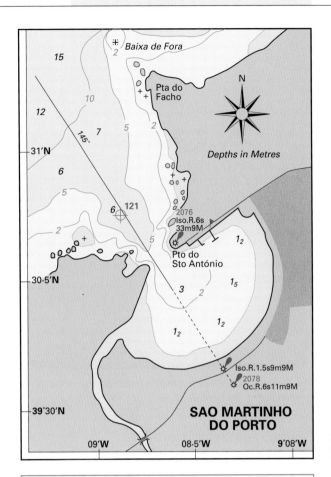

⊕120	39°32´.6N	9°10´.5W	São Martinho do Porto approach
⊕121	39°30´.76N	9°08´.9W	São Martinho do Porto entrance

Shallow but attractive fair-weather anchorage

Once a small fishing port but now a growing tourist town, São Martinho do Porto has a most attractive setting. The sea has widened a breach in the hard cliffs and excavated a crescent-shaped bay out of the softer rock behind. A foot tunnel runs through the cliff just short of the Ponta de Santo António, debouching onto a rocky shore where the unwary can get soaked.

Even though many of the buildings are new and most along the seafront are of four or five storeys, the town is surprisingly attractive with an almost Mediterranean feel to its architecture and pavement cafés and tourist shops to match. The shallow, sheltered waters of the bay ensure a warmer than average swimming temperature.

The bay is shallow and should only be entered in calm, settled weather. Once inside there is little movement even when breaking crests fill the entrance, but leaving in such weather would be impossible.

Approach and entrance

If coastal sailing much of that written about Nazaré, page 155, also applies. On closing São Martinho keep outside the enclosing headlands until the entrance is clearly seen. In particular, beware the rocks 300m off the unlit Ponta do Facho. This promontory, if one is close inshore to the northeast, masks Ponta do Santo António and its light, 0.5M to the south.

From offshore (though this would be unwise in less than perfect conditions), ⊕120 lies 2.2M northwest of the entrance, a course of 146° leading to ⊕121 in the final approach.

The leading marks, on 145°, consist of two red and white banded columns 9m and 11m in height, which may be difficult to pick out against the sand and scrub background. Use them for the approach, but enter midway between Ponta do Santo António and Ponta Santana. Several dozen small white buoys are scattered across and just inside the entrance, presumably marking fish pots but posing an obvious hazard to propellers.

In even moderate weather, though the anchorage may be tenable a boat can be trapped by the swell at the exit. If the fishermen leave *en masse* it may be wise to follow.

Anchorage

Anchor outside the moorings in the northeast part of the harbour in about 2m over sand. The quay leading round from Ponta de Santo António has no more than this at its head, shoaling towards the town, and has underwater projections in places. There are two short jetties where one could land by dinghy, but there seems little point when the alternative is clean, sandy beach.

Formalities

Call at the *Policía Marítima* office at the northeast corner of the beach (easily identified by its mast and lights) with passports and ship's papers.

The narrow entrance to São Martinho do Porto's semicircular bay   *AH*

Facilities and communications

The Clube Náutico de São Martinho do Porto has newly enlarged premises on the north quay. Water could doubtless be had for the asking, but there is no fuel available.

The town has reasonable shopping, banks, restaurants, bars etc, together with a post office and telephones. Taxis abound, and buses and trains (a branch line between Lisbon and Coimbra) run further afield – should one be happy to leave the boat for any length of time.

Not feasible – Lagõa de Obidos

The Lagõa de Obidos (39°26′N 9°14′W), just south of Foz de Arelho and about halfway between São Martinho do Porto and Cabo Carvoeiro, may appear on glancing at Admiralty as a possibility. However the mouth is almost totally blocked by sandbars and the tide runs swiftly through the gaps. Unlike the rather similar Esposende, there are no offlying hazards.

Looking southeast across the shallow bay at São Martinho do Porto from Ponta do Santo António   *AH*

Peniche to Cascais, including Ilha da Berlenga

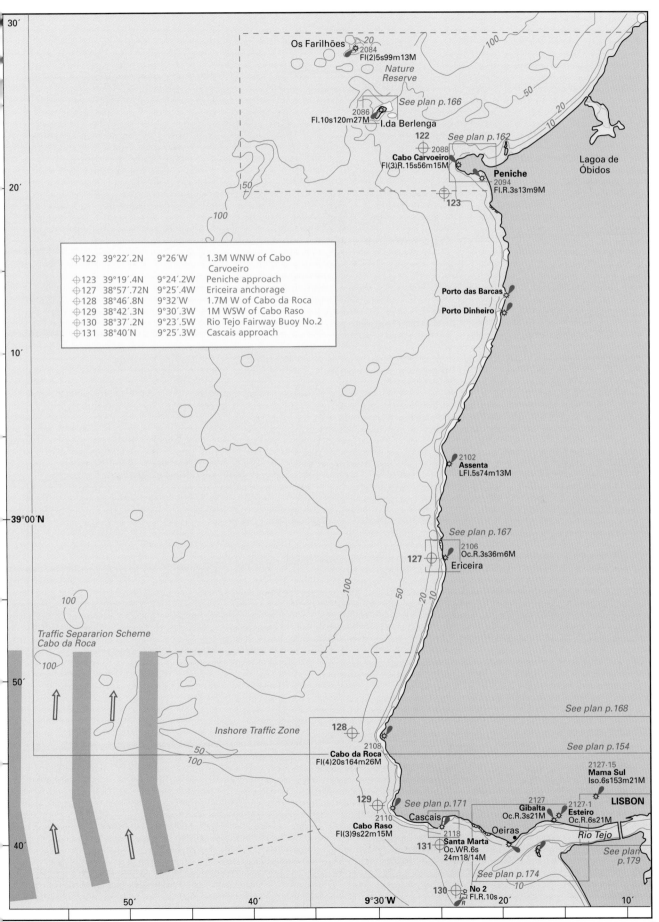

Os Farilhões
2084
Fl(2)5s99m13M

Nature Reserve

See plan p.166

2086
Fl.10s120m27M
I.da Berlenga

⊕122

2088
Cabo Carvoeiro
Fl(3)R.15s56m15M

See plan p.162

Lagoa de Óbidos

Peniche
2094
Fl.R.3s13m9M

⊕123

⊕122	39°22′.2N	9°26′W	1.3M WNW of Cabo Carvoeiro
⊕123	39°19′.4N	9°24′.2W	Peniche approach
⊕127	38°57′.72N	9°25′.4W	Ericeira anchorage
⊕128	38°46′.8N	9°32′W	1.7M W of Cabo da Roca
⊕129	38°42′.3N	9°30′.3W	1M WSW of Cabo Raso
⊕130	38°37′.2N	9°23′.5W	Rio Tejo Fairway Buoy No.2
⊕131	38°40′N	9°25′.3W	Cascais approach

Porto das Barcas

Porto Dinheiro

2102
Assenta
LFl.5s74m13M

See plan p.167

2106
Oc.R.3s36m6M

⊕127
Ericeira

Traffic Separarion Scheme Cabo da Roca

Inshore Traffic Zone

See plan p.168

⊕128

2108
Cabo da Roca
Fl(4)20s164m26M

See plan p.154

2127·15
Mama Sul
Iso.6s153m21M

⊕129

2110
Cabo Raso
Fl(3)9s22m15M

See plan p.171

Cascais

2127
Gibalta
Oc.R.3s21M

2127·1
Esteiro
Oc.R.6s21M

LISBON

Oeiras

2118
Santa Marta
Oc.WR.6s
24m18/14M

⊕131

Rio Tejo

See plan p.179

See plan p.174

⊕130
No 2
Fl.R.10s

R

39°00′N

30′

20′

10′

50′

40′

50′

40′

9°30′W

20′

10′

PORTUGAL – THE WEST COAST

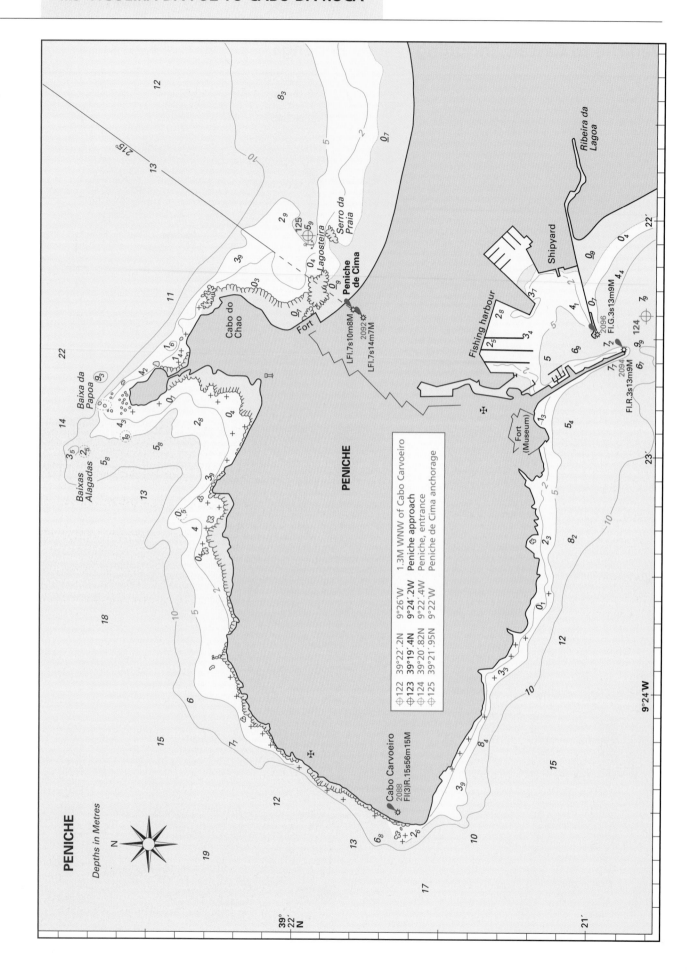

PENICHE

Depths in Metres

N

PENICHE

⊕122	39°22'.2N	9°26'W	1.3M WNW of Cabo Carvoeiro
⊕123	39°19'.4N	9°24'.2W	Peniche approach
⊕124	39°20'.82N	9°22'.4W	Peniche, entrance
✧125	39°21'.95N	9°22'W	Peniche de Cima anchorage

Cabo Carvoeiro
2088
Fl(3)R.15s56m15M

Peniche de Cima
2092 ✧
LFl.7s10m8M
LFl.7s14m7M

Serro da Praia

Ribeira da Lagoa

Shipyard

Fishing harbour

2096
Fl.G.3s13m9M

2094
Fl.R.3s13m9M

124 ⊕

Fort (Museum)

Fort

Cabo do Chao

Lagosteira

Baixa da Papoa

Baixas da Alagadas

46. Peniche

Waypoints
⊕122 – 39°22′.2N 9°26′W (1.3M WNW of
Cabo Carvoeiro)
⊕123 – 39°19′.4N 9°24′.2W (approach)
⊕124 – 39°20′.82N 9°22′.4W (entrance)
⊕125 – 39°21′.95N 9°22′W (Peniche de Cima
anchorage)
⊕126 – 39°24′.8N 9°30′.1W (Ilha Berlenga anchorage)
⊕127 – 38°57′.72N 9°25′.4W (Ericeira anchorage)

Courses and distances
⊕118 (Nazaré) – ⊕123 (via ⊕122) = 22.9M, 227°&153°
or 333°&047°
⊕123 – ⊕124 = 2M, 045° or 225°
⊕123 – ⊕126 = 7.1M, 320° or 140°
⊕124 – ⊕126 = 7.2M, 304° or 124°
⊕123 – ⊕127 = 21.7M, 182° or 002°
⊕123 – ⊕130 (Rio Tejo Fairway Buoy No.2, via
⊕128 & ⊕129) = 45.2M, 191°&164°&134° or
314°&344°&011°
⊕123 – ⊕131 (Cascais, via ⊕128 & ⊕129) = 42.4M,
191°&164°&120° or 300°&344°&011°
⊕127 – ⊕130 (Rio Tejo Fairway Buoy No.2, via ⊕128
& ⊕129) = 24.2M, 205°&164°&134° or
314°&344°&025°

Tides
Standard port Lisbon
Mean time differences
HW –0025 ±0010; LW 0000 ±0005
Heights in metres

MHWS	MHWN	MLWN	MLWS
3.5	2.7	1.3	0.6

Or refer to EasyTide at www.ukho.gov.uk (see page 2)

Charts	Approach	Harbour
Admiralty	3635	
Imray	C19, C49	C49
Portuguese	36, 23202, 24202, 24203,	
	26405	26405
Ilhas das Berlengas	26405	
Ilhéus dos Farilhões	26405	
Ericeira	(27501)	

Principal lights
2094 **West breakwater** Fl.R.3s13m9M Siren 120s
White tower, red bands 8m
2096 **East breakwater** Fl.G.3s13m9M
White tower, green bands 8m

Night entry
Well lit, and without problems other than in strong
southerlies. However space at the marina is often
limited.

Maritime radio station
Montejunto (39°10′.5N 9°03′.5W)
Remotely controlled from Lisbon)
Manual – VHF Ch 16, 24, 25, 27. *Autolink* – VHF Ch 86.

Harbour communications
Port Authority ☎ 262 784109 *Fax* 262 784225
Email japcpen@mail.telepac.pt
VHF Ch 11, 16 (call *Capimarpeniche*) (0900–1200,
1400–1700 weekdays only)
Marina da Ribeira ☎ 262 781153, VHF Ch 11, 16

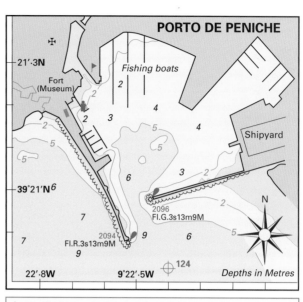

PORTO DE PENICHE

| ⊕123 | 39°19′.4N | 9°24′.2W | Peniche approach |
| ⊕124 | 39°20′.82N | 9°22′.4W | Peniche, entrance |

Busy fishing harbour with small yacht marina

Possibly settled by Phoenicians, and the scene of a
landing in 1589 by an English force, Peniche today
is an important fishing port with a large harbour.
The town is of greater interest than many along this
coast and the museum in the 16th century Fortaleza,
later converted into a political prison, is particularly
recommended. Until the 15th century Peniche was
effectively an island, and the defensive walls which
protected its shoreward side still run unbroken from
north to south.

The port is large and well sheltered from the
prevailing northerlies with an easy entrance, but it is
not picturesque, though the comings and goings of
the fishing fleet certainly add interest (and wash), as
do the Ilha da Berlenga tourist ferries. The festival of
Nossa Senhora da Boa Viagem takes place over the
first weekend in August and includes harbour
processions and blessing of the fishing fleet.

Although the small (140 berth) Marina da Ribeira
has been in existence for the better part of a decade,
the ambitious plans for a second and much larger
facility in the eastern part of the harbour mentioned

PORTUGAL – THE WEST COAST

Peniche from a little east of south, with the small Marina
da Ribeira tucked behind the breakwater on the left

Peniche's Marina da Ribeira with visiting yachts rafted on both sides of the outer pontoon. Fishing boats line the concrete moles in the background

in the previous edition of this book appear to have been shelved. Although a large new basin has been dredged over the past few years, its uses are entirely commercial. The friendly Clube Naval de Peniche hopes to lay a couple of additional pontoons for members, but such is the waiting list that no berths are likely to be vacated in the marina.

Approach

If coastal sailing from the north, most navigators will opt for the 5.5M wide channel between Ilha da Berlenga and Cabo Carvoeiro (⊕122), though tidal streams between the islands and the mainland may make for a rough passage. When seen from some distance to the north, Peniche can be mistaken for the island it once was. Also viable is the narrower, 3M gap between Ilha da Berlenga and Os Farilhões, though there are offlying rocks on both side and care is needed as the current sets south onto the larger island.

From Cabo Carvoeiro to Cabo da Roca, 33M to the south, the coast has steep cliffs with the occasional beach. A Traffic Separation Zone is situated off Cabo da Roca, 7M wide and approximately 10M from the headland. The major light en route is Assenta, 1M south of Ponta da Lamparoeira.

On closing Peniche, ⊕123 lies 2M due southwest of the entrance, a course of 045° leading to ⊕124, close outside the harbour mouth.

Entrance

On final approach from the west around Cabo Carvoeiro, the east breakwater light appears to the north of the west breakwater light. Approach the west breakwater within 50–100m and round in – the entrance is a little over 100m wide.

Peniche is a busy fishing port for vessels both large and small, and a greater than usual concentration of fish pots should be anticipated within 10–15M of the entrance. Some are well marked but the majority are not – be warned!

Berthing and formalities

Visiting yachts should secure to the long outer pontoon which shelters the marina proper, choosing a berth as space allows. Five or six yachts can moor in line ahead on the outside, rafting up from then on, while a few lucky ones may find places on the inside, though note that the northernmost inside berth is reserved for the *GNR–Brigada Fiscal* vessel. All berths alongside finger pontoons are private. At least 5m should be found throughout.

The marina is reasonably well protected, particularly at its northern end, though may suffer from swell in winds out of the south. More of a problem is the constant wash from fishing boats approaching and leaving their three long jetties to the northeast, at all hours of the day and night and almost invariably at speed – despite the 3 knot limit prominently displayed on the eastern breakwater end. Generous fendering is therefore essential, and particular care should be taken that masts are staggered to avoid rigging becoming entangled should two boats roll together. (In September 2004 a yacht lost her mast in this way, while on others crewmembers have been injured whilst attempting to fend off.)

The marina office shares premises at the root of the breakwater with the Ilha da Berlenga ferry booking offices, and is normally open 0700–0745, 0930–1200 and 1600–1830 weekdays, 0700–1200 and 1600–1800 weekends and holidays. If arriving outside these hours the skipper should in theory either walk round to the Instituto Portuário do Centro office at the main port gate, or call them on ☎ 262 781153, but it is unlikely that any English will be spoken. It may be simpler to await the arrival of a marina official or security guard, who amongst other things will issue a card to work the electronic gate (in 2002 it was reported that a deposit of €25 was required – or failing that the ship's documents). *GNR–Brigada Fiscal* and *Polícia Marítima* officials may also visit.

If going ashore before a card is issued it is essential for someone to remain inside the gate to let others back in. Even the most agile would have a tough

Fish drying outside a house in Peniche   *AH*

A fishing boat alongside the breakwater in Peniche   *AH*

Fishing nets on the quayside in Peniche   *AH*

time getting around the guard wires, and at least one entire crew is reported to have spent an uncomfortable night marooned only yards from their yacht (surprisingly, it seems that no-one was willing to take a midnight dip. . .)

In 2005 the high season rate for a visiting yacht of 10–12m was around €23 per night, rising to €27 for 12–15m, inclusive of water, electricity and tax. Multihulls paid a 50% surcharge. Payment must be made in cash – no credit cards are accepted.

Anchorage

Anchoring is not permitted in the harbour, but in winds from the northern quadrant good holding over sand is to be found south of the east breakwater.

Facilities

Boatyard Several boatyards with marine railways operate near the root of the east breakwater, backed by mechanical, electrical and electronic engineering workshops. Though more accustomed to fishing boats, in an emergency yachts can also be hauled – at a price.

Electronic and radio repairs Estêvão Alexandre Henriques Lda, ☎ 262 085536 *Email* estevaoah@netvisao.pt www.estevaoah.com two streets back from the harbour on Rua José Estêvão, sell and repair marine electronics of all kinds. Most of their trade comes from the fishing fleet but the engineers (some of whom speak English) are happy to visit yachts.

Chandlery Estêvão Alexandre Henriques Lda (see above) stock a limited amount of general chandlery and are willing to order.

Water On the pontoons.

Showers Two toilet/shower cubicles behind the marina office.

Launderette Next to the above – one washer but no dryer.

Electricity On the pontoons.

Fuel Diesel and petrol pumps at the head of the jetty opposite the marina office, administered by the Clube Naval de Peniche (see below). Long hoses run down to the berth, which has black fendering and is frequently occupied by small fishing boats. Fuel is available during office hours only (which vary) so check well in advance. Payment must be made in cash.

Bottled gas Camping Gaz available in the town, but no refills.

Clube naval The Clube Naval de Peniche currently has its headquarters in the small fort near the root of the west breakwater, beyond the red-doored lifeboat house. However new premises are to be built on a spit of land further east (see plan), hopefully by 2006.

Weather forecast Posted daily on the back of the large display board near the Ilha da Berlenga ferry offices, but generally in Portuguese text only (ie no synoptic chart). An English translation may be available from the marina office.

Banks In the town, nearly all with cash dispensers.

Shops/provisioning Good provisioning and general shopping, including a large supermarket in a new housing development northeast of the harbour.

Produce market In the town.

Cafés, restaurants and hotels Many, though sadly the tradition of grilling sardines on charcoal braziers by the roadside appears to have succumbed to modern hygiene regulations.

Medical services Hospital etc in the town.

Communications

Post office In the town.

Mailing address The marina office will hold mail for visiting yachts – c/o Instituto Portuário e dos Transportes Marítimos, Porto de Pesca de Peniche, 2520 Peniche, Portugal. It is important that the envelope carries the name of the yacht in addition to that of the addressee.

Internet access At the On Line Cybercafé on Rua Antonio Cervantes (very close to the harbour), but understood to be open evenings only.

Public telephones Kiosks on the root of the breakwater and elsewhere.

Fax service At the marina office, *Fax* 261 784225.

Car hire/taxis In the town. Taxis can be ordered via the marina office.

Buses Regular bus service to Lisbon (about 1hour 45 minutes) and elsewhere – a visit to the mediaeval walled town of Obidos is particularly recommended.

Ferries Tourist ferries to Ilha da Berlenga – and not a bad way to visit if one wishes to explore without the responsibility of a yacht at anchor (see below).

Air services International airport at Lisbon.

Looking southeast across Ponta da Papoa towards the anchorage at Peniche de Cima

Adjacent anchorages

1. **Peniche do Cima** (⊕125 – 39°21′.95N 9°22′W) on the north side of the peninsula southeast of Cabo do Chao. There are leading marks on 215° but they appear to lead straight onto a rocky shoal. Keep well east, sounding in to anchor close to the above position in 5–6m over sand. The entire bay is open to the north, and any northwesterly swell will also work around the corner.

⊕126 39°24′.8N   9°30′.1W   Ilha da Berlenga anchorage

2. **Ilha da Berlenga** (⊕126 – 39°24′.8N 9°30′.1W) remains desolate and largely unspoilt, despite the numerous tourist boats which ply from Peniche. The entire island, together with its offlying rocks and the seabed out to the 3m contour, is a nature reserve frequented by seabirds including gulls, puffins and cormorants. For this reason parts of the island are off-limits to visitors – many of whom in any case appear unwilling to venture far from the landing quay at Carreiro do Mosteiro. (For those who enjoy their wildlife small but inquisitive, a small investment of damp bread will swiftly entice the resident lizards out of their crevasses, while walkers should watch out for their kamikaze brethren who dash across paths almost underfoot.)

Approach from the southeast or south in order to avoid offliers which fringe the island in all other directions, making for either Carreiro do Mosteiro or Carreiro da Fortaleza – in which stands the distinctive Forte de São João Batista – on the southeast coast or Cova do Sono to the southwest (taking care to avoid the offlying Baixo do Sota Cataláo). All three anchorages call for careful 'eyeball' pilotage in good light, made easier by the crystal clear water.

Both Carreiro do Mosteiro and Carreiro da Fortaleza have beaches at their heads, and in the former landing can also be made by dinghy at the stone quay used by the tourist ferries. It would be unwise to leave the yacht unattended for long in any but the calmest conditions, but a short tour by dinghy will be amply rewarded, viewing the impressive Forte de São João Baptista – built in the 17th century by monks, tired of their undefended monastery being ransacked by pirates – and exploring the natural tunnels and caves. Once ashore, the small settlement of Bairro dos Pescadores overlooking the quay offers a café/restaurant and a small shop, the latter apparently selling little beyond ice cream.

The second possible anchorage, in the entrance to Cova do Sono in 8–10m over sand and rock, is

Ilha da Berlenga from the southeast, with the Ilhas Medas and Ilhas Estelas clearly visible behind

The centre part of the Ilha da Berlenga with, from left to right, Forte de São João Batista, the island's 29m lighthouse, and the inlet and village of Carreiro do Mosteiro

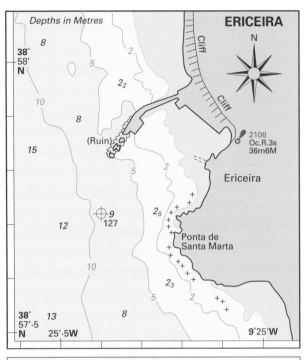

⊕127 38°57′.72N 9°25′.4W   Ericeira anchorage

somewhat better protected and has been used overnight in settled weather. However, although it is possible to land on the surrounding boulders, only a mountaineer – and one willing to ignore the bylaws which forbid roaming off the marked paths – could attain the island's virtually flat summit.

All official paths start and end at the quay in Carreiro do Mosteiro, but if intent on seeing the island in detail – and unless the crew is large enough to leave a person aboard at all times – it might be better to visit by ferry from Peniche, where several companies compete for business at the root of the main quay. A single day will be long enough to cover all the approved paths, but it is also possible to stay overnight, either in chalets or on the approved campsite – enquire at the tourist office in Peniche.

The Ilhéus dos Farilhões, some 4M north-northwest of Ilha da Berlenga, offer no feasible anchorages.

The small, exposed harbour at Ericeira, looking southeast. Extensive storm damage to the breakwater underlines the fact that only one thing separates Portugal's west coast from America – sea!

3. **Ericeira** (⊕127 – 38°57′.72N 9°25′.4W), 6M south of Assenta light and 11.5M north of Cabo da Roca, lies some 2M south of Cabo Carvoeiro and offers a possible daytime anchorage in calm, settled weather. However the single breakwater provides absolutely no shelter from onshore winds or swell, and local craft are kept ashore on the wide slipway – not for nothing is the area popular with surfers from all over Europe. No large scale chart is currently available for the area, which is admitted to be poorly surveyed. Though lit, approach after dark would be most unwise.

Close the land keeping well clear of the breakwater head, which lost its outer section to a winter storm nearly a decade ago and has yet to be rebuilt. Although the outer block shows at all states of the tide, underwater rubble lies scattered in all directions. Best anchorage is to be found in the entrance to the bay, south of the breakwater head, in 5–6m over rock and sand. There is little depth off the small quay, though it has steps convenient for landing by dinghy.

Once a clifftop village – though now dwarfed by the inevitable high-rise buildings – the old town centre has nevertheless retained much of its character and is renowned for its shellfish restaurants. The Clube Naval de Ericeira has a small clubhouse below the cliffs and there are several beach cafés, while the town itself offers the usual banks, shops, post office etc.

In 1910 Portugal's last king, Dom Manuel II, chose Ericeira as his port of departure after a military revolt and following the assassination of his father and elder brother. One can only wonder whether it was the little harbour's apparent unsuitability which prompted his choice.

PORTUGAL – THE WEST COAST

II.4 Approaches to the Rio Tejo and Lisbon

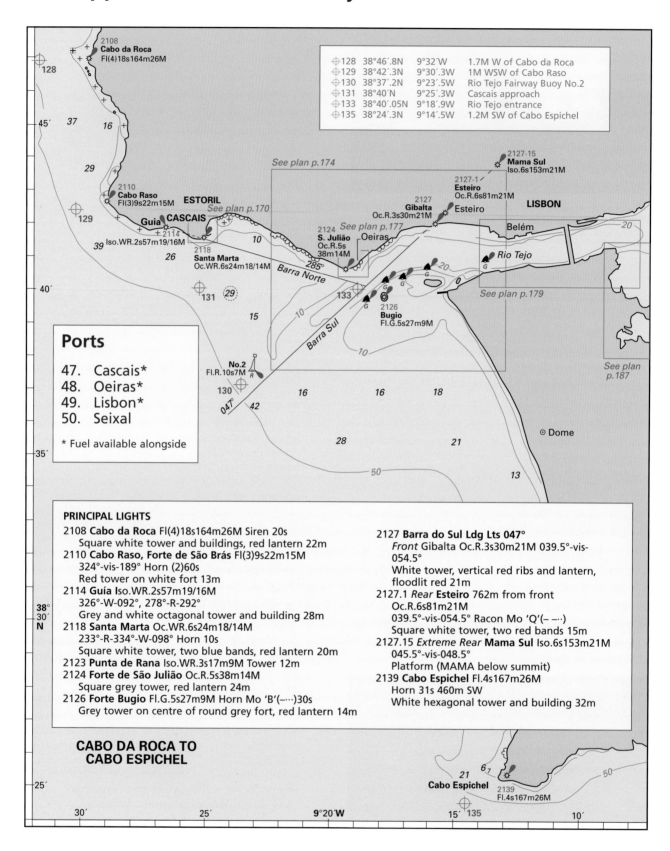

⊕128	38°46′.8N	9°32′W	1.7M W of Cabo da Roca
⊕129	38°42′.3N	9°30′.3W	1M WSW of Cabo Raso
⊕130	38°37′.2N	9°23′.5W	Rio Tejo Fairway Buoy No.2
⊕131	38°40′N	9°25′.3W	Cascais approach
⊕133	38°40′.05N	9°18′.9W	Rio Tejo entrance
⊕135	38°24′.3N	9°14′.5W	1.2M SW of Cabo Espichel

Ports

47. Cascais*
48. Oeiras*
49. Lisbon*
50. Seixal

* Fuel available alongside

PRINCIPAL LIGHTS

2108 **Cabo da Roca** Fl(4)18s164m26M Siren 20s
  Square white tower and buildings, red lantern 22m
2110 **Cabo Raso, Forte de São Brás** Fl(3)9s22m15M
  324°-vis-189° Horn (2)60s
  Red tower on white fort 13m
2114 **Guía** Iso.WR.2s57m19/16M
  326°-W-092°, 278°-R-292°
  Grey and white octagonal tower and building 28m
2118 **Santa Marta** Oc.WR.6s24m18/14M
  233°-R-334°-W-098° Horn 10s
  Square white tower, two blue bands, red lantern 20m
2123 **Punta de Rana** Iso.WR.3s17m9M Tower 12m
2124 **Forte de São Julião** Oc.R.5s38m14M
  Square grey tower, red lantern 24m
2126 **Forte Bugio** Fl.G.5s27m9M Horn Mo 'B'(–···)30s
  Grey tower on centre of round grey fort, red lantern 14m

2127 **Barra do Sul Ldg Lts 047°**
  Front Gibalta Oc.R.3s30m21M 039.5°-vis-054.5°
  White tower, vertical red ribs and lantern, floodlit red 21m
2127.1 *Rear* **Esteiro** 762m from front
  Oc.R.6s81m21M
  039.5°-vis-054.5° Racon Mo 'Q'(– –·)
  Square white tower, two red bands 15m
2127.15 *Extreme Rear* **Mama Sul** Iso.6s153m21M
  045.5°-vis-048.5°
  Platform (MAMA below summit)
2139 **Cabo Espichel** Fl.4s167m26M
  Horn 31s 460m SW
  White hexagonal tower and building 32m

CABO DA ROCA TO CABO ESPICHEL

The Rio Tejo estuary
Outer approaches to Cascais, Oeiras, Lisbon and the Rio Tejo

Waypoints
⊕100 – 38°45′N 10°05′W (27.7M W of Cabo da Roca)
⊕128 – 38°46′.8N 9°32′W (1.7M W of Cabo da Roca)
⊕129 – 38°42′.3N 9°30′.3W (1M WSW of Cabo Raso)
⊕130 – 38°37′.2N 9°23′.5W (Fairway Buoy No.2)
⊕133 – 38°40′.05N 9°18′.9W (Rio Tejo entrance)
⊕135 – 38°24′.3N 9°14′.5W (1.2M SW of Cabo Espichel)

Courses and distances
⊕123 (Peniche) – ⊕130 (via ⊕128 & ⊕129) = 45.2M, 191°&164°&134° or 314°&344°&011°
⊕127 (Ericeira) – ⊕130 (via ⊕128 & ⊕129) = 24.2M, 205°&164°&134° or 314°&344°&025°
⊕100 – ⊕130 = 33.4M, 103° or 283° (not advised due to the Traffic Separation Scheme off Cabo da Roca)
⊕130 – ⊕131 (Cascais) = 3.1M, 333° or 153°
⊕130 – ⊕133 = 4.6M, 052° or 332°
⊕130 – ⊕136 (Sesimbra, via ⊕135) = 21.6M, 151°&089° or 269°&331′
⊕130 – ⊕139 (Setúbal, via ⊕135) = 25.2M, 151°&090° or 270°&331°
⊕130 – ⊕142 (Sines, via ⊕135) = 48M, 151°&152° or 328°&329°

Charts	Approach	Entrance
Admiralty	3635, 3636	3220
Imray	C19, C49	C19, C49
Portuguese	23203, 24203, 24204, (26406)	(26406), 26303, 26304

Navtex
Monsanto Identification letters 'R' and 'G'
Transmits on 518kHz in English; 490kHz in Portuguese
Weather bulletins and navigational warnings for Galicia, Portugal and Andalucía: English – 0250, 0650, 1050, 1450, 1850, 2250 UT; Portuguese – 0100, 0500, 0900, 1300, 1700, 2100 UT

Weather bulletins and navigational warnings
Algés (38°44′N 9°11′W)
Weather bulletins in Portuguese and English for Galicia, Portugal and Andalucía: 2657kHz and VHF Ch 11 at 0905, 2105 UT
Navigational warnings in Portuguese and English within 200 miles offshore: 2657 kHz and VHF Ch 11at 1905, 2105 UT

Maritime radio station
Lisbon (38°44′.1N 9°11′.3W) *Digital Selective Calling* MMSI 002630100
MF Transmits on 2182, 2582, 2693, 2780kHz
Receives 2182kHz
VHF Manual – Ch 16, 23, 25, 26. *Autolink* – VHF Ch 83

Approach
From the north, keep 1M off the high cliffs of Cabo da Roca (⊕128) and the lower headland of Cabo Raso (⊕129) off which there is a Traffic Separation Zone 7M wide and approximately 10M from the headland.

From the south, Cabo Espichel is clear of offlying hazards, though all three headlands can produce nasty seas in wind over tide conditions.
See continuation page 175.

Cabo da Roca, with its prominent lighthouse and associated buildings, seen from the south

PORTUGAL – THE WEST COAST

47. Cascais

Waypoints
⊕131 – 38°40′N 9°25′.3W (approach)
⊕132 – 38°41′.65N 9°24′.75W (entrance)

Courses and distances
⊕123 (Peniche) – ⊕131 (via ⊕128 & ⊕129) = 42.4M,
91°&164°&120° or 300°&344°&011°
⊕130 (Rio Tejo Fairway Buoy No.2) – ⊕131 = 3.1M,
333° or 153°
⊕131 – ⊕132 =1.7 M, 015° or 095°
⊕132 – ⊕133 (Rio Tejo entrance) = 4.9M, 109°/289°
⊕131 – ⊕136 (Sesimbra, via ⊕135) = 24.7M, 152°&089°
or 269°&332°
⊕131 – ⊕139 (Setúbal, via ⊕135) = 32.3M, 152°&046°
or 226°&332°
⊕131 – ⊕142 (Sines, via ⊕135) = 51.1M, 152°&152°
or 332°&332°

Tides
Standard port Lisbon
Mean time differences
HW –0035 ±0010; LW –0010 ±0005
Heights in metres

MHWS	MHWN	MLWN	MLWS
3.5	2.7	1.5	0.7

Or refer to EasyTide at www.ukho.gov.uk (see page 2)

Charts	*Approach*	*Harbour*
Admiralty	3635	3220
Imray	C19, C49	C19, C49
Portuguese	23203, 24203, 24204, (26406)	26303

Principal lights
2118 Oc.WR.6s24m18/14M Horn 10s White tower, blue
bands, red cupola 233°-R-334°-W-098°
2121 **Praia da Ribeira** Oc.R.4s6m6M 251°-vis-309°
White metal column, red bands 5m
2122 **Albatroz** Oc.R.6s12m5M
Lantern on verandah of Hotel Albatroz 6m
2119 **Marina southeast breakwater** Fl(3)R.4s7m6M
Red post, white bands, on concrete base 3m
2119.1 **Marina north mole** Fl(2)G.4s7m3M
Green post, white bands 5m

Night entry
Should not present problems in any but the strongest
onshore conditions

Harbour communications
Marina de Cascais ☎ 214 824800/824857
Fax 214 824860 *Email* reception2@marinacascais.pt
www.marinacascais.pt (in Portuguese only)
VHF Ch 09, 16 (0900–2000 May to September
inclusive, otherwise 0900–1800)

Large marina with good facilities and shelter

There is no denying that Cascais is a pretty town, especially when seen from offshore and, being effectively a suburb of Lisbon, it has most of the facilities a visiting yachtsman might require – not least quick (and remarkably cheap) access to the city centre. Not surprisingly, it has for many years been a popular anchorage in the prevailing northerly winds.

Although the large Marina de Cascais opened in August 1999 though parts of the shoreside infrastructure still appear unfinished and fewer than half the retail premises are occupied. It is said that the 638 berths have yet to be fully occupied, though this can only be a matter of time.

It is a good 20 minutes' walk from the marina into the town centre, though buses run regularly from the main gate. Alternatively, a walkway has been completed along the walls above the Clube Naval de Cascais, giving excellent views and cutting the time considerably. An unexpected bonus is the very pleasant leafy park right opposite the marina's landward gates, complete with children's playground (a supervised indoor adventure play area is provided in the marina itself). There is also a small maritime museum nearby.

Approach

If coastal sailing from the north, between Cabo da Roca (⊕128) and Santa Marta there are steep rocky cliffs and fishing nets may be laid at least 0.5M offshore.

From the south, the track between Cabo Espichel and Cascais lies along 331°, leaving the Rio Tejo Fairway Buoy No.2 about 1M to port and thus crossing the Barra Sul at close to a right-angle. Considerable traffic should be anticipated at this point, and it is not a route to choose in poor visibility unless radar is carried. If approaching from the south at night, the light on São Julião will probably be picked up before that on Santa Marta. The bright shore lights may mask fishing boats, another time when radar will be useful.

From offshore, ⊕131 lies 1.7M south-southwest of the entrance, a course of 015° leading to ⊕132, close outside the harbour mouth.

The Marina de Cascais seen from just west of south, with the anchorage and town in the background

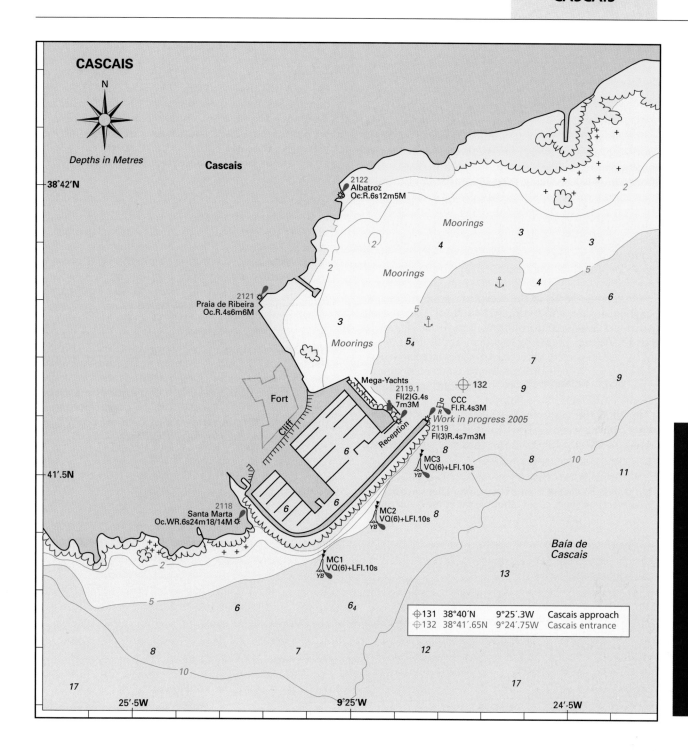

CASCAIS

N

Depths in Metres

Cascais

38°42′N

2122
Albatroz
Oc.R.6s12m5M

Moorings

3

4

3

2

Moorings

2

5

6

2121
Praia de Ribeira
Oc.R.4s6m6M

Moorings

3

5

4

Moorings

5 4

7

9

9

Mega-Yachts
2119.1
Fl(2)G.4s
7m3M

132

9

Fort

CCC
Fl.R.4s3M

Cliff

Reception

Work in progress 2005

2119
Fl(3)R.4s7m3M

8

8

10

6

6

MC3
VQ(6)+LFl.10s
YB

41′.5N

6

6

MC2
VQ(6)+LFl.10s
YB

8

11

2118
Santa Marta
Oc.WR.6s24m18/14M

Baía de
Cascais

2

MC1
VQ(6)+LFl.10s
YB

13

5

6

6 4

| ⊕131 | 38°40′N | 9°25′.3W | Cascais approach |
| ⊕132 | 38°41′.65N | 9°24′.75W | Cascais entrance |

8

7

12

10

17

17

25′.5W

9°25′W

24′.5W

Entrance

The bay is entered between the Cidadela de Cascais, prominently situated on the headland 300m behind the Marina de Cascais, and the Forte de Santo António da Barra, 1.5M to the east. Three south cardinal buoys and a single red can buoy are positioned some 100m from the marina's main breakwater, supposedly keeping yachts off a second, submerged wall which lies some distance outside the visible one. The marina entrance faces northeast with a fetch of no more than 0.4M, and for a yacht with a reliable engine (there is little protection from strong south or southwest winds until inside) should remain feasible in almost all conditions. Towage is available if necessary.

In 2005 work started to extend the southeast breakwater by 100m or so – about as far as the red can buoy shown on the above plan – and presumably the port-hand light will be moved in due course. In the meantime the area should be given generous clearance. Once the extra protection is in place the fuel pontoon is to be moved east to form a right-angle with the reception pontoon.

Berthing

A reception berth will be found on the starboard hand on entry, immediately below the marina office. Hours are from 0900–2000 from May to September inclusive, 0900–1900 during the rest of the year. Mega-yachts – those over 40m or so – berth on a pontoon outside the north mole, west of the fuel pontoon, where they lie stern-to (with buoys provided) in a least depth of 7m. In 2005 this pontoon was also being used by tourist boats, and a new mega-yacht pontoon was planned for slightly further east. All 638 berths inside the marina are alongside finger pontoons (with thoughtfully rounded ends), with access to each main walkway controlled by the usual card-operated electronic gate. Depths throughout the marina are in excess of 6m.

On arrival, berth at the reception pontoon on the starboard side under the windows of the marina office to complete formalities and be allocated a berth. Visiting yachts of less than about 14m (46ft) LOA are generally directed to the southern basin, which is both well-protected and convenient to the main gate. In 2005 all the office staff spoke good English and were most helpful.

In 2005 the high season (May to September) rate for a visiting yacht of 10–12m was €34.18 per night, rising to €46.02 for 12–15m, inclusive of electricity and water (including showers). In the low season this dropped to €14.53 per night (€372.23 per month) for 10–12m, or €19.82 per night €507.60 per month) for 12-15m. Though quoted by the marina ex-IVA – the equivalent of VAT – this has been added to the above figures for easy comparison with other harbours. Multihulls paid a surcharge of between 50% and 100%, according to beam. Most major credit cards are accepted, including VISA and MasterCard.

Anchorage

It is still possible to anchor in Cascais bay, though the area occupied by smallcraft moorings is increasing steadily. However the marina provides some additional protection from the southwest to compensate. Pick any spot outside the moorings so long as it does not impede the fairway to the fishermen's quay or the marina entrance. Holding is generally good over sand and light mud (though there are a few rocky patches), but much of the bay is foul and a tripline is a wise precaution. The bay is frequently rolly and there may be downdraughts off the surrounding hills. Dinghies can normally be left on the inside of the marina fuel pontoon (the mega-yacht pontoon is closed off by security gates), though for shopping trips it may be more convenient to land on the slightly dirty town beach.

The Marina de Cascais from the east. Work has since begun to extend the southeast breakwater by 100m or so – about as far as the red buoy at bottom right

Formalities

All formalities are handled in the reception block, initially in the marina office where the standard multipart form must be completed. The *GNR–Brigada Fiscal, Polícia Marítima* and *Alfândega* also have offices in the building, and may chose to inspect a yacht either while she lies at the reception pontoon or after a berth is allocated.

Those anchored in the bay should also visit the authorities at their offices in the marina reception building.

Facilities

Boatyard PortFair Yacht Service ☎ 214 847025, *Fax* 214 847026, handles general maintenance and repairs in all materials including GRP, timber and metal, as well as antifouling etc.

Travel-lift 70-tonne capacity lift in the boatyard area, with pressure hoses, etc. – book at the marina office. Maximum beam is currently 6.5m, but there are plans to increase this.

Engineers, mechanics, electronic and radio repairs All available via PortFair, who are authorised dealers for a number of international suppliers. Alternatively try Enervolt, mobile 91 4006 990, who sell and service solar panels, batteries, switch panels etc.

Sailmaker, sail repairs Vela Sailmaker Service, mobile 91 7429 107 *Fax* 218 847490 *Email* info@oficinadavela.com, handles sail repairs and canvaswork. If considering a new purchase it might be worth going further afield – see page 184.

Chandlery There are three chandleries in the central block: NautiStar, ☎ 214 846628 (open 1000–1300, 1430–1900 Tuesday to Sunday, closed Monday), which stocks general chandlery, galleyware and some books (and has a branch overlooking the Doca de Alcântara in Lisbon); Mar Masters Lda, ☎ 214 847490 (open 0900–1300, 1400–1800) which carries hardware such as rope, anodes and paint; and Motor & Sail, ☎ 214 845656 (open 1030–1300, 1400–2100), with general chandlery and clothing. In addition there is a good hardware/tool shop in the town.

Charts Available in Lisbon – see page 184.

Water On all pontoons.

Showers Three shower blocks, two in the central part of the complex and one at the reception building.

Launderette In the reception building (a longish walk from the southern basin). A 24 hour service wash is available if required.

Electricity On all pontoons, with plugs etc available at the marina office (deposit required).

Fuel Fuel pontoon (diesel and petrol) outside the north mole. Open marina office hours, with credit cards accepted. Fuel can also be obtained out of hours by prior arrangement and on payment of a surcharge.

Bottled gas Camping Gaz cylinders can be exchanged at both the NautiStar chandlery and the fuel pontoon.

Clube naval The Clube Naval de Cascais has premises immediately north of the marina, but there is no direct access.

Weather forecast Posted daily in the marina office.

Banks At least one automatic card machine in the marina complex, with banks in Cascais.

Shops/provisioning The was no supermarket – not even a source of fresh bread – in the marina complex as of 2005, but excellent grocery and other shopping will be found in Cascais itself.

A classically handsome American yacht lies alongside the reception pontoon at the Marina de Cascais *AH*

Produce market In Cascais, plus fish sold on the beach in the late afternoon. A general market is held every Wednesday and every second Sunday.

Cafés, restaurants and hotels More than a dozen restaurants and cafés in the marina complex, with plenty more of all three in the town.

Medical services First aid centre at the marina office, with full medical facilities (including English-speaking doctors) in the town.

Communications

Post office In Cascais.

Mailing address The marina office will hold mail for visiting yachts – c/o Marina de Cascais, Edifício Controle, 2750–800 Cascais, Portugal. It is important that the envelope carries the name of the yacht in addition to that of the addressee.

Public telephones Kiosks around the marina complex as well as in the town.

Internet access There is no longer a cybercafé in the marina complex but there are several in the town, including Net Phone & Fun which has branches on the corner of Rua Frederico Aronca and Rua das Flores, and on Rua Sebastião José de Carbalho e Melo. Rates (the same at both) are high.

Fax service At the marina office *Fax* 214 824899.

Car hire/taxis Can be arranged through the marina office.

Buses Buses into Cascais from outside the main entrance.

Trains Frequent trains from Cascais to Lisbon's Cais do Sodré station, close to the city centre. The journey, via Estoril and Belém, takes about 30 minutes.

Air services Lisbon International Airport is less than an hour away by train and taxi.

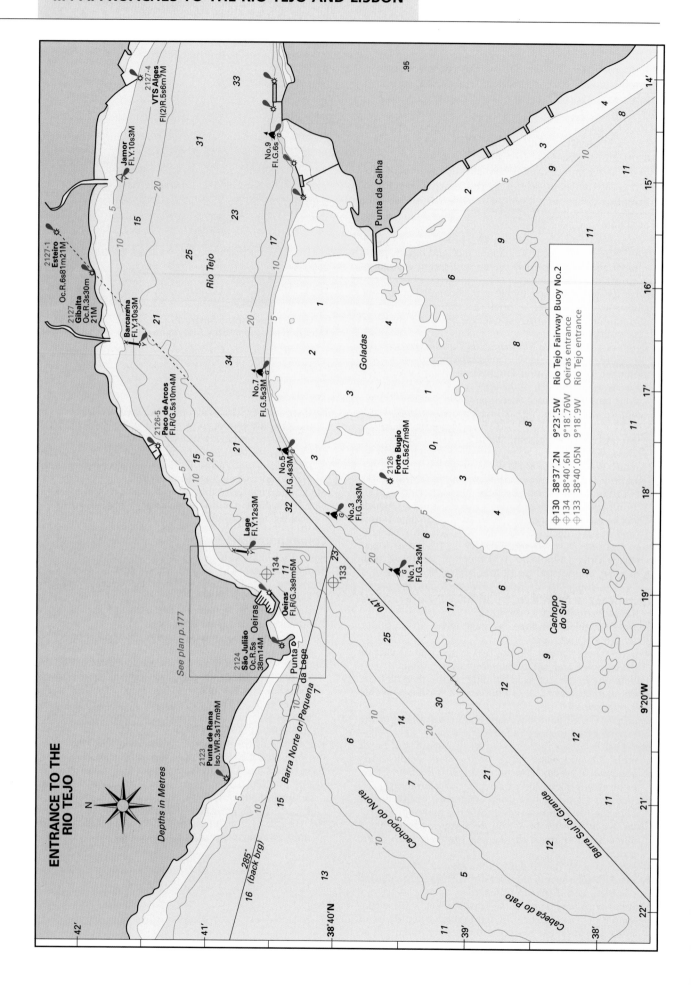

ENTRANCE TO THE RIO TEJO

N

Depths in Metres

⊕130	38°37'.2N	9°23'.5W	Rio Tejo Fairway Buoy No.2
⊕134	38°40'.6N	9°18'.76W	Oeiras entrance
⊕133	38°40'.05N	9°18'.9W	Rio Tejo entrance

VTS Alges
2127·4 Fl(2)R.5s6m7M

2127·4 Jamor Fl.Y.10s3M

No.9 Fl.G.6s G

Punta da Calha

2127·1 Esteiro Oc.R.6s81m21M

2127 Gibalta Oc.R.3s30m 21M

Barcaréna Fl.Y.10s3M

Rio Tejo

Goladas

No.7 Fl.G.5s3M G

2126·5 Paco de Arcos Fl.R.G.5s10m4M

No.5 Fl.G.4s3M G

2126 Forte Bugio Fl.G.5s27m9M

No.3 Fl.G.3s3M G

Lage Fl.Y.12s3M

134 Oeiras 11 Oeiras Fl.R/G.3s9m5M

No.1 Fl.G.2s3M G

133

See plan p.177

2124 São Julião Oc.R.5s 38m14M

Punta da Lage

Cachopo do Sul

2123 Punta de Rana Iso.WR.3s17m9M

Barra Norte or Pequena

Cachopo do Norte

Barra Sul or Grande

285° (back brg)

Cabeça do Pato

The Rio Tejo

Approach

If heading for Oeiras or Lisbon the choice is between the main Barra Sul (or Grande) and the shallower but less defined Barra Norte (or Pequena). Depths of the Cachope do Norte, which separates the two channels, shoal to less than 5m and seas may break even in low swell. As the greatest danger to a well-navigated yacht is probably from shipping, the northern route on 105° (or a back bearing of 285° on Santa Marta and Guia lights, see plan page 168) may be the best choice, particularly in poor visibility if not equipped with radar. At night however, shore lights tend to hide fishing boats which often display inadequate navigation lights or sometimes none at all.

If approaching from offshore or from the south the Barra Sul will be more direct, joining near Fairway Buoy No.2 (⊕130) and following the leading line on 047°. It is also the safest route if any swell is running. Note, however, that shipping may approach from any direction, joining the Barra Sul well inside Fairway Buoy No.2 or crossing en route to the designated ship anchorage which lies directly between Fairway Buoy No.2 and Cascais. Tidal streams in the Barra Sul can attain 3 knots at springs – more on the ebb after heavy rain – creating heavy seas during strong southwesterlies.

Entrance

The Rio Tejo is entered between Punta de Lage (Fort de São Julião) on the northern shore and Fort Bugio to the southeast, and yachts are advised to remain on or slightly north of the leading line as traffic dictates (⊕133) until well up to Gibalta before turning upriver. Tidal streams reach 2 or 3 knots either way at springs, not always running parallel to the shore, but are somewhat less powerful near the northern bank. This should be given an offing of at least 300m until the unmistakable Tôrre de Belém has been passed, but beyond that can be approached within 100m in good depths. The Ponte 25 de Abril suspension bridge has a clearance of 70m – unlikely to worry any yacht! – but spare a glance for the towering statue of Christ near its southern end.

Forte Bugio, on the south side of the mouth of the Rio Tejo. Not very long ago it was surrounded by drying banks at all states of the tide

Looking northeast into the wide mouth of the Rio Tejo. The new marina at Oeiras can be seen on the left and Forte Bugio and its associated shoals at right of centre

48. Oeiras

Waypoints
⊕133 – 38°40'.05N 9°18'.9W (Rio Tejo entrance)
⊕134 – 38°40'.6N 9°18'.76W (Oeiras entrance)

Courses and distances
⊕130 (Rio Tejo Fairway Buoy No.2) – ⊕133 = 4.6M, 052° or 332°
⊕132 (Cascais) – ⊕133 = 4.9M, 109° or 289°
⊕133 – ⊕134 = 0.6 M, 011° or 191°

Tides
Standard port Lisbon
Mean time differences
HW –0020 ±0500; LW –0005 ±0500
Heights in metres

MHWS	MHWN	MLWN	MLWS
3.7	2.9	1.4	0.6

Charts

	Approach
Admiralty	3635, 3220
Imray	C19, C49
Portuguese	(26406), 26303

Principal lights
2126.2 **South breakwater** Fl.R.3s9m5M
White tower, red bands, 5m
2126.25 **North mole** Fl.G.3s9m5M
White tower, green bands, 4m
North inner spur Fl(2)4s Green post 3m

Night entry
Feasible with care in light weather, but best avoided in stronger onshore winds

Harbour communications
Puerto de Recreio Oeiras ☎ 214 401510,
Fax 214 401515, *Email* precreio@oeirasviva.pt,
www.oeirasviva.pt
VHF Ch 09

Looking west over the new marina at Oeiras before the pontoons were installed with, from front to rear, Ponta da Lage dominated by the Forte de São Julião, Ponta da Rana, and the wide Baía de Cascais

Brand new marina close west of Lisbon

After more than five years in the building, the Puerto de Recreio Oeiras officially opened in September 2005. Some of the shoreside infrastructure was still under construction when visited the following February, but all was expected to be in place for the 2006 season.

While for many the chief attraction of Oeiras will undoubtedly be its proximity to Lisbon – door to door in 40 minutes or so, less if taxi-ing to the station – the marina is flanked by an outstanding beach and large sports complex including swimming pools, the old town centre is pleasant, and there are several attractions in the vicinity including the palace of Sebastião José de Carvalho e Melo, later Marquês de Pombal.

Approach

For outer approaches see The Rio Tejo estuary, pages 168/9, and pages 174/5.

If coastal sailing from Cascais, no more than 5M to the west, the Barra Norte (or Pequena) is the logical choice – see plan page 168. Either continue until ⊕133 is reached before turning onto 011° for 0.6M or, after rounding Punta de Lage and the prominent Fort de São Julião, steer by eye until the marina entrance is open before rounding to port.

Entrance

The marina entrance is narrow with a pronounced dog-leg – difficult for less manoeuvrable yachts and almost impossible under sail other than for the very skilled. The (well-fendered) reception/fuel berth is starboard-to on the west side of the north inner spur. At least 5m will be found in the entrance and 4m at the reception berth.

The inner spur, it should be said, appears almost 100% efficient in preventing surge entering the marina, even in established easterlies.

Berthing

A marina official will often meet a yacht at the reception berth, otherwise walk up to the office near the root of the spur. It shares premises with a helpful turismo desk and is nominally open 24 hours per day – though only 0800–2200 in summer and 0800–1800 in winter are guaranteed, with security staff on duty at other times. All personnel speak some English, with those in the office near fluent. Security is via the usual card-operated gates – if arriving after hours be sure to leave someone inside to operate the gate (via a button 10m or so down the walkway) if no official is to be found.

Visitors are normally berthed on the westernmost two of the six pontoons, with larger yachts near the root of the north inner spur. Twenty-three of the 274 slots are reserved for visitors (defined as a stay of less than 30 days), all able to accommodate 10m or more overall in a minimum of 2m. Four of the nine berths able to take yachts of 15–20m are also currently reserved for visitors. All berths are alongside finger pontoons.

In both 2005 and 2006 the high season (May to September) rate for a visiting yacht of 10–12m was €30.94 per night, rising to €46.41 for 12–15m, inclusive of electricity and water (including showers). In the low season this dropped to €19.04 per night (€404.60 per month) for 10–12m or €29.75 per night (€606.90 per month) for 12–15m. Though quoted by the marina ex-IVA – the equivalent of VAT – this has been added to the figures above for easy comparison with other harbours. Multihulls paid a surcharge of between 50% and 100%, according to beam. Most major credit cards are accepted, including VISA and MasterCard.

Formalities

All formalities are handled in the marina office, whose staff pass copies of the usual multipart form to the local *GNR–Brigada Fiscal*, *Polícia Marítima* and *Alfândega* (who may eventually open offices in the building). Should any officials wish to visit the yacht – most probable if either boat or crew are of non-EU origin – it is their responsibility to make the first move.

Facilities

The Puerto de Recreio Oeiras does not aspire to provide shoreside facilities for a yacht with serious problems, but these are near at hand in Cascais, Lisbon and Seixal.
Boatyard/travel-lift Not anticipated.
Engineers/electronics Contractors are expected to move on site during 2006.
Chandlery Anticipated for the 2006 season. Otherwise Lisbon's excellent chandleries are close at hand.
Water On the pontoons.
Showers In the reception block, with further toilets by the shops and cafés.
Launderette To be operational for the 2006 season.
Electricity On the pontoons.
Fuel Diesel and petrol at the reception berth, nominally 24 hours per day. Credit cards are accepted.
Bottled gas Nothing nearby, though check at the chandlery.
Weather forecast Posted daily at the marina office.

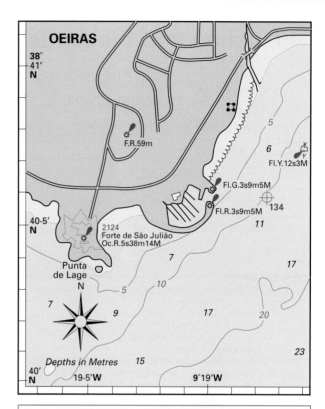

⊕133 38°40′.05N 9°18′.9W   Rio Tejo entrance
⊕134 38°40′.6N   9°18′.76W Oeiras entrance

Banks In the town, about 20 minutes on foot.
Shops/provisioning A small general store is to open in the marina complex during 2006.
Cafés, restaurants and hotels Several cafés and restaurants are anticipated for the marina complex, and there are numerous hotels nearby. Overlooking the beach west of the marina is the unusual Carruagem Bar in an old (and very plush) railway carriage.
Medical services First aid centre in the sports complex, with full services in the town.

Communications

Post office In the town centre, about 20 minutes on foot.
Mailing address The marina office will hold mail for visiting yachts – c/o Puerto de Recreio de Oeiras, Empresa Municipal OeirasViva EM, Estrada Marginal – Praia da Torre, 2780-267 Oeiras, Portugal. It is important that the envelope carries the name of the yacht in addition to that of the addressee.
Internet access There is a single (but fast) terminal at the tourist desk in the marina office, which visitors can use without charge for up to 20 minutes. Idenfication is required. Wireless broadband is available throughout the marina, but there is no shoreside phone socket through which laptops can be connected.
Public telephones In the sports complex.
Fax service At the marina office, Fax 214 401515.
Car hire/taxis Can be arranged via the marina office.
Trains Frequent (and cheap) trains to Lisbon's Cais do Sodré station, close to the city centre. Closest station is Santo Amaro, about 15 minutes on foot – Oeiras station is a little further. Walk east beside the beach, crossing the busy road via the underpass, and the station is 100m or so north. The journey takes about 20 minutes.
Air services Lisbon International Airport is less than an hour away by train and taxi.

PORTUGAL – THE WEST COAST

ATLANTIC SPAIN AND PORTUGAL   **177**

49. Lisbon and the Rio Tejo

Waypoints
⊕133 – 38°40′.05N 9°18′.9W (Rio Tejo entrance)

Courses and distances
⊕130 (Rio Tejo Fairway Buoy No.2) – ⊕133 = 4.6M,
052° or 332°
⊕132 (Cascais) – ⊕133 = 4.9M, 109° or 289°

Tides
Standard port Lisbon
Heights in metres

MHWS	MHWN	MLWN	MLWS
3.8	3.0	1.4	0.5

Or refer to EasyTide at www.ukho.gov.uk (see page 2)

Charts

	Entrance	*River*
Admiralty	3220	3221, 3222
Imray	C49	C49
Portuguese	(26406), 26303, 26304,	(26406), 26305,
		26306, 26307

Principal lights
2127.4 **VTS Algés** Fl(2)R.5s6m7M
    Red post, white bands 2m
2127.4 **Doca de Pedroucos, west mole**
    Fl.R.6s12m2M Metal mast 7m
2127.6 **Doca de Pedroucos, east mole**
    F.G.12m4M Metal mast 7m
Note Although some publications give light details for
both the Doca do Bom Sucesso and the Doca de Belém,
neither have had functional lights for some years
2130.4/5 **Ponte 25 de Abril, north pillar**
NW and NE sides Fl(3)G.9s7m6M
    Green column, ▲ topmark, 2m
SW and SE sides Fl(3)R.9s7m6M Horn (2)25s
    Red column, ■ topmark, 2m
Top Fl.R.10s189m Summit of pillar
2130.6/7 **Ponte 25 de Abril, south pillar**
NW and NE sides Fl(3)G.9s7m6M Horn 25s
    Green column ▲ topmark, 2m
SW and SE sides Fl(3)R.9s7m6M
    Red column, ■ topmark, 2m
Top Iso.R.2s189m Summit of pillar

Both pillars NW and SW lights 000°-vis-180°
    NE and SE lights: 180°-vis-000°
2132 **Doca da Marinha, W side** F.R.10m2M Post 7m
2132.2 **Doca da Marinha, E side** F.G.10m2M Post 7m
2136.1 **Seixal, north bank** Fl.G.3s7m5M Green column 5m
2136 **Seixal, south pillar** Fl.R.3s5m6M
    Red and white pillar on concrete plinth 2m
Plus many other lights throughout the harbour and
further upriver

Night entry
Probably best avoided if new to the area, though
perfectly feasible in all normal conditions. Tides run
strongly at springs

Harbour communications
Lisboa Port Control ☎ 213 922026 (for leisure craft
berthing instructions) *Fax* 213 922028
Email admin.junqueira@porto-do-lisboa.pt
porto-de-lisboa.pt*
VHF Ch 12, 14, 16, 68, 74 (call Lisbon Control) (24 hours)
Administração do Porto de Lisboa ☎ 213 611000
Fax 213 611005
Email Ecardoso@portodelisboa.pt
www.portodelisboa.com *(the same site as the above,
in Portuguese only, and mainly about the commercial
port)
VHF Ch 12 (0900–1300, 1400–1800 daily)
Tagus Yacht Center – see Seixal, page 186
Marinas
Doca de Bom Sucesso ☎ 213 013027 *Fax* 213 020092
Email doca.bomsucesso@porto-de-lisboa.pt
Doca de Belém ☎ 213 631246 Fax 213 624578
Email doca.belem@porto-de-lisboa.pt
Doca de Santo Amaro ☎ 213 922011 *Fax* 213 922038,
Email doca.stamaro@porto-de-lisboa.pt
Doca de Alcântara ☎ 213 922048 *Fax* 213 922085
Email doca.alcantara@porto-de-lisboa.pt
A little surprisingly, the individual marinas are not
equipped with VHF
Pedestrian bridge *Ponte Movél*, Doca de Alcântara VHF
Ch 68.

A historic capital city with good (though crowded) facilities for yachts

A capital city remarkable for its slightly dilapidated
beauty and the reverberations of its maritime past –
its people, its way of life and its architecture all show
influences far removed from Europe. In medieval
times it was one of Europe's busiest ports, tracing its
roots back to the Romans and very probably the
Phoenicians. Much of the city was rebuilt after a
serious earthquake and fire in November 1755 in
which more than 40,000 people died.

Amidst enough sights to occupy a month, perhaps
the most memorable are the Belém area to the west
of the city, which includes the fairytale Tôrre de
Belém and the Museu de Marinha (maritime
museum) housed in the western wing of the
impressive Mosterio dos Jerónimos, and the old
Alfama district on its hill to the east, dominated by
the Moorish Castelo de São Jorge. A guidebook is
almost a necessity.

In a guide for yachtsmen the Museu de Marinha,
housed in the west wing of Belém's spectacular
Mosterio dos Jerónimos, deserves special mention.
Its model collection is particularly fascinating,
covering traditional sailing craft as well as yachts

and naval vessels. There is also a comprehensive
collection of navigational instruments and much
attention to Portugal's great age of maritime
discoveries. In the western hall an assortment of
royal barges, sailing dinghies and seaplanes are on
display – with all descriptive labels in English as well
as Portuguese. Allow three hours minimum. The
museum is open 1000–1800 in summer and
1000–1700 in winter, the latter starting Tuesday of
the week which includes 1 October. All public
buildings in the Belém area are closed on Mondays.

Tôrre de Belém, built to command the mouth of the Rio Tejo

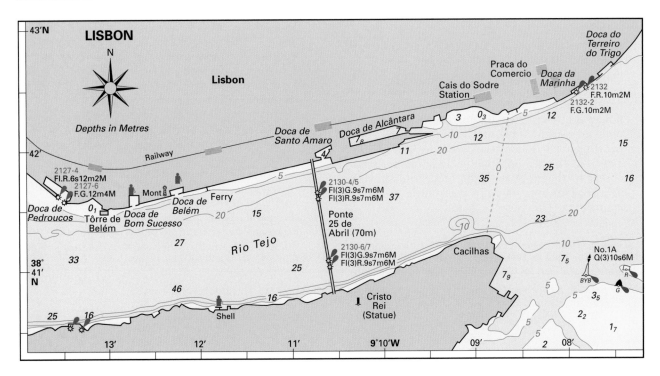

Berthing

At the end of 2005 there were four operational marinas in Lisbon, all on the north bank of the Rio Tejo. Two lie between the Tôrre de Belém and the Ponte 25 de Abril and two immediately above the bridge. All are run by the Administração do Porto de Lisboa (APL) and thus share characteristics such as good security with card-operated access gates, and similar working hours and price structure. All are popular with local yachtsmen, but space for a visitor can usually be found somewhere though it is strongly advised to make contact before arrival – apart from other considerations, none of the marinas have reception pontoons. Standard office hours are 0900–1300 and 1400–1800 daily throughout the year. Fluent English is spoken at both the main office at the Doca de Santo Amaro and at the individual marina offices.

In 2005 the overnight APL rate for a visiting yacht of 10–12m at any time of year was €24.10 per night or €340.70 per calendar month, rising to €37.14 per night or €529.16 per calendar month for 12–15m, inclusive of water, showers and electricity. Though prices are quoted ex-IVA, this has been added to the above figures for easy comparison with other harbours. Some credit and debit cards are accepted, but not all – check the current situation on arrival.

Note that the current in the river runs swiftly and that, with the possible exception of the Doca de Alcântara, all the marina basins can have awkward crosscurrents at the entrance. Not only will these set the yacht sideways – they may also tend to slew her round during those seconds when the bow is in the stationary water of the entrance and the stern still in the moving river.

Formalities

At the Administração do Porto de Lisboa marinas it is only necessary to complete a standard form at the office, copies of which are distributed to the *GNR–Brigada Fiscal*, *Polícia Marítima* and *Alfândega* (customs). Whether any or all chose to visit will be based on the yacht and crew's nationalities and her last port of call.

Fountains, gardens and historic architecture – in this case the 16th century Mosterio dos Jerónimos – are amongst the things that Portugal does supremely well   *AH*

Marinas

1. **Doca do Bom Sucesso** – a short distance upstream from the (floodlit) Tôrre de Belém. Once the marina to which foreign yachts were directed, it is now crowded with local yachts and unlikely to have space for a visitor unless a long-term berth-holder is known to be absent. The 163 berths (all with finger pontoons) are limited to 12m LOA, but dredging has increased depths to 3.5m. Fuel is available, the fuel pontoon being in the northeast corner of the basin with the office and showers nearby. However there is very little room to manoeuvre. The entrance is unlit.

Looking upstream towards the Ponte de 25 Abril bridge from near the Doca de Belém, with the statue of Christ on its towering plinth at far right   *AH*

2. **Doca de Belém** – 700m east of the Doca do Bom Sucesso and immediately beyond the prominent Padrão dos Descobrimentos (Monument to the Discoveries) which resembles a ship's prow. Contrary to what is shown on Admiralty 3221 the entrance is not lit.

Again the 194 berths are reserved for residents and, as in the Doca do Bom Sucesso, there is unlikely to be room for a visiting yacht except on a very temporary basis. Previously rather shallow, dredging has now ensured depths of at least 3m throughout. The marina office lies at the northeast corner of the basin with showers etc in the same block, both adjacent to a thriving boatyard (see *Facilities*, below). A welcome and imaginative touch, when new workshops were being built for boatyard contractors, was to place a café/restaurant on their roofs ensuring both cool breezes and interesting views.

Lisbon's Doca de Belém and Doca do Bom Sucesso looking a little north of west, with the Padrão dos Descobrimentos (Monument to the Discoveries) prominent in the centre. At far right is the Mosterio dos Jerónimos, which houses the extensive Museu de Marinha (maritime museum). Jutting out to sea at far left is the fairytale Tôrre de Belém

3. **Doca de Santo Amaro** – 150m beyond the suspension bridge and dredged to a nominal 4m, though reported to carry considerably less than this over a very soft bottom. Second largest of the four with 388 berths all equipped with finger pontoons, it is nevertheless crowded with local craft though a visiting yacht can sometimes be squeezed in. The entrance is narrow and unlit, but there is a convenient pontoon just inside on the port hand (though short on mooring cleats as it is not technically a reception pontoon but the property of the local rowing club). The marina office, labelled APL Docas de Recreio, is at the northeast end of the basin at the east end of the row of cafés and restaurants.

The only real drawback to the Doca de Santo Amaro – should space be available at all – is that it is not quiet. Traffic passing over the bridge sounds like a swarm of bees and could become irritating in time, but more importantly the area has become a popular centre for Lisbon nightlife with the bars and restaurants overlooking the basin remaining lively until 0400 or beyond. Of course more energetic crews may well consider this a plus . . .

The Doca de Santo Amaro close east of the Ponte de 25 Abril suspension bridge

Entry to the Doca de Alcântara is through a relatively narrow passage crossed by a pedestrian bridge. In the background is the long approach to the Ponte de 25 Abril bridge

PORTUGAL – THE WEST COAST

4. **Doca de Alcântara** – is a much larger basin than any of the others, entered about 1M upstream of the suspension bridge via an entry channel which, rather surprisingly, is not lit. A pedestrian bridge – or *Ponte Móvel* – crosses the entrance, reinstated late in 2005 after at least six years out of commission. It is normally left open, closing being signalled by lights and a horn. The control booth (when manned) operates on VHF Ch 68. The bridge is positioned well inside the entrance proper, and though a waiting pontoon is not provided there are normally plenty of moored vessels alongside which a yacht could lie for a short time.

Until a decade or so ago the Doca de Alcântara was purely commercial with yachts admitted only on sufferance. It is still used by the occasional trawler or other small commercial vessel and for this reason can sometimes be oily. Originally concentrated at the west end of the 0.5M long basin, the marina has now grown to 442 berths on ten pontoons and is said to have spread as far east as it can. It is the most likely spot for a visiting yacht to find space, though creative berthing solutions are sometimes necessary. Space is most likely to be at a premium in the early autumn, when many visitors are passing through yet long-term berth-holders are also present – in summer many of the latter are away cruising. Yachts of up to 30m can normally be berthed in the basin, probably alongside the wall, but the seriously large are expected to stay outside and will be treated as the ships they are. Depths throughout the entire basin are considerable.

The marina office and related services are situated about half way along the marina on the north side inside a gated compound, for which a security code is needed, and which provides the only access to the pontoons.

Problems with metal debris blown down off the Ponte 25 de Abril have occasionally been reported in westerly winds. The bridge – including the roadway – is constructed entirely of steel, meaning that even the smallest fragment swiftly turns to rust. In these conditions boat-proud owners may wish to hose down daily.

The long, narrow Doca de Alcântara from slightly west of south. It is by far the most likely place for a visitor to locate a berth

The surroundings to the Doca de Alcântara are still in transit from their commercial past as warehouses to new uses as shops, offices, restaurants and nightclubs, with the attendant and inevitable noise. However, unlike the Doca de Santo Amaro where wooden decking literally overhangs the marina, the Doca de Alcântara has a relatively wide paved area between buildings and basin. All the better for outdoor tables, of course . . .

The restored Portuguese East Indiaman *D Fernando II e Glória* (see page 149), is permanently berthed in the basin and is open to the public. In addition APORVELA, the Associação Portuguesa de Treino de Vela (sail training association), are in the process of moving from their old home at the Doca do Terreiro do Trigo and already keep several of their recreated caravels in the basin. It is possible that a small maritime museum will soon be added to the attractions.

The dome of the church of São Miguel seen over the rooms of the ancient Alfama district   *AH*

Berthing – past and future

Just a few years ago there were six marinas on the north bank of the Rio Tejo, all in old, stone-walled basins. The fifth marina, the Doca do Terreiro do Trigo, until recently the domain of the Portuguese sail training association APORVELA, has been effectively unusable for at least five years due to silting and is now back in the control of the Administração do Porto de Lisboa (APL). Rather than maintaining it as a marina, which would entail repeated dredging, it is likely to be put back into use for tugs and other vessels whose propeller wash will keep the basin clear – as the original designer apparently intended.

The short-lived sixth marina – the much-vaunted MarinaExpo, close to the site of Lisbon's very well organised Expo 98 – did not enjoy the protection of solid dock walls and was bedevilled from the start by major silting problems. When winter gales damaged the pontoons the marina had to be vacated in haste and has never reopened. Argument has raged for the past five years as to whether it should be reopened, though the estimated cost of €25 million cannot help. The Associação Náutica da Marina do Parque das Nações runs a detailed website at www.anmpn.pt – but without, unfortunately, an English version.

Other undated 'projects' are for a large marina in the river-mouth southeast of Esteiro lighthouse and the Boa Viagem beacon, in the vicinity of 38°42′N 9°15′W, and an equally large facility on the south shore of the river, somewhere east of the Ponte 25 de Abril suspension bridge. However neither have got beyond the planning stage – aptly described by one Portuguese official as the 'dreaming' stage – and are unlikely to come on-stream before the end of the decade, if at all.

The piles and surrounding walls of the ill-fated MarinaExpo, currently closed to yachts while arguments rage as to whether it can ever be reopened

Anchorages

There is no yacht anchorage convenient to Lisbon itself, though there are a number of possibilities further upriver where it widens into the Mar de Palha (literally 'Sea of Straw', or reeds). Large-scale Portuguese charts or electronic charts will be required for this area. The main channel of the Rio Tejo runs past the ferry landings, container terminal and commercial docks, is well buoyed and carries 5m to beyond the impressive Vasco da Gama motorway bridge.

For Seixal and Canal do Montijo see page 186.

The 17km Ponte Vasco de Gama, which opened to traffic in 1998 and is effectively the head of navigation for most yachts

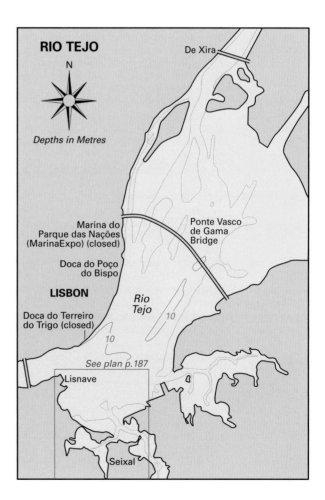

PORTUGAL – THE WEST COAST

Facilities

Many harbours have their 'Mr Fixit', in this case a gentleman known as Carlos, mobile 91 9868 807, has been consistently recommended as able to either handle or at least advise on almost anything. A yachtsman himself, he is well aware of what visitors may need. Carlos speaks several languages including fluent English.

Boatyard Next to the Doca de Belém and administered by APL, with all work carried out by sub-contractors who have to satisfy APL of their competence. There is a large area of secure hard-standing where owners can, if they wish, do their own work and are generally permitted to live on board while the boat is ashore (though this must be confirmed with APL on an individual basis). It would also be a possible venue for winter lay-up.

If professional services are required the best place to start is undoubtedly Técniates Yacht Services, ☎ 213 623362/649147 *Fax* 213 623367 *Email* tecniates.volvo @mail.sapo.pt www.tecniates.com (in Portuguese only), who have premises near the east end of the row of office/workshops and have been highly praised by more than one visiting skipper. As well as being an agent for Volvo Penta they can also handle repairs in GRP and timber, painting, osmosis treatment etc. Where a job is outside their sphere they can generally recommend a suitable contractor. Good English is spoken.

For details of the well-equipped Tagus Yacht Center near Seixal on the south bank of the Rio Tejo, see page 186.

Travel-lift The 20-tonne capacity lift at the Doca de Belém is operated by Técniates Yacht Services (see above) though owned by APL, and bookings must be made at the marina office. Due to depth restrictions it can operate only about six hours in twelve, but urgent cases are given priority. Yachts are generally placed in cradles backed up by additional props.

A 70-tonne capacity hoist with about 7m width, operable at all states of the tide, is to be found at the Tagus Yacht Center – see page 186.

Engineers Técniates Yacht Services at the Doca de Belém (see above) are Volvo Penta agents/engineers and may be willing to tackle more general problems. Otherwise they will advise who best to contact. See also Tagus Yacht Center, page 186.

Electronic and radio repairs NautiRadar Lda, ☎ 213 005050 *Fax* 21 3005059 *Email* tecnica@nautiradar.pt www.nautiradar.pt (in Portuguese only), at Gare Marítima da Rocha, Rocha Conde de Óbidos, 1350–352 Lisboa, sell and repair radar, autopilots, GPS, generators etc and stock both whole units and spares for all the familiar names including Raytheon, Garmin, Mastervolt etc. Open 0900–1300 and 1400–1800 weekdays, closed weekends. They are to be found on the south side of the Doca de Alcântara close to its eastern end and so quite a long walk, though a courtesy bus runs a shuttle service as far as the passenger terminal. They are willing to visit yachts in Cascais as well as in any of the Lisbon marinas, and can generally respond within 24 hours. See also Tagus Yacht Center, page 186.

Dimofel, on the first floor at Avenida de Liberdade 85, has been recommended as selling a good range of electronic components, with other shops in Rua São Jose, a block to the east.

Sailmaker/sail repairs Vela-Rio ☎/*Fax* 212 155994, at Rua D João de Castro, 15-B Santo André, 2830-186 Barreiro, Lisboa, makes and repairs sails and will also handle general canvaswork such as sprayhoods and awnings. The owner, Antonio Martines, speaks good English.

Chandleries Lisbon is well served for chandleries, with five in the Doca de Alcântara/Cais do Sodré area alone. All are short on display space with much more stock in store, so if you don't see what you want it is well worth asking – good English is spoken in all five. Listed alphabetically they are:

Azimute Lda ☎ 213 920730 *Fax* 213 974494 *Email* azimute@azimuteam.pt www.azimuteam.pt at Avenida Gomes de Araújo 11–A, Edifício Bartolomeu Dias, Doca de Alcântara, 1350-355 Lisboa, on the south side of the Doca de Alcântara at its eastern end and so quite a long walk, though a courtesy bus runs a shuttle service as far as the passenger terminal. Their extensive stock ranging from anchors right through to weatherproof matches. Open are 0900–1230 and 1400–1800 weekdays, irregular hours on Saturday. (From 2006 it would be worth checking to see whether a planned move to more convenient premises near the northwest end of the basin has taken place.)

J Garraio & Ca Lda ☎ 213 473081 *Fax* 213 428950 *Email* info@jgarraio.pt www.jgarraio.pt opposite the Cais do Sodré station at Avenida 24 de Julho 2–1°, 1200–478 Lisboa, open 0900–1230 and 1400–1900 weekdays, 0900–1230 Saturday. Particularly strong on pilot books in both Portuguese and English, but also with some general stock.

Luíz Godinho Lda ☎ 213 421001 *Fax* 213 016 658 *Email* luizgodinho@iol.pt (note 'iol' not 'aol'), at Avenida 24 de Julho 1 F/G, 1200–478 Lisboa (in the next block to J Garraio), open 0900–1900 weekdays, 0900–1300 Saturday. A conventional yacht chandler with good stocks of rope, chain, rigging wire and terminals (plus a swage machine) and other hardware, but few electronics and no books.

Marítima ☎ 213 979598 *Fax* 213 979 572 *Email* raul@maritimaonline.com at Doca de Santo Amaro, 1350–353 Lisboa (at the west end of the Doca de Santo Amaro, right under the suspension bridge), open 1000–1930 Monday to Saturday, with a good range of clothing and boots, as well as hardware (including windlasses), teak fittings, paint, rope and galleyware.

NautiStar Lda ☎ 213 941144/5 *Fax* 213 941143 *Email* info@nautistar.pt www.nautistar.pt, at Galerias Gonçalves Zarco 6, Doca de Alcântara, 1350–049 Lisboa, overlooking the marina from the north. Advertised hours are 1000–1800 Monday to Saturday, but it is often open much later. The Lisbon branch (there is also one at Cascais) is quite small and has limited stock on site, but the helpful staff will order from an impressive stack of catalogues. Good English is spoken.

Finally, sharing the Associação Naval de Lisboa clubhouse at the Doca de Belém is the tiny GeoNáutica ☎ 213 618761 *Email* geonautica@ geonautica.pt open 1300–1700 weekdays, 1000–1500 weekends, which appears to specialise in clothing, including oilskins and boots.

General hardware Rua da Boavista, which runs behind the main produce market, contains a number of small hardware shops and is a good bet for non-standard items. In particular, plugs for the Doca de Alcântara electricity supply are available there.

Charts Surprisingly, only two companies on the Atlantic coast of Portugal are licensed to sell Portuguese charts – Azimute Lda and J Garraio & Ca Lda – see above for locations. It may be worth noting that, whilst Admiralty charts are not cheap, Portuguese charts are even more expensive, even when bought in Lisbon (though there is some variation based on size and publication date) and are unlikely to be corrected to date. Charts can no longer be purchased directly from the Instituto Hidrográfico.

Liferaft servicing Both Azimute and NautiStar can arrange for servicing of most makes. Alternatively contact Orey-Técnica Naval e Industrial Lda ☎ 213 610890 *Fax* 213 640144 *Email* orey-tecnica@orey-tecnica.pt, at Rua María Isabel Saint-Léger 20, 1300-442 Lisboa, who supply and service liferafts as well as other safety equipment including flares, lifebuoys etc.

Water On the pontoons in all the marinas.

Showers At all the marinas, though in busy periods the six provided at the Doca de Alcântara are hardly adequate for its size.

Launderette No machines at any of the marinas, but many in the surrounding city. Alternatively NautiStar Lda can arrange for laundry to be done, but check the price first.

Electricity On the pontoons in all the marinas.

Fuel Diesel and petrol pumps at both the Doca do Bom Sucesso and the Doca de Belém (the latter is more accessible, with depths of at least 3m), operational during office hours (0900–1300 and 1400–1800 daily). In summer they may stay open later, but this should be confirmed beforehand. Credit cards including VISA are accepted.

Bottled gas Camping Gaz exchanges at Marítima (see above) and elsewhere. Butane and propane refills can be organised by NautiStar (see above) as well as by Carlos (see head of section), who can also arrange for diving bottles to be recharged.

Clube naval The Associação Naval de Lisboa has premises next to the Doca de Belém, where visiting yachtsmen are made welcome.

Weather forecast Posted daily at all the marina offices.

Banks All over Lisbon, almost invariably with at least one cash dispenser outside. Banks are normally open 0830–1200 and 1345–1430, weekdays only.

Shops/provisioning Absolutely everything available, as befits a capital city. Most convenient for provisioning if in the Doca de Santo Amaro/Alcântara complex is the large Pingo Doce supermarket reached via a pedestrian tunnel under the road and railway (ask at the marina office for directions).

Produce market Impressive, air-conditioned produce market almost opposite the Cais do Sodré station east of the Doca de Alcântara (and thus very close to the Garraio and Godinho chandleries), open 0600–1400 and 1500–1900. A vast area of fruit and vegetables is surrounded by flowers, eggs, meat and fish – all meticulously clean and with much ice in evidence. The large, two-storey building is decorated with beautiful azulejos (painted tiles) and surmounted by a distinctive dome, and is well worth a visit even if not buying.

Cafés, restaurants and hotels Many and varied, at all prices. Some bars and restaurants feature live fado singing.

Medical services If berthed in an APL marina one has access to the Administração do Porto de Lisboa's own Medical Centre, close to the Doca de Santo Amaro/Alcântara complex. More extensive medical services of all kinds are available in the city.

Communications

Post office Large post office just west of the Praça Comerçio, plus many others.

Mailing address Mail for a yacht hoping to stay in one of APL's marinas is best sent to the head office: Administração do Porto de Lisboa, Nautica de Recreio, Doca de Santo Amaro, 1399–012 Lisboa, Portugal. It is important that the envelope carries the name of the yacht in addition to that of the addressee.

Internet access Many possibilities throughout the city – the Tourist Office on Praça dos Restauradores can supply a current list. As of 2005 those closest to the Doca de Santo Amaro/Alcântara complex were Espaço Agora at Rua da Cintura do Porto de Lisboa, Armazém 1 Naves 3–5, open 0900–0330 Monday–Saturday, 0900–2200 Sunday; and Hiper Net in the Fundação das Comunicações (Communications Museum) at 22 Rua D Luis I, open 1000–1230 and 1400–1730 weekdays, closed weekends and holidays. The useful online Lisbon Guide at www. lisbon-guide.info also carries a listing in its Essential Information section.

Public telephones Kiosks handy to all marinas, plus many throughout the city.

Fax service At the APL marinas, *Fax* 213 922038 (actually the head office's number, but the best initial bet).

Car hire Many companies in the city, though APL receive a discount from AVIS which they passed on to the hirer. But be warned – the normally easygoing Portuguese appear to suffer a character change behind the wheel, and some city driving is manic. At the very least, pay the extra charge for collision damage waiver.

Taxis No shortage. Taxis can generally be ordered via the marina office.

Buses/trams The city's well-organised bus and tram service is particularly useful near the waterfront, linking all four marinas with the city centre. A ride in one of the small, pre-war trams is a Lisbon 'must', and most visitors also enjoy the various 'elevadors' which give access to the city's different levels. For the Doca de Santo Amaro/Alcântara complex take the E15 or E18 tram from the Praça Comerçio, getting off at Infante Santo and walking over the brightly painted footbridge.

Tickets covering travel by bus, tram, elevador and metro (see below) can be bought individually, by the day, or for longer periods, the latter often representing a considerable saving.

Trains and Metro Regular and frequent rail service from the Cais do Sodré station to Cascais and other points west. Most other trains depart from Rossio station at the south end of the Avenida da Liberdade. Both stations are notorious for pickpockets and other non-violent crime – be warned!

Lisbon's *metro* was given a facelift for the 1998 Expo, making it the quickest way to reach city destinations away from the waterfront. However finding a city centre station can be a real challenge – they tend to be very poorly signed.

Ferries Frequent ferries across the Rio Tejo to Cacilhas, from which one can get a bus up to the prominent statue of Christ near the south end of the 25 de Abril suspension bridge, as well as to Seixal and Montijo.

Air services International airport in the northeast part of the city, with scheduled flights to all parts of the world.

50. Seixal

38°38′.9N 05°06′W (entrance)
Principal lights
2136.1 **Seixal, north bank** Fl.G.3s7m5M
  Green column, 5m
2136 **Seixal, south pillar** Fl.R.3s5m6M
  Red and white pillar on concrete plinth 2m
Harbour communications
  Tagus Yacht Center ☎ 212 276400 *Fax* 212 210097
  Email taguscenter@hotmail.com
  www.tagusyachtcenter.com (note the spelling of
  'center')

Quiet anchorage with impressive, full-service boatyard

There are two main reasons for visiting Seixal. One is to enjoy a peaceful, free anchorage within easy reach (by ferry) of Lisbon; the second is to visit the Tagus Yacht Center, an enterprise which looks set to meet the maintenance needs of all but the very largest cruising yachts.

Approach (Canal do Barreiro)

Round Ponta de Cacilhas, on the south bank of the Rio Tejo 1.5M east of the suspension bridge, and head 150° past the prominent Lisnave shipyard to cross the Canal do Alfeite near buoys No.3AB and No.4AB. Continue down the Canal do Barreiro, which is well buoyed but has quite heavy ferry traffic, some of it at high speeds. Buoy No.13B marks the junction of the Canal do Seixal with the Canal do Barreiro, from which can be seen the relatively narrow entrance to the Canal do Judeu.

The final buoyage may not be not quite as shown on Admiralty 3222, with starboard hand pillar buoy in place of the east cardinal shown. In either case leave it to starboard. At one time a bridge crossed the narrow entrance, and its central support is now occupied by the port-hand light structure. At least 2.5m should be found throughout the approach and entrance.

Anchorage

Anchor opposite the town in 3–4m over sand and mud. Holding is said to be good. The area is surprisingly peaceful despite its proximity to the city and there is relatively little traffic (the ferry berths outside the entrance). There is currently no charge for anchoring.

Facilities

Seixal has an attractive waterfront with a small sandy beach and several sets of steps suitable for dinghy landing. All the usual shops will be found, as well as cafés, restaurants, post office and public telephones. A ferry connects the town with Lisbon's Cais Terreiro do Paço, running every 25 minutes between 0610 and 2330 and taking about 15 minutes for the trip.

Boatyard

Although worth a short visit on its merits alone, Seixal's attraction for yachts is enhanced by the relatively new Tagus Yacht Center. Office hours are normally 0800–1200 and 1300–1700 weekdays only.

Established in 2002 as an offshoot of the Venamar shipyard – the two are headed by brothers Nuno and Rafael Venâncio – Tagus Yacht Center has impressive facilities including a 70-tonne capacity travel hoist with about 7m width, plus a 40-tonne capacity crane, both of which can operate at all states of the tide. A floating dock provides a third option for large yachts and multihulls.

Almost any yacht-related task can be tackled, from straightforward painting to creating unobtainable parts from scratch (for which the shipyard's extensive machine-shop is utilised). Repairs can be carried out in GRP, wood and all types of metal, a large team of engineers have experience of virtually all makes of engine, and electricians and electronics experts can be called in from the shipyard as required.

The yard is reached via a buoyed channel, approximately 40m wide and dredged to carry a minimum of 3m at all times. There is a small waiting pontoon – though most would probably prefer to wait at anchor, as described above – and although the yard expects to handle major work, owners are welcome to carry out other tasks while their boat is ashore and can live aboard if they wish (toilets and showers are provided). There are small shops nearby for daily needs, with a large supermarket a few kilometres away. If coming by land, the 113 bus from the Seixal ferry terminal passes close to the yard.

As a final bonus, the brothers are outstandingly pleasant and helpful and both speak excellent English.

The narrow entrance to the Canal do Judeu at Seixal from the north, seen on a hazy day. The isolated block in the centre – an old bridge support – must be left to port on entry

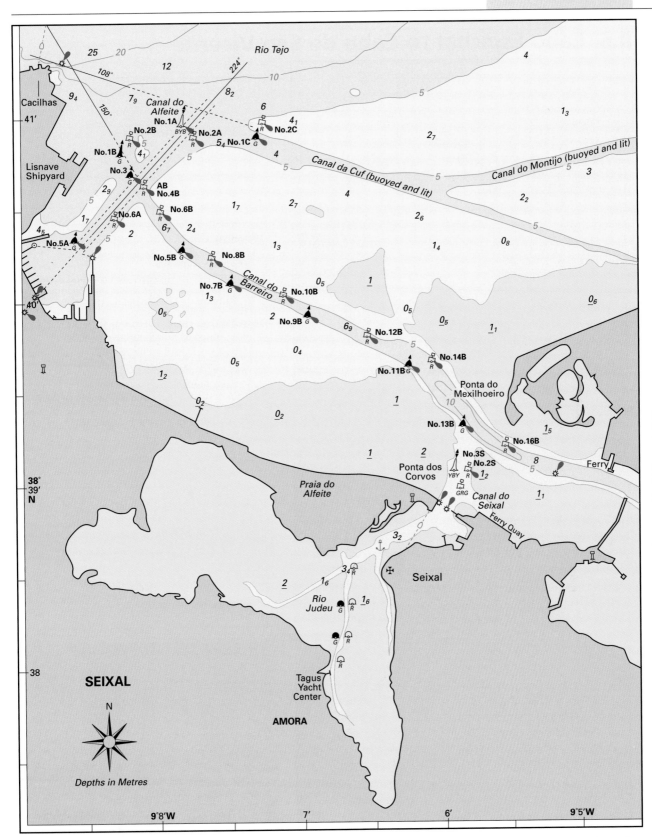

Canal do Montijo anchorages

Round Ponta de Cacilhas and head 108° into the buoyed Canal da CUF (Companhia União Fabril). The Canal do Montijo (also buoyed) leads off at 073° just over 1M from the entrance of the Canal da CUF. At high water it appears to be a large bay, but at low water mud and sandbanks define the channel accurately. The airfield on the low headland to the north is military, and landing is prohibited.

Montijo itself is not particularly attractive and has little room, but there are pleasant anchorages to be found by soundings along the channel or its southern offshoots. A current copy of either Admiralty 3222 or Portuguese 26305 is essential. There are no facilities.

II.5 Cabo Espichel to Cabo de São Vicente

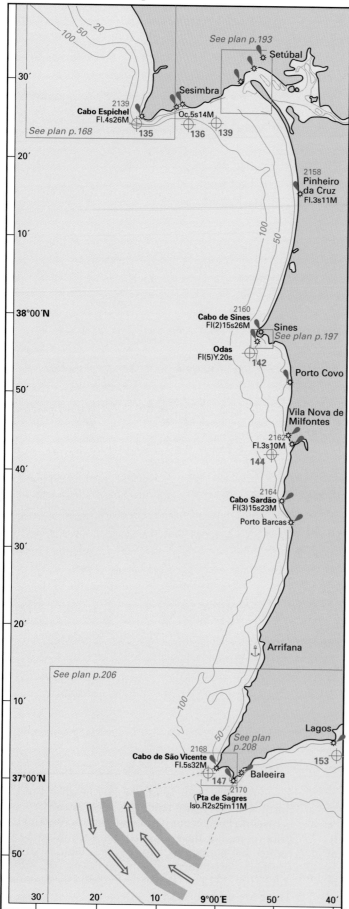

⊕135 38°24′.3N 9°14′.5W 1.2M SW of Cabo Espichel
⊕136 38°24′.4N 9°05′.7W Sesimbra approach
⊕139 38°24′.3N 9°01′.1W Setúbal & the Rio Sado approach
⊕142 37°54′.8N 8°54′.8W Sines approach
⊕144 37°42′.2N 8°50′.5W Vila Nova de Milfontes approach
⊕147 37°01′N   9°00′.7W 1M SW of Cabo de São Vicente
⊕153 37°03′.8N 8°39′.2W 1.1M SE of Ponta da Piedade (Lagos approach)

PRINCIPAL LIGHTS

2139 **Cabo Espichel** Fl.4s167m26M
    Horn 31s 460m SW
    White hexagonal tower and building 32m
2140 **Forte do Cavalo** Oc.5s34m14M Red tower 7m
2158 **Pinheiro da Cruz** Fl.3s66m11M
    White column, red bands
2160 **Cabo de Sines** Fl(2)15s55m26M
    001°-obscd-003° and 004°-obscd-007°
    White tower and building 28m
2162 **Milfontes (Rio Mira)** Fl.3s22m10M
    Turret on white building 5m
2164 **Cabo Sardão** Fl(3)15s67m23M
    Square white tower and red-roofed building 17m
2168 **Cabo de São Vicente** Fl.5s85m32M
    Horn(2)30s
    Off-white tower, red lantern, and building 28m

Ports

51.   Sesimbra*
52.   Setubal*
53.   Sines*
54.   Vila Nova de Milfontes

* Fuel available alongside

One of the few remaining double-ended trading vessels which used to ply the Sado estuary under sail. Most now take tourists on river trips   *AH*

51. Sesimbra

Waypoints
⊕135 – 38°24´.3N 9°14´.5W (1.2M SW of Cabo Espichel)
⊕136 – 38°24´.4N 9°05´.7W (approach)
⊕137 – 38°26´.3N 9°06´.2W (entrance)
⊕138 – 38°28´.6N 8°58´.7W (Portinho de Arrábida anchorage)

Courses and distances
⊕130 (Rio Tejo ⊕airway Buoy No.2) – ⊕136 (via ⊕135) = 21.6M, 151°&089° or 269°&331°
⊕131 (Cascais) – ⊕136 (via ⊕135) = 24.7M, 152°&089° or 269°&332°
⊕136 – ⊕137 = 1.9M, 348° or 168°
⊕136 – ⊕138 = 7M, 053° & by eye or by eye & 133°
⊕136 – ⊕139 (Setubal) = 3.6M, 092° or 272°
⊕136 – ⊕142 (Sines) = 30.8M, 164° or 344°

Tides
Standard port Lisbon
Mean time differences
HW –0035 ±0010; LW –0015 ±0005

Heights in metres

MHWS	MHWN	MLWN	MLWS
3.4	2.6	1.4	0.6

Or refer to EasyTide at www.ukho.gov.uk (see page 2)

Charts

Charts	Approach	Harbour
Admiralty	3635, 3636	
Imray	C19, C49	C49
Portuguese	23203, 24204, 26407	26407

Principal lights
2140 **Forte do Cavalo** Oc.5s34m14M Red tower 7m
2142 **Ldg Lts 003°** *Front* LFl.R.5s9m7M
  Red lantern on SW turret of fortress 10m
2142.1 *Rear* 34m from front LFl.R.5s21m6M
  Red lantern on NW turret of fortress 17m
Note These lights do NOT lead into the harbour but to a point on the shore about 0.5M to the east. Two sets of three lights in line (Fl.R and Fl) close east of Sesimbra mark a submarine cable area and again are NOT leading lights.
2144 **Breakwater** Fl.R.3s12m8M
  White tower, red bands 7m

Night entry
Straightforward in most conditions, though it would be wise to anchor until daylight rather than to attempt berthing alongside.

Harbour communications
Marina de Sesimbra (run by the Clube Naval de Sesimbra) ☎ 212 233451 *Fax* 212 281039
Email secretaria@naval-sesimbra.pt
www.naval-sesimbra.pt (in Portuguese only)
VHF Ch 11, 16, 72 (0900–1200, 1400–1700)

Busy fishing harbour sheltering a small, club-run marina

The town of Sesimbra lies 2km from its harbour, the whole dominated by a large Moorish castle from which there are wonderful views. Its economy is based on fishing and tourism but is also becoming a dormitory for Lisbon, doubtless the reason for the large number of new (and unsightly) buildings springing up on the surrounding hills.

The harbour is very much a working port, with brightly painted fishing boats clustered alongside a newly expanded unloading wharf. It is well protected by a 900m breakwater and, despite having limited space for visiting yachts, makes an interesting port of call for those not overly concerned about a lack of marina comforts.

Sesimbra from the southeast

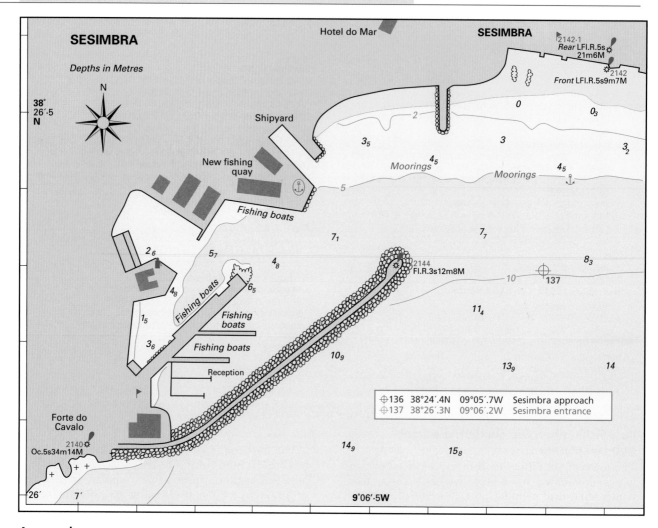

Approach

The major mark from north or south is Cabo Espichel. Forte do Cavalo, 6.5M east of Cabo Espichel, marks the landward end of the outer harbour mole. If coastal sailing, the coast between the two should be given an offing of at least 0.5M and after rounding Cabo Espichel there is still some southing to be made to get round Ponta da Pombeira.

The bluff trending east from Cabo Espichel rises from 160m near the cape to 500m towards Setúbal. Running up the hillside immediately east of Sesimbra are two sets of three lights in line: both sets flash 2.5s front, 3s centre, 3.5s rear, with a range of 2M; the western set on 030° flashes red and the eastern, on 000°, white. They mark submarine cables and anchoring within their limits is prohibited. In addition, three outfalls lie within a 0.5M radius of the breakwater head. Each is marked by a yellow post, × topmark, plus a nearby yellow spherical buoy, also × topmark. The pairs are lit, Fl.Y.8s3M, Fl.Y.6s3M and Fl.Y.4s3M respectively.

From offshore, ⊕136 lies 1.9M south-southeast of the entrance, a course of 348° leading to ⊕137, close outside the harbour mouth.

Entrance

The entrance is straightforward, though it would be unwise to cut the outer molehead too closely in case of fishing vessels exiting at speed.

Berthing

Initially the small (130 berth) marina run by the Clube Naval de Sesimbra was happy to accept visiting yachts, as is clearly stated in their brochure while the hammerhead on the northern of its two pontoons is prominently labelled as a reception berth. However, when visited early in 2005 staff in the Clube Naval de Sesimbra office claimed that the marina was full to capacity with local boats and that short-term visitors were no longer welcome, the minimum period of stay being a month. Whether this will be enforced in practice – particularly if local yachts are away and berths are empty – is uncertain, but if hoping to use the marina it would obviously be wise to make contact before arrival.

Fees are relatively steep, at more than €20 per night for a yacht of 10–12m during the high season, despite the lack of shoreside facilities at the *clube naval's* small premises opposite the entrance to the fishing boat wharves (they also have more formal premises on the seafront near the fort). This lack of facilities may be rectified by the 2006 season, however, as a new and futuristic clubhouse was taking shape at the extreme west end of the harbour, overlooking the marina.

Anchorage

Sesimbra is an extremely busy fishing port and there is nowhere inside the harbour that a visiting yacht can conveniently anchor. Local yachts and smallcraft lie on moorings off the beach between the shipyard and the short east mole, and the only possible anchorage is to the east of them in 5–6m, exposed to the south and southeast. Holding is variable over kelp and rock with sand patches – the excellent sandy beach fronting the harbour and town is at least partially man-made.

Sesimbra has a deserved reputation for strong local northerlies which get up in the late afternoon and die in the small hours – lay ground tackle accordingly.

Formalities

The *Polícia Marítima* have premises on the new fishing wharf and there is a *GNR–Brigada Fiscal* office in the town. In theory it is the skipper's duty to seek them out immediately on arrival, but in view of the walk involved it would be worth checking at the *clube naval* whether this is still considered necessary. Alternatively one or both may come to the yacht.

Facilities

Boatyard Fast Boats Repair Lda ☎ 212 686540 *Email* fastboats@iol.pt www.fboatrepair.com in the Zona Técnica da Marina, Doca de Sesimbra, 2970 Sesimbra, advertise their services for all kinds of maintenance and repair to wood and GRP, including painting and antifouling.
Travel-lift Not as such, though there are several cranes in the fishing quay.
Engineers, mechanics, electronic and radio repairs Available, though more used to working on fishing vessels. Enquire at the *clube naval*.
Water On the pontoons, and from a tap near the fuel pumps.

Showers At the *clube naval*.
Electricity On the pontoons.
Fuel Diesel and petrol are available from pumps on the old fishing quay (see plan) via long hoses. However depths alongside have not been verified and it would be wise to check by dinghy first – in any case, the wall is high and a visit at high water would make good sense.
Bottled gas Camping Gaz exchanges at several hardware stores in the town (a longish walk), but no refills.
Weather forecast Displayed daily outside the *clube naval*.
Clube naval As already noted, the Clube Naval de Sesimbra should be moving into its new premises during 2006.
Banks In the town.
Shops/provisioning/produce market In the town.
Cafés, restaurants and hotels No shortage. Many of the former specialise in seafood, including an outdoor café opposite the new fishing quay.
Medical services In the Sesimbra.

Communications

Post office In the town.
Telephones There does not appear to be a kiosk in the harbour area though there are plenty in the town.
Internet access Several cybercafés in Sesimbra.
Car hire/taxis In the town.
Buses Bus station near the market (about an hour to Lisbon), with minibuses running a frequent service into town from a stop at the root of the fishing mole.

Adjacent anchorages

1. In an unnamed bay 1.5M east of Cabo de Ares – which has an offlying rock requiring at least 0.5M clearance – over sand off a pleasant beach. The bottom shoals steadily towards the shore at the west end of the beach.

2. **Portinho de Arrábida** (⊕138 – 38°28′.6N 8°58′.7W – see plan page 193), a wooded bay backed by high cliffs some 6M east of Sesimbra, and one of the most scenic anchorages in all of Portugal. Although fully open to the south a surprising number of smallcraft lie on summer moorings in the western part of the bay.

   The approach from the west is complicated by a drying sandbank, the Baixo de Alpertuche, off Forte Arrábida. Keep 0.4M offshore until lightbeacon No.2 bears 090°, before altering to 033° to clear Forte Arrábida by 150–200m. This should give a least depth of 2.2m at low water springs but the bank may grow and/or move. Admiralty 3259 will be found useful and the water is crystal clear. Anchor outside the moorings over weed and hard sand – there are rocks and a small offlying island, Anixa, at the east end of the bay.

   There are no facilities other than a telephone kiosk behind the beach, half a dozen waterfront restaurants, and an oceanographic museum in Forte Arrábida on the western headland. Much of the surrounding area, including Anixa island, is a nature reserve.

Portinho de Arrábida seen from the southeast, with Ilha Anixa on the right and the Baixo do Alpertuche clearly visible in the foreground. Many claim that it is the most spectacular anchorage in all Portugal

52. Setúbal and the Rio Sado

Waypoints
⊕139 – 38°24′.3N 9°01′.1W (approach)
⊕140 – 38°26′.62N 8°58′.72W (leading line)
⊕141 – 38°29′.22N 8°55′.9W (entrance)

Courses and distances
⊕130 (Rio Tejo Fairway Buoy No.2) – ⊕139 (via F135) = 25.2M, 151°&090° or 270°&331°
⊕131 (Cascais) – ⊕139 (via F135) = 32.3M, 152°&046° or 226°&332°
⊕136 (Sesimbra) – ⊕139 = 3.6M, 092° or 272°
⊕139 – ⊕140 = 3M, 039° or 219°
⊕140 – ⊕141 = 3.4M, 040° or 220°
⊕139 – ⊕142 (Sines) = 29.9M, 170° or 350°

Tides
Standard port Lisbon
Mean time differences
HW –0015 ±0005; LW 0000 ±0005
Heights in metres

MHWS	MHWN	MLWN	MLWS
3.4	2.7	1.3	0.5

Or refer to EasyTide at www.ukho.gov.uk (see page 2)

Charts

	Approach	*Entrance/estuary*
Admiralty	3635, 3636	3259, 3260
Imray	C19, C49	C49
Portuguese	23203, 24204	26308, 26309

Principal entrance lights
2151 **Ldg Lts 040°** *Front* **Fishing harbour E jetty**
Iso.Y.6s13m22M
Red and white striped metal structure 9m
2151.1 *Rear* **Azêda** 1.7M from front Iso.Y.6s60m22M
038.3°-vis-041.3° White tower, red bands 31m
Difficult to distinguish against the lights of the city

2150.22 **Lightbeacon No.2** Fl(2)R.10s13m9M
Racon Mo 'B'(–···)15M Red post, white lantern
2150.26 **Lightbeacon No.4** Fl.R.4s13m4M
Red and white chequered column 5m
2150 **Forte de Outão** Oc.R.6s33m12M
Red hexagonal tower and lantern 11m
2150.28 **Lightbeacon No.5** Fl.G.4s13m4M
Black post and platform 5m
2150.4 **Forte de Albarquel** Iso.R.2s15m6M
Red lantern on S corner of fort
2152.1 **Anunciada** Iso.R.4s22m15M Red lantern
2152 **Algarve Exportador** Oc.R.4s14m15M Red lantern

Night entry
While entrance to the estuary should present no problems in light conditions and good visibility (when the leading lights will come into their own), it would be wise to await daylight before entering the marina

Harbour communications
Administração dos Portos de Sesimbra e Setúbal
☎ 265 542000, *Fax* 265 230992
Email geral@portodesetubal.pt
www.portodesetubal.pt (mainly concerned with commercial activity, and almost entirely in Portuguese)
VHF Ch 11, 16
Doca de Recreio das Fontainhas ☎ 265 542076
Fax 265 230992 *Email* geral@portodesetubal.pt
www.portodesetubal.pt (in Portuguese and English).

As of 2005 the marina had no VHF capability and none was planned, however prior contact by telephone to check whether a berth will be available is strongly advised.

The Península de Troiá and entrance to the Rio Sado seen from the southwest over some of the extensive offlying sandbanks. The Setúbal waterfront is clearly visible beyond

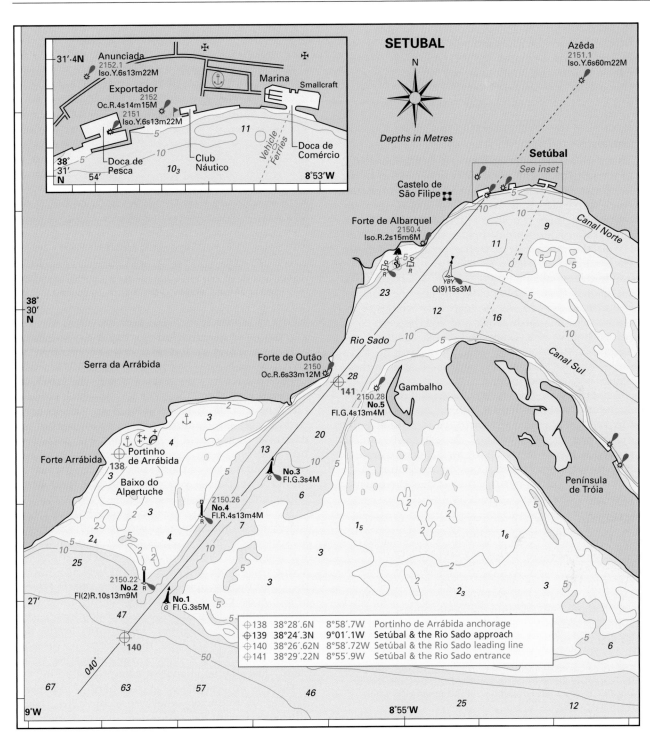

Commercial port with limited space for visiting yachts

Setúbal lies more than 1M inside the entrance to the Rio Sado, but its associated industries start with the cement works at the narrows and extend to the large shipyard and ore wharf 5M upstream. It is the country's third largest port and cannot claim to be attractive, though areas of the city have some charm. The entrance channel is narrow but well marked, but yachts are advised not to attempt it other than in fine weather and on the flood – the spring ebb can run at more than 3 knots – and certainly not in onshore winds of any strength.

The smallcraft basins are crowded and a visiting yacht is in competition with the residents, the fishing boats and the Península de Tróia ferries. However it is possible to anchor throughout much of the estuary, and though large areas dry there is a navigable channel as far as Alcacer do Sal, 24M upstream – or at least to the railway bridge below it. A second channel, supposedly in use as far back as Roman times, runs inside the Península de Tróia.

Approach

If coastal sailing from the direction of Sesimbra, note that Cabo de Ares has an offlying rock – keep at least 0.5M clear all along the coast. From the south,

PORTUGAL – THE WEST COAST

the course from Cabo de Sines of 353° stands away from the unbroken low sand hills of the Tróia shore. In either case head for lightbeacon No.2 (⊕140), which marks the southwest end of the approach channel.

From offshore ⊕139 lies 3M southwest of ⊕140, after which see below.

Entrance

The entrance channel lies between lightbeacon No.2 to the northwest and buoy No.1 about 600m to the southeast, widening out somewhat after lightbeacon No.4 is passed. It is essential to stay within the channel as there are shoals and drying banks on either side and, once past lightbeacon No.4, best to favour the north side if traffic permits. There are leading lights on 040°.

While it would be unwise to rely solely on GPS, the course from ⊕140, close outside the channel entrance, to ⊕141, in the gap between Forte de Outão on the north bank and lightbeacon No.5 (which marks the Gambalho bank), follows the leading lights down 040° (220° if departing), for a distance of 3.4M. It must be stressed that both these figures are over the ground.

Before reaching Forte de Albarquel the estuary opens up to the southeast. 800m southeast of the fort the Cabeça do João Farto west cardinal buoy marks the western end of an extensive middle ground. Leave it to starboard for Setúbal or well to port to run down the east side of the Península de Tróia. Most of the north shore west of the town is lined with moorings.

Berthing

There are three basins in addition to the commercial shipping docks – from east to west the Doca de Pesca (fish dock), that of the Clube Náutico de Setúbal, and the Doca de Comércio (commercial dock) or Doca de Recreio das Fontaínhas which contains a small marina in addition to fishing boats and the embarkation point for the Península de Tróia ferries. Yachts are not welcome in the fish dock, the *clube*

The three basins at Setúbal are, from west to east, the Doca de Pesca, the Clube Náutico, and the Doca de Comércio or Doca de Recreio das Fontaínhas, which houses the small marina

Setúbal's Doca de Comércio or Doca de Recreio das Fontaínhas from the southeast, with the marina pontoons on the left, the Península de Tróia ferry terminal in the middle and smallcraft moorings on the right. The latter may soon be moved, allowing the marina to expand

náutico harbour is tiny and very crowded, and the marina is frequently full to capacity – another harbour where it is essential to make contact prior to arrival.

Take particular care when entering the basin, as although two of the three car ferries which connect the Península de Tróia to Setúbal are small one is considerably larger, and to meet any of them in the narrow entrance could be unpleasant. The port-hand turn into the basin is swiftly followed by a second turn through an even tighter gap between the end of the west wall and a very solid concrete ferry berth dolphin, neither of which are lit.

The marina, or Doca de Recreio das Fontaínhas, is run by the Administração dos Portos de Sesimbra e Setúbal whose head office is nearby. It occupies the western half of the basin, and provides berthing for about 150 yachts and smallcraft as well as a few of the traditional double-ended trading vessels typical of the Sado estuary. All berths on the three long pontoons are alongside fingers and depths are said to be 3–3.5m throughout. Only three berths are reserved for visitors, and though one of these is nominally of 15m, if space is tight a smaller yacht clearly has a better chance of being squeezed in.

There is no designated arrivals berth – ask when making prior contact, otherwise secure where space allows and visit the office for advice. Hours are 0900–2100 daily from May to October, 0900–1900 at other times. As of early 2005 the marina manager spoke good English and was extremely helpful. Security in the marina is particularly good, with uniformed guards in addition to the usual electronic gate, and the water appears surprisingly clean bearing in mind that the basin is shared with fishing boats and ferries.

In 2005 the daily rate for a visiting yacht of 10–12m was €18.91 per night, rising to €24.30 for 12–15m, inclusive of water, electricity and tax. Multihulls paid a 50% surcharge. Payment had to be made in cash, with no credit cards accepted.

During the next few years the Administração dos Portos de Sesimbra e Setúbal (APSS) plans to move the small fishing boats which currently occupy the east end of the basin to the Doca de Pesca, so freeing up space for another 120 yacht berths. In the longer term it is hoped that a major new yacht harbour will be constructed southwest of Forte de Arbarquel in an area known locally as Toca de Pia Lopes.

Anchorages

There is a designated fishing and smallcraft anchorage southeast of the conspicuous Castelo de São Felipe in 10–12m, but it is some distance from all facilities. Alternatively it is possible to anchor off the *clube náutico* basin, convenient for shopping and where a dinghy can be left. Both these positions are exposed to the southern quadrant – should the wind shift into the south or southwest (unlikely in summer) move to the east side of the ferry landing stage at Punta do Adoxe on the Península de Tróia.

Formalities

The *GNR–Brigada Fiscal* have a desk in the marina office building, with the *Alfândega* and *Polícia Marítima* nearby. Copies of the marina paperwork are circulated to all three, and it is no longer necessary for most skippers to visit them in person. The marina manager will advise if this is required – most probably due to non-EU yacht registration or crew.

Facilities

Boatyard The somewhat ramshackle boatyard at the west end of the town waterfront may be able to work on a yacht, but its marine railways would be unsuitable for hauling a deep-keeled yacht.

Travel-lift No travel-lift, though a mobile crane capable of lifting up to 40 tonnes is situated at the Doca de Recreio das Fontaínhas. There are no boatyard facilities on site and it should only be regarded as an emergency measure. The Clube Náutico de Setúbal (see below) has a 5-tonne crane.

Chandlery A branch of Azimute Lda (see page 184) has recently opened at 80 Rua Praia da Saúde, ☎/*Fax* 265 534014 *Email* azimute.setubal@azimuteam.pt. Anything not in stock can be ordered from Lisbon.

Water On the marina pontoons.

Showers Shower block near the marina office, with card access (for which a deposit is required).

Launderette In the city.

Electricity On the marina pontoons.

Fuel Diesel and petrol pumps will be found on a pontoon in the eastern end of the basin beyond the ferry berths, open 0900–1200 and 1400–1800 in season. Payment must be made in cash. Small amounts of fuel can be bought from a filling station opposite the marina.

Bottled gas The filling station above sells only Portuguese gas cylinders, though Camping Gaz is understood to be available elsewhere in the city.

Clube náutico The Clube Náutico de Setúbal has premises overlooking the small basin west of the marina, with the usual bar and restaurant.

Weather forecast Displayed daily at the marina office.

Banks In the city.

Shops/provisioning Large supermarket one road inland from the *clube náutico*, and doubtless many others, as well as good general shopping in the city proper.

Produce market Fish and produce market adjacent to the supermarket above.

Cafés, restaurants and hotels Many throughout the city, including several waterside restaurants in the nearby public gardens.

Medical services In the city.

Communications

Post office In the city.

Mailing address The marina office will hold mail for visiting yachts – c/o Administração do Porto de Setúbal, Doca de Recreio das Fontaínhas, Praça da República, 2904–508 Setúbal, Portugal. It is important that the envelope carries the name of the yacht in addition to that of the addressee.

Internet access At least one cybercafé in the city, but at some distance from the marina.

Public telephones On the rear wall of the marina office.

Fax service The marina office can receive faxes but cannot send them.

Car hire/taxis In the city.

Buses and trains Services to Lisbon and elsewhere.

Ferries Shuttle service for foot passengers and vehicles to the Península de Tróia from inside the Doca de Recreio das Fontaínhas.

Air services Lisbon airport is some 35km distant.

Adjacent anchorages

1. In the shallow bay west of Forte de Albarquel, if space can be found amongst the moorings. Beware the double rock, Arflor, to the west, though this is now buoyed.

2. Along the eastern shore of the Península de Tróia, the northern 3M of which is quite steep-to. There are few facilities other than a tourist development near the ferry landing. Plans have been announced for the construction of 'two small leisure docks' a short distance to the east, but it is far from clear what these will consist of – or when.

3. Among the rice fields on the upper Rio Sado, well beyond the commercial wharves and shipyards. A large-scale Portuguese chart (best obtained in Lisbon – see page 184), a reliable echo sounder and plenty of time are all essentials.

The entrance to the Doca de Comércio / Doca de Recreio das Fontaínhas in Setúbal. It is essential to approach with caution, as a car ferry may be on the point of departure *AH*

53. Sines

Waypoints
⊕142 – 37°54′.8N 8°54′.8W (approach)
⊕143 – 37°55′.98N 8°52′.74W (entrance)

Courses and distances
⊕130 (Rio Tejo Fairway Buoy No.2) – ⊕142 (via ⊕135) =
48M, 151°&152° or 328°&329°
⊕131 (Cascais) – ⊕142 (via ⊕135) = 51.1M, 152°&152°
or 332°&332°
⊕136 (Sesimbra) – ⊕142 = 30.8M, 164° or 344°
⊕139 (Setúbal) – ⊕142 =29.9M, 170° or 350°
⊕142 – ⊕143 = 2M, 054° or 234°
⊕142 – ⊕144 (Vila Nova de Milfontes) = 13M, 165° or 345°
⊕142 – ⊕147 (Cabo de São Vicente) = 54M, 185° or 005°

Tides
Standard port Lisbon
Mean time differences
HW –0040 ±0010; LW –0015 ±0005
Heights in metres

MHWS	MHWN	MLWN	MLWS
3.3	2.6	1.3	0.6

Or refer to EasyTide at www.ukho.gov.uk (see page 2)

Charts

	Approach	*Harbour*
Admiralty	3636	3224
Imray	C19, C49, C50	C19, C49, C50
Portuguese	23203, 24204, 24205	26408

Principal harbour lights
2160 **Cabo de Sines** Fl(2)15s55m26M
001°-obscd-003° and 004°-obscd-007°
White tower and building 28m
Note Numerous nearby red lights mark chimneys,
radio masts etc

2160.16 **West breakwater** Fl.3s20m12M
White tower, red bands 8m
Note Lies about 500m SHORT of the breakwater end,
which is marked by a buoy
2160.3 **Terminal Ldg Lts 358°**
Front Iso.R.6s17m5M Post 6m
2160.31 *Rear* 579m from front
Oc.R.5.6s28m3M Post 20m
2160.36 **Fishing harbour (NW) mole** Fl.R.6s6M
White tower, red bands 4m
2160.37 **Marina (SE) mole** Fl.G.4s4M
White tower, green bands 5m
2160.08 **Southeast breakwater, NW corner** LFl.G.8s16m6M
White column, green bands 7m
Other lights exist within the commercial harbour

Night entry
Well-lit and straightforward, with the option to anchor
off the beach until daylight if desired

Maritime radio station
Atalaia (38°10′.3N 8°38′.6W)
Remotely controlled from Lisbon
Manual – VHF Ch 16, 23, 24, 25. *Autolink* – VHF Ch 85

Harbour communications
Administração do Porto do Sines ☎ 269 860600
Fax 269 860690 *Email* geral @portodesines.pt
www.portodesines.pt
VHF Ch 12, 16 (call *Sines Port Control*) (24 hours)
Marina de Sines ☎ 269 860631 *Fax* 269 860691
Email/website as above, but no VHF.

Small but highly-praised marina in large commercial harbour complex

Birthplace of Vasco da Gama and until 1971 a
relatively quiet fishing port, Sines – pronounced
'cinch' – can now handle 500,000-tonne tankers and
has heavy industry as well as petrochemicals
supporting its economy. However, although it can be
identified from well offshore by its many chimneys,
many either lit or smoking, once in the anchorage or
marina the industrial areas are masked behind the
attractive old town and are soon forgotten.
Surprisingly, not only is water quality off the beach
excellent, but there are no signs of air pollution either.

The Marina de Sines, which lies behind a
substantial stone mole southeast of the fishing
harbour, has received a unanimous thumbs up from
all who have reported on it since it opened in 1996
– an almost unique accolade.

Approach

Sines is most conveniently placed, being the only all-
weather harbour between Lisbon, some 50M to the
north, and Cabo de São Vicente, nearly 60M to the
south.

For 35M north of Cabo de Sines the coast is an
unbroken line of low sand hills – one long beach.
The theoretical ranges of Cabo Espichel and Cabo
de Sines lights overlap, but there are no other major
lights in between. Cabo de Sines has offlying rocks
and islands but 0.5M provides safe clearance.

From the south, the last major light is Cabo
Sardão 13M distant, with a less powerful light Vila

Nova de Milfontes. The coast between Cabo Sardão
and Sines is rocky with cliffs, though there are sandy
beaches around Vila Nova de Milfontes and Porto
Covo (the latter about 7M southeast of Sines and
identifiable by its water tower).

From offshore, ⊕142 lies 2M southwest of the main
breakwater, a course of 054° leading to ⊕143 in the
centre of the wide harbour mouth. A considerable
amount of commercial and fishing traffic should be
anticipated on closing the coast, and watch kept
accordingly.

Entrance

The entrance lies 1.5M south of Cabo de Sines and
is protected by a long breakwater, the southern end
of which has been in ruins for some years and is
partially submerged – note that the breakwater light
is situated almost 500m SHORT of the breakwater
end, which is marked by a (lit) red pillar buoy. DO
NOT CUT INSIDE this buoy.

From the south the entrance is wide and should
present no problems, though ships *en route* to the
commercial terminals in the southeastern part of the
harbour must be given ample space to manoeuvre.

Berthing

The small but welcoming Marina de Sines, run by
the Administração do Porto do Sines, occupies the
bight between the south inner breakwater and a
steep rocky outcrop. Initially the outer pontoons
were removed for the winter, but this is no longer
deemed necessary and the marina can now

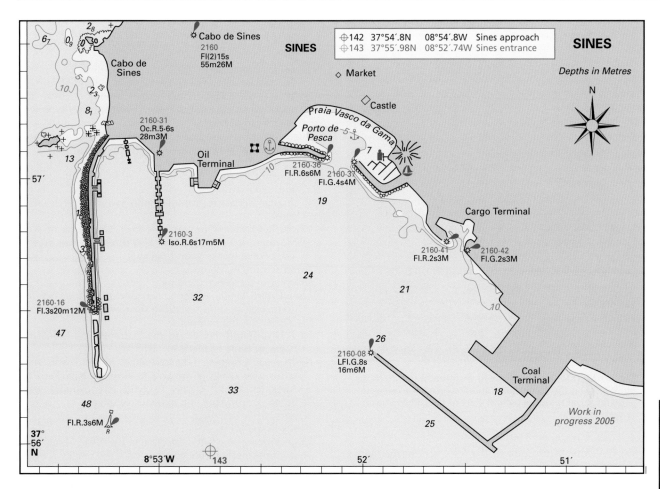

SINES

⊕142 37°54'.8N   08°54'.8W   Sines approach
⊕143 37°55'.98N   08°52'.74W Sines entrance

SINES

Depths in Metres

Cabo de Sines
2160
Fl(2)15s
55m26M

Cabo de Sines

Market

Castle

Praia Vasco da Gama

2160·31
Oc.R.5·6s
28m3M

Oil Terminal

Porto de Pesca

2160·36
Fl.R.6s6M

2160·37
Fl.G.4s4M

2160·3
Iso.R.6s17m5M

Cargo Terminal

2160·41
Fl.R.2s3M

2160·42
Fl.G.2s3M

2160·16
Fl.3s20m12M

2160·08
LFl.G.8s
16m6M

Coal Terminal

Work in progress 2005

Fl.R.3s6M

Looking across the wide harbour at Sines from the south-southwest. The rubble remains which lie off the end of the main breakwater show clearly at left, with the fishing harbour and marina on the right

accommodate 230 yachts year-round, including two or three of more than 20m overall. The portacabin which houses the office, showers etc is being replaced with permanent buildings, due for completion by 2007 at the latest, after which it is hoped that other services including shops, restaurants and a chandlery will also move on site.

On arrival yachts should secure to the hammerhead below the rock, which also serves as a fuelling pontoon. The marina office – currently a white portacabin – is some distance away up a steep flight of steps and is manned around the clock by notably helpful and friendly staff, all of whom speak English. In place of the more usual gated pontoons the entire marina area is fenced off, with security guards making regular patrols.

28 berths are reserved for yachts in transit, normally on the northwestern pontoon (the approach to which can be exciting when the *nortada* is blowing). This is the first part of the marina to be affected by swell and storm surge, when visitors will be moved further in if space allows. Depths vary from 3–8m, with 5m or more throughout the visitors' area, and all berths are alongside finger pontoons.

In 2005 the high season (June–September inclusive) rate for a visiting yacht of 10–12m was €14.26 per night, rising to €20.71 for 12–15m, inclusive of water, electricity and tax. In the low season this dropped to €9.92 per night (€173.48 per month) for 10–12m, or €14.75 per night (€262.92 per month)

PORTUGAL – THE WEST COAST

Sines harbour looking southwest, with the fishing harbour and marina in the foreground and the recently extended cargo and coal terminal behind. Part of the old town can be seen at far left

for 12–15m. Multihulls paid a 50% surcharge. Most major credit cards are accepted for berthing, though fuel must be paid for in cash.

Anchorage

Yachts are still permitted to anchor off the Praia Vasco da Gama, in 3–5m over sand and a little weed, provided they keep well clear of both fishing vessels and the marina approach. Being open to the southwest the anchorage is seldom without a slight roll, but the marina could not be closer should the wind shift onshore. Dinghies can be landed on the beach, which is cleaned and raked daily and is very popular with local residents.

Anchoring is charged at 35% of the marina equivalent (€5.00 for 10–12m and €7.25 for 12–15m in the 2005 high season), with no increase for multihulls. This entitles the crew to use marina facilities such as showers, launderette and internet (both the latter at the standard rate), and take on unlimited water. Payment should be made at the marina office.

Formalities

Whether at anchor or in the marina, take passports and ship's papers to the office to complete the usual form, copies of which are then circulated to the *GNR–Brigada Fiscal*, *Alfândega* and *Polícia Marítima*. The *GNR–Brigada Fiscal* operate from the small wooden hut near the slipway which the skipper should visit, following which officials may decide to visit the yacht, particularly if there are non-EU nationals aboard. In due course they will have an office in the new building mentioned above.

Facilities

Boatyard In the fishing and commercial areas, but as yet nothing specifically for yachts.

Travel-lift None as of 2005, though the dock is in place. The marina has a 6.3-tonne static crane, supplemented by a much larger mobile crane brought in from the docks when necessary. There is also a slipway where yachts can dry out.

Engineers, electronic and radio repairs In the fishing and commercial areas – enquire at the marina office.

Chandlery Sinaútica ☎ 269 635670, on Rua Teófila Braga, sells some chandlery in addition to inflatables and outboards. Also one near the fishing harbour, though naturally geared more towards commercial needs.

Charts Local charts are available from Nautisines on Rua Marquês de Pombal, which also offers internet access. The owner speaks good English.

Water On the pontoons.

Showers In the office building.

Launderette Single washing machine plus dryer at the marina office, plus several in the town.

Electricity On the pontoons.

Fuel Diesel and petrol at the hammerhead pontoon. Payment must be made in cash.

Bottled gas Camping Gaz exchanges in the town, with refills available via the GALP shop on Rua Pero de Alenquer. GALP claims to refill any cylinder with butane or propane, but allow three days.

Weather forecast Posted daily at the marina office.

Banks In the town.

Shops/provisioning Good selection in the town, about 2km from the marina (though a lot less if the dinghy is used, when nearly all the carrying will be downhill). No shops at all near the marina, though see *Berthing*, above.

Produce market Small but good open market in the old town.

Cafés, restaurants and hotels Small bar next to the marina office, which may eventually expand. In the meantime the old town is well supplied with restaurants and hotels.

Medical services In the town.

Communications

Post office In the town.

Mailing address The marina office will hold mail for visiting yachts – c/o Administração do Porto do Sines, Porto de Recreio, Apartado 16, 7520–953 Sines, Portugal. It is important that the envelope carries the name of the yacht in addition to that of the addressee.

Internet access Those berthed in the marina or paying to anchor can use one of the office computers for a small fee. Alternatively try Nautisines (see *Charts* above), open 1730–1900, or the pay-as-you-go terminal in the main post office on Praça Tomás Ribeiro. Wireless broadband is reported to be available throughout the marina, but this has not been verified.

Public telephones At the marina office and in the town.

Fax service Faxes can be received at the marina office, *Fax* 269 860891, but not sent.

Car hire/taxis In the town, or can be arranged via the marina office.

Buses Local buses, with long distance services to Lisbon (just under 3 hours) and elsewhere from the bus station in the eastern part of the old town.

Trains Sines no longer has a passenger rail service.

54. Vila Nova de Milfontes

Waypoints
⊕144 – 37°42´.2N 8°50´.5W (approach)
⊕145 – 37°42´.7N 8°48´.2W (entrance)
⊕146 – 37°17´.5N 8°52´.3W (Arrifana anchorage)

Courses and distances
⊕142 (Sines) – ⊕144 = 13M, 165° or 345°
⊕144 – ⊕145 = 1.9M, 075° or 255°
⊕142 – ⊕146 = 37.7M, 180° & by eye or by eye & 000°
⊕144 – ⊕146 = 25M, (186°) & by eye or by eye & (006°)
⊕144 – ⊕147 (Cabo de São Vicente) = 42M, 191° or 001°
⊕146 – ⊕147 (Cabo de São Vicente) = 17.8M, (202° or 002°)

Tides
Standard port Lisbon
Mean time differences Milfontes
HW –0035 ±0005; LW No data
Heights in metres Milfontes

MHWS	MHWN	MLWN	MLWS
3.7	2.9	1.5	0.7

Or refer to EasyTide at www.ukho.gov.uk (see page 2)

Charts

	Approach	River
Admiralty	3636	
Imray	C19, C50	
Portuguese	23203, 24205	(27501)

Principal lights
2162 **Milfontes (Rio Mira)** Fl.3s22m10M
Turret on white building 5m

Night entry
Not possible under any circumstances – the bar calls for eyeball pilotage in good overhead light.

Beautiful, unspoilt river with challenging entrance

Reputedly used by Hannibal and once rich enough to be sacked by Algerian pirates, pretty little Vila Nova de Milfontes on the Rio Mira shows scant evidence of its former importance. Despite much recent holiday development the white and tile village on the north bank has retained much of its character and mercifully escaped the high-rise blocks which mar so many Portuguese tourist resorts. There are superb beaches both inside and outside the entrance and the area's peace and tranquillity are a real treat – but first you must pick your way in.

Though viable for a keelboat in the right conditions the Rio Mira is shallow and, in common with many other Portuguese rivers, has a bar with a reported depth of no more than 1m at datum – considerably less if any swell is running. Once inside protection is excellent but flat weather, and particularly an absence of swell, are essential for both entry and departure. About a mile from the entrance there is a road bridge with a clearance of some 12m, but it is possible to explore the river by dinghy for many kilometres beyond.

As indicated above, in late 2005 there was still no reliable, large-scale chart of the area available.

The shallow bar at Vila Nova de Milfontes, seen from the southwest. The challenge of entering the Rio Mira is exacerbated by the fact that no reliable chart is available

A panoramic shot taken from near the Rio Mira light, looking up upstream towards the town and bridge. Again, the V-shaped middle ground shows up as a pale, sandy shadow   *AH*

Approach

The coast between Cabo de Sines to the north and Cabo Sardão to the south consists of rocky cliffs. There is a sandy beach at Porto Covo about 8M to the north, identifiable by its water tower.

From offshore ⊕144 lies 1.9M west-southwest of the rivermouth, a course of 075° leading to ⊕145 on the 10m line, about 0.7M from the entrance. This is the time to decide whether it is viable to investigate further or whether, perhaps regretfully, to alter course for the next destination.

Entrance

Since Vila Nova de Milfontes calls for careful eyeball pilotage, enter only in calm weather on a rising tide, preferably in the afternoon with the sun behind the boat. The entrance is marked by the Rio Mira light, shown from the corner of a square white building with a tiled roof on the north side of the entrance.

Approach to about 600m with the light bearing 050° and, with luck, a local fisherman will lead the way across the bar (though this is considerably less likely now that most of the local smallcraft have moved the mile north to Portinho do Canal). Failing this, turn east and keep the reef which extends southwards from the light about 60m off on the port hand. Although part is exposed it extends for some distance underwater as a brownish–purple area – be guided by the colour of the water.

Just inside the entrance best water is found relatively close under the light, but further upstream there is an unmarked middle ground, drying at low water springs, below and downstream from the fort. Its shape – a wide V with the apex pointing upstream – makes it particularly dangerous and it would be only too easy to find oneself in a blind alley. In 2000 a deep channel led south of the middle ground, but by 2005 it appeared less defined with the bank's southern arm apparently reaching almost to the shoreline. Minimum depths over this inner shoal could not be ascertained. Fishing nets suspended from buoys are sometimes laid inside the river.

Anchorage

There is plenty of room to anchor in the river, either in the northwest bight just inside the mouth (depths are shallow), or further upstream off the fishermen's quay in 4m or more. The ebb tide runs at up to 3 knots with the spring flood only marginally less, and it may be wise to set two anchors.

Formalities

The arrival of a foreign yacht in the river is a sufficiently rare event that it would almost certainly attract a visit from the authorities. Failing that there is a *GNR–Brigada Fiscal* office up the steps at the downstream end of the quay and, supposedly, a *Policía Marítima* office in the building supporting the single light.

Facilities

Quay with steps for dinghy landing, with a café/restaurant ashore and a public tap opposite. The town contains a range of shops from supermarkets to souvenirs, as well as banks, restaurants, a post office and several telephone kiosks. Buses run to Sines and elsewhere.

Looking out to sea from the Rio Mira light structure, with all kinds of rocks and reefs in the foreground   *AH*

Adjacent harbours and anchorages

1. **Porto Corvo, Portinho do Canal and Porto das Barcas** – if coastal sailing, the sharp-eyed may spot Porto Corvo at 37°51′N, Portinho do Canal at 37°44′.4N and/or Porto das Barcas at 37°33′.2N. Though all three are lit, to call any of them a 'port' is highly misleading and none could be entered by even the smallest yacht. Neither are there viable anchorages in their offings – sail on by.

2. **Arrifana** (⊕146 – 37°17′.5N 8°52′.3W), a bay surrounded by dramatic cliffs giving shelter from north and east, lies 26M south of Vila Nova de Milfontes and 18M north of Cabo de São Vicente. Though isolated and remote it can be a useful passage anchorage, particularly if beating into the prevailing *nortada*. However, with any swell rolling in, the surfing community arrive in force – and they know where to find waves . . .

   The coast is rocky and steep-to with offlying stacks and islands. The ruins of an old fort stand on the cliff to the north with a cairn, Pedra da Agulha, to the south. Beneath both are rocky islets – those under the fort are lumpy while those under the cairn have needle-like angularity.

   Approaching from the southwest, the islets off the fort stand out from the land and the white cottages behind the sandy beach become plain. Anchor off the beach in 10–12m over sand, avoiding the northern area which is peppered with rocky shoals. Pots or net floats may be encountered anywhere in the bay.

   A miniature harbour, home to half-a-dozen small fishing boats, nestles amongst the rocks at the north end of the beach. However it has nothing to offer in terms of facilities – not even a water tap – and is considerably further from the village by road than is the beach. A café/restaurant overlooks the latter, with a public telephone about 50m up the steep cobbled road to the village. Other than dramatic views and a few more restaurants there is little to justify the climb.

3. **Carrapateira** (37°11′.3N 8°54′.8W), lying 6.5M south of Arrifana and 11M north of Cabo de São Vicente, may also suggest itself as a possible anchorage in northeasterly winds. However shelter is considerably poorer than at Arrifana and there are numerous rocks both in the approach and off the beach.

The wide bay at Arrifana offers potential anchorage on the long haul between Sines and Cabo de São Vicente. Fully open to the west, however, it is also a popular spot with surfers   *AH*

PORTUGAL – THE WEST COAST

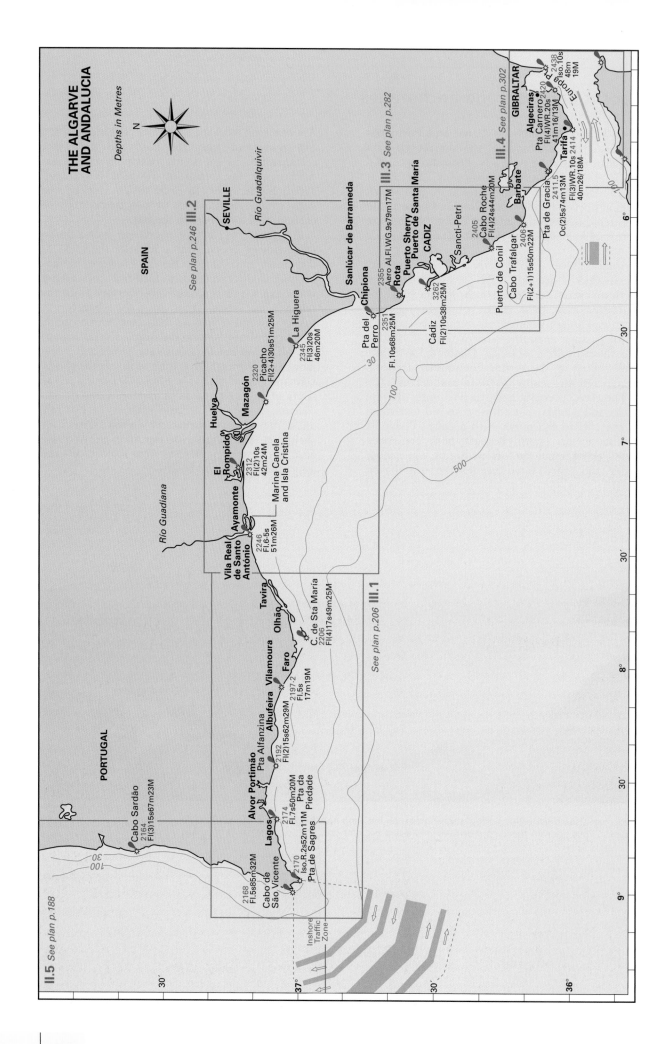

Depths in Metres

N

II.5 See plan p.188

PORTUGAL

SPAIN

See plan p.246 III.2

SEVILLE

Río Guadalquivir

Cabo Sardão
2164
Fl(3)15s67m23M

Río Guadiana

Alvor Portimão
Pta Alfanzina
2192
Fl(2)15s62m29M

Albufeira Vilamoura
2197.2
Faro
Fl.5s
17m19M

Lagos
2170
Iso.R.2s52m11M
Pta de Sagres

2174
Fl.7s50m20M
Pta da
Piedade

2168
Fl.5s85m32M
Cabo de
São Vicente

Vila Real
de Santo
António
Ayamonte
2246
Fl.6-5s
51m26M

El
Rompido
2312
Fl(2)10s
42m24M

Marina Canela
and Isla Cristina

Huelva
Mazagón
2320
Picacho
Fl(2+4)30s51m25M

La Higuera
2345
Fl(3)20s
46m20M

Tavira
Olhão
C. de Sta María
2206
Fl(4)17s49m25M

See plan p.206 III.1

Sanlúcar de Barrameda

Chipiona
Pta del
Perro

2351
Fl.10s68m25M

Rota
2355
Aero Al.Fl.WG.9s79m17M

Puerto Sherry
Puerto de Santa María
CADIZ

Cádiz
3262
Fl(2)10s38m25M

Sancti-Petri

Puerto de Conil

Cabo Roche
2405
Fl(4)24s44m20M

Cabo Trafalgar
2406
Fl(2+1)15s50m22M

Pta de Gracia
2411.5
Oc(2)5s74m13M

Barbate

III.3 See plan p.282

III.4 See plan p.302

GIBRALTAR

Algeciras
Pta Carnero 2420
Fl(4)WR.20s
41m16/13M

Tarifa
Fl(3)WR.10s 2414
40m26/18M

2438
Iso.10s
48m
19M
Europa

Inshore
Traffic
Zone

30

100

500

III. The Algarve and Andalucía

Cabo de São Vicente to Gibraltar

Rounding Cabo de São Vicente is a significant milestone on the voyage south
Alan Taylor

Gibraltar 'The Rock' looking north, with Europa Point lighthouse at bottom right and nearer it – very distinctive from the sea – the white-painted mosque with its tall minaret   *PR*

Punta del Perro lighthouse, built in 1867. The lower floors are sometimes open to the public   *AH*

Cabo de São Vicente to Gibraltar

Both ends of this stretch offer spectacular scenery with impressive cliffs. In the middle, these give way to sandy beaches often backed by lagoons – staging posts for migrant birds – including the Parque Natural de Ria Formosa around Faro and Olhão and the Parque Nacional de Doñana west of the Rio Guadalquivir. The western Algarve has been intensively developed for the tourist and in places the shoreline is littered with high-rise blocks and time-share estates, though these decrease as one approaches the border. In Spain, the stretch east of Cádiz is the least developed piece of coast between Portugal and France. Human activity can be traced back for millennia, with Faro, Seville, Cádiz and other settlements dating back to Phoenician or Roman times.

In contrast to the west coast there are a number of good estuary and river anchorages, generally over good holding. From São Vicente to the Guadalquivir the bottom is sand. From Cádiz onwards it is usually mud, often glutinous, providing good holding but needing a deck pump (or mop and bucket) when the anchor is brought in. Anchoring off any beach is possible in fine, settled weather when there is no swell.

This is as well, since marina fees reflect the generally high level of facilities on offer. In the Algarve the owner of a yacht of between 10–12m would, in 2005, have paid between €33 and €41 per night for marina berthing, the equivalent charge for a yacht of 12–15m being between €48 and €57. Prices in the low season dropped considerably, ranging from €12 to €21 for 10–12m, and €18 and €33 for 12–15m. All the marinas accepted credit cards and offered discounts for longer stays. Prices in the coastal marinas of Andalucía were somewhat lower, ranging in the high season from €18.00 in El Puerto de Santa María up to €29 in Puerto Sherry for a boat of 10–12m. Comparable fees for a 12–14m vessel varied from €25.00 to €34.86 in the same harbours. Low season rates for boats of similar size varied from less than €10 to around €15, and €13 to around €18. Again, credit cards were generally accepted.

All yachts, both locally-owned and visitors, spending more than 183 days in Portuguese waters are liable for a 'long stay' tax, calculated using a formula based on displacement in metric tons, engine capacity and age. In 2003 (the last date for which figures were available) a yacht of 8 tons displacement with a 40hp engine would have paid €121.92 if registered in 1986 or earlier, €74.80 if registered since 1986. Figures for a yacht of 16 tons displacement with a 90hp engine were €304.72 and €176.56 respectively. Collection is in the hands of the local *GNR–Brigada Fiscal*, and though non-payment can in theory lead to a fine of around €150.00 it is often poorly publicised. A certificate and receipt are issued on payment, valid for one year from the date of arrival in Portuguese waters (including the Azores and Madeira).

Caution

Nearly all charts of the area, both British Admiralty and Portuguese, still use ED50 datum, whereas both the plans and waypoints in the following pages have been converted to WGS84 (the necessary shift is generally stated on a published chart, and in addition several hundred known positions were verified by handheld GPS during research).

Great care has been taken over the creation of waypoints, together with their associated courses and distances. However it remains the responsibility of the individual navigator to satisfy him or herself of each one's validity before placing any reliance on it.

Hazards – tunny nets, fish cages and artificial reefs

Between March and early autumn *almadrabas* or tunny (tuna) nets tough enough to foul the screw of a freighter can be a considerable hazard, and may stretch several miles offshore. It is not advisable to sail over one, and officially vessels should not pass between the inner end of a net and the shore (though local fishermen habitually do so). At one time tunny nets were set as far west as Vilamoura, but over the past decade only five or six have been laid annually, all in the 30M between Puerto de Conil and Tarifa. However if the fish return elsewhere doubtless the nets will too. Further details of dates, locations and buoyage will be found under the notes for the nearest harbour, and annual positions are often displayed on marina notice boards. Note that the cardinal buoys used to mark the nets are frequently very undersized – sometimes less than 2m in height, including topmark – and should not be relied upon, particularly at night.

More prevalent though less worrying are the nets laid for other fish – less worrying because they generally lie too far beneath the surface to bother a yacht. When first laid they are inspected and must be correctly marked – two red or orange flags at the western end (anywhere from south-southwest to north) and a single green flag at the eastern end (north to south-southeast). In addition, white flags should be set at 1M intervals. At night each flag should be replaced by a yellow light (so two lights at the western end). However with the passage of time both lights and flags may disappear, to be replaced at random if at all.

In a few places floating fish cages may be encountered, and again details are included in the text. Most are indicated by yellow buoys and lights, and positions are indicated on current Admiralty and other charts. Finally, a number of artificial reefs have been constructed off the coast to provide fish havens, reducing the charted depth by up to 2.5m. However since these seldom lie in less than 10m and more often straddle the 20m line – and assuming that while yachtsmen may fish by line they seldom tow a trawl – they can safely be ignored.

Swell

Though less of a problem than along the west-facing coast, heavy swell can be produced either by an Atlantic disturbance or by a *levanter* blowing through the Strait of Gibraltar, and the shallower entrances should be avoided in such conditions.

Winds

In summer north and northeast winds predominate in the west, but the further offshore the more variable they become. Further east, the influence of the Portuguese trade winds gradually dies away. Like the Atlantic coast, the Algarve is also subject to stiff afternoon sea breezes. From early summer onwards these start to blow at around 1400, regularly reaching force 6 and occasionally force 7 (25 or 30 knots) within an hour and continuing until sundown. Typically they pick up from the southwest, moving through west to west-northwest or northwest by evening.

East of Cádiz, the effect of the Strait becomes increasingly marked with 80% of winds in the Strait from either west (*poniente*) or east-northeast (*levante*). Gales are unlikely in the height of summer but *levanters* with winds of 50–60 knots are not unknown, visibility dropping to 1M or less. They are not seasonal, generally last for two to three days, and blow up with little or no warning from the barometer – though sometimes a deep purple bank of haze in the morning or a sudden fast steep swell may give a clue. The *poniente* is generally less strong than the *levanter* but may last five days or more. Squalls can occur at any time in the Bay of Gibraltar if the wind is between northeast and southeast.

Visibility

Poor visibility, less than 2M, is more common (2–5%) in summer than in winter. Fog is infrequent but not unknown in the Algarve, while the Cádiz area has a reputation for fog in certain conditions associated with a *levanter*.

Shelter

In a *levanter* (easterly) shelter in the Strait is limited to the Cádiz complex, west of the Tarifa causeway, and Gibraltar. In a *poniente* (westerly) it is limited to the Cádiz complex, Tarifa itself, and Gibraltar.

Currents

Along the Algarve coast the set is predominantly east of southeast, running at about 0.5 knot. By the time it reaches the Strait it is running east at 1–1.5 knots, compensating for water lost from the Mediterranean through evaporation. However this pattern can be upset by the wind – a southeasterly gale in the south

of the area can produce a west-going stream along the coast as far as Cabo de São Vicente, while persistent strong westerlies, coupled with the regular current, can produce an easterly set of 4 knots.

Tides

Tidal predictions for the Algarve use Lisbon as the Standard Port; those for Andalucía use either Lisbon, Cádiz or Gibraltar. When calculating Spanish tides using Lisbon data, note that allowance has already been made for the difference in time zones (Spanish time being UT+1, Portuguese time UT, both advanced one hour in summer – see page 8.) Volume 2 of the Admiralty *Tide Tables: The Atlantic and Indian Oceans including tidal stream predictions (NP 202)*, published annually, covers the entire coastline. Alternatively consult the UK Hydrographic Office's EasyTide programme at www.ukho.gov.uk – see page 2 – which gives daily tidal data for all major harbours.

Tidal range decreases eastward, from 2.8m at springs and 1.2m at neaps at Lagos, to 0.9m and 0.4m respectively at Gibraltar – see individual harbours. There is no reliable information about tidal streams along the coast, though 2–3 knots has been reported in some places, notably around Faro and Olhão. In the centre of the Straits the east-going stream starts shortly after HW Gibraltar and the west-going stream about six hours later, though the closer inshore, the earlier the change takes place – see diagrams pages 302 and 304. In addition a great deal of detailed, practical advice on how best to tackle the Straits of Gibraltar – including clear current and tidal flow diagrams – will be found in Colin Thomas's *Straits Sailing Handbook*, published annually by Ocean Marine Ltd, Gibraltar, *Email* straits.sailing@gibtelecom.net.

Cruising the Algarve is much more pleasant if it can be timed to coincide with morning and evening high tides (in practice a few days before neaps). Otherwise the typically shallow river entrances – which in many cases are dependant on at least half flood and good daylight – can complicate departure and arrival times.

Climate

Most rain falls between the end of October and the beginning of April with virtually none in July and August. Cool in winter, hot in summer, Lagos has a mean of 36°C in July with Gibraltar capable of 40°C in a *levanter*. Sea temperatures at Gibraltar range from 21°C in summer to 14°C in winter.

Maritime radio stations and weather/navigational services

Many Portuguese Maritime radio stations and those broadcasting weather and navigational information are situated between, rather than at, ports or harbours. Details will be found under the nearest harbour to the station. All are remotely controlled from Lisbon. In Andalucía, all Maritime radio stations are remotely controlled from Málaga. Broadcast times are quoted in UT, but all other times (office hours etc) are given in LT.

III.1 Cabo de São Vicente to Tavira

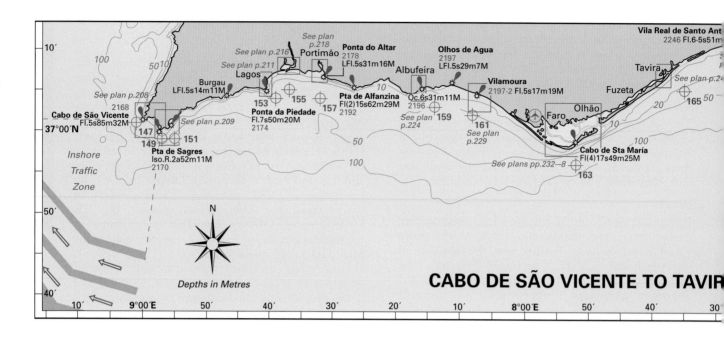

⊕147	37°01′N	9°00′.7W	1M SW of Cabo de São Vicente
⊕149	36°58′.8N	8°56′.9W	0.9M S of Ponta de Sagres
⊕151	36°59′N	8°53′.8W	Baleeira approach
⊕153	37°03′.8N	8°39′.2W	1.1M SE of Ponta da Piedade (Lagos approach)
⊕155	37°04.9N	8°36′.9W	Alvor approach
⊕157	37°04′.4N	8°31′.9W	Portimão approach
⊕159	37°03′.4N	8°13′.5W	Albufeira approach
⊕161	37°02′N	8°07′.8W	Vilamoura approach
⊕163	36°55′.6N	7°51′.9W	2.2M S of Cabo de Santa María
⊕165	37°04′.6N	7°35′.4W	Tavira approach
⊕167	37°06′.2N	7°24′.2W	Río Guadiana approach

PRINCIPAL LIGHTS

2168 Cabo de São Vicente Fl.5s85m32M Horn (2)30s
Off-white tower, red lantern, and building 28m
2170 Ponta de Sagres Iso.R.2s52m11M
Square white tower and building 13m
2174 Ponta da Piedade Fl.7s50m20M
Square yellow tower on building 5m
2178 Ponta do Altar LFl.5s31m16M 290°-vis-170°
Square white tower and building 10m
2192 Ponta de Alfanzina Fl(2)15s62m29M
Square white tower and building 23m
2196 Albufeira Oc.6s31m11M White column, red bands
2197 Olhos de Agua LFl.5s29m7M
White column, red bands
2206 Cabo de Santa María Fl(4)17s49m25M
White tower and building 46m
2246 Vila Real de Santo António Fl.6.5s51m26M
White tower, narrow black rings, red lantern 46m

Ports

54. Baleeira
55. Lagos*
56. Alvor
57. Portimão*
58. Albufeira*
59. Vilamoura*
60. Faro and Olhão
61. Tavira

* Fuel available alongside

Fish are landed, cleaned, cooked and eaten on the quayside at Ferragudo, across the river from Portimão. Researching a cruising guide does have its compensations ...

54. Cabo de São Vicente, Ponta de Sagres and Baleeira

Waypoints
⊕147 – 37°01′N 9°00′.7W (1M SW of Cabo de São Vicente)
⊕148 – 37°01′.5N 8°59′W (Enseada de Belixe anchorage)
⊕149 – 36°58′.8N 8°56′.9W (0.9M S of Ponta de Sagres)
⊕150 – 37°00′.05N 8°56′.55W (Enseada de Sagres anchorage)
⊕151 – 36°59′N 8°53′.8W (Baleeira, approach)
⊕152 – 37°00′.71N 8°55′.15W (Baleeira entrance)

Courses and distances
⊕142 (Sines) – ⊕147 = 54M, 185° or 005°
⊕147 – ⊕149 = 3.8M, 126° or 306°
⊕147 – ⊕153 (Lagos, via ⊕149) = 18.8M, 126°&071° or 251°&306°
⊕149 –⊕152 = 2.4M, 036° or 216°
⊕151 – ⊕152 = 2M, 328° or 148°
⊕151 – ⊕153 (Lagos) = 12.7M, 068° or 248°

Tides
Standard port Lisbon
Mean time differences (at Enseada de Belixe)
HW –0040 ±0010; LW –0015 ±0005
Heights in metres

MHWS	MHWN	MLWN	MLWS
4.1	3.2	1.7	0.8

Or refer to EasyTide at www.ukho.gov.uk (see page 2)

Charts	Approach	Anchorages
Admiralty	3636, 91, 89	
Imray	C19, C50	
Portuguese	23203, 23204, 24205, 24206	27502

Principal lights
2168 **Cabo de São Vicente** Fl.5s85m32M Horn (2)30s
Off-white tower, red lantern, and building 28m
2170 **Ponta de Sagres** Iso.R.2s52m11M
Square white tower and building 13m
2171 **Baleeira breakwater**
Fl.WR.4s12m14/11M 254°-W-355°-R-254°
White tower, red bands 6m

Warning
Long surface nets, lit or unlit, may be laid throughout the area and particularly in the vicinity of Baleeira, in addition to shorter nets and individual fish pots

Night entry
All three anchorages can be approached after dark in the right conditions, but very careful watch must be kept for the nets mentioned above

Maritime radio station
Sagres – *Digital Selective Calling* (MF)
MMSI 002630400 (planned)
Foia (37°18′.9N 8°36′.3W)
Remotely controlled from Lisbon
Manual – VHF Ch 16, 23, 24, 28. *Autolink* – VHF Ch 27.

Settled weather anchorages below spectacular cliffs

Cabo de São Vicente and Ponta de Sagres make a formidable pair, wild and windswept, sometimes seen for miles but, even in summer, sometimes heard before seen.

A few miles east of the headlands lies Baleeira, a relatively undeveloped harbour overlooked by a growing tourist resort. Its origins as a whaling centre are given away by its name and today a small fishing fleet still operates from the quay, along with a number of tourist boats. The beach close north of the harbour can be dirty, but Praia do Martinhal a little further east is well up to the Algarve's usual high standard.

Cabo de São Vicente from almost due south, with the lighthouse on the left and the Enseada de Belixe anchorage beneath the pale cliffs at centre right

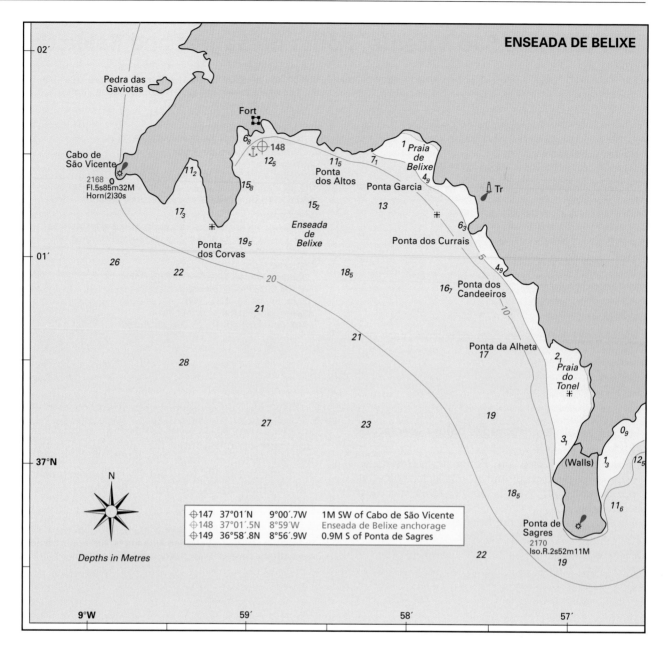

⊕147	37°01′N	9°00′.7W	1M SW of Cabo de São Vicente
⊕148	37°01′.5N	8°59′W	Enseada de Belixe anchorage
⊕149	36°58′.8N	8°56′.9W	0.9M S of Ponta de Sagres

Cabo de São Vicente and Ponta de Sagres – approach

When coastal sailing from the north the last major light is Cabo Sardão and from the east it is Ponta de Piedade south of Lagos. The 36M of coast between Cabo Sardão and Cabo de São Vicente is rocky and steep, and trends west of south. The 15M between Ponta de Sagres and Ponta de Piedade is similar, but trending southwest.

On passage southwards in the prevailing *nortada* both wind and waves are likely to increase noticeably on approaching Cabo de São Vicente, a combination of gusts off the cliffs and reflected swell. Both Cabo de São Vicente and Ponta de Sagres should be allowed a generous 2M clearance in these conditions, though much flatter water will generally be found east of Ponta de Baleeira. Equally, yachts heading west and north may expect to encounter rapidly deteriorating conditions on rounding Ponta

de Baleeira, and should prepare accordingly. It may be necessary to stay 2M or more offshore until 5–6M north of Cabo de São Vicente in order to avoid the worst. By far the best time to make the passage is early in the morning before the *nortada* reaches its full strength, especially if heading north.

If making landfall from offshore, particular care must be taken whilst crossing the Traffic Separation Zone which rounds Cabo de São Vicente and Ponta de Sagres – in fact there is much to be said for avoiding it altogether. The zone is up to 22M in width, its inshore edge nowhere less than 14M from the coast (older charts will show it as considerably closer in, the above change having come into force on 1 July 2005). On closing the headlands, ⊕147 lies 1M southwest of Cabo de São Vicente, ⊕149 about 0.9M south of Ponta de Sagres. The distance between the two is 3.8M on a course of 126°/306°.

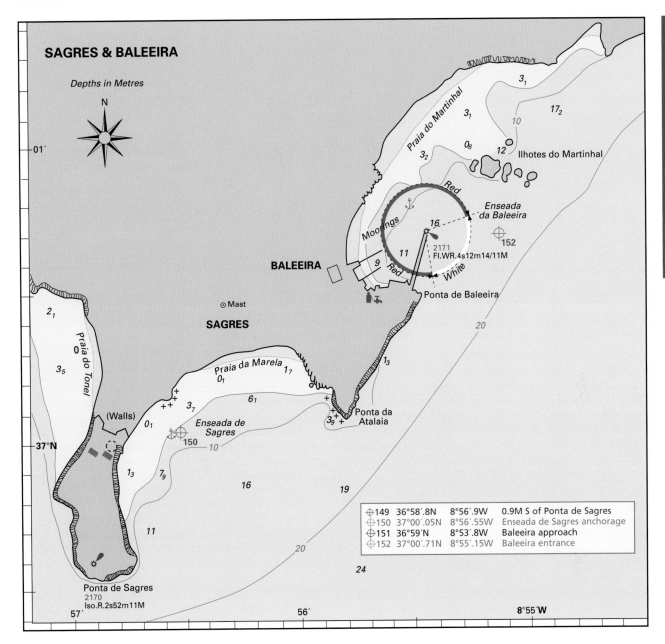

SAGRES & BALEEIRA

Depths in Metres

N

⊕149	36°58′.8N	8°56′.9W	0.9M S of Ponta de Sagres
⊕150	37°00′.05N	8°56′.55W	Enseada de Sagres anchorage
⊕151	36°59′N	8°53′.8W	Baleeira approach
⊕152	37°00′.71N	8°55′.15W	Baleeira entrance

Three anchorages can be useful if waiting for the usual strong afternoon *nortada* to die before heading north around Cabo de São Vicente, and though none give much protection from the south in these conditions most crews will, in any case, be wanting to press on.

Cabo de São Vicente and Ponta de Sagres – adjacent anchorages

1. **Enseada de Belixe** (⊕148 – 37°01′.55N 8°59′W) is wide open to the west and south, with entry straightforward day or night using the loom of Cabo de São Vicente light. If coming from the north pass outside the tall rock off the headland and continue beyond the first, small, wedge-shaped bay until Enseada de Belixe opens up round Pontal dos Corvos.

   Anchor in the western part of the bay in 14m, or for more shelter in the cove under the old fort where there is good holding in 9m about 100m from the shore. However beware the tidal rock some 200m south of the east end of the Praia de Belixe, which rises almost sheer out of 9m to show only at low water. Very little will be found ashore.

2. **Enseada de Sagres** (⊕149 – 36°58′.8N 8°56′.9W) is open to the southeast, with easy entry and excellent shelter from west through north to northeast. Anchor off the beach in good holding over sand. There is a growing tourist development at the top of the hill with supermarkets, shops, banks and restaurants.

Baleeira – approach

Two fish farms lie northeast of Baleeira, a potential hazard if on passage to or from Lagos or beyond. One is marked by four yellow can buoys, all Fl.Y.14s4M, and is centred on 37°01′.1N 8°53′.5W,

Looking west across Baleeira harbour towards the Ponta de Sagres. The walls of Prince Henry the Navigator's one-time headquarters can be seen near the root of the long promontory

the other by four spherical yellow buoys, all Fl.Y.5s3M, and is centred on 37°01′.5N 8°52′.6°. In addition long nets may be set at an angle to the shore, normally indicated by lit yellow buoys (powered by solar panels) and supported by yellow floats. These nets are not connected to the shore and, with due care, yachts can pass on either side.

From offshore make for ⊕151, 2M to the south-southeast of the harbour, from which a course of 328° leads in to ⊕152 close off the entrance. From ⊕149 to ⊕152 – there is no reason to head back offshore to ⊕151 – is 2.4M on 036°.

The harbour itself is sheltered by a high breakwater around 400m in length running northeast from Ponta de Baleeira, leaving it open to the east and with a fetch of nearly 1M to the northeast. The breakwater light is sectored, with its red area covering the Ilhotes do Martinhal, a group of large rocks about 500m to the northeast. Although it is possible to pass between the islands and the shore, the area is littered with rocks and strictly a case for eyeball navigation.

Baleeira – harbour and anchorage

Baleeira (⊕152 – 37°00′.71N 8°55′.15W off entrance) provides slightly more protection than the foregoing, being open only to the east. Anchor outside the moorings, northwest or north of the breakwater head, in 6–10m. Holding is patchy and the bottom is reported to be very foul – a tripline is recommended.

There are several ladders and a ramp convenient for landing, but if possible avoid going ashore at low water as the bottoms of the ladders are seriously dilapidated and the lower part of the ramp lethally slippery. The *Polícia Marítima* have an office in the Doca de Pesca building and may well intercept the skipper and crew as they come ashore – bring ship's papers and passports, in case. The *GNR–Brigada Fiscal* are also likely to check on any foreign flag yacht.

Facilities in the harbour are limited to diesel and water on the fishermen's quay, and a telephone kiosk at the top of the steps up from the harbour. There is an old-style boatyard just north of the jetties where fishing boats are brought ashore for work, but the (elderly) cradle would not suit a deep keeled yacht and in all but sinking condition it would be worth continuing to Lagos. Engineering and other skills may well be available, but again it would be much safer to head for a more yacht-orientated harbour.

The tourist development at the top of the steep road offers shops (including several supermarkets), banks, a post office and innumerable cafés, restaurants and hotels. Baleeira lies on the bus route from Lagos out to Sagres and Cabo de São Vicente, both popular tourist destinations.

Further afield

Navigators will wish to visit the site of Prince Henry's famous 'school of navigation' on the cliffs at Ponta de Sagres – complete with an (allegedly) 15th century *rosa dos ventos* (wind compass) in the courtyard – but may be disappointed that, with the exception of a small chapel and the northern wall, little else remains. (Sir Francis Drake must take a share of the blame, though the final havoc was wrought by the 1755 earthquake which devastated much of the Algarve.) An 'interpretative centre' has been set up within the vast Fortaleza, but inevitably the information presented (in several languages) is aimed at a very broad public and sadly the buildings are ugly and do not add to the general ambience. The energetic may also fancy the tramp as far as Cabo de São Vicente to watch the sun set, though the walk itself is somewhat boring.

55. Lagos

Waypoints
⊕153 – 37°03′.8N 8°39′.2W (1.1M SE of Ponta da
Piedade or Lagos approach)
⊕154 – 37°05′.86N 8°39′.68W (entrance)

Courses and distances
⊕147 (Cabo de São Vicente) – ⊕153 (via ⊕149) =
18.8M, 126°&071° or 251°&306°
⊕151 (Baleeira) – ⊕153 = 12.7M, 068° or 248°
⊕153 – ⊕154 = 2.1M, 349° or 169°
⊕154 – ⊕156 (Alvor entrance) = 2.3M, 064° or 244°
⊕154 – ⊕158 (Portimão entrance) = 6.4M, 085° or 265°

Tides
Standard port Lisbon
Mean time differences
HW –0025 ±0010; LW –0030 ±0005
Heights in metres

MHWS	MHWN	MLWN	MLWS
3.3	2.6	1.3	0.6

Or refer to EasyTide at www.ukho.gov.uk (see page 2)

Charts

	Approach	Harbour
Admiralty	3636, 91, 89	
Imray	C19, C50	C19, C50
Portuguese	23203, 23204, 24205, 24206	27502

Principal lights
2175 West breakwater
Fl(2)R.6s5M White tower, red bands 7m
2176 East breakwater Fl(2)G.6s5M
White tower, green bands 6m

Warning
Long surface nets, lit or unlit, may be laid in the bay
near the entrance to the harbour, in addition to shorter
nets and individual fish pots

Night entry
Straightforward other than in strong onshore winds.
The reception pontoon is not lit, but there is sufficient
ambient light for all practical purposes

Harbour communications
Port Authority ☎ 282 762826
Marina de Lagos ☎ 282 770210 *Fax* 282 770219
Email marina@marlagos.pt
www.marinadelagos.pt
VHF 09, 16 (0800–2200 1 June–15 Sept, otherwise
0900–1900)
Weather information VHF Ch 12 at 1000 and 1600 daily
from 16 July to 31 August.

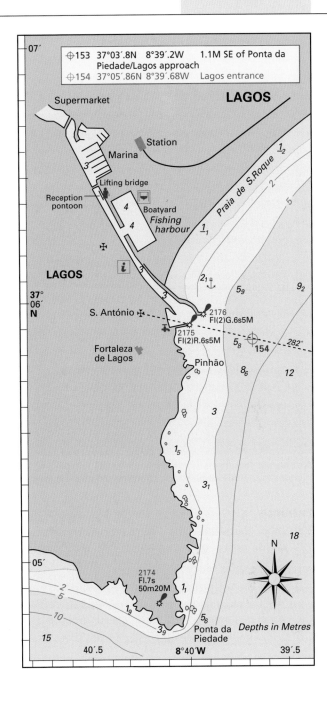

Large, well-protected marina adjacent to lively tourist resort

Lagos, on the banks of the Rio Bensafrim, is a crowded and active trading, tourist and fishing town. Its fairs, held in mid August and mid October, are lively events. It once had the only slave market in Portugal, and still has many notable buildings as well as an interesting museum and good nightlife.

The large and impressive Marina de Lagos has been awarded both the European Blue Flag and Euromarina Anchor Award. In addition to celebrating its 10th anniversary during 2004, it also welcomed its 20,000th visitor. It is a safe and popular place to leave a yacht brought south during the summer before a late autumn passage to the Canaries or beyond, since facilities are good and security excellent. For those in transit there is also the option of anchoring off. The Meia Praia, one of the Algarve's finest beaches, lies close east of the harbour.

Approach

Lagos lies in the lee of Ponta da Piedade, itself at the east end of a stretch of dramatic coastline noted for its cliffs and caves (see Adjacent anchorages, page 214). West of Ponta da Piedade the coast is rocky with cliffs and caves, but to the east, there are beaches past Alvor to Portimão, backed at their eastern end by low cliffs. Lights to the east include Ponta do Altar and Ponta de Alfanzina. If approaching Lagos from the east and on the wind (as is likely), the transit formed by the end of the west breakwater and the church of Santo António on 282° is useful.

From offshore ⊕153 lies 2.1M south of the entrance and a good mile from the rocks of Ponta da Piedade, a course of 349° leading to ⊕154 outside the harbour mouth.

An unusual view from the northeast over the entrance to Lagos, showing the cliffs and islands which add drama to the coastline to Ponta da Piedade and beyond

Entrance

Entrance between the twin breakwaters is straightforward, and though a bar periodically builds up southeast of the breakwater heads there is seldom less than 2.5m above datum. Even so, seas can build up in onshore winds. Once through the entrance the channel has a least depth of 3m, as does the marina. There is a 3 knot speed limit in the entrance channel and throughout the marina.

The roof the Mercado Municipal gives excellent views across the channel and fishing harbour – now partially occupied by tourist boats – towards the Sopromar boatyard with its pale blue travel-lift and large acreage of hardstanding   *AH*

Berthing

The marina lies about 0.7M inside the entrance. Secure to the 80m reception pontoon, close downstream of the lifting pedestrian bridge, to arrange a berth and complete formalities. Otherwise the bridge normally opens on demand (VHF Ch 09) during office hours (see above), seven days a week. When a train is due to depart or arrive – the station lies just behind the marina – the bridge remains closed for 15 minutes before or after, respectively. Multihull owners should note that the bridge has a limiting width of 11m.

The marina can take 462 yachts of up to 30m LOA, with room always found for visitors. All berths are alongside finger pontoons, with exceptionally large yachts occupying the seven hammerheads. The marina has been popular with British yachtsmen ever since it opened, and has a small but growing (and very loyal) band of long-term residents. It is also a frequent choice for owners wishing to over-winter in the Algarve, whether living aboard or returning home with occasional visits when the northern climate becomes too unpleasant. The staff – all of whom appear to speak some English – are particularly helpful.

In 2005 the overnight rate for a visiting yacht of 10–12m was €38.12 in the high and mid seasons (16 June–30 September) and €20.57 (or €401.12 per month) in the low season. The equivalent rates for a yacht of 12–15m were €56.27, €33.28 and €651.00 respectively. Multihulls paid a 100% surcharge in the high season (16 July–31 August) and 50% at other times. Rates listed in the marina brochure include water and electricity but not IVA (the equivalent of VAT) currently charged at 21%. However this has been added to the above figures for easy comparison with other harbours. Most major credit cards are accepted.

Anchorage

Anchor northeast of the east breakwater in 5–6m over good holding in hard sand. The corridor off the beach a little further east, indicated by a number of small yellow buoys, serves the local windsurfing centre and should be left clear. The anchorage is very exposed to south and east, and a southwesterly swell may also work its way around Ponta da Piedade. Land on the beach near the Clube de Vela de Lagos or in the small harbour overlooked by the turretted Fortaleza. There is no possible anchorage inside the harbour itself – the large fishing boat basin may look tempting, but the authorities would not agree.

Formalities

The *GNR–Brigada Fiscal, Polícia Marítima* and *Alfândega* all have offices in the marina reception building – enquire on first arrival whether or not it is necessary to visit them. If anchored off, the skipper should call at all three offices with ship's papers, passports etc.

Facilities

Boatyards After a number of years during which the lack of a good, secure boatyard was one of Lagos's few failings, yachtsmen are now well provided for by Sopromar Lda ☎ 282 763889 *Fax* 282 792135 *Email* sopromar@mail.telepac.pt   www.sopromar.com   a family-run concern which has been highly praised by numerous owners. Yard hours are officially 0830–1200 and 1300–1800 Monday to Saturday, closed Sunday, but in practice at least one member of the Pereira family is nearly always on site. English, French, German and Spanish are all spoken in addition to Portuguese. Many of the services offered – engineering, electronics, osmosis treatment with the Hotvac system, painting, rigging etc – are detailed below, but there is a very good chance that even if a particular service is not mentioned, Sopromar will be able to handle it.

Other services, including regular checking of unattended yachts left afloat in the marina, are offered by various long-term marina residents and local people – consult the noticeboard in marina reception.

Travel-lift 36-tonne capacity (6m beam) lift at Sopromar, with two waiting pontoons, a wide slipway and a scrubbing grid. The approach through the fishing boat harbour is said to carry adequate depths at all states of the tide and a 30m crane is available for mast removal.

Ashore there is secure lay-up space for at least 140 yachts plus 2000 sq metres of undercover workshops and storage. The hardstanding is well provided with water and electricity points, and ladders (or substantial steps for the less agile) can be borrowed. Owners are

The Marina de Lagos opened in 1994 and has become a popular wintering spot among owners from northern Europe

welcome to live aboard (there are immaculate toilets and showers on site), and to do their own work. 15 CCTV cameras monitor the area day and night. There are plans for a 70-tonne travel-lift, but no date has been set.

Engineers Sopromar has an extensive engine repair shop, handles welding in all materials and is agent for Volvo Penta, Yanmar and Mercruiser. Pedragosa Engineering ☎ 282 688056, *Mobiles* 96 7965 481 and 96 9018 894 *Email* mgsnook@bigfoot.com advertise their services for all types of work in stainless-steel and aluminium, including making one-off fittings from scratch. Finally Bluewater Yacht Services (though based mainly in Portimão, see page 222), still have engineers in Lagos who are happy to visit yachts in the marina. Their Lagos office, handling mainly brokerage, will be found on the first floor of the main commercial block.

Electronic and radio repairs At both Sopromar and Bluewater Yacht Services. In addition John Holloway, *Mobile* 91 4902 538 *Email* nojfairchild@hotmail.com handles all kinds of electrical and electronic work including radar etc.

Diver Francisco, *Mobile* 91 8287 551, will change anodes etc.

Sailmaker/sail repairs Fofovelas, ☎ 282 799425, *Mobile* 91 7550 960, *Email* fofovelas@sapo.pt, fofovelas@mail.pt, make and repair sails, as well as being agent for several well-known names.

Rigging Sopromar has a swage machine and stocks wire of all sizes.

Chandleries The chandlery at Sopromar – open 0900–1200 and 1430–1800 weekdays, 0900–1200 Saturdays – is one of the largest in Portugal, and items not in stock can generally be ordered within 48 hours. AlaRede, ☎/*Fax* 282 792238 *Email* alarede@sapo.pt at the north end of the fishing boat basin carries some general chandlery in addition to fishing and diving equipment. There are several good ironmongery and hardware stores in the town.

Charts Local charts are available from both the marina office and AlaRede (see above). The latter will order Portuguese charts from Lisbon if required.

Water At all berths. Yachts anchored off may be able to get water in the small western harbour (but check depths in advance).

Showers Single block – but large and very well kept – at the north end of the marina's café/shops complex. Crews of yachts anchored off may be able to shower at the *clube de vela* (see below).

Launderette At the north end of the marina's café/shops complex. Tokens are available at the marina office.

Electricity At all berths, with a variety of voltages available.

Fuel Petrol and diesel pumps on the reception pontoon below the bridge, run by the marina and available during office hours only. Credit cards are accepted but a 5% surcharge may be levied.

Bottled gas Camping Gaz cylinders can be exchanged either at Sopromar or at a hardware shop near the bus station in town. Sopromar can also arrange for other cylinders to be refilled with either propane or butane. A third possibility is the PB service station about 1km along the Portimão road, on the north side, where American yachtsmen have had propane cylinders refilled.

Clube náutico The Clube de Vela de Lagos ☎ 282 762256 *Fax* 282 764277 www.cvlagos.org has premises near the root of the west breakwater.

Weather forecast Posted daily at the marina reception and, during the high season, broadcast on VHF Ch 12 at 1000 and 1600.

Banks Several in the town, plus two cash dispensers in the marina complex.

Shops/provisioning Several large supermarkets, including an enormous Pingo Doce near the road bridge north of the marina (trolleys can be wheeled back and left at one of several designated 'trolley areas' for collection). Good general shopping in the older town on the west bank (direct access over the pedestrian bridge). Limited shopping in the marina complex – mostly tourist items and newspapers, including one supplying UK titles on day of issue.

Produce market Large produce and fish market on the west bank of the river (with great views from the roof terrace).

Cafés, restaurants and hotels Dozens if not hundreds, including several overlooking the marina itself.

Medical services LuzDoc ☎ 282 780700, a private medical clinic which also handles dental problems, has an office in the marina at Núcleo Gil Eanes 13 and a larger facility in the town, where there is also a public hospital.

Communications

Post office In the town.

Mailing address The marina office will hold mail for visiting yachts – c/o Marina de Lagos, Edificio da Administração, Sítio da Ponte, 8600–780 Lagos, Portugal. It is important that the envelope carries the name of the yacht in addition to that of the addressee.

Public telephones Several around the marina complex.

Internet access Owners can connect their own laptop at the marina office, or use wireless broadband from on board (the necessary cards are on sale at reception). Alternatively there are public terminals at the Regatta Club Bar.

Fax service At the marina office *Fax* 282 770219.

Car hire/taxis Can be arranged via the marina office or in the town.

Trains Brand new station just behind the marina complex, the western end of the (distinctly slow) Algarve coastal line.

Air services Faro international airport is about 50 minutes by taxi or, at a fraction of the taxi fare, 90 minutes by train (though a taxi will still be needed between the station and the airport).

Adjacent anchorages

1. Off the beach at Senhora da Luz (37°05′N 8°44′W), 3.5M west of Ponta da Piedade. Reported to be a pleasant anchorage in settled conditions off a small slipway, but fully exposed to the south.

2. Close east of Ponta da Piedade (37°05′N 8°40′W), and a good spot from which to explore the maritime caves and blow holes. If paddling ashore by inflatable, beware the high-speed tourist ferries which appear to hold their course regardless.

56. Alvor

Waypoints
⊕155 – 37°′04.9N 8°36′.9W (approach)
⊕156 – 37°06′.87N 8°37′.06W (entrance)

Courses and distances
⊕154 (Lagos entrance) – ⊕156 = 2.3M, 064° or 244°
⊕155 – ⊕156 = 2M, 356° or 176°
⊕156 – ⊕158 (Portimão entrance) = 4.3M, 097° or 277°

Tides
See Lagos, page 211

Charts	Approach	Harbour
Admiralty	3636, 91, 89	
Imray	C19, C50	
Portuguese	23203, 23204, 24205, 27502 24206	

Principal lights
2176.2 **West breakwater** Fl.R.4s8m7M
White tower, red bands 4m
2176.4 **East breakwater** Fl.G.4s8m7M
White tower, green bands 4m

Night entry
Not feasible due to shifting shoals which call for eyeball navigation. Any buoys encountered are likely to be unlit.

The Alvor breakwaters and entrance from the southeast, with a number of yachts in the lower anchorage

Attractive, windswept anchorage flanked by some tourist development

Until relatively recently Alvor was little more than a small fishing village reached via a shallow, sandy lagoon almost impassable by yachts. However construction of twin breakwaters at the entrance during the early 1990s, allied to extensive dredging within, has opened the Rio Alvor to the cruising yachtsman. Even so, care is still required and the entrance should not be attempted at low water, when swell is running, in onshore winds, on the ebb tide or at night.

The town is touristy (apparently aimed largely at the British market) but attractive, with good shops, restaurants and cafés, and the anchorage a pleasant change from fishing harbours and marinas – and a paradise for birdwatchers.

The waterfront has been prettied up considerably over the past five years, with cobbles and neat little cafés replacing the mud and fishermen's stores – the latter having been banished to their own area a little to the south – but continuing pride in the area's maritime heritage is confirmed by the flawless condition in which the village's old rowing and sailing lifeboat is maintained. The red doors to her boathouse can hardly be missed, and now feature a glass panel through which she can be admired when they are closed.

THE ALGARVE & ANDALUCIA

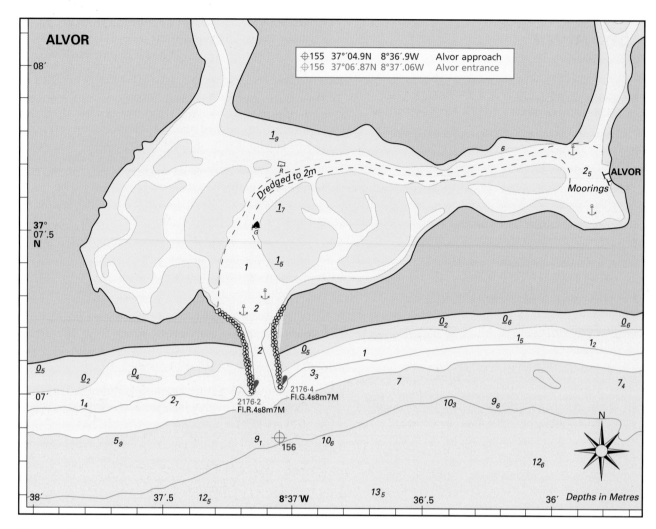

ALVOR

| ⊕155 | 37°04.9N | 8°36′.9W | Alvor approach |
| ⊕156 | 37°06′.87N | 8°37′.06W | Alvor entrance |

Dredged to 2m

ALVOR

Moorings

2176·4
Fl.G.4s8m7M

2176·2
Fl.R.4s8m7M

156

Depths in Metres

Approach

If coastal sailing, Alvor lies 2.3M east of Lagos and 4.3M west of Portimão, surrounded by sandy beaches – the Meia Praia, one of the Algarve's finest, stretches between Lagos and Alvor. The nearest major lights are Ponta da Piedade west of Lagos, and Ponta de Altar, close east of Portimão – Alvor no longer has a major light of its own, though both breakwaters are lit. High man-made sand dunes (created from dredged material) stand close each side of the entrance with conspicuous high-rise apartments further east.

From offshore ⊕155 lies 2M south of the entrance, a course of 356° leading to ⊕156, close outside the harbour mouth.

Entrance

Parallel breakwaters bracket the entrance, which was originally dredged to a nominal 4m. However considerable silting is reported to have taken place and by 2005 it was understood to carry no more than 2m at MLWS, shoaling further once inside. Enter on the half flood keeping to the middle of the narrow channel on a bearing of approximately 352°.Once inside, the estuary opens out and it is possible to anchor in the pool just inside the entrance, where at least 2m should be found at all times.

A bar carrying no more than 1m over datum is reported to have formed well inside the entrance (see plan). In 2005 a British yacht grounded at 37°07′.46N 8°37′.2W when attempting to leave at LWS and could not be got off for nearly three hours. Although no damage was done the owner comments that, had a southerly swell built up in the meantime, it might have been a very different story.

The narrow, dredged channel leading up to the basin off the town is most easily followed below half tide when the fringing sandbanks are uncovered. Both channel and basin carry a nominal 2m at MLWS, but if in doubt the dinghy could be sent ahead to recce. In 2005 the channel was marked by a number of small, unlit buoys, but it is understood that these were laid unofficially and may be removed.

Anchorage

Anchor near the entrance, as described above, or off the village to the north of the moorings – an area which, in summer, may become very crowded. Shelter in the basin is excellent and holding good over muddy sand. Nearly a decade ago it was reported that pontoons were to be installed for visiting yachts, but these have not materialised and in 2005 visiting yachts were still swinging happily to their own anchors. A small charge is sometimes

Looking northeast over the shallow lagoon at Alvor, backed by the channel leading to the anchorage off the town

made. The fairway leading to the fishermen's quay is clearly defined by smallcraft moorings and must not be impeded.

There are two pontoons with floating hammerheads, and though both are adorned with notices stating that it is 'Forbidden to place arts of fishing and to park any kind of boats', both are colonised by flocks of dinghies. A long painter would clearly be an advantage.

Facilities

Water by can from one of the waterfront cafés, with supermarkets, general shopping and a vast choice of restaurants in the town (the local shellfish is reputed to be particularly good). Services include a post office, public telephones, taxis and buses (at the roundabout), and Portimão station about 5.5km away.

The anchorage off Alvor town – no longer a village! – with the new fishermen's wharf at centre and the fast-growing tourist development on the right

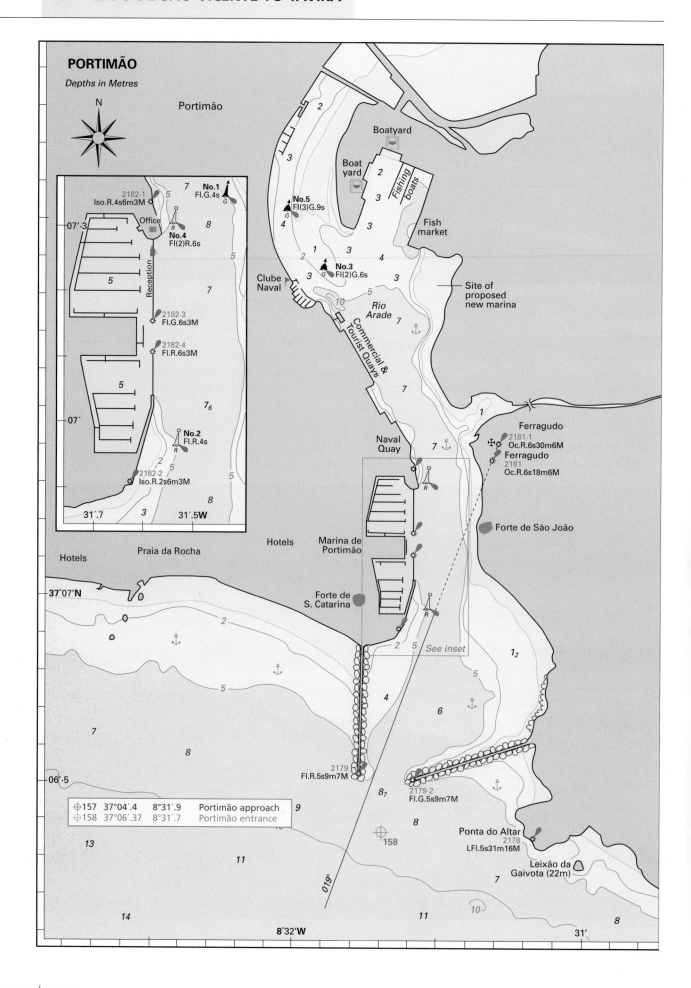

PORTIMÃO

Depths in Metres

N

Portimão

Portimão

2

Boatyard

3

Boat yard

2

No.5
Fl(3)G.9s
4

3

Fishing boats

3

Fish market

No.1
Fl.G.4s
7
G

2182·1
Iso.R.4s6m3M
5

Office

07'·3

No.4
Fl(2)R.6s
8
R

1
3

3
No.3
Fl(2)G.6s
G

3
4

Site of proposed new marina

5

Clube Naval

5

Rio Arade

10

7

5

7

2182·3
Fl.G.6s3M

Commercial & Tourist Quays

7

2182·4
Fl.R.6s3M

5

1

07'

No.2
Fl.R.4s
R

7₆

Ferragudo
2181·1
Oc.R.6s30m6M
Ferragudo
2181
Oc.R.6s18m6M

Naval Quay

7

2

2182·2
Iso.R.2s6m3M

5

5

Forte de São João

31'·7

3

31'·5W

2

8

Hotels

Marina de Portimão

Hotels

Praia da Rocha

Forte de S. Catarina

2

5

See inset

1₂

37°07'N

0

2

4

5

O

5

6

7

2179
Fl.R.5s9m7M

8₇

2179·2
Fl.G.5s9m7M

06'·5

8

8

| ⊕157 | 37°04'.4 | 8°31'.9 | Portimão approach |
| ⊕158 | 37°06'.37 | 8°31'.7 | Portimão entrance |

9

13

11

019°

158

Ponta do Altar
2178
LFl.5s31m16M

Leixão da Gaivota (22m)

7

14

11

10

8

8°32'W

31'

57. Portimão

Waypoints
⊕157 – 37°04′.4N 8°31′.9W (approach)
⊕158 – 37°06′.37N 8°31′.7W (entrance)

Courses and distances
⊕154 (Lagos entrance) – ⊕158 = 6.4M, 085° or 265°
⊕156 (Alvor entrance) – ⊕158 = 4.3M, 097° or 277°
⊕157 – ⊕158 = 2M, 005° or 185°
⊕157 – ⊕159 (Albufeira) = 14M, 096° or 276°
⊕157 – ⊕161 (Vilamoura) = 19.5M, 097° or 277°

Tides
Standard port Lisbon
Mean time differences
HW –0025 ±0010; LW –0030 ±0005
Heights in metres

MHWS	MHWN	MLWN	MLWS
3.3	2.6	1.4	0.7

Or refer to EasyTide at www.ukho.gov.uk (see page 2)

Charts

Charts	Approach	Harbour
Admiralty	3636, 91, 89	83
Imray	C19, C50	C50
Portuguese	23203, 23204, 24206	26310

Principal lights
2178 **Ponta do Altar** LFl.5s31m16M 290°-vis-170°
Square white tower and building 10m
2181 **Ldg Lts 019° Front** *Ferragudo* Iso.R.6s18m6M
White tower, red bands 4m

2181.1 *Rear* 54m from front Iso.R.6s30m6M
White tower, red bands 5m
2179 **West breakwater** Fl.R.5s9m7M
White tower, red bands 7m
2179.2 **East breakwater** Fl.G.5s9m7M
White tower, green bands 7m
2182.2 **Marina, southeast**
Iso.R.2s6m3M White column, red bands
2182.4 **Marina south pontoon head**
Fl.R.6s3M White column, red bands
2182.3 **Marina north pontoon head**
Fl.G.6s3M White column, green bands
2182.1 **Marina, northeast**
Iso.R.4s 6m3M White column, red bands

Night entry
No problem – spacious, well lit and with generous depths.

Harbour communications
Marina de Portimão ☎ 282 400680 *Fax* 282 400681
Email marinaportimao@mail.telepac.pt
www.marina-portimao.com
VHF Ch 09, 16 (0830–2100 1 July to 31 August, otherwise 0900–1800)
Weather information in Portuguese and English
VHF Ch 09 at 1000 daily from 1 July to 31 August

Portimão from the southwest. The anchorage inside the east breakwater
clearly remains popular, despite the appeal of the new Marina de Portimão

All-weather entrance leading to large, modern marina

Portimão on the Rio Arade has long been a busy fishing harbour, also handling small naval and commercial vessels. However in May 2000 the waterfront on the west side near the entrance was transformed with the opening of the large Marina de Portimão. From being one of those harbours where transients rafted four or five abreast wherever they could, and where few facilities were available, almost overnight Portimão began to rival Lagos and Vilamoura in its provision of berths and other services for visiting yachts. In 2005 all the marina staff spoke English and the attitude was helpful, friendly and very ready to consider reasonable requests. Amongst the non-profitmaking services on offer was a small but growing bookswap, with a surprising percentage of the titles in English.

The town of Portimão, on the west bank nearly 2M from the harbour mouth, is old and agreeable but undistinguished, and the beach resort of Praia da Rocha somewhat brash. The region's undoubted gem is the waterside village of Ferragudo on the east side of the estuary. If settled in the marina make the effort to launch the dinghy, cross the river, and enjoy a lunch of *sardinhas* grilled on a charcoal brazier on the tiny quay with seagulls wheeling overhead. A stroll through the village's steep cobbled alleys (mostly impassable to cars) will work off any resulting somnolence.

Approach

If inshore sailing, from Lagos to Portimão the coast consists of sandy beaches with a backdrop of hills. East of Portimão there are a few small sandy beaches but the shore is mainly rocky with cliffs. There are no off-lying hazards.

From offshore ⊕157 lies 2M south of the entrance, a course of 005° leading to ⊕158 close outside the harbour mouth.

The Marina de Portimão looking east towards the high-rise blocks of Praia da Rocha

Entrance

Entrance is safe in all but the heaviest onshore conditions, and should present no problems by day or night. The ends of the breakwaters are lit – these lights line up on 097° for those coming from Lagos. The charted leading line to enter the harbour itself is 019° (two red and white striped posts close east of Ferragudo church). However this leads close to a growing shoal around the head of the west breakwater, and about equidistant between the two heads offers better depths. From there leave buoy No.2 close to port before ducking through the marina entrance (both sides of which are lit) and securing to the inner side of the north pontoon.

If venturing further upstream, the buoyage is straightforward with a pair of lit buoys and then two unlit starboard hand buoys. The channel as far as Ponta São Francisco has a least depth of around 7m, but soundings shoal rapidly outside the buoyed channel.

Looking across the river towards the Forte de São João, with port hand buoy No.4 in the foreground   *AH*

Berthing

Nearly all the inner side of the marina's north pontoon is used for reception, though during office hours a yacht which makes contact via VHF or mobile phone may well be routed directly to a berth in the marina proper. Even when the tide is running at spring ebb it is claimed that the marina remains unaffected and securing is never a problem (the manager is himself a yachtsman, so speaks with more knowledge than some), though it has been reported that swell works into the north basin in southerly winds. Reception is housed in the circular orange building overlooking the pontoon and operates 0830–2030 from 1 July to 31 August and 0900–1800 at other times.

With a total capacity of 620 berths including one 50m slot, nearly all in 5m or more depths, the marina is already running at 80% capacity with the larger berths filling up particularly fast. Its only real downside is its sheer size – those berthed centrally face a lengthy walk to shops, toilets and showers (a bicycle would quickly prove its worth), while those in the south basin, though conveniently near most of the facilities, may be kept awake far into the night by music from the bars and karaoke joints. In compensation, there is an excellent beach nearby and plans to build a seawater swimming pool for hotel and marina users. Security throughout the marina is excellent, with two guards patrolling at all times in addition to card access gates and facilities.

In 2005 the high season (16 June–30 September) rate for a visiting yacht of 10–12m was €35.34 per night, rising to €52.36 for 12m–15.5m, inclusive of water, electricity and tax. The low season equivalents were €14.40 per night (€334.89 per month) and €20.94 per night (€511.87 per month) respectively, with further discounts for longer stays. Though quoted by the marina ex-IVA – the equivalent of VAT – this has been added to the above figures for easy comparison with other harbours. Multihulls paid a 50% surcharge during the high season, but this might be waived at other times. Most major credit cards were accepted.

As of 2005 there was no other visitors' berthing option on the Rio Arade – the upstream basin near the new *clube naval* building was reserved for local smallcraft, and visitors were no longer welcome on the old yacht pontoon just below the bridge. Tales of a 'new marina' beyond the bridge relate to a private leisure club with a single, equally private, pontoon for small motorboats, limited by an air height of 5m beneath the old road bridge.

Plans to build a second yacht marina on the east side of the river just upstream of Ferragudo were submitted to the authorities late in 2004 by the owners of the Marina de Portimão. If these come to fruition a further 330 berths for vessels of up to 50m and 5m draught will become available, though not until 2008 at the earliest.

With little unused space near the marina, a sizeable boatyard has been established upriver in the old fishing harbour. The old centre of Portimão can be seen across the river at right, with the Clube Naval de Portimão and smallcraft basin (not open to visitors) at left

Anchorage

The anchorage inside the east breakwater is secure with good holding in sand, though sometimes affected by swell and/or wash. It would be a safe choice if arriving by night, but note that the bottom shelves steeply between the 5m and 2m contours. Alternatively anchor off Ferragudo near the fishing boat moorings, in 3–4m over mud. Be sure to leave the marked channel clear as the fishing fleet appears to leave en masse in the hours before daybreak (if the throb of their engines does not wake you, their wash will). No charge is made for anchoring in either spot.

A dinghy can safely be left at the marina, for which a charge is made, but this involves a long walk into the town. Upstream possibilities are limited, though it would certainly be worth asking both at the smallcraft basin and at the Clube Naval de Portimão (where, if permission is granted, it would clearly be tactful to patronise the bar).

Formalities

All paperwork is carried out in the marina office with copies passed to the usual officials. None need to be seen, but non-EU registered yachts, or those carrying non-EU citizens, may be visited by one or more sets of officials in the days after arrival.

Facilities

Boatyard The marina's boatyard is some distance away in the old fishing harbour just short of the old road bridge (see plan), with the compensation of almost unlimited lay-up area. Security is good, with high fences, gates locked overnight and regular patrols. Lockerage can be rented if required.

While lifting, pressure-hosing and chocking-up are carried out by marina employees, all other work is done by specialist contractors – see below. DIY is permitted, and owners may live aboard whilst ashore (the yacht area is provided with a single, rather basic, shower and toilet). There is a supermarket within walking distance.

Travel-lift Choice of two at the boatyard, of 50-tonne and 300-tonne capacity respectively. The latter is believed to be the largest travel-hoist in mainland Portugal. Book at the marina office.

Engineers, electronics, and general maintenance Amongst the four or five contractors who regularly work in the yard, Bluewater Yacht Services, ☎ 282 432404 *Mobile* 96 9064 618 *Fax* 282 432406 *Email* info@bluewateralgarve.com www.bluewateralgarve.com, who also have an office near the marina's northern basin, appear to offer by far the widest range of services. Owner Paul Mallett is an engineer (as well as an Ocean Yachtmaster) and other members of the eight permanent staff can handle electrical work and electronics (installation and repair of water-makers and refrigeration are specialities), repairs in all materials, osmosis treatment (including slurry blasting and peeling), painting – in fact all disciplines necessary to keep yachts of up to 20m or so in good working order. Unattended yachts can be collected from and returned to the marina, and finally all work – or damage, should one be so unlucky – can be overseen/assessed by a fully qualified surveyor, recognised by Lloyds.Languages spoken currently include English, Portuguese, Spanish, German, Dutch and some French, and Paul and his team are happy to travel throughout southern Portugal and Spain to carry out work on boats in situ.

Sailmaker/sail repairs Marine Canvas, ☎ 967 084927, in the boatyard area make covers, awnings etc, and can handle minor sail repairs. While not sailmakers themselves, Bluewater Yacht Services have contacts throughout the Algarve and can arrange for sails of almost any size to be made or repaired.

Rigging Bluewater Yacht Services can supply and fit all sizes of rigging, and have in the past replaced entire rigs on yachts in the 20m range.

Chandlery Good selection at Aradenáutica Lda in the boatyard area. Failing that, the resources of Lagos and Vilamoura are both within reach by train.

Charts A stock of local charts is held by the marina office, while Portuguese charts for more distant waters can be ordered overnight from Lisbon.

Liferaft servicing Another item in the Bluewater Yacht Services portfolio

Water Throughout the marina, and in the boatyard.

Showers Two blocks in the marina complex, with card access (but quite a long walk from some berths). Problems can arise if a larger crew have only one access card between them.

Launderette Next to the marina office, with six washers and three dryers all token-operated, open 0900–1800. Again, a long walk from some berths.

Electricity Throughout the marina, and in the boatyard.

Fuel Two each diesel and petrol pumps near the root of the north pontoon, operational during office hours. Fuel should be paid for in cash – though a credit card will be accepted in an emergency, a surcharge will be imposed (and note that it is a long walk from the fuel berth to the marina's single cash dispenser).

There is a second yacht fuelling berth just upstream of the *clube naval*, but operating times and other details are not known.

Bottled gas Camping Gaz is available in the town, and it has been reported that other cylinders can be refilled at the BP service station (ask for directions at the tavira desk). Allow several days for the latter.

Weather forecast Posted daily at the marina office and during the high season, broadcast on VHF Ch 09 at 1000.

Clube naval The Clube Naval de Portimão has smart new premises complete with their own pontoon on the Quai Vasco da Gama, just upriver of the smallcraft basin.

Banks In Praia da Rocha and Portimão, with a cash dispenser near the southwest corner of the marina's south basin.

Shops/provisioning In Praia da Rocha and Portimão, though considerably better (and cheaper) in the latter – see also under *Buses*, below.

Limited shopping in Ferragudo. There is a mini-market near the southwest corner of the marina, opposite the cash dispenser. Nearby are the usual range of tourist shops and newsagents.

Produce markets In Portimão and Ferragudo.

Cafés, restaurants and hotels Every second building in Praia da Rocha, if not even more, with a large hotel fronting much of the marina. The waterfront restaurant on the end of the central spur is said to be good.

Medical services In Praia da Rocha and Portimão – contact is best made via the marina office.

Communications

Post offices In Praia da Rocha and Portimão.

Mailing address The marina office will hold mail for visiting yachts – c/o Marina de Portimão, Edificio Administrativo, 8500 Portimão, Portugal. It is important that the envelope carries the name of the yacht in addition to that of the addressee.

Telephones Several kiosks around the marina complex, and in the town.

Internet access Wireless broadband was being installed throughout the marina in early 2005, and there is a desk in the reception building with telephone points to which laptops can be connected. Failing this there is free internet access at the library in the old town, plus several cybercafés in nearby Praia da Rocha.

Fax service At the marina – ☎/*Fax* 282 400681.

Car hire/taxis No shortage. Both can be ordered via marina reception.

Buses Frequent if slow. A minibus runs daily from the reception area to the Modelo supermarket and the old town – enquire at the marina office for times.

Trains Station north of Portimão, and a convenient way to reach Faro airport.

Air services Faro International Airport is about 55km away.

Adjacent anchorage

Off Praia da Rocha, west of Portimão's west breakwater. A shoal patch carrying less than 2m extends 70m southeast from the southernmost of the two rocks off Ponta dos Castelos, itself 0.7M west of the breakwater. Suitable for daytime use only, and open to the south.

58. Albufeira

Waypoints
⊕159 – 37°03′N 8°14′.5W approach
⊕160 – 37°04′.82N 8°15′.24W (entrance)

Courses and distances
⊕157 (Portimão) – ⊕159 = 14M, 096° or 276°
⊕159 – ⊕160 = 1.9M, 342° or 162°
⊕159 – ⊕161 (Vilamoura) = 5.5M, 101° or 287°

Tides
Standard port Lisbon
Mean time differences
HW –0010 ±0025; LW 0000 ±0005
Heights in metres

MHWS	MHWN	MLWN	MLWS
3.6	2.8	1.5	0.7

Charts

	Approach	Harbour
Admiralty	91, 89	
Imray	C19, C50	
Portuguese	(90), 23203, 23204, 24206	(27503)

Principal lights
2196 **Albufeira** Oc.6s31m11M White column, red bands
2196.02 **North breakwater** Fl(2)G.5s9m4M
    White column, three green bands 3m
2196.01 **South breakwater** Fl(2)R.5s9m4M
    White column, two red bands 3m
Inner channel, north side Fl.2.G
    White column, three green bands 3m
Inner channel, south side Fl.2.R
    White column, three red bands 3m

Night entry
Though narrow, the entrance is well lit and should present no problems in normal conditions. However swells may build up outside in strong southerlies, making close approach in darkness unwise

Harbour communications
Marina de Albufeira ☎ 289 514282 *Fax* 289 514292
Email info@amarinadealbufeira.com
www.amarinadealbufeira.com
VHF Ch 09 (0900–2100 1 June–15 September, 0900–1800 1 November–31 March, 0900–1900 at other times).

The new harbour and marina at Albufeira from the southeast. The bulk of the tourist development stretches away to the right

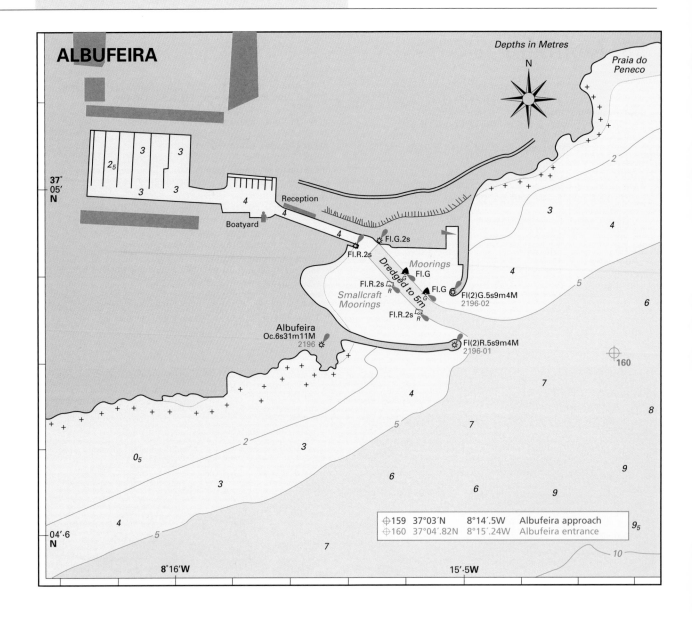

ALBUFEIRA

Depths in Metres

Praia do Peneco

N

37°05'N

Reception

Boatyard

Fl.G.2s

Fl.R.2s

Dredged to 5m

Moorings
Fl.G

Fl.R.2s

Smallcraft
Moorings

Fl.G

Fl.G

Fl(2)G.5s9m4M
2196·02

Fl.R.2s

Albufeira
Oc.6s31m11M
2196

Fl(2)R.5s9m4M
2196·01

160

04'·6 N

| ⊕159 | 37°03'N | 8°14'.5W | Albufeira approach |
| ⊕160 | 37°04'.82N | 8°15'.24W | Albufeira entrance |

8°16'W

15'·5W

Brand new marina some distance from the main tourist area

Berthed in the Marina de Albufeira it is hard to believe that the somewhat brash tourist resort of the same name is less than 2km away. Due at least in part to its position in a natural amphitheatre, the complex forms its own enclosed world, subtly emphasised by the quirky architecture and unusual colours of the surrounding buildings (referred to locally, and somewhat irreverently, as 'Legoland').

The marina opened for business late in 2003, and though still lacking some of the usual services was making impressive progress when visited in February 2005. The buildings lining either side of the basin were complete, though many were still untenanted, with development about to start on land at the rear of the basin. This is expected to take several more years, and some noise and dust are inevitable. When the shoreside infrastructure is fully established the inner basin will be overlooked by apartments, villas, shops restaurants and bars, so though never a secluded spot it promises to be a lively one.

Approach

The marina lies just under 15M east of Portimão and 5M west of Vilamoura. The approach is straightforward and without hazards, marked by Ponta Baleeira light on the cliffs close south in addition to the two breakwater lights. However by day the stone breakwaters may be difficult to pick out against the cliffs behind, particularly with an afternoon sun. Currently the marina lies at the southwest end of the considerable Albufeira conurbation, but it can only be a matter of time before this leapfrogs onto the ochre cliffs to the southwest. Several fishing floats were observed in the approach, a potential hazard to a yacht's propeller, particularly after dark.

From offshore ⊕159 lies 2M southeast of the entrance, a course of 316° leading to ⊕160, close outside the harbour mouth.

Entrance

The marina's outer entrance is just over 100m wide and faces almost due east. Although this may well make entry in southerly winds more feasible than is the case with some of its neighbours, it should still be approached with caution in these conditions. The slightly angled channel through the outer harbour is indicated by four good-sized buoys, all of which are lit, and is dredged to 5m. Smallcraft lie to moorings on either side of the channel.

The long, relatively narrow cutting which gives access to the inner basin carries 4m along its length, as does the small intermediate basin where larger yachts are berthed. The long reception pontoon lies on the starboard hand near the far end of this passage, with the marina office behind. Surge may affect the reception pontoon even in relatively light conditions making generous fendering wise.

Berthing

The Marina de Albufeira contains 475 berths, including one for a yacht of 30m or more, all alongside finger pontoons. Around 80 berths are reserved for visiting yachts in depths which decrease from 4m near the entrance to 2.5m in the western part of the basin. Once inside, shelter is excellent, though some surge may penetrate as far as the larger yacht berths. Security is also taken seriously, with CCTV and security patrols in addition to card access to the pontoon gates (most of which are, thoughtfully, provided with a small plan of the marina with essential services marked).

Secure to the reception pontoon on arrival – office hours are 0900–2100 in summer (1 June–15 September), 0900–1800 in winter (1 November–31 March), and 0900–1900 in spring and autumn. Unsurprisingly, during its first season the marina

was never totally full, but this can only be a matter of time and there is no obvious spot where short-term visitors might be rafted up. The office staff speak Spanish and some French in addition to English.

In 2005 the overnight rate for a visiting yacht of 10–12m was €33.32 in the high season (1 June–15 September), €11.90 in the low season (1 November–31 March), and €26.19 at other times. The equivalent rates for a yacht of 12–15m were €47.84, €18.39 and €38.02 respectively. Most unusually there is no weekly or monthly berthing rate, the shortest 'long term' it is possible to book for being nine months. Multihulls paid a 50% surcharge in the low season, rising to 100% at other times. Rates listed in the marina brochure include water and electricity but not IVA (the equivalent of VAT), but this has been added to the above figures for easy comparison with other harbours. Most major credit cards are accepted.

Formalities

As of 2005 none of the usual triumvirate of officials – the *GNR–Brigada Fiscal*, *Polícia Marítima* and *Alfândega* – had offices on site, though copies of the paperwork were circulated to them electronically. For skippers of EU-registered vessels with EU crews arriving from within Portugal, that was the end of the matter. Others might receive a visit from *Imigração* (immigration) or perhaps *Alfândega* (customs), though the onus was on the officials to visit the yacht rather than vice versa. Marina officials will advise.

Anchorage

Anchoring in the outer harbour is not permitted – in any case there would be no room to swing between the moored smallcraft – and though in theory one could drop a hook outside in the wide bay running east to Albufeira resort there is little protection.

The marina basin at Albufeira. The reception pontoon can be seen at the head of the narrow approach channel

Facilities

Boatyard Contractors operate within the boatyard area to the south of the intermediate basin. Only two are currently installed, occupying less than a quarter of the large, green-sided workshop building. For services see below.

Travel-lift 70-tonne capacity lift plus 6.3 tonne crane – book at reception. The marina does not provide props, which are currently available only from boatyard contractors.

Engineers, electronics and maintenance Although PowerCool *Mobile* 91 7966 373 *Fax* 289 587005 *Email* info@powercool.org www.powercool.org, specialises in generators and air-conditioning (Kohler and Dometic respectively), British owner Michael Killeen is cheerfully flexible and happy to handle anything from engineering (he spent ten years working on large aircraft engines) through electronics to antifouling and polishing. They are also a Volvo Penta agent and service centre. Some spares are held in stock, while others can be ordered direct from the manufacturer or, failing that, fabricated locally. Should a task be outside PowerCool's scope, Michael will almost certainly 'know a man who can'.

Ben Smith (see Chandlery, below) is also an experienced marine engineer, formerly based in Vilamoura.

General maintenance Riominho Náutica *Mobile* 96 8492 215 *Email* albufeira@riominho.com www.riominho.com handles yacht valeting and straightforward maintenance including painting/antifouling and minor GRP repairs. Alternatively Peter Heitman, *Mobile* 91 7262 359, offers carpentry services.

Diver Available via the marina office.

Sailmaker The boatyard buildings contain a purpose-built sail loft, but by late 2005 it still had no tenant. However Vilamoura is not far up the road . . .

Chandlery Tudo Marine Services Lda, *Mobile* 91 8608 809 and 91 2556 134, *Email* tudomarine@yahoo.co.uk, run by Ben Smith and Gavin Hawkins has premises in the boatyard area. Stock focuses on general chandlery and engine spares.

Nearby is Santa María Artigos Náuticos, whose other shop overlooks the smallcraft marina at Faro. General chandlery, lifejackets and some clothes are likely to feature, with good English spoken.

Water At all berths.

Showers Temporarily housed in portacabins on the central spur, with two permanent shower blocks planned for the north side of the basin.

Launderette A launderette is likely to be built in due course, but in the meantime laundry can be left at the marina office to be done elsewhere.

Electricity At all berths.

Fuel Diesel and petrol pumps on a pontoon on the port side, opposite and slightly beyond the reception pontoon, open during office hours. Credit cards are accepted.

Holding tank pump-out At the fuel pontoon.

Bottled gas Camping Gaz exchanges at a filling station in the town, but no refills. It would also be worth enquiring at the chandlery.

Weather forecast Posted daily at the marina office.

Clube náutico Planned for the central spur, though building has yet to start.

Bank A cash dispenser is promised for the marina complex by the end of 2005.

Shops, provisioning Mini-market in the marina complex,

Looking across the approach channel towards the reception pontoon with a large ketch tucked in behind it. The pastel 'Legoland' buildings add welcome colour on a cloudy day

with other shops about 400m (most of it uphill) to the northeast.

Cafés, restaurants and hotels Several cafés and restaurants already up and running in the buildings overlooking the inner basin (some of which offer discounts to berth-holders and/or will deliver to yachts). A hotel is to be included in the second phase of the development – distinctly coals to Newcastle!

Medical services First aid clinic in Albufeira and hospital in Faro – the office will be happy to advise.

Communications

Post office Planned, but not a priority. Several in Albufeira.

Mailing address The marina office will hold mail for visiting yachts – c/o Marina de Albufeira, Sítio da Orada, 8201-918 Albufeira, Portugal. Envelopes should give both the name of the yacht and that of the addressee.

Telephones Numerous kiosks dotted around the marina complex.

Internet access Visitors can either use one of the office computers to check Email, or bring their own laptop to the reception building. Wireless broadband may be installed in the longer term.

Fax service At the marina office, *Fax* 289 514292.

Car hire/taxis Can be ordered via the marina office.

Buses Bus stop at the roundabout not far from the reception building.

Trains Station at Ferreiras, about 6km distant.

Air services Faro airport is 30km away – about 30 minutes by taxi.

Throughout the Algarve one finds disused well shafts, a reminder that piped water came late to much of the area   *AH*

59. Vilamoura

Waypoints
⊕161 – 37°02′N 8°07′.8W (approach)
⊕162 – 37°04′N 8°07′.35W (entrance)

Courses and distances
⊕157 (Portimão) – ⊕161 = 19.5M, 097° or 277°
⊕159 (Albufeira) – ⊕161 = 5.5M, 101° or 287°
⊕161 – ⊕162 = 2M, 010° or 190°
⊕161 – ⊕163 (Cabo de Santa María) = 14.3M, 117° or 297°
⊕161 – ⊕165 (Tavira, via ⊕163) = 30.3M, 117°&056° or 236°&297°
⊕161 – ⊕167 (Río Guadiana, via ⊕163) = 38.9M, 117°&064° or 244°&297°

Tides
Standard port Lisbon
Mean time differences (at Albufeira)
HW –0010 ±0025; LW 0000 ±0005
Heights in metres

MHWS	MHWN	MLWN	MLWS	
3.6	2.8	1.5	0.7	

Charts	Approach	Harbour
Admiralty	91, 89, 93	
Imray	C19, C50	C50
Portuguese	23203, 23204, 24206	(27503)

Principal lights
2197.2 **Vilamoura** Fl.5s17m19M
   Red framework on cream and red control tower 16m
Vilamoura marina
2197.3 **West breakwater** Fl.R.4s13m5M
   White tower, red bands 7m
2197.4 **East breakwater** Fl.G.4s13m5M
   White tower, green bands 7m
Quarteira (fishing) harbour
2198.1 **West mole** Fl.R.3s12m6M
   Red tower, white bands 6m
2198.2 **West mole spur** Fl(2)R.4s9m3M
   Red tower, white bands 4m
2198.3 **East mole** Fl.G.3s12m6M
   Green tower, white bands 6m

Night entry
   Straightforward other than in strong southerlies.

Harbour communications
   Port Authority ☎ 289 313214 *Fax* 289 310580
   Marina de Vilamoura ☎ 289 310560 *Fax* 289 310580
   Email marinavilamoura@lusotur.pt
   www.vilamoura.net
   VHF Ch 09, 16 (call *Vilamoura Radio*) (24 hours)
   Weather information in Portuguese and English: VHF Ch 12 at 1000 daily.

The approach to Vilamoura Marina with the reception pontoon in the centre, the boatyard on the left and the large V-shaped basin behind

Large, well-established marina backed by vast tourist complex

In 2004 the Marina de Vilamoura celebrated its 30th anniversary, making it the longest-established marina in southwest Iberia. The complex also claims to be Europe's largest private tourist development.

The marina and its adjacent boatyard are surrounded by a large tourist complex which includes four golf courses, a casino and countless hotels, and offers a wide choice of open-air cafés, boutiques, souvenir shops etc. In contrast, a serious effort is being made to establish a 200 hectare Environmental Park just west of the marina to preserve the wetland home of many species of birds. There are also Roman ruins close by, together with a small museum or, for the less culturally inclined, an excellent beach within a short dinghy ride – in walking distance if berthed on the west side of the basin.

Vilamoura is a popular and secure place to leave a yacht, either long-term or for a few months – perhaps between a summer passage southwards and the late autumn passage to Madeira, the Canaries and beyond – in which case its proximity to Faro airport is an obvious advantage.

Approach

The coast on both sides of Vilamoura is low and rocky and the breakwaters may be difficult to pick out, but the marina is surrounded by conspicuous tower blocks, particularly to the east where a large pale pink hotel stands close to the entrance. A small fishing harbour lies a few hundred metres east of the entrance, with the tower blocks of Quarteira beyond. There is no excuse for confusing the two entrances – Vilamoura to the west is considerably larger, and though the light characteristics of each breakwater pair are surprisingly similar the marina has its own major light close to the reception quay – but nevertheless more than one arriving yacht has managed to end up in the wrong place.

From offshore ⊕161 lies 2M south of the entrance, a course of 010° leading to ⊕162, on the 5m line close to the harbour mouth.

Entrance

The entrance is about 100m wide, between breakwaters which stretch a good 500m from the shore, and can be dangerous in strong southerly winds (true of most Algarve harbours). Previously congested with moored fishing boats, for the past five years – effectively since the neighbouring fishing harbour opened – the outer basin has remained empty. Anchoring is not permitted.

Head for the 60m wide channel leading to the inner basin and secure to the long reception pontoon beneath the control tower and offices. Depths in the outer harbour are approximately 4m, decreasing to 3.3m off the reception pontoon and in the southern part of the basin and 2m in the northeast section. Although silting is an ongoing problem, particularly in the outer basin, periodic dredging has largely kept it at bay.

The inner basin at Vilamoura Marina seen from almost due east, with the reception area and boatyard at upper left

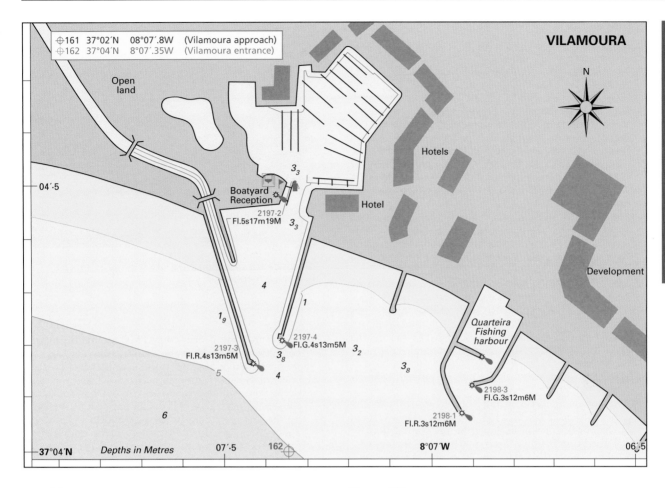

⊕161 37°02′N 08°07′.8W (Vilamoura approach)
⊕162 37°04′N 8°07′.35W (Vilamoura entrance)

Open land

VILAMOURA

N

Hotels

04′·5

Boatyard Reception

3_3

Hotel

2197·2
Fl.5s17m19M

3_3

Development

4

1

Quarteira Fishing harbour

1_9

2197·3
Fl.R.4s13m5M

2197·4
Fl.G.4s13m5M

3_8

3_2

3_8

5

4

2198·3
Fl.G.3s12m6M

6

2198·1
Fl.R.3s12m6M

37°04′N Depths in Metres 07′·5 162 8°07′W 06′·5

THE ALGARVE & ANDALUCIA

Berthing

The Marina de Vilamoura contains around 1000 berths (the exact number appears to be flexible) and can take vessels of 60m or more. On arrival secure to the reception pontoon until clearance procedures have been completed and a berth allocated. If arriving outside office hours – 0830–2130 1 June–15 September; 0830–1930 1 April–31 May and 16 September–31 October; 0830–1830 1 November–31 March – it will be necessary to remain there until the offices open in the morning. Water and electricity are both available on the reception pontoon. Security throughout the marina is assured by CCTV, frequent patrols and pontoon gates operated by electronic cards.

In 2005 the overnight charge for a visiting yacht of 10–12m was €40.90 in the high season (1 July–31 August), €39.69 in the mid seasons (1–30 June and 1–30 September) and €14.88 (or €404.14 per month) in the low season (October to May inclusive). The equivalent rates for a yacht of 12–15m were €57.11, €54.57, €21.05 and €580.80 respectively. Multihulls paid a 50–100% surcharge, and larger yachts might be charged an additional fee for heavy use of electricity. Rates listed in the marina brochure include water and electricity but not IVA (the equivalent of VAT), but this has been added to the above figures for easy comparison with other harbours. Most major credit cards are accepted.

Formalities

All paperwork (for which ship's papers, passports and evidence of insurance are required) is carried out in the marina office overlooking the reception pontoon. After many years dogged by somewhat tedious officialdom, by 2005 is was no longer necessary for the skipper of an EU-registered yacht carrying a crew of EU-nationals to visit either *Imigração* (immigration) or *Alfândega* (customs), although both have offices in the same building. Where non-EU nationals and/or yachts were involved it was still necessary for the skipper to visit *Imigração*, while the *Alfândega* were most interested in yachts which had arrived from outside Portugal and particularly from outside the EU. Both offices open seven days a week, maintaining the same hours as the marina office itself.

The outer breakwaters of Vilamoura Marina seen from the southwest with Quarteira fishing harbour in the background

Facilities

Boatyard Services are provided by a range of different contractors, or owners can do their own work. Largest is probably BEB Carpentry Services, ☎ 289 302797 *Mobile* 96 9097 580 *Fax* 289 302721 *Email* bebcarpentry@hotmail.com www.boat-carpenters.com run by Brian Brennan – English spoken! – which has been working at Vilamoura for over ten years and can handle almost anything in timber or GRP. Others include Heitmann Yacht Services, ☎ 289 360610; Tecnimaritima Lda, ☎ 289 301070; Lacomar Lda, ☎ 289 312471; and Emmanuel Bosch, *mobile* 96 8308 735, who between them offer carpentry services, painting and GRP repairs.

Travel-lifts 30- and 60-tonne capacity hoists, plus two smaller cranes. The concreted hardstanding, which can take a maximum of 200 yachts, has good security, and DIY is not a problem. There is also a tidal grid for boats drawing less than 2m.

Engineers In 2005 no less than seven engineering workshops were established in the boatyard area, including agents for Volvo and Yanmar and others specialising in welding and fabrication. A full list, including contact numbers, is included in the marina brochure (available on request from mid February onwards).

Electrical, electronic and radio repairs Janusz Oszczepalski, ☎ 289 322615

Sailmaker/sail repairs The J P Velas-Doyle loft ☎ 289 321155 *Fax* 289 3221159 *Email* peter@jp-velas.pt www.jp-velas.pt will be found on the second floor of the reception building. Peter and Joanne Keeping, who together with their team speak seven languages, will build new sails from scratch, repair old ones, and handle canvaswork including spray hoods and biminis. They also supply roller furling gears and running rigging.

Chandlery A branch of Náutica Capitalcar, ☎ 289 314764, overlooks the boatyard area – well-stocked and carrying a good range of maintenance materials. Open 0900–1200 and 1400–1800 weekdays, 0900–1230 Saturday. Other chandleries exist around the marina basin, but tending towards the decorative rather than the practical.

Charts Both Admiralty and Portuguese charts can be ordered from Lisbon via the marina office.

Water At all berths and the reception/fuel pontoon.

Showers Behind the marina office (effectively in the boatyard compound) plus two other blocks around the marina basin, all with card access.

Holding tank pump-out A very useful free service, though almost unique in this area, is the provision of a pump-out barge to empty a yacht's holding tank without the need for her to leave the berth. Arrange via marina reception.

Launderettes One on each side of the marina basin.

Electricity At all berths and the reception/fuel pontoon.

Fuel Diesel and petrol pumps will be found at the north end of the reception pontoon, open marina office hours and with credit cards accepted.

Bottled gas Camping Gaz cylinders can be exchanged at the chandlery, where it may also be possible to get other bottles refilled.

Clube náutico The Clube Náutico de Vilamoura has premises next to the marina office, overlooking the reception pontoon. Crews of visiting yachts are made welcome.

Weather forecast Posted daily at the marina office and broadcast on VHF Ch 12 at 1000.

Alongside the reception / fuel berth in the entrance to Vilamoura Marina   *AH*

Banks Several cash dispensers (ATMs) around the marina complex, with banks in the tourist area.

Shops/provisioning Several small supermarkets, mostly a street or two back from the marina, which meet daily needs (and will sometimes deliver) but are inadequate for serious passage provisioning. For serious stocking-up the best bet would be the big Modelo supermarket about 15 minutes away by car (ask at the marina office for directions). Dozens of tourist and general shops overlook the marina basin.

Produce market Well-stocked markets in Quarteira and Lidl.

Cafés, restaurants and hotels Dozens of the former right beside the marina (including one at the *clube náutico*), with lots more, plus several luxury hotels, within walking distance.

Medical services Medical centre (including dentists) in the tourist area, best contacted with the assistance of marina reception. Hospital in Faro.

Communications

Post Office In the tourist complex behind the marina.

Mailing address The marina office will hold mail for visiting yachts – c/o Marina de Vilamoura, 8125–409 Quarteira, Algarve, Portugal. It is important that the envelope carries the name of the yacht in addition to that of the addressee.

Public telephones Several around the marina complex, including one beside the reception quay and another in the boatyard compound.

Fax service At the marina office *Fax* 289 310580.

Internet Free access via a computer in the marina office, plus a phone socket to which laptops can be connected. Wireless broadband is also available throughout the marina, with the necessary cards on sale at reception. Lastly, there are several cybercafés in the tourist resort.

Taxis/car hire In the commercial area, or via the marina office. Note that sign-posting within the tourist complex is poor – allow for a few wrong turnings if hiring a car to catch or meet a plane etc.

Buses Bus service to Faro (about 40 minutes) and elsewhere, from stops in the tourist complex. Ask at the marina office for directions.

Air services Faro international airport is about 20 minutes by taxi, 40 minutes by bus (though a taxi will be needed from town to airport).

60. Faro and Olhão

Waypoints
⊕163 – 36°55′.6N 7°51′.9W (2.2M S of
  Cabo de Santa María)
⊕164 – 36°57′.55N 7°52′.25W
  (Cabo de Santa María, entrance)

Courses and distances
⊕161 (Vilamoura) – ⊕163 = 14.3M, 117° or 297°
⊕163 – ⊕164 = 2M, 352° or 172°
⊕163 – ⊕165 (Tavira) = 16M, 056° or 236°
⊕163 – ⊕167 (Río Guadiana) = 24.6M, 064° or 244°

Tides
Standard port Lisbon
Mean time differences (at Cabo de Santa María)
HW –0040 ±0010; LW –0010 ±0005
Heights in metres

MHWS	MHWN	MLWN	MLWS
3.4	2.6	1.3	0.6

Or refer to EasyTide at www.ukho.gov.uk (see page 2)

Charts

	Approach	*Channels*
Admiralty	91, 89, 93	83
Imray	C19, C50	
Portuguese	23204, 24206	26311

Principal lights
2206 **Cabo de Santa María**
  Fl(4)17s49m25M
  White tower and building 46m
2208 **West breakwater** Fl.R.4s9m6M
  White tower, three red bands 5m
2209 **East breakwater** Fl.G.4s9m6M
  White tower, three green bands 5m
2206.1 **Ldg Lts on 021°** *Front* Barra Nova Oc.4s8m6M
  White column, red stripes
2206 Rear 512m from front **Cabo de Santa María** (above)
2211 **Ilha de Cultra,** training wall
  Oc.G.5s6m3M Metal column on building 6m
Canal de Faro
2212 **First Ldg Lts 099°** (a back bearing if entering)
  Front **Mar Santo** Oc.R.5s9m5M
  White column, red bands 5m
2206 Rear 244m from front **Cabo de Santa María** (above)
2214 **Second Ldg Lts 328°**
  Front **Casa Cubica (Fabrica Fritz)** Fl.R.3s11m6M
  Lantern on south wall of building 5m
2214.1 Rear 731m from front Oc.R.6s63m6M
  Lantern on church tower 21m
Canal de Olhão
2222 **Cais Farol** Fl.G.3s7m6M Green metal column 5m
2221 **First Ldg Lts 220°** (a back bearing if entering)
  Front **Golada** LFl.R.5s6m6M
  White over red cylinder on three white columns 6m
2221.1 Rear 447m from front Oc.R.5s8m7M
  White over red cylinder on three white columns 7m
2218 **Ponte do Carvão, Ilha de Culatra**
  Fl.5.5s6m6M Green column 4m
2219 **Ponte Cais, Ilha de Culatra**
  Oc.G.4s6m5M Green column

2224 **Second Ldg Lts 125°** (back bearing if entering)
  Front Arraiais Iso.G.1.5s7m5M
  Black and white striped column, ▲ topmark 5m
2224.1 *Rear* 226m from front Oc.G.3s13m5M
  Black and white striped column, ▲ topmark 8m
2225 **Third Ldg Lts on 352°** *Front* Murtinas
  LFl.R.5s7m7M White column, red bands
2225.1 *Rear* 301m from front Oc.R.5s13m7M
  White column, red bands
2226 **Fourth Ldg Lts 044°** *Front* **Cais de Olhão**
  Iso.R.6s8m7M White column, red bands 7m
2226.1 *Rear* **Igreja** 360m from front Oc.R.4s20m6M
  Church tower 12m
Many other lit buoys and beacons exist in the Canal de
Faro, Canal de Olhão and Canal da Assetia. However
none should be relied upon implicitly, and any or all
may be moved if the channels shift

Night entry
The entrance is well lit, but tidal currents – and eddies
– can be powerful. If unfamiliar with the channels it
would be wise to anchor at the first opportunity and
await daylight

Maritime radio station
Estoi (37°06′.1N 7°49′.8W)
Remotely controlled from Lisbon)
Manual – VHF Ch 16, 24, 27, 28. *Autolink* – VHF Ch 86
Weather bulletins and navigational warnings
Weather bulletins in Portuguese and English for Cabo
Carvoerio to the Rio Guadiana within 20 miles
offshore VHF Ch 11 at 0805, 2005 UT
Navigational warnings in Portuguese and English
within 200 miles offshore: VHF Ch 11at 0805, 2005 UT

Harbour communications
Faro – Port Authority ☎ 289 803601 *Fax* 289 860666
Email portfaro@mail.telepac.pt
VHF Ch 11, 16 (call *Postradfaro*) (24 hours)
Olhão – Port Authority ☎ 289 703160
VHF Ch 11, 16 (call *Capimarolhão*) (0900–1230,
1400–1730 weekdays only)
Olhão – Marina ☎ 289 703519.

A single entrance leading to many anchorages and a new marina

Both Faro and Olhão (pronounced 'Oh-le-ow') are
sizeable towns, but for many the greater appeal lies
with the tidal lagoons which run along the coast for
some 30M between the mainland and the sea. The
offlying islands, together with the coastal fringes,
form the Parque Natural de Ria Formosa – certain
restrictions apply but the bird life, including storks
and various waders, is abundant. To take full
advantage of the geography a sailing dinghy or a

shoal-draught boat able to take the ground is
preferable, but there is water enough in the main
channels for deep-draught yachts.

The entrance at Cabo de Santa María is well
marked and the way through the sand defined by
breakwaters. A stream of fishing boats may give a
useful lead when they return with their catch in the
early morning, but the bar – which is dredged from
time to time – presents few problems in fine weather.
Once inside, the channels are well buoyed, but if
going to Olhão beware the wash of passing fishing

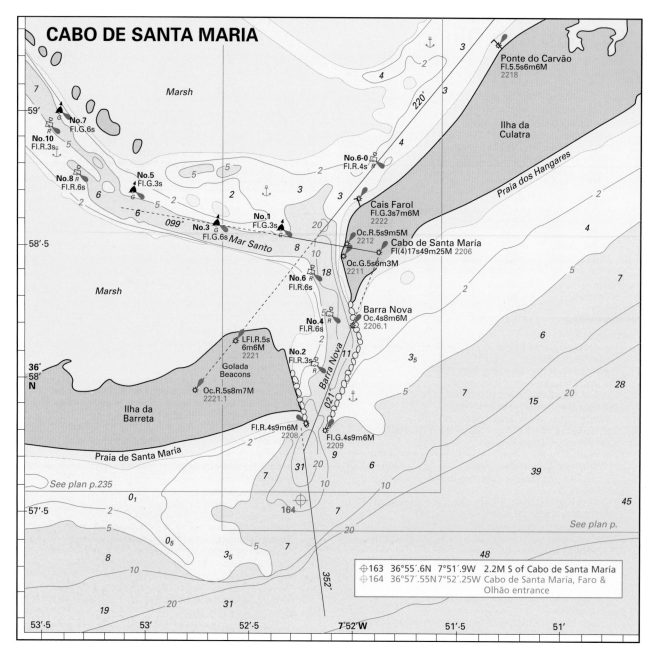

CABO DE SANTA MARIA

Marsh

No.7
Fl.G.6s
No.10
Fl.R.3s
No.8
Fl.R.6s
No.5
Fl.G.3s
No.3
Fl.G.6s
No.1
Fl.G.3s
099°
Mar Santo

Marsh

LFl.R.5s
6m6M
2221
No.6
Fl.R.6s
No.4
Fl.R.6s
No.2
Fl.R.3s
Golada
Beacons
Oc.R.5s8m7M
2221.1

Ilha da
Barreta

Praia de Santa María

Fl.R.4s9m6M
2208

Fl.G.4s9m6M
2209

See plan p.235

Ponte do Carvão
Fl.5.5s6m6M
2218

Ilha da
Culatra

Praia dos Hangares

No.6-0
Fl.R.4s

Cais Farol
Fl.G.3s7m6M
2222
Oc.R.5s9m5M
2212
Cabo de Santa María
Fl(4)17s49m25M 2206
Oc.G.5s6m3M
2211

Barra Nova
Oc.4s8m6M
2206.1

Barra Nova

021°

352°

⊕163 36°55'.6N 7°51'.9W 2.2M S of Cabo de Santa María
⊕164 36°57'.55N 7°52'.25W Cabo de Santa María, Faro &
Olhão entrance

See plan p.

boats. The ferries, too, are not over-considerate. Another potential problem throughout the area is the prevalence of floating weed, which tends to clog engine water filters, and small crustaceans which take up residence in log impellers. Both will need clearing regularly.

Approach

The coast is very low-lying and currents of up to 3 knots may set along it. The 50m contour runs at 1M offshore at the point, further away on either side. The major light of Cabo de Santa María is on the sandspit about 1.3M northeast of the most southerly point of the cape and 0.7M north-northeast of the breakwaters. From a distance it looks like a needle on a sandy island.

Coming along the shore from the west, the beach starts a few miles east of Vilamoura and is backed by tourist villages. It becomes deserted to the southeast

and 8M from Santa María the lagoon starts, with an occasional shallow entrance across the sand, and Faro airport behind. The 5m line runs 600–700m offshore, except southwest of the entrance where it turns south to a point, very steep-to (shoaling from 30m down to 5m within 50m or less) more than 0.5M offshore. A short distance further west the 2m contour does much the same, forming a southwest facing bank over which the water shoals from 15m to 2m in little more than 100m. Either of these may cause a southwesterly swell to break. Remain at least 0.7M offshore until the west breakwater bears 352°.

To the east, the lagoon and its protecting banks extend 20M with some wide – but generally shallow – gaps. Opposite Fuzeta, 5M east of Olhão and identified by a distinctive church, the 50m line runs about 2M offshore. Since 2003 a floating fish cage has been anchored south of Fuzeta at 37°00'.5N 7°44'.45W. It is marked by two buoys, both Fl.Y., on

Built in the 1930s, the 49m light on Cabo de Santa María flashes its warning to vessels up to 25M out to sea. Nearby stands the white and red lifeboat house   *AH*

Entrance

From a point at least 0.7M south of the entrance, steer 352° until the end of the east breakwater just opens to the east of a line with Santa María light. There can be a marked set across the entrance and it is important to remain on the leading line. Although there is adequate depth to enter at any state of the tide the spring ebb may run at 7 knots through the entrance. In these circumstances hug the west mole – there is good water within 15m of it and the ebb will be reduced to about 4 knots – but be ready for powerful eddies and keep a careful watch for fish-traps (often marked by black flags). There are three port-hand buoys before the channels to Faro and Olhão divide. Local yachtsmen frequently cut inside these, not least to escape the tide, but new arrivals may feel happier leaving them close to port.

Both channels are buoyed, and though in the past buoys were frequently reported to be out of position this is no longer common, particularly during the summer. A corrected copy of either Portuguese 26311 or Admiralty 83 is almost essential, but even so the banks shift continually and yachts have reported grounding well within the marked channel. As always, best water is to be found on the outsides of bends.

Note Vessels drawing more than 2.5m may not use the channel at night (not recommended for the visitor, in any case), and vessels are forbidden to cross each other's bows at the junction of the channels – those outward bound should remain outside the channel and let inward bound vessels pass.

the same latitude and at 7°44´.8W and 7°44´.1W respectively. All vessels are requested to give the cage and buoys at least 500m clearance. Tunny nets used to be laid in this area though none have been in place recently, and if they return are certain to be buoyed and lit.

From offshore ⊕163 lies 2M south of the entrance, a course of 352° down the leading line linking with ⊕164, 500m south of the entrance.

Looking northwest over the long breakwater at Cabo de Santa María towards the city of Faro. The west end of Ilha de Culatra lies on the right

Anchorages near Cabo de Santa María and Ilha da Culatra

There are several possibilities in this area, most of them weather dependent and all requiring an anchor light to be displayed if remaining after dark. (Several yachts have been fined in this area in recent years for not displaying either an anchor ball or a light, as appropriate).

In settled northerlies yachts occasionally anchor outside, east of the east breakwater and south of Santa María light (1). In southerlies shelter will be found inside, either north-northwest of buoy No.1 (2 – see plan page 232), or in the Praça Larga north of the Ponte Cais on Ilha da Culatra (3 – see plan page 238). Holding in both areas is good over sand, though wind against tide conditions can set up quite a chop and also cause yachts on single anchors to yaw considerably. Two anchors (both from the bow) may be wise if planning to stay for any length of time. It is also possible to enter or leave the Praça Larga from the east, via the Barra Grande (also known as the Barra Velha), but the shifting banks are not reliably buoyed and this route is not recommended without local knowledge.

In 2005 there were reckoned to be around 3000 permanent residents on Isla de Culatra, mostly in Ponte Cais though the village close to Cabo de Santa María (referred to locally as Farol – literally, 'lighthouse' – is also growing at speed. There are no roads – and no cars – though a few tractors plough their way through the loose sand, and mains water and electricity are very new arrivals. Even so Ponte Cais has several shops including a small but surprisingly well-stocked supermarket, a cash point (said to 'run dry' rather frequently), numerous restaurants and bars, and both post and telephone offices. Ferries run between Ponte Cais, Farol and Olhão – two or three a day in winter and far more in summer.

Close east of Ponte Cais is a tidal lagoon, a favourite wintering spot with both locals and liveaboard owners of multihulls and bilge-keelers, some of whom have been there more than a decade. There are no facilities as such, but no charges either, and daily needs can easily be met in Ponte Cais. However local people naturally feel they should have first rights to the limited foreshore space, and as of late 2005 there was little room to spare. If interested, anchor off and prospect first by dinghy, both to check depths in the northeast-facing entrance and to ensure that space will be available, either on the beach or at anchor.

There is talk of building a marina on Ilha da Culatra, but no plans have yet been drawn up and no date set.

The lagoon on Ilha de Culatra, a popular wintering hole for bilge-keelers and multihulls   *AH*

Looking northwest over marsh and mudflat towards the main yacht anchorage at Faro, with the city on the right

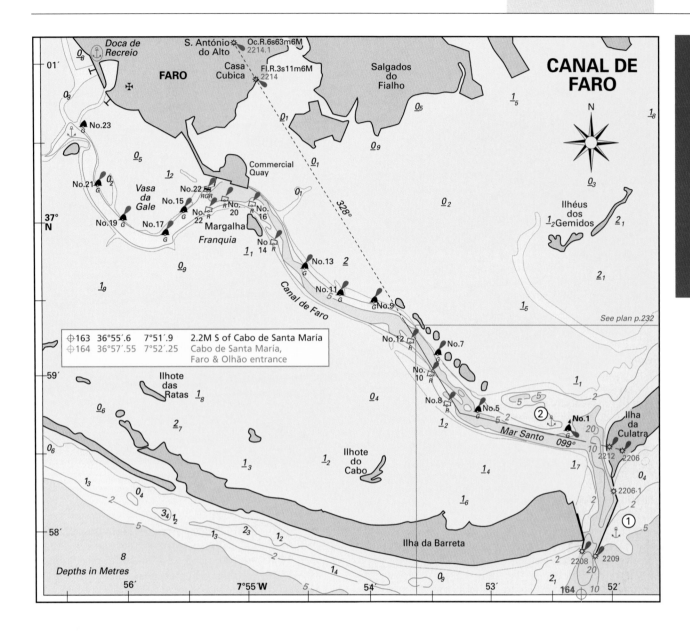

60a Faro

37°00′.8N 7°56′.2W

Not to be confused with the tourist sprawl behind the beaches to the west of the city, Faro's walled Cidade Velha (old town) right next to the small Doca de Recreio should not be missed, providing welcome shade on a hot day and superb views over the estuary and town from the belltower of the Sé (cathedral). Pause to watch the storks on their untidy nests – on the cathedral tower, above the Cidade Velha's neo-classical Arco de Vila, on lamp posts overhanging the city's streets ... everywhere. Until recently they flew south to Morocco for the winter, but it seems that global warming has encouraged them to stay year-round.

Approach and anchorage

Again there is no option but to anchor, the favoured spot being the pool formed at the junction of the creeks, with the railway bridge covering the entrance to the Doca de Recreio bearing about 040° in 3–4m. Although now largely occupied by moorings it may be possible to find space in the channel leading southwest, where there is at least one deep pool, though two anchors (both from the bow and laid upstream and downstream respectively) may be required to limit swinging room.

When approaching the junction, favour the port side of the channel past buoys No.17 and No.21, switching to the starboard hand when the latter is 100m or so astern to avoid an extensive sand spit running out from the port bank (visible until mid-tide and sometimes marked by a small blue buoy). The deep channel here carries 4m or more depth but is a bare 15m wide. The photographs on pages 234 and 237, though taken at more than half flood, may be helpful.

A single-track railway links Faro in the west to Vila Real de Santo António in the east, looping around the old city of Faro only feet from the water's edge　　*AH*

Faro is famous for its storks – this pair have set up home on neo-classical Arco de Vila which gives access to the old city　　*AH*

Land either at the Doca de Recreio, passing under the railway bridge (about 1m clearance at high water), or at one of the three jetties outside (the northernmost is probably the best bet). If landing in the basin note that the pontoons are closed off by individual security gates, and that the entire east side is reserved for fishermen. The office of the Capitania – where the *Policía Marítima* are often to be found – overlooks the north end of the basin, sharing its premises with a small maritime museum (open 1430–1630). A weather forecast is posted outside.

Facilities and communications

Facilities include water from taps beside the slipway on the quay between the basin and the marshes, and the possibility of showers at the Ginásio Clube Navale next door (which also has a snack-bar and upstairs restaurant – the only thing it does not appear to have is much to do with sailing!). In the same building is Nautifaro, previously a chandlery but now specialising mainly in outboard engines and

Perhaps the most aristocratic of the Faro storks are the pair which nest on the belltower of the Sé (cathedral). Though watchful, they seem unworried by human presence　　*AH*

their needs. Santa María Artigos Náuticos ☎ 289 804805 *Email* santamarianautica@mail.telepac.pt (open 0900–1300 and 1500–1800 weekdays, 1000–1300 Saturday) a little way down the same quay has filled the gap. Good English is spoken and the helpful owner, a local yachtsman, is happy to order as necessary. Diesel is available by can from a filling station on the landward side of the basin, though there is nowhere that a yacht can fill tanks directly. Camping Gaz bottles can be exchanged at several hardware stores in the city, but it is not possible to get other cylinders refilled.

Faro is the regional capital and has facilities to match, including banks, shops of all kinds, wining and dining spots, and medical services. Communications include a post office and numerous telephone kiosks, several internet cafés (including three terminals and two phone booths with jack plugs at the Western Union office directly opposite the smallcraft basin, plus a cybercafé on the nearby Praça Ferreira de Almeida), taxis, car hire, buses, trains (the station is close north of the smallcraft basin) and of course Faro International Airport, a couple of kilometres northwest as the egret flies, though rather more by road. Perhaps surprisingly, the aircraft noise is not intrusive and there appears to be little flying at night. In any case, any problems are more than offset by the proximity of the airport for crew changes and visiting friends.

Boatyard and storage ashore

If wishing to haul out for work or dry storage it would be well worth investigating the Quinta do Progresso boatyard ☎ *Mobile* 919 317171 *Fax* 289 822506 *Email* jbotas@vodaphone.pt which is an unpretentious but well-run concern some distance north of the anchorage. 'Bruce', the helpful Portuguese owner/manager, speaks English, French, Spanish and some German and Dutch, while engineer John grew up in the United States. There are on-site workshops for engineering, electronics, spars and rigging, GRP work and painting, though owners are welcome to do their own work, and stout metal cradles are available. Owners of yachts ashore are welcome to live aboard if they wish, with water and electricity throughout the yard and showers provided. Supermarkets and other shops are within walking distance, and an on-site chandlery is planned.

Due to environmental concerns – it is on the northern fringes of the Parque Natural de Ria Formosa – it has taken more than five years to obtain permission to dredge a channel up to the yard, but by 2006 at least 1.6m should be found at LWS and up to 4.4m at HWS. At the same time a massive 100-tonne capacity travel-lift is to replace the slightly elderly 24-tonne lift currently in use. While it is outside the scope of this book to give

Yachts wintering at Faro, seen from a rooftop in the city centre   *AH*

boatyard prices, as of 2005 Quinta do Progresso claimed to offer the best value in the Algarve, together with a friendly attitude and quiet surroundings (liveaboard pets are welcome too).

Longer term possibilities include a small marina, with around 180 berths in 2m or so. However as of 2005 this was at the very early planning stage and it has yet to overcome the obvious environmental concerns.

The yacht anchorage at Faro – though to be accurate, many of these yachts actually lie to moorings – with the small craft basin behind and the red roofs of the old city to the right

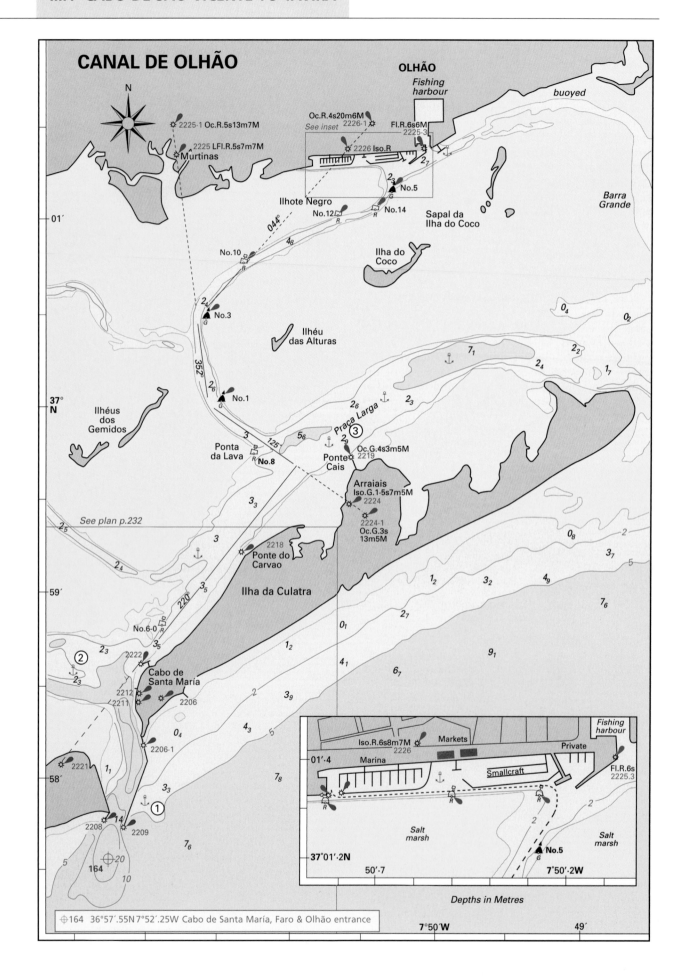

CANAL DE OLHÃO

OLHÃO

Fishing harbour

buoyed

Oc.R.4s20m6M
See inset 2226·1
FI.R.6s6M
2225·3

2225·1 Oc.R.5s13m7M

2225 LFI.R.5s7m7M
Murtinas

2226 Iso.R

No.5

Barra Grande

044°

Ilhote Negro

No.12
No.14

Sapal da Ilha do Coco

No.10

Ilha do Coco

No.3

Ilhéu das Alturas

352°

No.1

Praça Larga

Ilhéus dos Gemidos

Ponta da Lava
No.8

125°

Ponte Cais

Oc.G.4s3m5M
2219

Arraiais
Iso.G.1·5s7m5M
2224

2224·1
Oc.G.3s 13m5M

See plan p.232

2218
Ponte do Carvao

Ilha da Culatra

220°

No.6-0

Cabo de Santa María

2222

2212
2211
2206

2206·1

2221

2208
14
2209

164
20

Fishing harbour

Iso.R.6s8m7M
2226

Markets

Private

FI.R.6s
2225.3

01'·4
Marina

Smallcraft

Salt marsh

Salt marsh

No.5

37°01'·2N

50'·7

7°50'·2W

Depths in Metres

164 36°57'.55N 7°52'.25W Cabo de Santa María, Faro & Olhão entrance

7°50'W
49'

Olhão's new small craft harbour and marina seen from the southeast, with the Grupo Naval's small basin and the much larger fishing dock on the right

60b Olhão

37°01′.3N 07°50′.5W

Work finally started on Olhão's long-awaited marina in 2001. Construction was overseen by the Instituto Portuário e dos Transportes Marítimos do Sul (IPTM) who intended, on completion, to turn the running of the project over to a commercial company. By 2004 the structure was effectively finished and local smallcraft began to fill the inner berths. At the same time, word spread among the cruising community that no charges were being made and Olhão became a popular – and free – winter residence. As of late 2005 the situation was still unresolved though charges were being levied. There was little remaining space for visitors and the minimum length of stay was one month. If intending to arrive by yacht, there is much to be said for first anchoring off Ponte Cais and taking the ferry over to Olhão to assess the current situation.

Olhão itself is a pleasant, non-touristy town with superb markets on the waterfront surrounded by public gardens and a small children's play area.

Approach

Although it is perfectly possible to negotiate the channel up to Olhão at low water, most skippers will feel happier at around half flood. From the Praça Larga turn northwest leaving buoy No.8 to port, and either steer the courses indicated on the plan opposite or follow the buoyage as far as starboard hand No.5. Almost continuous dredging is required to keep this channel clear and yachts must not, under any circumstances, anchor in the fairway.

From a position close west of buoy No.5 steer directly for the hammer-head ferry pier, swinging west only just short of it to skirt the smallcraft pontoons and leave buoy No.2-P well to port. Beyond it will be seen No.4-P and, in the distance, No.6-P. All are spherical red buoys with topmarks and are lit, though this is no place to be on the move after dark. Continue west, staying as close to the smallcraft pontoon as conditions allow, repeating the process past the marina proper. On no account err to the south, as the edge of the dredged channel is too steep to give any warning before impact (though too soft to do much damage). The marina is entered at its western end, as indicated on the inset plan.

Berthing

The marina comprises two separate sections, the eastern berthing local smallcraft on two long east/west pontoons, the western providing around 270 berths for yachts of up to 17m, in 3m depths. 250 of these berths are on the eleven inner pontoons, which run on a north/south axis from a single pontoon which parallels the shore. The remaining berths – and the only ones which may be accessible to a visitor, as there is already a 140-boat waiting list for inner berths – lie inside the long 'shelter' pontoon. It seems likely that this pontoon was never intended to provide more than short-term berthing as it is not provided with water and electricity points, though cleats are provided on the inner side. It is reported that, during strong southerlies, it becomes distinctly lively as soon as the rising tide covers the mudbanks to the south. A full-scale southerly gale has yet to be experienced.

On arrival, unless allocated a berth in advance the best bet will probably be to raft alongside a yacht of suitable size on the inside of the long south pontoon. However this is frowned on by the authorities and the boat should not be left unattended even with the consent of those on the inside yacht. Security is via the usual card (and more necessary than in some areas, due to the traveller encampment to the west of the town). Apparently there are plans to build a hotel on this land, but no one knows when.

In 2005 the monthly rate for a visiting yacht of 10–12m was €94.46, rising to €116.27 for 12–15m, including tax. Payment was made at the IPTM office (see below), and had to be made in cash.

Anchorage

It may be possible for two or three yachts to anchor in the western part of the gap between the two parts of the marina, though space is tight due to moored smallcraft. Holding is good in about 3m over mud.

Formalities

All formalities are currently handled at the office of the Instituto Portuário e dos Transportes Marítimos do Sul (IPTM), which overlooks the west side of the large fishing boat basin, open 0800–1200 and 1300–1630 weekdays. The *Capitania* and *Polícia Marítima* share an office on the corner opposite the Grupo Naval, easily distinguished by its array of radio aerials, with the *GNR–Brigada Fiscal* between the two.

Facilities

Boatyard Nearest is the Quinta do Progresso yard at Faro (see page 237).

Travel-lift A dock has been incorporated into the large paved area close west of the marina, but it is likely to be some time before a travel-lift arrives. There is a wide slipway in the same area.

Engineers, mechanics, radio repairs At the fishing harbour.

Chandlery Sulcampo on the seafront road sells some general chandlery and electronics in addition to fishing tackle and diving equipment. Cabrita Lda, opposite the market buildings, is similar. The larger Sulnáutica, on the road behind the IPTM office, stocks outboards, batteries, inflatables, some chandlery and the inevitable fishing gear.

Water No access to water on the outer pontoon, though supplied to the inner berths. Several public taps and water fountains nearby, however.

Showers Nothing at the marina, but several local *residencials* are willing to let yachtsmen use showers for a small fee.

Launderette Several in the town.

Electricity Not available on the outer pontoon.

Fuel By can from a filling station near the root of the ferry jetty.

Olhão's new marina before the three port-hand buoys were laid. The extent of the nearby mudbank is clearly visible below the surface

The narrow approach to Olhão marina, seen from the ferry pier to the east. It is essential to leave all three buoys to port   *AH*

Olhão marina seen from the west before the port-hand buoys were laid. At low water springs the abrupt edge of the mudbank is obvious   *AH*

Bottled gas Camping Gaz exchanges at the Casa Jóvale hardware store close northwest of the market buildings, and at Cabrita Lda (see above) but no refills.

Clube naval The Grupo Naval de Olhão has its own basin east of the ferry pier, but there is no space for visitors.

Banks In the town, with a cash dispenser almost opposite the market buildings.

Shops, provisioning Small supermarket up the road opposite the market buildings, plus a large Lidl supermarket within (longish) walking distance. Good general shopping in the town.

Produce market Excellent – and spotlessly clean – produce and fish markets virtually overlooking the marina. As always, at their best in the early morning.

Cafés, restaurants and hotels The usual wide variety, with some particularly good fish restaurants on the road behind the market buildings.

Medical services In the town.

Communications

Post office In the town, close to the church.

Telephones Several public kiosks near the market buildings with others in the town.

Internet access Provided by the town authorities on a street one back from the waterfront (go down the wide road opposite the market buildings, turn left and then left again), open 1000–2200 Monday–Thursday, 1000–1300 and 1500–1800 Thursday–Friday, 1000–2000 Saturday, closed Sunday. The first half hour is free, but there are likely to be long queues outside school hours.

Car hire In the town, or from Faro airport.

Taxis A few in the town.

Buses & trains To Faro, Tavira and beyond.

Ferries Regular ferries to Ilha Armona and Ilha de Culatra

Air services Major airport at Faro, about 10km to the west as the gull flies, though considerably further by land.

Fuzeta

37°01´.3N 07°50´.5W

The inlet of Fuzeta, 15M east of Cabo de Santa María, might be described as a smaller version of Olhão a couple of decades ago, tucked behind broadly similar banks. Though very appealing it is feasible only for shoal-draught yachts or multihulls able to enlist local assistance for the approach. The inner banks appear to be largely of sand, rather than the mixture of mud and sand encountered further west, making drying out much more pleasant. The small town has all the usual facilities, including fuel at the fishermen's quay (up the narrow inlet, marked by prominent red/white and green/white banded towers), and nearby shops and produce market. A small and somewhat ramshackle boatyard lies near the head of the creek.

Since 2003 a floating fish cage has been anchored south of Fuzeta at 37°00´.5N 7°44´.45W. It is marked by two buoys, both Fl.Y, on the same latitude and at 7°44´.8W and 7°44´.1W respectively. All vessels are requested to give the cage and buoys at least 500m clearance. Tunny nets used to be laid in this area though none have been in place recently, and if they return are certain to be buoyed and lit.

The small inlet at Fuzeta east of Olhão, seen from the southeast. It can only be approached by shoal-draught yachts or multihulls, or perhaps by dinghy from larger yachts anchored further west

The eastern entrance to Fuzeta should not be tackled without local knowledge – and this is why...

61. Tavira

Waypoints
⊕165 – 37°04´.6N 7°35´.4W (approach)
⊕166 – 37°06´.38N 7°36´.63W (entrance)

Courses and distances
⊕161 (Vilamoura) – ⊕165 (via ⊕163) = 30.3M,
  117°&056° or 236°&297°
⊕163 (Cabo de Santa María) – ⊕165 = 16M, 056° or
  236°
⊕165 – ⊕166 = 2M, 331° or 151°
⊕165 – ⊕167 (Río Guadiana) = 9.1M, 080° or 260°

Tides
See Vila Real de Santo António, Río Guadiana, page
247

Charts

Charts	Approach	Harbour
Admiralty	91, 89, 93	
Imray	C19, C50	
Portuguese	23204, 24206	(27503)

Principal lights
2234 **Ldg Lts 326°** *Front* Armação Fl.R.3s6m4M
  White post, red bands 5m
2234.1 *Rear* 132m from front Iso.R.6s9m5M
  White post, red bands 5m
2235 **West breakwater** Fl.R.2.5s7m7M
  White column, red bands 4m
2235.2 **East breakwater** Fl.G.2.5s5m6M
  White column, green bands 4m

Night entry
Though perfectly feasible, entry in darkness calls for
settled conditions, a rising tide (half-flood or more)
and considerable confidence.

Attractive and unspoilt river anchorage with limited facilities

A very old town – one of its bridges claims Roman
origins, and the only Greek inscription to be found
in Portugal was discovered in nearby Santa Luzia –
Tavira is still heavily dependant on fishing and in
spite of an ever-growing tourist trade has managed
to retain much of its character. Some of its old walls
and many of its tiled houses remain, with wrought
iron balconies and original decoration, overlooked
by floodlit churches and a ruined castle.

The anchorage is connected to the town by a 2km
causeway flanked by salt pans and parking areas –
very popular with the land-cruiser brigade – and by
the Rio Gilão which at high tide is navigable by
dinghy. Once in the anchorage there is good
protection from the sea, though little from the wind,
and the current runs strongly. The area is part of the
Parque Natural de Ria Formosa and the
birdwatching possibilities are endless.

Approach

Between Cabo de Santa María and Tavira the coast
comprises a low sandbank, broken east of Olhão
and again off Fuzeta. A floating fish cage is
positioned south of Fuzeta – see page 242 – and at
certain times of year tunny nets may be laid up to
1.5M offshore, but otherwise there are no natural
hazards.

The entrance is dredged every few years, most
recently in 2001 when 4m was to be found along the
leading line. It is likely that it has silted to some
degree since then. The leading marks, a pair of red
and white banded poles, can be difficult to identify –
if in doubt err to the east, as a shoal extends beyond
the end of the west breakwater.

From offshore ⊕165 lies 2M south-southeast of the
entrance, a course of 331° leading to ⊕166 on the
10m line outside the harbour mouth.

Entrance

Do not enter before half flood or at all if the swell is
heavy – if wind and/or swell are onshore conditions
become rougher on the ebb. The best time for either
entering or for leaving is about one hour before high

Tavira from west-southwest. The Ria Formosa is a
deservedly popular anchorage with cruising yachtsmen

Yachts anchored off the Quatro Aguas ferry jetty in the Ria Formosa. The main channel – though not the ferry passage – is indicated by pairs of stout, lit posts

water. When taking the sharp turn to port into the anchorage give the (unlit) tourist ferry quay and its off-lying post a generous berth (floating lines may trail from it), and keep a sharp lookout for the small ferries, some of which move at surprising speed.

Anchorage

The channel west past Quatro Aguas ('four waters') towards Santa Lucia is indicated by pairs of very solid posts, all nominally lit, and though some local boats remain moored in what appears to be the fairway it would be most unwise to anchor in it – at the very least one would regularly be disturbed by wash from passing fishing boats. In summer it may be difficult to find sufficient space for a larger yacht to swing, in which case (and for all yachts at spring tides) it would be prudent to set two anchors, both from the bow and laid upstream and downstream respectively. The bottom is foul in places and a tripline advised. Holding is good over sand, but the

A local fishing boat heads out to sea past the breakwaters at Tavira   *AH*

current runs strongly enough at springs for most yachts to remain tide-rode even in contrary winds of 20 knots.

Shallow draught vessels have the option of continuing southwest along the Ria Tavira towards Santa Lucia, again anchoring well clear of the fairway which is used by fishing boats day and night. The lower reaches are marked by lit posts.

Formalities

There is a manned *GNR–Brigada Fiscal* office next to the ferry jetty, but Tavira is not a port of entry/exit and passports cannot be stamped for departure (which in any case should only be necessary in the case of non-EU citizens). The Capitania is located in the town, close west of the fishing quay.

Facilities and communications

At the anchorage: water by can from the Clube Náutico de Tavira, which also has showers and a small bar (seek permission before helping oneself to either of the former, as a small fee may be charged), plus several other bars and restaurants but no shops. Fresh shellfish can be bought from a counter at the rear of wholesaler Tomé Mariscos, housed in a large yellow building west of the *clube náutico*.

A square concrete barge against which it is possible to dry out lies on the beach immediately opposite the ferry jetty. However it appears to be settling into the sand and now covers at high water springs. The smallcraft harbour on the west bank just inside the Rio Gilão is too small, shallow and crowded to be feasible for a visiting yacht, and landing by dinghy at the single pontoon is impractical due to a locked security gate. There is a lay-up area for local yachts (maximum about 8m) behind the *clube náutico*, and though there is no possibility of hauling a larger keel-yacht this would undoubtedly be the place to start enquiries if faced with a major problem.

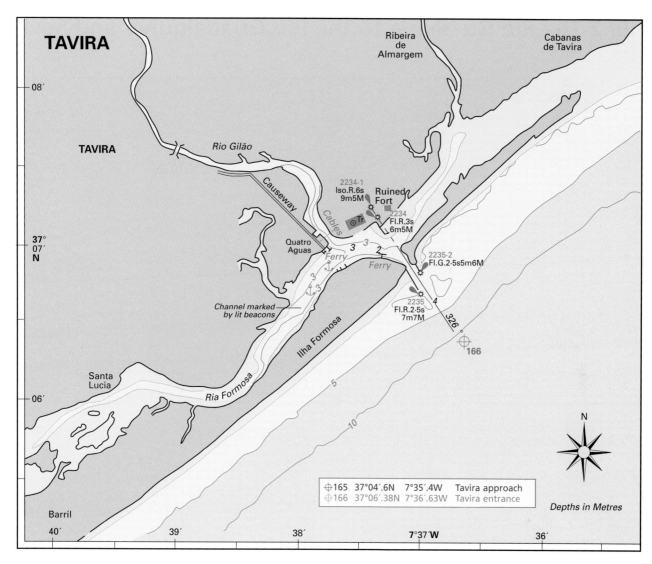

TAVIRA

THE ALGARVE & ANDALUCIA

TAVIRA

Rio Gilão

Ribeira
de
Almargem

Cabanas
de Tavira

Causeway

Cables

2234·1
Iso.R.6s
9m5M

Ruined
Fort

2234
Fl.R.3s
6m5M

Tr

Quatro
Aguas

3   3   2

Ferry

Ferry

2235·2
Fl.G.2·5s5m6M

3

3

Channel marked
by lit beacons

Ilha Formosa

2235
Fl.R.2·5s
7m7M

4

326

166

Santa
Lucia

Ria Formosa

5

10

N

Barril

⊕165 37°04'.6N 7°35'.4W   Tavira approach
⊕166 37°06'.38N 7°36'.63W   Tavira entrance

Depths in Metres

There is a phone kiosk near the ferry jetty and the area is served by Tavira's 'land train' – popular with younger crewmembers as well as older ones encumbered with shopping. Heading in the other direction there is a passenger ferry to Ilha Tavira which operates on demand.

On Ilha Formosa: camp site with several cafés and restaurants, a phone kiosk and a cash dispenser but, rather surprisingly, no shop.

In the town: good shopping (including a vast Pingo Doce on the east bank near the new bridge), banks with cash dispensers, restaurants, hotels etc. Diesel can be transported by can from a waterside filling station just upstream of the new bridge (accessible by dinghy). There are several hardware stores at which Camping Gaz bottles can be exchanged (but not refilled), plus one near the east end of the cast-iron bridge which sells limited chandlery. Runabouts, outboards and inflatables are displayed in a showroom on the west bank near the filling station.

A post office, telephones and several cybercafés will be found (the latter including one on the east bank of the river between the two old bridges, which

Dos and don'ts in the Parque Natural de Ria Formosa   *AH*

has ten or twelve computers plus multiple sockets for laptop users). Transport options include taxis, buses (including the road train mentioned previously) and a station just north of the town. Faro airport is about 30km down the coast.

III. 2 The Río Guadiana to the Río Guadalquivir and Seville

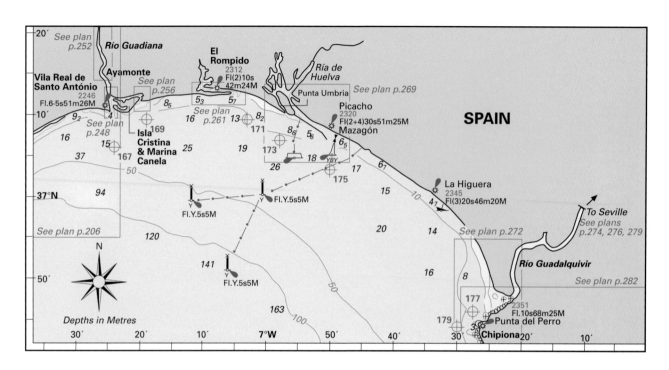

⊕167	37°06'.2N	7°24'.2W	Río Guadiana approach
⊕169	37°08'.6N	7°18'.6W	Marina Canela & Isla Cristina approach
⊕171	37°09'.2N	7°03'.3W	El Rompido approach
⊕173	37°06'.7N	6°57'.7W	Punta Umbría approach
⊕175	37°03'.3N	6°49'.7W	Mazagón approach
⊕177	36°46'N	6°28'W	Chipiona & the Río Guadalquivir approach
⊕179	36°44'N	6°30'.3W	3.1M W of Punta del Perro

PRINCIPAL LIGHTS

2246 **Vila Real de Santo António** Fl.6.5s51m26M
White tower, narrow black rings, red lantern 46m
2312 **El Rompido** Fl(2)10s42m24M
White tower, single red band 29m
2320 **Picacho** Fl(2+4)30s51m25M
White tower with brick corners, as has building, 25m
2345 **Higuera** Fl(3)20s46m20M
White tower and lantern 24m
2351 **Punta del Perro (Chipiona)** Fl.10s68m25M
Stone tower on building 62m

Ports

62. Vila Real de Santo António*
    and Ayamonte (Río Guadiana)
63. Islas Canela* and Cristina*
    (Ría de la Higuerita)
64. El Rompido*
65. Punta Umbría
66. Mazagón*
67. Chipiona*
68. The Río Guadalquivir and Seville*

* Fuel available alongside

Yachts in Marina Isla Canela

62. The Río Guadiana, Vila Real de Santo António (Portugal) and Ayamonte (Spain)

Waypoints
⊕167 – 37°06′.2N 7°24′.2W (approach)
⊕168 – 37°08′.15N 7°23′.83W (entrance)

Courses and distances
⊕161 (Vilamoura) – ⊕167 (via ⊕163) = 38.9M, 117°&064° or 244°&297°
⊕163 (Cabo de Santa María) – F167 = 24.6M, 064° or 244°
⊕165 (Tavira) – ⊕167 = 9.1M, 080° or 260°
⊕167 – ⊕168 = 2M, 009° or 189°
⊕167 – ⊕169 (Islas Canela & Cristina) = 5.1M, 062° or 242°
⊕167 – ⊕175 (Mazagón) = 27.8M, 096° or 276°

Tides
Standard port Lisbon
Mean time differences (Portuguese time zone)
HW –0035 ±0020; LW –0020 ±0020
Heights in metres

MHWS	MHWN	MLWN	MLWS
3.2	2.5	1.3	0.5

Or refer to EasyTide at www.ukho.gov.uk (see page 2)
Both Vila Real and Ayamonte are listed, on the Portuguese and Spanish pages respectively

Charts

Charts	Approach	River
Admiralty	91, 89, 93	
Imray	C19, C50	C50
Portuguese	23204, 24206	26312
Spanish	44B, 440	440A

Principal lights

Entrance
2246 **Vila Real de Santo António** Fl.6.5s51m26M
White tower, narrow black rings, red lantern 46m
2249 **West breakwater** Fl.R.5s7m4M
White lattice tower, red bands 5m
2250 **East (submerged) training wall** Fl.G.3s4M
Black tower on concrete base

Vila Real de Santo António (Portugal)
2247 **Marina south mole, angle** Fl.R.2M Grey post 2m
2247.1 **Marina south mole, head** Fl.R.2M Grey post 2m
2247.2 **Marina north mole, head** Fl.G.2M Grey post 2m
2247.3 **Marina north mole, root** Fl.G.2M Grey post 2m
2249.5 **Fishermen's quay** F.R. Red post, white bands 2m

Ayamonte (Spain)
Marina basin south side
Fl.G.1M Green column
Marina basin north side
Fl.R.1M Red column
2305 **Baluarte** Fl.G.3s2m3M
Black and green framework tower, masonry base 4m

Night entry
Perfectly feasible in light conditions on a flood tide, but nevertheless not advised unless familiar with the area. See also the warning regarding the ferry jetty under on page 249

Harbour communications
VHF Ch 09
(See also individual marinas, pages 249 and 251).

The long west breakwater at the mouth of the Río Guadiana, seen from south-southwest. Vila Real de Santo António (Portuguese) and Ayamonte (Spanish) lie on either bank, with the tall suspension bridge visible in the distance

Scenic river with two small marinas, plus yacht pontoons and anchorages upstream

The Río Guadiana forms part of the border between Portugal and Spain. A suspension bridge spans the river about 2M north of the twin towns of Vila Real de Santo António and Ayamonte, though a diminutive car ferry (which at first glance looks more like a fishing boat) still carries local traffic between the two. The river, which has strong currents, is navigable to Pomarão some 25M upstream and can make a pleasant change to seafaring. It has been reported that the upper valley of the Río Guadiana remains noticeably cooler than the surrounding areas even during the height of summer, possibly due to the chill of the river water which comes straight off the mountains inland.

Over the past decade facilities for yachts have improved dramatically, with small marinas at Vila Real de Santo and Ayamonte (the latter run by the Empresa Pública de Puertos de Andalucía (see page 255). Some provision for yachts is also in place upriver, primarily at Alcoutim (Portuguese) and Sanlúcar de Guadiana (Spanish).

Approach

Either side of the Río Guadiana the coast consists of a low sandbank broken by gaps giving access to the lagoons which run from west of Cabo de Santa María to 2M east of the Río Guadiana. Further east the sand continues unbroken for another 12M. If coastal sailing, note that depths between the Río Guadiana and the Ría de la Higuerita are very shoal, with drying patches up to 1M offshore. The 5m line generally runs more than 1.5M offshore, making 2M a safe distance off. Fishing nets may be laid several miles offshore.

Approaching from the west, two conspicuous marks are the high-rise buildings of Monte Gordo 2M west of the entrance and the tall Vila Real light (white with narrow black bands). From the east, the tower blocks of Isla Cristina stand out. The twin pillars of the suspension bridge can also be seen for many miles.

From offshore ⊕167 lies 2M south of the entrance, a course of 009° leading to ⊕168, about 0.6M southwest of the outer entrance buoys.

Entrance

Do not attempt to enter other than at half flood or above (manoeuvring in the marina at Vila Real de Santo António is least traumatic at slack water), and be especially careful if there is any swell.

The river is canalised between a breakwater and a submerged training wall running 335°, their ends 550m apart and lit. Seaward of the walls are two pairs of port and starboard hand buoys, all lit (though the starboard hand buoys in particular have a reputation for unreliability and long periods off station).

Pass between the buoys and then head for the west breakwater, keeping it slightly open on the port bow. The east training wall is almost totally submerged, with a concrete tower marking its seaward end. Keep about 50m off the breakwater, remaining on the west side until off the town of Vila Real de Santo António.

The bar can be rough on the ebb, particularly if there is any swell running, and is hazardous in onshore weather. When planning departure, allow time to reach the bar before the ebb gathers speed.

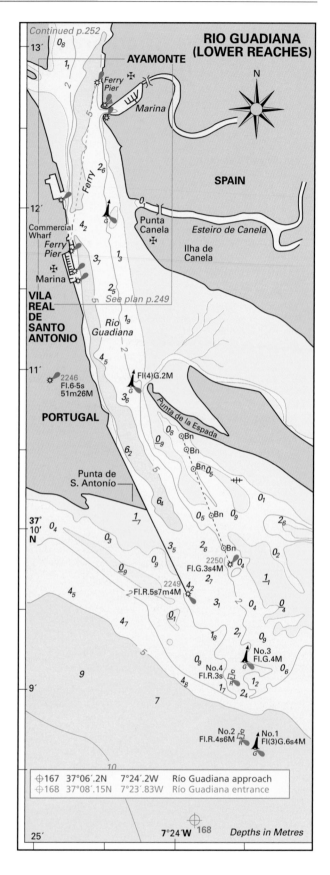

| ⊕167 | 37°06′.2N | 7°24′.2W | Río Guadiana approach |
| ⊕168 | 37°08′.15N | 7°23′.83W | Río Guadiana entrance |

Looking upstream towards the suspension bridge, with one of the diminutive car ferries in the foreground   *AH*

Vila Real de Santo António (Portugal)

Port Authority
☎ 281 512035/513769 *Fax* 281 511140
Email anguadiana@mail.telepac.pt
VHF Ch 11, 16 (call *Capimarvireal*) (24 hours)
Porto de Recreio do Guadiana
☎ 281 541571 VHF Ch 09

The town of Vila Real was largely rebuilt in the 18th century, following destruction in the 1755 earthquake and tidal wave which decimated Lisbon as well as much of the Algarve. It follows a strict grid plan of wide avenues and open squares, often paved with black and white cobbles in intricate patterns. Even the much newer suburbs follow these lines – less interesting perhaps than the winding lanes of the older villages, but with considerably less scope for getting lost. A large part of the centre is a pedestrian area, making Vila Real a very pleasant town in which to wander. As a final bonus it has, for some inexplicable but happy reason, been very largely overlooked by foreign tourists.

The Porto de Recreio do Guadiana opened in late 1997 and contains about 360 berths for yachts of up to 20m, all against with finger pontoons. A high proportion of these are nominally reserved for visitors, but the definition of 'visitor' is necessarily vague and the marina is frequently full in the high season. It is claimed that space will nearly always be found for new arrivals, but sometimes only for a single night. Even when the marina is full, yachts are not permitted to berth in the old Doca de Pesca about 0.5M upstream.

In late 2005 it was stated that a hotel, leisure park and marina were to be built in the largely undeveloped Ponta da Areia district south of the town. However work had not started and little appeared to be known about the project locally.

The Porto de Recreio do Guadiana at Vila Real de Santo António looks across the river towards Spain. The regular layout of the 18th century town, and not least the chequered paving in the main square, is both unusual and striking

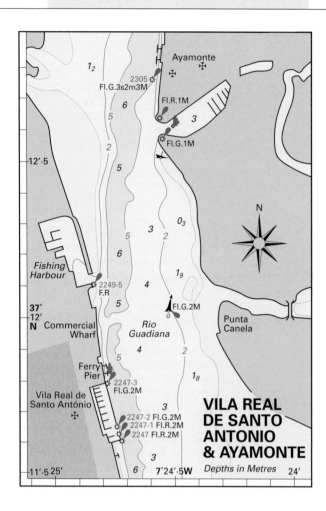

Entrance and berthing

The narrow marina entrance – less than 20m wide – is situated at its downstream end, with a reception area just inside on the starboard hand. When this is occupied the fuel pontoon (between the marina and the ferry pier) may be pressed into service as a reception berth, at other times arriving yachts may be directed straight to a berth by marina staff. The staff cannot, of course, allow for the handling characteristics of individual craft, and at periods of strong tide it may occasionally be necessary to be deaf to directions and secure wherever possible until the flow diminishes. If planning to leave other than at slack water it would also be wise to turn the yacht in her berth in advance. If manoeuvring in the river at night, note that although the pylons to which the ferry jetty is secured both carry lights, the jetty itself – which is painted matt black and projects a further 10m out into the stream – is totally unlit.

Both entrance and marina are subject to strong tidal cross-currents – flow in the river itself can reach 3 knots on the ebb and 2 knots on the flood – making slack water by far the best time to manoeuvre. Once inside space is tight. Both sides of the entrance, as well as the upstream end of the fuel pontoon, are lit but movement at night is to be avoided as it will be difficult to estimate and allow for the cross-current. When new, the marina carried 4m or more in the southern part of the basin, decreasing slightly to the north, but silting has been

Fishing in the traditional way – azulejos (painted tiles) on the wall of the *Capitania* at Vila Real de Santo António *AH*

an ongoing problem and in early 2005 dredging was in progress. It was stated that this would provide 10m beside the river, 8m down the middle and 6m next to the street. Even allowing for the silting which seems certain to follow, depths should remain adequate for quite a few years.

The marina office, open 0900–1230 and 1430–1800 in winter or 1930 in summer, closed weekends, occupies a smart portacabin at the north end of the basin with the services alongside. Both services and pontoons are secured by locked gates with the usual card access.

In 2005 the overnight charge for a visiting yacht of 10–12m was €19.04 in the high season (16 June–15 September), €13.50 in the mid seasons (16 March–15 June and 16 September–15 November) and €9.00 (or €216.00 per month) in the low season. The equivalent rates for a yacht of 12–15m were €28.50, €18.50, €12.50 and €331.00 respectively. Multihulls paid a 50% surcharge. Rates quoted by the marina included water but not electricity (an additional €2.50 per day or €21.00 per month – less in summer) or IVA (VAT), though the latter has been added to the above figures for easy comparison with other harbours. Most major credit cards were accepted.

Formalities

If the yacht is registered in the EU, and all her crew are EU nationals, completion of the usual multi-part form in the marina office is sufficient. Otherwise it may be necessary to visit the offices of the *Polícia Marítima* and *Imigração* at the *Capitania*, about 50m south of the marina.

Facilities

Boatyard There are a number of boatyards downstream from the marina which serve local fishing boats. At least one works in GRP, but none have the means to lift a keel yacht from the water (though see below). Levant Nav, ☎/*Fax* 281 513294 *Email* geral@levantnav.com near the station (not on the waterfront) also moulds and repairs in GRP.

Travel-lift None on the whole river, though the Associacão Naval do Guadiana have a 5-tonne crane at their premises at the south end of the marina basin plus a slipway where it might be possible to dry alongside. Enquire at the office overlooking the slipway, where English is usually spoken.

This could be about to change, as Rino Johansen of Náutica Levante SYS, long established in the boatyard

area at Puerto Deportivo Isla Cristina (see page 256), plans to open a second centre at Vila Real among the boatyards mentioned above. When complete the yard should contain a 50-tonne travel-lift and a dry dock capable of taking yachts of up to 50m LOA and 6.7m beam, backed by his established team of engineers and maintenance staff, with hardstanding available for winter storage ashore.

Engineers None on site, but staff in the office mentioned above will advise who to contact.

Chandlery Nautiguadiana, opposite the marina, carries fishing tackle and some general chandlery. Marinautica, a little further down the road, stocks the above plus some electronics, stainless steel fittings, paint etc. The Boutique Náutica at the *clube naval* sells some chandlery in addition to clothing.

Water On the pontoons.

Showers In well-kept portacabins next to the marina office.

Launderette In the town – ask at the office for directions.

Electricity On the pontoons.

Fuel Diesel from a fuelling berth extending upstream from the marina, with petrol available by can from a pump ashore. Payment must be made in cash.

Bottled gas Camping Gaz exchanges are available in the town but it is not possible to get other cylinders refilled.

Weather forecast Posted daily outside the marina office and in the window overlooking the slipway.

Clube naval The Associação Naval do Guadiana, which now occupies a blue-tiled building at the south end of the marina basin, has a terrace bar and restaurant open to non-members.

Banks In the town, with a cash dispenser directly opposite the marina.

Shops/provisioning/produce market Good shopping of all kinds in the town, including a supermarket four blocks directly inland from the marina.

Cafés, restaurants and hotels An abundance of the former nearby, with a comfortable if somewhat traditional hotel right opposite.

Medical services In the town.

Communications

Post office In the town.

Mailing address The marina office will hold mail for visiting yachts – c/o Associação Naval do Guadiana, Doca de Recreio, Apartado 40 Avenida da República, 8901-909 Vila Real de Santo António, Algarve, Portugal. It is important that the envelope carries the name of the yacht in addition to that of the addressee.

Public telephones Several nearby.

Internet access Directly opposite the marina in the foyer of the Hotel Guadiana (small fee payable), at the public library (free, but often busy) and elsewhere.

Fax service At the marina office *Fax* 281 511140.

Car hire/taxis In the town or via the marina office.

Buses Bus station beyond the ferry pier, itself next to the marina. Ten minutes ride northward is the attractive riverside village of Castro Marim, with two castles and a unusually imaginative children's playground.

Trains Vila Real is the eastern terminus of the Algarve coastal line, with a sleepy station close to the fishing harbour in the northern part of the town.

Ferries The diminutive passenger and car ferry departs every hour for Ayamonte, returning on the half hour.

Air services Faro International Airport is some 60km by road or rail.

Ayamonte (Spain)

Puerto Deportivo del Ayamonte
☎ 959 321294 Fax 959 320767
Email ayamonted@eppa.es
www.eppa.es
VHF Ch 09

Ayamonte is, in its way, just as attractive as its Portuguese rival and certainly as historic. Parts of the original 16th century walls are still visible, there is an attractive church, and several exuberantly tiled squares where all generations congregate in the early evening. With fewer tourists to cater for than in the Algarve the shops are better stocked with practical, everyday items and the cafés are thronged with local people.

The old fishermen's basin contains the westernmost of the string of yacht marinas and sport fishing harbours run by the Empresa Pública de Puertos de Andalucía – see page 255. Opened in April 1998 and able to take 173 yachts on its five pontoons, seven years later considerable expansion was in progress – and not before time as the marina was often full even though 25% of berths were nominally reserved for yachts in transit. However it was claimed that by 2006 the entire basin would be dredged to a minimum of 3m and that four additional pontoons would be in place, doubling capacity to around 350 berths, most of them for yachts of between 20m and 18m in length and all alongside finger pontoons.

The Puerto Deportivo Ayamonte from the southeast, with the suspension bridge (clearance at least 20m) at upper right

Entrance and berthing

The entrance to the basin is some 60m wide and subject to strong cross-currents, but complete protection is gained once inside. Both sides are lit, though arrival after dark is not recommended until the modifications are complete (see also *Fuel*, below). Preferably call on VHF Ch 09 before entering the basin, otherwise secure to the westernmost hammerhead or, failing that, choose a suitable berth on the westernmost pontoon.

Weekdays office hours are 0930–1330 and 1600–1700, closed Saturday and Sunday afternoons in winter. However there is 24 hour security in addition to electronic pontoon access gates. Charges are at the standard EPPA rate – see page 255.

Formalities

As is usual in Spain formalities are very relaxed. After completing the usual paperwork in the marina office it is possible that an official may visit the yacht, though this is unlikely in the case of an EU yacht and crew.

Facilities

Boatyard Fishermen's yard near the ferry pier, but nothing for yachts.
Engineers Some mechanical skills available – enquire at the marina office.
Chandlery Not as such, but try the Camilo hardware store (or take the ferry across the river to Vila Real).
Water On the pontoons.
Showers In a portacabin next to the marina office.
Electricity On the pontoons
Fuel A 'fuel pontoon' has been in position near the entrance to the basin for at least five years – completely bereft of pumps or even shore access. It is hoped that the marina expansion will finally see it come on-stream, but in the meantime it is a real hazard to yachts entering after dark being grey, low-lying, and totally unlit.
Bottled gas Camping Gaz exchanges in the town, but no refills.
Weather forecast Posted daily outside the marina office.
Banks In the town.
Shops/provisioning Good shopping in the town, plus a supermarket one block to the east of the marina basin.
Produce market In the town.
Cafés, restaurants and hotels Plenty in the town, but nothing at the marina itself.
Medical services In the town.

Communications

Post office In the town.
Mailing address The marina office will hold mail for visiting yachts – c/o Puerto Deportivo Ayamonte, 21400 Ayamonte, Huelva, España. It is important that the envelope carries the name of the yacht in addition to that of the addressee.
Public telephones Beside the marina office and elsewhere.
Internet access At Todoapc on the north side of the basin near the entrance, which also advertises computer maintenance and repairs.
Fax service At the marina office, ☎/*Fax* 959 321694.
Car hire/taxis/buses In the town.
Ferries Small but frequent passenger and car ferry to Vila Real de Santo António.
Air services Faro International Airport is some 65km distant by road, Seville approximately twice as far.

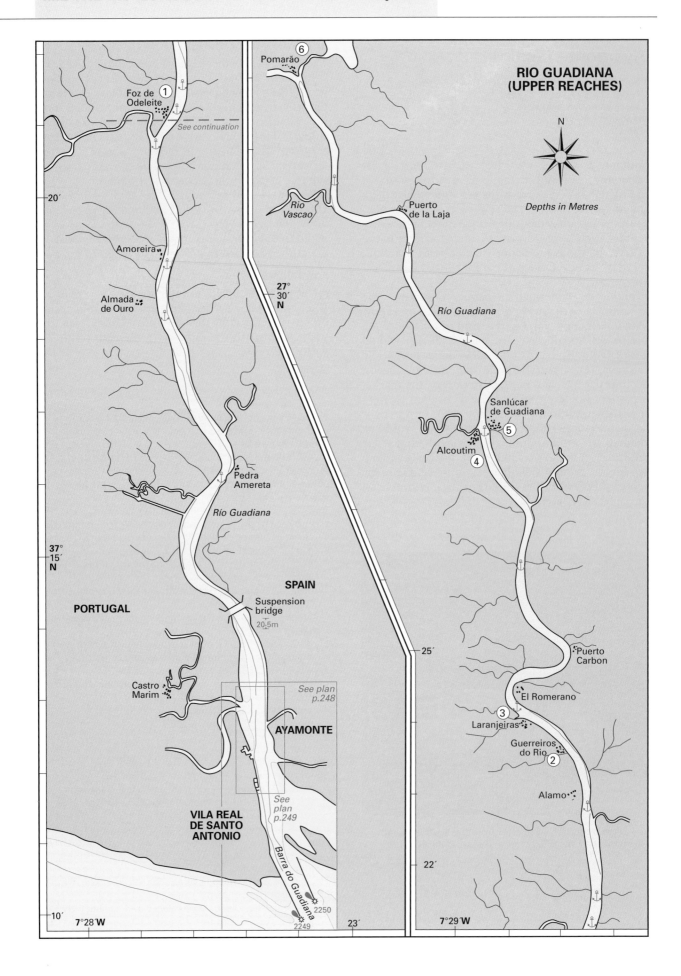

RIO GUADIANA
(UPPER REACHES)

N

Depths in Metres

Pomarão ⑥

Foz de
Odeleite ①

See continuation

20′

*Rio
Vascao*

Puerto
de la Laja

Amoreira

27°
30′
N

Río Guadiana

Almada
de Ouro

Sanlúcar
de Guadiana

Alcoutim ④ ⑤

Pedra
Amereta

Río Guadiana

37°
15′
N

Puerto
Carbon

SPAIN

PORTUGAL

Suspension
bridge
20.5m

25′

El Romerano

Castro
Marim

*See plan
p.248*

Laranjeiras ③

AYAMONTE

Guerreiros
do Rio ②

*See
plan
p.249*

VILA REAL
DE SANTO
ANTONIO

Alamo

22′

Barra do Guadiana

2250

10′   7°28′W

2249   23′   7°29′W

Upriver

There is general agreement that the upper reaches of the Río Guadiana are not to be missed, particularly by birdwatchers. White storks can often be seen on the lower reaches of the river above Ayamonte, and other interesting birds include cattle egrets, black-winged stilts and kingfishers. Red-rumped swallows, hoopoes, golden orioles and bee-eaters may be seen further upriver, and a flock of azure-winged magpies live close upstream of Alcoutim/Sanlúcar.

If heading upriver, leave at low water, favouring the starboard side while passing Ayamonte to avoid the muddy shoal which extends nearly halfway across the river north of Vila Real. There is relatively little traffic other than regular ferries, excursion boats in summer and a few fishing vessels.

After passing under the rather elegant suspension bridge (clearance approximately 20.5m at high water, 23m at low water) the Río Guadiana is quiet, pretty and deep but has a current to be reckoned with – approaching 2 knots on the flood and 3 knots on the ebb. With the aid of the former it is possible the make the 20M or so up to Portuguese Alcoutim and Spanish Sanlúcar de Guadiana on one tide. The river is not buoyed, other than a single red can marking shallows just downstream from the bridge, and in 2005 the channel was not always obvious. However with a little care a minimum of 3.5m – and a maximum of 20m – may to be found as far as Alcoutim/Sanlúcar even at dead low water. The channel generally runs deepest on the outside of bends, often only 20–50m from the bank, but shoals may be found off the mouths of many tributaries. Straight stretches usually offer the best anchorages, with 6–8m depths and good holding over mud. High water at Alcoutim/Sanlúcar occurs about 2 hours after Vila Real, high water at Pomarão about 2.5

The pontoon at Foz de Odeleite (1), the first settlement one passes when venturing up the Río Guadiana   *AH*

The second pontoon lies off the Portuguese village of Guerreiros do Rio (2,) where there is a small river museum   *AH*

hours later. In both cases tidal range is marginally reduced compared to the entrance.

Avoid venturing upstream immediately after heavy rain further inland which, as well as adding to the already strong current, can send large items of floating debris such as branches, bamboo canes etc careering downstream. It should be mentioned that in November 1997 a flash flood caused serious damage along the length of the river (apparently, due to lack of consultation, sluice gates were opened on both Portuguese and Spanish sides simultaneously) and many yachts were wrecked. However the lesson has been learned and it is unlikely that this particular hazard will recur.

The Spanish side is sparsely inhabited as far as Sanlúcar, but there are several small villages on the Portuguese bank, including Foz de Odeleite (37°21´.22N 7°26´.46W, Guerreiros do Rio (37°23´.85N 7°26´.8W) and Laranjeiras (37°24´.23N 7°27´.48W). All three have short pontoons – also used by tourist boats running day excursions up the river from Vila Real – to which

The third Portuguese village to have its own pontoon is Laranjeiras (3), where there is also a good anchorage   *AH*

The town of Alcoutim (4) on the Portuguese bank, which has three pontoons (one reserved for commercial craft) and is a favourite spot for over-wintering   *AH*

Both have good pontoons, three on the Portuguese side and a single long one on the Spanish, all with functioning water and electricity (though Alcoutim's central pontoon is intended for tourist boats rather than yachts). Adjacent to the Sanlúcar pontoon are purpose-built showers and toilets for the use of berth-holders (key from the nearby Capitania). In 2005 a flat rate of €8 per night was collected from all yachts lying alongside, irrespective of size, though lying to a buoy was understood to be free, as was anchoring. In common with the other Portuguese villages, Alcoutim has a three night berthing rule throughout the year. Although sometimes relaxed out of season it is rigorously enforced during the summer. Sanlúcar nominally allows a maximum of two weeks alongside, but this is seldom enforced.

yachts can secure for no more than three nights. All three pontoons are nominally equipped with water and electricity though not, as of early 2005, actually delivering. Depths alongside have not been verified, but appear generous. Although it was reported a few years ago that visitors moorings had been laid off the villages, these were not in evidence by 2005. None has much in the way of shoreside facilities beyond a bar or two, though a van selling bread and basic foodstuffs makes regular visits, but all are served by the bus which runs north from Vila Real to Alcoutim and beyond. A 'river museum' can be visited at Guerreiros do Rio, while a Roman villa is being excavated near Laranjeiras (yachts too large for the pontoon will find good anchorage opposite the village in 4–5m).

Portuguese Alcoutim (37°28′.29N 7°28′.25W) and Spanish Sanlúcar de Guadiana (37°28′.37N 7°28′.11W), linked by pedestrian ferry, are an entirely different matter to the villages downstream.

Both towns have cafés, restaurants, limited shopping (including pharmacies), banks with cash dispensers and public telephones, while Alcoutim also has a small hospital and internet access in the public library (booking advised). Squat stone castles peer at each other across the river, but most would agree that the Castelo de San Marcos on the Spanish side – with origins dating back to the 13th century – has the visual edge over its Portuguese rival, though the latter contains a small museum. Younger crewmembers will enjoy the *praia fluvial* (river beach) on a narrow tributary just north of Alcoutim, complete with sand, safe paddling/swimming, and a nearby play area. On the Portuguese side buses run to south to Vila Real and north (twice weekly) as far as Mértola, an old walled town complete with obligatory castle and museums.

At least two dozen visitors of all nationalities chose to winter at Alcoutim/Sanlúcar in 2004/5, five or six alongside, a few on moorings and the majority

Opposite Alcoutim is the Spanish town of Spanish Sanlúcar de Guadiana (5), dominated by its hilltop castle. A pedestrian ferry plies between the two towns   *AH*

Pomarão (6), on the Portuguese bank, is as far up the Río Guadiana as most yachts can penetrate, though care is needed on the approach   *AH*

at anchor. (If planning to stay at anchor for any length of time it would be wise to lay two, the heaviest upstream and a second – but more than a kedge – downstream, secured together at a point deep enough for the yacht to swing).

A muddy shoal runs out from the west bank just north of Alcoutim – local advice is to keep well to starboard of the line of mooring buoys if heading upriver. With persistence most yachts can get as far as Pomarão (37°33′.28N 7°31′.57W), on the Portuguese side about 7M upstream of Alcoutim. This takes one past disused mine workings and derelict piers once used by sizeable ore-carriers, but the river narrows and has silted in places (best water will generally be found on the eastern side). Particular caution should be exercised in the approach to Pomarão, which has numerous offlying rocks and boulders. Two short pontoons, both provided with water and electricity, lie beneath the village, which has a seasonal café but little else. There is a short pontoon on the south side but nothing whatsoever ashore. (Some road maps show a bridge at Pomarão, but it is long gone – if it ever existed at all – and there is no sign of supports or other remains.) If anchoring in the vicinity of Pomarão it is best to avoid the area off the old ore-loading jetty immediately west of the pontoons, which is reported to be fouled with chains, and to continue about 200m upstream before dropping. Even so a trip line might be adviseable.

Intrepid explorers may wish to continue beyond Pomarão towards Mertola, a sizeable Portuguese town, though currently a sand and shingle bar halts yachts a few miles downstream of the town, not even allowing sufficient depth to proceed by dinghy. This last stretch of the river runs between stony cliffs and is totally undeveloped. However rocks and sandbanks abound, the latter most often around the mouths of small tributary creeks, and navigation is strictly visual. The water comes straight off the mountains and is clear but very cold.

The Empresa Pública de Puertos de Andalucía marinas

One cannot cruise for very long on the Andalucían coast without encountering the string of yacht marinas and sport fishing harbours financed, built and run by the Empresa Pública de Puertos de Andalucía (formerly the Junta de Puertos de Andalucía) in Seville, ☎ 955 007200 *Fax* 955 007201 *Email* eppa@eppa.es www.eppa.es (in Spanish only).

As of early 2005 they ran nine yacht harbours to the west of Gibraltar as well as several in the Mediterranean. From west to east these comprised: Ayamonte, Isla Cristina, Punta Umbría, Mazagón, Chipiona, Rota, Puerto América (Cádiz), Sancti Petri and Barbate, only 35M west of Gibraltar.

A single sheet, supposedly available in several languages, covered all nine, featuring an aerial photograph of each marina together with a plan showing the location of facilities such as fuel, travel lift, showers etc. Much the same information was available on their website (above), though often in Spanish only.

Prices are standard for the entire chain, despite widely differing facilities and appeal, but it appears that some discretion is allowed when it comes to charging for use of water and electricity (listed at €1.48 per day). In 2005 the high season (1 June to 30 September) rate for a visiting yacht of 11–12m was €19.14 per night, rising to €25.91 for 12–15m. Low season rates for yachts of similar dimensions were €9.57 and €12.96 respectively (exactly half the high season tariff). Multihulls are subject to a 50% surcharge. If a berth of the correct length is not available and a yacht is forced to occupy a larger berth this is charged for, irrespective of the actual length of the boat.

Though quoted by the marina ex-IVA at 16%, this has been added to the above figures for easy comparison with other harbours. A 10% discount is available for a stay of a month or more, 15% for three months and 30% for six months (the latter not including July or August). All payment must be made in advance, with most major credit cards accepted. Evidence of insurance may be required, but does not need to be translated into Spanish.

All the marinas appear well maintained and nearly all offices include at least one English-speaker, often fluent. The office attitude is nearly always helpful, though not always as flexible as might be the case with a privately-run concern. Where facilities include a travel-lift and hardstanding these also appear to be well-maintained and efficiently handled, with boats ashore normally placed in robust cradles with additional props. However, while owners are welcome to work on their own boats while ashore, living aboard – even for a single night – is totally forbidden. (Rumour has it that an inhabited yacht blew over during a gale in 2003, and though no one was injured it led to the rule – which had been on the books for several years but largely ignored – being taken out, dusted down, and strictly enforced). Security gates are locked at night (usually 2200–0700) and in some harbours there may be no access at weekends. Check when booking.

It has been calculated that by 2115 – less than a decade away – 15,000 new berths will be needed in Andalucía if demand is to be satisfied. Although this includes the Mediterranean coast as far east as Almería new marinas, both public and private, are likely to open on the Atlantic coast at regular intervals. Information on many of these will appear on the Empresa Pública de Puertos de Andalucía's own website at www.eppa.es, and will also be included in the ongoing supplement to this book carried on the publishers' website – www.imray.com – as it becomes available. Reports on new marina developments in the area would be particularly welcome (see back cover for publisher's contact details).

63. Islas Canela and Cristina (Ría de la Higuerita)

Waypoints
- ⊕169 – 37°08´.6N 7°18´.6W (approach)
- ⊕170 – 37°10´.45N 7°18´.93W (entrance)

Courses and distances
- ⊕167 (Río Guadiana) – ⊕169 = 5.1M, 062° or 242°
- ⊕169 – ⊕170 = 1.9M, 352° or 172°
- ⊕169 – ⊕171 (El Rompido) = 12.3M, 087° or 267°
- ⊕169 – ⊕173 (Punta Umbría) = 17M, 096° or 276°
- ⊕169 – ⊕175 (Mazagón) = 23.7M, 103° or 283°

Tides
See Río Guadiana, page 247

Charts

	Approach	River
Admiralty	91, 89, 93	
Imray	C19, C50	C50
Spanish	44B, 440	440A

Principal entrance lights
2308 **Ldg Lts 313°** *Front* Q.W.8m5M
   Aluminium framework tower 7m
2308.1 *Rear* 100m from front Fl.4s13m5M
   Aluminium framework tower 12m
2307 **West breakwater** VQ(2)R.5s8m4M
   Red framework tower 4m
2309 **Pantalán del Moral, head** F.W
Note The tall white building on Punta del Caimán is NOT a light structure but an apartment block

Night entry
As with the (much wider) Río Guadiana, while night entry is perfectly possible in the right conditions it is best avoided by those unfamiliar with the area

Harbour communications
VHF Ch 09 (see also marinas, pages 258 and 259).

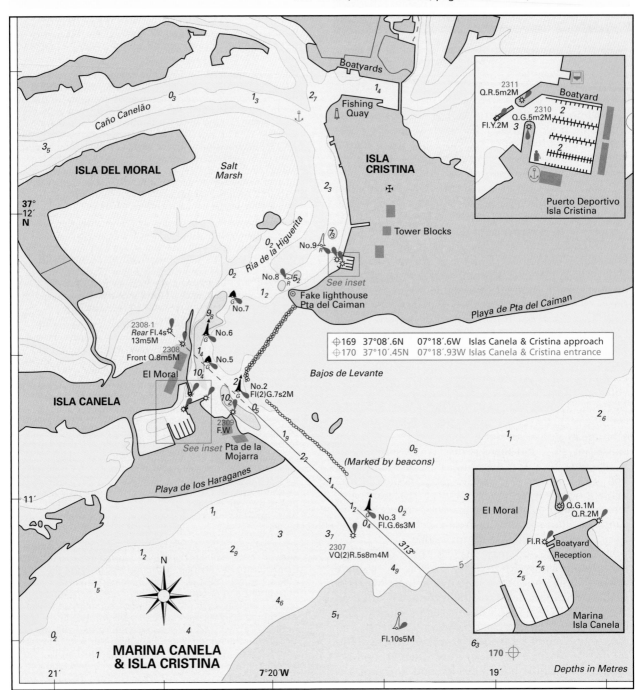

| ⊕169 | 37°08´.6N | 07°18´.6W | Islas Canela & Cristina approach |
| ⊕170 | 37°10´.45N | 07°18´.93W | Islas Canela & Cristina entrance |

MARINA CANELA & ISLA CRISTINA

Depths in Metres

Two well-run marinas surrounded by windswept salt marsh

Marina Isla Canela and the Puerto Deportivo Isla Cristina represent very contrasting styles of Spanish marina development. The former, opened in 2001, is of the 'marina village' style and while quiet and secure lacks any shoreside atmosphere. The old fishermen's quarter at Punta del Moral on the north side of the basin is being swallowed up by new development, while much of the area to the south, while rather attractive with its moorish architecture – some of it atop old castle walls – and well-kept grounds, is emphatically private. It is only a short walk to a superb beach, however.

In contrast Isla Cristina, on its long sandspit to the east of the Ría de la Higuerita, is one of the most important fishing ports in Andalucía. Although tourism – much of it Spanish – is a growing industry, the old town a short walk away is attractive and the waterfront north of the marina interesting, particularly the thriving fishing harbour with its bustling market. An illustrated notice in three languages gives some explanation for the visitor. The Puerto Deportivo Isla Cristina was one of the first built by the Empresa Pública de Puertos de Andalucía (see page 255) and is best suited to smaller yachts, being relatively shallow and with few berths able to accommodate more than 10m overall.

Approach

If coastal sailing, note that depths between the Rio Guadiana and the the Ría de la Higuerita are very shoal, with drying patches up to 1M offshore. The 5m line generally runs more than 1.5M offshore, making 2M a safe distance off.

From offshore ⊕169 lies 1.9M south of the entrance, a course of 352° leading to ⊕170 on the leading line and about 0.7M from the west breakwater head. Fishing nets may be laid several miles offshore, and in 2005 a fish farm was in place marked by two yellow pillar buoys with × topmarks, both lit Q.Y., centred on 37°08'.12N 7°17'.53W.

Although the shore on either side of the entrance is low-lying, the new development at Punta de la Mojarra (generally referred to as Isla Canela, though correctly this is the island close north) and long, pale buildings at Isla Cristina show up well from seaward. Near the southwest corner of Punta del Caimán will be seen a tall beige building complete with domed superstructure, looking for all the world like a rather fancy lighthouse. In fact it is yet another apartment block – but a fine daymark. An older tower, the Torre Catalán, lies halfway between Isla Cristina and Rompido.

Entrance

Approach from the south, preferably at between half and three-quarter flood, and turn in to run parallel with the west breakwater. The deeper water is on the western side of the channel. Follow the leading marks on 313° – the grey framework towers resemble electricity pylons and can be difficult to distinguish from offshore.

Upriver

Above the marinas and fishing wharves the channel becomes sinuous and shoal, flanked by salt marsh and ancient, abandoned hulks. It is possible to anchor in the entrance to the Caño Canelão (though rolly from fishing boat wash), but otherwise this is an area to be explored by dinghy, and with an eye to the tide-tables. Not surprisingly, the bird watching possibilities are endless.

The mouth of the Ría de la Higuerita looking north, with Marina Isla Canela and its associated development on the left and Isla Cristina further upstream on the right. The distinctive 'fake lighthouse' stands just to the right of centre

Marina Isla Canela

Principal lights
2309 **Pantalán del Moral, head** F.W
2308.2 **South mole** Q.R.2M Red post 2m
2308.3 **North mole** Q.G.1M Green post (not working 2005)
2308.4 **Travel-hoist dock** Fl.R.1M Red post

Communications
☎ 959 479000 *Fax* 959 479020
Email marina@islacanela,es
www.islacanela.es and www.islacanela.co.uk
VHF Ch 09

As already mentioned, Marina Isla Canela is of the 'marina village' type, though it appears that relatively few berths have been sold to apartment owners and, as of early 2005 – its fourth year of operation – it had never been completely full. The surrounding buildings have a distinctly north African character – perhaps related to the fact that 'canela' means 'cinnamon'. The initial phase contains 231 berths in minimum depths of 2.5m. Only 24 of these can take yachts of more than 11m overall – including three hammerheads, each rated for 24m – but there is room for expansion to the west, where dredging will one day create space for a further 305 berths.

Entrance and berthing

The entrance is well marked and is lit to port, but as of early 2005 the triangular green base on the starboard hand was without lens or light. The reception berth requires a second turn to port, lying just beyond the travel-lift and crane and below the blue and white marina office. The four pontoons lie beyond, well sheltered from fishing boat wash and other disturbance, with the largest yachts to the southwest and smallest to the northeast – access requires the usual electronic card. Office hours are 0900–1400, 1600–2000 from June to September and 0900–1400, 1500–1800 throughout the rest of the year, Monday to Saturday only. In early 2005 the staff were helpful and efficient, and excellent English was spoken.

In spite of being able to accommodate yachts of well over 12m, this is the maximum length for which set charges are advertised. In 2005 the overnight charge for a visiting yacht of 11–12m was €23.71 in the high season (June to September inclusive), dropping to €10.76 in the low season. Multihulls paid a 50% surcharge. Water was included but electricity was metred and charged in addition – as was IVA, though the latter has been added to the above figures for easy comparison with other harbours. Discounts were available for longer stays if paid in advance. Most major credit cards are accepted.

Formalities

Whether arriving from Spain or Portugal a single-sheet form is completed at the marina office, a copy of which is automatically passed to the authorities.

Facilities

Boatyard Generous (if slightly exposed) area of secure, concreted hardstanding on which yachts are propped but not, as of 2005, in cradles. Several contractors operate workshops in the area, including Náutica Avante, ☎ 959 479013, *Fax* 479530. DIY work is permitted, but this is restricted to office hours (so no work on Sunday) and owners are not allowed to live aboard a yacht while she is ashore.
Travel-lift 32-tonne capacity lift in the boatyard.
Engineers, electronic and radio repairs In the boatyard (or visit Náutica Levante SYS at Puerto Deportivo Isla Cristina, see opposite).
Chandlery Náutica Avante (see above) operate a small chandlery in the commercial centre but it is almost totally given over to fishing tackle.
Water On the pontoons.
Showers In the blue and white reception building.
Launderette Neither available nor planned.
Electricity On the pontoons.
Fuel Diesel and petrol available 24 hours a day from pumps near the office.
Bottled gas Not available.
Weather forecast Posted daily at the marina office.
Club náutico Already established in the reception building, though how much it is a true club and how much a commercial organisation is difficult to say.
Bank No bank, but at least one cash dispenser in the commercial area.
Shops, provisioning Two small supermarkets in the commercial area. For more serious shopping it would be necessary to visit either Ayamonte or Isla Cristina.
Cafés, restaurants and hotels A wide choice in the commercial centre, with a few more in the old town to the north.
Medical services Can be summoned from Ayamonte via the marina office.

Communications

Post office Not as such – not even a post box! – but the supermarket sells stamps and mail for despatch can be left at the marina office.
Mailing address The marina office will hold mail for visiting yachts – c/o Marina Isla Canela, 21409 Isla Canela, Ayamonte, Huelva, España. It is important that the envelope carries the name of the yacht in addition to that of the addressee.
Telephones In the marina office and commercial centre.
Internet access Cybercafé in the commercial centre.
Fax service At the marina office, *Fax* 959 479020.
Car hire At least one agency in the commercial centre.
Taxis Order via the marina office.
Buses Bus stop a little way down the road.
Air services International airports at Faro (Portugal) and Seville (Spain).

Puerto Deportivo Isla Cristina

Principal lights
2310 **South mole** Q.G.5m2M Green column 2m
2311 **North mole** Q.R.5m2M Red column 2m
Wavebreak pontoon Fl.Y.2M Column 2m
Communications
☎ 959 343501 *Fax* 959 343511
Email islacristinad@eppa.es www.eppa.es
VHF Ch 09

Puerto Deportivo Isla Cristina from the east. The wavebreak pontoon, installed to deflect the wash of passing fishing boats, shows up very clearly

Shortly after passing the entrance to Marina Isla Canela the channel bends to starboard around a drying middle ground marked by several starboard hand buoys (do not be tempted to emulate local craft which may take a short cut across the shallows). A port-hand buoy opposite the 'lighthouse' and a second almost opposite the marina entrance mark a second shoal. A 90m wavebreak pontoon was laid off the marina entrance in 1998 in a partially successful attempt to deflect the considerable wash from passing fishing boats, few of which take any notice of the 4 knot speed limit.

Entrance and berthing

The relatively narrow entrance to Puerto Deportivo Isla Cristina lies inside the shelter pontoon described above. Although the latter is lit, particular care should be taken if entering after dark. Depth in the entrance is 2.5m, decreasing to 2m inside. Secure to the reception/fuel pontoon immediately to starboard to be allocated a berth, preferably having already called up on VHF Ch 09 – a wise precaution in any case, since only 20 of the marina's 203 berths are able to take yachts of more than 10m overall. These are all on the northernmost pontoon, with all berths now alongside finger pontoons.

Office hours vary from summer to winter, being 0800–2000 daily in summer, 0930–1330 and 1600–1730 in winter, closed weekend afternoons. Berthing staff are on duty from 0700–2200 and there is 24 hour security, as well as electronic gates to individual pontoons and the boatyard area. In 2005 all the staff on duty were exceptionally helpful and friendly, and several spoke good English.

Formalities

Whether arriving from Spain or Portugal a single-sheet form is completed at the marina office, a copy of which is automatically passed to the authorities. Nothing further needs to be done, even if arriving from outside the EU, though occasionally the *Guardia Civil* may visit the yacht in her berth.

Facilities

Boatyard An area of gated hardstanding near the travel-lift enables owners to do their own maintenance or to call in one of the contractors in the area. By far the largest – and longest established – is Náutica Levante SYS, ☎ 959 332730 *Mobile* 60 9508 204 *Fax* 959 332797 *Email* info@nauticalevante.com www.nauticalevante.com (Spanish only), which handles repairs and maintenance in all materials, osmosis treatment, painting etc. Norwegian owner Rino Johansen speaks fluent English as well as several other languages.

Travel-lift 32-tonne capacity lift. In 2005 all yachts were placed in cradles with additional shores.
Engineers, electronics and radio repairs Náutica Levante SYS, as above.
Sail repairs Can be arranged via Náutica Levante SYS, though an entire new sail would have to be ordered from further afield.
Chandlery Well-stocked chandlery in the commercial block – another Náutica Levante SYS enterprise. Items not available can be ordered, usually within 24 hours.
Liferaft servicing Náutica Levante are an agent/service centre for Zodiac, but will also handle other makes.
Water On the pontoons.
Showers At the rear of the commercial block.
Launderette At the rear of the commercial block.
Electricity On the pontoons.
Fuel Diesel and petrol available at the fuel/reception berth, open 0700–1900 daily. Exact payment must be made in cash – no change is given.
Bottled gas Camping Gaz available in the town, but no refills.
Weather forecast Posted daily at the marina office.
Banks In the town.
Shops/provisioning All usual shops in the town, a short walk from the marina, but no food shops on site.
Cafés, restaurants and hotels Small café overlooking the marina, but no restaurant. However both are to be found in the older part of the town, with hotels mainly centred in the newer beachside areas.
Medical services In the town.

Communications

Post office In the town.
Mailing address The marina office will hold mail for visiting yachts – c/o Puerto Deportivo Isla Cristina, Officina del Puerto, Bda Punta del Caiman s/n, 21410 Isla Cristina, Huelva, España. It is important that the envelope carries the name of the yacht in addition to that of the addressee.
Public telephones Kiosk near the marina office, with others in the town.
Internet access Several places in the town, including a cybercafé on the ground floor of the 'lighthouse' building.
Fax service At the marina office, *Fax* 959 345501.
Car hire/taxis Available in the town or via the marina office.
Buses To Ayamonte, Huelva and beyond.
Air services International airports at Faro (Portugal) and Seville (Spain).

64. El Rompido

Waypoints
⊕171 – 37°09′.2N 7°03′.3W (approach)
⊕172 – 37°11′.32N 7°02′.73W (entrance)

Bearings and distance
⊕169 (Islas Canela and Cristina) – ⊕171 = 12.3M, 087° or 267°
⊕171 – ⊕172 = 2.2M, 012° or 192°
⊕171 – ⊕173 (Punta Umbría) = 5.1M, 119° or 299°
⊕171 – ⊕175 (Mazagón) = 12.4M, 118° or 298°

Tides
See Mazagón, page 268

Charts *Approach*   *River*
Admiralty   91, 89, 93
Imray   C19, C50
Spanish   44B, 440   441A

Principal lights
2312 **El Rompido** Fl(2)10s42m24M
   White tower, red band 29m
buoy **Fairway No.1** LFl.10s5M
   Red and white vertical striped pillar buoy, • topmark
Note At least a dozen further buoys should indicate the channel (see plan).

Shallow, challenging entrance leading to windswept coastal lagoon

Most cruising yachtsmen would agree that El Rompido is one of the most attractive spots along this stretch of the coast, but before gaining its tranquil interior the difficult, twisting bar must be negotiated – see Entrance, below. That it has been inhabited since pre-Roman times comes as no surprise, the long sandspit of the Punta del Gato (*rompeolas* = breakwater) making the protected waters of the Río Piedras seem more like a lagoon than a river.

Caution
Both the position of and depths over the bar alter frequently, and local yachtsmen are now responsible for relocating the buoyage in response to these changes. Current positions of the first ten buoys are listed on the marina website (*recalada* translates as fairway or landfall buoy), but it should be noted that they are expressed in degrees, minutes and seconds and given in EU50 datum (which places each buoy about 190m from its WGS84 position). All in all it appears wisest to trust current local knowledge as reflected in the buoys themselves.

Night entry
Unsuitable for night entry by a keel yacht under any circumstances.

Harbour communications
Puerto Marina El Rompido, ☎ 959 399614
Email info@puertoelrompido.com
www.puertoelrompido.com VHF Ch 09
Varadero Río Piedras SA, ☎ 959 399026,
Fax 959 399034, *Email* varadero@vianwe.com,
VHF Ch 09
Club Náutico Río Piedras, ☎/Fax 959 399349,
VHF Ch 09

However, after millennia with few changes, development has been rapid over the past twelve years. In 1994 El Rompido was a small, picturesque, riverside village with limited facilities other than an excellent boatyard. Visiting yachts – once safely over

The shallow bar at the mouth of the Río Piedras, looking northwest. The positions of the numerous buoys change frequently

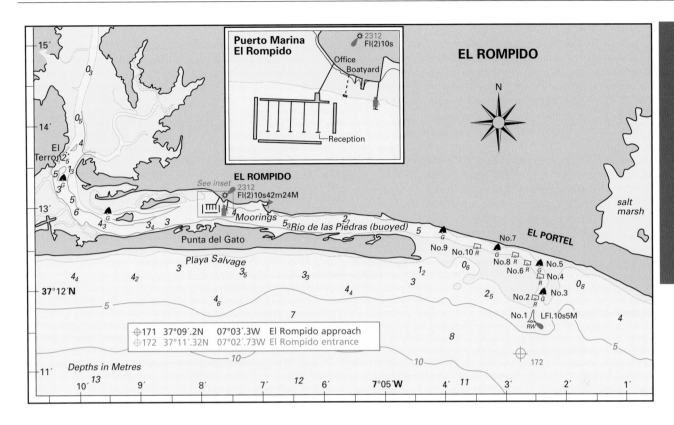

the bar – could anchor or perhaps rent a mooring. Ten years later it had become a popular holiday destination for Spaniards from Seville and elsewhere, backed by a large new hotel to serve the 36 hole golf course and crowded with moored yachts and smallcraft. There was little space left for anchoring. The latest – and perhaps most unexpected – innovation is the construction of a 350 berth marina, close to the long-established *Varadero Río Piedras SA* boatyard and some 4.5M from the river entrance.

Approach

From the west, the shoreline is unbroken between Isla Cristina and El Rompido with a daymark, the Torre Catalán, on the higher dunes west of the point where the Río de las Piedras turns inland. From this tower to the entrance – some 7.5M – the river runs parallel to the shore behind the Punta del Gato and Playa Salvage. To the east the beach is backed by dunes rising up to 40m and topped by umbrella pines.

From offshore ⊕171 lies 2.2M south-southwest of the entrance, a course of 012° leading to ⊕172, nearly 0.5M south of the fairway buoy but already in depths of less than 5m. This is the time to decide whether it is safe to press on, or whether conditions are less than perfect and it would be more prudent to turn west for Portugal or east for Mazagón and beyond.

A fish haven centred on a spot about 3M south of the entrance and measuring a good 2M square is shown on Admiralty Charts 89, 90 and 92, but as clearance over is at least 5m it should not concern many yachts.

Entrance

Note the *Caution* opposite. The bar alters continuously in both shape and depth, but as of 2005 local knowledge claimed about 1m at MLWS. With a spring range of 2.5m (and neap range of 1.3m) most cruising yachts should be able to enter with reasonable care, particularly if local assistance is forthcoming. For this reason yachtsmen are strongly recommended to contact marina manager Wolfgang Michalsky (who speaks fluent English) for up-to-date information prior to arrival. With sufficient notice it may even be possible to arrange to be 'talked in' via mobile phone by an English-speaking assistant dispatched to the entrance by car.

The marina website includes a link to EasyTide – see page 2 – which shows the current predicted tidal height above datum at nearby Huelva. However strong northwesterly winds in the Strait of Gibraltar may reduce predicted levels.

Berthing

Due to open during 2006, the new Puerto Marina El Rompido will contain some 350 berths, 40 percent of them reserved for yachts in transit and half of these for short-stay visitors. Although long-term berths will be limited to yachts of 14m or less, a few 30m visitor berths are planned. Depths will be limited at 2–3m, but in practice any yacht able to negotiate the bar will be able to berth in the marina.

The structure is unusual, with a single pontoon secured by piles projecting some distance into the river and giving access to the marina's five projecting fingers. All berths are against finger pontoons. Detached floating wavebreaks made from recycled tyres are secured up and downstream, with a third (concrete) pontoon to the south. These will obviously do nothing to decrease the tidal flow, and newcomers would be well advised to avoid manoeuvring during the height of the ebb or, to a lesser extent the flood, particularly at springs.

A reception berth is planned for the hammerhead of one of the two downstream pontoons. However the office will be ashore, near the head of the access pontoon.

The 2006 high season (June to September) rate for a visiting yacht of 10–12m is set at €19.40 per night, rising to €23.71 for 12–14m, inclusive of water but not electricity (which will metered). In the low season prices will be exactly half the above. Multihulls are to pay a surcharge of 50%. Though quoted by the marina ex-IVA (the equivalent of VAT), this has been added to the above figures for easy comparison with other harbours. Most major credit cards will be accepted.

Anchorage and moorings

Anchor on the north side of the river as moorings and draught permit. There are hundreds of moorings further downstream but nearly all are occupied by local craft. It may be possible to lie alongside for a short period on the east end of the fuel jetty hammerhead, which is equipped with suitable cleats.

Multihulls and other shoal draught vessels may be able to work upstream as far as El Terrón, where there is a busy fishermen's quay and a shallow pontoon for local smallcraft. Holding is said to be good over mud. Water, telephones, restaurants and basic shopping will be found ashore, and fuel is available at the quay (though depths alongside have not been verified). There are information boards about the *Paraje Natural 'Marismas del Río Piedras y Flecha de El Rompido'*, an area covering the Punta del Gato sandspit and much of the Río Piedras estuary. For those with yachts already on a secure mooring it would make an interesting dinghy excursion.

The highly praised Varadero Río Piedras at El Rompido, which has recently changed hands for the first time since it was established in 1981   *AH*

The brand new Puerto Marina El Rompido as it looked in early February 2006. It was expected to be operational in good time for the 2006 season   *WM*

Major changes have been taking place on the water at El Rompido since this photograph was taken. The three jetties remain – the nearest one holds the fuel pumps – but beyond them a new marina will soon be open for business

Facilities

Boatyard, engineers, electronic and radio repairs The Varadero Río Piedras SA ☎ 959 399026 *Fax* 959 399034 *Email* varadero@vianwe.com, is tucked between the long hammerhead jetty and the new marina, almost directly below the lighthouse. After 25 years, founder owner Wolfgang Michalsky has recently sold up in order to become marina manager. New owners are Christian and Borja, a German/Spanish couple who have every intention of continuing the yard's excellent reputation for helpfulness and efficiency.

   Employees or subcontractors can handle repairs in timber, GRP and metals including stainless steel and aluminium. Alternatively owners can do their own work. There are on-site mechanical and electronics workshops, plus an agency for Volvo, Nautech and Lewmar. The yard would be an excellent place for winter lay-up, though space is limited.

Travel-lift The boatyard's marine railway can handle vessels of up to 100 tonnes and 6m beam.

Sailmaker Olivier Plisson of Vop Sails, ☎/*Fax* 959 399025 *Email* info@vopsails.com www.vopsails.com who has premises just outside the Varadero Río Piedras, makes and repairs sails and will handle canvaswork of all kinds.

Chandlery Small chandlery at the boatyard, with further items ordered as required.

Water Available on the marina pontoons, or by can from the boatyard or the Club Náutico Río Piedras (where there is a coin-operated tap on the pontoon).

Showers At the marina. Otherwise at the boatyard or the *club náutico*, both of which make a small charge.

Launderette To be installed at the marina. In the meantime, there is a washing machine at the boatyard (timing and fee negotiable).

Electricity On the marina pontoons.

Fuel At the hammerhead jetty east of the boatyard, open 0900–1530 Tuesday to Thursday, 0900–1500, 1600–1900 Friday and Saturday, 0900–1500 Sunday, closed Monday. ☎ 62 0922 969.

Nets – and some oversize blocks – cover the fishermen's wharf at El Terrón on the Río Piedras   *AH*

The 42m lighthouse at El Rompido stands in attractive surroundings some distance from the shoreline, but is nevertheless an important light   *AH*

Club náutico The Club Náutico Río Piedras ☎ 959 399349 *Fax* 959 399217 occupies a slightly isolated site some distance downstream from the town and has its own hammerhead pontoon, plus a very pleasant terrace bar/restaurant.

Weather forecast At the marina office. May also be available at the boatyard on request.

Bank In the town, including a cash machine at the west end of the old quarter.

Shops/provisioning Several small supermarkets, including one near the church. A small supermarket is planned for the marina.

Produce market On the main square.

Cafés, restaurants A profusion in the old part of the town, including restaurants serving excellent seafood. Hotels are mostly to be found in the newer area to the east. Cafés, restaurants etc are planned for the new marina complex.

Medical services Clinic and pharmacy in the town, but no hospital.

Communications

Post office Backing onto the church.

Mailing address The marina office will hold mail for visiting yachts – c/o Puerto El Rompido, E 21459 El Rompido, Cartaya/Huelva, España. It is important that the envelope carries the name of the yacht in addition to that of the addressee.

Public telephones Several throughout the town.

Internet access Wireless broadband is available throughout the marina, with additional connection facilities in the office.

Fax service At the boatyard, *Fax* 959 399034, by arrangement.

Taxis Best ordered by phone.

Buses To Huelva, for connection with trains to Seville etc.

Air services International airports at Faro and Seville.

65. Punta Umbría

Waypoints
⊕173 – 37°06′.7N 6°57′.7W (approach)
⊕174 – 37°08′.71N 6°56′.91W (entrance)

Courses and distances
⊕169 (Islas Canela & Cristina) – ⊕173 = 17M, 096° or 276°
⊕171 (El Rompido) – ⊕173 = 5.1M, 119° or 299°
⊕173 – ⊕174 = 2.1M, 017° or 197°
⊕173 – ⊕175 (Mazagón) = 7.3M, 118° or 298°

Tides
See Mazagón, page 268

Charts

	Approach	River
Admiralty	91, 93	73
Imray	C19, C50	
Spanish	44B, 441	4411

Principal lights
2315 **Breakwater head** VQ(6)+LFl.10s9m5M
    Black tower, yellow top 4m
2316 **Real Club Marítimo jetty** Fl(3)G.15s6m3M Green post 3m

Night entry
Though well lit, in view of depths at the bar night entry is not recommended for those unfamiliar with the area

Harbour communications
Real Club Marítimo y Tennis de Punta Umbría
☎ 959 311899
VHF Ch 09, 16
Puerto Deportivo de Punta Umbría
☎ 955 314304/959 314298
Fax 959 314706
Email puntaumbriad@eppa.es
www.eppa.es
VHF Ch 09
Club Deportivo Náutico Punta Umbría
☎/*Fax* 959 659049
Email clubdeportivonp@terra.es
VHF Ch 09

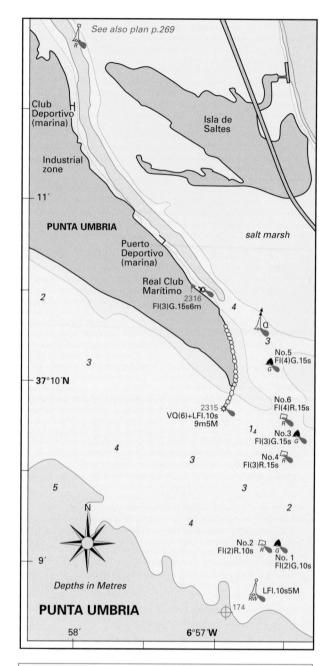

⊕173	37°06′.7N	6°57′.7W	Punta Umbría approach
⊕174	37°08′.71N	6°56′.91W	Punta Umbría entrance

Attractive river with increasing amenities for yachts, inside a shallow entrance

Once a small fishing village, of which there are still traces to be found upstream from the busy fishing quay, and with some elegant (and a few ostentatious) houses lining the riverbank, Punta Umbría is a growing tourist resort, thanks largely to its excellent beaches. The town is now said to be one of the fastest-growing in Andalucía.

Its advantages for the visiting yachtsman include convenient food shopping, with at least one large supermarket close to the river. However there are still few places where a larger yacht can berth, the channel is too narrow and full of moorings to anchor opposite the town, and the lower reaches may not prove as peaceful as expected as the fishing fleet start leaving soon after 0400 and keep passing until dawn.

Approach

Approaching from the west, low, sandy, pine-topped cliffs stretch from the lighthouse at El Rompido all the way to Punta Umbría. From the east, the coast from Matalascañas as far as Mazagón is backed by

sand dunes, while the final 7M from Mazagón is formed almost entirely of the impressive Juan Carlos I breakwater, against which a low-lying sandy beach – the Playa de Espigón – has built up. A restricted area containing a tanker loading berth and associated pipeline extends almost 5M offshore about 2M east of the entrance. Anchoring and fishing are banned in its vicinity, but vessels may pass inside or between the buoys.

From offshore ⊕173 lies 2.1M south-south-west of the entrance, a course of 017° leading to ⊕174, close to the red and white landfall buoy.

Approaching Punta Umbría from south-southeast, with the shoal which runs out from the western promontory just visible beneath the surface

Entrance

The breakwater is about 0.5M in length, though much of this is masked from the west by an accretion of sand. Both the position and depth of the channel is unpredictable, but in August 2005 the plan opposite was considered accurate. Depths at the bar were no more than 1m at chart datum (4.2m at MHWS or 3.5m at MHWN), with eight buoys indicating the channel. With so much river traffic there would be an excellent chance of following a local vessel in, though allowance must be made for the probable difference in draught.

Once past the root of the mole the channel begins to deepen, after which 5m or more should be found about 100m from the western bank.

Berthing and moorings

There are three berthing possibilities, though all are distinctly limited.

1. The **Real Club Marítimo y Tennis de Punta Umbría** occupies a maroon building off which lies its double pontoon (though the outer, detached one is clearly intended more to provide shelter from fishing boat wash than as a serious berthing prospect). Although there is unlikely to be space alongside the club does control some adjacent moorings – if one can stand the incessant disturbance. Water and electricity are installed on the inner pontoon, and the club has the usual bar and restaurant (where the usual 'club' formalities should be observed).

2. The **Puerto Deportivo de Punta Umbría** is one of EPPA's newest marinas having only opened in 2002, and one of its smallest in all senses of the word. It also lacks many of the shoreside facilities found at its larger peers. Even though depth is not an issue – there is a minimum of 2.5m throughout – only a dozen of the 197 berths can take vessels of more than 10m and the vast majority are occupied by diminutive runabouts. At first glance the long outer pontoon appears spacious and tempting, but any direction to secure to it should be resisted strenuously – a detached wave-break pontoon is positioned downstream of the marina, but the outer pontoon receives no protection whatsoever from the wash of speeding fishing boats. The entire marina heaves and groans alarmingly as each one passes, and few fishermen appear to pay even lip service to the 5 knot speed limit. When several boats follow each other in close succession and their washes combine, damage may occur.

The marina office is open from 1000–1330 and 1630–2000 daily in summer, closing at 1730 during the winter (when it is also shut on weekend afternoons). When visited in 2005 little English was spoken. Water and electricity are available on the pontoons, with showers ashore (but no launderette). A weather forecast is posted daily, and fuel is available nearby (see *Facilities*, below), but little else appears to be on offer. Charges are at the standard Empresa Pública de

Looking straight up the main channel at Punta Umbría, with the pontoons of the Real Club Marítimo y Tennis de Punta Umbría nearest the camera, the new EPPA-run Puerto Deportivo de Punta Umbría at centre and the larger Club Deportivo Náutico Punta Umbría in the distance

Puertos de Andalucía rate – see page 255.

Surprisingly, despite jutting much further into the channel than any of the other jetties, the southeast corner of the marina appears to be unlit.

3. The **Club Deportivo Náutico Punta Umbría**, formed in 1995, laid its first pontoons in 2000 and now operates the only true marina on the river. Being upstream of the fishermen's quay it is also by far the most peaceful. Although private and normally full of members' boats, space for a visiting yacht of up to 10m can usually be found alongside the long outer pontoon in depths of 5–6m, if only for a night or two. The club also controls a number of moorings able to take up to 12m. In both cases it would be wise to make contact before arrival (though no English was spoken when visited in 2005).

The club has extensive grounds (clearly popular with the local goat fraternity) and a sizeable clubhouse featuring the usual bar and restaurant. The secretary's office will be found upstairs, having entered at the rear of the building, and is open 1100–1400 and 1600–2000 Monday to Saturday inclusive. There appears to be no fixed price structure for visiting yachts, another thing to enquire about when booking. Water and electricity are available on the pontoons, including the outer one, and there are doubtless showers in the clubhouse, but there are no other facilities on site. However it is only a short walk into the town, and even shorter to the supermarket in the industrial zone (see *Facilities*, below).

Anchorage

The channel is largely occupied by moorings, with very little space left in which to anchor anywhere near the town. The best bet would almost certainly be to continue past the Club Deportivo Náutico, beyond which the moorings thin out. Though most fishing boats go no further than the wharf just upstream of the EPPA-run Puerto Deportivo, some traffic should be anticipated and the fairway left clear. An anchor light should be displayed at night. In all cases allow for the strength of the ebb tide, which may reach 4–5 knots at springs even close in to the shore.

Facilities

Boatyard Náuticas Punta Umbría SA operate a large, gated boatyard in the industrial area north of the Puerto Deportivo and the fishing wharf, where many local yachts are wintered ashore. Although served by a good-sized marine railway, in 2005 the maximum size appeared to be around 10m. Nauti-Ria SL, ☎/*Fax* 959 315590, handle repairs to smaller vessels, with an anonymous GRP fabricator opposite. Other yards build and repair tugs and small military/official vessels, mostly in steel, with yet another building sizeable timber fishing boats. All are on the well-named '*Calle Veraderos*' (shipyard road) between the industrial area and the river.

Travel-lift None (though see above).

Engineers, electronics Náuticas Punta Umbría SA is able to handle most types of yacht and engine maintenance.

Sailmaker/sail repairs Shanty Sails, ☎ 959 310700, *Fax* 959 310696, close to Náuticas Punta Umbría in the industrial zone, make and repair sails and handle general canvaswork.

Chandlery Náuticas Punta Umbría SA (open 1000–1330, 1630–2030, closed Saturday afternoon and all day Sunday) has a well-stocked chandlery adjacent to its boatyard.

Water On all three pontoons.

Showers At all three clubhouses/offices.

Launderette In the town.

Electricity On all three pontoons.

Fuel Diesel and petrol from a pontoon between the Puerto Deportivo and the fishermen's quay. Hours are not specified.

Bottled gas Camping Gaz exchanges available in the town, but no refills.

Weather forecast At the Puerto Deportivo office.

Club náutico The long-established Real Club Marítimo y Tennis de Punta Umbría and the much newer Club Deportivo Náutico Punta Umbría. See under Berthing, above.

Banks In the town, with cash dispensers.

Shops/provisioning Large and cavernous supermarket (the Spanish equivalent of a Cash and Carry) one block in from the boatyards mentioned above. General shopping of all kinds in the town.

Cafés, restaurants and hotels At the two clubs, with dozens more throughout the town.

Medical services In the town.

Communications

Post office In the town.

Mailing address Both the Puerto Deportivo (Puerto Deportivo de Punta Umbría, Plaza Pérez Pastor Punta Umbría, 21100 Huelva, España) and the Club Deportivo Náutico (Club Deportivo Náutico Punta Umbría, Prolongación Avenida de la Marina s/n, Apartado de Correos No 78, 21100 Huelva, España) will hold mail for visiting yachts, by prior arrangement only. In both cases it is important that the envelope carries the name of the yacht in addition to that of the addressee.

Telephones Close to the Puerto Deportivo office and elsewhere.

Car hire Several offices in the town.

Taxis In the town, or order via the berthing office.

Buses In the town, connecting with trains at Huelva.

Air services About equidistant between Faro (Portugal) and Seville (Spain).

A porcupine of fish marker buoys on the shore at Punta Umbría. One can only wonder at the choice of flag colours . . .   *AH*

66. Mazagón

Waypoints
  ⊕175 – 37°03′.3N 6°49′.7W (approach)
  ⊕176 – 37°05′.25N 6°49′W (entrance)

Courses and distances
  ⊕167 (Río Guadiana) – ⊕175 = 27.8M, 096° or 276°
  ⊕169 (Islas Canela & Cristina) – ⊕175 = 23.7M,
    103° or 283°
  ⊕171 (El Rompido) – ⊕175 = 12.4M, 118° or 298°
  ⊕173 (Punta Umbría) – ⊕175 = 7.3M, 118° or 298°
  ⊕175 – ⊕176 = 2M, 016° or 196°
  ⊕175 – ⊕177 (Chipiona and the Río Guadalquivir) =
    24.6M, 135° or 315°

Tides
  Standard port Lisbon
  Mean time differences (at Huelva bar)
  HW +0010 ±0010; LW +0035 ±0005
  (allowing for one hour difference in time zones)
  Heights in metres
  MHWS   MHWN   MLWN   MLWS
   3.2   2.5   1.2   0.4
  Or refer to EasyTide at www.ukho.gov.uk (see page 2)

Charts	Approach	Harbour
Admiralty	91, 93	73
Imray	C19, C50	C50
Spanish	44B, 441	4411

Principal lights
River entrance
2321 **Breakwater head** Fl(3+1)WR.20s30m12/9M
  165°-W-100°-R-125° Racon Mo 'K'(–·–)12M
  White tower, red band 27m
2324.05 **Dir Lt 339.2°** DirWRG.60m8M
  337.5°-G-338°-R-338.6°-Oc.G-339.1°-W-339.3°-Oc.R-
  339.8°-R-340.4°-R-340.9° White tower 15m
Note The deep channel shifts from time to time and
buoys are moved accordingly.
Marina
2325 **Southwest breakwater head** Q.G.8m2M
  Grey framework on green base 4m
2325.2 **Northeast breakwater head** Q.R.6m2M
  Grey framework on red base 4m
2325.5 **Southwest breakwater spur** Fl.G.5s4m1M
  Grey framework on green base 4m
2325.7 **Reception quay** Fl.R.5s4m1M
  Grey framework on red base 3m

Night entry
  The approach to Mazagón and Huelva is buoyed and lit
  for large commercial vessels – a yacht should have no
  trouble in any but the worst conditions.

Coast radio station
  Huelva *Digital Selective Calling*
  MMSI 002241012
  VHF Ch 10, 16, 26
  Weather bulletins and navigational warnings
  Weather bulletins and navigational warnings in Spanish
  and English: VHF Ch 10 at 0415, 0815, 1215, 1615, 2015
  UT

Harbour communications
  Puerto Deportivo Mazagón ☎ 959 536251/959 376550
  Fax 959 376237 *Email* mazagon@eppa.es
  www.eppa.es
  VHF Ch 09, 16

Modern, purpose-built yacht marina with good facilities but little character

Another of the new harbours built and run by the Empresa Pública de Puertos de Andalucía, Puerto Deportivo Mazagón is somewhat larger than most. It opened in July 1993 and has slowly expanded until by early 2005 it contained more than 500 berths, including 25 reserved for visiting yachts. Two more pontoons were soon to be added, bringing the total up to nearly 600. The marina is also home to various 'official' craft including the smaller Huelva pilot boats, fishery protection vessels and a *Guardia Civil* RIB.

There is an excellent beach right next to the marina, with the quiet and leafy town a steepish walk up the road.

Approach and entrance

Approaching from the west, low, sandy, pine-topped cliffs stretch from the lighthouse at El Rompido to the tower blocks at Punta Umbría. From this point, the last 7M of very low shore is backed by Juan Carlos I breakwater – one of the longest in Europe. A restricted area containing a tanker loading berth and associated pipeline extends almost 5M offshore about 4.5M west of the rivermouth. Anchoring and fishing are banned in its vicinity, but vessels may pass inside or between the buoys.

To the east, for some 16M the shore is backed by sand dunes ending at the resort town of Matalascañas which has prominent radio aerials. A firing range – which is not marked on the Admiralty chart – exists inshore from about 5M southeast of Mazagón almost as far as Matalascañas. When active, a Range Safety Vessel will call up any craft straying into the area on VHF Ch 16 with instructions to keep clear.

A gas pipeline nearly 25M in length and fed by at least two production wells comes ashore about 4M southeast of Mazagón. Two yellow buoys with topmarks, both Fl.Y.5s5M, indicate its western and southern extremes at 36°59′.5N 7°11′.4W and 36°51′N 7°05′.3W respectively. A further two buoys, identical to the above, mark the junction at 37°09′.9N 6°59′.7W. Anchoring and mooring are prohibited in the vicinity, but there are no restrictions on sailing over it.

From offshore ⊕175 lies about 2.5M south-southwest of the entrance, a course of 016° leading to ⊕176, itself some 750m from the (west cardinal) fairway buoy and on the 339° leading line for the main channel.

Once in the channel, Mazagón marina will be seen on the starboard hand about 1.5M inside the breakwater end. The entrance, which is lit, carries at least 4.5m as far as the reception pontoon, which is on the port hand below the prominent tower housing the marina office.

Berthing

Secure to the long reception pontoon, which doubles as a fuelling berth (avoid securing in the centre for this reason). If arriving outside office hours (1000–1300, 1600–1730 daily in winter, rather

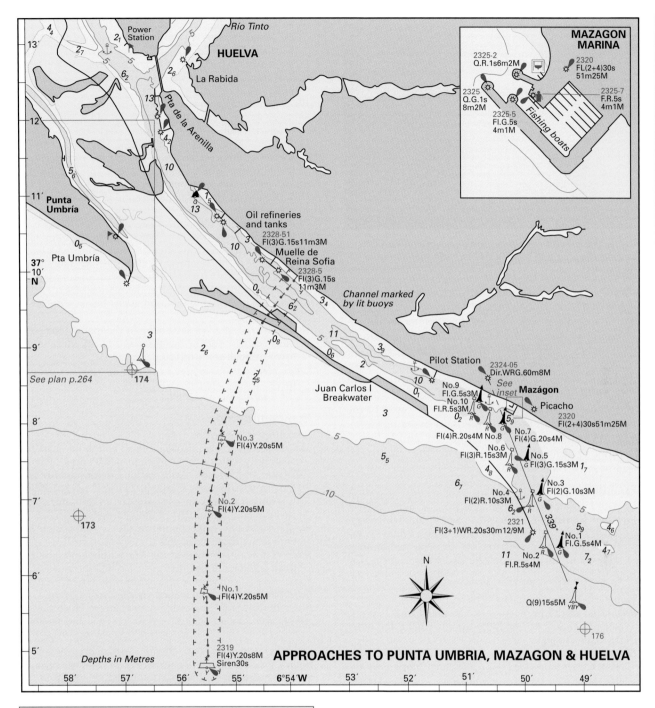

MAZAGON MARINA

2325·2 Q.R.1s6m2M
2320 FL(2+4)30s 51m25M
2325 Q.G.1s 8m2M
2325·5 FI.G.5s 4m1M
2325·7 F.R.5s 4m1M

Fishing boats

Río Tinto

Power Station

HUELVA

La Rabida

Pta de la Arenilla

Punta Umbría

Pta Umbría

37° 10′ N

Oil refineries and tanks

2328·51 FI(3)G.15s11m3M

Muelle de Reina Sofia

2328·5 FI(3)G.15s 11m3M

Channel marked by lit buoys

Pilot Station

2324·05 Dir.WRG.60m8M

See inset

Mazágon

Picacho

Juan Carlos I Breakwater

No.9 FI.G.5s3M
No.10 FI.R.5s3M
2320 FI(2+4)30s51m25M

No.7 FI(4)G.20s4M

FI(4)R.20s4M No.8

No.6 FI(3)R.15s3M

No.5 FI(3)G.15s3M

No.4 FI(2)R.10s3M

No.3 FI(2)G.10s3M

No.3 FI(4)Y.20s5M

No.2 FI(4)Y.20s5M

174

See plan p.264

173

2321 FI(3+1)WR.20s30m12/9M

No.1 FI.G.5s4M

No.2 FI.R.5s4M

339°

Q(9)15s5M YBY

176

No.1 FI(4)Y.20s5M

2319 FI(4)Y.20s8M Siren30s

Depths in Metres

APPROACHES TO PUNTA UMBRIA, MAZAGON & HUELVA

⊕173	37°06′.7N	6°57′.7W	Punta Umbría approach
⊕174	37°08′.71N	6°56′.91W	Punta Umbría entrance
⊕175	37°03′.3N	6°49′.7W	Mazagón approach
⊕176	37°05′.25N	6°49′W	Mazagón entrance

longer in summer), security staff will allocate a berth, or leave the yacht where she is if no berth is available. A total of eleven pontoons (all with fingers) take yachts of up to 20m in 4m depths throughout. Yachts of more than 20m are normally berthed alongside the southwest breakwater, the outer part of which appears to have been colonised by fishing boats. Charges are at the standard Empresa Pública de Puertos de Andalucía rate – see page 255 – and, as at nearly all their marinas, the staff are helpful and efficient though in 2005 relatively little English was spoken.

Anchorages

Anchoring in the Ría de Huelva is possible but not encouraged. The tide runs strongly – heavy ground tackle is required – and it is essential to display a riding light as there is considerable fishing boat traffic at night as well as large freighters which pass each other in the channel.

In southwesterly winds yachts have successfully anchored close north of the breakwater, about 400m in from the end. Considerable wash from passing traffic should be anticipated and this is a distinctly short-term solution. In all but strong southerlies a better bet would be either off the beach northwest of the marina (taking care to avoid the sewage outfall, marked by an unlit yellow post with an × topmark) or about 1M further up the channel beyond the pilot

Puerto Deportivo Mazagón seen from south-southwest beyond the long and elegant curve of the Juan Carlos I breakwater

station. Both offer good holding over sand, but again may be uncomfortable due to wash. It is essential to keep well clear of the channel itself.

Finally, yachts occasionally venture up the channel to Huelva, anchoring opposite the Real Club Marítimo de Huelva, an angular white building just upstream of the Río Tinto bridge and prominent Columbus statue. The club has extensive moorings and it may be necessary to anchor to the west of the buoyed channel in order to maintain swinging room. The western bank remains completely undeveloped, making a pleasant contrast to the industrial buildings of Huelva itself.

Facilities

Boatyard Not as such, though there is a large area of rather windswept hardstanding and several workshops run as individual enterprises, with more currently being built. Alternatively owners are welcome to do their own work, but cannot live aboard whilst ashore. The gates are locked from 2100 until 0900, with card access at other times.

Travel-lift 32-tonne capacity hoist.

Engineers In addition to selling chandlery, Náutica Raggio, *Mobile* 609 814805, handles engine and other mechanical repairs.

Electronic and radio repairs Alfamar, ☎ 959 377825, who have premises in the commercial block near the marina office, is agent for Simrad, Furuno, Trepat, Raymarine etc, and also handles repairs. However in early 2005 no English was spoken.

Sailmaker/sail repairs The marina office will contact Shanty Sails, ☎ 959 310700, in Punta Umbría.

Chandlery An unexpected variety, all in the commercial block on the northwest side of the marina and all quite small. In alphabetical order: Broker de Servicios Náuticos SL ☎ 959 376221, sells general chandlery and clothes in addition to yacht brokerage. Idamar Náutica ☎ 959 536160, *Email* nautica@grupo-idamar.com stocks general chandlery and fishing equipment. A branch of the much larger Idamar Group, they are also agents for Bénéteau and for RFD inflatables (see also *liferaft servicing*, below). Titulaciones Náuticas, ☎ 959 376292, is a Jeanneau agent and also stocks some chandlery, clothing and shoes. Náutica Raggio (see above) sells fishing equipment and some chandlery.

Charts Spanish charts are available in Huelva from

Valnáutica SL–Idamar SA ☎ 959 250999 *Fax* 959 250214 at Avenida Enlace 16, and from the Instituto Geográfico Nacional ☎ 959 281967 at Vázquez López 12.

Liferaft servicing Idamar Náutica is agent for RFD but will repair and service all makes of liferaft and inflatable dinghy.

Water On the pontoons.

Showers At the rear of the commercial block, and on the southeast mole.

Launderette In a block on the southeast mole, so a long walk for those berthed near the marina office. Access by electronic card.

Electricity On the pontoons.

Fuel Diesel and petrol at the reception/fuel berth during office hours.

Club náutico The blue and white tiled Club Náutico de Mazagón looks strangely like an up-ended swimming pool (which it has, plus a tennis court, both available to visitors for a nominal fee). It also offers the more usual restaurant etc.

Weather forecast Posted daily at the marina office.

Banks Cash dispenser in the commercial block, with banks in the town.

Shops/provisioning No food shop in the marina complex, but one close outside the gates and plenty more in the town (though some distance away).

Cafés, restaurants and hotels Several cafés and restaurants in the marina complex, with more in the town.

Medical services In the town.

Communications

Post office In the town.

Mailing address The marina office will hold mail for visiting yachts – c/o Oficina del Puerto, Puerto Deportivo Mazagón, Avda. de los Conquistadores, s/n, Mazagón, Palos de la Frontera, 21130 Huelva, España. It is important that the envelope carries the name of the yacht in addition to that of the addressee.

Public telephone Single phone in the commercial block with many more in the town.

Internet access Cybercafé at the Amena phoneshop in the town (up the hill and turn right beyond the park).

Fax service At the marina office, *Fax* 959 376237.

Car hire/taxis Can be arranged via the marina office.

Buses In the town, connecting with trains at Huelva.

Air services About equidistant between Faro and Seville.

Puerto Deportivo Mazagón looking northwest towards Huelva. At least two more pontoons have been laid against the wall nearest the camera since this picture was taken

67. Chipiona

Waypoints
⊕177 – 36°46′N 6°28′W (approach – also for the
Río Guadalquivir)
⊕178 – 36°45′.2N 6°26′.2W (entrance)
⊕179 – 36°44′N 6°30′.3W (3.1M W of Punta del Perro)

Courses and distances
⊕175 (Mazagón) – ⊕177 = 24.6M, 135° or 315°
⊕177 – ⊕178 = 1.7M, 119° or 299°
⊕177 – ⊕181 (Rota, via ⊕179 & ⊕180) = 14.3M,
223°&149°&107° or 287°&329°&043°
⊕177 – ⊕183 (Cádiz, via ⊕179 & ⊕180) = 16M,
223°&149°&121° or 301°&329°&043°

Tides
Standard port Lisbon
Mean time differences (at Río Guadalquivir bar)
HW 0000 ±0005; LW +0025 ±0005
(allowing for one hour difference in time zones)
Heights in metres

MHWS	MHWN	MLWN	MLWS
3.2	2.5	1.3	0.4

Or refer to EasyTide at www.ukho.gov.uk (see page 2)

Charts	*Approach*	*Harbour*
Admiralty	91, 93	85
Imray	C19, C50	C50
Spanish	44B, 44C, 442, 443	4422-II

Principal lights
2351 **Punta del Perro (Chipiona)** Fl.10s68m25M
Stone tower on building 62m
2352 **Breakwater head** Fl(2)G.10s5m5M Green tower 5m
2354 **East mole** Fl(4)R.11s3m3M Red tower 3m
2354.5 **Breakwater spur** Fl(3)G.9s3m1M Green tower 3m

Night entry
Not recommended for those unfamiliar with the area,
due to shoals near the entrance.

Harbour communications
Puerto Deportivo Chipiona ☎ 956 373844
Fax 956 370037
Email chipiona@eppa.es
www.eppa.es
VHF Ch 09

Well-run marina backed by pleasant holiday town

One of the first of the new harbours built by the Empresa Pública de Puertos de Andalucía – see page 255 – Puerto Deportivo Chipiona was created by extending the old fishing harbour and opened in 1992. The north basin is now largely occupied by larger yachts and those in transit, with local boats in the south basin and fishing vessels along the breakwater. Facilities are good and Chipiona is an obvious place to wait for a fair tide up the Río Guadalquivir, as well as to top up with fuel.

The town is pleasant and shady with many restaurants, supermarkets and shopping precincts, and is well worth exploring. Punta del Perro lighthouse, built in 1867, is particularly worth a visit as the lower floors are sometimes open to the public, despite apparently still having several keepers in residence. The low cliffs between the two feature a number of restaurants and cafés, nearly all with local seafood on the menu.

If intending to venture up the Río Guadalquivir, note the paragraph on page 275 regarding Ricardo Franco's *La Navegación de Recreo por el Río de Sevilla* (Leisure Navigation on the River of Seville). Though now out of print, a copy of this impressive work can be consulted at the marina office.

Looking northeast into the mouth of the Río Guadalquivir. Punta del Perro lighthouse is in the foreground, with the Puerto Deportivo Chipiona directly behind

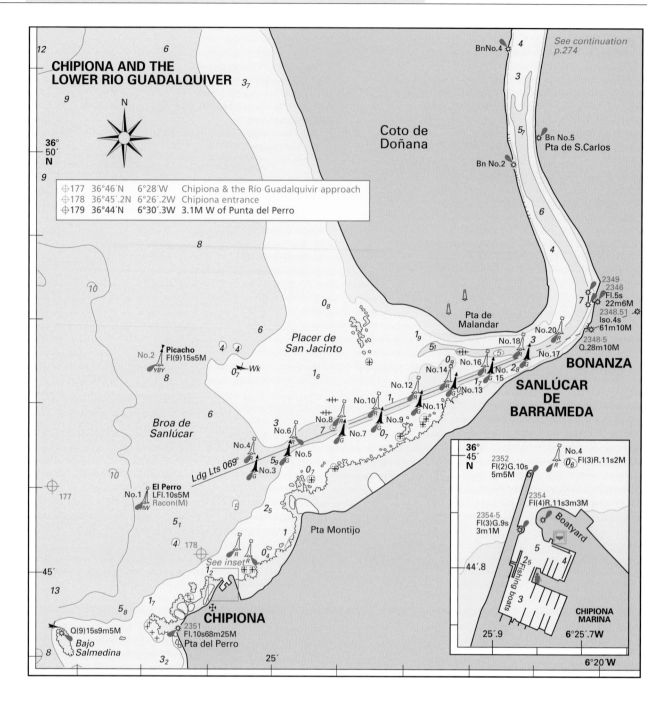

Chart labels (Chipiona and the Lower Río Guadalquivir):

12　6

**CHIPIONA AND THE
LOWER RIO GUADALQUIVER**

3₇

9

N

36°
50′
N

9

Coto de
Doñana

BnNo.4　4

*See continuation
p.274*

3

5₇　Bn No.5
Pta de S.Carlos

Bn No.2

6

⊕177　36°46′N　6°28′W　Chipiona & the Río Guadalquivir approach
⊕178　36°45′.2N　6°26′.2W　Chipiona entrance
⊕179　36°44′N　6°30′.3W　3.1M W of Punta del Perro

8

4

10

2349
2346　Fl.5s
7　22m6M
2348.51　Iso.4s
61m10M

0₈

6

Placer de
San Jacinto

1₉

Pta de
Malandar

5₁

No.18　3　No.20
No.17

2348·5
Q.28m10M

BONANZA

4　4　Picacho
Fl(9)15s5M
No.2　YBY
8

0₇　Wk

1₆

No.16　(5)
No.14　0₉
No.12　No.15　2₈
1₇
No.13

**SANLÚCAR
DE
BARRAMEDA**

6

**Broa de
Sanlúcar**

3
No.6
No.8
No.10
No.11
No.9
1₁
0₇

7

No.7

36°
45′
N

No.4
0₆　Fl(3)R.11s2M

No.4
No.5
No.3
5₉

0₇

Ldg Lts 069°

2352
Fl(2)G.10s
5m5M

2354
Fl(4)R.11s3m3M

10

El Perro
No.1　LFl.10s5M
Racon(M)
RW

5₁

0₇

2₅

Pta Montijo

2354·5
Fl(3)G.9s
3m1M

44′.8

Boatyard

5

2₅

Fishing boats

4

177

4　178
R

1

**CHIPIONA
MARINA**

3

−45′

13

1₂

See inset

5₈　1₇

CHIPIONA

25′.9

6°25′.7W

Q(9)15s9m5M

*Bajo
Salmedina*

8

2351
Fl.10s68m25M
Pta del Perro

3₂

25′

6°20′W

Approach – Chipiona and the Río Guadalquivir

If coastal sailing towards the Río Guadalquivir from Mazagón the first 20M is backed by sand dunes, but southeast of Matalascañas the coastline flattens. A firing range – which is not marked on the Admiralty chart – exists inshore from about 5M southeast of Mazagón almost as far as Matalascañas. When active, a Range Safety Vessel will call up any craft straying into the area on VHF Ch 16 with instructions to keep clear.

In good visibility a course can be shaped directly for No.2 buoy, a west cardinal guarding Bajo Pichaco rock. Though the buoy is sometimes difficult to see against the land, the wreck which has lain on the rock for more than a decade is still prominent. At half tide and above it is possible for a yacht to cut inside the wreck, but without large-scale charts this is not recommended. In poor visibility it would be wise to stand on for ⊕177, see below.

Approaching from Bahía de Cádiz or other points south, the 10m line lies up to 1.75M from the coast between Rota and Punta del Perro. Off the latter lies the dangerous Bajo Salmedina, extending almost 1.6M offshore and marked by a west cardinal tower – plus several wrecks. If in doubt head for ⊕179, some 3M offshore. Having rounded Bajo Salmedina, remain a minimum of 0.5M offshore while working northeast for Chipiona as multiple obstructions – some natural, some artificial – extend at least 600m out from the shore for most of the distance. Do not turn in for Chipiona until the marina entrance bears at least 110°.

The interior of Chipiona harbour, seen from near the fish market at the southwest corner of the basin. The Puerto Deportivo now occupies the entire eastern side *AH*

Several new fish havens have recently been established off Punta del Perro and in the approaches to Bahía de Cádiz, but as all lie outside the 10m contour they pose no danger to yachts.

From offshore head for ⊕177, just under 1M west-northwest of El Perro No.1 buoy, a large red and white pillar. From ⊕177 a course of 119° for 1.7M leads to ⊕178, 0.5M from the Chipiona breakwater. Alternatively, 081° for 2.2M places one directly between channel buoys Nos.3 and 4 and on the 069° leading line for Bonanza and, eventually, Seville.

Entrance – Chipiona

If approaching from any point west of north the entrance is hidden until very close in. Make for the breakwater head with its bright green tower, leaving the two smallish red pillar buoys to port (in 2005 they were much closer to the entrance than indicated on Admiralty 85), finally swinging southwest to enter. A few years ago the entrance was reported to have silted to less than 2.5m at MLWS, but following dredging in 2005 a minimum of 4m should be found at all times.

Berthing

Secure to the long reception pontoon at the head of the central mole – the Muelle de Espera – directly beneath the marina office. Visitors are usually berthed in the northeast basin (now dredged to 4m), convenient for the shops and restaurants, with finger pontoons throughout. One or two seriously large yachts – up to 40m – can lie alongside the west side of the outer pontoon, but it is essential to contact the marina office well in advance. All the marina's 412 berths are often full in the high season, though a smaller visitor may be found space in the south basin among the locals in 2.5–3m depths.

Weekdays office hours are 1000–1330 and 1600–1730 in winter, closed Saturday and Sunday afternoons, but remaining open later in summer with no weekend closing. In 2005 staff were helpful with good English spoken. Charges are at the standard Empresa Pública de Puertos de Andalucía rate – see page 255. As in most of EPPA marinas there is 24 hour security, with card-operated gates to the pontoons.

Puerto Deportivo Chipiona seen from the northwest, with port-hand buoy No.4 (see inset plan) just out of the picture on the left

Facilities

Boatyard On the northeast arm, with a generous area of concreted hardstanding behind a high security fence. Yachts from several nations over-wintered there in 2004/5, all generously propped – essential when there is so little protection from the wind. The gates are locked from 2200 until 0700 and living aboard is forbidden (see page 255). In 2005 there appeared to be several contractors working on site, including Náutica Bahía Blanca (general maintenance and painting) and Náutica Motosanlucar (GRP and inflatable repairs, osmosis treatment, etc).

Travel-lift 45-tonne capacity lift in the boatyard area – book at the marina office.

Engineers, electronic and radio repairs Náutica Motosanlucar and others in the boatyard area.

Chandleries Two in the boatyard area – Náutica Bahía Blanca, *Mobile* 63 6165 368, which has a strong emphasis on the practical, and Náutica Motosanlucar, which stocks general chandlery. Larger than either is F Medina Náutica, ☎ 956 374772, opposite the southeast corner of the south basin, open 0930–1400 and 1630–1900 weekdays, closed Saturday afternoon and Sunday.

Water On the pontoons.

Showers In the block overlooking the north basin, with access via electronic card.

Launderette Near the marina office.

Electricity On the pontoons.

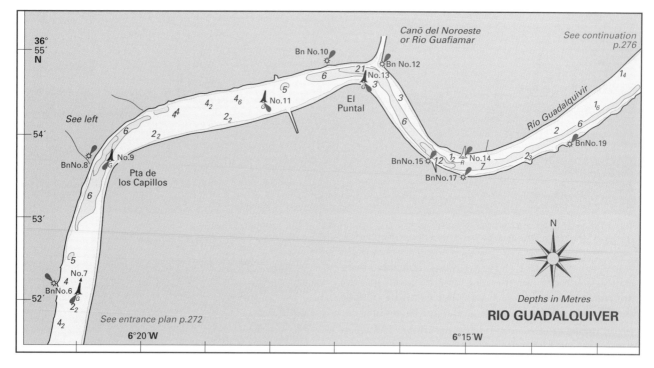

Fuel Diesel and petrol at the reception pontoon, 0800–1300 and 1630–1930 weekdays, 0830–1400 weekends.

Bottled gas Camping Gaz exchanges are available in the town, but no refills.

Weather forecast Posted daily at the marina office.

Banks In the town, but no cash dispenser at the marina.

Shops/provisioning Small general shop in the block overlooking the north basin, otherwise the nearest food shop is a supermarket some 300m distant, with plenty more in the town proper. The lonja (fish market) at the southwest corner of the basin also sells retail, and is well worth a visit.

Cafés, restaurants and hotels A good range – Chipiona has long been a popular holiday resort among Spaniards – with several small café/restaurants overlooking the north basin.

Medical services In the town.

Communications

Post office In the town.

Mailing address The marina office will hold mail for visiting yachts – c/o Oficina del Puerto, Puerto Deportivo Chipiona, Avda Rocío Jurado s/n, 11550 Chipiona, Cádiz, España. It is important that the envelope carries the name of the yacht in addition to that of the addressee.

Public telephones Two in the marina complex, plus many in the town.

Fax service At the marina office, Fax 956 370037.

Car hire/taxis Best organised via the marina office.

Buses To Rota, Seville (about 2 hours) etc.

Air services International airport at Seville, national airport at Jerez for connections to Madrid etc.

The wide mouth of the Río Guadalquivir looking northeast, with several pairs of channel buoys clearly visible. Sanlúcar de Barrameda is on the right, with the long breakwater off Bonanza in the distance

68. The Río Guadalquivir and Seville

Waypoints
As for Chipiona, page 271

Tides
Standard port Lisbon
Mean time differences (at Río Guadalquivir bar)
(allowing for one hour difference in time zones)
HW 0000 ±005; LW +0025 ±0005
Heights in metres

MHWS	MHWN	MLWN	MLWS
3.2	2.5	1.3	0.4

Mean time differences (at Bonanza)
HW +0030 ±0010; LW +0070 ±0010
(allowing for one hour difference in time zones)
Heights in metres

MHWS	MHWN	MLWN	MLWS
3.0	2.4	1.1	0.5

Mean time differences (at Seville)
HW +0415 ±0015; LW +0530 ±0020
(allowing for one hour difference in time zones)
Heights in metres

MHWS	MHWN	MLWN	MLWS
2.1	1.8	0.9	0.5

Or refer to EasyTide at www.ukho.gov.uk (see page 2)

Charts

	Approach	*River*
Admiralty	91, 93	85
Imray	C19, C50	
Spanish	44B, 44C, 442	4421,
		4422-II to 4422-XVIII

Principal lights
Entrance
2348.5 **Ldg Lts 069°** *Front* Q.W.28m10M
   White structure with red and white chequers 22m
2348.51 *Rear* 0.6M from front Iso.4s61m10M
   White structure with red and white chequers 30m
Eight pairs of lit pillar buoys, plus one extra port-hand buoy, mark the channel as far as Bonanza
Bonanza
2346 **Bonanza** Fl.5s22m6M Brick tower, white lantern 20m
2349 **Detached breakwater, S end** Fl(2+1)G.21s6m5M
   Green column, red band, over diagonal stripes 2m
2349.1 **Detached breakwater, N end** Fl.G.5s6m5M
   Green column 2m
Many other lit buoys and beacons mark the Río Guadalquivir up to Seville – see plans opposite, and on pages 276 and 279
Night entry
   The river is well buoyed and lit as far as Bonanza, making a pre-dawn start upstream entirely feasible
Harbour communications
   Port Authority ☎ 954 247300/298271
   Fax 954 247333/615548 *Email* comercial@apsevilla.com
   www.apsevilla.com
   VHF Ch 12 (24 hours)
   Puerto Gelves ☎ 955 761212 *Fax* 955 761583
   Email info@puertogelves.com
   puertogelves@terra.es
   www.puertogelves.com
   VHF Ch 09, 16
   Marina Yachting Seville ☎ 954 230326 *Fax* 954 230172
   Club Náutico Sevilla ☎ 954 454777 *Fax* 954 284693
   Email nauticosevilla@nauticosevilla.com
   www.nauticosevilla.com
   VHF Ch 09
   Seville lock ☎ 954 454196 VHF Ch 12
   Puente de las Delicias lifting bridge
   ☎ 954 247630, 247640 VHF Ch 12

Historic city with a lengthy river approach

Seville is one of the foremost cities of Spain, steeped in history and with something unexpected around every corner. The old part appears to have far more than its fair share of monuments and historic buildings, including a stunning cathedral and several royal palaces. A guide book and street plan are almost necessities. A yacht provides a most convenient base for exploration, but as summer temperatures can rise above 40°C (102°F) the best time to visit is in spring or autumn – though Seville is also becoming an increasingly popular place to winter on board. In April 2005 yachts from at least nine different nations were to be seen in the city's three marinas, most having clearly been there for several months. Highlights of the year are the Easter processions of *Semana Santa* and the vast *Feria* which is held two weeks later on a site adjacent to the Club Náutico Sevilla.

In common with most large cities Seville has a reputation for petty crime, including pickpockets, but a purposeful air, valuables tucked away out of sight and avoidance of secluded areas after dark should give reasonable protection. It is not a place to hire a car – traffic is frequently grid-locked and parking next to impossible – but several (brave) yachtsmen and women have recommended bicycles as a practical means of transport. A stout chain is recommended.

The approach up the Río Guadalquivir (from the *Arabic Wadi-al-Kabir* or 'big river'), while tedious at times, is not without interest. In particular, the *Parque Nacional de Doñana* on the west bank is world famous for its birds and other wildlife and it is usually possible to spot some of its residents. In 1998 the park suffered an ecological disaster when the failure of a major dam upstream released nearly 7 million cubic metres of lead-zinc slurry into the river system, killing most of the fish and many of the birds which depended on them. It has been estimated that it will take up to 50 years for the region to recover fully, but in the meantime much of the wildlife has already made a remarkable comeback.

If spending a few days in Chipiona prior to tackling the river, ask marina officials for a chance to study their copy of *La Navegación de Recreo por el Río de Sevilla* (Leisure Navigation on the River of Seville). This fascinating volume, first published in 1981 and revised in 1998 by master mariner and Guadalquivir pilot Ricardo Franco, is already out of print despite its €62.00 price tag. Beautifully presented in a dark blue box cover, profusely illustrated by aerial photographs and detailed charts, and with detailed and authoritative text in English as well as Spanish, it would well repay study with a notebook and the current chart to hand. While in the office it would also be worth confirming that the lock and bridge-opening times given over the next few pages are still current – the helpful Chipiona staff should have all the details to hand.

Approach

As for Chipiona – see page 271.

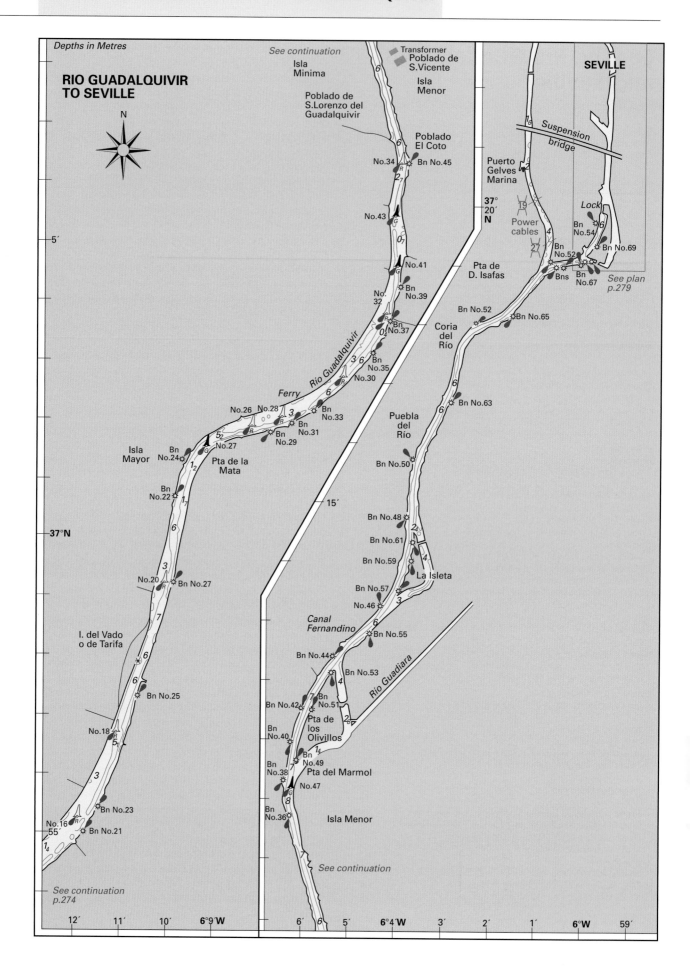

Depths in Metres

RIO GUADALQUIVIR TO SEVILLE

N

See continuation
Isla Minima

Transformer
Poblado de S.Vicente

Isla Menor

SEVILLE

Poblado de S.Lorenzo del Guadalquivir

Poblado El Coto

No.34 Bn No.45

2₇

No.43

0₇

No.41

No.32 Bn No.39

Bn No.37

3 6 Bn No.35

No.30

Ferry

No.26 No.28

No.27

3 Bn No.33

Bn No.31

Bn No.29

5₂

Isla Mayor Bn No.24

Pta de la Mata

1₂

Bn No.22

1₇

6

15′

7

3

No.20 Bn No.27

7

I. del Vado o de Tarifa

6

6 Bn No.25

No.18

5₁

3

Bn No.23

No.16

55′ Bn No.21

1₄

See continuation p.274

Rio Guadalquivir

Puerto Gelves Marina

37° 20′ N

Pta de D. Isafas

19

Power cables

27

Bn No.52

Coria del Río

Bn No.65

6

Bn No.63

6

Puebla del Río

Bn No.50

Bn No.48

2₄

Bn No.61

Bn No.59

4

La Isleta

Bn No.57

No.46

3

6

Canal Fernandino

Bn No.55

Bn No.44

Rio Guadiara

Bn No.53

7

Bn No.42

Bn No.51

4

2

Bn No.40

Pta de los Olivillos

Bn No.49

1₄

Bn No.38

Pta del Marmol

No.47

8

Bn No.36

Isla Menor

7

See continuation

Suspension bridge

1₆

2

Lock

Bn No.54

4

Bn No.52

Bn No.69

Bns Bn No.67

See plan p.279

12′ 11′ 10′ 6°9′W 6′ 6′ 5′ 6°4′W 3′ 2′ 1′ 6°W 59′

37°N

Entrance (see plan page 272)

The channel close to the mouth is wide and very well buoyed, but can become dangerously rough when strong west or southwest winds oppose the spring ebb and cause short steep seas to build. The 'service centre' for the Río Guadalquivir's buoyage is at Bonanza and, perhaps as a result, maintenance is generally excellent.

The river

It is about 55M from the mouth to Seville. Starting an hour or so before the beginning of the flood (which a yacht can ride upriver for at least 9 hours – see *Tides* above) most yachts will be able to make it on one tide. To catch one's breath before heading upriver and to top up with fuel, a stop in the marina at Chipiona (page 271) would be convenient. Alternatively in light weather it is possible to anchor off Sanlúcar de Barrameda, where there is a large and stylish yacht club, a superb beach and, perhaps of greatest interest, the visitors' centre for the *Parque Nacional de Doñana* housed in the old ice factory – itself worth a visit for its imaginative tilework. In 1519 Sanlúcar was the departure point for Magellan's fleet and the port to which, three years later, the 18 survivors returned.

Little more than 1M further upriver lies Bonanza, where a yacht may be able to secure temporarily to the inside of the long detached concrete breakwater – quite unmistakable with its downstream end painted in diagonal red and green stripes – while the fishing fleet is at sea. Other possibilities are to anchor north of the moorings well out of the powerful current, or on the west bank around the corner 1M above Bonanza, again well out of both the fairway and the current. Even at neaps the ebb may run at 3 knots in the centre of the channel, and is considerably stronger at springs. The flood never attains anything like the same rates. It is said that owners of wooden vessels should avoid Bonanza due to its reputation for shipworm, said to breed in the old hulks which litter the surrounding shores. Thefts of dinghies, oars and outboards have also been reported.

The old ice factory at Sanlúcar de Barrameda now houses the visitors' centre for the Parque Nacional de Doñana – highly recommended   *AH*

All the many lights and buoys on the Río Guadalquivir are serviced from the quay at Bonanza, overlooked by the handsome – and still working – lighthouse   *AH*

Above Bonanza

After passing the tall, shining heaps of locally-produced salt just upstream of Bonanza the river winds through flat and somewhat featureless countryside – a passage described with feeling as 'very long and boring' – until close to Seville, progress best being marked by simply ticking off the buoys and beacons as they are passed. There is good water the whole way – 6000-tonne freighters visit the city – but the channel is not always in the centre of the river. Where beacons run down one side they indicate the main channel, seldom less than 5m though down to 4m on the reach north of Bonanza (where the channel follows the west side) and above the first starboard turn (where the channel is to the north). A few red and green buoys also give guidance. The river carries such a heavy load of silt that echo-sounders are generally unable to cope – typical performance is to give no sensible reading for tens of minutes, then briefly read the correct depth for a minute or two, and then go haywire again. Probably of more concern is the commercial traffic, with ships apparently maintaining full speed both day and night.

There are several possible anchorages to be found out of the fairway, but none are very convenient and the current can be strong.

Returning downstream, unless one can make at least 7 knots the passage will take more than one tide – low water at Bonanza occurs nearly 4.5 hours earlier than at Seville, so for every mile made downstream the ebb will finish that much earlier. Leave Seville about 3 hours before local high water, and after about 2 hours of foul tide pick up the ebb. If unable to make 7 knots it will be necessary either to push against the flood – though this seldom exceeds 2 knots even at springs – or to anchor en route.

Seville

Refer to page 280 for marina, lock and bridge communications

The Río Guadalquivir divides on the southern outskirts of the city to form an island, the two branches rejoining some 6M further upstream (or more correctly vice versa, of course). The tidal western branch which contains the Puerto Gelves marina is in fact artificial, and was created to enable the eastern, commercial branch to be canalised. The latter – the Canal de Alfonso XIII – offers yachts a choice of two very contrasting places to berth, in addition to containing the city's surprisingly extensive cargo-handling wharves. These are the modest Marina Yachting Sevilla and, further up, the far more upmarket Club Náutico Sevilla.

Air height to both branches is determined by power cables. The single set which cross the eastern arm carry 44m so are unlikely to trouble any yacht, but the northern of the two sets which cross the western channel carry only 19m at high water (Admiralty 85 shows 16.5m, but the Spanish authorities confirm the slightly higher figure, as does an indicator board on the western bank). This has on occasion inconvenienced larger yachts, which may have to pass under at low water and then anchor before catching the ebb downstream, but this is rare. The cables encountered about 0.6M further downstream on the same channel carry a more generous 27m.

1. **Puerto Gelves** (37°20´.4N 6°01´.4W) is the centrepiece of a small marina village, planned in conjunction with EXPO '92 but not completed for a further two years. Even then it was a further ten years or so before the final (downstream) block neared completion. The river carries 4–5m other than very close to the banks, but the marina is effectively the limit of navigation for sailing yachts as several low road and rail bridges cross the river less than a mile upstream.

   The marina, which contains 133 pontoon berths for yachts of up to 16m plus many more smallcraft 'dry-sailed' from the boatyard area, has in the past suffered from chronic silting which has reduced low water depths in the basin to less than 2m (though the underlying mud is extremely soft). However the management have recently acquired their own small dredger so hope to keep abreast of the problem. The river water appears basically clean but distinctly soupy.

   On arrival secure to the reception pontoon on the starboard side of the entrance – in spite of the marina's relatively small size it is claimed that space is always available for visitors – and call at the portacabin office at the root of the north wall. In 2005 several of the staff spoke English or other European languages. Hours are 0900–1430 and 1630–1930 weekdays, 0900–1400 Saturday, closed Sunday, though uniformed *marineros* are

Puerto Gelves marina from the north. The amount of suspended silt in the river water is very apparent

on duty at all times (some of it spent monitoring the CCTV). The entrance is lit, with appropriately painted beacons on either side, but navigating in the river after dark would be unwise.

In 2005 the rate for a visiting yacht of 11–12m was €10.67 per night, rising to €14.08 for 13m–14m, inclusive of water and tax. (Though quoted by the marina ex-IVA, this has been added to the above figures for easy comparison with other harbours). Electricity was billed separately, at €1.68 per day. Monthly rates were not quoted, but quarterly rates for yachts of these dimensions were €827.75 and €1092.27 respectively with further discounts available for longer stays. Multihulls paid a 50% surcharge. Unusually, tariffs did not vary throughout the year.

Facilities at and around Puerto Gelves are listed on page 281.

Adjacent anchorage

It is possible to anchor in the river just upstream of the marina entrance, where maximum tidal range is 1.6m and holding generally good in soft mud – but note that after heavy rain inland the current has been known to attain 8 knots! On payment of a small fee, those at anchor can use the marina's showers, launderette, etc.

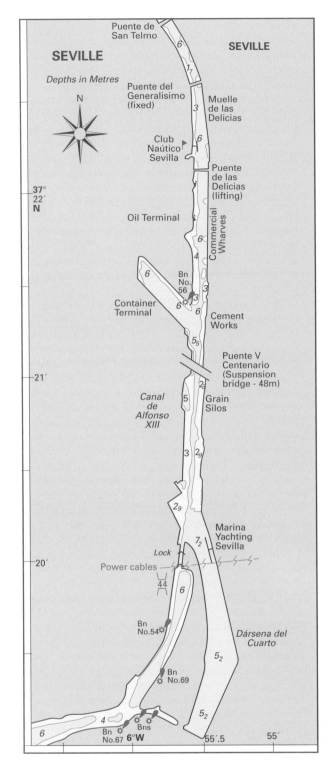

The view upstream from the Canal de Alfonso XIII lock is dominated by the Puente V Centenario suspension bridge (48m clearance), with the Puente de las Delicias lifting bridge beyond   *AH*

Approaching the lock which controls water levels in the Canal de Alfonso XIII, with the Marina Yachting Seville on the right. The Puente V Centenario suspension bridge crosses the canal at upper left

Canal de Alfonso XIII

Water levels in the Canal de Alfonso XIII are controlled by lock gates. In 2005 the lock – which displays a green light when it is clear to enter – opened at 0100, 0400, 0700, 1000, 1100, 1300, 1600, 1900 and 2100 daily throughout the year. When tidal heights permit, both gates are left open for considerable periods though entry is still controlled by the lights. The lock-keepers monitor VHF Ch 12 and speak some English. There are no bollards inside the lock, though some loops of rope are provided at the upstream end or yachts may secure to the ladders. Reports of fuel pumps at the lock are unfounded.

Below the Canal de Alfonso XIII lock the Río Guadalquivir is almost entirely rural   *AH*

2. **Marina Yachting Sevilla** (37°20′N 5°59′.5W) is situated hard round to starboard from the lock amidst rural if somewhat bleak surroundings. Although established in the early 1990s it does not appear to have developed much in that time and facilities remain poor. Noise from the nearby shipyard, combined with the lock loudspeaker, can also be a problem. Its final disadvantage for visitors is that it is some 3.5km from the city centre, tucked behind an industrial area and far from either shops or public transport – though there is no reason why the enterprising crew should not commute into the city by dinghy . . .

The marina comprises a single pontoon with yachts berthed alongside. Depths range from 3–6m. Secure in any available space, and if an attendant does not appear call at the small office, open 0930–1900 weekdays, closed weekends (though with 24 hour security). In 2005 the staff, while helpful, spoke almost no English. Charges are calculated on a length x breadth basis and do not alter throughout the year. In 2005 the overnight rate for a beamy monohull of just under 12m LOA was €27.84 for the first seven nights, dropping to €13.92 per night thereafter. Further reductions were available for longer stays. Water and electricity were included, and although quoted ex-IVA this has been added to the above figures for easy comparison with other harbours.

Facilities at and around Marina Yachting Sevilla are listed on page opposite.

3. **The Club Náutico Sevilla** (37°22′.2N 5°59′.6W) unquestionably offers by far the most convenient berthing in the city as well as excellent shoreside facilities. The club lies on the west bank just upstream of a lifting bridge, backed by extensive and well-kept grounds containing tennis courts, mini-golf and several swimming pools, all of which may be used by visiting crews. It is freely admitted that only a small percentage of the 8000

or so members own – or have any real interest in – boats. In April 2005 yachts from eight different nations were seen there, some clearly having over-wintered, and for those not overtly worried about the budget it would make a tempting choice.

To reach the club it is necessary to negotiate not only the lock but also the Puente de las Delicias lifting bridge (which replaces the now demolished Puente Alfonso XIII, though still shown on Admiralty 85). The previous twice-daily opening was cut back drastically a few years ago, and it now opens only on Monday, Wednesday and Friday at 2000, and on Saturdays and holidays at 0830 and 2000 (substituting 1730 for 2000 between November and March). It remains closed throughout the day on Sunday, Tuesday and Thursday. There are several jetties below the bridge where it may be possible to secure whilst waiting.

The majority of berthing is stern-to off one of two long pontoons (haul-off lines are provided, tailed to the pontoon). That furthest upriver is reserved for club members, the lower one is mainly used for visitors and can take 27 yachts of 12m or less, including a few against its inner side. Further downstream again is a section of wall against which can be fitted a maximum of 14 yachts of between 12m and 24m overall (fewer if a high proportion are very beamy), lying to their own bower anchors. At least 4m is found throughout. Perhaps surprisingly, space is nearly always available other than during the April *Feria*, when for a few days the prices treble, but even so it is wise to make contact in advance, either by phone from downriver or at the very least on VHF before passing through the bridge.

The club office is to be found upstairs in the main building, open 0900–1900 weekdays, 0900–1300 Saturday, closed Sunday. Although many of the notices throughout the club's premises are in English as well as Spanish, surprisingly little is actually spoken. Charges are calculated on a length x breadth basis and do not alter throughout the year (other than at the time of Seville's great April *Feria*). In 2005 the overnight rate for a beamy monohull of just under 12m LOA was €35.52 for the first 15 nights, decreasing to €33.12 for the next 15 and with further reductions thereafter. Water, electricity, IVA and 'port tax' (which comprises nearly one-third of the total) were all included.

Facilities at and around the Club Náutico Sevilla are listed opposite.

The extensive grounds of the Club Náutico Sevilla – with its pools, tennis courts and two yacht pontoons – looking southeast

Facilities

Boatyard Astilleros Magallanes ☎/Fax 955 760545 and at Puerto Gelves offers a wide range of services including osmosis treatment, steelwork, welding etc. It appears to be the only facility of its kind in the area. Limited English is spoken, but one of the marina office staff may be willing to translate.
Email info@astillerosmagallanes.com
www.astillerosmagallanes.com

Travel-lift 25-tonne capacity hoist at Puerto Gelves, booked via the marina office, backed by a generous area of hardstanding where owners are welcome to do their own work.

Engineers, electronics and radio repairs Spoilt for choice at Puerto Gelves, with Astilleros Magallanes, Náutica Vergara and Didier Boat Broker (see *Chandlery*, below) all having workshops either on site or nearby. Albea, a short distance up the road, deals mainly with cars but will handle boat electrics and is a good source for 12 volt batteries. Ask at the marina office if in search of less usual items or services – eg they can recommend a company to re-galvanise anchor chain.

There is a well-equipped engineering workshop at Marina Yachting Sevilla, workshop ☎ 954 230208, while the office at the Club Náutico Sevilla will call in mechanics and other specialists as necessary.

Sail repairs and canvaswork Sun Sails has premises near Puerto Gelves, where some chandlery is also stocked. Opening hours are irregular and initial contact is best made via the marina office.

Chandlery Náutica Vergara at Puerto Gelves ☎ 955 761063 *Fax* 955 761053 *Email* nauticavergara @vianwe.com, holds limited stock but are happy to order (most items arrive within 48 hours). As of 2005 one member of staff spoke fluent English. Also based at Puerto Gelves is Didier Boat Broker, ☎/Fax 955 761792 whose range tends towards spares and hardware. Didier himself is French.
Email info@didierboatbroker.com
www.didierboatbroker.com

NáutiSevilla SL (see *Charts*, below) occupies premises in the city itself where limited stocks are held. Hours are 1000–1330, 1630–2000 weekdays, 1000–1330 Saturday. In 2004 the manager spoke good English.

Charts NáutiSevilla SL, ☎ 954 414832 *Fax* 954 422056 at Calle Recaredo 14, and the Instituto Geográfico Nacional ☎ 955 569324 at Avenida San Francisco Javier 9, No.8, mod 7, both stock Spanish charts.

Water On the pontoons at all three marinas. The Club Náutico Sevilla has separate taps for drinking water and for boat washing – do not confuse them!

Showers At all three marinas.

Launderette Washing machines next to the shower block at Puerto Gelves, but no laundry facilities at the Club Náutico Sevilla (though the office can arrange for it to be done elsewhere). The latter does not appear to have a washing line ban, however . . .

Electricity On the pontoons at all three marinas.

Fuel Diesel and petrol pumps at Puerto Gelves, on the port side on entry, the only convenient source of yacht fuel in the entire city.

Bottled gas Camping Gaz exchanges at most hardware stores, including one almost opposite the Puerto Gelves entrance, but little chance of getting other cylinders refilled.

Club náutico The Club Náutico Sevilla is worth a visit even if not staying on its pontoons. A reasonable standard of dress is expected in the clubhouse.

Weather forecast Posted at the Puerto Gelves office at weekends – during the week it is necessary to ask, and daily at the Club Náutico Sevilla.

Banks Throughout the city and at Gelves.

Shops/provisioning Excellent in the city, as one would expect, but no shops anywhere near Marina Yachting Sevilla, and some distance to walk from the Club Náutico Sevilla (fortunately, several of the larger city supermarkets have delivery services). Puerto Gelves boasts a handy mini-market just around the corner from the marina bar, with more shops within walking distance.

Produce markets Near the river north of the bullring and on Calle Alfarería in the Triana district (about 20 minutes' walk from the Club Náutico Sevilla), plus a weekly market at Gelves.

Cafés, restaurants and hotels Thousands, at all price levels, with only the Marina Yachting Sevilla apparently lacking. The Club Náutico Sevilla has a particularly pleasant terrace bar overlooking its yacht pontoons.

Medical services All aspects including major hospitals. Doctor and dentist at Gelves.

Communications

Post office Throughout the city and at Gelves.

Mailing address All three marina offices will hold mail for visiting yachts – c/o Puerto Gelves, Autovía Sevilla–Coria, km 3.5, 41120 Gelves, Sevilla, España; c/o Marina Yachting Sevilla SA, Carretara del Copero s/n, Punta del Verde, 41012 Sevilla, España; or c/o Club Náutico Sevilla, Avda Sanlúcar de Barrameda s/n, Apartado de Correos 1003, 41011 Sevilla, España. It is important that the envelope carries the name of the yacht in addition to that of the addressee.

Public telephones Next to the chandlery at Puerto Gelves, and several in the grounds of the Club Náutico Sevilla. There is no longer a public telephone at Marina Yachting Sevilla.

Internet access Numerous possibilities throughout the city, with Sevilla@Internet almost opposite the Cathedral particularly recommended – fast computers, reasonably quiet and, being on the first floor, generally quite cool and airy.

Compustation, near Puerto Gelves, does not offer internet access but does handle computer repairs as well as selling consumables such as inkjets.

Fax service At Puerto Gelves, *Fax* 955 761583, and the Club Náutico Sevilla, *Fax* 954 284693.

Car hire/taxis Readily available in the city (though the rush hour is even worse than most). The office staff at all three marinas are happy to telephone for taxis.

Buses Buses run every 20 minutes from just outside Puerto Gelves into the centre of Seville (about 15 minutes), and from near the Club Náutico Sevilla.

Trains Good services throughout Spain (eg 2.5 hours to Madrid). Seville's new metro line, due for completion in 2006, features a stop little more than 1km from Puerto Gelves which will provide a handy link with the city centre.

Air services International airport just outside the city, served by Iberia, BA and, more recently, Ryanair.

III.3 The Río Guadalquivir to Cabo Trafalgar

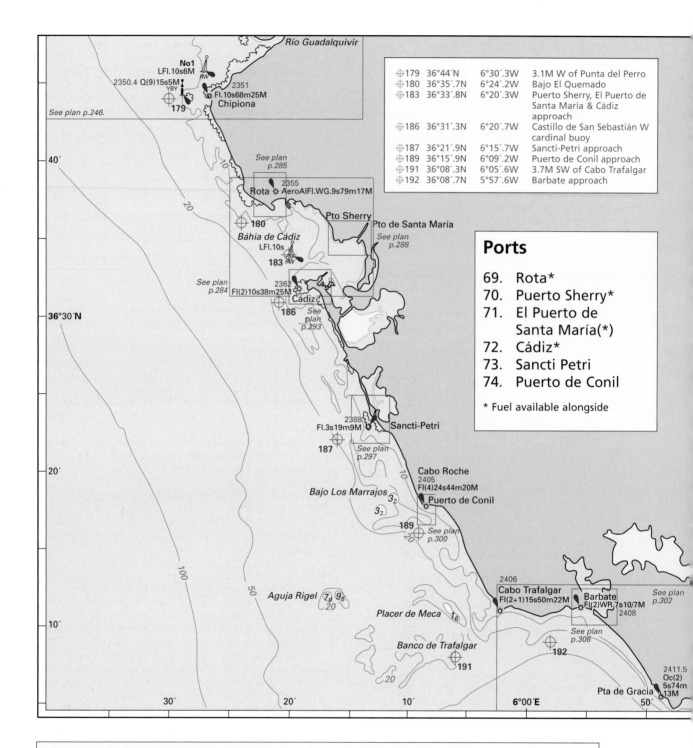

⊕179	36°44′N	6°30′.3W	3.1M W of Punta del Perro
⊕180	36°35′.7N	6°24′.2W	Bajo El Quemado
⊕183	36°33′.8N	6°20′.3W	Puerto Sherry, El Puerto de Santa María & Cádiz approach
⊕186	36°31′.3N	6°20′.7W	Castillo de San Sebastián W cardinal buoy
⊕187	36°21′.9N	6°15′.7W	Sancti-Petri approach
⊕189	36°15′.9N	6°09′.2W	Puerto de Conil approach
⊕191	36°08′.3N	6°05′.6W	3.7M SW of Cabo Trafalgar
⊕192	36°08′.7N	5°57′.6W	Barbate approach

Ports

69. Rota*
70. Puerto Sherry*
71. El Puerto de Santa María(*)
72. Cádiz*
73. Sancti Petri
74. Puerto de Conil

* Fuel available alongside

PRINCIPAL LIGHTS

2351 **Punta del Perro (Chipiona)** Fl.10s68m25M
  Stone tower on building 62m
2350.4 **Bajo Salmedina** Q(9)15s9m5M
  West cardinal tower, ⊥ topmark
2355 **Rota Aeromarine Aero** AlFl.WG.9s79m17M
  Red and white chequered spherical tank 49m
2362 **Cádiz, Castillo de San Sebastián** Fl(2)10s38m25M
  Horn Mo 'N'(–·)20s Aluminium tower on castle 37m

2388 **Castillo de Sancti-Petri** Fl.3s19m9M
  Square tower 16m
2405 **Cabo Roche** Fl(4)24s44m20M
  Square pale yellow tower, silver lantern 20m
2406 **Cabo Trafalgar** Fl(2+1)15s50m22M
  White conical tower and building 34m

Bahía de Cádiz (Cádiz Bay)

Approaches to Rota, Puerto Sherry, Santa María and Cádiz

Waypoints
⊕180 – 36°35′.7N 6°24′.2W (Bajo El Quemado)
⊕181 – 36°35′.1N 6°21′.8W (Rota, approach)
⊕183 – 36°33′.8N 6°20′.3W (Puerto Sherry, El Puerto de Santa María and Cádiz, approach)
⊕186 – 36°31′.3N 6°20′.7W (Castillo de San Sebastián west cardinal buoy)

Courses and distances
⊕177 (Chipiona & Río Guadalquivir) –⊕181 (via ⊕178 & ⊕179) = 14.3M, 223°&149°&107° or 287°&329°&043°
⊕177 (Chipiona & Río Guadalquivir) – ⊕183 (via ⊕178 & ⊕179) = 16M, 223°&149°&121° or 301°&329°&043°
⊕181 – ⊕183 = 1.8M, 137° or 317°
⊕181 – ⊕187 (Sancti-Petri, via ⊕186) = 14.1M, 167°&157° or 337°&347°
⊕181 – ⊕191 (Cabo Trafalgar, via ⊕186) = 29.9M, 167°&152° or 332°&347°
⊕183 – ⊕187 (Sancti-Petri, via ⊕186) = 12.7M, 187°&157° or 337°&007°
⊕183 – ⊕191 (Cabo Trafalgar, via ⊕186) = 28.5M, 187°&152° or 332°&007°

⊕183 – ⊕192 (Barbate, via ⊕186 & ⊕191) = 35M, 187°&152°&086° or 266°&332°&007°

Charts

	Approach	Bay
Admiralty	91, 93	86
Imray	C19, C50	C19, C50
Spanish	44B, 44C, 443, 443A, 443B	

Principal lights
2355.2 **Rota old lighthouse** Oc.4s33m13M
  Off-white tower, red band 28m
2355 **Rota Aeromarine Aero** AlFl.WG.9s79m17M
  Red and white chequered spherical tank 49m
2362 **Cádiz, Castillo de San Sebastián** Fl(2)10s38m25M
  Horn Mo 'N'(–·)20s Aluminium tower on castle 37m
Harbours and marinas – listed individually.

Coast radio station
Cádiz (remotely controlled from Málaga)
Digital Selective Calling MMSI 002241011
VHF Ch 16, 26, 74
Weather bulletins and navigational warnings
Weather bulletins in Spanish and English: VHF Ch 74 at 0315, 0715, 1115, 1515, 1915, 2315 UT
Navigational warnings in Spanish and English: on receipt

Part III.3 covers an area which witnessed one of the most significant naval battles ever fought. At the beginning of the 19th century, Napoleon's ambitions to invade Britain depended on his navy being able to protect his Grande Army as they crossed the English Channel. The English fleet under Admiral Nelson, charged to prevent this, attempted to blockade the French and then followed their fleet across to the Caribbean and back to Europe. By October 1805 the combined fleet of French (Admiral Villeneuve) and Spanish ships (Admiral Gravina) were anchored under the protection of the forts of Cádiz.

On 20th October the combined fleet under Admiral Villeneuve sailed from Cádiz heading in line to the southeast in a light wind. He was unaware that the watching English frigate HMS *Sirius* acted, through a line of relay ships, as eyes for Nelson's force, which gave chase. Nelson briefed his captains on his unconventional plan of

attack. On the morning of the 21st Villeneuve turned his fleet back north towards Cádiz. Nelson made his memorable flag signal 'England expects every man to do his duty', and at 1215 gave his final message to the Fleet – 'Engage the enemy more closely'.

Nelson's 27 ships attacked the combined fleet of 33 ships in two columns. His Flagship HMS *Victory* (Captain Hardy) led the weather column, HMS Royal *Sovereign* (Captain Collingwood) the lee. By late afternoon the battle was over, the combined fleet was destroyed or scattered without loss of a single English ship, and Nelson had been shot by a French marine from the fighting top of the *Redoubtable*. Napoleon's invasion plans were thwarted and Britain controlled the seas – 'Trafalgar' shaped the course of European history for 100 years.

Nelson, a national hero, was buried in St Paul's Cathedral. His famous statue on its column overlooks Trafalgar Square. The second ship in line behind HMS *Victory* at Trafalgar remains immortalised as *The Fighting Temeraire* – the most popular work by WM Turner who painted her in 1838 as she was tugged upriver to be broken up.

Two hundred years after the battle, French and Spanish vessels formed a substantial part of an international naval fleet which joined the Royal Navy in a Fleet Review and festival in the Solent off Portsmouth in summer 2005. On 21st October 2005, members of several yacht clubs laid wreaths off Cabo Trafalgar and gathered on the beach to honour the heroism, and the loss of life, on all sides in this greatest of sea battles   *MW*

HMS *Victory*, launched in 1765 and the only surviving 18th century ship of the line in the world, remains in service in Portsmouth Dockyard with her masts towering above the modern navy   *MW*

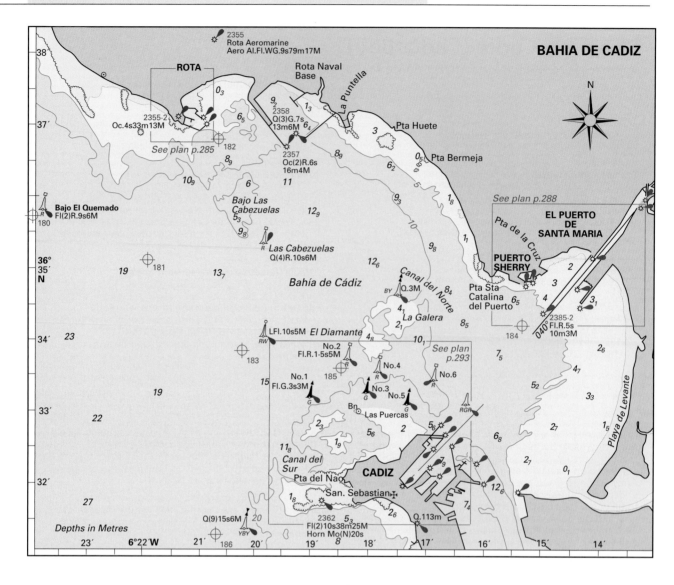

BAHIA DE CADIZ

⊕180	36°35'.7N	6°24'.2W	Bajo El Quemado
⊕181	36°35'.1N	6°21'.8W	Rota approach
⊕182	36°36'.78N	6°20'.76W	Rota entrance
⊕183	36°33'.8N	6°20'.3W	Puerto Sherry, El Puerto de Santa María & Cádiz approach
⊕184	36°34'.2N	6°15'.3W	Puerto Sherry & El Puerto de Santa María entrance
⊕185	36°33'.57N	6°18'.42W	Cádiz entrance
⊕186	36°31'.3N	6°20'.7W	Castillo de San Sebastián W cardinal buoy

Approach

The Bahía de Cádiz is more than 5M wide across its mouth and gives access to the harbours of Rota, Puerto Sherry and El Puerto de Santa María as well as to Cádiz itself.

From the northwest, the 10m line lies up to 1.75M from the coast between Punta del Perro and Rota. Off the former lies the dangerous Bajo Salmedina, extending almost 1.6M offshore and marked by a west cardinal tower. If in doubt, ⊕179 lies some 3M offshore. Having rounded Bajo Salmedina remain a minimum of 1.3M offshore until south of 36°36'N. In poor weather head for ⊕180, Bajo El Quemado, and follow the waypoints as above.

From the south, an offing of at least 2M is necessary to clear the various offshore hazards. In particular, do not be tempted to take any short cuts around the peninsula of Cádiz itself – the reefs and shoals running westwards from the Castillo de San Sebastián have claimed many vessels over the years. Unless very confident it would be wise to come in on the west cardinal buoy about 1M southwest of the Castillo, from there shaping a course of 030° for Los

Cochinos buoy No.1 and so entering the Canal Principal. Alternatively a course of 332° from ⊕191 (Cabo Trafalgar) to ⊕186, followed by 007° to ⊕183 takes one well clear of all hazards en route to any of the bay's three southeastern harbours.

From offshore the approach to both ⊕181 and ⊕183 is straightforward, the marine farm previously centred on 36°34'.3N 06°26.1W and marked by four cardinal buoys having been removed early in 2004.

Further information on the final approaches to each harbour will be found in that harbour's notes.

69. Rota

Waypoints
⊕180 – 36°35′.7N 6°24′.2W (Bajo El Quemado)
⊕181 – 36°35′.1N 6°21′.8W (approach)
⊕182 – 36°36′.78N 6°20′.76W (entrance)

Courses and distances
⊕177 (Chipiona & Río Guadalquivir) – ⊕181 (via ⊕179
  & ⊕180) = 14.3M, 223°&149°&107° or
  287°&329°&043°
⊕181 – ⊕182 = 1.9M, 027° or 207°
⊕181 – ⊕183 = 1.8M, 137° or 317°
⊕181 – ⊕187 (Sancti-Petri, via ⊕186) = 14.1M,
  167°&157° or 337°&347°
⊕181 – ⊕191 (Cabo Trafalgar, via ⊕186) = 29.9M,
  167°&152° or 332°&347°

Tides
Standard port Cádiz
Mean time differences
HW –0010; LW –0015 ±0005
Heights in metres
MHWS MHWN MLWN MLWS
3.1   2.4   1.1   0.4
Or refer to EasyTide at www.ukho.gov.uk (see page 2)

Charts   *Harbour*
Admiralty   86
Imray   C19, C50
Spanish   4431

Principal lights
2355.2 **Rota old lighthouse** Oc.4s33m13M
  Off-white tower, red band 28m
2355.4 **Southwest breakwater** Fl(3)R.10s9m9M
  Red post on short concrete tower 3m
2355.5 **Northeast breakwater** F.G Green metal post
  (Close to floodlit statue of the Virgin and Child)

Night entry
  Without problem provided no corners are cut – literally.
  Although the entrance is relatively narrow it is well lit,
  with the reception berth directly opposite.

Harbour communications
  Puerto Deportivo Rota ☎ 956 840069
  Fax 956 813811 *Email* rota@eppa.es
  www.eppa.es
  VHF Ch 09

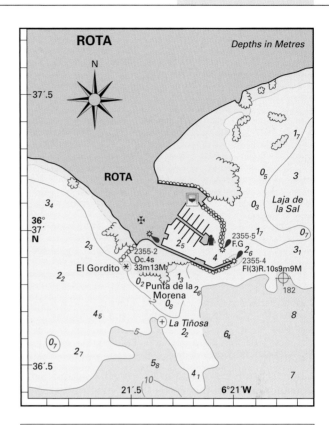

| ⊕181 | 36°35′.1N | 6°21′.8W | Rota approach |
| ⊕182 | 36°36′.78N | 6°20′.76W | Rota entrance |

A well-kept, expanding marina close to an interesting old town

The northwesternmost of the Bahía de Cádiz harbours, Rota is an attractive old town with strong Moorish influences, not least in the massive stone archways which span its narrow streets. Like many Spanish towns it is best explored on foot. Excellent beaches fringe its harbour on both sides, and the tall slim lighthouse with its single red band which stands near the root of the south breakwater makes identification certain by day or night. Rota is becoming an increasingly popular place for liveaboards to winter afloat, with foreign yachts from at least five different nations seen in April 2005.

Like a number of other harbours run by the Empresa Pública de Puertos de Andalucía, Rota combines the functions of yacht and fishing harbour, though the latter have now been banished to the southwest breakwater. It is occasionally referred to as Puerto Astaroth, but is more normally known by

the less romantic but much more descriptive title of Puerto Deportivo Rota. It should on no account be confused with the much larger Rota Naval Base which lies about 1M further east.

In April 2005 major construction work was taking place ashore. Other than a single bar/restaurant all the units were untenanted, though it was understood that a variety of shops and the local *club náutico* were due to move in shortly.

Approach and entrance

For outer approaches from the northwest and southeast refer to Bahía de Cádiz.

Once ⊕180 is reached – or when south of 36°36′N if sailing closer inshore – head due east until the southwest breakwater head bears 030° or less before altering course to round its end. Allow generous clearance as sand has built up beyond the light. The north breakwater will open up behind – for maximum protection the entrance was built facing northeast – with the prominent white statue of the Virgin and Child close to its end. From the south or southeast the breakwater head can be approached direct. The entrance forms a dogleg and is relatively narrow, but otherwise presents no problems.

From offshore ⊕181 lies 1.9M south-southwest of the entrance, a course of 027° leading to ⊕182 close outside the harbour mouth.

Puerto Deportivo Rota looking east. More pontoons have been installed in the south basin since this photograph was taken   *AH*

Berthing

The reception/fuel pontoon lies directly opposite the entrance against the end of the diamond-shaped hammerhead, with the marina office close by. With a total of 509 berths on eleven pontoons, 144 of them able to take yachts of 12m or more, space for a visitor can nearly always be found, if only for a couple of nights (though note EPPA's policy that if a berth of the correct length is not available and a yacht occupies a larger berth this will be charged for, irrespective of the actual length of the boat). If staying long-term and offered a choice, the northeast basin is considerably more protected than that to the southwest which, during gales, suffers both from surf breaking over the breakwater and swell from the entrance. Depths shoal gradually from 4m near the hammerhead to 2.5m along the northwest perimeter.

Weekdays office hours are 1000–1330 and 1600–1730 in winter, closed Saturday and Sunday afternoons, but remaining open later in summer with no weekend closing. In 2005 the office staff were particularly helpful, with good English spoken by several. Charges are at the standard Empresa Pública de Puertos de Andalucía rate – see page 255. As in most of EPPA marinas there is 24 hour security, with card-operated gates to the pontoons.

Facilities

Boatyard On the north side of the marina, with a large area of secure (but somewhat windy) hard standing. All larger occupy cradles, with additional shores. Laying-up ashore in Rota is becoming increasingly popular.

Travel-lift 32-tonne capacity lift at the boatyard.

Engineers, electronic and radio repairs Available at or via the boatyard. For more major jobs specialists may be called in from Puerto Sherry.

Chandlery Small chandlery, outboard repairs etc at Náutica Pepito ☎ 956 143353, by the entrance to the boatyard. Limited English is spoken. A branch of Náutica Vergara – see *Seville*, page 281 – was due to open later in 2005.

Water On the pontoons.

Showers On the hammerhead (in the building which also houses the fuel berth office), and in an anonymous cream building with grey doors near the root of the central mole, both well-kept.

Launderette In the anonymous cream building.

Electricity On the pontoons.

Fuel Diesel and petrol at the reception pontoon on the central hammerhead, 0800–1400 and 1500–1900.

Bottled gas Camping Gaz in the town, but no refills.

Weather forecast Posted daily outside the marina office.

Club náutico Due to move into new premises overlooking the marina during 2005.

Banks In the town, with cash dispensers.

Shops/provisioning Good shopping in the town only a short walk from the marina.

Produce market Directly opposite the marina.

Cafés, restaurants and hotels The usual holiday town variety, plus bar/restaurant near the root of the mole.

Medical services In the town.

Communications

Post office In the town.

Mailing address The marina office will hold mail for visiting yachts – c/o Oficina del Puerto, Puerto Deportivo Rota, Calle Higuereta 1, 11520 Rota, Cádiz, España. It is important that the envelope carries the name of the yacht in addition to that of the addressee.

Public telephones Around the marina with more in town.

Internet access At least four points in the town, including free access at the library.

Fax service At the marina office, *Fax* 956 813811.

Car hire/taxis Can be organised via the marina office.

Buses To Chipiona, El Puerto de Santa María, Seville etc.

Air services Airports at Seville and Jerez, both served by Ryanair among others.

Rota Naval Base

36°37′N 6°19′W

A major naval harbour prohibited to yachts

This large harbour about 1M east of the Puerto Deportivo Rota is a restricted military area used by both the Spanish and the US navies. Approach or entry by unauthorised vessels, including yachts, is strictly forbidden.

70. Puerto Sherry

Waypoints
⊕183 – 36°33´.8N 6°20´.3W (approach, also for
  El Puerto de Santa María and Cádiz)
⊕184 – 36°34´.2N 6°15´.3W (entrance, also for
  El Puerto de Santa María)
⊕185 – 36°33´.57 6°18´.42 (Cádiz entrance)

Courses and distances
⊕177 (Chipiona & Río Guadalquivir) – ⊕183 (via ⊕179
  & ⊕180) = 16M, 223°&149°&121° or
  301°&329°&043°
⊕183 – ⊕184 (via ⊕185) = 4.1M, 099°&076°
  or 256°&279°
⊕183 – ⊕187 (Sancti-Petri, via ⊕186) = 12.7M,
  187°&157° or 337°&007°
⊕183 –⊕191 (Cabo Trafalgar, via ⊕186) = 28.5M,
  187°&152° or 332°&007°

Tides
See El Puerto de Santa María, page 290

Charts

	Harbour
Admiralty	86
Imray	C19, C50
Spanish	4431

Principal lights
2385.2 **Santa María, West training wall, head**
  Fl.R.5s10m3M Red metal tower 6m
2382 **South breakwater** Oc.R.4s4M
  Wide cream tower with attached arches 15m
2382.3 **East mole, SE corner** Oc.G.5s3M
  Green block on wall
2382.5 **Inner harbour, W side** Q.R.1M
  Squat red structure 2m
2382.4 **Inner harbour, E side** Q.G.1M
  Squat green structure 2m

Night entry
Straightforward but narrow. Swing wide and head up
the centre to avoid shallows to port and an unlit
concrete spur opposite

Harbour communications
Puerto Sherry ☎ 956 870103 *Fax* 956 873902
Email puertosherry@puertosherry.com
www.puertosherry.com (in English and Spanish)
VHF Ch 09 (24 hours)

Large, purpose-built marina with a good onsite boatyard but lack-lustre surroundings

Puerto Sherry is by far the largest, oldest and in some
ways the best equipped marina on the Atlantic coast
of Andalucía. Planned as a true 'marina village' with
construction begun in 1985, many of the apartments
and hotels still remain unfinished twenty years on.
There is no true village ashore, the marina complex
being backed by carefully landscaped villas and golf
courses.

The overall impression is still of a large building
site, with some of the completed buildings already
beginning to peel. It would be fair to say that few
cruising yachtsmen spend time in Puerto Sherry for
pleasure, but more than one has found its well-
equipped boatyard and concentration of specialised
skills to be a veritable lifesaver in time of need.

Approach

For outer approaches from the northwest and
southeast refer to Bahía de Cádiz, page 284.

Once in the bay, from north of west approach via
Las Cabezuelas buoy and the Canal del Norte,
passing no more than 1M off Punta Santa Catalina
del Puerto in order to avoid the La Galera and El
Diamante banks which shoal to 2–1m. From south
of west, follow the directions for Cádiz – page 293 –
diverging from the Canal Principal after passing El
Diamante port hand buoy No.4. From there a direct
course of 063° leads to the marina entrance.

From offshore, on reaching ⊕183 (also the
approach waypoint for Puerto Sherry and Cádiz)
either continue on 099° to ⊕185 before altering to
076° for ⊕184 or, in flat conditions and with due
care, sail the direct course of 084° for 4.1M, crossing
the edge of the El Diamante shoal en route. ⊕184
lies about 800m south of the south breakwater head
– on no account steer directly for the south
breakwater from ⊕183, unless happy to cross the
La Galera shoal which carries 2.1m at datum.

From all directions the cream 'lighthouse' building
at the end of the south breakwater, which houses the
marina office, makes a conspicuous daymark.

Entrance

The 100m-wide entrance faces slightly south of east
and is well sheltered, but care must be taken due to
the extensive shoal which has formed around and
inside the end of the south breakwater. In 2005 it
was marked by eight pink buoys – some of them
actually several small buoys tied in clusters – none of
which were lit. A concrete spur, also unlit, juts out
from the wall opposite. A minimum of 3m at low
water is claimed in the centre of the entrance.

There is no longer a designated reception pontoon
– the pontoon on the inside of the south breakwater is
reserved for large yachts only – and, if no response is
received by mobile phone or VHF, arriving yachts
should secure to the fuel pontoon on the port side of
the entrance to the inner basin to be allocated a berth.

Berthing

Puerto Sherry contains nearly 800 berths for craft of
up to 60m (provided they can cope with the 3m
depths) in totally sheltered conditions, and it would
be rare for space not to be available for a visitor. All
pontoons are equipped with fingers – those
immediately overlooked by the two hotels are
somewhat public, those to the south are quieter but
entail a longer walk. In fact the size of the complex
is such that, if berthed on one of the western
pontoons and needing to visit the boatyard area, it
might well be worth launching the dinghy.

The marina office is open 0800–1900 weekdays
and 0800–1500 weekends, and when visited in 2005
some English was spoken. In 2005 the overnight rate
for a visiting yacht of 11–12m was €28.97 in the
high season (1 June–30 September) and €14.48 (or
€260.68 per month) at other times. The equivalent
rates for a yacht of 13–14m were €34.86, €17.43
and €313.75 respectively. Multihulls paid a 50%
surcharge. These figures did not include water,
electricity or IVA, though this latter has been added
for easy comparison with other harbours. Most
major credit cards are accepted.

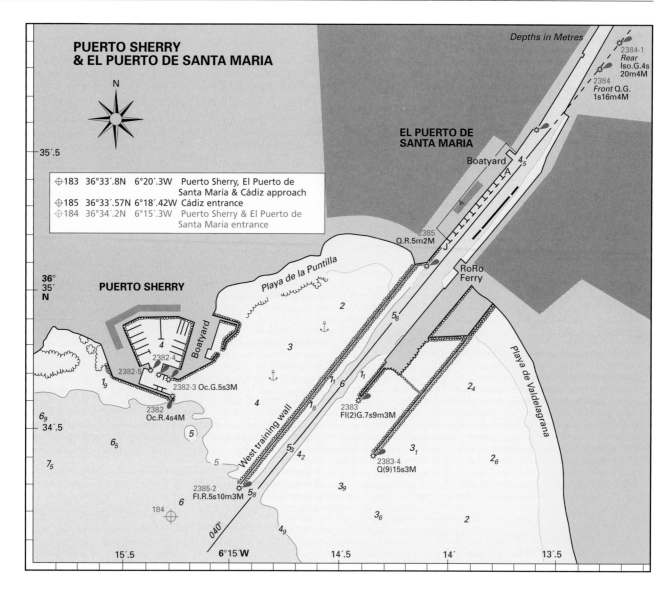

PUERTO SHERRY & EL PUERTO DE SANTA MARIA

Depths in Metres

⊕183 36°33′.8N 6°20′.3W Puerto Sherry, El Puerto de
                            Santa María & Cádiz approach
⊕185 36°33′.57N 6°18′.42W Cádiz entrance
⊕184 36°34′.2N 6°15′.3W Puerto Sherry & El Puerto de
                            Santa María entrance

Facilities

Boatyard There is a large area of gated hardstanding on the wide east mole, with work carried out by a number of companies – see below. Security is relaxed during the day but doubtless better at night. DIY work is permitted, but owners cannot live aboard yachts which are ashore.

Travel-lift 50-tonne capacity lift for which bookings must be made at the marina office. No shortage of shores and some cradles.

Engineers, electronic and radio repairs, chandlery Several companies share the workload in the boatyard, and each appears to have its own chandlery. As a result the range is good, prices are competitive, and all will order items not in stock. Taken alphabetically they are: Industria Náutica del Sur SL ☎ 956 874001 *Fax* 956 874000, *Email* info@nauticadelsur.e.telefonica.net which handles hull and engine maintenance and repairs, osmosis treatment, painting etc; Náutica Sherry, ☎ 956 861416 *Fax* 956 861417 *Email* nauticasherry@yahoo.es which again handles mechanical repairs and general maintenance and has a well-stocked chandlery (English-speaking staff are more likely to be on duty in the morning); and Puerto Náutica SL, ☎ 956 540878, which focuses largely on mechanical and electrical work, with less general

chandlery stocked (they have a second outlet on the road into Santa María, mostly selling nautical nick-nacks but with some galleyware and clothes).

Julio Romero Náutica ☎/*Fax* 956 870392, which operates from a portacabin near the northeast corner of the inner basin, is a much smaller concern specialising in outboard repair. In 2005 limited English was spoken.

Sailmaker/sail repairs Velas Climent SL, ☎/*Fax* 956 870539, occupies a rather anonymous white building with blue trim in the boatyard area. They are experienced sailmakers, as well as handling repairs and general canvaswork.

Rigging Industria Náutica del Sur handles rigging, with a specialist brought in from Valencia if necessary.

Chandleries See above.

Water On the pontoons.

Showers Several shower blocks around the marina complex.

Launderette Near the marina office.

Electricity On the pontoons. However large, non-standard adapter plugs are necessary and the marina office does not always have enough to lend or rent to visitors.

Fuel Petrol and diesel pumps on the west side of the entrance to the inner harbour. In theory fuel can be bought at any time of the day or night, and credit cards are accepted.

Puerto Sherry marina seen from the southwest, with the training walls of the Río Guadalete leading to El Puerto de Santa María visible in the distance. Although taken in 1999 – restrictions on private flying have since been introduced around Rota Naval Base – remarkably little has changed *AH*

Bottled gas Not available.

Weather forecast Posted daily at the marina office.

Bank Not only no bank, but no card machine in the entire complex. Berthing can be paid for by credit card, but not an ice-cream or a cup of coffee . . .

Shops/provisioning Small supermarket on the west side of the inner basin, though it would be necessary to go into El Puerto de Santa María (and take a taxi back) for serious storing up.

Cafés, restaurants and hotels Several cafés and restaurants along the west side of the inner basin, with a large hotel to the north, but no longer a café in the boatyard area.

Medical services First aid point in the marina, with more serious facilities in nearby Puerto de Santa María.

A local yacht leaves Puerto Sherry marina between the unlit concrete spur and the 'lighthouse' building. The small pink buoys mark a growing shoal – see text   *AH*

Communications

Post office In El Puerto de Santa María.

Mailing address The marina office will hold mail for visiting yachts – c/o Puerto Sherry, Marina Puerto de Santa María SA, Apartado de Correos 106, 11500 - El Puerto de Santa María, Cádiz, España. It is important that the envelope carries the name of the yacht in addition to that of the addressee.

Public telephones A generous number dotted around the marina complex.

Internet access Laptops can be connected via a metered socket in the hotel, but there is no internet café closer than El Puerto de Santa María. Rumours of wireless broadband at the marina are unfounded.

Fax service At the marina office, *Fax* 956 873902.

Car hire/taxis Can be arranged via the marina office. The walk along the beach to El Puerto de Santa María should take well under an half an hour.

Air services Airports at Seville and Jerez, both served by Ryanair among others.

Adjacent anchorage

Yachts of modest draught can anchor off Playa de la Puntilla, east of Puerto Sherry marina and north of the Puerto de Santa María training wall, sheltered from all directions other than southwest. The beach shoals gently and fairly evenly, though there are a few shallower patches, with holding good over sand and mud.

71. El Puerto de Santa María

See plan page 288

Waypoints
⊕183 – 36°33'.8N 6°20'.3W (approach, also for Puerto Sherry and Cádiz)
⊕184 – 36°34'.2N 6°15'.3W (entrance, also Puerto Sherry)
⊕185 – 36°33'.57 6°18'.42 (Cádiz entrance)

Courses and distances
⊕177 (Chipiona & Río Guadalquivir) – ⊕183 (via ⊕179 & ⊕180) = 16M, 223°&149°&121° or 301°&329°&043°
⊕183 – ⊕184 (via ⊕185) = 4.1M, 099°&076° or 256°&279°
⊕183 – ⊕187 (Sancti-Petri, via ⊕186) = 12.7M, 187°&157° or 337°&007°
⊕183 – ⊕191 (Cabo Trafalgar, via ⊕186) = 28.5M, 187°&152° or 332°&007°

Tides
Standard port Cádiz
Mean time differences
HW –0005 ±0010; LW –0005 ±0010
Heights in metres

	MHWS	MHWN	MLWN	MLWS
	3.2	2.6	1.1	0.4

Or refer to EasyTide at www.ukho.gov.uk (see page 2)

Charts
	Harbour
Admiralty	86
Imray	C19, C50
Spanish	4431

Principal lights
2384 **Ldg Lts 040°** *Front* Q.G.16m4M
Aluminium framework tower 14m
2384.1 *Rear* 255m from front Iso.G.4s20m4M
Aluminium framework tower 18m
2385.2 **West training wall, head** Fl.R.5s10m3M
Red tower 6m
2383.4 **East outer breakwater** Q(9)15s3M
West cardinal tower 3m
2383 **East inner breakwater** Fl(2)G.7s9m3M
Green tower 4m
2385 **West training wall, root** Q.R.5m2M Red tower 3m

Night entry
Not recommended in a strong southwesterly, otherwise well lit and without hazards

Harbour communications
Real Club Náutico de Santa María
☎ 956 852527, 852861 *Fax* 956 874400
Email rcnpuerto@ono.com
www.rcnpsm.com
VHF Ch 09 (0830–2130, not Sunday).

Small, welcoming, club-run marina

El Puerto – the Santa María was added relatively recently – is a pleasant town and a very old port which formerly handled all the produce of Jerez, brought down the Río Guadalete on barges. Whitewashed sherry *bodegas* (warehouses) still line parts of the river and most producers offer tours – check with the tourist office. In Elizabethan times, at least one planned attack on Cádiz went awry when English sailors on forays ashore discovered the stored liquor and drank themselves to a standstill.

The Real Club Náutico de El Puerto de Santa María prides itself on its friendly atmosphere, a welcome contrast to the somewhat impersonal feel of many marinas. In common with many Spanish yacht clubs it has a small but attractive garden and sports facilities including a gymnasium, tennis courts and open-air swimming pool, which visiting yachtsmen are welcome to use for a small fee.

The river, which is relatively narrow, still carries some commercial traffic and there is no space to anchor.

Approach and entrance

For outer approaches from the northwest and southeast refer to Bahía de Cádiz, page 284.

Once in the bay, from north of west approach via Las Cabezuelas buoy and the Canal del Norte, passing no more than 1M off Punta Santa Catalina del Puerto in order to avoid the La Galera and El Diamante banks which shoal to 2.1m. From south of west, follow the directions for Cádiz – page 293 – diverging from the Canal Principal after passing El Diamante port hand buoy No.4. From there a direct course of 073° leads into the entrance channel, which itself runs 040°, parallel to the training west wall.

From offshore, on reaching ⊕183 (also the approach waypoint for Puerto Sherry and Cádiz) either continue on 099° to ⊕185 before altering to 076° for ⊕184 or, in flat conditions and with due care, sail the direct course of 084° for 4.1M, crossing the edge of the El Diamante shoal en route. ⊕184 lies about 500m from the end of the west training wall.

Berthing

The beautifully kept Real Club Náutico, founded in 1920, administers an equally shipshape marina capable of berthing around 175 yachts and smallcraft, including a few vessels of up to 25m. Other than at the innermost berths, depths are generous at 5m or more. Shelter from wind and waves is excellent, but wash from fishing boats may sometimes cause movement. About 20 berths are normally reserved for visitors, all of them on the ten hammerhead pontoons approached from the northwest bank – the three detached pontoons on the southeast side of the channel are reserved for club members. Regattas are held during August at which time the pontoons are likely to be full, but a visiting yacht can nearly always be found space at other times.

Preferably make contact 24 to 48 hours before arrival, otherwise call on VHF Ch 09 on approach – at least one of the office staff speaks excellent English. Failing that secure to any hammerhead and enquire at the white control tower or the office (near the road gate and turnstile) for a berth. The office is open 0830–2130 Monday to Saturday and – most unusually for Spain – does not close for siesta. Security is excellent, with a uniformed guard when the office is closed and card-operated turnstiles into the grounds. The club's *marineros* will keep an eye on any unattended yacht.

In 2005 the overnight charge for a visiting yacht of 10–12m was €18.00 for the first ten nights and €17.00 for the following twenty, decreasing by increments down to €14.00 for nights 91 to 180. Equivalent figures for a yacht of 12–14m overall were €25.00, €23.50 and €19.00. All were inclusive of water, electricity and tax and, unusually, tariffs did not vary throughout the year.

The Real Club Náutico de El Puerto de Santa María, seen here from the southeast, has changed little in the past decade and offers one of the most attractive ports of call in Andalucía   *AH*

Looking down the Río Guadalete over the pontoons of the Real Club Náutico de El Puerto de Santa María   *AH*

Facilities

Boatyard Small boatyard at the upstream end of the premises with limited hardstanding mostly occupied by members' yachts.

Travel-lift Not as such, but a 25-tonne marine railway and 5-tonne crane lift members' yachts.

Engineers Some mechanical capabilities at the boatyard. For serious problems it may be necessary to go to Puerto Sherry.

Water On the pontoons.

Showers Spotless showers in the Real Club Náutico.

Laundry/launderette The office can arrange to have laundry collected, otherwise there are launderettes in the town.

Electricity On the pontoons.

Fuel After many years without, diesel and petrol pumps were due to be installed during 2005.

Bottled gas Camping Gaz available at hardware stores in the town, but no refills.

Weather forecast Available at the office on request.

Banks In the town, with cash dispensers.

Shops/provisioning/produce market Good shopping of all kinds in the town, with a busy market a few blocks west of the Real Club Náutico.

Cafés, restaurants and hotels Very pleasant restaurants at the Real Club Náutico, both terrace and indoor (the latter more formal), with plenty more in the town and along the beach.

Medical services In the town.

Communications

Post office In the town.

Mailing address The Real Club Náutico will hold mail for visiting yachts – c/o Real Club Náutico de El Puerto de Santa María, Avenida de la Bajamar 13, 11500 - El Puerto de Santa María, Cádiz, España. It is important that the envelope carries the name of the yacht in addition to that of the addressee.

Public telephones Several on the Real Club Náutico premises.

Internet access There are reported to be several cybercafés in the town, as well as free connection at the library. Great choice of hardware and (Spanish) software at the enormous PC City computer superstore a few km out of town on the road to Jerez.

Fax service At the Real Club Náutico office, *Fax* 956 874400.

Car hire/taxis In the town, or can be arranged via the office.

Buses and trains To Cádiz, Jerez, Seville (about an hour) and elsewhere.

Ferries Passenger ferries to Cádiz (and not a bad way to visit that city).

Air services Airports at Seville and Jerez, both served by Ryanair among others.

72. Cádiz

Waypoints
⊕183 – 36°33´.8N 6°20´.3W (approach, also for Puerto Sherry and El Puerto de Santa María)
⊕185 – 36°33´.57N 6°18´.42W (entrance)
⊕186 – 36°31´.3N 6°20´.7W (Castillo de San Sebastián west cardinal buoy)

Courses and distances
⊕177 (Chipiona & Río Guadalquivir) – ⊕183 (via ⊕179 & ⊕180) = 16M, 223°&149°&121° or 301°&329°&043°
⊕183 – ⊕185 = 1.5M, 099° or 279°
⊕183 – ⊕187 (Sancti-Petri, via ⊕186) = 12.7M, 187°&157° or 337°&007°
⊕183 – ⊕191 (Cabo Trafalgar, via ⊕186) = 28.5M, 187°&152° or 332°&007°
⊕183 – ⊕192 (Barbate, via ⊕186 & ⊕191) = 35M, 187°&152°&086° or 266°&332°&007°

Tides
Standard port Cádiz
Heights in metres

MHWS	MHWN	MLWN	MLWS
3.3	2.5	1.2	0.5

Or refer to EasyTide at www.ukho.gov.uk (see page 2)

Charts

	Harbour
Admiralty	86, 88
Imray	C19, C50
Spanish	4430

Principal lights
2362 **Cádiz, Castillo de San Sebastián** Fl(2)10s38m25M Horn Mo 'N'(‒·)20s Aluminium tower on castle 37m

Dique Mar de Levante Fl(4)G.10s12m3M Green post
2367 **North breakwater** Fl.G.3s10m5M Green triangular column 6m
2368 **East breakwater** Fl.R.2s11m5M Red triangular column 5m
2370 **Marina southeast breakwater** Fl(4)G.16s1M Green post 2.5m
2370.2 **Marina northwest mole** Fl(4)R.16s1M Red post 2.5m
Plus many other lights in the commercial harbour

Night entry
The Canal Principal is very well lit, and used by ferries and other large vessels day and night. Care should be taken on approaching the marina until all work is finished (scheduled for 2007)

Harbour communications
Port Authority ☎ 956 240400 *Fax* 956 240476
Email cadiz@puertocadiz.com
www.puertocadiz.com
VHF Ch 16, 74
Marina Puerto América ☎ 956 223666 *Fax* 956 224220
Email puertoamerica@eppa.es
www.eppa.es
VHF Ch 09
Real Club Náutico de Cádiz ☎ 956 213262
Fax 956 221040 VHF Ch 09
Centro Náutico Elcano ☎ 956 290012 *Fax* 956 290099,
Email cnelcano@teleline.es VHF Ch 09
Puerto de Gallineras ☎ 956 486626.

Well-run marina within walking distance of one of Spain's oldest cities

Cádiz is an ancient and fascinating city, founded by the Phoenicians over 3000 years ago. It has long been a major port, with a fine defensive position and good shelter, and for many years handled nearly all the lucrative trade with the New World. This led to great wealth, the results of which can still be seen in the scale of its public and private buildings, many of which date back to the 18th century. The commercial area extends along the peninsula to the southeast, less impressive architecturally but containing good shopping, restaurants and hotels.

Until the early 1990s Cádiz was a difficult city to visit by yacht, the docks devoted to fishing and commercial use and the pontoons in the Real Club Náutico de Cádiz basin packed with local craft. The opening of the Marina Puerto América overcame this problem, and though set amidst bleak surroundings nearly a kilometre from the old city walls it offers good shelter and security for the yacht whilst the crew explore elsewhere.

The Cádiz peninsula looking northeast. In the foreground are the Castillo de San Sebastián, lighthouse and surrounding reefs, with the old city and harbour beyond. In the distance the entrance to El Puerto de Santa María can just be made out   *AH*

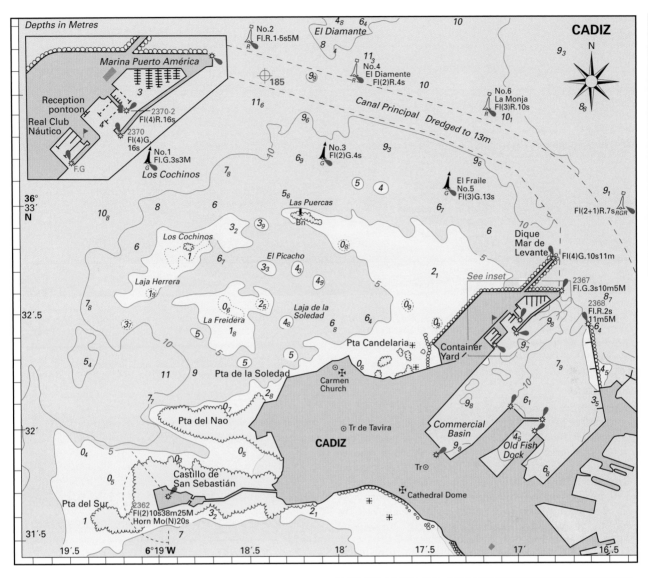

Approach

For outer approaches from the northwest and southeast refer to Bahía de Cádiz, page 284.

From offshore ⊕183 (also the approach waypoint for Puerto Sherry and El Puerto de Santa María) lies 1.5M to the west, a course of 099° leading to ⊕185 in the entrance to the Canal Principal.

The final approach is best made via the Canal Principal, which is well buoyed and lit and may safely be used by day or night. After identifying Los Cochinos buoy No.1, in normal weather it is safe to make direct for buoy No.5 (starboard hand) on 094°, passing close south of buoy No.3 in a least depth of 5m. Do not, however, be tempted to cut much south of buoy No.1 for fear of the unmarked Los Cochinos shoal. From buoy No.5 a course of 115° leads well clear of the end of the new Dique Mar de Levante (labelled Dique Mar de Leva on Admiralty 88), around which the north breakwater head, will be seen. In heavy weather, or when a large swell is running, it would be wise to remain in the Canal Principal which has a dredged depth of 13m.

Fishermen may be seen using a passage close northwest of the peninsula, which uses bearings on

⊕183	36°33'.8N	6°20'.3W	Puerto Sherry, El Puerto de Santa María & Cádiz approach
⊕185	36°33'.57N	6°18'.42W	Cádiz entrance
⊕186	36°31'.3N	6°20'.7W	Castillo de San Sebastián W cardinal buoy

various buildings in Cádiz itself to plot a course between the various rocks and shoals. However this is definitely one for the experienced navigator possessing both fair weather and a current large-scale chart – or, of course, detailed local knowledge.

Entrance

On rounding the north breakwater the marina entrance will be seen to starboard about 500m to the southwest with – unless or until moved – an enormous grey crane beyond. In 2005 the marina's outer breakwater was being extended, which in addition to allowing for expansion should greatly improve protection in the north basin, which previously suffered from both swell and wash. A reception pontoon is to be installed in the southwest corner of the southern basin – if this is not in place secure to the fuel pontoon on the northwest (inner) mole.

A somewhat low-angled shot of the Puerto América marina at Cádiz, taken while the marina's southeast breakwater was being extended. Shelter in the marina is much improved as a result

Berthing

The expansion mentioned above – which should be completed in 2006 or early 2007 – will increase capacity from 175 berths to nearer 300, many of the new slots able to take yachts of 12m or more. (Currently there are 59 berths rated for 12m and ten for up to 15m). As in all EPPA marinas, all berths will be alongside individual fingers. The marina is rarely full, but even so it is best to make contact by phone in advance, calling on VHF on closer approach.

Office hours are 0930–1300 and 1700–2000 daily in summer, 1000–1330 and 1600–1730 in winter, remaining closed in the afternoon on Wednesday, Saturday and Sunday. In 2005 the marina manager – who has been in post for several years – was outstandingly helpful and pleasant and spoke excellent English (an opinion confirmed in feedback from numerous visiting skippers). His somewhat elderly portacabin office is due for replacement within the next few years but is likely to stay in much the same place near the root of the inner mole. As in all EPPA marinas, security is good with guards outside office hours and individual card-operated gates to pontoons and services. Berthing charges are at the standard Empresa Pública de Puertos de Andalucía rate – see page 255.

Other berthing in the Cádiz area

The following are included largely for interest and to dispel any possible hopes, since none have much to offer a visiting yacht.

1. **The Real Club Náutico de Cádiz** lies next to Puerto América (though threatened with displacement to make way for a container park), where it has a 182-berth basin packed with member's own vessels. Visitors are welcome to visit the bar and waterside restaurant.

The restructured entrance to the Puerto América marina at Cádiz   *AH*

2. **The Centro Náutico Elcano** (36°30´.1N 6°15´.3W) is a relatively new, private marina situated just north of the main (bascule) bridge. Depths are less than 2m and maximum length 9m, though most craft berthed there are considerably smaller. No provision is made for visitors and it is doubtful whether space could be found for an overnight stay.

3. **Puerto de Gallineras** (36°26´.2N 6°12´.1W) is a somewhat ambitious name for the single pontoon run by the Club Náutico de Gallineras to which a number of smallcraft are secured. On the shallow waterway which links Cádiz with Sancti-Petri, controlling depths are no more than 1m and there are several bridges if approached from the north.

Facilities

Boatyard There is a large gated area of hardstanding, but no boatyard as such.

Travel-lift None at present, though it is hoped that one will be in situ for 2007. There is a 10-tonne crane on site, and in an emergency a mobile crane can be brought in from the commercial docks – a very expensive process.

Lord Byron declared Cadíz to be 'the most beautiful town I ever beheld'. Though few would go that far, he did have a point *AH*

Engineers, mechanics, general maintenance Náutica Benítez ☎/Fax 956 220244 *Email* nautica@nautica.benitez.com www.nauticabenitez.com has premises overlooking the new south basin where mechanical and other repairs are carried out.

Chandlery Some chandlery, mostly of a practical nature and including an impressive range of engine spares, at Náutica Benítez.

Charts The Spanish Instituto Hidrográfico de la Marina has its national headquarters in Cádiz, but does not sell direct to the public. Instead try either Libreria 'Alfa 2' (also known as Papelería Manuel Pereira González, open 0930–1330 and 1730–2030, closed Saturday afternoon and Sunday) at Calle Pelota 14, in a pedestrian area close to the cathedral; or JL Gándara y Cia SA ☎ 956 270443 *Fax* 956 272207 *Email* cadiz@gandara-sa.com at Calle La Línea de la Concepción 11 in the Zona Franca industrial area.

Water On the pontoons.

Showers A smart new shower block has recently been completed on the main breakwater overlooking the north basin.

Launderette Planned for 2006, adjacent to the new shower block.

Electricity On the pontoons.

Fuel Diesel and petrol pumps on the end of the northwest (inner) mole.

Bottled gas Camping Gaz available in the city, but no refills.

Club náutico The Real Club Náutico de Cádiz, close south of the marina, welcomes reasonably tidy visitors to its terrace bar and restaurant.

Weather forecast Posted daily in the marina office, as are warnings of firing exercises.

Banks Many in the city, but no cash dispenser at the marina.

Shops/provisioning/market Excellent shopping and a good produce market in the city, but all at some distance from the marina. It is hoped that in due course a supermarket and other shops will open on the large empty space nearby.

Cafés, restaurants and hotels Snack bar next to the marina office plus a small restaurant at the Real Club Náutico. For those with transport (or happy to walk) there is a wide choice in the old city.

Medical services In the city.

Communications

Post office In the city. Stamped mail can be left at the office for posting.

Mailing address The marina office will hold mail for visiting yachts – c/o Puerto América, Punta de San Felipe s/n, 11004 - Cádiz, España. It is important that the envelope carries the name of the yacht in addition to that of the addressee.

Public telephone Next to the marina office, otherwise a booth at the Real Club Náutico plus many in the city.

Internet access At the Real Club Náutico, plus several cybercafés in the city – ask for directions at the office. Informática Gaditana SA on the road behind the ferry basin sells computers and consumables such as inkjets.

Fax service At the marina office, *Fax* 956 224220.

Car hire/taxis Can be organised via the marina office.

Buses and trains Links to Jerez, Seville etc from the city, but no public transport near the marina.

Ferries Passenger ferries to El Puerto de Santa María – and to the Canaries!

Air services Airports at Seville and Jerez, both served by Ryanair among others.

The small marina at the Centro Náutico Elcano is limited to 9m overall and 2m draught *AH*

72. Sancti-Petri

Waypoints
⊕187 – 36°21′.9N 6°15′.7W (approach)
⊕188 – 36°22′.3N 6°13.16W (entrance)

Courses and distances
⊕181 (Rota) – ⊕187 (via ⊕186) = 14.1M, 167°&157°
  or 337°&347°
⊕183 (Cádiz) – ⊕187 (via ⊕186) = 12.7M, 187°&157°
  or 337°&007°
⊕187 – ⊕188 = 2.1M, 079° or 249°
⊕187 – ⊕189 (Puerto de Conil) = 8M, 139° or 319°
⊕187 – ⊕192 (Barbate, via F191) = 22.4M,
  149°&086° or 266°&329°

Tides
See Cádiz, page 292

Charts	Approach	River
Admiralty	91, 93	
Imray	C19, C50	C50
Spanish	44B, 44C, 443, 443B	4438

Principal lights
2387 **Punta del Arrecife** Q(9)15s8m3M
  West cardinal beacon, ⌁ topmark
2388 **Castillo de Sancti-Petri** Fl.3s19m9M
  Square tower 16m
2398 **Ldg Lts 050°** *Front* Fl.5s13m6M
  Aluminium framework tower 10m
2398.1 *Rear* 45m from front Oc(2)6s17m6M
  Aluminium framework tower 10m
2404 **Ldg Lts 346°** *Front* Punta del Boquerón
  Fl.5s12m6M Aluminium framework tower 6m
2404.1 *Rear* 60m from front Oc(2)6s22m6M
  Aluminium framework tower 10m
2404.4 **Bajo de Poniente** Fl.R.5s8m2M Red pillar
2404.5 **Piedra Larga** Fl.G.5s8m2M Green pillar

Night entry
Not recommended under any circumstances. However
in light conditions it would be possible to anchor close
south of the outer buoys and await daylight

Harbour communications
Puerto Deportivo Sancti-Petri ☎ 956 496169
Fax 956 496102 *Email* sanctipetri@eppa.es
www.eppa.es
VHF Ch 09
Club Náutico de Sancti-Petri ☎ 956 495428
Fax 956 495434 *Email* spetri@infonegocio.com
VHF Ch 09.

Attractive, windswept anchorage with few facilities

The sandy and windswept lagoon at Sancti-Petri
provides a peaceful port of call for those confident of
their pilotage and not too worried about facilities
ashore. Other than an active *club náutico* and a few
summer-only cafés the village which occupies the
eastern peninsula is almost entirely deserted, with
most of the buildings either falling into ruin or being
demolished. Even so the majority are clearly
identifiable, and in 2005 work was in hand to
restore the little church. Street lamps run down the
cobbled streets and benches recline in the shade of
palm trees around the square – only missing are the
people.

History is divided as to whether Sancti-Petri died
after the tunny fishing company which provided
nearly all its employment closed down, or whether it
was forcibly emptied during the Franco years for use

as a military training area. When first included in
this volume in 1994 it was entirely deserted – almost
ghostly – though by 1997 some of the houses in the
southern part of the village were being renovated by
Spanish families while others appeared to be
occupied by squatters. By 1999 work had come to a
halt, with little change six years later. However by
2005 a new *paseo* and fishermen's quay had been
constructed along the southeast side of the
peninsula, so plans are plainly afoot. Try to visit
Sancti-Petri before it is rediscovered and 'developed'
as bijou residences.

Facilities for yachts are improving, though it is
highly unlikely that a cruising yacht will be able to
find a slot in either of the marinas. A mooring is a
possibility, though many visitors prefer to lie to their
own anchors. The stone quay is used by fishing
vessels and ferries out to the tiny, rocky Isla de
Sancti-Petri, which has been inhabited since
prehistoric times. It is claimed that the remains of a
temple to Hercules can still be seen, along with more
recent fortifications and the square-sided lighthouse.
Alternatively explore further up the estuary where
the bird life is a twitcher's dream, particularly during
the winter when large flocks of flamingoes are to be
seen.

Approach

Coastal sailing towards Sancti-Petri from Cádiz or
other points north the coastline appears low and
somewhat featureless, consisting of marshes and
saltpans. Remain outside the 10m line in order to
avoid a small, unmarked, isolated rock about 2M
north of Punta del Arrecife, at the north end of the
reef which extends more than 1M north from the
Isla de Sancti-Petri. Punta del Arrecife is marked by
a lit west cardinal column with topmark – on no
account attempt to cut inside it, but instead give the
island generous clearance until able to pick up either
the outer pair of buoys or the outer leading marks on
050° as detailed below.

Coming from the south, beware the long, rocky
shoal which runs southwest from Cabo Trafalgar,
culminating in the dangerous Bajo Aceitera more
than 1.5M offshore. In heavy weather the Placer de
Meca bank, 3.2M to the west, may break and should
also be avoided. A race can form up to 8M offshore
in these conditions, particularly when east-going
current and tidal stream oppose the *levanter*. North
of the cape a direct course for Sancti-Petri takes one
uncomfortably close to the 1.2m shoal of Lajas de
Conil – keep a good 2.5M offshore until
approaching Cabo Roche. Once past the headland
with its square lighthouse there are no hazards other
than the isolated Laja Bermeja about 1M south of
the entrance – remain outside the 10m line until able
to pick up either the outer pair of buoys or the outer
leading marks on 050° as detailed below.

From offshore care must be taken to avoid the Hazte
Afuera/Cabezo de la Pasada bank, a long narrow
ledge which shoals to 3.1m in places. The bank,
which lies parallel to the coast about 2.5M off,

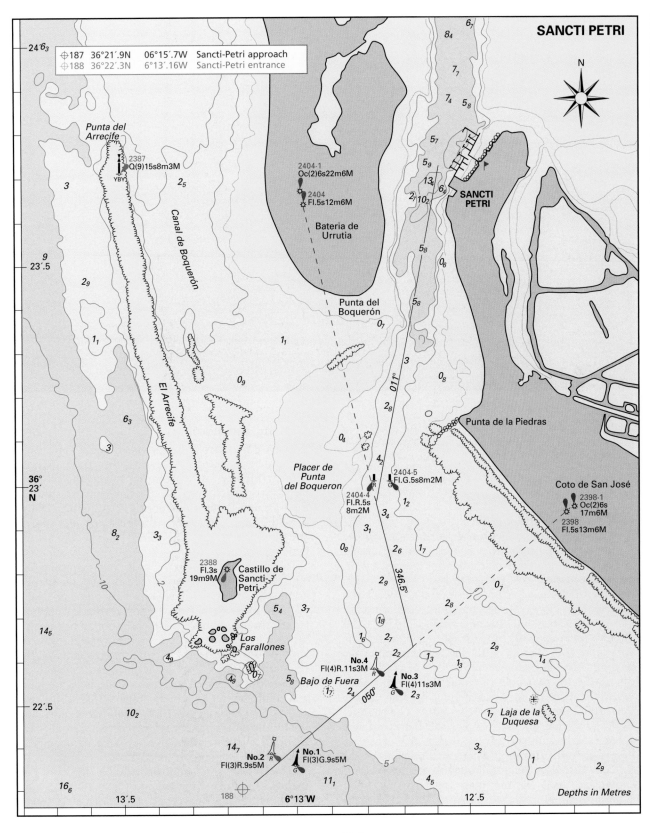

| ⊕187 | 36°21′.9N | 06°15′.7W | Sancti-Petri approach |
| ⊕188 | 36°22′.3N | 6°13′.16W | Sancti-Petri entrance |

SANCTI PETRI

Punta del Arrecife

2387
Q(9)15s8m3M
YBY

Canal de Boquerón

El Arrecife

2404·1
Oc(2)6s22m6M

2404
Fl.5s12m6M

Bateria de Urrutia

SANCTI PETRI

Punta del Boquerón

011°

Punta de la Piedras

Placer de Punta del Boqueron

2404·5
Fl.G.5s8m2M
G

2404·4
Fl.R.5s 8m2M
R

Coto de San José

2398·1
Oc(2)6s 17m6M

2398
Fl.5s13m6M

2388
Fl.3s 19m9M

Castillo de Sancti-Petri

346.5

Los Farallones

No.4
Fl(4)R.11s3M
R

No.3
Fl(4)11s3M
G

Laja de la Duquesa

Bajo de Fuera

050°

14₇

No.2
Fl(3)R.9s5M
R

No.1
Fl(3)G.9s5M
G

188

6°13′W

Depths in Metres

13′.5

6°13′W

12′.5

extends for more than 3M from end to end. ⊕187
lies off the northern end of the bank, a course of
079° for 2.1M leading to ⊕188 and the outer
entrance buoys.

In onshore swell the offshore banks may break, in
which case any thoughts of entering Sancti-Petri
should be forgotten.

Entrance

Though protection once inside is good, the entrance
should only be attempted on a rising tide, in fair
weather and in good visibility. If in doubt wait for a
local vessel to give a lead in. The bar is believed to
carry at least 2m at MLWS, but an onshore swell can
create very dangerous conditions and the

Sancti-Petri entrance from south-southwest. The island castle stands on the left, from which the Los Farallones reef runs out towards the pair of entrance buoys. At near low water the Placer de Punta del Boqueron sandbank shows clearly, with Sancti-Petri village behind

surrounding sandbanks shift with every gale. The current runs strongly, with a good 2 knots on the flood and more on the ebb. Night approach should not be contemplated, even though the entrance is lit.

Having made a position southwest of the Castillo de Sancti-Petri as described above, pass between the outer pair of buoys, at the same time picking up the Coto de San José outer leading marks on 050° – the aluminium framework towers are not conspicuous and tend to blend in with the vegetation. After passing between the inner buoys (one of which was off station for part of 2005) alter course onto 346° when the Batería de Urrutia inner leading marks (also aluminium towers) come into line. The channel shifts from time to time, and if the buoys do not agree exactly with the leading marks it is probably best to trust the former. (Although all four buoys are officially listed as being pillars with topmarks (and shown as such on the plan on page 297), in September 2004 and again in April 2005 they were confirmed to be much smaller and without topmarks, though of the correct colour).

Continue on 346° until about 100m short of the gate formed by Bajo de Poniente and Piedra Larga (identical red and green columns with lattice baskets surrounding their lights), turning slightly to starboard through the gap. Continue upriver on 011°, favouring the starboard side. A minimum of 3m should be found within the river.

Berthing and mooring

There are two sets of pontoons at Sancti-Petri, both so modest as hardly to justify the name marina. Those further downstream form the Puerto Deportivo Sancti-Petri, by far the smallest affair in the Empresa Pública de Puertos de Andalucía chain, those beyond – together with the many moorings – are administered by the Club Náutico de Sancti-Petri.

The Puerto Deportivo Sancti-Petri contains 87 berths for boats of up to 12m, but of the 25 nominally reserved for visitors only one can take a yacht of more than 10m. Depths of 5m are claimed for the three hammerheads, where it may be possible to lie for a short period to fill water tanks etc. Should one secure a berth, charges are at the standard Empresa Pública de Puertos de Andalucía rate – see page 255. The marina office is located in a new building on the quay, open 1000–1330 and 1600–1830 weekdays, 1000–1330 weekends, and some English is spoken. Access to the marina is via an electronic gate (though it is hard to imagine a safer place), making it unsuitable for landing by dinghy. However it may be possible for crews at anchor to obtain, on payment of a small fee, a card which will also give access to the immaculate toilets and showers.

As of early 2005 the Club Náutico de Sancti-Petri no longer accepted visiting yachts on its pontoons, which were full to capacity with locally-owned boats, though it may be possible to rent a mooring out of season. Again, pontoon access is via an electronic gate, limiting dinghy landing possibilities unless a card is forthcoming. The *club náutico*, which also houses the obligatory bar/café, occupies the only two story building on the waterfront. Office hours are basically 0900–1400 and 1600–1930 daily, but closing at 1900 on Monday and Tuesday and not opening until 0930 on weekends and holidays. In 2005 the office staff spoke little English, but several club members were happy to interpet.

Anchorage

It is possible to anchor almost anywhere in the estuary as depth permits, but note that at times the ebb can run at 3 knots or more. Fortunately holding is excellent over sand and mud. It is understood that 2m can be carried right up to the jetty at San Fernando, some 3M into the lagoon.

In the absence of a card to give access to one of the pontoons, the best prospect for dinghy landing is on the muddy beach at the head of the peninsula, also used by local fishermen. If coming in by outboard watch out for numerous underwater obstructions.

Facilities

Boatyard The *club náutico* has a walled compound near the quay where members lay up yachts to 11m or so. However a crane must be brought in for the purpose as there is no travel-lift or marine railway.

Engineers Enquire at the *club náutico* .

Chandlery Nautime Jet ☎ 956 495975, has premises on the quay, mainly concerned with jet skis but also selling a limited range of general chandlery, clothes and electronics.

Water On both sets of pontoons – yachts on moorings may be able to lie alongside briefly to fill tanks.

Showers On the quay for *puerto deportivo* users, or in the *club náutico* .

Electricity On both sets of pontoons.

Fuel The diesel pump previously on the *club náutico* jetty was not in situ in April 2005, and it was not clear whether it would be reinstated.

Club náutico Small and friendly club, with few facilities but helpful members.

Weather forecast Posted daily outside both offices.

Banks Several in Chiclana de la Frontera about 7km inland, and at least one cash dispenser in Costa Sancti-Petri about 2km away.

Shops/provisioning/market Other than a kiosk selling cold drinks and ice-creams there is no shop in Sancti-Petri of any kind. The nearest serious shopping is in Chiclana de la Frontera, though basic needs can be met in Costa Sancti–Petri.

Cafés, restaurants and hotels Bar/café at the *club náutico* with restaurants on either side, plus other cafés and restaurants on the east side of the peninsula.

Medical services Red Cross post operational in summer only, otherwise in Chiclana de la Frontera.

Communications

Post office In Chiclana de la Frontera. No box either, though harbour staff may be willing to post stamped mail for visitors. Alternatively hand to the postman on his daily visit.

Mailing address Both offices will hold mail for visiting yachts – c/o Oficina del Puerto, Puerto Deportivo Sancti-Petri, Poblado de Sancti-Petri, 11139 Chiclana de la Frontera, Cádiz, España; or Club Náutico de Sancti-Petri, Apdo de Correos 118, Chiclana de la Frontera, Cádiz, España. It is important that the envelope carries the name of the yacht in addition to that of the addressee.

Public telephones On the quay and in the *club náutico*.

Internet access In Chiclana de la Frontera and understood to be available in Costa Sancti–Petri, though this has not been verified.

Fax service At the *puerto deportivo* office, ☎/Fax 956 496169, or the *club náutico* , ☎/Fax 956 495434.

Taxis Organise via either office.

Buses About every two hours from a stop near the quay (check the return timetable before departure).

Most visitors must anchor at Sancti-Petri, as both the EPPA-run Puerto Deportivo Sancti-Petri and the pontoons of the Club Náutico de Sancti-Petri are generally full

73. Puerto de Conil

Waypoints
⊕189 – 36°15′.9N 6°09′.2W (approach)
⊕190 – 36°17′.5N 6°08′W (entrance)
⊕191 – 36°08′.3N 6°05′.6W (3.7M SW of Cabo Trafalgar)

Courses and distances
⊕183 (Cádiz) – ⊕189 (via F186) = 20.2M, 187°&149° or 329°&007°
⊕187 (Sancti-Petri) – ⊕189 = 8M, 139° or 319°
⊕189 – ⊕190 = 1.9M, 031° or 211°
⊕189 – ⊕192 (Barbate, via ⊕191) = 14.6M, 159°&086° or 266°&339°

Tides
Standard port Cádiz
Mean time differences (at Cabo Trafalgar)
HW +0015 ±0010; LW –0005 ±0010
Heights in metres

MHWS	MHWN	MLWN	MLWS
2.4	1.9	0.9	0.4

Charts   *Approach*
Admiralty   91, 93
Imray   C19, C50
Spanish   44B, 44C, 105, 444

Principal lights
2405 **Cabo Roche** Fl(4)24s44m20M
     Square pale yellow tower, silver lantern 20m
2405.4 **Southwest breakwater**
     Fl.R.6s10m5M Red tower 6m
2405.6 **Northeast mole** LFl.G.7s7m3M Green tower 3m
2405.8 **Inner mole** Fl(2)R.8s8m2M Red tower 4m

Night entry
In light conditions it would be possible to anchor east of the harbour, having taken care to avoid the tunny nets detailed below.

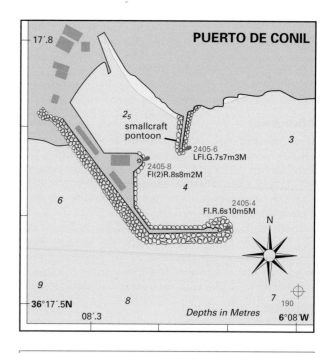

⊕189	36°15′.9N	06°09′.2W	Puerto de Conil approach
⊕190	36°17′.5N	06°08′W	Puerto de Conil entrance

Busy fishing harbour with possible anchorage outside

Puerto de Conil lies tucked behind the headland of Cabo Roche, almost midway between the Isla de Sancti-Petri and Cabo Trafalgar. A colourful, busy and obviously thriving fishing harbour, with all the associated smells and interest, but there are few facilities on site. The harbour is situated several kilometres from the town of the same name, and there is literally nothing outside the harbour gates other than miles of open heathland.

Puerto de Conil from a little west of south. The small harbour has nowhere for a visiting yacht to lie alongside, but there is good anchorage just outside

Hundreds of rusty fisherman anchors are stored behind the harbour, to be used when the tunny (tuna) nets are set – see page 204 – and in April 2005 a shapely wooden fishing boat was in build – framed but not yet planked – opposite the slipway. There is a major fossil bank near the root of the east mole.

Approach

If coastal sailing, approaching Cabo Roche from northwards presents no particular hazards in fair weather, though in any swell the 3.4m and 3.7m offshore banks may well break. In such conditions it would be wise to stay well outside the 20m line and continue for Barbate or beyond. Coming from the south, rocky shoals run southwest from Cabo Trafalgar culminating in the dangerous Bajo Aceitera more than 1.5M offshore. In heavy weather the Placer de Meca bank, 3.2M to the west, may break and should also be avoided. A race can form up to 8M offshore in these conditions, particularly when east-going current and tidal stream oppose the *levanter*. An inside passage is used by fishermen, but it should not be attempted without local knowledge. Careful pilotage remains necessary after rounding the cape to pass either inside or outside the 1.2m Lajas de Conil – in this case the inside passage is more than a mile wide and carries 8m or more – but see also the *Caution* below.

From offshore ⊕189 lies 1.9M south-southwest of the entrance, a course of 031° leading to ⊕190, about 200m from the breakwater head.

Caution

A large marine farm has been established just over 4M west of Puerto de Conil, centred on 36°17′.5N 6°13′.3W but covering an area almost 5M square. Its perimeter is marked by six yellow buoys with × topmarks, all lit Fl.Y.1.5s3M.

In early 2002 a 48m cable, supported by buoys and lying 2m below the surface, was laid in a northeasterly direction from 36°17′.1N 6°08′.2W (about 0.7M south of Cabo Roche). It was marked by a single west cardinal buoy with topmark, Q(9)15s2M. Although described as 'experimental' it was still in position in late 2005.

Finally, an *almadraba* or tunny (tuna) net known as *El Palmar* is laid from March to August or September each year between Cabo Roche and Cabo Trafalgar. It has been in much the same position for the past decade, and in 2005 was marked by four lit cardinal buoys:

buoy **North** 36°14′.9N 6°07′.3W
   Q.3M North card, ↑ topmark
buoy **East** 36°15′N 6°06′.8W
   Q(3)10s3M East card, ◆ topmark
buoy **South** 36°14′.2N 6°08′.2W
   Q(6)+LFl.15s3M South card, ▼ topmark
buoy **West** 36°14′.6N 6°08′.9W
   Q(9)15s3M West card, topmark

Fishing boats rafted four and five abreast in Puerto de Conil on a quiet Sunday afternoon   *AH*

Berthing and anchorage

Until the late 1990s Puerto de Conil consisted only of a single short breakwater, but the addition of an angled extension plus a short opposing mole has much increased its size. Even so all the inner walls other than the fishing quay are rubble-fronted (dinghies and other smallcraft lie on haul-out moorings), and a yacht would almost certainly have to remain outside the entrance. The Club Náutico de Conil's smallcraft pontoon just inside the north mole is already full to capacity with no possible space for even the smallest cruising yacht, while security gates limit its practicality for dinghy landing.

Anchor east of the short northeast mole in 3–5m over sand, protected from southwest through north to east but fully exposed to south and southeast. There is a reported 2.5m inside the harbour.

Facilities

Little more than a small bar and several water taps, though it might be possible to take on diesel from the fishermen's pump. There is a 10-tonne capacity travel-lift, but propping up a deep-keeled yacht would pose a challenge.

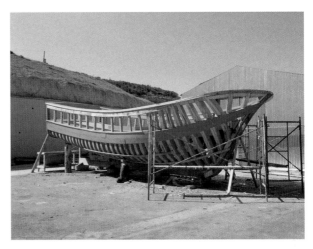

A traditional wooden fishing vessel in build at Puerto de Conil   *AH*

III.4 Cabo Trafalgar to Gibraltar

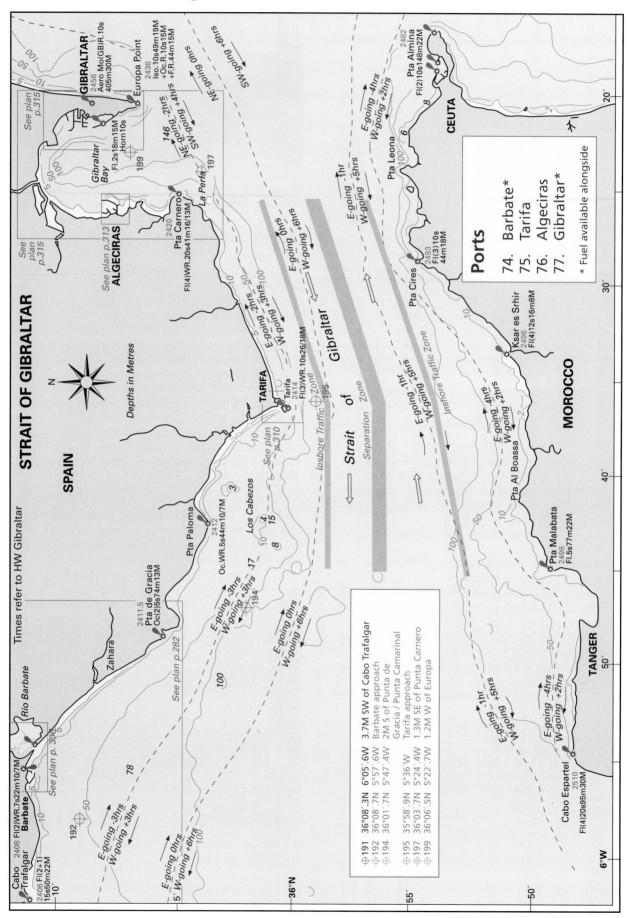

Ports

74. Barbate*
75. Tarifa
76. Algeciras
77. Gibraltar*

* Fuel available alongside

Times refer to HW Gibraltar

Depths in Metres

⊕191	36°08'.3N	6°05'.6W	3.7M SW of Cabo Trafalgar
⊕192	36°08'.7N	5°57'.6W	Barbate approach
⊕194	36°01'.7N	5°47'.4W	2M S of Punta de Gracia / Punta Camarinal
⊕195	35°58'.9N	5°36'.4W	Tarifa approach
⊕197	36°03'.7N	5°24'.4W	1.3M SE of Punta Carnero
⊕199	36°06'.5N	5°22'.7W	1.2M W of Europa

PRINCIPAL LIGHTS

Europe

2406 **Cabo Trafalgar** Fl(2+1)15s50m22M
White conical tower and building 34m

2411.5 **Punta de Gracia (Punta Camarinal)**
Oc(2)5s74m13M Masonry tower 20m

2412 **Punta Paloma** Oc.WR.5s44m10/7M
010°-W-340°-R-010° (over Bajo de Los Cabezos)
Two-storey building 5m

2414 **Tarifa** Fl(3)WR.10s40m26/18M
089°-R-113°-W-089° (over Bajo de Los Cabezos)
Racon Mo 'C'(-·-·)20M White tower 33m
Siren (3)60s Masonry structure 10m

2420 **Punta Carnero** Fl(4)WR.20s41m16/13M
018°-W-325°-R-018° (Red sector covers La Perla
and Las Bajas shoals) Siren Mo 'K'(-·-)30s
ellow tower, green base, silver lantern 19m

2438 **Europa Point, Gibraltar**
Iso.10s49m19M 197°-vis-042°, 067°-vis-125°
Oc.R.10s15M and F.R.15M 042°-vis-067°
(Red sector covers La Perla and Las Bajas shoals)
Horn 20s White tower, red band 19m

Africa

2510 **Cabo Espartel** Fl(4)20s95m30M
Yellow square stone tower

2498 **Pta Malabata** Fl.5s77m22M
White square tower on white dwelling

2496 **Ksar es Srhir** Fl(4)12s16m8M
Column on metal framework tower

2493 **Pta Cires** Fl(3)10s44m18M Round tower

2482 **Pta Almina** Fl(2)10s148m22M
White tower and building

Traffic Separation Zone

There is a Traffic Separation Zone in the Strait of
Gibraltar between 5°25′.5W and 5°45′W – see plan
opposite. The Inshore Traffic Zone to the north is
nowhere less than 1.7M wide (off the Isla de Tarifa)
and generally more than 2M. Tarifa Traffic monitors
VHF Ch 16 and 10 and vessels are advised to maintain
a listening watch whilst in the area. Weather and
visibility information for an area including the Traffic
Separation Zone is broadcast on VHF Ch 10 and 67 as
detailed over.

Warning If enjoying a fine spinnaker run into the
Straits from the west be aware that winds in excess
of 30 knots are said to blow at Tarifa for 300 days
of the year.

Surface flow in the Strait

Surface water flow through the Strait is the product of a
combination of current and tidal stream, the former
dominant for at least eight hours out of the twelve.

A permanent, east-going current sets through the Strait,
compensating for water lost from the Mediterranean
through evaporation. Strength varies from 1 knot close to
the northern shore to approaching 2 knots in the centre
and southern part of the channel, with a decrease to 1.5
knots or less near the Moroccan shore. However this
pattern can be upset by the wind, and persistent strong
westerlies, coupled with the regular current, can produce
an easterly set of up to 4 knots. Conversely, the entire flow
may reverse after prolonged easterly winds, though in
practice this seldom happens.

Tidal streams, though capable of exceeding 3 knots at
springs and more off the major headlands, must be
worked carefully if attempting to make progress
westwards – riding the stream eastwards is generally not a
problem unless faced with a strong *levanter*. Streams turn
earlier near the coast – see plan opposite – but bear in
mind that even then the current may prove stronger than
the tide for a considerable part of the cycle. In the middle,
the tidal stream runs directly through the Strait, but
inshore it tends to follow the coastline. Where the
boundary between east and west-moving water lies with a
west-going tide depends on the relative strengths of the
two forces, and in stronger winds may be readily
detectable by the sea state. Tidal races may form off Cabo
Trafalgar, the Bajo de Los Cabezos west of Tarifa, and Isla
de Tarifa itself, typically when east-going current and tidal
stream oppose the *levanter*.

Over the course of the passage, particularly in a slower
yacht or if beating, it may be possible to extend the
duration of favourable tide available by moving from one
tidal band into another. For example: leaving Gibraltar at
HW+0300 to head west, using the west-going stream
inshore until it turns east at HW–0300, then moving
offshore to gain a further three hours of west-going
stream until HW Gibraltar (though it should be noted that
this tactic will take a yacht from the Inshore Traffic Zone
into the main west-going shipping channel). See also
overleaf.

A great deal of detailed, practical advice on how best to
tackle the Straits of Gibraltar – including clear current and
tidal flow diagrams – will be found in Colin Thomas's
highly recommended *Straits Sailing Handbook*, published
annually by Ocean Marine Ltd Gibraltar
Email straits.sailing@gibtelecom.net.

Cabo Trafalgar – possibly the most famous headland in the world? – seen from
the southeast. The 50m lighthouse can be seen 22M away

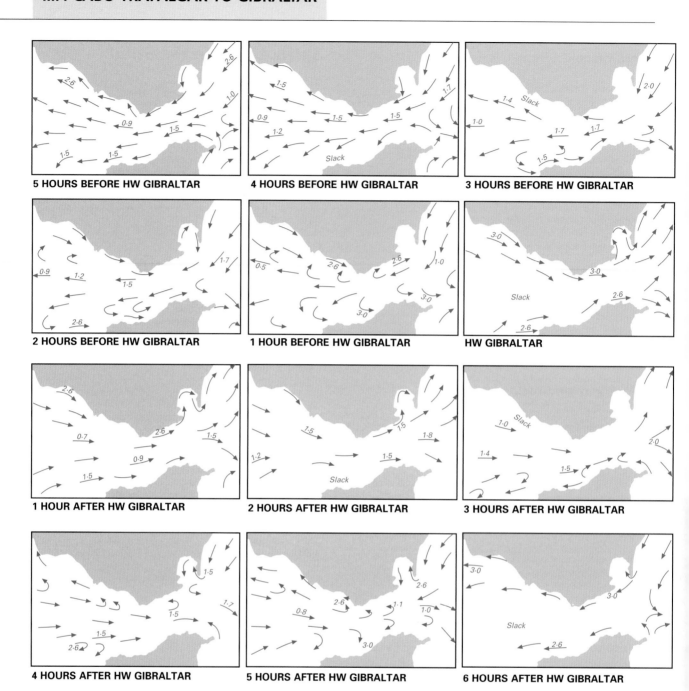

5 HOURS BEFORE HW GIBRALTAR   **4 HOURS BEFORE HW GIBRALTAR**   **3 HOURS BEFORE HW GIBRALTAR**

2 HOURS BEFORE HW GIBRALTAR   **1 HOUR BEFORE HW GIBRALTAR**   **HW GIBRALTAR**

1 HOUR AFTER HW GIBRALTAR   **2 HOURS AFTER HW GIBRALTAR**   **3 HOURS AFTER HW GIBRALTAR**

4 HOURS AFTER HW GIBRALTAR   **5 HOURS AFTER HW GIBRALTAR**   **6 HOURS AFTER HW GIBRALTAR**

These diagrams are published with the kind permission of Dr M Sloma, editor of *Yacht Scene*. Under no circumstances will *Yacht Scene* or the RCC Pilotage Foundation be liable for any accident or injury which may occur to vessels or persons whilst using the above current predictions.

Graham Hutt, author of RCCPF *North Africa*, who knows the Strait well, offers the following strategy:

Eastbound vessels

For yachts entering the Strait from the west, there is no real problem going eastwards, unless there is a strong easterly wind, in which case passage will be rough, especially around Tarifa, where winds often reach 40 knots. If strong winds are forecast, stay in Barbate (or Tanger) until it drops or anchor in the lee of Tarifa if strong east winds are encountered once on passage. The best time to depart for the trip east is soon after LW.

Westbound vessels

In strong westerlies is is almost impossible to make progress west, due to the combined east-going current that can, with unfavourable tide, reach 6 knots or more – with steep swell and overfalls off Tarifa, Ceuta Point and Punta Malabata.

In good conditions, to make use of the favourable current, set off from Gibraltar 2 hours after HW. Keeping close inshore, a foul current of around a knot will be experienced off Punta Carnero. A favourable west-going current 4 hours after HW will assist passage during springs, although this is weak and east-going at neaps. If heading south out of Gibraltar for Tanger, it is usually wise to use the engine to cross from Tarifa making a fast passage to counter the increasing east-going current – or anchor in the shelter of Tarifa and wait for the next favourable tide, around LW, to make the crossing.

74. Barbate

Waypoints
⊕192 – 36°08'.7N 5°57'.6W (approach)
⊕193 – 36°10'.56N 5°55'.8W (entrance)
⊕194 – 36°01'.7N 5°47'.4W (2M S of Punta de Gracia or Punta Camarinal)

Courses and distances
⊕183 (Cádiz) – ⊕192 (via ⊕186 & ⊕191) = 35M, 187°&152°&086° or 266°&332°&007°
⊕187 (Sancti-Petri) – ⊕192 (via ⊕191) = 22.4M, 149°&086° or 266°&329°
⊕191 (Cabo Trafalgar) – ⊕192 = 6.5M, 086° or 266°
⊕192 – ⊕193 = 2.4M, 038° or 218°
⊕192 – ⊕195 (Tarifa, via ⊕194) = 20.5M, 130°&107° or 287°&310°
⊕192 – ⊕200 (Queensway Quay, Gibraltar, via ⊕194, ⊕195 & ⊕197) = 35.7M, 130°&107°&063°&022° or 202°&243°&287°&310°
⊕192 – ⊕201 (Marina Bay, Gibraltar, via ⊕194, ⊕195 & ⊕197) = 36.6M, 130°&107°&063°&017° or 197°&243°&287°&310°

Tides
Standard port Cádiz
Mean time differences
HW +0005 ±0000; LW +0015 ±0000
Heights in metres

MHWS	MHWN	MLWN	MLWS
1.9	1.5	1.0	0.6

Or refer to EasyTide at www.ukho.gov.uk (see page 2)

Charts

Charts	Approach	Harbour
Admiralty	91, 773, 142	
Imray	C19, C50	C50
Spanish	44C, 105, 444	4441

Principal lights
2408 **Barbate** Fl(2)WR.7s22m10/7M 281°-W-015°-R-095°
White tower, dark red bands 18m
2409 **South breakwater** Fl.R.4s11m5M
Red conical tower 2m
2409.2 **Ldg Lts 297°** *Front* Q.2m1M
280.5°-vis-310.5°White pillar 3m
2409.21 *Rear* 385m from front Q.7m1M
280.5°-vis-10.5°
White pillar, red bands, on perimeter wall 6m
2410 **East breakwater** Fl(2)G.7s7m2M Green tower 2m
Anti-swell barrier, SE end Fl(2+1)R.21s1M
Red post, green bands
2411.25 **Marina, south mole** Fl.R.4s2M Red column 4m
2411.2 **Marina, north mole** Fl.G.2M Green column 4m
Note The leading lights on 058.5° close east of the marina entrance lead into the shallow Río Barbate. Yachts are advised to keep well clear

Night entry
Straightforward in normal conditions, taking care to avoid both the tunny nets detailed below and the low-lying anti-swell barrier inside the harbour itself (see plan)

Harbour communications
Puerto Deportivo Barbate ☎ 956 431907
Fax 956 431918 *Email* barbated@eppa.es
www.eppa.es VHF Ch 09.

The large harbour at Barbate looking northeast. A pair of channel buoys may be seen inside the harbour entrance, with infilling taking place in the nearby fishing and commercial area

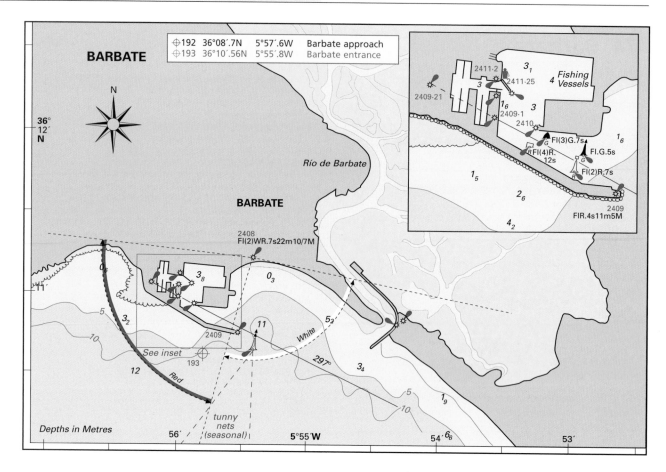

The last – or first – marina west of Gibraltar,
so very useful, if slightly soulless

Formerly known as Barbate de Franco (pronounced
'Barbartay', with the 'de Franco' now dropped), the
old town has been swallowed up by new
development and has no great appeal, though the
marina is useful as a refuge from the strong winds
characteristic of the Straits. The harbour, in which
fishing boats berth to the east and yachts to the west,
covers a large area and is the easternmost (in the
Atlantic) of the string of harbours and marinas
financed, built and run by the Empresa Pública de
Puertos de Andalucía in Seville – see page 255. In
2005 part of the eastern harbour was being filled in,
but this does not affect the marina.

The shallow Río Barbate about 0.4M to the east is
used by local boats, but the entrance is difficult and
depths within are less than 2.5m.

Approach and entrance

If inshore sailing from the west, swing wide around
Cabo Trafalgar to clear the rocky shoal which runs
southwest from Cabo Trafalgar – which at only 20m
or so appears low-lying compared to the hills 2km to
the northeast – culminating in the dangerous Bajo
Aceitera more than 1.5M offshore. In heavy weather
the Placer de Meca bank, 3.2M to the west, may
break and should also be avoided. A race can form
up to 8M offshore in these conditions, particularly
when east-going current and tidal stream oppose the
levanter. An inside passage is used by fishermen, but
it should not be attempted without local knowledge.

From the southeast, Punta Camarinal cuts the
direct line from Tarifa (off which a race may also
form). Note also the dangerous Bajo de Los Cabezos
shoal, 5M west of Tarifa and 2M south of Punta
Paloma, on which waves break even in calm weather.
Between Punta Camarinal and Barbate the coast is
relatively steep-to. In either case take care to avoid
the two tunny nets laid in the area each year – see
below.

From offshore ⊕192 lies 2.4M southwest of the
entrance, a course of 038° leading to ⊕193, close
outside the harbour mouth. This course clears the
western edge of tunny nets referred to below.

Caution

Three *almadrabas* or tunny (tuna) nets are laid
annually in the vicinity of Barbate. The Ensenada de
Barbate net is laid from March to September each
year very close to the harbour entrance – it is stated
that vessels should not pass between the inner end of
the net and the shore, but local fishermen habitually
do so. For the past ten years it has been set in
roughly the same position, and in 2005 was marked
by four lit cardinal buoys:

buoy **North** 36°10'.8N 5°55'.4W
   (about 200m SE of the south breakwater head)
   Q.3M North cardinal, ⮝ topmark
buoy **West** 36°09'.3N 5°56'.3W
   Q(9)10s3M West cardinal, ⮞ topmark
buoy **South** 36°08'.9N 5°57'.1W (March to June)
   36°08'.1N 5°55'.1W (June to September)
   Q(6)+LFl.12s3M South cardinal, ⮟ topmark
buoy **East** 36°08'.9N 5°55'.4W
   Q(3)10s3M East cardinal, ⬥ topmark

The Puerto Deportivo Barbate lies at the west end of the harbour, seen here from the southeast. The anti-swell pontoon which lies at an angle off the entrance is poorly lit and a potential hazard if entering at night

Between September and February the Ensenada de Barbate net is replaced by a floating fish cage some 270m by 60m, marked by two lit buoys. In 2005 these were:

buoy **West** 36°09′.2N 5°55′.8W
    Q(9)10s3M **West** cardinal, ✕ topmark
buoy **East** 36°09′N 5°55′.4W
    Q(3)10s3M **East** cardinal, ♦ topmark

The Cabo Plato tunny net is laid from March to August each year off the small village of Zahara some 4.5M southeast of Barbate. Again it appears to maintain much the same position, and in 2005 it was marked by three lit cardinal buoys:

buoy **West No.1** 36°07′.5N 5°52′.1W
    Q(9)15s3M **West** cardinal, ✕ topmark
buoy **West No.2** 36°06′.4N 5°52′.1W
    Q(9)15s3M **West** cardinal, ✕ topmark
buoy **South** 36°06′.3N 5°50′.6W
    Q(6)+LFl.15s3M **South** cardinal, ♥ topmark

Finally, and a more recent addition, the Ensenada de Bolonia net is laid about halfway between Barbate and Tarifa off the village of that name (worth visiting for its Roman ruins). In 2005 it too was marked by three lit cardinal buoys:

buoy **West** 36°04′.2N 5°46′.3W
    Q(9)15s3M **West** cardinal, ✕ topmark
buoy **South** 36°03′.7N 5°47′.1W
    Q(6)+LFl.15s3M **South** cardinal, ♥ topmark
buoy **East** 36°04′N 5°45′.8W
    Q(9)15s3M **West** cardinal, ✕ topmark

Entrance

Entrance is straightforward, though in 2005 a shoal had built up around the head of the south breakwater – give it generous clearance. Two pairs of lateral buoys should then be seen, though the starboard hand inner buoy is seldom on station. A minimum of 2m should be found in the channel at MLWS.

Berthing

The marina is reached through a narrow entrance leading almost due west from the main harbour, with a reception pontoon on the port hand under the office building and fuel opposite. A low yellow and black anti-swell barrier runs out from the northern side – see plan. The weakish red light on its end is said to be unreliable – take particular care at night. The marina consists of two separate and almost completely enclosed basins, one leading out of the other, with pontoons laid around their perimeters and down the centre of the larger western basin. There are 314 berths in total, 120 of them able to take yachts of more than 11m and 18 for more than 15m. There is always room for visitors, who are usually berthed near the marina office. Hours are 1000–1330 and 1600–1730 daily in summer, closed weekend afternoons in winter, and in early 2005 good English was spoken. Berthing charges are at the standard Empresa Pública de Puertos de Andalucía rate – see page 255.

Facilities

Boatyard, engineers, electronic and radio repairs Talleres Gonzalez-Guerra, ☎ 956 431903, handle general and mechanical repairs from their premises just outside the boatyard on the north side of the marina, and also fabricate in stainless steel.

Travel-lift 45-tonne capacity lift handling both yachts and fishing boats, with a large area of fenced (but windy) hardstanding. Book at the marina office.

Chandlery A good range of general chandlery at Talleres Gonzalez-Guerra, open 0900–1400 and 1530–1830 weekdays, 0900–1330 Saturday. They are happy to order if necessary, and some English is spoken.

Water On the pontoons.

Showers In the office building.

Launderette In the office building.

Electricity On the pontoons (but using non-standard plugs which are available from the marina office).

Fuel Available during office hours at the fuelling pontoon on the north side of the entrance.

Bottled gas Camping Gaz available in the town about 2km distant.

Club náutico Near the fishing harbour.

Weather forecast Posted daily at the marina office.

Bank In the town.

Shops/provisioning Good supermarket on the road behind the harbour, with more in the town. In early 2005 there were no shops at the marina, but the large new 'commercial building' may rectify this. Meanwhile a bicycle would be useful . . .

Produce market In the town.

Cafés, restaurants and hotels Small café/bar at the marina serving tasty food in relaxed surroundings. Plenty of all three in the town.

Medical services In the town.

Communications

Post office In the town.

Mailing address The marina office will hold mail for visiting yachts – c/o Puerto Deportivo Barbate, Oficina del Puerto, Avda del Generalisimo s/n, 11160 Barbate, Cádiz, España. It is important that the envelope carries the name of the yacht in addition to that of the addressee.

Public telephones Several kiosks around the marina.

Internet access At least one cybercafé in the town.

Fax service At the marina office, Fax 956 431918.

Car hire/taxis Book via the office.

Buses Bus service to Cádiz, Algeciras and La Línea.

Air services International airport at Gibraltar, a short walk across the border from La Línea. Alternatively Jerez or Seville.

Looking north across the narrow entrance to the Puerto Deportivo Barbate, with the fuel pontoon opposite and the yellow and black anti-swell barrier on the right   *AH*

75. Tarifa

Waypoints
⊕195 – 35°58′.9N 5°36′W (approach)
⊕196 – 36°00′.24N 5°36′.14W (entrance)

Courses and distances
⊕192 (Barbate) – ⊕195 (via F194) = 20.5M, 130°&107°
or 287°&310°
⊕195 – ⊕196 = 1.3M, 355° or 175°
⊕195 – ⊕198 (Algeciras, via ⊕197) = 14M, 063°&346°
or 166°&243°
⊕195 – ⊕200 (Queensway Quay, Gibraltar,
via ⊕197) = 15.2M, 063°&022° or 202°&243°
⊕195 – ⊕201 (Marina Bay, Gibraltar,
via ⊕197) = 16.1M, 063°&017° or 197°&243°

Tides
Standard port Gibraltar
Mean time differences
HW –0040; LW –0040
Heights in metres

MHWS	MHWN	MLWN	MLWS
1.4	1.0	0.6	0.3

Or refer to EasyTide at www.ukho.gov.uk (see page 2)

Charts	Approach	Harbour
Admiralty	91, 773, 142	142
Imray	C19, C50	C50
Spanish	44C, 105, 445, 445B	4450

Principal lights
2414 **Tarifa** Fl(3)WR.10s40m26/18M
089°-R-113°-W-089° (over Bajo de Los Cabezos)
Racon Mo 'C'(–·–·)20M White tower 33m
Siren (3)60s Masonry structure 10m
2415 **Isla de Tarifa**, NE 36°00′.3N 5°36′.3W
Fl.R.5s11m3M Square red and white tower 2m
2416 **East breakwater** Fl.G.5s10m5M 249°-vis-045°
Green lattice tower on white base 5m

(Dwarfed by square stone pillar surmounted by
statue of man, approximately 55m)
2417 **Breakwater elbow** Q(6)+LFl.15s10m3M
255°-vis-045° South cardinal column, ⍗ topmark, 2M
2418 **West Mole** Fl(2)R.7s6M1M
Red lantern on white hut 4m

Night entry
Not advised, at least until an area in the harbour is
designated for visiting yachts.

Navtex
Tarifa Identification letters 'G' and 'T'
Transmits 518kHz in English; 490 in Spanish
Weather bulletins for Cabo de São Vicente to
Gibraltar and the Western Mediterranean within 450
miles of the coast: English – 0900, 2100; Spanish –
0710, 1910
Navigational warnings for the Rio Guadiana to
Gibraltar: English – 0100, 0500, 1300, 1700; Spanish –
0310, 0710, 1110, 1510, 1910, 2310

Coast radio station
Tarifa (remotely controlled from Málaga)
Digital Selective Calling MMSI 002240994
MF Transmits/receives: 2182kHz
VHF Ch 10, 16, 67, 74
Weather bulletins and navigational warnings
Weather bulletins and visibility (fog) warnings in
Spanish and English for Bahía de Cádiz, Strait of
Gibraltar and Alborán: VHF Ch 10, 67 at 0015, 0215,
0415, 0615, 0815, 1015, 1215, 1415, 1615, 1815, 2015,
2215 UT
Navigational warnings in Spanish and English for the
Strait of Gibraltar: VHF Ch 10, 67 on receipt

Commercial and fishing harbour with little provision for yachts

Tarifa is the most southerly city of mainland Europe
and, at barely 8M distant, considerably closer to
North Africa than is Gibraltar. It is famous for its
frequent strong winds, which together with excellent
beaches have made it the boardsailing capital of Europe.

Reputedly where the Moors landed on their
European invasion, the older part of the town still
shows a strong North African influence, particularly
in the well preserved streets around the harbour. It
has an active (but not over-obtrusive) tourist
industry and consequently is well provided with
shops, restaurants and hotels. Unfortunately the Isla

Looking northeast over Isla de Tarifa, with the busy fishing and ferry harbour on the right

THE ALGARVE & ANDALUCIA

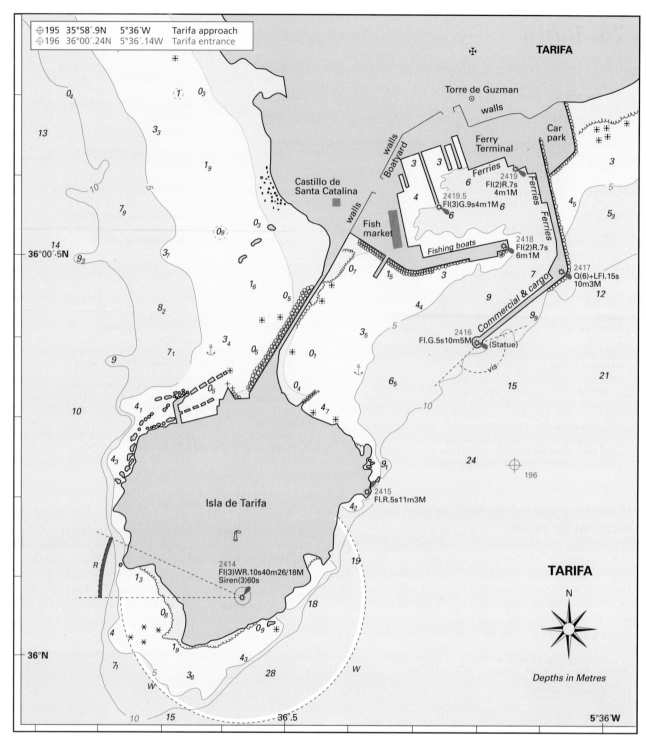

| ⊕195 | 35°58′.9N | 5°36′W | Tarifa approach |
| ⊕196 | 36°00′.24N | 5°36′.14W | Tarifa entrance |

de Tarifa is a military area and closed to the public, as is the handsome old Castillo de Santa Catalina to the northwest, but the road between Tarifa and Algeciras is worth traversing if possible for its dramatic views of both Gibraltar and the Strait.

Approach

If coastal sailing from the west, Tarifa light stands high on its promontory clear of the land. Chief danger is the Bajo de los Cabezos, 5M west of Tarifa and 3M south of Punta Paloma. The bank is marked by broken water even in calm weather, and several wrecks are reputed to lie close to the surface. From

the east, there are dangers up to 1M offshore between Punta Carnero and Punta de Cala Arenas, but once west of the latter the shore is generally steep to. There is a prominent wind farm on the hills northeast of the town.

There is no true offshore approach due to the busy Traffic Separation Zone – see page 303 – but if coasting further out ⊕195 lies 1.3M almost due south of the entrance, a course of 355° leading up the east side of the Isla de Tarifa to ⊕196, close off the entrance.

A race may form off Isla de Tarifa when east-going current and tidal stream oppose the *levanter*.

Caution

An *almadraba* or tunny (tuna) net known as *Lances de Tarifa* is laid between March and July each year northwest of Isla de Tarifa. It has been in much the same position for the past decade, and in 2005 was marked by three lit cardinal buoys:

buoy **Northwest** 36°01′.1N 5°38′.3W
  Q(9)15s3M West cardinal, ✗ topmark
buoy **Southwest** 36°00′.9N 5°38′.1W
  Q(9)15s3M West cardinal, ✗ topmark
buoy **South** 36°00′.7N 5°37′.6W
  Q(6)+LFl.15s3M South cardinal, ⵎ topmark

Entrance

The harbour entrance faces southwest towards the Isla de Tarifa and its connecting causeway. Head for the conspicuous statue at the end of the east breakwater, before making the dogleg into the harbour.

Note In a *levanter* this approach becomes a lee shore and it may be wiser to use the second of the anchorages mentioned below – or to press on for Barbate or beyond.

Berthing

Tarifa is far from yacht-orientated and there is no designated spot where visiting yachts may berth, though the best bet would almost certainly be amongst the local craft which lie bow or stern-to the concrete moles to the northwest. Some command of Spanish would be a major advantage.

The east wall is no longer viable, being entirely taken up with ferries and small cargo vessels. Constant comings and goings by the fishing fleet make for almost continuous movement.

Formalities

The *Policía* and *Inmigración* both have offices in the ferry terminal (*Estación Marítima*) at the root of the east breakwater and should be visited if arriving from outside Spain. Foreign yachts are also a sufficient rarity that the Capitania is likely to visit. Several years ago a charge of around €15.00 was levied for an overnight visit by an 11.5m yacht, despite the almost total lack of facilities.

Considerably nearer to North Africa than Algeciras or Gibraltar, Tarifa is primarily a commercial harbour with, as yet, no provision for yachts

Facilities

Virtually nothing, other than a few water taps. There is no yacht fuel and no possibility of getting electricity aboard. The small boatyard (with marine railway) in the northwest corner of the harbour is geared to fishing boats but could doubtless carry out minor yacht repairs if necessary.

A café/bar will be found on the southwest arm, otherwise the town has shops of all kinds, a produce market, banks, restaurants and hotels.

Communications

Post office in the old part of town, with telephones around the harbour etc. Several internet cafés, one (slightly northwest of the harbour) combining operations with a launderette! Taxis in surprising numbers. Buses to Cádiz, Algeciras and La Línea, from which it is a short walk to the international airport at Gibraltar.

Adjacent anchorages

A *Parque Natural* has been established along the coast between Punta de Gracia in the west and Punta Carnero in the east, extending more than 1M offshore. However although some fishing and diving activities are prohibited there appears to be no ban on anchoring in the area.
1. In the clean sandy bay northeast of Isla de Tarifa, between the causeway and the harbour entrance, in 4–5m over sand. The area is popular with both divers and boardsailors, but a yacht may attract curiosity from the authorities.
2. Just north of a derelict mole on the northwest side of Isla de Tarifa, with shelter from easterly seas (though not the wind) given by the causeway. Good holding over sand in 3–4m.

76. Algeciras

Waypoints
⊕197 – 36°03′.7N, 5°24′.4W (1.3M SE of Punta Carnero)
⊕198 – 36°06′.95N 5°25′.43W (entrance)

Courses and distances
⊕195 (Tarifa) – ⊕198 (via ⊕197) = 14M, 063°&346° or 166°&243°
⊕197 – ⊕198 = 3.4M, 346° or 166°
⊕198 – ⊕200 (Queensway Quay, Gibraltar) = 2.7M, 068° or 248°
⊕198 – ⊕201 (Marina Bay, Gibraltar) = 3.2M, 051° or 231°

Tides
Standard port Gibraltar
Mean time differences
HW –0010; LW –0010
Heights in metres

MHWS	MHWN	MLWN	MLWS
1.1	0.9	0.4	0.2

Or refer to EasyTide at www.ukho.gov.uk (see page 2)

Charts

	Approach	Harbour
Admiralty	91, 773, 142, 3578, 1448	1455
Imray	C19, C50	
Spanish	44C, 45A, 105, 445, 445A	4451

Principal lights
Commercial Harbour
2425 **Northeast breakwater** Fl(2)R.6s10m8M Red tower 8m
Note In 2005 major land reclamation and infilling was in progress around the Isla Verde.
Dársena del Saladillo (yacht basin)
2423 **South breakwater** Fl(3)R.9s6m3M
White post, red top 6m

Night entry
Not advised, since all three marinas in the Dársena del Saladillo are private and anchoring is forbidden.

Coast radio station
Algeciras *Digital Selective Calling*
MMSI 002241001 VHF Ch 16, 74
Weather bulletins and navigational warnings
Weather bulletins in Spanish and English: VHF Ch 74 at 0315, 0515, 0715, 1115, 1515, 1915, 2315 UT
Navigational warnings in Spanish and English: on request

Harbour communications
Port Authority ☎ 956 585400/585431
Fax 956 585443/585431 *Email* comercial@apba.es
www.apba.es
VHF Ch 08, 13, 16, 68, 74 (call *Algeciras Tráfico*)
Real Club Náutico de Algeciras VHF Ch 09, 16

Major commercial harbour, with three private marinas in a separate basin

Algeciras is primarily an industrial and ferry port, through which passes many of the guest-workers returning to Africa with roof racks bending under their loads.

Yachts have their own basin – the Dársena del Saladillo – south of the main harbour, where three separate clubs run three separate marinas. Sadly none welcome visiting yachts – See Berthing, below. The following approach and entrance instructions are given for the Dársena del Saladillo in the hope that this situation may one day change.

Approach

The approaches to Algeciras are extremely busy with commercial traffic of all sizes. In particular, a sharp watch needs to be kept for the many high-speed ferries, including hydrofoils, which run between Algeciras and Morocco. These are notorious for maintaining their course and speed at all times, presumably adhering to the 'might is right' principle.

Coming from the west, there are dangers up to 1M offshore between Punta de Cala Arenas and Punta Carnero. On rounding this headland the city and harbour will be seen some 3M to the north behind a mile-long breakwater terminating with a light. Various ledges run out from the headlands between Punta Carnero and the entrance to the Dársena del Saladillo (also lit).

If approaching from Gibraltar or other points east, the entrance to the Dársena del Saladillo should be easily seen south of the oil tanks on the commercial quay and it can be approached directly.

If approaching from the south, possibly from Ceuta or elsewhere in Morocco, ⊕197 lies in clear water southeast of Punta Carnero, a course of 346° for 3.4M leading to ⊕198 in the approaches to the Dársena del Saladillo, passing close to a spherical yellow ODAS buoy off Punta Calero en route.

Yachts can safely cut inside the east cardinal buoy placed nearly a mile offshore, though an offing of at least 0.5M should be maintained. Further ledges lie both north and south of the entrance, and the three buoys marking the approach should under no circumstances be ignored. In 2005 major infilling work was taking place to the north of the Saladillo entrance (see plan), marked by additional buoys. Keep well clear.

Entrance

The dogleg entrance to the Dársena del Saladillo has been very well designed, such that when visited in a 30 knot easterly wind no swell at all was entering. As noted above, three buoys mark the final approach, after which the entrance itself is straightforward.

Berthing

As stated above none of the three marinas in the Dársena del Saladillo accept visitors. Taken clockwise on entry these are the Real Club Náutico de Algeciras, which previously had premises in the main harbour, the Club Náutico Saladillo and the Club Deportivo El Pargo. The first (southern) marina is also the largest by a considerable margin, and would undoubtedly be the best one to try in an emergency. It is also the club where some English is most likely to be spoken, and visitors are also welcome to dine in the Real Club Náutico's restaurant.

Facilities

The Real Club Náutico marina is provided with all the usual facilities, including a fuel berth on the end of the breakwater which forms its eastern limit.

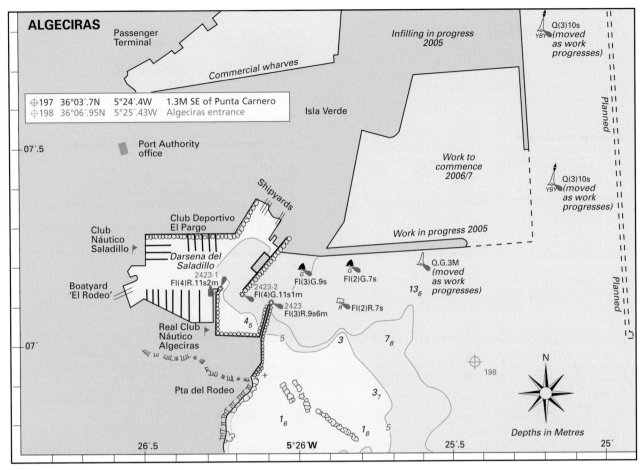

ALGECIRAS

| ⊕197 | 36°03′.7N | 5°24′.4W | 1.3M SE of Punta Carnero |
| ⊕198 | 36°06′.95N | 5°25′.43W | Algeciras entrance |

The Dársena del Saladillo at Algeciras, seen from east-southeast. Although the Real Club Náutico de Algeciras, the Club Náutico Saladillo and the Club Deportivo El Pargo all have pontoons in the harbour, none currently accept visitors

The west side of the basin is home to Astilleros y Varaderos 'El Rodeo', ☎ 956 600511, a shipyard primarily engaged with work on steel fishing vessels and other commercial craft, though with at least one larger steel yacht ashore when visited in 2005. Almost opposite, across the busy harbourside road, will be found Náutica Iberia, where a limited range of chandlery is on sale in addition to smallcraft and jet-skis. Spanish charts may be obtained either from SUISCA SL ☎ 902 220007 *Email* admiraltycharts@suiscasl.com or in the Centro Blas Infante; or from Valnáutica SL ☎ 956 570677 at Avenida 28 de Febrero 33.

All the usual shops, banks, restaurants and hotels are to be found in the city, but at some distance, together with a post office, telephones, car hire and taxis. Trains run to many destinations including Madrid, and buses to La Línea, from which it is a short walk to the international airport at Gibraltar.

77. Gibraltar

Waypoints

⊕199 – 36°06′.5N 5°22′.7W (Gibraltar Bay, SE)

⊕200 –36°08′N 5°22′.3W (South Gap, for
    Queensway Quay)

⊕201 – 36°08′.98N 5°22′.35W (North Mole, for
    Marina Bay)

Bearings and distance

⊕192 (Barbate) – ⊕200 (via ⊕194, ⊕195 & ⊕197) =
    35.7M, 130°, 107°, 063° & 022° or 202°, 243°,
    287°&310°

⊕192 (Barbate) – ⊕201 (via ⊕194, ⊕195 and ⊕197) =
    36.6M, 130°, 107°, 063°&017° or 197°, 243°,
    287°&310°

⊕195 (Tarifa) – ⊕200 (via ⊕197) = 15.2M, 063°&022°
    or 202°&243°

⊕195 (Tarifa) – ⊕201 (via ⊕197) = 16.1M, 063°&017°
    or 197°&243°

⊕198 (Algeciras) – ⊕200 = 2.7M, 068° or 248°

⊕198 (Algeciras) – ⊕201 = 3.2M, 051° or 231°

⊕199 – ⊕200 = 1.5M, 012° or 198°

⊕199 – ⊕201 = 2.5M, 007° or 187°

Tides

Standard port Gibraltar
Heights in metres

MHWS	MHWN	MLWN	MLWS
1.0	0.7	0.3	0.1

Or refer to EasyTide at www.ukho.gov.uk (see page 2)

Charts

Charts	Approach	Harbour
Admiralty	91, 773, 142, 3578, 1448	144, 45
Imray	C19, C50, M1	C19, C50
Spanish	44C, 45A, 105, 445, 445A	4452

Principal lights

Approach

2420 **Punta Carnero** Fl(4)WR.20s41m16/13M
    018°-W-325°-R-018° (Red sector covers La Perla
    and Las Bajas shoals) Siren Mo 'K'(–.–)30s Yellow tower,
    green base, silver lantern 19m

2456 **Gibraltar Aeromarine** Aero Mo GB(––./–...)R.10s405m30M
    Obscd on westerly bearings within 2M

2438 **Europa Point, Gibraltar** Iso.10s49m19M
    197°-vis-042°, 067°-vis-125°
    Oc.R.10s15M and F.R.15M 042°-vis-067°
    (Red sector covers La Perla and Las Bajas shoals) Horn 20s
    White tower, red band 19m

Harbour

2442 **South mole, north end (A Head)** Fl.2s17m15M Horn 10s
    White tower 15m

2445 **Detached mole, south end (B Head)** Q.R.8m5M Metal
    structure on concrete building 11m

2450.7 **Cormorant Camber, south end** 2F.R(vert) 4m, 1m apart

2451.5 **Coaling Island, north mole** 2F.G(vert)

2446 **Detached mole, north end (C Head)** Q.G.10m5M
    Metal structure on concrete building 11m

2448 **North mole, southwest arm (D Head)** Q.R.18m5M
    Tower 17m

2449.2 **North mole, northwest elbow (E Head)**
    F.R.28m5M Tower

Airport runway, SW corner VQ.9M (Occas)

Airport runway, NW corner VQ.9M (Occas)

Airport runway, south spur F.R.9M

2436.8 **La Linea, breakwater** Fl(2)G.7s7m4M White
    tower, green bands 4m

2437.2 **La Linea, north mole** Q.R.6m2M White tower,
    red bands 5m

Plus other lights in the interior of the harbour and to
the north.

Night entry

Not a problem in normal conditions, but best left until
daylight in strong west or northwesterlies.

Weather bulletins and navigational warnings

Gibraltar Broadcasting Corporation

*Weather bulletins in English for waters within 5 miles
of Gibraltar:* 91.3, 92.6, 100.5MHz and 1458kHz at
0530, 0630, 0730, 1030, 1230 UT Mon–Fri; 0530, 0630,
0730, 1030 UT Sat; 0630, 0730, 1030 UT Sun

British Forces Broadcasting Service, Gibraltar

*Storm and gale warnings in English for the Gibraltar
area:* 93.5, 89.4, 97.8, 99.5MHz on receipt

*Weather bulletins and tidal information in English for
waters within 5 miles of Gibraltar:* 93.5, 97.8MHz at
0745, 0845, 1005, 1605 LT weekdays; 0845, 0945, 1202
LT Sat; 0845, 0945, 1202, 1602 LT Sun

*Weather bulletins and tidal information in English for
waters within 5 miles of Gibraltar:* 89.4, 99.5MHz at
1200 LT weekdays

Harbour communications

Port Authority ☎ 72514/78134/77004 *Fax* 77011
VHF Ch 06, 12, 13, 14, 16 (all vessels, including yachts,
should listen on VHF Ch 12 while in the area)

Queen's Harbour Master ☎ 350 55901 *Fax* 55981
VHF Ch 08 (0800–1630 Mon–Thu, 0800–1600 Fri)

Marina Bay ☎ 73300 *Fax* 42656
Email pieroffice@marinabay.gi
www.marinabay.gi
VHF Ch 71 (0830–2130 summer, 0830–2030 winter)

Queensway Quay Marina ☎ 44700 *Fax* 44699
Email qqmarina@gibnet.gi
www.taywood.gi
VHF Ch 71 (0830–2145 summer, 0830–2015 winter)

Sheppard's ☎ 75148/77183, *Fax* 42535.
Email admin@sheppard.gi
www.sheppard.gi

The 'gateway to the Mediterranean', with excellent facilities for yachts and considerable interest ashore

Gibraltar is a safe and convenient stopping point for
yachts entering or leaving the Mediterranean, as well
as being a duty-free port. All facilities are available
for repairs and general maintenance, and both
general and ship's stores of every kind can be
obtained in Gibraltar or by air from England (for
some items it may be cheaper, if more effort, to
arrange for delivery from England marked 'For
Yacht – in Transit' and therefore duty free, rather

than to buy off the shelf once there). Both the pound
sterling and the Gibraltar pound (at parity) are legal
tender.

Long popular with English-speaking yachtsmen,
the marinas are busy and it is almost essential to
book ahead. They are, currently, Queensway Quay,
approached via the south entrance and closest to the
town, and Marina Bay, close south of the airport
runway, which is convenient for crew changes but
can be noisy. In 2007 the new Ocean Village Marina
is expected to come onstream, but it now seems as
though Sheppard's marina is unlikely to re-open.

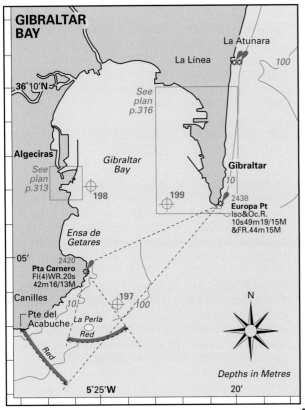

See plan p.316

See plan p.313

⊕197	36°03′.7N	05°24′.4W	(Punta Carnero)
⊕198	36°06′.95N	05°25′.43W	(Algeciras entrance)
⊕199	36°06′.5N	05°22′.7W	(Gibraltar Bay, SE)

Unless in a tearing hurry, a tour of the Rock itself must be *de rigeur*, and the museum – with displays of Gibraltar in prehistoric, Phoenician and Roman times – is also recommended. Crossing the border into Spain also is quick and easy on foot, though a passport should be carried, but another matter entirely by car. It is normal to queue in either direction, but while the wait to come in seldom exceeds ten minutes it is not unusual to queue for an hour or more to leave – considerably longer during the rush hour. A phone call to 42777 will give the current outward waiting time. If telephoning from Spain, or by mobile phone in either country, include the Spanish access code of 956-7.

Approach

By day the massive Rock is visible for many miles, though if approaching from the west it opens fully only after rounding Punta Carnero into Gibraltar Bay. Almost without exception the coastline is steep to, but beware of squalls and sudden windshifts in the bay, particularly during a *levanter*. The coast is fringed with wrecks from all eras, many popular as dive sites – any vessel flying International Code Flag 'A' (white with a blue swallowtail) should be given generous clearance. Yachts must also give way to naval and commercial vessels at all times.

By night, Gibraltar advertises its presence by flashing its red GB to the heavens and by a lesser light at Europa Point. The precipitous east face is largely dark; the west, where the town and harbours lie, is like a Christmas tree. This can be confusing even in good visibility and make lights difficult to identify – apart from those mentioned above, the most conspicuous are likely to be those on the south mole's A Head and north mole's D Head.

If approaching in poor visibility beware the amount of traffic in the vicinity. From ⊕199 in the southeast part of the Bay a course of 012° for 1.5M leads to ⊕200, for approach to Queensway Quay, or 007° for 2.5M to ⊕201, for approach to Marina Bay.

Formalities

For many years it was necessary for all yachts to clear customs and immigration at the Waterport Wharf opposite Marina Bay, but this requirement was dropped early in 2006 and now all formalities are handled at the marinas. Particulars of vessel and

⊕199	36°06′.5N	5°22′.7W	1.2M W of Europa Point, Gibraltar
⊕200	36°08′N	5°22′.3W	Gibraltar South Gap, for Queensway Quay
⊕201	36°08′.98N	5°22′.35W	North Mole, for Marina Bay

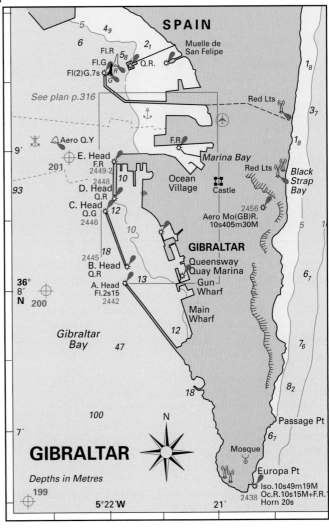

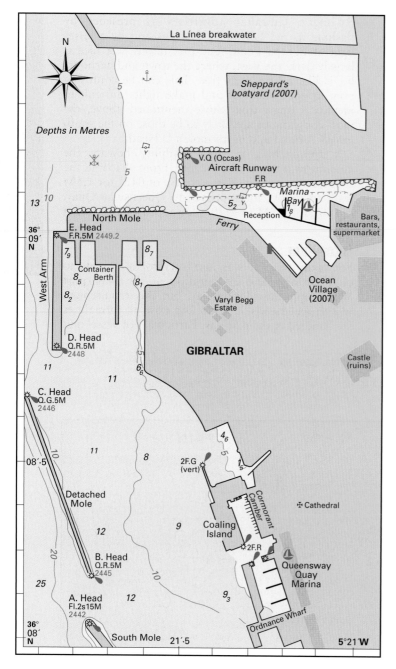

Entrance and berthing

By late 2007 three marinas should be operating in Gibraltar – Marina Bay, Ocean Village and Queensway Quay. Sheppard's Marina is not expected to reopen but their their boatyard and excellent chandlery continue to function – see under Facilities for details.

1. Marina Bay

☎ 73300 *Fax* 42656 VHF Ch 71
Email: pieroffice@marinabay.gi
www.marinabay.gi

Marina Bay is the largest of the marinas with about 200 berths able to take vessels of up to 70m or 4.5m draught, and is approached by rounding the North Mole's E Head. At night a row of red lights at the end of the airport runway mark the north side of the channel. Note that yachts MAY NOT MOVE IN THE VICINITY while the runway lights are flashing. There is also a height restriction of 23m. Arrivals berth alongside the office, towards the outer end of the main pier, having first called at Waterport (see above) for inward clearance. Hours are 0830–2200 daily in summer, 0830–2030 in winter. Berthing is Mediterranean-style – bow or stern-to with a buoy and lazy-line provided to the pontoon.

In 2005 the high season (1 May–31 October) rate for a visiting yacht of up to 12m was £11.50 per night, rising to £18.00 for 12–15m. In the low season this dropped to £7.00 and £10.00 respectively, with discounts available for stays of a month or more. Electricity and water were charged in addition. Payment could be made by credit card, though better discounts were available to those who used cash. Multihulls paid a 50% surcharge.

2. Ocean Village (due to open 2007)

Ocean Village Marina is currently under construction on the site of the old Sheppard's. It is said that it will contain berths for 140 yachts of between 10m and 30m (other sources mention berthing for 'super-yachts'), but how many berths will be sold along with the surrounding houses and apartments is not known. All the usual facilities and amenities are promised.

crew will be required, bearing in mind that Gibraltar is not part of the EU and therefore visa requirements are different to those of Spain and Portugal. It will speed the process up if a crew list giving names, nationalities, passport numbers etc is prepared before arrival.

Anchorage

Anchoring is permitted (and free) in the gap between the airport runway and the La Linea breakwater, northwest of Windsock Island – see plan. Holding is good in 4–5m over sand. As this area is British territory it is first necessary to clear customs and immigration, which may create a problem now that these are handled only by the marinas.

Looking down onto the pontoons of Marina Bay from the northwest. Sheppard's Marina, at upper right, has closed since this photograph was taken

La Línea   Site of new Sheppard's boatyard   Marina Bay   Fuel,   Ocean Village Marina (2007)

Looking due east towards Gibraltar airport runway in September 2004. A number of changes have taken place since that time

Gibraltar harbour looking southeast, with the West Arm at left and the Detached and South Moles on the right. Major changes have been made at Queensway Quay marina since this photograph was taken

3. Queensway Quay Marina

☎: 44700 *Fax* 44699 VHF Ch 71
Email qqmarina@gibnet.gi www.taywood.gi
Queensway Quay Marina has the advantage over the northern marinas of greater distance from the dust and noise of the airport, and being barely five minutes from the town centre.

It opened in March 1994 with some 120 berths, including several for yachts of up to 35m. The interior layout was redesigned in the late 1990s in an attempt to overcome problems of surge and swell in westerly winds, reducing numbers to around 100 but making space for a few mega-yachts of up to 90m. However this was only partially successful, and over the winter of 2005/6 the marina entrance was moved from west to north with a new 'island' created between marina and harbour. At the same time the marina was dredged to 4m throughout. When work is complete the marina will contain around 150 berths, some of which will be allocated to the owners of the houses to be built on the 'island'. Surprisingly, the marina does not have a website on which one can monitor progress.

The marina is approached through the main harbour via either of the two passes, continuing towards the gap between Coaling Island and the new 'island' which forms the west side of Queensway Quay (soon to be colonised by sizeable houses). On passing through this gap the entrance lies to starboard. The buildings overlooking the marina are floodlit.

Berth at the reception pontoon on the east side of the new entrance on first arrival. The marina office is to be relocated to overlook the area but in the meantime is situated near the root of the north mole. Hours are 0830–2200 daily in summer, 0830–2100 in winter. Berthing is Mediterranean-style, with the bow or stern-to with a buoy and a lazy-line provided to the pontoon.

In 2005 the high season (1 May–31 October) rate for a visiting yacht of up to 12m was £8.42 per night, rising to £12.05 for 12–15m. In the low season this dropped to £7.21 and £8.42 respectively, with discounts available for stays of a month or more. Electricity and water were charged in addition. Payment could be made by credit card, though better discounts were available to those who used cash. Multihulls paid a 50% surcharge.

The anchorages north of the runway and off La Línea, photographed in September 2004. Infilling has since taken place on the left – the site of Sheppard's new boatyard. In the foreground is the border crossing

The new entrance layout at Queensway Quay Marina, introduced to overcome problems with surge. Houses and apartments are to be built on the new 'island' to the west

A family of Barbary Apes at home on the Rock   *AH*

Adjacent anchorage

The long, hooked breakwater at Spanish La Línea (literally 'the line' – an allusion to its military role during the various sieges of the Rock) north of Gibraltar encloses a large area of water where it is possible to anchor. Holding is good over sand and shingle in 3–4m – it is essential to avoid anchoring in the fairway, dredged to a nominal 6.5m. There has long been talk of a marina being built in the southeast corner of the harbour – in addition to the 'Puerto Chico' smallcraft pontoons to the northeast – but no start had been made by 2006 although the road layout for the adjoining shopping and leisure centre was in place. Unless dredged, much of the facility will lie inside the 2m line. There is good shopping, including a large supermarket and excellent produce market in the town of La Línea, but note that it is necessary to show one's passport to cross into Gibraltar, even on foot.

Facilities

It has been said that if you can't buy it or get it fixed in Gibraltar, you probably can't buy it or get it fixed anywhere. Though perhaps a slight exaggeration there is much truth in the remark and the following list cannot claim to be comprehensive.

Boatyard During 2006 the Sheppard's workshops, ☎ 76895, *Fax* 71780, *Email* yachtrep@gibnet.gi, were in temporary accommodation on Coaling Island (see plan), due to move to new premises north of the runway late in 2007. Services include painting, osmosis treatment and GRP repairs, plus those listed individually below. While the new premises will provide berthing for yachts under repair they will not comprise a marina.

Travel-lift Pending completion of their new facility north of the runway, Sheppard's can haul vessels of up to 30 tonnes at the North Mole and up to 10m or 6.5 tonnes at Coaling Island. Book through the workshop office, above. Once established in their new premises they will again be able to lift up to 40 tonnes.(Ceuta has installed a 250–tonne travel hoist and opened a yard near the marina. Contact yard ☎ 511985 or *Mobile* 629 675605. See Imray/RCCPF *North Africa* for pilotage details.

Engineers Sheppard's can handle light engineering, welding, engine servicing and repairs to most makes, and are Volvo Penta agents. Also Marine Maintenance Ltd ☎ 78954 *Fax* 74754 *Email* fred@gibnet.gi (Perkins and Yanmar) at Marina Bay, and Medmarine Ltd ☎ 48888 *Fax* 48889, (Yamaha) at Queensway Quay.
   Tempco Marine Engineering ☎ 74657 *Fax* 76217, specialise in refrigeration etc.

Electronic & radio repairs Sheppard's workshops (as above) or ElectroMed ☎ 77077 *Fax* 72051 *Email* mail@electro-med.com www.eletro-med.com, at Queensway Quay, who can supply and repair equipment from most major manufacturers.

Sailmaker/sail repairs J & F Sailmakers, ☎ 41469 in South Pavilion Road, who also handle general canvaswork and upholstery. Alternatively Magnusson Sails ☎ 952 791241 *Fax* 952 791241, about 35 miles away in Estepona, who may be willing to deliver/collect. Canvaswork and sprayhood (but not true sailmaking) is also undertaken by MF Balloqui & Sons ☎ 78105 *Fax* 42510, at 39/41 City Mill Lane.
   Rigging Sheppard's workshops, as above.

Liferaft servicing GV Undery & Son ☎ 73107/40402 *Fax* 46489 *Email* compass@gibtelecom.net (who are also compass adjusters).

Chandleries Though there are small chandleries at both Marina Bay and Queensway Quay marinas, these pale into insignificance beside Sheppard's, which is to remain in its current position opposite Marina Bay and adjacent to the new Ocean Village development. A full list of items available will be found online at www.sheppards.gi – sufficient to say here that they stock makes and items from Avon to Zodiac and adhesives to ventilators. Should an item not be in stock it can be ordered from the UK elsewhere (delivery takes between 3 days and 3 weeks on a speed = cost basis). Open 0900–1300 and 1430–1800 weekdays, 1000–1300 Saturday.

Charts Fully corrected Admiralty charts and other publications from Gibraltar Chart Agency Ltd ☎ 76293 *Fax* 77293 *Email* gibchartag@gibtelecom.net at 11A Block 5, Watergardens. Open 0900–1800 weekdays. Yacht Scene Publications *Fax* 79385, are official agents for Spanish charts.

Water On the pontoons at all marinas.

Showers At all marinas. Queensway Quay has particularly good disabled facilities.

Launderettes At Marina Bay and Queensway Quay, the latter incorporating a dry cleaners. Others in the town.

Electricity On the pontoons at all marinas.

Fuel Diesel and petrol at the fuelling berth inshore of the customs berth (0800–1800 daily). It is not yet known what the fuelling situation will be at Queensway Quay following its redesign.

Bottled gas All bottled gas is imported from Spain by Rumagas ☎ 70296, and sold through outlets including the Shell office at the fuel berth and most filling stations. There is, however, an ongoing shortage of small cylinders. Those staying any length of time and able to accommodate larger bottles can buy the necessary adaptor at Sheppard's chandlery; short-stay visitors are advised to arrive with enough gas for their stay.

Yacht club The old-established Royal Gibraltar Yacht Club ☎ 78897, welcomes visiting yachtsmen.

Weather forecast Posted daily at all marinas. An online report is available at www.gibraltarweather.com.

Banks In the town.

Shops/provisioning Neither Marina Bay nor Queensway Quay have supermarkets on site, but in any case for serious storing–up most people descend on the vast Morrisons near the new Ocean Village site. Good general shopping in the town.

Duty-free stores are available via Albor Ltd ☎/*Fax* 73283, at Marina Bay – which doubles as a newsagent, bookshop and cybercafé – where one can order almost anything in almost any quantity for a yacht in transit.

Produce market Excellent produce market over the border at La Línea.

Cafés, restaurants & hotels Bars and restaurants overlooking both Marina Bay and Queensway Quay, with many more in the town. Hotel accommodation on the Rock tends to be both limited and (compared with Spain) expensive.

Medical services There is a casualty and general hospital at St Bernards (casualty ☎ 73941) able to deal with most medical and surgical conditions. There is a GP Centre in Casemate Square, and a private clinic and pharmacist at Marina Bay. UK residents are eligible for NHS treatment on the production of a passport.

Communications

Post office On Main Street.

Mailing address Both Marina Bay and Queensway Quay will hold mail for visiting yachts – c/o Marina Bay Complex Ltd, Marina Bay, PO Box 80, Gibraltar; and c/o Queensway Quay Marina, PO Box 19, Ragged Staff Wharf, Gibraltar. The envelope must carry the name of the yacht in addition to that of the addressee.

Public telephones Convenient to all three marinas, and in the town.

Internet access Both Marina Bay and Queensway Quay offer wireless broadband (Wi-Fi). Alternatively there are many cybercafés on the Rock, including one at Albor Ltd overlooking Marina Bay and another on Queensway Road, between Marina Bay and Queensway Quay.

Fax service At both marina offices: Marina Bay – *Fax* 42656; Queensway Quay – *Fax* 44699.

Car hire/taxis No shortage of taxis and rental cars (which may be taken into Spain).

Buses Buses to the frontier for onward connections.

Ferries Weekly ferry to Tanger.

Air services Frequent air services to several UK destinations – but no flights to Spain.

Appendix

I. Charts

Charts and other publications may be updated annually by reference to the Admiralty *List of Lights and Fog Signals Volume D (NP 77)* or weekly via Admiralty or other *Notices to Mariners.*

British Admiralty charts and publications, are available from:

Imray Laurie Norie & Wilson Ltd
Wych House St Ives Huntingdon
Cambridgeshire PE27 5BT England
☎ 01480 462114 *Fax* 01480 496109
www.imray.com

Note Large-scale charts are only shown on index diagrams where the scale permits.

British Admiralty

Chart	Title	Scale
45	Gibraltar harbour	3,600
73	Puerto de Huelva and Approaches	25,000
83	Ports on the south coasts of Portugal and Spain	
	Porto de Portimão	20,000
	Approaches to Faro and Olhão	
85	Río Guadalquivir	40,000
	Puerto de Sevilla	15,000
	Barra del Río Guadalquivir	20,000
86	Bahia de Cádiz	25,000
87	Cabo Finisterre to the Strait of Gibraltar	1,000,000
88	Cádiz	12,500
89	Cabo de São Vicente to Río de Las Piedras	175,000
91	Cabo de São Vicente to the Strait of Gibraltar	350,000
93	Cabo de Santa María to Cabo Trafalgar	175,000
142	Strait of Gibraltar	100,000
	Tarifa	25,000
144	Gibraltar	10,000
773	Strait of Gibraltar to Isla de Alborán	300,000
1094	Rías de Ferrol, Ares, Betanzos and La Coruña	25,000
1110	La Coruña and Approaches	10,000
1111	Punta de la Estaca de Bares to Cabo Finisterre	200,000
1113	Harbours on the northwest coast of Spain	
	Ría de Camariñas	30,000
	Ría de Corme y Lage	40,000
1117	Puerto de Ferrol	10,000
1118	Ria de Ferrol	10,000
1448	Gibraltar Bay	30,000
1455	Algeciras	10,000
1730	Ría de Vigo	25,000
	Ensenada de San Simón	25,000
1731	Vigo	10,000
1732	Ría de Pontevedra	25,000
1733	Marin and Pontevedra	10,000
1734	Approaches de Ría de Arousa	25,000
1755	Plans in Ría de Arousa	
	Santa Uxia de Arousa	7,500

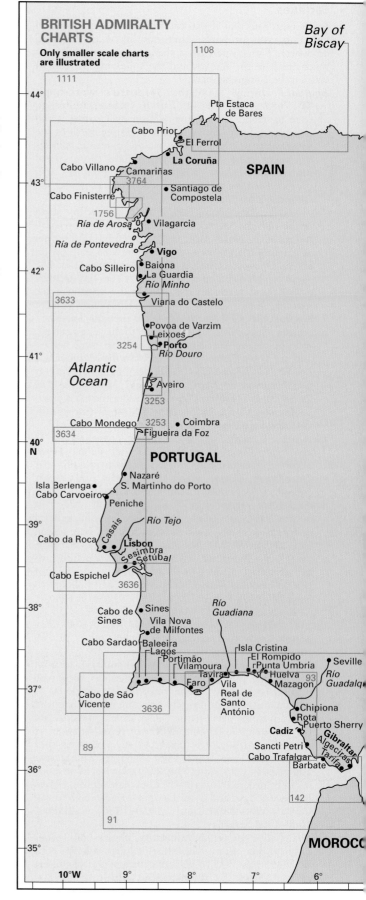

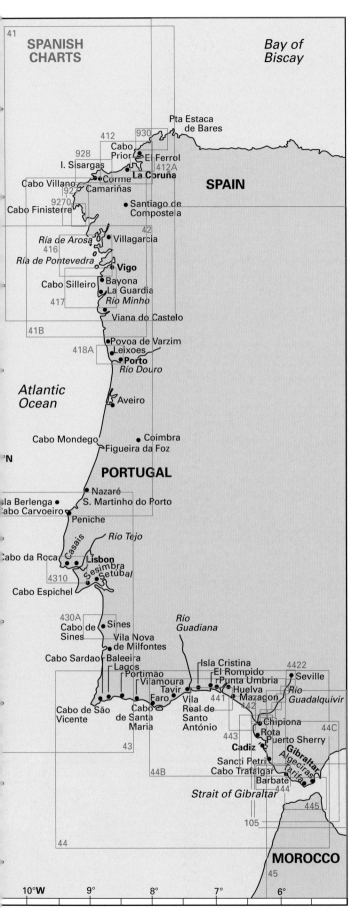

	A Pobra do Caramiñal	75,000
	Vilanova de Arousa and	
	San Xulian de Arousa	10,000
	Cambados and San Martin de O Grove	10,000
1756	Ría de Muros	40,000
1762	Vilagarcia de Arousa	7,500
1764	Ría de Arousa	25,000
3220	Entrance to Rio Tejo including	
	Baia de Cascais	15,000
3221	Lisboa, Paco de Arcos to Terreiro do Trigo	15,000
3222	Lisboa, Alcântara to Canal do Montijo	15,000
	Alfeite	7,500
	Azinheira	7,500
	Montijo	15,000
3224	Approaches to Sines	30,000
	Sines	12,500
3227	Aveiro and Approaches	30,000
	Port of Aveiro	12,500
	Continuation to Aveiro	12,500
3228	Approaches to Figueira da Foz	30,000
	Figueira da Foz	7,500
3257	Viana do Castelo and Approaches	30,000
	Viana do Castelo	7,500
3258	Approaches to Leixóes and	
	Barra do Rio Douro	30,000
	Porto de Leixões and Barra do Río Douro	10,000
3259	Approaches to Setubul	15,000
3260	Setubul, Carraca to Ilha do Cavalo	15,000
3578	Eastern Approaches to the Strait	
	of Gibraltar	150,000
3633	Islas Sisargas to Montedor	200,000
3634	Montedor to Cabo Mondego	200,000
3635	Cabo Mondego to Cabo Espichel	200,000
3636	Cabo Espichel to Cabo de São	
	Vicente	200,000
3764	Cabo Toriñana to Punta Carreiro	40,000

Spanish Hydrographic Institute

Chart	Title	Scale
41	De Cabo de la Estaca de Bares a	
	Río Lima	350,000
41A	De Puerto de San Ciprián a Cabo	
	Finisterre	200,000
41B	De las islas Sisargas a la desembocadura del rio	
	Miño	175,000
42	Del rio Miño a Lisboa	350,000
43	De Cabo Carvoeiro a Cabo de San	
	Vicente	350,000
44	De Cabo de San Vicente al Estrecho	
	de Gibraltar	350,000
44B	De Cabo de Santa María a Cabo	
	Trafalgar	175,000
44C	Estrecho de Gibraltar	175,000
45	Estrecho de Gibraltar y Mar de Alborán	350,000
105	Estrecho de Gibraltar. De Cabo Roche	
	a punta de la Chullera y de Cabo Espartel	
	a Cabo Negro	100,000
412A	Rías de El Ferrol, Ares, Betanzos y	
	La Coruña	25,000
415B	Aproches de la Ría de Arosa y	
	Corrubedo	25,000
	Isla Sálvora	25,000
415C	Ría de Arosa	25,000
416	De la Peninsula del Grove a Cabo	
	Silleiro	60,000
416A	Ría de Pontevedra	25,000
416B	Ría de Vigo	25,000
417	De Islas Cies a Río Miño	60,000
	Plano inserto Puerto de la Guardia	5,000

APPENDIX

418	Aproches de puerto Leixoes	30,000
430A	Aproches del puerto de Sines	30,000
441	Del Ria de Las Piedras al arroyo del Loro	50,000
441A	Río de las Piedras	25,000
442	Del arroyo del Loro al puerto de Rota	50,000
443	De Chipiona a Cabo Roche	50,000
443A	Aproches del Puerto de Cádiz – Zona Norte	25,0004
43B	Aproches del Puerto de Cádiz – Zona Sur	25,000
444	De Cabo Roche a punta Camarinal	50,000
445	Estrecho de Gibraltar. De punta Camariñal a punta Europa y de Cabo Espartel a punta Almina	60,000
445A	Bahía de Algeciras	25,000
445B	Bajo de los Cabezos e Isla de Tarifa	25,000
453	De punta Europa a la Torre de las Bóvedas	50,000
927	De Cabo Villano a Monte Louro	50,000
928	De las Islas Sisargas a Cabo Villano	50,000
	Plano inserto Fondeadero de las Islas Sisargas	15,000
4122	Acceso a la Ría de El Ferrol	10,000
4123	Puerto de El Ferrol	10,000
4125	Rías de Ares y Betanzos	10,000
4126	Ría y Puerto de La Coruña	10,000
4152	Vilanova de Arousa y San Xultan de Arousa	10,000
	Santa Uxia de Ribeira	7,500
	A Podora do Caramiñal	7,500
	Cambados y San Martin de O Grove	10,000
4153	Puerto de Villagarcía de Arosa y Villajuan	7,500
4162	Puerto de Marín	5,000
4165	Ría de Vigo (Hoja I)	7,500
4167	Puertos de Panjón y Bayona	10,000
4219	Puerto de Aveiro	10,000
4310	Desembocadura del Río Tejo y Puerto de Lisboa	40,000
4311	Barra y puerto de Huelva	25,000
4421	Broa de Sanlúcar de Barrameda y fondeadero de Bonanza	12,500
4422	Río Guadalquivir. De la Broa de Sanlúcar a Sevilla	
	Hoja I – Indice gráfico del Río Guadalquivir	200,00
	Hoja II – Broa de Sanlúcar y fondeadero de Bonanza	25,000
	Hoja III – Barra del Río Guadalquivir (Fifteen further sheets, Hojas IV to XVIII, cover the Río Guadalquivir as far as Puerto de Sevilla)	12,500
		12,500
4430	Puerto de Cádiz	12,500
4433	Puerto de la Base Naval de Rota	5,000
4437	Arsenal de La Carraca y accesos al mismo	5,000
4438	Barra de Sancti-Petri	5,000
4441	Puerto de Barbate	10,000
4450	Puerto de Tarifa	7,500
4451	Bahía de Algeciras { Zona Oeste	10,000
4452	Bahía de Algeciras { Zona Este	10,000
	Bahía y Puerto de Tánger	4,360
4461	Puertos de Tánger, El Aaraich y Asilah	15,000
	Bahía y Puerto de Tanger	15,000
	Puerto do Asilah	10,000
	Barra y puerto de El Aaraich	10,000
9270	De Cabo de la Nave a Monte Louro	30,000

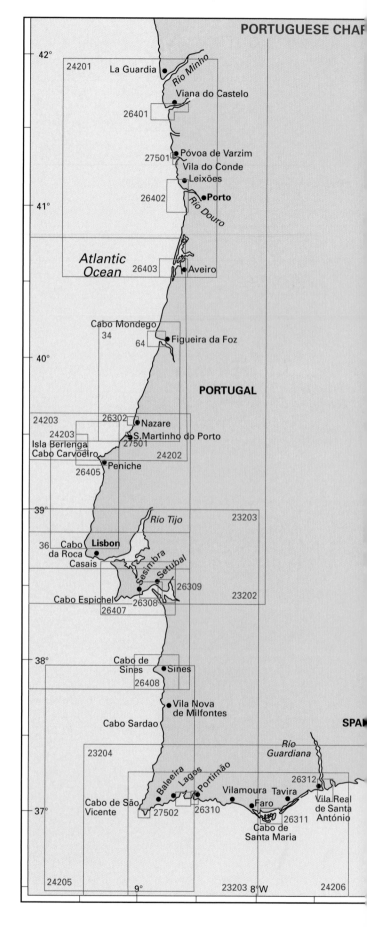

Portuguese Hydrographic Institute

(Brackets imply that the chart is anticipated but not yet published)

34	Cabo Mondego à Nazaré	75,000
	Plano São Martinho do Porto	10,000
36	Cabo Carvoeiro ao Caso da Roca	75,000
	Plano Ericeira	10,000
51	Barra e Porto de Caminha	10,000
64	Barra e Porto da Figueira da Foz	10,000
(90)	Enseada de Albufeira	10,000
(23201)	Vigo a Leixões	200,000
23202	Cabo Silleiro ao Cabo Carvoeiro	350,000
23203	Lisboa a Cabo de São Vicente	300,000
23204	Cabo de São Vicente ao Estreito de Gibraltar	350,000
24201	Carminha a Aveiro	150,000
24202	Aveiro a Peniche	150,000
24203	Nazaré a Lisboa	150,000
	Plano Ilha Berlenga	30,000
24204	Cabo da Roca ao Cabo de Sines	150,000
24205	Cabo de Sines a Lagos	150,000
24206	Cabo de São Vicente à Foz do Guadiana	150,000
(26301)	Barra e Porto de Caminha	10,000
26302	Porto da Nazaré	7,500
	Plano Porto da Nazaré	3,000
26303	Barras do Porto de Lisboa e Baia de Cascais	15,000
26304	Porto de Lisboa (de Paço de Arcos ao Terreiro do Trigo)	15,000
26305	Porto de Lisboa (de Alcântra à Cala do Montijo	15,000
	Plano do Alfiete	7,500
	Plano da Azinheira	7,500
	Plano Montijo	15,000
26306	Porto de Lisboa (do Cais do Sodré a Sacavém)	15,000
26307	Rio Tejo (de Sacavém a Vila Franca de Xira)	15,000
26308	Barra e Porto de Setúbal	15,000
26309	Porto de Setúbal (da Carraca à Ilha do Cavalo)	15,000
26310	Barra e Porto de Portimão	7,500
26311	Barra e Portos de Faro e Olhão	15,000
26312	Barra e Portos de Vila Real de Santo António e Ayamonte	15,000
26401	Aproximações a Viana do Castelo;	30,000
	Plano Barra e Porto de Viana do Castelo	7,500
26402	Aproximações a Leixões; Porto de Leixões e Barra do Rio Douro	30,000
	Plano Porto de Leixões e Barra do Rio Douro	10,000
26403	Aproximações a Aveiro	30,000
	Plano Barra e Porto de Aveiro	12,500
(26404)	Figueira da Foz	30,000
26405	Peniche e Ilhas Berlengas	50,000
	Plano do Porto de Peniche	10,000
	Plano de Farilhões	25,000
	Plano das Berlenga	25,000
(26406)	Cascais a Vila Franca de Xira Barras do Porto de Lisboa	50,000
26407	Sesimbra	40,000
	Plano Porto de Sesimbra	7,500
26408	Aproximações ao Porto de Sines	30,000
	Plano do Porto de Sines	10,000
(27501)	Portos da Costa Oeste	
	Barra e Porto de Esposende	7,500
	Porto de Póvoa de Varzim	7,500
	Porto de Vila do Conde	7,500
	Baia de São Martinho do Porto	10,000
	Porto de Ericeira	7,500
	Barra de Vila Nova de Milfontes	7,500
27502	Portos de Enseadas (Costa Sul – Zona Oeste)	15,000
	Plano das Enseadas de Belixe, Sagres e Baleeira	15,000
	Plano da Ponta da Piedade à Praia do Vau	15,000
(27503)	Portos da Costa Sul	10,000
	Enseada de Albufeira	10,000
	Vilamoura	10,000
	Barra de Tavira	15,000
	Barra de Fuzeta	15,000

Imray charts

Chart	Title	Scale
C18	**Western Approaches to the English Channel and Biscay** WGS 84	1:1,000,000
C19	**Portuguese Coast Passage Chart Cabo Finisterre to Gibraltar** WGS 84	758,800
	Plans Bayona, Viana do Castelo, Figueira da Foz, Approaches to Lisbon, Lagos, Bahía de Cádiz, Strait of Gibraltar, Gibraltar	
C48	**La Coruña to Porto** WGS 84	1:350,000
	Plans Ría de Vivero, Ria de Cedeira, Rías de Ares and Betanzos, La Coruña, Ría de Camariñas, Riía de Muros, Ría de Arosa Ría de Vigo, Viana do Castelo, Rías de Corme and Lage, Ría de Pontevedra, Póvoa de Varzim, Leixões	
C49	**Ría de Aveiro to Sines** WGS 84	1:350,000
	Plans Figuera da Foz, Nazaré, Cascais, Lisboa, Sines, Porto de Peniche, Setúbal, Rio Sado, Sesimbra	
C50	**Sines to Gibraltar** WGS 84	1:350,000
	Plans Sines, Portimão, Vilamoura, Vila Real de St António, Lagos, Isla Christina, Mazagón, Chipiona, Puerto Sherry, Sancti-Petri, Barbate, Tarifa, Rota, Bahía de Cadiz, Gibraltar, Strait of Gibraltar	
M10	**Western Mediterranean – Gibraltar to the Ionian Sea** WGS 84 WGS 84	1:2,750,000
M11	**Mediterranean Spain – Gibraltar to Cabo de Gata & Morocco** WGS 84	1:440,000
	Plans Strait of Gibraltar, Gibraltar, Ceuta, Almeria, Estepona, Puerto de Almerimar	

II. Waypoints

Waypoints are listed by part sections. Users are reminded that they are offered as an aid to navigation. Whilst every effort has been made to ensure their accuracy none has been proved at sea, no assumption may be made that direct passage is possible between any two (unless the text specifically states that it may) and all should be used in conjunction with visual or other observation.

Positions

Although a few official charts of this area have yet to be converted from Datum ED50, skippers should note that all positions in this book are to WGS84. All were derived using C-Map electronic charts and Admiralty charts. Harbour positions have been verified using a handheld GPS. Waypoints have not been verified at sea. They have been included to help with planning and orientation. Much of this coast demands visual pilotage and skippers must satisfy themselves that it is safe to sail directly between any two waypoints.

Part I Galicia

⊕	Lat N	Long W	Description
1	44°00′	08°00′	14M N Cabo Ortegal
2	43°43′	08°28′	10M NW Cabo Prior
3	43°31′	08°25′.5	4.2M W Cabo Prioriño
4	43°24′.8	08°28′.5	Outer App West La Coruña
5	43°26′	08°22′	App El Ferrol
6	43°24′	08°16′	App for Ares and Marina Sada
7	43°23′.2	08°22′.1	Ría de la Coruña
8	43°21′.9	08°22′.2	off breakwater La Coruña
9	43°25′	08°42′	3M N Bajos de Baldaya
10	43°19′.3	08°48′	Malpica
11	43°25′	08°52′	3.5M N Islas Sisargas
12	43°18′	09 00′.05	1.5M NW Pta del Roncudo
13	43°15′	09 00′.05	Río de Corme
14	43°15′	08°59′.0	S Bajo de la Averia
15	43°15′.55	08°57′.75	Corme
16	43°13′.4	08°59′.7	Laxe
17			Not allocated
18	42 33′.9	08°50′.75	App. Vilanova
19	43°14′	09°17′	5M NW Cabo Villano
20	43°09′.6	09°14′.4	Outer NW App. Camariñas
21	43°08′.6	09°13′	NE Las Quebrantes
22	43°07′.2	09°13′	App. Camariñas
23	43°07′	09°14′.2	Outer W App. Camariñas
24	43°06′.9	09°11′.2	0.75M SW Camariñas
25	43°07′.4	09°10′.6	Camariñas
26	43°06′.5	09°12′.4	App. Muxia
27	43°05′	09°24′.4	5M WNW Cabo Toriñana
28	42°52′.8	09°24′	5.5M W Cabo Finisterre
29	42°51′	09°16′	1.7M S Cabo Finisterre
30	42°54′.5	09°15′	Finisterre
31	42°53′.8	09°12′.4	Seno de Corcubin
32	42°53′.7	09°10′.9	0.6M S Carrumeiro Chico
33	42°54′.5	09°10′.1	0.5M E Carrumeiro Chico
34	42°56′.5	09°11′	Corcubión
35	42°43′.5	09°19′	9M WSW Pta Insua
36	42°47′.2	09°11′.0	0.8M SW Las Minarzos
37	42°44′.5	09°07′.7	1.8M S Pta Insua
38	42°43′.0	09°05′	Entrance Ría de Muros
39	42°45′.3	09°01′.5	Centre Ría de Muros
40	42°46′.75	09°03′.1	Muros
41	42°46′.7	08°57′	0.25M SE Pta Cambrona
42	42°47′.5	08°56′.58	App Freixo
43	42°47′.6	08°54′.6	App Noia channel
44	42°46′	08°57′	Portosin
45	42°43′.9	09°00′.2	Puerto del Son
46	42°34′.5	09°12′.4	5M W Cabo Corrubedo
47	42°30′	09°10′	9M WSW Cabo Corrubedo
48	42°33′.6	09°04′.4	0.6M S Corrubedo
49	42°27′.3	09°01′.03	0.7M SW Isla Salvora
50	42°30′.95	09°03′.85	0.6M WNW Islas Sagres
51	42°30′.55	09°01′.40	0.7M WSW Aguino
52	42°30′.4	08°59′.5	0.3M E Piedras Del Sagro
53	42°28′.9	09°03′	App Canal del Norte
54	42°29′.9	09°01′.4	W App Passo Salvora
55	42°28′.85	08°59′.5	E App Passo Salvora
56	42°27′.5	08°58′.5	Canal Principal Arosa
57	42°30′	08°58′	1.5M NW Roca Pombeiriño
58	42°33′.3	08°58′.4	0.7M SE Sta Uxia de Riveira
59	42°33′.7	08°59′	App. Sta Uxia de Riveira
60	42°32′.8	08°55′.7	0.5M ESE Isla Rua
61	42°35′	08°54′	1.0M WNW Pta Barbafeita
62	42°36′.7	08°54′	0.5M W Puerto Cruz
63	42°35′.5	08°50′.9	3M WSW Vilagarcia
64	42°38′	08°49′.5	Rianxo
65	42°36′.2	08°46′.6	Vilagarcia
66	42°31′.2	08°53′	1.7M NW O Grove
67	42°30′.5	08°52′	0.7M NNW O Grove
68	42°30′.9	08°50′.0	Ensenada de Cambados
69	42°26′	08°55′.3	0.9M S Pta Miranda
70	42°27′	08°54′.35	App. São Vicente
71	42°23′	09°07′	7M SW Isla Salvora
72	42°24′.5	08°53′.47	Canal de la Fagilda
73	42°17′	09°00′	Outer App. Ría de Pontevedra
74	42°20′.2	08°53′	Entrance Ría de Pontevedra
75	42°23′.4	08°48′.6	Porto Novo/Sanxenxo
76	42°24′.1	08°42′.6	App. Marin
77	42°25′.5	08°42′	App. Combarro
78	42°22′.8	08°44′.0	Aguete
79	43°20′.2	08°47′.2	Bueu/Beluso
80	42°15′.65	08°53′.3	N Canal Del Norte
81	42°14′.45	08°52′.65	S Canal Del Norte
82	42°13′.4	08°53′.8	Islas Cies
83	42°13′.2	08°49′	Ría de Vigo
84	42°14′.55	08°44′.75	Abeam Vigo
85	42°15′.5	08°46′.7	Cangas
86	42°15′.65	08°42′.55	Abeam Punta Lagoa
87	42°17′.3	08°39′.7	Vigo high bridge (de rande)
88	42°10′	08°52′.7	Canal Del Sur
89	42°08′.5	08°58	Outer App Canal Del Sur
90	42°08′.7	08°54′	1M W Islotes Las Serralleiras
91	42°07′.95	08°53′	0.8M SSW Islotes Las Serralleiras
92	42°08′	08°51′	0.3M WNW Punta del Buey
93	42°07′.6	08°50′.3	App. Baiona
94	42°07′.5	08°54′.8	1M NW Cabo Silleiro
95	42°06′.5	8°56′.6	2M W of Cabo Silleiro
96	41°45′.5	8°55′.1	1.6M WNW La Guardia
97	41°54′	8°53′	La Guardia
98	42°22′	8°50′	Ría de Pontevedra
99	42°22′	8°47′	S Morrazán

Part II Portugal – The West Coast

⊕	Lat N	Long W	Description
100	38°45′	10°05′	27.7M W of Cabo da Roca
101	41°51′.3	8°54′.9	Foz do Minho approach
102	41°51′.04	8°52′.48	Foz do Minho entrance
103	41°39′.2	8°52′.5	Viana do Castelo approach
104	41°40′.34	8°50′.43	Viana do Castelo entrance
105	41°21′.2	8°48′.7	Póvoa de Varzim approach
106	41°22′.15	8°46′.14	Póvoa de Varzim entrance
107	41°19′.7	8°47′.5	Vila do Conde approach
108	41°20′.1	8°44′.88	Vila do Conde entrance
109	41°09′.2	8°44′.7	Leixões approach
110	41°10′.2	8°42′.35	Leixões entrance
111	41°08′.4	8°43′	Porto & the Rio Douro approach
112	41°08′.7	8°40′.8	Porto & the Rio Douro entrance
113	40°37′.6	8°48′.5	Ria de Aveiro approach
114	40°38′.41	8°46′.11	Ria de Aveiro entrance
115	40°11′.4	8°56′.5	1.7M W of Cabo Mondego
116	40°08′.4	8°55′.2	Figueira da Foz approach
117	40°08′.67	8°52′.62	Figueira da Foz entrance
118	39°35′.7	9°07′.2	Nazaré approach
119	39°35′.48	9°04′.74	Nazaré entrance
120	39°32′}6	9°10′}5	São Martinho do Porto approach
121	39°30′}76	9°08′}9	São Martinho do Porto entrance

⊕	Lat N	Long W	Description
122	39°22′.2	9°26′	1.3M WNW of Cabo Carvoeiro
123	39°19′.4	9°24′.2	Peniche approach
124	39°20′.82	9°22′.4	Peniche, entrance
125	39°21′.95	9°22′	Peniche de Cima anchorage
126	39°24′.8	9°30′.1	Ilha da Berlenga anchorage
127	38°57′.72	9°25′.4	Ericeira anchorage
128	38°46′.8	9°32′	1.7M W of Cabo da Roca
129	38°42′.3	9°30′.3	1M WSW of Cabo Raso
130	38°37′.2	9°23′.5	Rio Tejo Fairway Buoy No.2
131	38°40′	9°25′.3	Cascais approach
132	38°41′.65	9°24′.75	Cascais entrance
133	38°40′.05	9°18′.9	Rio Tejo entrance
134	38°40′.6	9°18′.76	Oeiras entrance
135	38°24′.3	9°14′.5	1.2M SW of Cabo Espichel
136	38°24′.4	9°05′.7	Sesimbra approach
137	38°26′.3	9°06′.2	Sesimbra entrance
138	38°28′.6	8°58′.7	Portinho de Arrábida anchorage
139	38°24′.3	9°01′.1	Setúbal & the Rio Sado approach
140	38°26′.62	8°58′.72	Setúbal & the Rio Sado leading line
141	38°29′.22	8°55′.9	Setúbal & the Rio Sado entrance
142	37°54′.8	8°54′.8	Sines approach
143	37°55′.98	8°52′.74	Sines entrance
144	37°42′.2	8°50′.5	Vila Nova de Milfontes approach
145	37°42′.7	8°48′.2	Vila Nova de Milfontes entrance
146	37°17′.5	8°52′.3	Arrifana anchorage
147	37°01′	9°00′.7	1M SW of Cabo de São Vicente

Part III The Algarve and Andalucía

⊕	Lat N	Long W	Description
148	37°01′.5	8°59′	Enseada de Belixe anchorage
149	36°58′.8	8°56′.9	0.9M S of Ponta de Sagres
150	37°00′.05	8°56′.55	Enseada de Sagres anchorage
151	36°59′	8°53′.8	Baleeira approach
152	37°00′.71	8°55′.15	Baleeira entrance
153	37°03′.8	8°39′.2	1.1M SE of Ponta da Piedade/Lagos approach
154	37°05′.86	8°39′.68	Lagos entrance
155	37°04.9	8°36′.9	Alvor approach
156	37°06′.87	8°37′.06	Alvor entrance
157	37°04′.4	8°31′.9	Portimão approach
158	37°06′.37	8°31′.7	Portimão entrance
159	37°03′.03	8°14′.5	Albufeira approach
160	37°04′.82	8°15′.24	Albufeira entrance
161	37°02′	8°07′.8	Vilamoura approach
162	37°04′	8°07′.35	Vilamoura entrance
163	36°55′.6	7°51′.9	2.2M S of Cabo de Santa María
164	36°57′.55	7°52′.25	Cabo de Santa María, Faro & Olhão entrance
165	37°04′.6	7°35′.4	Tavira approach
166	37°06′.38	7°36′.63	Tavira entrance
167	37°06′.2	7°24′.2	Río Guadiana approach
168	37°08′.15	7°23′.83	Río Guadiana entrance
169	37°08′.6	7°18′.6	Islas Canela & Cristina approach
170	37°10′.45	7°18′.93	Islas Canela & Cristina entrance

⊕	Lat N	Long W	Description
171	37°09′.2	7°03′.3	El Rompido approach
172	37°11′.32	7°02′.73	El Rompido entrance
173	37°06′.7	6°57′.7	Punta Umbría approach
174	37°08′.71	6°56′.91	Punta Umbría entrance
175	37°03′.3	6°49′.7	Mazagón approach
176	37°05′.25	6°49′	Mazagón entrance
177	36°46′	6°28′	Chipiona & the Río Guadalquivir approach
178	36°45′.2	6°26′.2	Chipiona entrance
179	36°44′	6°30′.3	3.1M W of Punta del Perro
180	36°35′.7	6°24′.2	Bajo El Quemado
181	36°35′.1	6°21′.8	Rota approach
182	36°36′.78	6°20′.76	Rota entrance
183	36°33′.8	6°20′.3	Puerto Sherry, El Puerto de Santa Maria & Cádiz approach
184	36°34′.2	6°15′.3	Puerto Sherry & El Puerto de Santa Maria entrance
185	36°33′.57	6°18′.42	Cádiz entrance
186	36°31′.3	6°20′.7	Castillo de San Sebastián W cardinal buoy
187	36°21′.9	6°15′.7	Sancti-Petri approach
188	36°22′.3	6°13.16	Sancti-Petri entrance
189	36°15′.9	6°09′.2	Puerto de Conil approach
190	36°17′.5	6°08′	Puerto de Conil entrance
191	36°08′.3	6°05′.6	3.7M SW of Cabo Trafalgar
192	36°08′.7	5°57′.6	Barbate approach
193	36°10′.56	5°55′.8	Barbate entrance
194	36°01′.7	5°47′.4	2M S of Punta de Gracia/Punta Camarinal
195	35°58′.9	5°36′	Tarifa approach
196	36°00′.24	5°36′.14	Tarifa entrance
197	36°03′.7	5°24′.4	1.3M SE of Punta Carnero
198	36°06′.95	5°25′.43	Algeciras entrance
199	36°06′.5	5°22′.7	1.2M W of Europa Point, Gibraltar
200	36°08′	5°22′.3	Gibraltar South Gap, for Queensway Quay
201	36°08′.98	5°22′.35	North Mole, for Marina Bay

III. Facilities

The pamphlet *Galicia sailing facilities/installations nautiques*, provides a comprehensive list of the facilities available in all harbours and marinas in Galicia. It is available free in most major marinas or may be downloaded from www.turgalicia.es. In addition it includes maps, photographs contact telephone numbers and details of each region and local tourist highlights.

IV. Useful addresses

Spanish embassies and consulates
London (Embassy) 39 Chesham Place,
London SW1X 8SB
☎ 020 7235 5555 *Fax* 020 7259 6392
Email embespuk@mail.mae.es
London (Consulate) 20 Draycott Place,
London SW3 2RZ
☎ 020 7589 8989 *Fax* 020 7581 7888
Email conspalon@mail.mae.es
Manchester Suite 1a Brook House, 70 Spring Gardens,
Manchester M2 2BQ ☎ 0161 236 1262/33
Edinburgh 63 North Castle Street, Edinburgh EH2 3LJ
☎ 0131 220 1843 *Fax* 0131 226 4568

Washington DC 2375 Pennsylvania Ave DC 20037
☎ (202) 452 0100 *Fax* (202) 833 5670
New York 150 E 58th Street, New York, NY 10155
☎ 212 355 4080 *Fax* 212 644 3751

Portuguese embassies and consulates
London 11 Belgrave Square, London SW1X 8PP
☎ 020 7494 1441 *Fax* 0207 245 1287
Email london@portembassy.co.uk
www.portembassy.gla.ac.uk
Washington DC 2310 Tracy Place NW,
Washington DC 20008
☎ 202 332 3007
www.portugalemb.org

British and American embassies and consulates
In Spain
UK – *Madrid* Calle Fernando el Santo 16, 28010
Madrid. ☎ (34) 91 700 8200 or 319 0200
Fax (34) 91 700 8210
UK – *Seville* Plaza Nueva 87, 41001 Seville
☎ 954 228875
US – *Madrid* Calle Serrano 75, 28006 Ma-drid
☎ (34) 91 587 2200, *Fax* (34) 91 5872303
US – *Seville* Paseo de las Delicias 7, Seville
☎ 954 231883
In Portugal
UK – *Lisbon* Rua de São Bernado 33, 1249–082 Lisbon
☎ 213 924000
Email PPA.lisbon@fco.gov.uk
www.uk-embassy.pt
UK – *Porto* Travessa Barão de Forrester 10, 4400–034
Vila Nova de Gaia, Porto. ☎ 226 184789
Email britcon.oporto@sapo.pt
UK – *Portimão* Largo Francisco A Mauricio 7-1°, 8500
Portimão. ☎ 282 490750
Email britcon.portimao@mail.telepac.pt
US – *Lisbon* Avenida das Forças Armadas, 1600–081
Lisbon. ☎ 217 273300, *Fax* 217 269109

Spanish national tourist offices
London 22-23 Manchester Square, London W1M 5AP
☎ 0207 486 8077 *Fax* 0207 486 8034
www.tourspain.co.uk
New York 666 Fifth Avenue, New York, NY 10103
☎ 212 265 8822 *Fax* 212 265 8864

Portuguese national tourist offices
London 22–25A Sackville Street, London W1X 2LY
☎ 020 7494 5723 / 1441 *Fax* 020 7494 1868
brochure line 0845 355 1212
Email iceplond@aol.com
www.portugal.org
New York 590 Fifth Avenue, 4th Floor, New York
NY 10036–4704
☎ 212 354 4403 *Fax* 212 764 6137
Email tourism@portugal.org
www.portugal.org

V. Regulations, Tax and VAT

(The information below should not be considered definitive. Skippers of non VAT paid boats and those planning to stay for more than 183 days in a years are strongly advised to verify the regulations which will be applicable to them.)

Personal documentation
Spain – Currently EU nationals – including UK citizens – may visit for up to 90 days, for which a national identity card or passport is required but no visa. American, Canadian and New Zealand citizens may also stay for up to 90 days without a visa, though Australians need one for more than 30 days. EU citizens wishing to remain in Spain may apply for a *permiso de residencia* once in the country; non-EU nationals can apply for a single 90-day extension, or otherwise obtain a long-term visa from a Spanish embassy or consulate before leaving home. The website www.graysworld.co.uk/spanish-property/resident-tourist provides advice on this matter.

Certificate of competence
1. Given below is a transcription of a statement made by the Counsellor for Transport at the Spanish Embassy, London in March 1996. It is directed towards citizens of the UK but doubtless the principles apply to other EU citizens. One implication is that in a particular circumstance (paragraph 2a below) a UK citizen does not need a Certificate of Competence during the first 90 days of his visit.
2. a. British citizens visiting Spain in charge of a UK registered pleasure boat flying the UK flag need only fulfil UK law.
   b. British citizens visiting Spain in charge of a Spanish registered pleasure boat flying the Spanish flag have one of two options:
   i. To obtain a Certificate of Competence issued by the Spanish authorities. See *Normas reguladore para la obtención de titulos para el gobierno de embarcaciones de recreo* issued by the Ministerio de Obras Publicas, Transportes y Medio Ambiente.
   ii. To have the Spanish equivalent of a UK certificate issued. The following equivalencies are used by the Spanish Maritime Administration:
   Yachtmaster Ocean *Capitan de Yate*
   Yachtmaster Offshore *Patron de Yate de altura*
   Coastal Skipper *Patron de Yate*
   Day Skipper *Patron de Yate embarcaciones de recreo*
   Helmsman Overseas* *Patron de embarcaciones de recreo restringido a motor*

*The Spanish authorities have been informed that this certificate has been replaced by the International Certificate of Competence.

3. The catch to para 2(a) above is that, in common with other EU citizens, after 90 days a UK citizen is technically no longer a visitor, must apply for a permiso de residencia and must equip his boat to Spanish rules and licensing requirements.
   In practice the requirement to apply for a *permiso de residencia* does not appear to be enforced in the case of cruising yachtsmen who live aboard rather than ashore and are frequently on the move. By the same token, the requirement for a British skipper in charge of a UK registered pleasure boat flying the UK flag to carry a Certificate of Competence after their first 90 days in Spanish waters also appears to be waived. Many yachtsmen have reported cruising Spanish waters for extended periods with no documentation beyond that normally carried in the UK.
4. The RYA suggests the following technique to obtain an equivalent Spanish certificate:
   a. Obtain two photocopies of your passport
   b. Have them notarised by a Spanish notary
   c. Obtain a copy of the UK Certificate of Competence and send it to the Consular Department, The Foreign and Commonwealth Office, Clive House,

Petty France, London SW1H 9DH, with a request that it be stamped with the Hague Stamp (this apparently validates the document). The FCO will probably charge a fee so it would be best to call the office first ☎ 020 7270 3000.

d. Have the stamped copy notarized by a UK notary.
e. Send the lot to the Spanish Merchant Marine for the issue of the Spanish equivalent.

It may be both quicker and easier to take the Spanish examination.

Tax

Although the tax rules appear not to be applied evenly across Spain the following is offered as general advice to help individuals consider whether to seek more formal advice regarding their particular situation. The Spanish operate a self assessment system and can reclaim tax back for five years. Three types of taxes may apply specifically to yacht owners:

Tarifa G-5 This is broadly a port tax levied to help maintain the port. Its application appears to vary from harbour to harbour and province to province. It is likely to form part of a marina fee for short stays. If staying for long periods or over-wintering it would be wise to ensure that a contract with the marina is inclusive of all taxes,

Wealth tax This is a national tax but may be applied differently from region to region. A person staying in Spain for less than 6 months is not liable to wealth tax. However, if the 183 day limit is exceeded the rules of residency may apply and trigger a demand for the tax. It is the individual's time in Spain which is relevant, not the location of the boat.

Other taxes If staying beyond 183 days the full Spanish Legislation and tax rules apply – and could include such matters as income tax, property tax, local town tax.

Portugal Currently EU nationals need only a national identity card or passport to enter Portugal and can then stay indefinitely. American and Canadian citizens can remain for up to 60 days without a visa, Australians and New Zealanders for up to 90 days. Extensions are issued by the Sevico de Estrangeiros which has a branch in most major towns, or failing that by the local police. At least one week's notice is required.

VAT and temporary import

A boat registered in the EU and on which VAT has been paid in an EU country, or which was launched before 1 January 1985 and is therefore exempt on the grounds of age (and has the documents to prove it), can stay indefinitely in any other EU country without further VAT liability.

The time limit for which relief from customs duty and VAT is available to non-EU registered yachts visiting the EU is 18 months. The period for which a yacht must remain outside the EU before starting another 18 month period is not specified. Those affected are recommended to check current regulations which may be found on HM Customs and Excise website www.hmce.gov.uk Search under the words 'Pleasure craft'.

Spain A VAT paid (exempt) yacht may normally remain in the country almost indefinitely provided a '*Permiso Aduanero*' is first obtained, but may not be used commercially (i.e. for chartering).

Portugal There is no limitation on length of stay for a VAT paid or exempt yacht. An annual tax is levied on all yachts kept for long periods (over 183 days) in Portuguese waters irrespective of their VAT status, see pages 118 and 204.

Gibraltar As Gibraltar is not a part of the EU, VAT does not apply.

VI. Marina charges – Galicia

Berthing charges in Galicia tend to be by m² (max length x max beam x sqm rate) or by LOA. This appendix can give no more than a snap shot of the charges reported in 2005; marina contact details are given in the pilot if yachtsmen wish to check current rates before arrival.

Sailors may wish to be aware that seven of the marinas have formed *Group PdG* (*Puertos Deportivos de Galicia*) which offers, for €5, a *Pasaporte*; this entitles holders to discounted rates.

Participating Marinas are: PD Viveiro, Sada, La Coruña, Vilagarcia, Sanxenxo, Punta Lagoa, PD Baiona. Further details are available through www.marinasdegalicia.com

	(Low season/High season)
Rías Altas	
Puerto Deportivo Viveiro	€0.35/0.42
Ares	10-12m €28
Marina Sada	€0.22/0.43
Darseno Deportivo Coruña	€0.32/0.50
Camariñas	10–12m €15
Ría de Muros	
Club Nautico Portisin	10-12m €23.6, 12–14m €27.3
Ría de Arosa	
Riviera	10-12m €23, 12-14m €26.
Pobra do Caramiñal	10m €14.2, 12m €19.39, 14m €24.13
Marina Vilagarcia	€0.36/0.50
São Vicente	€0.13.33/23.77
Ría de Pontevedra	
Nauta Sanxenxo	€0.26/0.38
Ría de Vigo	
Punta Lagoa	€0.50/1.00
Puerto Deportivo Baiona	€0.453/0.453
MRCY	10–12m €24.7

VII. Portugal and Andalucía on the Net

Portugal

www.algarvenet.com – covers all of southern Portugal (though slightly dated in places) with pages for the Algarve Resident and Região Sul newspapers (the latter with English translation).

www.ana-aeroportos.pt – ANA Aeroportos de Portugal SA runs Portugal's three mainland airports. Daily arrival / departure times, and much more.

www.cp.pt – website of Comboios de Portugal (the national railway system), in Portuguese and English. Routes, timetables, fares and online booking in an impressively user-friendly layout.

www.flytap.com – website of the national airline, TAP Portugal. In most major languages with schedules, fares and online booking. Fast and user-friendly.

www.hidrografico.pt – website of the Portuguese Hydrographic Institute, with full chart catalogue. In Portuguese only, but easy enough to follow. No online sales, but links to two Lisbon chart agents

www.portugal.org – website of ICEP (Investment, Trade & Tourism Portugal) but a long way from the dry-as-dust site which might be expected. Vast amounts of useful information in several languages including English plus dozens (possibly hundreds) of relevant links. A great place to start.

www.portugal-info.net – a well-organised site carrying information on and/or links to pretty well every town of any size in the entire country. Useful maps, current weather conditions, telephone numbers etc. English language only.

www.portugalvirtual.pt – another general site worth investigating. A little more commercially-orientated than some, but if you want a plan of the Lisbon metro or opening times for the Palácio Nacional de Ajuda, it's all here. In Portuguese and English.

www.the-news.net – online edition of The Portugal News, an English-language national daily paper.

www.travel-images.com – thousands of downloadable pictures of the entire world, including Portugal and Spain, but with little accompanying text. Check the Utilities section for some quirky lists.

www.visitportugal.com – Portugal's official tourism website, in six languages including English. Well constructed and illustrated, and updated regularly with details of forthcoming events. Several short video clips. Recommended.

www.well.com/user/ideamen/portugal.html – subtitled 'a Collection of Home Pages about Portugal', a description which it would be hard to better – whatever your interest you'll find something here. Follow the 'Portuguese Gastronomy' link to www.geocities.com/TheTropics/4338/ana.html (or go there direct) for nearly 100 Portuguese recipes in both languages.

Andalucia

www.andalucia.com – commercial (and some might say superficial) site mainly slanted towards the Mediterranean part of the province.

www.andalucia.org – official website of the Andalucían Tourist Office, covering all the usual aspects plus (via the Sports Activities button) an unusually full and accurate list of the province's marinas and yacht harbours. In good English, with a useful search facility.

www.andalucia2.com – a very busy site with lots of facts, figures and useful phone numbers, but lacking any great appeal.

www.armada.mde.es/ihm – website of the Spanish Hydrographic Institute, with full chart catalogue as well as Avisos a los Navegants (Notices to Mariners). In Spanish only, but relatively easy to follow.

www.eppa.es – website of the Empresa Pública de Puertos de Andalucía which runs the majority of marinas in Andalucía. Other, non-EPPA marinas are also included. In Spanish and English, though not all pages are fully translated.

www.iberia.com – the Iberia website, in numerous languages (the United Kingdom is Reino Unido) and with all the usual bells and whistles.

www.idealspain.com – perhaps the most appealing of the Andalucían tourist sites, with maps and well-illustrated notes about many places of interest. Includes an image library and message board. English only.

www.renfe.es – fast but slightly forbidding site of RENFE, the Spanish rail network, in four languages including English.

VIII. Glossary

A more complete glossary is given in the *Yachtsman's Ten Language Dictionary* compiled by Barbara Webb and Michael Manton with the Cruising Association (Adlard Coles Nautical). Terms related to meteorology and sea state follow at the end of each section.

General and chartwork terms

English	Spanish	Portuguese
anchor, to	fondear	fundear
anchorage	fondeadero, ancladero	fundeadouro, ancoradouro
basin, dock	dársena	doca
bay	bahía, ensenada	baía, enseada
beach	playa	praia
beacon	baliza	baliza
beam	manga	largura, boca
berth	atracar	atracar
black	negro	preto
blue	azul	azul
boatbuilder	astillero	estaleiro
bottled gas	cilindro de gas, carga de gas	cilindro de gás, bilha de gás
breakwater	rompeolas, muelle	quebra-mar, molhe
buoy	boya	bóia
bus	autobús	autocarro
cape	cabo	cabo
car hire	aquilar coche	alugar automóvel
chandlery (shop)	efectos navales, apetrachamento	fornecedor de barcos, aprestos
channel	canal	canal
charts	cartas náuticas	cartas hidrográficas
church	iglesia	igreja
crane	grua	guindaste
creek	estero	esteiro
Customs	Aduana	Alfândega
deep	profundo	profundo
depth	sonda, profundidad	profundidade
diesel	gasoil	gasoleo
draught	calado	calado
dredged	dragado	dragado
dyke, pier	dique	dique
east	este	este
eastern	levante, oriental	levante, do este
electricity	electricidad	electricidade
engineer, mechanic	ingeniero, mecánico	engenheiro, técnico
entrance	boca, entrada	bôca, entrada
factory	fábrica	fábrica
foul, dirty	sucio	sujo
gravel	cascajo	burgau
green	verde	verde
harbourmaster	diretor do porto	capitán de puerto
height, clearance	altura	altura
high tide	pleamar, marea alta	preia-mar, maré alta
high	alto/a	alto/a
ice	hielo	gelo
inlet, cove	ensenada	enseada
island	isla	ilha, ilhéu
islet, skerry	islote	ilhota
isthmus	istmo	istmo
jetty, pier	malecón	quebra-mar

English	Spanish	Portuguese
knots	nudos	nós
lake	lago	lago
laundry,	lavandería,	lavanderia,
launderette	automática	automática
leading line, transit	enfilación	enfiamento
leeward	sotavento	sotavento
length overall	eslora total	comprimento
lighthouse	faro	farol
lock	esclusa	esclusa
low tide	bajamar,	baixa-mar,
	marea baja	maré baixa
mailing address	dirección de	endereço para
	correo	correio
marina,	puerto deportivo,	porto desportivo,
yacht harbour	dársena de yates	doca de recreio
medical services	servicios	serviços médicas
	médiocos	
mud	fango	lôdo
mussel rafts	viveros	viveiros
narrows	estrecho	estreito
north	norte	norte
orange	anaranjado	alaranjado
owner	propietario	propietário
paraffin	parafina	petróleo para
		iluminãçao
petrol	gasolina	gasolina
pier, quay, dock	muelle	molhe
point	punta	ponta
pontoon	pantalán	pontão
port (side)	babor	bombordo
Port of Registry	Puerto de	Porto de Registo
	Matrícula	
port office	capitanía	capitania
post office	oficina de correos	agência do
		correio
quay	muelle	molhe, cais
ramp	rampa	rampa
range (tidal)	repunte	amplitude
red	rojo	vermelho
reef	arrecife	recife
reef, spit	restinga	restinga
registration number	matricula	número registo
repairs	reparacións	reparações
rock, stone	roca, piedra	laxe, pedra
root (eg. of mole)	raíz	raiz
sailing boat	barca de vela	barco à vela
sailmaker,	velero,	veleiro,
sail repairs	reparacións velas	reparações velas
saltpans	salinas	salinas
sand	arena	areia
sea	mar	mar
seal, to	precintar	fechar
shoal, low	bajo	baixo
shops	tiendas, almacéns	lojas
shore, edge	orilla	margem
showers (washing)	duchas	duches
slab, flat rock	laja	laje
slack water,	repunte	águas paradas
tidal stand		
slipway	varadero	rampa
small	pequeño	pequeno
south	sur	sul
southern	meridional	do sul
starboard	estribor	estibordo
strait	estrecho	estreito
supermarket	supermercado	supermercado
tower	torre	tôrre
travel-lift	grua giratoria,	e pórtico, pórtico

English	Spanish	Portuguese
	pórtico elevador	elevador, içar
water (drinking)	agua potable	água potável
weather forecast	previsión/boletin	previsão de
	metereológico	tempo, boletim
		meteorológico
weed	alga	alga
weight	peso	pêso
west	oeste	oeste
western	occidental	do oeste
white	blanco	branco
windward	barlovento	barlavento
works (building)	obras	obras
yacht (sailing)	barca de vela	barco à vela
yacht club	club náutico	clube náutico,
		clube naval
yellow	amarillo	amarelo

Meteorology and sea state

English	Spanish	Portuguese
calm	calma	calma
(force 0, 0–1 kts)		
light airs	ventolina	aragem
(force 1, 1–3 kts)		
light breeze	flojito	vento fraco, brisa
(force 2, 4–6 kts)		
gentle breeze	flojo	vento bonançoso,
(force 3, 7–10 kts)		brisa suave
moderate breeze	bonancible	vento moderado,
(force 4, 11–16 kts)		brisa moderado
fresh breeze	fresquito	vento fresco,
(force 5, 17–21 kts)		brisa fresca
strong breeze	fresco	vento muito
(force 6, 22–27 kts)		fresco,
		brisa forte
near gale	frescachón	vento forte,
(force 7, 28–33 kts)	ventania moderada	
gale	duro	vento muito
(force 8, 34–40 kts)		forte,
		ventania fresca
severe gale	muy duro	vento
(force 9, 41–47 kts)		tempestuoso,
		ventania forte
storm	temporal	temporal,
(force 10, 48–55 kts)		ventania total
violent storm	borrasca,	temporal
(force 11, 56–63 kts)	tempestad	desfieto,
		tempestade
hurricane	huracán	furacão, ciclone
(force 12, 64+ kts)		
breakers	rompientes	arrebentação
cloudy	nubloso	nublado
depression (low)	depresión	depressão
fog	niebla	nevoeiro
gust	racha	rajada
hail	granizada	saraiva
mist	neblina	neblina
overfalls, tide race	escarceos	bailadeiras
rain	lluvia	chuva
ridge (high)	dorsal	crista
rough sea	mar gruesa	mar bravo
short, steep sea	mar corta	mar cavado
shower	aguacero	aguaceiro
slight sea	marejadilla	mar chão
squall	turbonada	borrasca
swell	mar de leva	ondulação
thunderstorm	tempestad	trovoada

General and chartwork terms

Spanish	English	Portuguese
Aduana	Customs	Alfândega
agua potable	water (drinking)	água potável
alga	weed	alga
almacéns	shops	lojas
alto/a	high	alto/a
altura	height, clearance	altura
amarillo	yellow	amarelo
anaranjado	orange	alaranjado
ancladero	anchorage	fundeadouro, ancoradouro
apetrachamento	chandlery (shop)	fornecedore de barcos, aprestos
aquilar coche	car hire	alugar automóvel
arena	sand	areia
arrecife	reef	recife
astillero	boatbuilder	estaleiro
atracar	berth	atracar
autobús	bus	autocarro
azul	blue	azul
babor	port (side)	bombordo
bahía	bay	baía, enseada
bajamar	low tide	baixa-mar, maré baixa
bajo	shoal, low	baixo
baliza	beacon	baliza
barca de vela	sailing boat, yacht	barco à vela
barlovento	windward	barlavento
blanco	white	branco
boca	entrance	bôca, entrada
boya	buoy	bóia
cabo	cape	cabo
calado	draught	calado
canal	channel	canal
capitanía	port office	capitania
carga de gas	bottled gas	cilindro de gás, bilha de gás
cartas náuticas hidrográficas	charts	cartas
cascajo	gravel	burgau
cilindro de gas	bottled gas	cilindro de gás, bilha de gás
club náutico	yacht club	clube náutico, clube naval
dársena de yates	marina, yacht harbour	porto desportivo, doca de recreio
dársena	basin, dock	doca
dique	dyke, pier	dique
direcçión de correo	mailing address	endereço para correio
diretor do porto	harbourmaster	capitán de puerto
dragado	dredged	dragado
duchas	showers (washing)	duches
efectos navales	chandlery (shop)	fornecedore de barcos, aprestos
electricidad	electricity	electricidade
enfilación	leading line, transit	enfiamento
ensenada	bay, inlet, cove	baía, enseada
entrada	entrance	bôca, entrada
esclusa	lock	esclusa
eslora total	length overall	comprimento
este	east	este
estero	creek	esteiro
estrecho	narrows, strait	estreito
estribor	starboard	estibordo
fábrica	factory	fábrica
fango	mud	lôdo
faro	lighthouse	farol
fondeadero	anchorage	fundeadouro, ancoradouro
fondear	anchor, to	fundear
gasoil	diesel	gasoleo
gasolina	petrol	gasolina
grua giratoria	travel-lift	e pórtico, pórtico elevador, içar
grua	crane	guindaste
hielo	ice	gelo
iglesia	church	igreja
ingeniero, mechanic	engineer, técnico	engenheiro, mecánico
isla	island	ilha, ilhéu
islote	islet, skerry	ilhota
istmo	isthmus	istmo
lago	lake	lago
laja	slab, flat rock	laje
lavandería, l. automática	laundry, launderette	lavanderia, l.automática
levante	eastern	levante, do este
malecón	jetty, pier	quebra-mar
manga	beam	largura, boca
mar	sea	mar
marea alta	high tide	preia-mar, maré alta
marea baja	low tide	baixa-mar, maré baixa
matricula	registration number	número registo
meridional	southern	do sul
muelle	breakwater, pier, quay, dock	quebra-mar, cais
molhe,		
negro	black	preto
norte	north	norte
nudos	knots	nós
obras	works (building)	obras
occidental	western	do oeste
oeste	west	oeste
oficina de correos	post office	agência do correio
oriental	eastern	levante, do este
orilla	shore, edge	margem
pantalán	pontoon	pontão
parafina	paraffin	petróleo para iluminãçao
pequeño	small	pequeno
peso	weight	pêso
piedra	rock, stone	pedra
playa	beach	praia
pleamar	high tide	preia-mar, maré alta
pórtico elevador	travel-lift	e pórtico, pórtico elevador, içar
precintar	seal, to	fechar
previsión/boletin metereológico	weather forecast	previsão de tempo, boletim meteorológico
profundidad	depth	profundidade
profundo	deep	profundo
propietario	owner	propietário
Puerto de Matrícula	Port of Registry	Porto de Registo
puerto deportivo	marina, yacht harbour	porto desportivo, doca de recreio

Spanish	English	Portuguese
punta	point	ponta
raíz	root (eg. of mole)	raiz
rampa	ramp	rampa
reparacións	repairs	reparações
repunte	tidal range, stand, slack water	águas paradas, amplitude
restinga	reef, spit	restinga
roca	rock	laxe
rojo	red	vermelho
rompeolas	breakwater	quebra-mar, molhe
salinas	saltpans	salinas
servicios médicos	medical services	serviços médicas
sonda	depth	profundidade
sotavento	leeward	sotavento
sucio	foul, dirty	sujo
supermercado	supermarket	supermercado
sur	south	sul
tiendas	shops	lojas
torre	tower	tôrre
varadero	slipway	rampa
velero, reparacións velas	sailmaker, sail repairs	veleiro, reparações velas
verde	green	verde
viveros	mussel rafts	viveiros

Meteorology and sea state

Spanish	English	Portuguese
calma	calm (force 0, 0–1 kts)	calma
ventolina	light airs (force 1, 1–3 kts)	aragem
flojito	light breeze (force 2, 4–6 kts)	vento fraco, brisa
flojo	gentle breeze (force 3, 7–10 kts)	vento bonançoso, brisa suave
bonancible	moderate breeze (force 4, 11–16 kts)	vento moderado, brisa moderado
fresquito	fresh breeze (force 5, 17–21 kts)	vento frêsco, brisa fresca
frêsco	strong breeze (force 6, 22–27 kts)	vento muito fresco, brisa forte
frescachón	near gale (force 7, 28–33 kts)	vento forte, ventania moderada
duro	gale (force 8, 34–40 kts)	vento muito forte, ventania fresca
muy duro	severe gale (force 9, 41–47 kts)	vento tempestuoso, ventania forte
temporal	storm (force 10, 48–55 kts)	temporal, ventania total
borrasca, tempestad	violent storm (force 11, 56–63 kts)	temporal desfieto, tempestade
huracán	hurricane (force 12, 64+ kts)	furacão, ciclone
aguacero	shower	aguaceiro
depresión	depression (low)	depressão
dorsal	ridge (high)	crista
escarceos	overfalls, tiderace	bailadeiras
granizada	hail	saraiva
lluvia	rain	chuva
mar corta	short, steep sea	mar cavado
mar de leva	swell	ondulação
mar gruesa	rough sea	mar bravo
marejadilla	slight sea	mar chão
neblina	mist	neblina

Spanish	English	Portuguese
niebla	fog	nevoeiro
nubloso	cloudy	nublado
racha	gust	rajada
rompientes	breakers	arrebentação
tempestad	thunderstorm	trovoada
turbonada	squall	borrasca

General and chartwork terms

Portuguese	English	Spanish
agência do correio	post office	oficina de correos
água potável	water (drinking)	agua potable
águas paradas, amplitude	tidal range, stand, slack water	repunte, repute
alaranjado	orange	anaranjado
alfândega	customs	aduana
alga	weed	alga
alto/a	high	alto/a
altura	height, clearance	altura
alugar automóvel	car hire	aquilar coche
amarelo	yellow	amarillo
areia	sand	arena
atracar	berth	atracar
autocarro	bus	autobús
azul	blue	azul
baía, enseada	bay, inlet, cove	bahía, ensenada
baixa-mar, maré baixa	low tide	bajamar, marea baja
baixo	shoal, low	bajo
baliza	beacon	baliza
barco à vela	sailing boat, yacht	barca de vela
barlavento	windward	barlovento
bôca, entrada	entrance	boca, entrada
bóia	buoy	boya
bombordo	port (side)	babor
branco	white	blanco
burgau	gravel	cascajo
cabo	cape	cabo
calado	draught	calado
canal	channel	canal
capitán de puerto	harbourmaster	diretor do porto
capitania	port office	capitanía
cartas hidrográficas	charts	cartas náuticas
cilindro de gás, bilha de gás	bottled gas	carga de gas, cilindro de gas
clube náutico, clube naval	yacht club	club náutico
comprimento	length overall	eslora total
dique	dyke, pier	dique
do oeste	western	occidental
do sul	southern	meridional
doca	basin, dock	dársena
dragado	dredged	dragado
duches	showers (washing)	duchas
e pórtico, pórtico elevador, içar	travel-lift	grua giratoria, pórtico elevador
electricidade	electricity	electricidad
endereço para correio	mailing address	dirección de correio
enfiamento	leading line, transit	enfilación
engenheiro, técnico	engineer, mechanic	ingeniero, mecánico
esclusa	lock	esclusa
estaleiro	boatbuilder	astillero

APPENDIX

Portuguese	English	Spanish
este	east	este
esteiro	creek	estero
estibordo	starboard	estribor
estreito	narrows, strait	estrecho
fábrica	factory	fábrica
farol	lighthouse	faro
fechar	seal, to	precintar
fornecedore de barcos, aprestos	chandlery (shop)	apetrachamento, efectos navales
fundeadouro, ancoradouro	anchorage	fondeadero, ancladero
fundear	anchor, to	fondear
gasoleo	diesel	gasoil
gasolina	petrol	gasolina
gelo	ice	hielo
guindaste	crane	grua
igreja	church	iglesia
ilha, ilhéu	island	isla
ilhota	islet, skerry	islote
istmo	isthmus	istmo
lago	lake	lago
laje	slab, flat rock	laja
largura, boca	beam	manga
lavanderia, l. automática	laundry, launderette	lavandería, l. automática
laxe	rock	roca
levante, do este	eastern	levante, oriental
lôdo	mud	fango
lojas	shops	almacéns, tiendas
mar	sea	mar
margem	shore, edge	orilla
norte	north	norte
nós	knots	nudos
número registo	registration number	matricula
obras	works (building)	obras
oeste	west	oeste
pedra	rock, stone	piedra
pequeno	small	pequeño
pêso	weight	peso
petróleo para iluminãçao	paraffin	parafina
ponta	point	punta
pontáo	pontoon	pantalán
Porto de Registo	Port of Registry	Puerto de Matrícula
porto desportivo, doca de recreio	marina, yacht harbour	puerto deportivo, dársena de yates
praia	beach	playa
preia-mar, maré alta	high tide	pleamar, marea alta
preto	black	negro
previsão de tempo, boletim meteorológico	weather forecast	previsión/boletin metereológico
profundidade	depth	profundidad, sonda
profundo	deep	profundo
propietário	owner	propietario
quebra-mar	jetty, pier	malecón
quebra-mar, molhe, cais	breakwater, pier, quay, dock	muelle, rompeolas
raiz	root (eg. of mole)	raíz
rampa	ramp, slipway	rampa, varadero
recife	reef	arrecife
reparações	repairs	reparacións
restinga	reef, spit	restinga

Portuguese	English	Spanish
salinas	saltpans	salinas
serviços médicas	medical services	servicios médicos
sotavento	leeward	sotavento
sujo	foul, dirty	sucio
sul	south	sur
supermercado	supermarket	supermercado
tôrre	tower	torre
veleiro, reparações velas	sailmaker, sail repairs	velero, reparacións velas
verde	green	verde
vermelho	red	rojo
viveiros	mussel rafts	viveros

Meteorology and sea state

Portuguese	English	Spanish
calma	calm (force 0, 0–1 kts)	calma
aragem	light airs (force 1, 1–3 kts)	ventolina
vento fraco, brisa	light breeze (force 2, 4–6 kts)	flojito
vento bonançoso, brisa suave	gentle breeze (force 3, 7–10 kts)	flojo
vento moderado, brisa moderado	moderate breeze (force 4, 11–16 kts)	bonancible
vento fresco, brisa fresca	fresh breeze (force 5, 17–21 kts)	fresquito
vento muito fresco, brisa forte	strong breeze (force 6, 22–27 kts)	fresco
vento forte, ventania moderada	near gale (force 7, 28–33 kts)	frescachón
vento muito forte, ventania fresca	gale (force 8, 34–40 kts)	duro
vento tempestuoso, ventania forte	severe gale (force 9, 41–47 kts)	muy duro
temporal, ventania total	storm (force 10, 48–55 kts)	temporal
temporal desfieto, tempestade	violent storm (force 11, 56–63 kts)	borrasca, tempestad
furacão, ciclone	hurricane (force 12, 64+ kts)	huracán
aguaceiro	shower	aguacero
arrebentação	breakers	rompientes
bailadeiras	overfalls, tide race	escarceos
borrasca	squall	turbonada
chuva	rain	lluvia
crista	ridge (high)	dorsal
depressão	depression (low)	depresión
mar bravo	rough sea	mar gruesa
mar cavado	short, steep sea	mar corta
mar chão	slight sea	marejadilla
neblina	mist	neblina
nevoeiro	fog	niebla
nublado	cloudy	nubloso
ondulação	swell	mar de leva
rajada	gust	racha
saraiva	hail	granizada
trovoada	thunderstorm	tempestad

IX. Abbreviations used on charts

Spanish	Portuguese	Meaning
F.	F.	Fixed
D.	Rl.	Flashing
Gp.D.	Rl.Agr.	Group flashing
F.D.	F.Rl.	Fixed and flashing
F.Gp.D.	F.Rl.Agr.	Fixed and group flashing
Ct.	Ct	Quick flashing
Gp.Ct.	Ct int	Interrupted quick flashing
Oc.	Oc.	Occulting
Gp.Oc.	Oc.Agr.	Group occulting
Iso	Is.	Isophase
Mo.	Morse	Morse
Colours		
am.	am.	Yellow
az.	azul	Blue
b.	br.	White
n.	pr.	Black
r.	vm.	Red
v.	vd.	Green
Seabed		
A	A.	Sand
Al	Alg	Weed
R.	R.	Rock
F	L.	Mud
Co.	B.	Gravel

APPENDIX

Index